Bhutan

Stan Armington

LONELY PLANET PUBLICATIONS
Melbourne • Oakland • London • Paris

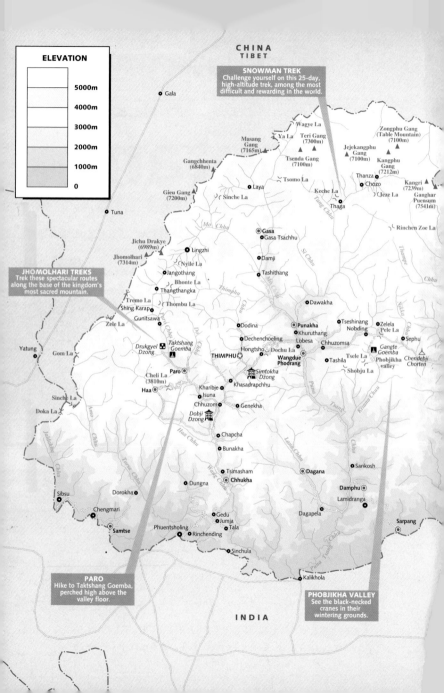

ELEVATION

5000m
4000m
3000m
2000m
1000m
0

CHINA
TIBET

SNOWMAN TREK
Challenge yourself on this 25-day, high-altitude trek, among the most difficult and rewarding in the world.

Gala

Wagye La

Masang Gang (7165m)
Ya La
Teri Gang (7300m)
Zongphu Gang (Table Mountain) (7100m)

Gangchhenta (6840m)
Tsenda Gang (7100m)
Jejekangphu Gang (7100m)
Kangphu Gang (7212m)

Tsomo La
Thanza
Chozo
Kangri (7239m)

Gieu Gang (7200m)
Laya
Keche La
Jeze La
Ganghar Puensum (7541m)

Tuna
Sinche La
Thaga
Rinchen Zoe La

Jichu Drakye (6989m)
Lingzhi
Gasa
Gasa Tsachhu

Jhomolhari (7314m)
Damji

JHOMOLHARI TREKS
Trek these spectacular routes along the base of the kingdom's most sacred mountain.

Nyile La
Tashithang

Jangothang
Bhonte La
Thangthangka

Tremo La
Thombu La
Dawakha

Shing Karap
Dodina
Punakha
Tseshinang
Zelela Pele La

Gunitsawa
Dechenchoeling
Khuruthang
Nobding
Sephu

Zele La
Hongtsho
Dochu La
Lobesa
Chhuzomsa
Gangte Goemba

Yatung
Gom La
Taktshang Goemba
THIMPHU
Wangdue Phodrang
Tashila
Tsele La
Phobjikha valley
Chendebji Chorten

Drukgyel Dzong

Cheli La (3810m)
Paro
Simtokha Dzong
Shobju La

Sinche La
Haa
Kharije
Khasadrapchhu

Doka La
Isuna
Chhuzom
Genekha

Dobji Dzong

Chapcha

Bunakha

Tsimasham
Dagana
Sarikosh

Sibsu
Chhukha
Damphu

Dorokha
Lamidranga

Chengmari
Dungna

Samtse
Gedu
Dagapela

Jumja
Phuentsholing
Tala
Sarpang

Rinchending
Dagapela

Sinchula

Kalikhola

PARO
Hike to Taktshang Goemba, perched high above the valley floor.

PHOBJIKHA VALLEY
See the black-necked cranes in their wintering grounds.

INDIA

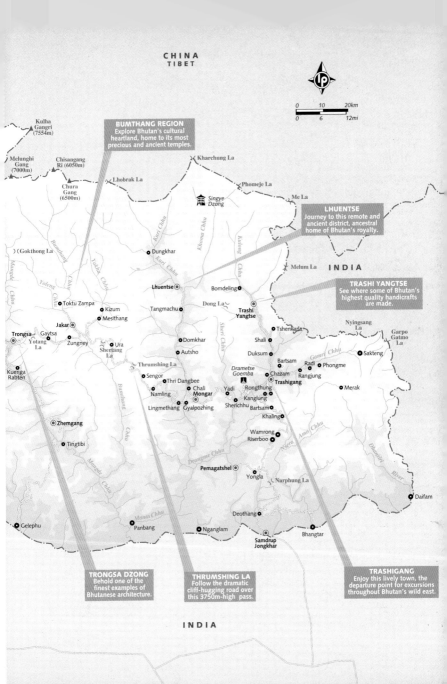

CHINA
TIBET

0   10   20km
0   6   12mi

Kulha
Gangri
(7554m)

Melunghi
Gang
(7000m)

Chisangang
Ri (6050m)

Lhobrak La

Kharchung La

Phomeje La

Me La

Chura
Gang
(6500m)

Singye
Dzong

BUMTHANG REGION
Explore Bhutan's cultural
heartland, home to its most
precious and ancient temples.

(Gokthong La)

Dungkhar

LHUENTSE
Journey to this remote and
ancient district, ancestral
home of Bhutan's royalty.

INDIA

Melum La

Toktu Zampa

Kizum

Lhuentse

Bomdeling

Mesithang

Tangmachu

Dong La

Trashi
Yangtse

TRASHI YANGTSE
See where some of Bhutan's
highest quality handicrafts
are made.

Jakar

Tshenkarla

Nyingsang
La

Garpo
Gatmo
La

Trongsa

Gaytsa

Yotang
La

Zungney

Ura

Domkhar

Shali

Sakteng

Sherteng
La

Autsho

Duksum

Bartsam

Radi

Phongme

Kuenga
Rabten

Thrumshing La

Sengor

Thri Dangbee

Chali

Mongar

Yadi

Drametse
Goemba

Rongthung

Chazam

Rangjung

Trashigang

Merak

Namling

Gyalpozhing

Kanglung

Sherichhu

Bartsam

Lingmethang

Zhemgang

Khaling

Tingtibi

Wamrong
Riserboo

Pemagatshel

Yongla

Narphung La

Daifam

Gelephu

Panbang

Nganglam

Deothang

Bhangtar

Samdrup
Jongkhar

TRONGSA DZONG
Behold one of the
finest examples of
Bhutanese architecture.

THRUMSHING LA
Follow the dramatic
cliff-hugging road over
this 3750m-high pass.

TRASHIGANG
Enjoy this lively town, the
departure point for excursions
throughout Bhutan's wild east.

INDIA

Bhutan
2nd edition – June 2002
First published – November 1998

Published by
Lonely Planet Publications Pty Ltd ABN 36 005 607 983
90 Maribyrnong St, Footscray, Victoria 3011, Australia

Lonely Planet offices
Australia Locked Bag 1, Footscray, Victoria 3011
USA 150 Linden St, Oakland, CA 94607
UK 10a Spring Place, London NW5 3BH
France 1 rue du Dahomey, 75011 Paris

Photographs
Many of the images in this guide are available for licensing from
Lonely Planet Images.
W www.lonelyplanetimages.com

Front cover photograph
The impressive Kurjey Lhakhang in Choskhor valley, central Bhutan
(Julia Wilkinson)

ISBN 1 86450 145 6

text & maps © Lonely Planet Publications Pty Ltd 2002
photos © photographers as indicated 2002

Printed through Colorcraft Ltd, Hong Kong
Printed in China

Contents – Text

2 Contents – Text

WESTERN BHUTAN   169

CENTRAL BHUTAN   201

EASTERN BHUTAN   226

TREKKING   248

LANGUAGE   299

GLOSSARY   303

INDEX   313

Contents – Maps

The Author

Stan Armington

Stan has been organising and leading treks in Nepal since 1971. A graduate engineer, he has also worked for the US National Park service in the Yellowstone and Olympic Parks, and served as a guide on Mt Hood in Oregon. He was one of Lonely Planet's first authors. His guide *Trekking in the Nepal Himalaya*, first published in 1979, won the Pacific Asia Tourism Association's 2002 PATA Gold Award award for its 8th edition.

Stan is a director of the American Himalayan Foundation, a fellow of the Royal Geographical Society and the Explorers Club, and a member of the American Alpine Club and the Alpine Stomach Club. He lives in Kathmandu, where he runs a trekking company and tries to keep up with all the changes to trekking routes in both Nepal and Bhutan.

FROM THE AUTHOR

I received an enormous amount of assistance with research for this edition from both Bhutanese and expatriates in Bhutan. Everyone was eager to help make this book accurate, not necessarily to attract more tourists to Bhutan, but to help readers come to understand this tiny, little-known and often misunderstood Buddhist Himalayan kingdom. The most important thank you is to Sangay Wangdi, Thuji Nadik and Tashi Peyden of the Department of Tourism, who allowed me to travel throughout the country and provided background information and advice. Dasho Ugyen Tshering, Lyonpo Dawa Tsering, Lyonpo C Dorje and Dasho Sangay Wangchug kindly clarified many government policies, as did Dasho Jigme Tshultrim (Mongar Dzongdag) and Nima Tsering (Bumthang Dzongdag). Sonam Wangmo and Rinzin Ongdra Wangchuk of Yu Druk Travels arranged travel facilities and answered an incredible number of questions. Thanks also to Robin Pradhan, Pem Tshomo, Tashi Tangbi, Justin Gurung and Dilu Giri. Special thanks to: Thsering Yonten, Dr Paolo Morisco, Tobgay S Namgyal of the Bhutan Trust Fund, Kunzang Choden of Ugyen Chholing Trust, Sithar Namgye (Surveyor General), and Rajni Chavda of the Urban Planning Division.

Kinley Dorji of *Kuensel*, Khendum Dorji of Chhundu Travels and Diana Myers provided cultural background. Piet van der Poel, Dr Gavin Jordan, David Thompson, Bart Jordans and Jan Pirouz Poulsen shared their knowledge and travel experience, as did Michael Vinding, James Roberts, George van Driem, Peter Schmidt, John Sanday and numerous denizens of Benez and Om Bar.

Many monks and caretakers shared their knowledge of the temples under their charge. Gangte Trulku was especially helpful, as was Lam Kezang of the Institute for Zorig Chusum in Trashi Yangtse.

Special thanks to Kunzang Dorji and Karma Ura for their insightful writings on Bhutanese culture. Nick Williams and Sonam Tobgay provided information about river running. 'Jungly John' reviewed the section on Himalayan Buddhism.

Rogier Gruys and Grant Bruce, Jim Williams, Lily Leonard, Ugyen Rinzin and Jurmin Wangdi helped with information on trekking routes. Adam Pain helped with the section on birds. Dorji Wangdi and Mindup Tshering organised some spectacular treks, and several drivers transported me back and forth across the country on incredibly winding roads.

Dr David Shlim provided advice on medical issues relevant to Nepal and Bhutan. The town maps and accurate trek elevations were produced with differentially corrected GPS data thanks to equipment and software provided by Trimble Navigation.

This Book

Stan Armington researched and authored both the first and second editions of *Bhutan*. The textiles special section, 'The Warp & the Weft', was written by Diana Myers, and Dr David Shlim was responsible for advice on healthy travel.

From the Publisher

John Hinman and Sarah Sloane were the coordinating editor and coordinating designer, respectively. Andrew Bain, Nancy Ianni, Shelley Muir and Jenny Mullaly assisted with editing and proofing; Isabelle Young helped with indexing. Mapping assistance was provided by Mandy Sierp, who also saw the book through layout; Shahara Ahmed compiled the climate charts. Chris Lee Ack provided cartography support and Glenn van der Knijff helped create the trekking profiles. Matt King coordinated the illustrations and Annie Horner sourced the photographic images for the book. The cover was designed by Karen Nettlefield and laid out by Maria Vallianos. Mark Germanchis provided expert Quark support through layout. Quentin Frayne lent his expertise to the Language chapter.

Thanks

Many thanks to the travellers who used the last edition and wrote to us with helpful hints, useful advice and interesting anecdotes:

Fabrizio Abrescia, Kathy Aubin, Jeanne DeGenova, ML Drayer, Linda Fessette, Arne Georgzen, Anita Gowers, Charles Harpole, A Van Hout, Sushi Karnik, Meenakshi Kher, Olya Khomenko, C Kim, Per Kjaer Johansen, Norm Land, Richard Leavitt, Delyan Manchev, Duncan McIntosh, Guy Michael Tkach, Gayle Prest, Brian Quinn, Esther Ratner, Jacob Russell, Michael Schudrich, Gideon Sheps, Mendy Shoval, J Simpson, Andrew Stott, Joanne Sugiono, Tenga Trepatsang, Jigme Tsering, Monique van Wijnbergen, Joselyn Weeds, Johan Westman

Foreword

ABOUT LONELY PLANET GUIDEBOOKS

The story begins with a classic travel adventure: Tony and Maureen Wheeler's 1972 journey across Europe and Asia to Australia. There was no useful information about the overland trail then, so the Wheelers published the first Lonely Planet guidebook to meet a growing need.

From a kitchen table, Lonely Planet has grown to become the largest independent travel publisher in the world, with offices in Melbourne (Australia), Oakland (USA), London (UK) and Paris (France).

Today Lonely Planet guidebooks cover the globe. There is an ever-growing list of books and information in a variety of media. Some things haven't changed. The main aim is still to make it possible for adventurous travellers to get out there – to explore and better understand the world.

At Lonely Planet we believe travellers can make a positive contribution to the countries they visit – if they respect their host communities and spend their money wisely. Since 1986 a percentage of the income from each book has been donated to aid projects and human rights campaigns, and, more recently, to wildlife conservation.

> Although inclusion in a guidebook usually implies a recommendation we cannot list every good place. Exclusion does not necessarily imply criticism. In fact there are a number of reasons why we might exclude a place – sometimes it is simply inappropriate to encourage an influx of travellers.

UPDATES & READER FEEDBACK

Things change – prices go up, schedules change, good places go bad and bad places go bankrupt. Nothing stays the same. So, if you find things better or worse, recently opened or long-since closed, please tell us and help make the next edition even more accurate and useful.

Lonely Planet thoroughly updates each guidebook as often as possible – usually every two years, although for some destinations the gap can be longer. Between editions, up-to-date information is available in our free, quarterly *Planet Talk* newsletter and monthly email bulletin *Comet*. The *Upgrades* section of our website (W www.lonelyplanet.com) is also regularly updated by Lonely Planet authors, and the site's *Scoop* section covers news and current affairs relevant to travellers. Lastly, the *Thorn Tree* bulletin board and *Postcards* section carry unverified, but fascinating, reports from travellers.

Tell us about it! We genuinely value your feedback. A well-travelled team at Lonely Planet reads and acknowledges every email and letter we receive and ensures that every morsel of information finds its way to the relevant authors, editors and cartographers.

Everyone who writes to us will find their name listed in the next edition of the appropriate guidebook, and will receive the latest issue of *Comet* or *Planet Talk*. The very best contributions will be rewarded with a free guidebook.

We may edit, reproduce and incorporate your comments in Lonely Planet products such as guidebooks, websites and digital products, so let us know if you don't want your comments reproduced or your name acknowledged.

How to contact Lonely Planet:
Online: e talk2us@lonelyplanet.com.au, W www.lonelyplanet.com
Australia: Locked Bag 1, Footscray, Victoria 3011
UK: 10a Spring Place, London NW5 3BH
USA: 150 Linden St, Oakland, CA 94607

Introduction

Describing his arrival in Bhutan in his *Lands of the Thunderbolt* (1923), the Earl of Ronaldshay wrote:

With our passage through the bridge, behold a curious transformation. For just as Alice, when she walked through the looking-glass, found herself in a new and whimsical world, so we, when we crossed the Pa-chhu, found ourselves, as though caught up on some magic time machine fitted fantastically with a reverse, flung back across the centuries into the feudalism of a mediaeval age.

Bhutan is not an ordinary place. It has one foot in the past and one in the future. Its far-sighted leaders recognise the necessity of being part of the modern world, but they realise that once their forests and culture are destroyed, they can never be recovered. They have maintained their traditional culture, yet they have adapted what they need from modern technology. You'll find monks transcribing ancient Buddhist texts into computers and traditionally dressed archers using the most modern high-tech bows and arrows.

Bhutan is a country of rolling hills and towering crags, with only small patches of cultivation and very little deforestation. It is often compared to Switzerland, not only because they are similar in size, but also because many parts of Bhutan look like the Swiss Alps, with green hills, houses that look like chalets and snow peaks sticking out of nowhere.

Bhutan holds many surprises and a visit to the country is a splendid adventure. English is widely spoken, and you can easily converse with school children and many

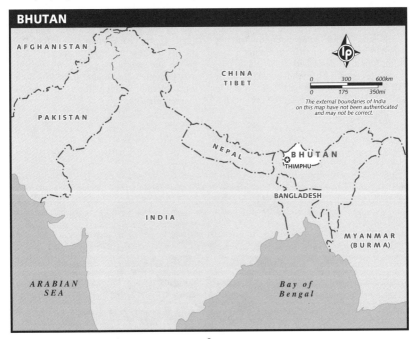

BHUTAN

AFGHANISTAN

CHINA
TIBET

0   300   600km
0   175   350mi

The external boundaries of India
on this map have not been authenticated
and may not be correct.

PAKISTAN

NEPAL

BHUTAN
THIMPHU

BANGLADESH

INDIA

MYANMAR
(BURMA)

ARABIAN
SEA

Bay of
Bengal

other people. The Bhutanese are very curious about life outside their mountain kingdom and are eager to hear stories about your country and how you live.

There are Western-style hotels and food throughout the country, but the best facilities are in Thimphu, the capital, and the town of Paro where the airport is located. If you travel to eastern Bhutan, be prepared for simple hotels and less familiar meals. To see the best of Bhutan, you should spend a week or more on foot, trekking through the great forested wilderness that covers most of the country.

Bhutan is a land replete with myths and legends, and many tales contribute to its undeserved reputation of being an impossible place to visit. While certainly isolated and remote, it is not in fact a difficult place to visit. There is no limit to the number of tourists who can visit and you do not need any special influence or 'pull'. Subject to some well-defined restrictions, it is actually easy to arrange a trip to Bhutan. You can even organise a journey as an independent traveller; you do not have to travel in a group.

Bhutan is a little-known country, and not much information is available. Sometimes it is inaccurately described as a 'living museum'. It does visibly maintain its traditions, but its temples and monasteries are active and viable institutions that are very much a part of the modern world. It is not a nation of saintly, ascetic, other-worldly monks; you will find Bhutan to be full of well-educated, fun-loving and vibrant people.

There are numerous contradictions in the various sources that describe Bhutan's history. Facts and figures are often missing or confusing. There is no authoritative list of place names, no list of mountain peaks, and population figures are based on estimates. The statistics and description of historical events presented here are based on credible sources, but many of these 'facts' are open to interpretation. Much of the information about temples, monuments and local history was provided by monks, caretakers and school teachers, who do not always agree with each other – or with the history books – about events, dates and other information.

Travel within Bhutan can be frustrating, but it is always an adventure because the unexpected continually happens. Sometimes this utter fortuitousness causes problems; at other times the surprises are the joy of friendship, understanding or unsurpassed beauty that will bring you back again and again. If you visit Bhutan, you will become one of the few who have experienced the charm and magic of the country, and you may become a proponent of the kingdom's tourism policy and its efforts to maintain its distinct identity.

Facts about Bhutan

HISTORY

Bhutan's early history is steeped in Buddhist tradition and mythology. It's said that a saint who had the ability to appear in eight different forms visited Bhutan and left the imprint of his body and his hat on rocks. Local schoolbooks describe demons that threatened villages and destroyed temples until captured through magic and converted to Buddhism. Tales abound of ghosts who destroyed temples, and angels who rebuilt them. Another story tells of a saint who flew on the back of a tiger and turned into a *garuda*, a bird that is a distant relative of the griffin.

The kingdom's more recent history is no less amazing, with intrigue, treachery, fierce battles and extraordinary pageantry all playing an important part.

Researchers have attached dates to many events, though these often do not seem to fit together into a credible and accurate chronology. When reading Bhutanese history, it's easier to let your imagination flow. Try visualising the spirit of the happenings rather than rationalising events as historical truth. This will, in part, help prepare you for a visit to Bhutan, where spirits, ghosts, yetis, medicine men, and lamas reincarnated in three different bodies are accepted as a part of daily life.

Bhutan's medieval and modern history is better documented than its ancient history, but is no less exotic. This is a time of warlords, feuds, giant fortresses and castles. The country's recent history begins with a hereditary monarchy that was founded in the 20th century and continued the country's policy of isolationism. It was not until the leadership of the third king that Bhutan emerged from its medieval past of serfdom and isolation. Until the 1960s the country had no national currency, and no telephones, schools, hospitals, postal service or tourists. Development efforts have now produced all these – plus a national assembly, airport, roads and a national system of health care. Despite the speed of moderni-

Origin of the Name 'Bhutan'

There is little agreement on the origin of the name 'Bhutan'. It may have evolved from the Sanskrit 'Bhot-ant', meaning 'the end of Tibet', or from 'Bhu-uttan' meaning 'high land'. Early British explorers called it Bootan or Bhotan, and they believed the name derived from 'Bhotsthan', meaning 'land of the Bhotias' (Bhotia is Sanskrit for people from Tibet). Whatever the origin, the name evolved into the current form of Bhutan, and the people are known as Bhutanese.

Although known as Bhutan to the outside world, the country has been known as Druk Yul, 'land of the thunder dragon', to its inhabitants since the 13th century. The people call themselves Drukpa, and the state religion is the Drukpa Kagyu lineage of Mahayana Buddhism.

sation, Bhutan has maintained a policy of careful, controlled growth in an effort to preserve its national identity. The government has cautiously accepted tourism, television and the Internet.

Early History

Many of the important events in the country's early history involved saints and religious leaders and were therefore chronicled only in scriptures. Most of these original documents were destroyed in fires in the printing works of Sonagatsel in 1828 and in Punakha Dzong in 1832. Much of what was left in the old capital of Punakha was lost in an earthquake in 1897 and more records were lost when Paro Dzong burned in 1907. Therefore much of the early history of Bhutan relies on reports from British explorers, on legend and folklore, and on a few manuscripts that were safely preserved in monasteries.

Archaeological evidence suggests Bhutan was inhabited as early as 1500 BC, or possibly even 2000 BC. Its first inhabitants were nomadic herders who lived in low-lying valleys in winter and moved their animals to high pastures in summer; many Bhutanese still live this way today. The river valleys of Bhutan provided relatively easy access across the Himalaya, and it is believed that the Manas River valley was used as a migration route from India to Tibet.

India, particularly the kingdom of Cooch Behar in what is now West Bengal, influenced Bhutan from the early days. The rulers of Cooch Behar established them-selves in Bhutan, but their influence faded in the 7th century AD as the influence of Tibet grew after the introduction of Buddhism.

Some of the early inhabitants of Bhutan were followers of Bon (known as Ben cho in Bhutan), the animistic tradition that was the main religion throughout the Himalayan region before the advent of Buddhism. It is believed that the Bon religion was introduced in Bhutan in the 6th century AD.

Buddhism was probably introduced to Bhutan as early as the 2nd century, although

Guru Rinpoche

Guru Rinpoche is also known by the names Padmasambhava, Precious Master and Ugyen Rinpoche. *Padma* is a Sanskrit word meaning 'lotus flower' and is the origin of the Tibetan and Bhutanese name Pema; *sambhava* means 'born from'. He is a historical figure of the 8th century, and his birth was predicted by Sakyamuni, the Historical Buddha. He is regarded as the second Buddha and had miraculous powers, including the ability to subdue demons and evil spirits.

Guru Rinpoche is credited with many other magical deeds and is regarded as the founder of Nyingma Buddhism. He is one of the most important of Bhutan's religious figures and his visit to Bumthang is recognised as the true introduction of Buddhism to Bhutan. He left an impression of his body on the rock upon which he meditated near the head of the Choskhor valley in Bumthang. On this site the temple of Kurjey Lhakhang was built, and Guru Rinpoche's body print can still be seen there. His statue appears in almost all temples built after his visit to Bhutan in AD 746.

His birthplace was Uddiyana in the Swat valley of what is now Pakistan. Uddiyana is known in Dzongkha as Ugyen, and some texts refer to him as Ugyen Rinpoche. He travelled in various manifestations throughout Tibet, Nepal and Bhutan, meditating in numerous caves, which are regarded as important 'power places'. He preserved his teachings and wisdom by concealing them in the form of *terma* (hidden treasures) to be found by enlightened treasure discoverers called *tertons*. His biographer, Yeshe Chhogyel, urges us not to regard Guru Rinpoche as a normal human being, because by doing so we will fail to perceive even a fraction of his enlightened qualities.

Bhutanese and Tibetans differ over a few aspects of his life; the following description reflects the Bhutanese tradition.

Eight Manifestations

The Guru is depicted in eight forms (Guru Tshen-gay). These are not really different incarnations, but representations of his eight main initiations, in which he assumed a new personality that was symbolised by a new name and appearance. Because initiation is equivalent to entering a new life, it is a form of rebirth. The eight forms follow the chronology of Guru Rinpoche's life.

He emerged as an eight-year-old from a blue lotus on Lake Danakosha in Uddiyana, and was adopted by King Indrabodhi. Then he was called Tshokye Dorji (diamond thunderbolt born from a lake). He later renounced his kingdom and went to receive teachings and ordination from the master Prabhahasti in the cave of Maratrika (near the village of Harishe in eastern Nepal), becoming Sakya Senge (lion of the Sakya clan). In this form he is identified with Sakyamuni, the Historical Buddha.

After studying the teachings of the Vajrayana and mastering the sciences of all Indian pundits, he obtained full realisation and was able to see all the gods and deities. Then he was called Loden Chogsey (possessor of supreme knowledge). He took as his consort Mandarava, the daughter of historians say the first Buddhist temples were built only in the 7th century AD. See the boxed text 'The Ogress in Tibet' in the Western Bhutan chapter for the story of the construction of these temples.

Visits of Guru Rinpoche

In AD 746 Sendha Gyab (also know as Sindhu Raja), the king of Bumthang, became possessed by a demon, and it required a powerful tantric master to exorcise it. He sent for the great teacher Padmasambhava, better known as Guru Rinpoche (Precious Master). The Guru captured the demon and converted it to Buddhism. For good measure, he also converted the king and his rival, restoring the country to peace. (For a complete description of Guru Rinpoche's efforts, see the boxed text 'The Story of Kurjey Lhakhang' in the Central Bhutan chapter.)

The Guru visited Tibet at the invitation of Trisong Detsen, the second of the three great religious rulers of Tibet, where he introduced Nyingma Buddhism and overcame

Guru Rinpoche

the king of Zahor (in the Mandi district of Himachal Pradesh, India). This enraged the king, who condemned them both to be burned, but through his powers the Guru turned the pyre into a lake and converted the kingdom to Buddhism. Then he was called Pema Jugney (Padmasambhava).

He returned to Uddiyana to convert it to Buddhism, but was recognised as the prince who had renounced his kingdom and was burned, along with his consort. He was not consumed by the fire and appeared sitting upon a lotus in a lake. This lake is Rewalsar, also called Tsho Pema (the lotus lake), in Himachal Pradesh, and is an important pilgrimage spot. His father, King Indrabodhi, offered him the kingdom and he became Padma Gyalpo (the lotus king), remaining for 13 years and establishing Buddhism.

When he was preaching in the eight cremation grounds to the *khandroms* (female celestial beings), he caught the life force of the evil deities and he turned them into protectors of Buddhism. Then he was called Nyima Yeozer (sunbeam of enlightenment). Later, 500 heretic masters tried to destroy the doctrine of Buddha, but he vanquished them through the power of his words and brought down a thunderbolt destroying the non-Buddhists in a flash of hail and lightning. He was then called Sengye Dradrok (roaring lion).

When he came to Bhutan the second time and visited Singye Dzong in Kurtoe and Taktshang in Paro, he was in the form of Dorji Drakpo (fierce thunderbolt). He subdued all the evil spirits hindering Buddhism and blessed them as guardians of the doctrine. In this form, Guru Rinpoche rides a tigress.

Statues of Guru Rinpoche

Most statues of Guru Rinpoche are in his manifestation as Padmasambhava, wearing royal robes and holding the insignia of spiritual realisation. His hat is known as the 'lotus cap' and is adorned with a crescent moon, the sun and a small flame-like protuberance that signifies the union of lunar and solar forces. The hat is surmounted by a *dorji* (thunderbolt) and also an eagle's feather, which represents the Guru's soaring mind, penetrating the highest realms of reality.

Often the statues of Padmasambhava are flanked by statues of two female devotees. These are the Indian princess Mandarava, the lady of wisdom, and the Tibetan khandroma Yeshe Chhogyel, who is regarded as an incarnation of Saraswati, the goddess of knowledge. She was gifted with such a perfect memory that she was able to remember the Guru's every word and became his sole biographer. She is depicted as a white, heavenly being with traditional ornaments and flying scarves; Mandarava is usually depicted as an Indian hill princess.

Guru Rinpoche's celestial abode or paradise is a copper-coloured mountain named Zangto Pelri. The guardians of the four directions guard the four gates, and in the centre is a three-roofed pagoda, with Guru Rinpoche enthroned on the ground level, flanked by his two consorts.

the demons that were obstructing the construction of Samye Monastery.

He returned to Bhutan via Singye Dzong in Lhuentse and visited the districts of Bumthang, Mongar and Lhuentse. At Gom Kora, in eastern Bhutan, he left a body print and an impression of his head with a hat. He flew in the form of Dorji Drakpo (one of his eight manifestations) to Taktshang in Paro on a flaming tigress, giving the famous Taktshang monastery the name 'Tiger's Nest' (see Taktshang Goemba under Around Paro in the Western Bhutan chapter).

It is believed that Guru Rinpoche also made a third visit to Bhutan during the reign of Muthri Tsenpo, the son of Trisong Detsen.

Medieval Period

The grandson of Trisong Detsen, Langdharma, ruled Tibet from AD 836 to 842. He banned Buddhism, destroyed religious institutions and banished his brother, Prince Tsangma, to Bhutan. It is believed that many monks fled from Tibet and took refuge in Bhutan during this period. Despite the assassination of Langdharma and the reintroduction of Buddhism, Tibet remained in political turmoil and many Tibetans migrated to Bhutan and settled in the western part of the country.

Between the 9th and 17th centuries numerous ruling clans and noble families emerged in different valleys throughout Bhutan. The various local chieftains spent their energy quarrelling among themselves and with Tibet, and no important nationally recognised political figure emerged during this period.

The Bhutanese Form of Buddhism

Back in Tibet, Lama Tsangpa Gyarey Yeshe Dorji (AD 1161–1211) founded a monastery in the town of Ralung, just east of Gyantse, in AD 1180. He named the monastery Druk (Dragon), after the thunder dragons that he heard in the sky as he searched for an appropriate site upon which to build a monastery. The lineage followed here was named after the monastery and became known as Drukpa Kagyu.

In the 11th and 12th centuries there was a further large influx of Tibetans into Bhutan. Many Drukpa lamas left Tibet because of persecution at the hands of the followers of the rival Gelug lineage. Most of these lamas settled in the western part of Bhutan and established branches of Drukpa monastic orders. Western Bhutan became loosely united through the weight of their teachings. Charismatic lamas emerged as de facto leaders of large portions of the west, while the isolated valleys of eastern and central Bhutan remained separate feudal states.

One of the most important of these lamas was Gyalwa Lhanangpa, who founded the Lhapa Kagyu lineage. He established the Tango monastery on a hill above the northern end of the Thimphu valley and established a system of forts in Bhutan similar to the *dzongs* found in Tibet.

Lama Phajo Drukgom Shigpo (1184–1251), a disciple of Lama Tsangpa Gyarey, came to Bhutan from Ralung and defeated Lama Lhanangpa. He and his companions established the small Dohon Dzong on the west bank of the Wang Chhu and took control of the Tango monastery. Lama Phajo is credited with establishing the Bhutanese form of Buddhism by converting many people to the practice of the Drukpa Kagyu school. Other lamas resented his presence and success and they tried to kill him through magic spells. Phajo turned the spells back on the lamas, destroying several of their monasteries.

Many Bhutanese nobles are descended from Lama Phajo. Between the 13th and 16th centuries, the Drukpa Kagyu lineage flourished and Bhutan adopted a separate religious identity. Many more lamas from Ralung were invited to Bhutan to teach and build monasteries.

Among the visitors to Bhutan during this period was Lama Ngawang Chhogyel (1465–1540). He made several trips and was often accompanied by his sons, who established several *goembas* (Buddhist monasteries). They are credited with building the temple of Druk Choeding in Paro and Pangri Zampa and Hongtsho goembas near Thimphu. Another visitor was Lama Drukpa Kunley, the 'divine madman', who lived from 1455 to 1529 and established Chime Lhakhang near Punakha. (See the boxed text 'The Divine Madman' in the Western Bhutan chapter.)

Between the 11th and 16th centuries numerous terma hidden by Guru Rinpoche in caves, rocks and lakes were discovered, as he had prophesied, by tantric lamas called tertons. The tertons were important religious figures; the best known of these was Pema Lingpa, who recovered his first terma from the lake of Membartsho near Bumthang in 1475. Pema Lingpa constructed several monasteries in Bumthang and is one of the most important figures in Bhutanese history. (For more information see the boxed text 'Terton Pema Lingpa' in the Central Bhutan chapter.)

Rise of the Shabdrung

By the 16th century the political arena was still fragmented between many local chiefs, each controlling his own territory and en-gaging in petty feuds with the others. There were numerous monasteries competing for superiority, and the lamas of western Bhutan were working to extend their influence to the east of the country.

Everything changed in 1616 when Ngawang Namgyal (1594–1651) came to Bhutan from Ralung, the original home of the Drukpa Kagyu in Tibet. In his early years he studied religion and art and is said to have been a skilled painter. He was a descendent of Tsangpa Gyarey, the founder of Ralung. At age 12 he was recognised as the reincarnation of Pema Karpo, the prince-abbot of Ralung Monastery. This recognition was challenged by the ruler of another principality in Tibet, and Ngawang Namgyal found his position at Ralung very difficult. When he was 23, the protective deity Yeshe Goenpo (Mahakala) appeared to him in the form of a raven and directed him south to Bhutan. He travelled through Laya and Gasa and spent time at Pangri Zampa,

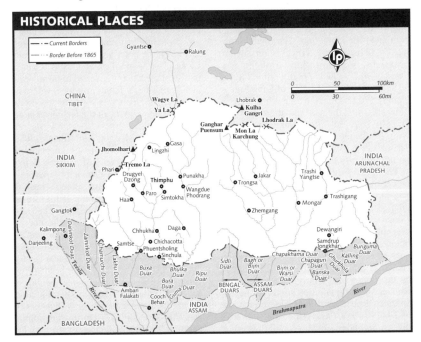

HISTORICAL PLACES

which was established by his great-great-grandfather, Ngawang Chhogyel.

As Ngawang Namgyal travelled throughout western Bhutan teaching, his political strength increased. Soon he established himself as the religious ruler of Bhutan with the title Shabdrung Rinpoche (precious jewel at whose feet one prostrates), thus becoming the first in the line of shabdrungs. He built the first of the present system of dzongs at Simtokha, just south of present-day Thimphu. While the primary function of earlier Bhutanese dzongs was to serve as invincible fortresses, the Simtokha Dzong also housed a monastic body and administrative facilities and fulfilled its defensive function. This combination of civil, religious and defensive functions became the model for all of Bhutan's later dzongs.

The Shabdrung's rule was opposed by the leaders of rival Buddhist lineages within Bhutan. They formed a coalition of five lamas under the leadership of Lama Palden and attacked Simtokha Dzong in 1629. This attack was repelled, but the coalition then aligned itself with a group of Tibetans and continued its opposition. The Shabdrung's militia defeated the Tibetans on several occasions, and the influence of the rival lineages diminished. Finally, after forging an alliance with the brother of King Singye Namgyal of Ladakh, the Shabdrung's forces defeated the Tibetans and their coalition ally. In 1639 an agreement was reached with the Tsang Desi in Tibet recognising Shabdrung Ngawang Namgyal as the supreme authority in Bhutan.

The Shabdrung further enhanced his power by establishing relations with neighbouring kings, including Rama Shah, the king of Nepal, and Raja Padmanarayan of Cooch Behar. It was at this time that the king of Ladakh granted the Shabdrung a number of sites in western Tibet for the purpose of meditation and worship. These included Diraphuk, Nyanri and Zuthulphuk on the slopes of the holy Mt Kailash. The Bhutanese administration of these monasteries continued until the Chinese takeover of Tibet in 1959. Other Tibetan monasteries that came under Bhutanese administration

were Rimpung, Doba, Khochag, and De Dzong, all near Gartok. A Bhutanese lama was sent as representative to Nepal, and Bhutanese monasteries were established at Bodhnath (Chorten Jaro Khasho) and Swayambhunath in Kathmandu. Bhutan administered Swayambhunath until after the Nepal-Tibet war of 1854–56, when it was retaken by Nepal on the suspicion that Bhutan had helped the Tibetans.

During his reign, Shabdrung Ngawang Namgyal ordered the construction of many monasteries and dzongs throughout Bhutan. Of these, the dzongs at Simtokha, Paro, Punakha and Trongsa are still standing. He established the first *sangha* (community of monks) at Cheri Goemba near Thimphu. When Punakha Dzong was completed in 1635, the sangha was moved there and became the *dratshang* (central monk body), headed by a supreme abbot called the Je Khenpo.

Invasions from Tibet

In the meantime, strife continued in Tibet, between the Nyingma (known as 'red hat') group of Buddhists and the Gelugpas ('yellow hat'); the latter are headed by the Dalai Lama. The Mongol chief Gushri Khan, a patron of the Dalai Lama, led his army in an attack on Tibet's Tsang province, where he overthrew the Rinpong dynasty and established the supremacy of the Gelugpas in the region.

In 1644 the Mongols and Tibetans, who were used to the extremely high plains of Tibet, launched an assault from Lhobrak into Bumthang, but found themselves overpowered by the forests and relative heat of Bhutan. Shabdrung Ngawang Namgyal personally led the successful resistance and several Tibetan officers and a large number of horses were captured. Much of the armour and many weapons that were taken during this battle are on display in Punakha Dzong. Drukgyel Dzong was built at the head of Paro valley in 1647 to commemorate the victory and to prevent any further Tibetan infiltration.

One of the strongest of Tibet's Dalai Lamas was the 'Great Fifth'. During his administration, he became jealous of the growing influence of the rival Drukpas on his southern border and mounted further invasions into Bhutan in 1648 and 1649. Each attempt was launched via Phari in Tibet, from where the Great Fifth's forces crossed the 5000m-high Tremo La pass into Paro valley. They were repelled, and again the Bhutanese captured large amounts of armour, weapons and other spoils. Some of this booty may still be seen in the National Museum in Paro. Legend relates that the Shabdrung built a *thos*, a heap of stones representing the kings, or guardians of the four directions, to subdue the Tibetan army. You may not find this one, but similar thos can still be seen in the courtyards of many of Bhutan's goembas.

Ngawang Namgyal's success in repelling the Tibetan attacks further consolidated his position as ruler. The large militia that he raised for the purpose also gave him effective control of the country. Mingyur Tenpa, who was appointed by the Shabdrung as *penlop* (governor) of Trongsa, undertook a campaign to unite all the valleys of the central and eastern parts of the country under the Shabdrung's rule, which he accomplished by about 1655. At this time the great dzongs of Jakar, Lhuentse, Trashi Yangtse, Shongar (now Mongar), Trashigang and Zhemgang were constructed.

A Bhutanese Identity Emerges

The Shabdrung realised that Bhutan needed to differentiate itself from Tibet in order to preserve its religion and cultural identity. He devised many of Bhutan's customs, traditions and ceremonies in a deliberate effort to develop a unique cultural identity for the country.

As a revered Buddhist scholar, he had both the astuteness and authority to codify the Kagyu religious teachings into a system that was distinctively Bhutanese. He also defined the national dress and instituted the *tsechu* festival.

The Shabdrung created a code of laws that defined the relationship between the lay people and the monastic community. A system of taxes was developed; these were paid in kind in the form of wheat, buckwheat, rice, yak meat, butter, paper, timber

and clothing. The people were subject to a system of compulsory labour for the construction of trails, dzongs, temples and bridges. These practices lasted almost unchanged until the third king eliminated them in 1956.

In the 1640s the Shabdrung created the system of Choesi, the separation of the administration of the country into two offices. The religious and spiritual aspects of the country were handled by the Shabdrung. The political, administrative and foreign-affairs aspects of the government were to be handled by the *desi* (secular ruler), who was elected to the post. The office of the Shabdrung theoretically had greater power, including the authority to sign documents relating to an important matter within the government. Under the system at that time, the Shabdrung was the spiritual ruler and the Je Khenpo was the chief abbot and official head of the monastic establishment. The Je Khenpo had a status equal to the desi and sometimes held that office.

The first desi was Tenzin Drugyey (1591–1656), one of the monks who came with Ngawang Namgyal from Ralung Monastery. He established a system of administration throughout the country, formalising the position of penlop as that of provincial governor. There were initially three districts: Trongsa in the centre, Paro in the west and Dagana in the south. The penlops became the representatives of the central government, which was then in Punakha. There were three officers called *dzongpens* (lords of the dzong) who looked after the affairs of the subdistricts of Punakha, Thimphu and Wangdue Phodrang.

Shabdrung Ngawang Namgyal went into retreat in Punakha Dzong in 1651. He didn't emerge again, and although it is likely that he passed away very early in the period of retreat, his death remained concealed until 1705. It is believed that the four successive desis who ruled during this period felt that the continued presence of the Shabdrung was necessary to keep the country unified and Tibet at bay. Nonetheless, Tibet mounted seven attacks on Bhutan between 1656 and 1730.

In 1668 Mingyur Tenpa was enthroned as the third desi. He ruled for 12 years, during which time he extended the boundaries of Bhutan westwards to Kalimpong, which is now part of India.

Civil Wars

When the Je Khenpo finally announced the death of the Shabdrung in 1705, he said that three rays of light emanated from the Shabdrung's body, representing the *ku sung thug* (body, speech and mind) of Ngawang Namgyal. This indicated that the Shabdrung would be reincarnated in these three forms, though only the reincarnation of the Shabdrung's mind was considered to be the head of state. Because the position of shabdrung was a continuing one, it was necessary for the mind incarnation to be reborn after the death of the previous incarnation.

This structure resulted in long periods when the shabdrung was too young to rule and the desi often became the de facto ruler. Because the desi was an elected position, there was considerable rivalry among various factions for the office. These factions also took advantage of uncertainty over which of the three incarnations of the Shabdrung was the 'true' incarnation. None of the successive incarnations had the personal charisma or political astuteness of Ngawang Namgyal.

The next 200 years were a time of civil war, internal conflicts and political infighting. While there were only six mind incarnations of the Shabdrung during this period, there were 55 desis. The longest-serving desi was the 13th incumbent, Sherab Wangchuk, who ruled for 20 years; and the most important was the fourth, Gyalse Tenzin Rabgye, who ruled from 1680 to 1694. Few of the rulers finished their term; 22 desis were assassinated or deposed by rivals.

The political situation became so unstable that some of the rival factions appealed to the Tibetans for assistance. In 1729 and 1730 Tibet took advantage of Bhutan's instability and invaded the country three times. The lamas in Tibet initiated a truce that eventually ended the hostilities. The rival Bhutanese factions submitted their case to the Chinese emperor in Beijing for mediation. But the issue was only finally resolved when several of the Bhutanese protagonists died, leaving the currently recognised mind incarnation of the Shabdrung as the ruler. At the same time, formal diplomatic relations were established between Bhutan and Tibet, which the late historian Michael Aris said 'helped to guarantee the fact of Bhutanese independence'.

Relations with Cooch Behar

In 1730 the 10th desi assisted Gya Chila, the ruler of Cooch Behar, to defeat invaders and to settle a family feud; Bhutan was then allowed to station a force in that southern kingdom. In 1768 the desi tried to suppress the influence of the religious establishment in Bhutan and to strengthen his own influence outside of the country. He established alliances with the Panchen Lama in Tibet and with King Prithvi Narayan Shah of Nepal. In 1772 the Bhutanese invaded Cooch Behar to help settle a feud over succession. They won, and kidnapped the crown prince and the queen of Cooch Behar. The Bhutanese also captured Raja Dhairjendra Narayan, the king of Cooch Behar, in the same year.

Involvement of the British

In his book, *Lands of the Thunderbolt*, the Earl of Ronaldshay wrote:

...it was not until 1772 that the East India Company became conscious of the existence, across its northern frontier, of a meddlesome neighbour.

The first contact the British had with Bhutan was when the claimants to the throne of Cooch Behar appealed to the East India Company to help drive the Bhutanese out of their kingdom.

Because the East India Company was a strictly commercial enterprise, its officers agreed to help when the deposed ruler of Cooch Behar offered to pay half of the revenues of the state in return for assistance. In December 1772 the British governor of

Bengal, Warren Hastings, sent Indian troops and guns to Cooch Behar and, despite suffering heavy losses, routed the Bhutanese and restored the king to the throne. However, Cooch Behar paid a very high price for this assistance. Not only did its rulers pay 50,000 rupees, but in 1773 they also signed a treaty ceding the kingdom to the East India Company.

The British pushed the Bhutanese back into the hills and followed them into Bhutan. The British won another major battle in January 1773 at the garrison of Chichacotta (now Khithokha) in the hills east of what is now Phuentsholing. A second battle was fought near Kalimpong in April 1773. The Bhutanese troops were personally led by the 16th desi but, after the second defeat, he was deposed by a coup d'etat.

First Treaty with the British

The new desi wanted to make an agreement with the British and appealed to the Panchen Lama in Tibet for assistance. The Panchen Lama then wrote what the British described as 'a very friendly and intelligent letter' that was carried to Calcutta (now called Kolkata) by an Indian pilgrim. The British, although more eager to establish relations with Tibet than to solve the issue of Bhutan, did agree to comply with the Tibetan request. The result was a peace treaty between Bhutan and the British signed in Calcutta on 25 April 1774. In this treaty the desi agreed to respect the territory of the East India Company and to allow the company to cut timber in the forests of Bhutan. The British returned all the territory they had captured.

The East India Company wasted no time in sending a trade mission to Tibet. In May 1774 George Bogle led a party through Bhutan to Tibet. The group spent a few weeks in Thimphu waiting for permission to go to Tibet, and eventually reached the seat of the Panchen Lama in Tashilhunpo in October. The written account of this mission provides the first Western view into the isolated kingdom of Bhutan and is described in the 'Exploration by Western Travellers' boxed text later in this chapter.

The 1897 Earthquake

One of the most devastating natural disasters in Bhutan was the great Assam earthquake that occurred at 5.06pm on 12 June 1897. The epicentre was about 80km south of Bhutan in Assam and had a magnitude of 8.7 on the Richter scale, which seismologists categorise as 'catastrophic'. Of course, there were no seismometers to measure the event, and the magnitude was estimated from its devastating effects. By comparison, the 1995 Kobe quake measured 7.2, the San Francisco earthquake of 1906 measured 8.3, and the Prince William Sound earthquake in 1964 had a magnitude of 9.2.

The earthquake destroyed the dzongs in Punakha and Lingzhi and severely damaged the dzongs of Wangdue Phodrang, Trongsa, Jakar and the *utse* (central tower) of Trashi Chhoe. Paro Dzong escaped largely unharmed.

This earthquake is famous not only because of its size, but because it was the first documentation of a quake producing vertical accelerations greater than 1G, which means that large boulders were actually lifted from their location and moved to a new spot without touching the ground.

The British in India attached their own names, derived from Sanskrit, to the titles used by the Bhutanese. They called the shabdrung the '*dharma raja*', and the desi '*deb raja*'. Raja is Sanskrit for 'king'; therefore the dharma raja was the king who ruled by religious law and the deb raja was the king who delivered wellbeing or material gifts. Deb is a corruption of the Sanskrit word *deva* or *devata* (the giver).

The Problem of the Duars

The political intrigue and civil wars continued in Bhutan, and there were numerous skirmishes over boundaries and trading rights. The British were engaged in the Burmese war of 1825–26. As a result of this war, the British gained control of Assam, the territory that forms the eastern half of Bhutan's southern border.

The area of plains between the Brahma-putra River up to and including the lowest of the hills of Bhutan was known as the *duars*, which means doors or gates (see the The Duars under Geography later in this chapter). The western part of this area, known as the Bengal Duars, had been annexed by the third desi, Mingyur Tenpa, in the late 17th century and the Bhutanese considered it their territory. The eastern part, the Assam Duars, had long been administered in a complex rental agreement between Bhutan and Assam.

After the Burmese war, the British took over the peculiar land rental arrangement for the Assam Duars, along with what were described as 'very unsatisfactory relations of the Assamese with the Bhutanese'. Major disagreements between the British and Bhutan resulted. In 1826 the British and Bhutanese came into conflict over the ownership of the duars. Other than the area's strategic importance, the British were attracted to the duars because they were excellent tea-growing country. However, they were also a malarial jungle, and the British had a very difficult time keeping the troops stationed there healthy.

Bhutan's existing agreement with the Assamese allowed the British to occupy the region from July to November, and the Bhutanese to occupy it the remainder of the year in return for payment in horses, gold, knives, blankets, musk and other articles. The new arrangement meant that Bhutan sent the payment to the British, who accused the Bhutanese of delivering piebald horses and other defective goods. The Bhutanese insisted that middlemen working for the British had substituted inferior goods.

Disagreements over payments and administration escalated between the British and the Bhutanese. The British annexed Buringma Duar in the far west, then returned it when Bhutan paid a compensation of Rs 2000. In 1836 the British mounted an attack on Dewangiri (now known as Deothang), in the east, to force the surrender of fugitives who had committed crimes in British territory. The dzongpen refused to comply and attacked the British detachment. The British won that battle and annexed Dewangiri and the entire Banska Duar. The following year, however, at the request of the desi, they agreed to return control of the duar to the Bhutanese.

The British annexed the two easternmost duars in 1840 and the rest of the Assam Duars in September 1841, agreeing to pay Bhutan an annual compensation of Rs 10,000. Lord Auckland wrote to the deb and dharma rajas that the British were:

...compelled by an imperative sense of duty to occupy the whole of the duars without any reference to your Highnesses' wishes, as I feel assured that it is the only course which is likely to hold out a prospect of restoring peace and prosperity to that tract of country.

Perhaps more revealing is a letter from Colonel Jenkins, the governor-general's agent, outlining the need for taking over the Assam Duars. He wrote:

Had we possession of the Dooars, the Bhootan Government would necessarily in a short time become entirely dependent upon us, as holding in our hands the source of all their subsistence.

This was the time of the Afghan War and the Anglo-Sikh wars. The British Indian administration had little time to worry about Bhutan, and major and minor conflicts and cross-border incursions continued. Although the British were making plans to annex the Bengal Duars, they were not able to follow through. Their troops were kept busy trying to suppress the Indian uprising of 1857, which was a movement against British rule in India.

Bhutan took advantage of the instability in the region and mounted numerous raids in the Bengal Duars. To compensate for their losses, the British deducted large sums from payments they owed the Bhutanese. In 1861 the Bhutanese retaliated by raiding Cooch Behar, capturing a number of elephants and kidnapping several residents, including some British subjects.

The Trongsa Penlop Gains Control

At this time the incumbent shabdrung was a youth of 18, and the affairs of state were handled by the Lhengyal Shungtshog (Council of Ministers), which consisted of the Trongsa and Paro penlops, several dzongpens and other officials. There was constant infighting and intrigue between the Paro and Trongsa penlops, both of whom were vying for power through attacks, conspiracy and kidnapping. When one gained control, he appointed a desi and enthroned him; soon the other penlop gained control, ejected the opposing desi and placed his own representative on the throne.

Through a series of shrewd alliances the Trongsa penlop, Jigme Namgyal (1825–82), gained the upper hand and established effective control of the country. This was the first time peace had prevailed since the time of the first shabdrung. Jigme Namgyal was working to strengthen his power and that of the central government when he had an inconvenient visitor.

The Humiliation of Ashley Eden

The British had managed to extend their influence into Sikkim, making it a British protectorate. They decided to send a mission to Bhutan to, among other things, establish a resident British representative promoting better communications with the rulers. According to the official account, the mission was designed:

...on a scale calculated to impress the Court with the importance which the British Government attaches to the establishment of clear and decisive relations with the Government of Bhootan, and the adoption of some means whereby the present unsatisfactory state of affairs on the Frontier may be put a stop to, and that the mutual rendition of persons charged with the commission of heinous crimes may be secured.

Despite reports of political chaos in Bhutan, Ashley Eden, the secretary of the government of Bengal, set out from Darjeeling in November 1864 to meet the desi, or deb raja. Ignoring numerous messages from the Bhutanese that the British mission was not welcome, Eden pushed on past Kalimpong, through Daling, Haa and Paro, reaching Punakha on 15 March.

It's not clear whether it was more by accident or by design, but Eden's party was jeered, pelted with rocks, made to wait long hours in the sun and subjected to other humiliations. Both Bhutanese and British pride suffered badly. As Eden describes it in *Political Missions to Bootan*:

The Penlow [penlop] took up a large piece of wet dough and began rubbing my face with it; he pulled my hair, and slapped me on the back, and generally conducted himself with great insolence. On my showing signs of impatience or remonstrating, he smiled and deprecated my anger, pretending that it was the familiarity of friendship, much to the amusement of the large assemblage of bystanders.

Eden exacerbated the situation by sending the Lhengyal Shungtshog a copy of a draft treaty with terms that he had been instructed to negotiate. His actions implied that this was the final version of the treaty that the Bhutanese were to sign without any discussion. The Bhutanese took immediate exception to Eden's perceived high-handedness and soon presented him with an alternative treaty that returned all the duars to Bhutan. One clause in the treaty stated:

We have written about that the settlement is permanent; but who knows, perhaps this settlement is made with one word in the mouth and two in the heart. If, therefore, this settlement is false, the Dharma Raja's demons will, after deciding who is true or false, take his life, and take out his liver and scatter it to the winds like ashes.

Reading this, it's little wonder that Eden feared for the safety of his party. He signed the treaty, but under his signature added the English words 'under compulsion', which, naturally, the Bhutanese could not read.

The Duar War of 1865

Although the British considered Eden's mission a failure, and reprimanded him for his conduct, they continued the dispute with Bhutan over payment for the Bengal Duars.

Exploration by Western Travellers

Some of the most interesting stories of Bhutan, and much of Bhutan's recorded history, came from the descriptions provided by early explorers. These records provide an insight into what they observed and reveal the extraordinary attitudes of some of the envoys Britain sent to negotiate with Bhutan.

Fathers Cacella & Cabral

The first Western visitors to Bhutan were two Portuguese Jesuit priests. In early 1627 Fathers Cacella and Cabral travelled from Calcutta to Bhutan en route to Shigatse in Tibet. They stayed for a few months in Cheri Goemba, north of Thimphu, with the Shabdrung. There is no complete written account of their journey, but one of their letters provides an interesting insight into Ngawang Namgyal's character:

He received us with a demonstration of great benevolence, signifying this in the joy which he showed on seeing us and on knowing where we had come from, where we were from, that is from what country or nation, and he asked the other questions normal at a first meeting.

...he is at the same time the chief lama...He is proud of his gentleness for which he is highly reputed, but less feared...He is also very celebrated for his abstinence in never eating rice or meat or fish maintaining himself only with fruit and milk...He occupied himself, as he told us, in praying and in his spare time he made various objects and he showed us one of them, which was the best, being an image of the face of God in white sandalwood, small but very well made and this is an art of which he is very proud, as also that of painter at which he is good...he also has a great reputation as a man of letters...

The Shabdrung has a long beard and some of its hairs reach his waist...

George Bogle

Some 150 years later, the first British expedition arrived in Bhutan in 1774, just after the first British treaties with Bhutan and Tibet were signed. The Court of Directors of the East India Company sent a mission to Tibet via Bhutan to find out about goods, 'especially such as are of great value and easy transportation'. The expedition team, led by George Bogle, planted potatoes wherever they went, providing a new food crop for Bhutan and a lasting legacy of this mission. They spent five months in Thimphu and then travelled on to Tibet. Bogle found the Bhutanese 'good-humoured, downright, and so far as I can judge, thoroughly trustworthy'. He did, however, note that the practice of celibacy by many monks led to 'many irregularities' and the cold resulted in 'an excessive use of spirituous liquors'.

Samuel Turner

In the next few years two small expeditions travelled to Bhutan. Dr Alexander Hamilton led a group to Punakha and Thimphu in 1776, and another in 1777, to discuss Bhutanese claims to Ambari Falakati and to consolidate transit rights through Bhutan to Tibet that had been negotiated by Bogle's mission.

The next major venture into Bhutan was in 1783, when Samuel Turner led a grand expedition with all the accoutrements of the British Raj. They travelled through the duars in palanquins (sedan chairs) and followed Bogle's route to Thimphu. They also visited Punakha and Wangdue Phodrang before crossing to Tibet. Among the members of the 1783 expedition was Samuel Davis, who was a draftsman and surveyor. His journal and outstanding paintings provide one of the earliest views of Bhutan. Much of Davis' material is presented in *Views of Mediaeval Bhutan* by Michael Aris.

Ashley Eden

Minor British expeditions to Bhutan were made in 1810 and 1812 and again in 1815 when an Indian officer, Kishen Kant Bose, was sent to try to settle frontier disputes. RB Pemberton led a mission in 1837 from eastern Bhutan to Punakha, where he tried, unsuccessfully, to resolve the conflict over the duars.

The Ashley Eden mission of 1863 was the next attempt to resolve the issue of the duars. Among the members of this expedition was Captain HH Godwin-Austen of the Indian Topographical

Exploration by Western Travellers

Survey. Godwin-Austen had explored Pakistan's Baltoro Glacier in 1861 and, on some maps, K2, the second highest peak in the world, is named after him.

Contradicting Bogle's impression, Eden said of the Bhutanese: 'They are totally untrustworthy, more faithless indeed than the worst savages on our Frontier'. In his journal he ridiculed Buddhist practices and described the ex-penlop of Paro as 'physically worn out with debauchery of every description'.

Eden's party crossed the Cheli La from Haa into Paro valley in February and had an extremely difficult time in the deep snow. Some years later, John Claude White suggested that Eden might have been given incorrect directions, perhaps on purpose. It is astounding that, even having admitted failure, Eden still viewed his as a 'friendly mission'. His report certainly was a major factor in British annexation of the duars. He advocated a punitive policy to teach the Bhutanese that they would not be allowed to 'treat our power with contempt'. He later went on to build the 'toy train' railroad to Darjeeling.

John Claude White

There were no formal expeditions to Bhutan for more than 40 years after Eden's, but the Survey of India sent several agents disguised as lamas and pilgrims to explore Bhutan and Tibet in 1883 and 1886.

By 1905 the Bhutanese and British were friends due to the assistance the penlop of Trongsa, Ugyen Wangchuck, had provided the 1904 Younghusband expedition to Lhasa. John Claude White, a British political officer, came to present the insignia of Knight Commander of the Indian Empire to the penlop. White had been a member of the 1904 expedition and was an old friend of Ugyen Wangchuck.

White and his large party travelled from the city of Gangtok, in Sikkim, into Haa and Paro, en route to the investiture ceremony in Punakha. Later, White and his party were guests of Ugyen Wangchuck at his new palace of Wangdichholing in Bumthang. The expedition later returned with the first photographs of dzongs and the court of Bhutan.

In 1906 White made a reconnaissance through eastern Bhutan to southern Tibet. He made a third trip, in 1907, when he was invited as the British representative to the coronation of Ugyen Wangchuck as the first king of Bhutan. As the party neared Punakha, his own contingent of British officers and their band of pipes and drums was met by a Bhutanese delegation. The Bhutanese escorted them to the dzong on mule back, accompanied by a marching band playing trumpets, drums and gongs. As they approached the dzong, they were greeted by a salute of guns and the procession was joined by dancers who twirled down the path in front of the British contingent.

A summary of White's account appeared in the April 1914 issue of the *National Geographic*, and made Bhutan known to the world for the first time.

Other British Political Officers

Between 1909 and 1947 the British government dealt with Bhutan in the same way as it did with other Indian princely states, but it never specifically defined its relationship with Bhutan. Starting with CA Bell in 1909, numerous British political officers visited Bhutan and presented the king with decorations.

In 1921 the Earl of Ronaldshay, who was described as a 'closet Buddhist', travelled to Bhutan as a guest of the first king. He travelled from Gangtok to Paro, where he was met with great fanfare. He described the procession:

...behind them [trumpeters] tripped the dancers, who brought the whole procession to a halt whenever they came to a piece of ground which they deemed suitable for the treading of a measure.

The party visited Taktshang and witnessed the Paro tsechu, but never met the king, who was in Punakha, ill with influenza.

In 1927 Lt Col FM Bailey attended the coronation of the second king and Lt Col JLR Weir travelled to Bumthang in 1931 to present the king with the insignia of Knight Commander of the Indian Empire. This journey was the basis for the book and television documentary *Joanna Lumley in the Kingdom of the Thunder Dragon*.

The Bhutanese, in turn, were furious the British had renounced the treaty Eden had signed. In November 1864 the British summarily annexed the Bengal Duars, and proceeded to occupy them, gaining effective control of the entire south of Bhutan. The Trongsa penlop mounted a carefully planned counterattack. His troops, protected by shields of rhinoceros hide, captured two British guns and drove the British forces out of Bhutan in January 1865.

The British regrouped and recaptured various towns, including Samtse (then called Chamurchi). A fierce battle at Dewangiri on 2 April essentially ended the war, with the British destroying all the buildings and slaughtering their captives. Negotiations continued through the summer. Eventually the Bhutanese returned the captured guns and accepted a treaty. The treaty of Sinchula was signed, under duress, by the Bhutanese on 11 November 1865. In it the Bhutanese ceded the duars to Britain forever and agreed to allow free trade between the two countries.

Through this treaty, Bhutan lost a major tract of valuable farmland and a large portion of its wealth. Its borders became the foot of the hills bordering the plain of India. It is often said that Bhutan's border is where a rock rolled down the hill finally stops. Among the important landmarks the Bhutanese lost were the town of Ambari Falakati, north-west of Cooch Behar, the town of Dewangiri (now called Deothang) in the east and the territory on the east bank of the Teesta River, including what is now the town of Kalimpong.

Back in Bhutan's heartland there were continuing civil wars, but the penlop of Trongsa, Jigme Namgyal, retained his power and in 1870 was enthroned as the 51st desi. The next 10 years were again a time of intrigue, treachery, power broking and continual strife. The penlop of Paro and the dzongpens of Punakha and Wangdue Phodrang conspired to challenge the position of Desi Jigme Namgyal and his successor, who was his half-brother. After he retired as desi, Jigme Namgyal remained in firm control of the country and in 1879 appointed his 17-year-old son, Ugyen Wangchuck, as Paro penlop. Michael Aris' book *The Raven Crown* gives a detailed description of this extraordinary period.

After Jigme Namgyal died, his son consolidated his own position following a feud over the post of penlop of Trongsa. At the age of 20, Ugyen Wangchuck marched on Bumthang and Trongsa and in 1882 was appointed penlop of Trongsa, while still retaining the post of penlop of Paro. Because his father had enhanced the powers of the office of the Trongsa penlop, this gave him much more influence than the desi. When a battle broke out between the dzongpens of Punakha and Thimphu, Ugyen Wangchuck tried to mediate the dispute.

He sent in his troops after unsuccessful negotiations and his forces defeated the troops loyal to both dzongpens and seized control of Simtokha Dzong. The monk body and the penlop of Paro tried to settle the conflict and in 1885 arranged a meeting at the Changlimithang parade ground in Thimphu. During the meeting a fight broke out, the representative of the Thimphu dzongpen was killed and the dzongpen fled to Tibet. Following the battle, Ugyen Wangchuck emerged as the most powerful person in the country, assumed full authority, installed his own nominee as desi, and reduced the post to a ceremonial one.

The First King

In order to re-establish Bhutan's sovereignty and help consolidate his position, Ugyen Wangchuck developed closer relations with the British. He accompanied Francis Younghusband during his invasion of Tibet in 1904 and assisted with the negotiations that resulted in a treaty between Tibet and Britain. The British rewarded the penlop by granting him the title of Knight Commander of the Indian Empire. In 1906 Sir Ugyen Wangchuck was invited to Calcutta to attend the reception for the Prince of Wales and returned to Bhutan with a better appreciation of the world that lay beyond the country's borders.

In 1907 the secular ruler, the desi, died and Ugyen Wangchuck was elected as the hereditary ruler of Bhutan by a unanimous vote of Bhutan's chiefs and principal lamas. He was crowned on 17 December 1907 and installed as head of state with the title Druk Gyalpo (Dragon King). He continued to maintain excellent relations with the British, partly in an effort to gain some security from the increasing Chinese influence in Tibet.

The Treaty of Punakha

British-Bhutanese relations were enhanced in the treaty of Punakha, which was signed in 1910. This treaty stated that the British government would 'exercise no interference in the internal administration of Bhutan'. It was agreed that Bhutan would 'be guided by the advice of the British Government in regard to its external relations'. The compensation for the duars was doubled to Rs 100,000 per year and Bhutan agreed to refer disputes with Cooch Behar and Sikkim to the British for settlement.

Bhutan still refused to allow the appointment of a British resident, and continued to maintain a policy of isolation aimed at preserving its own sovereignty in an era of colonisation. In 1911 King Ugyen Wangchuck attended the great durbar held by King George V at Delhi and was given the additional decoration of Knight Commander of the Order of the Star of India.

The Second King

Ugyen Wangchuck died in 1926 and was succeeded by his 24-year-old son, Jigme Wangchuck, who became the second hereditary king of Bhutan. He ruled during the time of the Great Depression and WWII, but these catastrophic world events did not affect Bhutan because of its barter economy and isolation.

Jigme Wangchuck refined the administrative and taxation systems and brought the entire country under his direct control. He made Wangdichholing Palace in Bumthang his summer palace, and moved the entire court to Kuenga Rabten, south of Trongsa, in the winter. Karma Ura's book *The Hero With a Thousand Eyes* gives a wonderful insight into the protocol and workings of the Bhutanese court in those days.

After India gained independence from Britain on 15 August 1947, the new Indian government recognised Bhutan as an independent country. In 1949 Bhutan signed a treaty with independent India that was very similar to their earlier treaty with the British. The treaty reinforced Bhutan's position as a sovereign state. India agreed not to interfere in the internal affairs of Bhutan, while Bhutan agreed to be guided by the government of India in its external relations. The treaty also returned to Bhutan about 82 sq km of the duars in the southeast of the country, including Dewangiri, that had been annexed by the British.

The Third King & the Modernisation of Bhutan

King Jigme Wangchuck died in 1952. He was succeeded by his son, Jigme Dorji Wangchuck, who had been educated in India and England and spoke fluent Tibetan, English and Hindi. To improve relations with India he invited the Indian prime minister, Jawaharlal Nehru, and his daughter, Indira Gandhi, to visit Bhutan in 1958.

When the Chinese took control of Tibet in 1959, it became obvious that a policy of isolationism was not appropriate in the modern world. The king knew that in order to preserve Bhutan's independence, the country had to become a member of the larger world community. In 1961 Bhutan emerged from centuries of self-imposed isolation and embarked on a process of planned development.

Bhutan joined the Colombo Plan in 1962. This gave it access to technical assistance and training from member countries in South-East Asia. The first 'five-year plan' for development was implemented in 1961 and India agreed to help finance and construct the large Chhukha hydroelectric project in western Bhutan. Not all Bhutanese approved of the pace of change. There were clashes between rival power groups; the prime minister, Jigme Palden Dorji, who was a leading proponent of change, was assassinated on 5 April 1964. After a period of confusion, the king assumed the duties of that post; the Council of Ministers still does not include the office of prime minister.

Bhutan joined the Universal Postal Union in 1969 and became a member of the United Nations in 1971. In the same year, Bhutan and India established formal diplomatic relations and exchanged ambassadors.

The king's domestic accomplishments were also impressive. In 1953, early in his reign, he established the Tshogdu (National Assembly) and drew up a 12-volume code of law. He abolished serfdom, reorganised land holdings, created the Royal Bhutan Army (RBA) and police force, and established the High Court. However, as he led Bhutan into the modern world, he emphasised the need to preserve Bhutanese culture and tradition.

The Present King

King Jigme Dorji Wangchuck died in 1972 at age 44. He was succeeded by his 16-year-old son, Jigme Singye Wangchuck. Like his father, he was educated in India and England, but he also received a Bhutanese education at the Ugyen Wangchuck Academy in Paro. He pledged to continue his father's program of modernisation and announced a plan for the country to achieve economic self-reliance. This plan took advantage of Bhutan's special circumstances – a small population, abundant land and rich natural resources. Among the development goals set by the king was the ideal of economic self-reliance and what he nicknamed 'gross national happiness'.

The coronation of King Jigme Singye Wangchuck as the fourth Druk Gyalpo on 2 June 1974 was a major turning point in the opening of Bhutan, and was the first time that the international press was allowed to enter the country. A total of 287 invited guests travelled to Thimphu for the event, and several new hotels were built to accommodate them. These hotels later provided the basis for the development of tourism in Bhutan.

The king has emphasised modernisation of education, health services, rural development and communications. He was the architect of Bhutan's policy of environmental conservation, which gives precedence to ecological considerations over commercial interests. He continued the reforms begun by his father in the areas of administration, labour and justice, including the introduction of a secret ballot and the abolishment of compulsory labour. He promotes national identity, traditional values and the concept of 'One Nation, One People'.

In 1988 the royal wedding solemnised the king's marriage to the sisters Ashi Dorji Wangmo, Ashi Tshering Pem, Ashi Tshering Yangdon and Ashi Sangay Choedon. The crown prince is Dasho Jigme Khesar Namgyal Wangchuck.

Problems in the South

Several political problems in the south of the country have affected Bhutan's relations with its neighbours.

Nepali-Speakers In the late 19th and the early 20th centuries many Nepalis migrated to Bhutan and settled in the south of the country. They now comprise much of the population in that region, to the extent that the term Lhotshampa (southern Bhutanese) is almost synonymous with Nepali-speaker.

Although the Nepali-speakers are from many ethnic groups, the majority of them are Hindus, with traditions that are different from those of the Drukpas who live in the north of the country. Some Nepalis asserted that they faced discrimination from the Drukpas and demanded political changes as long ago as the 1950s, when the now-defunct Bhutan State Congress Party was formed.

From the 1950s the Bhutanese government took steps to integrate the ethnic Nepalis. For the first time they were granted citizenship, represented in the National Assembly and admitted into the bureaucracy. Nepali was taught as a third language in primary schools in southern Bhutan and was made the second official language of the country. Also, recognition was given to the festivals, customs, dress and traditions of the Lhotshampas. The Nepalis remained culturally distinct from the Bhutanese of the northern valleys.

However, up until the 1980s, there seemed to be little or no conflict between the Drukpas and the Lhotshampas.

Major problems didn't really emerge until the late 1980s. At that time, the government began to focus on preserving what it saw as Bhutan's threatened national identity. It introduced a policy of *driglam namzha* (traditional values and etiquette) under which all citizens had to wear the national dress of *gho* and *kira* at schools, government offices and official functions. At the same time, as part of the implementation of the 'New Approach to Education', study of the Nepali language was eliminated from the school curriculum. Resentment began to stir among some Nepalis in the south, exacerbated by what the government now concedes was overzealous enforcement of the policies by some district officials.

Mindful of the country's extremely porous border – and Bhutan's attractiveness because of its fertile land, low population and free health and education facilities – in 1988 the government conducted a nationwide census. This was aimed partly at identifying illegal immigrants, defined as those who could not prove family residence before 1958. Thousands of ethnic Nepalis lacked proper documentation. A series of violent acts in the south, including robberies, assaults, rapes and murders – primarily against legitimate Bhutanese citizens of Nepali descent – created a sense of fear and insecurity that led to an exodus of Nepali-speakers from Bhutan. How much of the migration was voluntary remains a matter of fierce debate, but tens of thousands of Nepali-speakers left Bhutan between 1988 and 1993.

At the same time, a set of dissident leaders emerged charging human rights abuses in the treatment of Nepalis inside Bhutan and demanding full democracy and other political changes in the kingdom. This movement received some international attention.

By the end of 1992, some 80,000 Nepali-speakers who said they were from Bhutan were housed in seven camps in the Jhapa district of south-eastern Nepal, organised by the office of the United Nations High Commissioner for Refugees (UNHCR). By early 1993 the exodus had virtually stopped. Initially, all those who arrived were accepted into the camps as a group; in June 1993 the UNHCR established a screening centre at Kakarbhitta on the Nepal-India border. At the end of 1997 there were 93,674 people in the camps, 10% to 11% of whom were born there.

Bhutan and Nepal agreed that they would settle the problem on a bilateral basis. They have held several rounds of talks to try to identify which residents of the camps are legitimate citizens of Bhutan and to find an appropriate solution to this complex problem. After numerous meetings they agreed to a joint verification process which began in March 2001. The process was completed at the first camp, Khudanabari, in December 2001 and the goal was to close the camp on a mutually agreeable basis and continue the verification process at other camps, though the two governments were still negotiating the details as this book went to print.

The status of the people in the camps of Jhapa is protected by the UNHCR, which uses donor support to provide the survival rations and shelter. It is likely that if the support disappears, and if the two countries cannot agree on how to resolve the crisis, those in the camps, most of them former farmers, would enter the larger diaspora of Nepali-speakers in South Asia.

Bodo Groups & the United Liberation Front of Assam The north-eastern region of India has suffered years of separatist violence carried out by militants, some of whom have established bases in the jungles of southern Bhutan from which they mount assaults. The actions of these groups have claimed the lives of more than 20,000 people in the Indian state of Assam.

The Bodos are Mechey tribal people that have two militant groups, the Bodo Liberation Tiger Force and the Bodo Security Force, both of which are fighting for a Bodo homeland. The United Liberation Front of Assam, more commonly known as ULFA, is a separatist group formed in 1979 with the goal of an independent Assamese nation. They have staged numerous attacks, including derailing a train with a bomb, and attacking Indian vehicles and, in July and August 2001, buses carrying Bhutanese passengers through India.

The Indian Army has stationed 50,000 troops in Assam to try to deal with these groups. Bhutan does not have the capacity to aggressively patrol its long and open border with India; in any case, the Bhutanese forces' limited supply of weapons is no match for the high-tech weaponry that the rebels possess. The situation becomes even more complicated because, by treaty, nationals of Bhutan and India are allowed to cross freely into each other's country. Bhutan does not support the separatist groups and is negotiating with the leaders to get them to leave the country peacefully. The presence of these intruders has made travel in the south-eastern part of the country risky for both Bhutanese and tourists and is the reason for restrictions on visiting such places as Royal Manas National Park, Pemagatshel and Samdrup Jongkhar.

History of Tourism in Bhutan

Until the beginning of King Jigme Dorji Wangchuck's modernisation efforts in 1960, most of the non-Indian foreigners who entered Bhutan were the explorers covered earlier in the boxed text 'Exploration by Western Travellers'. A few foreigners were permitted into the country during the 1960s, but only the royal family had the authority to invite foreigners to Bhutan, so almost all visitors were royal guests.

The First Trekkers Early trekkers included Desmond Doig, a friend of the royal family who trekked in 1961 on assignment for *National Geographic*. In 1963 Professor Augusto Gansser travelled throughout the country studying geology, and in 1964 a group of British physicians, Michael Ward, Dr Frederic Jackson and R Turner, mounted an expedition to the remote Lunana region in the north-west.

Pioneering Tourists The coronation of the present king in 1974 was the first time that a large number of foreign visitors had

entered the kingdom. After the coronation, in another experiment with modernisation, small groups of tourists were allowed into the country and given permission to visit the dzongs and goembas in Thimphu and Paro. From these beginnings, the pattern for Bhutan's tourism industry evolved.

The first group of paying tourists arrived in 1974, organised and led by Lars Eric Lindblad, founder of Lindblad Travel in Connecticut, USA, one of the pioneers of modern-day group tours. Lindblad encouraged the government to limit tourism and to charge high fees. The government soon established a quota of 200 tourists a year, who had to travel in a group of six or more. The cost was set at US$130 per day – a lot of money at that time. Because there was no airport, entry was via road from India, through the southern border town of Phuentsholing. At that time, travellers needed a special 'inner line' permit to cross the northern part of India, and this took six weeks to arrange through the Indian foreign ministry in Delhi. At first, tourists were restricted to Phuentsholing, Paro and Thimphu. Visitors could enter Punakha and Wangdue Phodrang from 1978, and in 1982 Trongsa and Bumthang were added to the list. Trekking in western Bhutan was started in 1978, and by 1982 it was possible to trek in central Bhutan.

Paro airport was opened in 1983 and the newly formed national airline, Druk Air, operated flights from Kolkata using small turbo-prop Dornier aircraft. This meant travellers could avoid the long drive and time-consuming permit restrictions in India and be deposited in the heartland of Bhutan. The airport runway was extended in 1990 and Druk Air began operating a 72-passenger BAe-146 jet aircraft, with direct international connections.

Until 1991 all tourists were handled by the Bhutan Tourism Corporation, a government agency. Tourism was privatised that year and soon numerous agencies were established, most run by ex-employees of the now-disbanded government tourist company. Though they have to abide by government rates and standards, the tour operators are free to operate as independent profit-making concerns. The Department of Tourism, under the Ministry of Trade & Industry, is responsible for all aspects of tourism.

Mountaineering Although there are no 8000m-high peaks, mountains in Bhutan tend to be rugged and beautiful and are still largely unexplored. There is still much confusion and controversy over the name, location and height of many peaks. Jhomolhari was a famous landmark on the trip to Everest for early mountaineers. On the approach march for the 1921 British Everest Expedition, George Leigh Mallory described it as 'astounding and magnificent', but he remained 'cold and rather horrified' by the mountain. It was climbed from Tibet in 1937 by F Spencer Chapman and Passang Lama and again in 1970 by a joint Indian-Bhutanese team.

Michael Ward and Dr Frederic Jackson made an extensive survey of Bhutan's mountains in 1964–65. They climbed several peaks of between 5500m and 5800m and categorised the Bhutan Himalaya as a defined and integrated group of mountains.

Bhutan opened its mountains to climbers for a short period from 1983 to 1994. A Bhutanese expedition scaled the 4900m-high Thurigang, north of Thimphu, in 1983. Jichu Drakye was attempted three times before it was successfully climbed in 1988 by an expedition led by Doug Scott, the famous mountaineer. In 1985 Japanese expeditions climbed Kula Gangri (7239m), Kari Jang, Kang Bum and Masang Gang. Gangkhar Puensum (7541m) remains the highest unclimbed peak in the world after unsuccessful attempts by Japanese and British teams in the 1980s. The mountains, weather and snow conditions in Bhutan can be fierce. An American team, including some world-class high-altitude climbers, failed to get to the base of Gangkhar Puensum. Reinhold Messner also failed to climb anything in Bhutan, saying that 'climbing in the prevailing snow conditions would have been suicidal'.

The government decided to prohibit mountain climbing after villagers living near the peaks asked it to for religious reasons.

GEOGRAPHY
Bhutan is a landlocked country about 300km long and 150km wide, encompassing 46,500 sq km. It is bounded on the north-west and north by Tibet. The rest of the country is surrounded by India: on the east by the state of Arunachal Pradesh; on the south by Assam and West Bengal; and on the west by Sikkim. Tibet's Chumbi valley, the old trade and expedition route from India to Lhasa, lies between the northern parts of Bhutan and Sikkim.

Virtually the entire country is mountainous, and ranges in elevation from 100m to the 7541m Gangkhar Puensum peak on the Tibetan border. It can be divided into three major geographic regions: the high Himalaya of the north; the hills and valleys of the centre; and the foothills and plains of the south.

Greater Himalaya
A range of high Himalayan peaks forms part of the northern and western borders of the country. These giant peaks are the thrones of the gods; almost none have been climbed, many are virtually unexplored and some are not even named. There are several high mountain passes that cross the Himalaya, but for the most part it remains an impenetrable snow-clad barrier (20% of the country is under perpetual snow). The Himalayan range extends from Jhomolhari (7314m) in the west to Kulha Gangri, near the centre point of the northern border. A chain of lower peaks extends eastwards to the Indian state of Arunachal Pradesh.

The Lunana region, just south of the midpoint of Bhutan's border with Tibet, is an area of glacial peaks and high valleys that are snowbound during the winter. A range of high peaks forms the southern boundary of Lunana and isolates it from the rest of the country.

Inner Himalaya
South of the high peaks lies a maze of broad valleys and forested hillsides ranging from 1100m to 3500m in elevation. This is the largest region of Bhutan and all the major towns, including Thimphu, are here. This

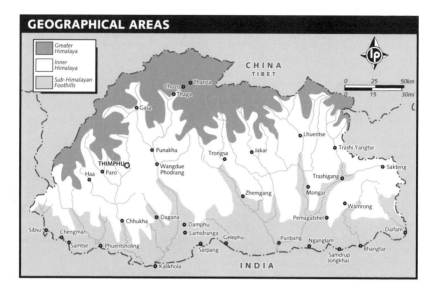

GEOGRAPHICAL AREAS

part of Bhutan is cut by deep ravines formed by fast-flowing rivers that have their source in the high Himalaya. The hillsides are generally too steep for farming; most have remained covered in virgin forest. There are significant differences between the western and eastern parts of this region. These are described below.

The West The greater part of Bhutan's western border is formed by the Himalayan range, including the peaks of Jhomolhari and Jichu Drakye. Several forested ridges extend eastwards from this range, and these define the large valleys of Thimphu, Paro, Haa and Samtse. Between Punakha and Thimphu lies a well-defined ridge that forms the watershed between Thimphu's Wang Chhu and Punakha's Puna Tsang Chhu. The east-west road crosses this ridge through a 3050m pass, the Dochu La.

A range called the Black Mountains lies to the east of the Puna Tsang Chhu watershed, forming the major barrier between eastern and western Bhutan. Pele La (3500m) is the most important pass across the Black Mountains and was an important mule track before the road was constructed.

Central Bhutan A north-south range of hills separates the Trongsa and Bumthang valley systems. The road crosses this ridge via Yotong La (3425m). Further east, the Donga range of hills follows the border that separates the Bumthang and Lhuentse districts, with Thrumshing La (3780m) as the crossing point for the road. Eastern Bhutan, which encompasses most of the Manas Chhu watershed, lies to the east of this range.

The East Thrumshing La provides the only road access across the Donga range, which drops precipitously on its eastern side to the Kuri Chhu. The steep Rodang La crosses the northern part of this range and there are few lower passes in the south that are still used by herders. The northern region just east of the Donga range is known as Kurtoe.

In the far east, another range of hills runs south from the Himalayan slopes to separate the Lhuentse and Trashi Yangtse valleys

Southern Foothills The plains in the south of the country are part of the region known as the Terai, which extends from Kashmir, through Nepal, to Bhutan. The foothills rise swiftly from the plains, and except for a very narrow band of flat land, this part of the country is either forest or terraced farmland.

The Duars At the south of Bhutan the hills end abruptly and the Indian plain begins. The fertile valleys that extend 15km to 30km from the hills to the Indian states of Assam and Bengal are known as the duars, as is the lower portion of Bhutan's foothills. Duar is a Sanskrit word meaning 'passes' or 'gates', and is the origin of the English 'door'. Before the British annexed Bhutan's southern regions, known as the duars in 1865, each was under the control of a Bhutanese dzongpen. As the duars were covered in malaria-infested jungle, they were unoccupied by the Bhutanese, who stayed in the northern hills.

Each duar is named after a river valley that leads out of Bhutan, though the duar itself is actually the land between two rivers. The land ranges from an elevation of about 100m to almost sea level at the Brahmaputra River, though the slope is barely perceptible. The fertile land supports tea gardens, huge rice paddies and a few protected forest areas such as the Buxa Tiger Reserve.

Seven of the duars abut the border of Assam between the Dhansiri (Durlah) and Manas Rivers. The remaining 11, from the Manas River to the Teesta River in the east, border on the state of Bengal.

Rivers

Rivers, or chhus, play an important role in Bhutan's geography, and their enormous potential for hydroelectric power has helped shape the economy. Flowing south, they have created deep valleys, making all east-west travel a tedious process of climbing over hills, descending to a river and climbing again to the next ridge. There are four major river systems in Bhutan, most known by several names as they flow through the country.

Most of the rivers have their headwaters in the high mountains of Bhutan, but the Himalaya are not a continental divide, and there are three rivers that actually flow through the mountains into the country. The Amo Chhu flows from Tibet's Chumbi valley across the south-western corner of Bhutan, where it becomes the Torsa Chhu, and exits at Phuentsholing. Two tributaries of the Manas, in eastern Bhutan, originate outside the country. The Kuri Chhu has its headwaters in Tibet (where it is known as the Lhobrak Chhu) and crosses into Bhutan at an elevation of only 1200m; the other tributary, the Gamri Chhu, rises in India's Arunachal Pradesh.

The Thimphu Chhu, known in its lower reaches as the Wang Chhu, powers the Chhukha and Tala hydroelectric projects and eventually becomes the Raidak River in India. The Pho Chhu and Mo Chhu join at Punakha to form the Puna Tsang Chhu, which drains the area between the Dochu La and the Black Mountains. This river is known as the Sankosh when it reaches India. The Manas is Bhutan's largest river, draining about two-thirds of the country; in its upper reaches it is known as the Drangme Chhu. The Mangde Chhu flows from Trongsa and joins the Manas Chhu just before it flows into India. Unlike most other rivers that flow from Bhutan into India, the Manas retains its original name when it crosses the border. All of Bhutan's rivers eventually flow through the duars to become part of the Brahmaputra, which is known in Tibet as the Yarlung Tsampo, with a source near Mt Kailash in the far west.

Because the central Himalaya of Bhutan receives the full brunt of the monsoon, Bhutan's rivers are larger and have created much broader valleys than rivers further to the west in Nepal and India. In their upper reaches, most Bhutanese rivers have created large fertile valleys such as those of Paro, Punakha, Thimphu, Haa and Bumthang. As the rivers pass through the centre of Bhutan, the valleys become steeper and narrower, and roads have to climb high on the hillside. In eastern Bhutan the Manas valley is generally broader, and some roads run alongside the river itself.

When they reach the plains, the rivers drop much of the glacial silt they have collected and follow a meandering course over gravel stream beds. There are several oxbow lakes in the plains where rivers have changed their course over the years.

GEOLOGY

Millions of years ago the space Bhutan occupies was an open expanse of water, part of the shallow Tethys Sea, and the Tibetan plateau, or 'roof of the world', was beach-front property. Some 60 million years ago the Indo-Australian plate collided with the Eurasian continent and was pushed under Eurasia. The earth's crust buckled and folded, and mountain building began. Ancient crystalline and sedimentary rocks were pushed upwards, and then folded into great ridges.

The new mountains blocked off rivers that once flowed unimpeded from Eurasia to the sea. However, on the southern slopes of the young mountains, new rivers formed as moist winds off the tropical sea were forced upwards until they cooled and shed their moisture. As the mountains continued to rise and the gradient became steeper, these rivers cut deeply into the terrain. The continual crunching of the two plates, augmented by phases of crustal uplifting, created additional new mountain ranges; once again the rivers' courses were interrupted and a few east-west valleys evolved.

The mountains are changing even today, not only through erosion and displacement of material downstream, but through plate movement pushing the ranges higher still. The geology of Bhutan is complex, but may be roughly categorised into the same three regions that are used to define the geography.

Greater Himalaya From north of Paro through the Thimphu valley to Trongsa is what Augusto Gansser, the authority on Bhutan's geology, defines as the 'main central thrust fault'. North of this fault is a crystalline mass of gneiss (coarse-grained metamorphic rock) that Gansser labelled 'Taktshang gneiss'. A large intrusion of tourmaline granite, which Gansser named 'Jhomolhari granite', forms the peak of Jhomolhari and the western portion of the Paro valley. Just north of this deposit is the Lingzhi valley, which is composed of a wide deposit of sedimentary rocks. Along Bhutan's northern border, a large granite mass forms the high Himalaya.

North of Bhutan is the plateau of Tibet, which is largely composed of uplifted sedimentary deposits.

Inner Himalaya Gansser has mapped a 'main boundary fault', which is the line at which the Indian plate pushed under the Eurasian plate. The fault extends across part of the far south of Bhutan, then enters India, passing south of Phuentsholing. It reenters Bhutan near Gelephu, passes north of Deothang and then continues east, back into India. Just north of the main boundary fault are several sedimentary deposits that have sheared, faulted and metamorphosed into a complex structure. The central region has layers of quartziferous sandstone, and the east has thin layers of coal. Other deposits found include quartzite, shale and dolomite.

South of the main central thrust fault the land is composed of a wide band of gneiss. South of the band of gneiss is the Paro metamorphic belt, a band which includes marble and quartzite. Iron is found in Paro and Punakha, and British explorers recounted how a magnet would pick up bits of iron from the soil.

Southern Foothills The region south of the boundary fault is mostly sandstone and ancient sedimentary deposits. The Geological Survey of India (GSI) has identified limestone deposits in Gelephu and talc in Samtse and Chhukha.

CLIMATE

Bhutan is at the same latitude as Miami and Cairo. The climate varies widely depending on the elevation. In the southern border areas it is tropical; at the other extreme, in the high Himalayan regions, there is perpetual snow. Temperatures in the far south range from 15°C in winter (December–February) to 30°C in summer (June–August). In Paro the range is from minus 5°C in January to 30°C in July, with 800mm of rain. In the high mountain regions the average temperature is 0°C in winter and may reach 10°C in summer, with an average of 350mm of rain.

Only in the high Himalayan regions does the snow remain year round – in the form of

For the majority of Bhutanese people, daily life is shaped by the rhythms of subsistence farming.

Archery, a favourite sport of the Bhutanese

Seeing the world through a *dzong* window

A quiet day of business in the remote western village of Lingzhi.

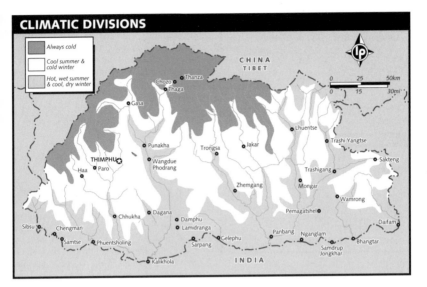

glaciers. Some snow falls in northern and central Bhutan but does not remain on the ground for long. As a general rule, snow melts immediately below 2400m, stays a short while (longer in shaded areas) between 2400m and 3500m, and remains on the ground until early March above 3500m.

Rain occurs primarily during the southwest monsoon season from June to September. Bhutan bears the brunt of the monsoon, receiving more rainfall than other Himalayan regions – up to 5.5m a year. Only 150km south of Bhutan, Cherrapunji in Assam has recorded the highest rainfall in the world, averaging 9.5m annually with a record of 19.7m, the height of a six-storey building.

Precipitation varies significantly with the elevation. The average rainfall is:

Himalayan regions	less than 500mm per year
Inner central valleys	500mm–1000mm per year
Southern foothills	2000mm–3500mm per year
Southern border area	3000mm–5000mm per year

During the monsoon, heavy rain falls almost every night; in the day there may be long periods without rain. Low clouds hang on the hills, obscuring views and, if they are too low, forcing the cancellation of flights at Paro airport. The 2000 monsoon was particularly severe, and caused widespread flooding and erosion in southern Bhutan, including damage to much of the Phuentsholing market area.

Very little rain falls during the autumn, from October to December, making this the ideal season for trekking and mountain viewing. On clear days during this period the mountain views are truly spectacular.

ECOLOGY & ENVIRONMENT

Thanks to its early isolation, small population and difficult terrain, Bhutan emerged into the 20th century with much of its forests and ecosystems intact. But now, with an increasing population, improved roads and communication and limited farming land, a major effort is required to protect the country's natural heritage.

Government Policy

Bhutan has consciously decided to forego immediate economic gain from exploitation of its natural resources in order to preserve its environment for long-term sustainable

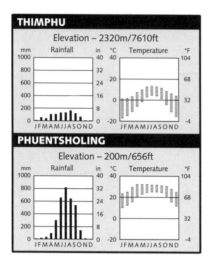

THIMPHU
Elevation – 2320m/7610ft

PHUENTSHOLING
Elevation – 200m/656ft

benefits. The commitment to conservation is reflected in a 1995 resolution of the National Assembly that at least 60% of the country must be maintained under forest cover in perpetuity.

Overall environmental policy is established by the National Environment Commission, while biological diversity and the parks are legislated and managed by the Ministry of Agriculture. As it does with every aspect of modernisation and development, the government is proceeding cautiously in an effort to integrate environmental concerns into all of its programs. The government also works with conservation organisations, both international and Bhutanese, to protect the environment, ensure a better quality of life for its people and preserve the country's heritage for future generations.

Environmental Issues

Bhutan's rapid urban growth and development activities have not come about without some negative impact on the environment. Natural-resource utilisation now has equal, if not more, ecological pressures from urban populations as from rural consumers. However, growing awareness of environmental issues has prompted appropriate conservation measures. Among these are requirements for environmental assessments for all new public or private investment projects, and nationwide bans on the commercial export of raw timber and the use of plastic bags. The government also intervenes in development projects if deemed necessary, as it did in 1996 to close down a major plywood factory because the plant was consuming too much wood.

Firewood Wood is used as fuel in rural areas and in most monasteries (in urban areas cooking gas or kerosene is used), and it was probably only Bhutan's low population that spared the forests before conservation planning was introduced. Managing firewood harvesting is a major problem. At almost 2.8 cubic metres per person, Bhutan's annual consumption of firewood is one of the highest in the world – and that represents about 375,000 trees. Wood accounts for 80% of energy consumption, and although the government is promoting electricity as an alternative source of energy, few rural households have electricity.

Grazing & Farming Practices Conservation issues centre on human-wildlife conflicts, such as crop and livestock depredation by wild predators, and the deterioration of high-altitude wildlife habitat from grazing pressure. There are now programs under way to balance the needs of traditional herders and farmers with wildlife protection.

A significant amount of shifting cultivation ('slash and burn', called *tseri* in Dzongkha) is practised in Bhutan, particularly in the east of the country. Villagers clear forests, grow corn and other crops for a few years, then abandon the fields and move on. The practice is officially banned and several methods, including education and fertiliser supply, are being implemented to change this practice.

Poaching While the Bhutanese generally observe their own conservation policies, the open southern and northern borders offer opportunities for poaching of both plant and animal life. Many species are sought for their alleged medicinal or other valuable properties. Killing and poaching are unacceptable in Buddhist tradition, but the high prices that wildlife products such as rhino horn, tiger bone, musk and *Cordyceps sinensis* (winter-worm summer-plant) command outside Bhutan present major challenges to conservationists.

The Department of Forestry Services (DFS) operates effective antipoaching programs designed to protect endangered plants and animals, enforce forestry rules, and control trade in wildlife parts and products. A national network of foresters regulates timber harvesting, and road checkpoints are operated throughout the country to monitor the transportation of forest products.

Urban Growth The central business districts of all the major towns are relatively new, with most of the construction and growth having occurred after 1970. Despite their newness, most were constructed without extensive town planning. It's estimated that the urban population will increase fourfold by 2020; plans have been instituted for proper city planning, sewage and water treatment and other related facilities in Thimphu and many other towns. Conservationists believe that Bhutan's urban growth could be creating a greater negative impact on the natural environment than subsistence farming by rural Bhutanese.

Biodiversity
Scientists have long considered the eastern Himalaya to be an area critically important to global efforts to preserve biological diversity. Bhutan has a tremendous diversity of plants, animals and ecosystems from subtropical ecosystems near sea level to high alpine habitats. The forests are believed to contain 5500 species of plants and 770 species of birds.

Due to its biological significance, Bhutan is included in a 1998 list of 18 global 'hotspots' of biological diversity. Although these hotspots collectively occupy only half of one percentage point of the earth's space, they are home to one-fifth of the world's

plant species, and two-thirds to three-quarters of the most endangered species of plants and animals.

Conservation Organisations
Bhutan Trust Fund The first of its kind globally, the Bhutan Trust Fund For Environmental Conservation (☎ 323846, fax 324214, W www.bhutantrustfund.org), PO Box 520, Thimphu, was established in 1991 as an innovative, long-term financing mechanism for conservation. With an endowment from conservation organisations, foundations and government aid agencies in various countries of more than US$30 million invested in the global capital markets, the trust fund uses its annual investment revenue to supplement and eventually replace external donor financing for Bhutan's environmental management.

The trust fund initially financed the revision and expansion of an ecologically representative system of nine protected areas, and leveraged management planning and external donor financing in at least five out of nine protected areas. At the time of research, through financial grants awarded to both government and nongovernment entities, it was enabling staff recruitment and training in the parks, building research capability in Sherubtse College and other educational institutions, providing institutional support for the Royal Society for Protection of Nature, and promoting rural community actions for sustainable conservation and development. Fully governed and managed by the Bhutanese themselves, the independent trust fund was also financing field research by qualified Bhutanese into critical environmental issues.

Department of Forestry Services
While overall biodiversity matters are overseen by the Ministry of Agriculture, the DFS is the government's main steward of the country's forests, wildlife and protected areas. The DFS nature conservation division (☎ 325042, fax 325475) provides policy and technical support to the protected areas and is also responsible for species conservation throughout the country.

Royal Society for Protection of Nature
Established in 1986, the Royal Society for Protection of Nature (RSPN; ☎ 326130, fax 323189, W www.rspn-Bhutan.org, PO Box 325, Thimphu) is Bhutan's only nonprofit, nongovernment environmental organisation. It played a major role in creating awareness of environmental issues among Bhutanese youth and the public, and has been an important partner to the government on many conservation initiatives.

Through its conservation education programs, RSPN established nature clubs in many schools and developed an innovative study course called 'follow that stream'. Under the guidance of RSPN-trained teachers, students observe the transformation in water quality and life forms as a stream passes through their village.

RSPN annually monitors the endangered black-necked cranes in the Phobjikha and Bomdeling valleys, and has also produced two documentary videos on the cranes.

WWF The global network of WWF, known in the US and Canada as World Wildlife Fund, and elsewhere as World Wide Fund for Nature, is represented in Bhutan through a program office established in 1992. The WWF (☎ 323528, fax 323518, W www .wwfbhutan.org.bt) became involved in the country in 1977 with training opportunities for Bhutanese conservationists, and today works closely with the government to support various wildlife conservation programs.

FLORA
Bhutan supports a great variety of plants, ranging from tropical species in the south to alpine tundra in the Himalayan regions in the north. Though the government policy is to maintain at least 60% of the land as forest, the present ratio is higher, with a remarkable 72% of the country covered in forests of fir, mixed conifers, and temperate and broadleaf species.

An astonishing array of plants grow in Bhutan: over 5000 species, including 300 species of medicinal plants and over 50 species of rhododendron. Of the more than 600 species of orchid, most are commonly found up to 2100m, although some hardy species thrive even above 3700m.

Bhutan's heavy rain encourages tree growth. Forests are found up to 4500m and serve not only as a source of fuel, timber and herbs, but also as a cultural resource, as they form the basis of many folk songs and ritual offerings to the gods in the form of wood, flowers and leaves. The trees of the far eastern Himalaya are very different from those of the western Himalaya of India and Nepal.

Because glaciation had no impact on the lower reaches of the Himalaya, these foothills remain repositories of plants whose origins can be traced back before the ice age. This area is home to some of the most ancient species of vegetation on earth.

In Bhutan the vegetation profile falls into five general classes:

Tropical	up to 1000m
Subtropical	900m to 1800m
Temperate	1800m to 3500m
Subalpine	3500m to 4500m
Alpine	4500m to 5500m

Tropical & Subtropical
Tropical evergreen forests growing below 800m are repositories of unique biodiversity, but much of the rich vegetation at these lower elevations has been cleared for pasture and terraced farmland. In the next vegetation zone are the subtropical grasslands and forests, found between 900m and 1800m, along with forests of oak, walnut and sal, and numerous varieties of orchid.

Forests of sal, a hardwood used for building construction, are found in the south. Sal grows at elevations as high as 1250m, and is the dominant species wherever it occurs. The evergreen Indian laburnum, which bears vivid yellow flowers between April and June, is also found here. The distinctive flame of the forest bears vivid orange flowers between February and May.

The easily identifiable hemp, with its five-pointed leaves, grows on the perimeters of cultivated land and along road edges, even in Thimphu. Hemp has, of course, many uses other than the obvious one, and has been traditionally woven into rope and cloth. In Bhutan hemp is considered a weed and is fed to the pigs – imagine a pig with the 'munchies'!

The chir pine is a tall, straight conifer that appears on sunny slopes in the subtropical zone. It has long, often bright green, needles and medium-sized, oval cones. You can easily distinguish it from its relative, the blue pine, because the needles of the chir pine are in groups of three and those of the blue pine are shorter and in groups of five. The wood is used for rough furniture and boxes. The chir can be harvested for its resin, which is used to make rosin and turpentine.

Temperate

The temperate zone is a region of great diversity, largely influenced by the elevation. The tropical vegetation of the lower zones gives way to dark forests of oak, birch, maple, magnolia and laurel. On most hills, the sunny south side is forested with broadleaf species such as oak, and the damp, shady north side with rhododendron and conifers.

Above 2400m is the spruce, hemlock and weeping cypress, and higher still, growing up to the tree line, is the east Himalayan fir. A high-altitude variety of oak is found between 2250m and 2850m and above this are substantial forests of birch.

Throughout this zone you'll also find the poplar, willow, walnut, ash, aspen and magnolia. Conifers include the blue pine, hemlock, larch and fir. In the autumn you will see the mauve or pinkish flowers of the Himalayan wild cherry blooming in the hills between 1200m and 3000m.

Between March and May the hillsides are ablaze with the deep red flowers of the etho metho, the country's most famous rhododendron. There are 46 species of rhododendron that occur throughout the country at altitudes between 1200m and 4800m and ranging from small shrubs to 20m-high trees.

The blue pine is found at altitudes up to 4000m and is often mixed with juniper and birch trees. The wood of the blue pine is often used for roofing shingles and the bark of the tree is often cut to collect resin.

Subalpine & Alpine

Between the tree line and the snow line at about 5500m are low shrubs, rhododendron, Himalayan grasses and flowering herbs. Junipers are found in a dwarfed form at altitudes over 4000m. Their distinctive foliage, short prickly needles and fleshy, berry-like fruit, should be unmistakable. Also in this region are lichens, mosses and alpine flowers such as the tiny rhododendron nivale, edelweiss and varieties of primula.

As the snows begin to melt at the end of the long winter, the high-altitude grazing lands are carpeted with a multitude of wildflowers, which remain in bloom until early summer. After the onset of the monsoon, in July, a second and even more vibrant flowering occurs, which extends until the end of the monsoon, in late August or early September. Some of the varieties found at these higher elevations include anemones, forget-me-nots, dwarf irises, dwarf rhododendrons, primulas, delphiniums and ranunculus.

Blue Poppy The blue poppy, Bhutan's national flower, is a delicate blue- or purple-tinged bloom with a white filament. In Dzongkha it is known by the name *euitgel metog hoem*. It grows to nearly 1m tall, on the rocky mountain terrain found above the tree line (3500m to 4500m elevation). The flowering season occurs during the early monsoon, from late May to July, and the seeds yield oil. It is a monocarpic plant, which means that it blooms only once. It grows for several years, then flowers, produces seeds and dies. Poppies can be found atop some high passes from the far eastern parts of the country all the way across to the west.

At one time the blue poppy was considered to be myth, along with the yeti, because its existence was not confirmed. In 1933 a British botanist, George Sherriff, who was in Bhutan studying Himalayan flora, found the plant in the remote mountain region of Sakteng in eastern Bhutan. Despite this proof that the flower exists, few people have seen one; a mystique surrounds the species in the same way it does the snow leopard.

Useful Trees & Shrubs

As well as sal and the other trees just mentioned, several other forest species in Bhutan are important for commercial, medicinal and domestic purposes. The east Himalayan fir is used for roofing shingles and its leaves have medicinal properties. The wooden bowls that are used in Bhutan are made from burs of a variety of trees, including maple. Birch is used for the carved wooden blocks used to print Buddhist texts. The national tree is the weeping cypress, which is valued as timber and for producing incense. Oak is used extensively for firewood.

Lemongrass is harvested for essential oil production. Bhutanese handmade paper is made from the daphne plant, which grows at higher elevations, or from a lowland plant known as edgeworthia. Both of these plants are known as *dhey shing* or *dheykap* in Dzongkha.

In deciduous forests in the duars grows sissoo, used in furniture, and semal, which is used for matches, plywood and paper. The two plants that produce the ingredients in *doma* (betel nut) are also found here. The nut comes from the khair, a palm-like tree, and the leaf used to wrap it comes from the betel leaf vine.

FAUNA

Bhutan has 165 species of mammals. The region near Royal Manas National Park is home to a large variety of well-known south Asian game species.

Takins

The takin (see boxed text) looks like a cross between a gnu and a musk deer. It has an immense face and a tremendously thick neck. Short, thick legs support its heavy body, which rises to more than 1m at the shoulder. Takins live in north-western and far north-eastern Bhutan, although the most likely place to see one is in the mini-zoo in Thimphu.

Monkeys

Several species of monkey are found in Bhutan. Rhesus monkeys, earth coloured with short tails, travel on the ground in large, structured troops, and are unafraid of humans. Langurs are arboreal, and have black faces, grey fur and long limbs and tails. The rhesus's habitat ranges from the duars to 2400m, while the langur's goes higher, up to 3600m. Assamese macaques range from dark to yellowish-brown and have a short tail with no hair on the face.

Bhutan is the only place in the world where the golden langur is found; this small primate's existence was not even known to the scientific community until the 20th century. Not surprisingly, its distinctive feature is its golden coat, which varies in lightness from season to season, as well as by region. Its range is from the Puna Tsang Chhu in the west to the Manas river system in the east. If you are fortunate enough to see a golden langur, it will undoubtedly be in the trees, probably in open forest. The animal has a specially adapted stomach that allows it to digest leaves.

Elephants

The Asian elephant roams in and around the Royal Manas National Park and in the rainy season may travel far into the hills to the north. Elephants are also known to maintain matriarchal societies, and females up to 60 years of age bear calves. Though able to reach 80 years of age, elephants' life spans are determined by their teeth: Their molars are replaced as they wear down, but only up to six times. When the final set is worn, the elephant dies of starvation.

Snow Leopards

The snow leopard's extraordinarily beautiful coat – soft grey with black or dark grey spots – has, unfortunately, been its downfall worldwide. It has been hunted relentlessly and is now in danger of extinction. Elusive and elegant, the big cat is almost entirely solitary, largely because a single animal's hunting territory is so vast (about 10,000 sq km) and prey is scarce throughout the very high-altitude areas in which it lives. However, when its favourite prey, the blue sheep, migrates to lower valleys in winter, the snow leopard follows. It is then that the sexes might meet, although the females are only receptive to mating for one week.

Tigers

Of the world's large predators, the tiger is perhaps the most spectacular. Tigers are strongly territorial, like domestic cats, and basically solitary. Each male's territorial range is up to 100 sq km, and a female's range is only a little smaller. Though they are mostly concentrated in and around Royal Manas National Park, tigers may be

The Takin – Bhutan's National Animal

The reason for selecting the takin as the national animal is based both on its uniqueness and its strong association with the country's religious history and mythology. When the great saint Lama Drukpa Kunley, the Divine Madman, visited Bhutan in the 15th century, a large congregation of devotees gathered from around the country to witness his magical powers. The people urged the lama to perform a miracle.

However, the saint, in his usual unorthodox and outrageous way (see the boxed text 'The Divine Madman' in the Western Bhutan chapter), demanded that he first be served a whole cow and a goat for lunch. He devoured these with relish and left only the bones. After letting out a large and satisfied burp, he took the goat's head and stuck it onto the bones of the cow. And then with a snap of his fingers he commanded the strange beast to rise up and graze on the mountainside. To the astonishment of the people the animal arose and ran up to the meadows to graze. This animal came to be known as the *dong gyem tsey* (takin) and to this day these rather clumsy animals can be seen grazing on the mountainsides of Bhutan.

The takin continues to befuddle taxonomists, who cannot quite relate it to any other animal. The famous biologist George Schaller called it a 'beestung moose', referring to its humped nose and similarity in size to the North American moose. Taxonomists have now put it into a class by itself, *Budorcas taxicolor*.

The takin's grazing and browsing behaviour further befuddles its taxonomic status. In the open meadows takins behave like herd animals, such as the wildebeest of the Serengeti plains of Africa: These physically large animals stay in a herd and have horns to defend themselves in the open and exposed meadows. In the forest they behave like animals adapted to dense forests: The herd scatters and most animals remain solitary, much like deer.

In summer, takins migrate to subalpine forests and alpine meadows above 3700m and graze on the luxuriant grasses, herbs and shrubs found there. By migrating they escape the leeches, mosquitoes, horseflies, and other parasites of the monsoon-swept lower valleys. This is also the time when the vegetation in the alpine region is richest in nutrients. Thus, takins can gain several kilograms of storable energy: Some males become massive, weighing as much as 1000kg or more. Summer is also the time when takins mate. The gestation period is between seven and eight months, and young – usually a single calf – are born between December and February. These are black, in contrast to the golden yellow and brownish coat of the adults. Sometimes the Himalayan black bear will follow a pregnant female takin and immediately after she has given birth, chase her away and eat the calf.

In late August takins start their slow descent to the lower valleys. They do this in stages, grazing as they descend. They arrive at the winter grazing grounds in temperate broadleaf forests between 2000m and 3000m by late October.

Hunting is banned by law, and poaching is limited since there is no high economic value placed on the body parts of the takin. In traditional medicine, however, the horn of the takin, consumed in minute amounts, is supposed to help women during a difficult childbirth.

The major threats that the takin faces are competition with domestic yaks for food in the alpine regions and loss of habitat in the temperate regions. In the temperate zones, logging may have detrimental effects on the takin's survival.

Tashi Wangchuk

found throughout Bhutan, even at high altitudes, and as far north as Jigme Dorji National Park.

Several tiger conservation measures already have been implemented in Bhutan and, coupled with the strong protected-areas system, has provided a favourable environment for the animal. The protected regions of Bhutan and India provide sufficient habitat to sustain viable breeding populations.

Other Cats

Several species of cat share the tiger's habitat; these include the Asiatic golden cat, fishing cat, clouded leopard, common leopard and marbled cat.

Rhinos

The greater one-horned rhino is the largest of the three Asian species of rhino and belongs to a totally different genus to that of the two-horned African varieties. It has poor eyesight and, though weighing up to two tonnes, is amazingly quick.

Bears & Pandas

The Himalayan black bear is omnivorous and a bane to farmers growing corn in the temperate forests. Bears do occasionally attack humans, probably because their poor eyesight leads them to interpret that a standing person is making a threatening gesture. If a bear approaches to attack, the best defence is not to run, but to lie face down on the ground.

Black bears are known to roam in winter instead of hibernating. The common black bear is found at elevations below 2000m.

The sloth bear is a medium-sized bear with a shaggy black coat and a white U- or V-shaped mark on its chest. It eats mostly termites.

The red panda, or cat bear, is known in Bhutan as *aamchu donkha* and is most commonly found near Pele La, Thrumshing La and parts of the Gasa district. It is about 50cm tall, bright-chestnut coloured and has a white face. It is largely herbivorous, eating leaves, roots and grasses. The red panda is nocturnal, sleeping in trees during the day and coming to the ground to forage at night.

Wild Dogs

Jackals and wild dogs can be found both inside and outside of the protected regions.

Deer

The sambar, with its large, imposing antlers, is the largest deer in Bhutan. The barking deer, or muntjac, usually makes its presence known by its sharp, one-note alarm call. Both are found in forested areas up to 2400m.

The unusual musk deer, with antelope-like features, is only 50cm high at the shoulder and is taxonomically stranded between deer and antelopes. The male has no antlers, but has oversized canine teeth that protrude from its mouth. The male also has a musk gland in its abdomen, and the high value of musk as an ingredient in perfume has accelerated the demise of the species. This diminutive deer is very secretive and prefers forest cover near the tree line.

Sheep, Goats & Antelopes

The blue sheep, or bharal, is genetically defined somewhere between goats and sheep. It turns a bluish-grey in winter and is found in the Himalayan region from 1800m to 4300m. You will see large herds of blue sheep on many trek routes.

The Himalayan tahr is difficult to classify, though its niche is that of a 'mountain goat'. Except during the winter rutting season, these animals are found in two different kinds of herds, male and female. The males are sometimes seen alone and have long flowing manes and coats, and short, curved horns.

The Tibetan gazelle is found at elevations above 5000m in a few of the higher valleys opening into Tibet.

The brown goral is found only in the eastern Himalaya. It has small, backwards-facing horns and lives at elevations between 900m and 2400m, though it occasionally moves higher.

The serow is a large, thick-set animal whose coat ranges in colour from almost black to a shade of red. Its preferred habitat is wooded areas between 1800m and 3000m elevation.

Other Mammals

Other large mammals include the wolf, yak, wild water buffalo, gaur and wild pig. Fat marmots whistle as you pass their burrows in the high alpine pastures.

Birds

Each year Bhutan's extensive bird list grows longer, a consequence of both Bhutan's biodiversity and the small amount of systematic birding that has been done in the kingdom.

So far, 675 species have been recorded. This reflects the kingdom's wide range of vegetation profiles – from subtropical to alpine – and its location at the northern edge of the zoogeographical Indomalayan (Oriental) region and the permeable and fluid (for birds) border with China.

The variety of birds can be highly variable over a short distance and is also very seasonal. Bhutan is famous for its wintering populations of the vulnerable black-necked crane. Less well known are the winter populations, mainly as solitary individuals, of the endangered white-bellied heron, for which there are about five records in the last five years, including one on the Mo Chhu above Punakha.

Some bird species are even more transient, migrating through Bhutan between Tibet and northern India in autumn and spring. Pailas' fish eagle, which is considered rare, is regularly seen migrating up the Punak Chhu near Wangdue Phodrang in spring. It is often in the company of ospreys, a wide range of ducks, waders such as the pied avocet, and other species that breed in Tibet.

As well as the seasonal migrants, there is widespread internal migration. Winter brings numerous species down to lower altitudes, including accentors, rosefinches, grosbeaks, snow pigeons and pheasants such as the satyr tragopan, the Himalayan monal and the blood pheasant. Observant early-morning walkers can often find these on the mountains and passes around Thimphu. In the east of Bhutan, the rare Blyth's

The Black-Necked Crane

The rare and endangered black-necked crane occupies a special place in Bhutanese hearts and folklore. Its arrival every autumn from Tibet inspires songs and dances; it usually heralds the end of the harvesting season and also the time when farm families start migrating to warmer climates.

Many legends and myths exist about the bird, which the Bhutanese call *thrung thrung karmo*. Wetlands of the high mountain valleys of Phobjikha, Bomdeling and Gaytsa serve as the winter habitat for about 360 birds. Like other cranes, these have an elaborate mating ritual, a dance in which pairs bow, leap into the air and toss vegetation about while uttering loud bugling calls. It can be difficult to distinguish the sexes because the coloration is so similar, but the females are slightly smaller. The crane's preferred delicacies include fallen grain, tubers and insects.

The world's entire population of 5600 to 6000 black-necked cranes breed in Tibet and Ladakh. They winter in south-central Tibet and north-eastern Yunan province in China, as well as in Bhutan.

SARAH JOLLY

tragopan has been recorded. The Khalij pheasant is relatively common throughout the year. In summer many lowland species move to higher altitudes to breed; these species include the exotic-looking hoopoe, various species of minivets, cuckoos (one can commonly hear at least five different species calling), barbets, warblers, sunbirds, fulvettas and yuhinas.

Given the density of forest cover and the steep vertical descents, the road is often the best place from which to watch birds, as the traffic volume is very low. Recommended stretches include the road down from Dochu La to Wangdue Phodrang (the adventurous can take the old trail, which is even better), from Wangdue Phodrang to Nobding (on the way to Pele La), and before Trongsa. For those who go east, the 2000m descent between Sengor and Lingmethang is spectacular: Ward's trogon and the Rufous-necked hornbill have been recorded in this area. Trekking will provide you with a greater chance of seeing high-altitude birds, including the lammergeier, the Himalayan griffon, the raven, the unique high-altitude wader – the ibisbill – and pheasants.

Even the casual observer can be sure to see the blue whistling thrush (usually diving into a culvert), yellow-billed blue magpies, the wallcreeper (in jerky, crimson-streaked flight), white-capped water redstarts, plumbeous water redstarts and spotted nutcrackers in pine forest, and red-billed choughs on the roofs of dzongs.

Several bird guides for Bhutan are listed in Books in the Facts for the Visitor chapter. If you wish to know the calls – and this is often the only way of identifying reclusive or hidden species – then Scott Connop's tape *Birds Songs of the Himalaya* covers the calls of 70 species. The tape can be ordered through Wildsounds (☎ 44-1263-741100) or by mail order (ⓔ nhbs@nhbs.co.uk).

Endangered Species

All animals in Bhutan are protected by the Buddhist ethic that prohibits killing. As further protection, the 1995 Forest & Nature Conservation Act defines several species as totally protected. These are the Asian elephant, clouded leopard, golden langur, musk deer, pangolin, pygmy hog, snow leopard, takin, tiger, wild buffalo, black-necked crane, monal pheasant, peacock pheasant, raven, Rufous-necked hornbill, golden mahseer, spotted deer, gaur, leopard, leopard cat, Himalayan black bear, red panda and serow.

NATIONAL PARKS & PROTECTED AREAS

Protected areas constitute 26% of the country. In 1999 an additional 3800 sq km was designated as a network of biological corridors linking the nine protected areas.

All but three of the protected areas encompass regions in which there is a resident human population. Preserving the culture and fostering local tradition is part of the mandate of Bhutan's national-park system. The government has developed zoning policies and an integrated conservation and development program to allow people living within a protected area to farm, graze animals, collect plants and cut firewood in harmony with conservation and park management policies.

Bhutan established its national-park system to protect important ecosystems, and they have not been developed as tourist attractions. You won't find the kind of facilities you may normally associate with national parks, such as entrance stations, campgrounds and visitor centres (or even signs). In many cases you won't even be aware that you are entering or leaving a national park.

Jigme Dorji National Park

Jigme Dorji National Park is the largest protected area in the country, encompassing an area of 4329 sq km. It protects the western parts of Paro, Thimphu and Punakha Dzongkhags (districts) and almost the entire area of Gasa Dzongkhag. Habitats in the park range from subtropical areas at 1400m to alpine heights at 7000m. The park management has to cope with the needs of both lowland farmers and seminomadic yak herders. Villagers are also allowed to harvest a wide variety of indigenous plants for use in incense and traditional medicines.

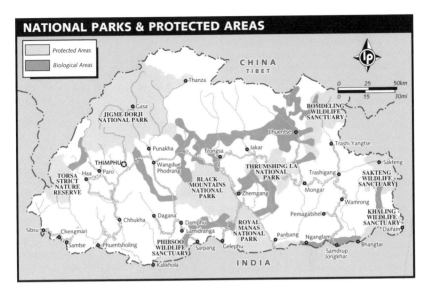

NATIONAL PARKS & PROTECTED AREAS

The park is the habitat of several endangered species, including the takin, snow leopard, blue sheep, tiger, musk deer, red panda, Himalayan black bear and serow. Other mammals to be found are leopard, wild dog, sambar, barking deer, goral, marmot and pika. More than 300 species of birds have been catalogued within the park.

Three of the country's major trekking routes pass through the park. Ecotourism guidelines have been established to prevent environmental damage. Management guidelines focus on overgrazing, sustainable harvesting of medicinal plants, firewood consumption, ecotourism and community development.

Royal Manas National Park

The 1023-sq-km Royal Manas National Park in south central Bhutan adjoins the Black Mountains National Park to the north and India's Manas National Park and Manas Tiger Reserve to the south. Together they form a 5000-sq-km protected area that runs from the plains to the Himalayan peaks.

The area has been protected as a wildlife sanctuary since 1966 and was upgraded to a national park in 1988. It is the home of

rhinos, buffalos, tigers, leopards, gaurs, bears, elephants and several species of deer. It is also home to several rare species, including the golden langur, capped langur, pygmy hog and hispid hare. The 362 species of birds in the park include four varieties of hornbills. Unfortunately, because of security problems related to separatist groups in India at the time of research, it was not safe to visit Manas.

Black Mountains National Park

The 1400-sq-km Black Mountains National Park protects the range of hills that separates eastern and western Bhutan. It is an important area because it includes virgin forests in an area that is generally known as the middle hills. This band of hills extends across the entire Himalayan foothills of Nepal and India and outside of Bhutan has largely been cleared of forests.

Plant life in the park includes a wide range of broadleaf species, conifers and alpine pastures. Animals include tigers, Himalayan black bears, leopards, red pandas, gorals, serows, sambars, wild pigs and golden langurs, and an amazing 449 species of birds have been catalogued. The Phobjikha valley,

Migoi – The Bhutanese Yeti

Naturally, Bhutanese yetis have different characteristics from yetis found (or not found) in Tibet and other Himalayan regions. The Bhutanese name for a yeti is *migoi* (strong man) and they are believed to exist throughout the northern part of the country.

The migoi is covered in hair that may be anything from reddish-brown to black, but its face is hairless, almost human. It is similar to the yetis of Nepal and Tibet in that the breasts of the female are large and sagging, and both sexes have an extremely unpleasant smell. But Bhutanese migoi are special because they have the power to become invisible, which accounts for the fact that so few people have seen them. Another feature that helps them escape detection is that the feet of many yetis face backwards, confusing people who try to follow them.

The book *Bhutanese Tales of the Yeti* by Kunzang Choden is a wonderful collection of tales told by village people in Bhutan who have seen, or have met people who have seen, a migoi.

wintering place of black-necked cranes, is included in the park.

Phibsoo Wildlife Sanctuary

A 278-sq-km area was set aside in 1974 as a wildlife reserve and upgraded to the Phibsoo Wildlife Sanctuary in 1993. On the southern border of Bhutan, about 50km east of Phuentsholing, it was established to protect the only remaining natural sal forest in Bhutan. Several protected species thrive in the sanctuary, including axis deer, chital, elephant, gaur, tiger, golden langur and hornbill.

Thrumshing La National Park

The 768-sq-km Thrumshing La National Park lies between Bumthang and Mongar. It was set aside to protect temperate forests of fir and chir pine. It is also home to red pandas and several endangered bird species including the Rufous-necked hornbill, Satyr tragopan and chestnut-breasted partridge.

Bomdeling Wildlife Sanctuary

The 1300-sq-km Bomdeling Wildlife Sanctuary protects most of the area of Trashi Yangtse Dzongkhag. Within the reserve is a large area of alpine tundra. The sanctuary protects the habitat of blue sheep, snow leopard, red panda, tiger, leopard, Himalayan black bear and musk deer. It also protects the Bomdeling area, which is an important roosting place of black-necked cranes. The sanctuary lies on the eastern border of Bhutan, adjoining a planned reserve in the Indian state of Arunachal Pradesh.

Sakteng Wildlife Sanctuary

The Sakteng Wildlife Sanctuary is unique because it is the only reserve in the world created specifically to protect the habitat of the yeti. It's in the easternmost part of the country, where 650 sq km of temperate forests of eastern blue pine and rhododendron are protected. This sanctuary lies on the Indian border and adjoins a planned national park in India.

Khaling Wildlife Sanctuary

In far south-eastern Bhutan, 273 sq km have been set aside as the Khaling Wildlife Sanctuary. Wild elephants, gaurs, pygmy hos, hispid hares and other tropical wildlife are protected here. This sanctuary adjoins a comparable reserve in India.

Torsa Strict Nature Reserve

The Torsa reserve is in the western part of the Haa district, where the Torsa river enters from Tibet. The 644-sq-km reserve was set aside to protect the temperate forests and alpine meadows of far west Bhutan and is the only protected area with no resident human population.

GOVERNMENT & POLITICS

The present form of the legislative, judicial and administrative systems in Bhutan was established in 1968 as part of the late King Jigme Dorji Wangchuck's modernisation program.

In many ways, the government has assumed a very protective role. This is possible because of the small population and compact size of the country. The king and senior government officials are very concerned about issues of development, education and health care, and environmental and cultural preservation.

This protectiveness also extends to various aspects of tourism. While many aspects of the tourism policy are designed to protect Bhutan's culture, economy and environment from excessive influence from tourists, some controls are intended to safeguard tourists themselves from harm. Most of the southern part of Bhutan is off-limits because of the danger of attacks from militant Indian separatist groups that have sought refuge inside Bhutan.

The government makes an effort to explain the reasoning behind the many rules and regulations it implements and people generally comply with established procedures for taxes, licensing and social standards. Even drivers follow the rules, though this is also the only way to survive when driving on Bhutan's narrow roads.

Bhutan's six development goals, as expressed by the present king, Jigme Singye Wangchuck, are:

- Self-reliance
- Sustainability
- Efficiency and development of the private sector
- People's participation and decentralisation
- Human-resource development
- Regionally balanced development

The National Assembly

The Tshogdu, or National Assembly, meets once a year. It has 150 members, all of whom serve three-year terms and fall into three categories. The largest group, with 105 members, are the *chimis*, representatives of Bhutan's 20 dzongkhags. Each household has a vote in village elections and the *gups* (village headmen or headpersons) elect the chimi. The *zhung dratshang* (clergy) elect 10 monastic representatives and another 35 representatives are senior civil servants nominated by the government. These appointees include the *dzongdags* (district governors), ministers, secretaries of various government departments and other high-ranking officials.

Bhutanese Symbols

The National Flag

The upper half of the flag is yellow, signifying the secular authority of the king. It is the colour of fruitful action, both in the affairs of religion and of the state.

The lower half of the flag is orange, representing the religious practice and spiritual power of Buddhism as it is manifested in the Kagyu and Nyingma lineages.

The *druk* (dragon) honours the thunder dragon after which the country is named. White represents purity and expresses the loyalty of the country's various ethnic and linguistic groups. The snarling mouth of the druk expresses the stern strength of the male and female deities protecting Bhutan. In the druk's claws are jewels representing the country's wealth and perfection.

The National Anthem

In the Thunder Dragon Kingdom adorned with sandalwood,
The protector who guards the teachings of the dual system,
He, the precious and glorious ruler, causes dominion to spread,
While his unchanging person abides in consistency,
As the doctrine of the Lord Buddha flourishes,
May the sun and peace of happiness shine on the people.

The Raven Crown

The crown of Bhutan is known as Usa Jaro Jongchen. Its brim is embroidered with a motif called Jachung and on the top is the head of a raven. This symbol is in recognition of the protective deity Mahakala. On the head of the raven are a sun and moon, together a symbol of longevity, steadfastness and enlightenment, and the Norbu, a sacred gem symbolising the fulfilment of right endeavour.

The Tshogdu elects a speaker who presides over the meetings and may call special sessions when the need arises. The Tshogdu enacts legislation and advises the government on all matters of national importance. Decisions are passed by a simple majority, though a secret ballot is sometimes used for certain issues. Any Bhutanese over the age of 25 can be a candidate for election as a chimi.

In June 1998 the king instituted major political reforms and devolved all executive authority to an elected council of ministers. He also pushed through a proposal to introduce a vote of confidence in the Druk Gyalpo, emphasising that it was vital for the present and future wellbeing of the nation. In December 2001, as part of the continuing evolution of Bhutan's political system, the king appointed a committee to draft Bhutan's first written constitution.

The Royal Advisory Council

A body known as the Lodey Tsokgdey, or Royal Advisory Council, was formally established in 1965 to advise the king and government ministers on important questions and to supervise the implementation of programs and policies laid down by the Tshogdu. The chairman is appointed by the king. There are six representatives of the people and two from the monk bodies.

The Council of Ministers

The Lhengyal Shungtshog, or Council of Ministers, is composed of the *lyonpos* (ministers) of the government departments and nine Royal Advisory Councillors. The seven ministries are: Home Affairs; Trade, Industry and Power; Health and Education; Finance; Foreign Affairs; Agriculture; and Communication. Until 1998 lyonpos were appointed by the king, and many served for extended periods, including Lyonpo Dawa Tshering, who holds a place in the *Guinness Book of Records* as the world's longest-serving foreign minister (1972–98). Since the political reforms of 1998, lyonpos are elected by the National Assembly. The chairmanship of the Lhengyal Shungtshog, and therefore the position of head of government, is held in rotation among the Lyonpos for one-year terms.

The Monastic Order

Religious institutions gain important patronage from the government. The state supports about 5000 monks in various monk bodies collectively known as the *sangha*. The Je Khenpo is the chief abbot of Bhutan and the head of the monastic establishment. The office is an elected one and the present incumbent is the 70th in an unbroken succession of Je Khenpos since the office was created by the Shabdrung in 1637. The Je Khenpo is chosen by members of the dratshang, who send the nomination to the king for his consent.

The dratshang is presided over by the Je Khenpo, who is the spiritual head of Bhutan. The Je Khenpo is the only person besides the King who wears the saffron scarf (see the boxed text 'Ceremonial Scarves' later in this chapter), an honour denoting his authority over all religious institutions.

The Judiciary

Bhutan's legal code, both civil and criminal, is based on that laid down by Ngawang Namgyal, the first Shabdrung. While a number of modifications have been made, the code preserves the spirit and substance of traditional Buddhist precepts. The present laws, called the Thrimshung Chenmo (Supreme Laws), were enacted by the National Assembly in 1957 and were updated when a comprehensive new legal code was adopted in July 2001.

Minor litigation is practically a national pastime in Bhutan. Most disputes are settled at the local level by gups or the chimi. The legal system encourages compromise and arbitration to avoid the expense of going to court. The Bhutanese legal system does not have a formal system of solicitors and lawyers, but it does permit those accused in criminal cases to appoint a trained paralegal counsel, called a *jambi*, to represent them.

The UN Commission on Human Rights operated a program in 1996 to train Bhutanese judges and paralegals on international standards of the administration of justice. Police officers also attended courses on human rights and law enforcement.

Each dzongkhag has its own *dzongkhag thrimkhang* (district court), which is headed by a *thrimpon* (district magistrate). The Thrimkhang Gongma (High Court) was established in 1968, with both original and appellate jurisdictions. The high court has eight judges, presided over by a chief justice. All citizens are treated equally in the eyes of the law, and if they feel they have been treated unfairly by the court system, everyone has the right to make an appeal to the king – and many people do.

Autonomous Bodies

The government includes several other independent institutions, some of which are unique to Bhutan.

National Commission for Cultural Affairs

Known as the Solzin Lhentshog, the National Commission for Cultural Affairs (NCCA), was established in 1985 and is responsible for preserving Bhutan's religious and cultural heritage. The council, under the chairmanship of the home affairs minister, administers the National Museum, National Library, Royal Academy of Performing Arts and the Textile Museum in Thimphu.

National Environment Commission

An independent national commission, the National Environment Commission (NEC), is charged with making and regulating policies to manage and preserve the country's natural resources and legislate the country's environmental management. The commission was created in 1989 and includes ministers and secretaries from several related government departments. The NEC developed an environmental strategy for Bhutan called the 'middle path' and recently formulated environmental-assessment legislation requiring environmental clearance for all development projects.

Council for Ecclesiastical Affairs

Known as the Dratshang Lhentshog, the nine-member Council for Ecclesiastical Affairs is presided over by the Je Khenpo. This body is responsible for preserving the purity of religious teaching, ensuring the wellbeing of the monk body and administering religious establishments.

Dzongkha Development Commission

An independent body advances Dzongkha, the national language, and coordinates all linguistic matters. Its activities include producing school textbooks and establishing standards for transliterating Dzongkha to English.

Royal Civil Service Commission

The Department of Manpower, which was established in 1973, was renamed the Royal Civil Service Commission in 1992 and is responsible for developing and implementing the civil service's personnel policies.

Royal Audit Authority

An independent commission, the Royal Audit Authority, is responsible for auditing the accounts of all ministries, divisions, dzongkhag administrations and projects.

Royal Monetary Authority

The functions of Bhutan's central bank are performed by the Royal Monetary Authority. It issues banknotes and coins and supervises Bhutan's two commercial banks.

Royal Institute of Management

Training and development of the country's public-administration system is performed by the Royal Institute of Management, based in Simtokha.

National Technical Training Authority

The NTTA oversees vocational training and administers the two technical schools in Kharbandi as well as the National Institute for Zorig Chusum (the national art institute) and the National Driver Training Institute.

Local Government

The dzongs are the focal points of every district's administration, as well as its economic, social and religious affairs. The country is divided into 20 administrative districts called dzongkhags, each with a district administrator, called a dzongdag, who is responsible to the home minister. *Rabdeys* (district monk bodies) are based in dzongs and are presided over by an abbot, who is called the *lam neten*.

DZONGKHAGS (ADMINISTRATIVE DISTRICTS)

Larger dzongkhags are divided into smaller subdistricts called *dungkhags*, which are presided over by a *dungpa*.

The lowest administrative level is the *gewog* (block), headed by an elected official known as a gup (pronounced to rhyme with 'cup'). A gup is elected by the people of the community for a three-year term. Because of regional linguistic differences, these officials are called *mandals* in the south. Village or block councils are called Gewog Yargay Tshokchung, commonly referred to by the initials GYT.

The next level of community forum is the dzongkhag development council, known as the 'Dzongkhag Yargay Tshokchung', or DYT. These are citizen groups that can make recommendations to the Tshogdu through their representative, the local chimi. Because Bhutan is such a small country, many issues that in other places would be strictly local matters are dealt with at the national level.

ECONOMY

The per-capita income in 2000 was US$656. One reason for the low figure is that 85% of the population is engaged in subsistence farming and has minimal cash income. Subsistence farming means just that; if the farmer doesn't take care of the crops, or there is some natural disaster, the family has no food.

Only 7.8% of the land is used for agriculture. Most of this is in the south and valleys up to 3000m. Crops are maize, rice, millet, wheat, buckwheat, barley, mustard, potatoes, vegetables, oranges, apples and cardamom. Most households raise cattle or, in the high country, yaks.

Though the vast majority of the population still farms, the agricultural sector's share of gross domestic product has dropped to less than 35% as sale of hydroelectric power has contributed a larger share of the national income.

The Department of Mines enforces the government's conservation policies that control mining and quarrying. Small mines, mostly in the south, produce gypsum, limestone, dolomite, coal, talc, marble and slate.

Hydroelectric Power

The export of power already provides 40% of government revenue. Bhutanese officials see the export of electricity as the key to gaining economic independence. The government's policy is that the future backbone of the economy will be power. Hydroelectric power is Bhutan's largest resource and is sustainable, renewable and environmentally friendly. The government wants to eventually fund the country's entire budget by selling power.

Bhutan's other resources include forests and minerals, but it has so far chosen not to exploit them in a big way. Its strategy gives priority to conservation, and its hydroelectric projects are based mainly on 'run of the river' designs rather than large dams. Although this type of hydro scheme avoids the submergence of land and forests and the forced relocation of residents that is often associated with major dam construction, it still has some environmental impact. During the winter months, when the river flow is low, a very high percentage of the total flow may be needed to power the turbines. This changes the volume and hydrology of the river system, and may affect silt clearance and fish breeding.

Power engineers estimate that the country has the potential to generate as much as 30,000MW. The Chhukha project is already generating 336MW, 78% of which is exported. The Tala project, also on the Wang Chhu, was started in 1996 and is planned to come on line in 2006 with a capacity of 1,020MW. Others include the 60MW project on the Kuri Chhu near Mongar and the 60MW Austrian-aided Basochhu project near Wangdue Phodrang.

Despite the abundance of hydroelectric power in Bhutan, many rural homes are without electricity. Because it is expensive to construct power transmission lines to small villages in the hills, a portion of the income from the sale of hydroelectric power goes to developing local sources of energy.

Micro-hydroelectric facilities are being constructed to serve rural communities throughout the country. The country has also embarked on a program of introducing solar power into remote areas. The government's rural energy unit has a goal of solar-electrifying all schools and monasteries where hydroelectric power is infeasible.

Exports

As well as electricity, Bhutan exports calcium carbide, wood products and cement. Its other major export is agricultural products, including apples, canned fruit and jam. A new cash crop being successfully exported is mushrooms. More than 457 varieties of mushrooms are grown in Bhutan, of which 137 varieties are edible. The *matsutake* mushroom, known in Bhutan as *sangay shamu*, is exported to Japan, Singapore, Thailand and India. These mushrooms are found in Thimphu, Bumthang, Haa and Paro. With the help of the National Mushroom Project, farmers are also cultivating shiitake mushrooms in Thimphu and the east.

Other exports include ferrosilicon and cement. Bhutan no longer exports unprocessed logs, but the Bhutan Board Company is producing high-quality furniture from chipboard. Large trading partners are India and Bangladesh.

Stamps One of Bhutan's more unusual exports is postage stamps. The post office has produced an extensive collection of exotic stamps, including some made of metal and silk, others with three-dimensional images and even stamps that are mini-phonograph records. Many of the stamps have Bhutanese themes – dzongs, flowers and animals are commonly portrayed. Other, peculiar collections portray things such as Roman emperors or Mickey Mouse and other Disney characters.

Essential-Oil Production Oil is extracted from lemongrass, a fast-growing plant found throughout eastern Bhutan. It is distilled in local factories using large stainless-steel boilers. The resulting oil is exported for use in perfume and as a deodorising agent in detergent and phenol. (For more information see the boxed text 'Essential Oil' in the Eastern Bhutan chapter.)

Development Policy
The government's policy is to restrain development to try to prevent failures, rather than allowing uncontrolled development and having to correct problems later.

Overall, Bhutan remains cautious about foreign influences. It allowed the American soft-drink manufacturer Pepsi to build a manufacturing plant only in 1997, and did not embrace television or the Internet until 1999.

Efforts are being made to develop growth centres in rural areas to discourage migration to the cities. The decision to locate the country's only college in the rural community of Kanglung in eastern Bhutan is an example of this strategy. Other schools and government facilities have been built in rural areas to encourage shopkeepers to look towards smaller markets rather than concentrating only on larger towns.

An ambitious ninth five-year plan was launched in 2001. The previous plan emphasised developing health, education, communication, roads and hydroelectric power. When it was implemented the king visited every district in the country and held meetings, at which each household was represented, to explain the plan to the people and to discuss their needs and problems.

Foreign Aid
In 1999 Bhutan received US$75 million in foreign grants and aid, most of it from India, Japan and Western Europe. Its total 1998–99 budget was Nu 7.28 billion (about US$167 million), with most going towards major construction efforts such as hydroelectric projects.

The government is quite concerned that socioeconomic development should not lead to deterioration of either the people's way of life or their traditional values. Each project is scrutinised and may be slowed or stopped if it affronts religious faith or adversely affects the environment.

A fancy pseudo–Bhutanese-style building north of the post office in Thimphu houses the various UN agencies that operate in Bhutan. The United Nations Development Programme (UNDP) in Bhutan focuses on poverty reduction, improving the public sector, supporting environmental management and energy development. It also works to promote gender equality in decision making at all levels as well as fostering public access to and use of information and communications technologies for economic and social development.

Other important international agencies are the Asian Development Bank, World Bank, WWF and several development agencies of the European Union. In addition to the large assistance provided by India, Bhutan has development ties with Japan, Switzerland, Denmark, Austria, the Netherlands, Canada, Australia and New Zealand.

POPULATION & PEOPLE
Population
The estimated population of Bhutan in 2001 was 690,000, with 42% of the population aged under 15. As a result of a family-planning advocacy campaign the population growth rate is 2.5% per year, down from 3.1% in 1994, which was then one of the highest in the world. As in many non-industrialised countries, the high infant mortality rate in the past induced people to have more children. With the introduction of better medical facilities, many more children now survive.

The government is keenly aware that an increased population will strain the country's resources. At present, Bhutan has a ratio of resources to population that provides adequate housing and food as well as an unspoiled environment. The government is working to introduce measures that will reduce the growth rate. They include birth control, provision of better education and increased employment opportunities for women.

The country is still predominantly rural and 66% of the population are farmers. An estimated 80% of the population lives more than an hour's walk from a road and as much as 50% lives more than one day of walking from a motorable road. The urban population is increasing and is now estimated at 21%.

There is some confusion over the discrepancy between a population figure of 1.2 million, which was published by the UN, and the current estimate of about 700,000.

In 1971, when Bhutan applied for UN membership, the population was estimated at just less than one million. No census data existed and government officials estimated the population as best they could, choosing to err on the high side in order to help gain world recognition. Over the years, this figure was adjusted upwards in accordance with estimates of Bhutan's population growth figures, finally reaching the 1.2 million figure. In some publications this total has even been listed at 1.5 million!

Ethnic Groups

The population can be categorised into three main ethnic groups.

The Sharchops, who live in the east of the country, are recognised as the original inhabitants of Bhutan. They are Indo-Mongoloid; it is still unclear exactly where they migrated from and when they arrived in Bhutan. Their name, Sharchop, is translated as 'people of the east'.

The Ngalop are descendants of Tibetan immigrants who arrived in Bhutan from the 9th century. These immigrants settled in the west of the country; Ngalops dominate the region west of the Black Mountains. The Ngalops and Sharchops are collectively known as Drukpas, and account for about 65% of the population.

The third group is the people of Nepali descent, who began settling in the south of Bhutan in the late 19th century. Called the Lhotshampa, they represent numerous Nepali-speaking ethnic groups – primarily Brahman, Chettri, Gurung, Rai and Limbu, but also Newars.

Several smaller groups, many with their own language, form about 1% of the population. Many of these groups comprise fewer than 1000 people. The most important of these groups are the Bumthap in Bumthang, the Mandhep in Trongsa, the Khyeng in the central region of Zhemgang,

and the Layap in the north-west. Other smaller groups are the Brokpa in the far eastern villages of Merak and Sakteng, the Doya and Lhopu in the southern district of Samtse, the Dagpa in the east, Tibetans in the central-west and north and the Lepcha in the west.

Health

Once ranked as having one of the world's poorest health standards, Bhutan has made great efforts to improve health facilities and now provides free health care to all its citizens. It has achieved a child immunisation rate of nearly 100%, iodine deficiency has been eliminated and 73% of the rural population has access to safe drinking water.

Life expectancy has increased from 47.4 years in 1984 to 66 years in 2000. Infant mortality was once the highest in the world, at 142 per thousand births; by 2001 it had been reduced to 60.5 per thousand births.

Health care in Bhutan is provided on a four-tiered network consisting of the National Referral Hospital in Thimphu, two regional referral hospitals and smaller hospitals in the headquarters of each district. Rural health care is provided through a network of Basic Health Units (BHUs) staffed by a health assistant, nurse-midwife and a basic health worker; 78% of the population has access to a BHU within a two-hour walk. These medical practitioners also serve a role similar to 'walking doctors' and provide services to more distant villages through a system of outreach clinics that they visit on a regular schedule.

EDUCATION

Until the 1950s the only education available in Bhutan was from the monasteries. To obtain a secular education, students travelled to schools in Darjeeling. While monastic education continues to play an important role in Bhutan, Western-style education has been expanded and is now available throughout the country. Literacy has increased from 28% in 1984 to 54% in 1996 and this is being further enhanced through adult education programs.

Primary & Secondary Education

The government's goal is to have 95% of the school-age population attending school, though a lack of teachers and a variety of cultural problems are making the goal difficult to achieve. Often children don't start school until they are eight or nine years old and there are still more boys than girls attending school. School time is 8.30am to 3.30pm and the annual holiday is in winter, from 17 December to 9 March.

Since 1961 the medium of instruction has been English. Dzongkha, the national language, is taught as a second language. One reason for this arrangement was the shortage of Bhutanese teachers when the educational system was established. It has proved to be a wise decision and has enabled Bhutanese students to gain an excellent, international-standard education at universities in Asia, Europe, Australia and the US.

Many of Bhutan's teachers are still hired from India, particularly the southern state of Kerala, but their numbers are diminishing as Bhutan produces more trained teachers.

The educational structure provides for 11 years of basic schooling: one year of pre-primary schooling, six years of primary, two years of junior high and two years of high school. Students have to undergo an examination to move from primary school to junior high, and another to graduate from junior high to high school, and an effort is made to channel those who fail into vocational training programs.

Education is aimed at providing basic literacy skills and a knowledge of Bhutan's history, geography and traditions. It is a very interesting reflection on Bhutan's value system to discover that the other important subjects are agriculture, environment, health, hygiene, population and moral science. The schools employ a contemporary system of activity-based learning to teach these subjects. There is even an emphasis on the use of computers in high schools.

Most villages in Bhutan have community or primary schools. There are 59 junior high schools, 26 high schools, one college and ten specialised training institutes. Several of the high schools also provide junior college

facilities. Free education and textbooks are provided to all students until they reach tertiary level. Morning prayers and the national anthem start the day for all students throughout the kingdom. It is quite a spectacle to see several hundred children in national dress lined up and singing in the morning sunshine.

One of the major issues facing Bhutan's education system – and perhaps the entire country – is described in the documents of the eighth five-year plan under the heading *Students' Expectations*:

One of the growing concerns facing the development of education in Bhutan is the increasing expectation among students for 'white-collar' employment in government. Related to this is the general reluctance to undertake any manual work and the preference, instead, for office-related jobs no matter how unproductive and lowly paid these may be. This has led to the disproportionate demand for academic education compared to training in technical and agricultural skills, which has further contributed to the emerging problems related to youth and rural-urban migration. While these problems are a reflection of wider social and economic influences, education is perceived as playing a pivotal role and, therefore, there is an increasing call from public and private sector institutions, as well as from parents, for the education system to tackle them.

Tertiary Education

A key aspect of Bhutan's development plan involves training doctors, engineers and other professionals. Tertiary education involves two years of junior college and a three-year undergraduate program. With only one college, the country relies heavily on donor assistance to send young graduates to foreign universities. Sherubtse College at Kanglung in eastern Bhutan is affiliated with Delhi University.

Teachers are trained in the National Institute of Education, which has facilities in Paro and Samtse.

Vocational Schools & Religious Training

The Royal Institute of Management (RIM) was established in 1968 to train government administrators. It also has an innovative

The First Rule

In a mountain village named Laya, I was standing in a schoolhouse and staring at a document entitled *Manual for Teachers of Mathematics*. What caught my eye was something offered as a 'first rule':

Always remember that you are a human being as well as a teacher, that your students are also human beings, and that you are here because you have something important to give them that they need.

It is not what one would expect as a first rule for maths teachers anywhere else in the world. But this is Bhutan, and in Bhutan, I am learning, people are not the abstract ciphers they can come to be in a more urban environment. They are human beings who, even in official matters, tend to deal with each other as human beings. 'I am not as much concerned about the Gross National Product', the king is supposed to have said, 'as I am about the Gross National Happiness'.

Robert Peirce

program that teaches accounting, typing and the use of computers to people who have left school without qualifications. It offers 11 one- or two-year training programs in fields such as accounting, auditing and administrative management. It runs special courses such as an Environmental Education and Awareness program for chimis and also conducts two four-week orientation courses per year for newly arrived international volunteers. RIM also provides a refresher course in traditional values and etiquette for university graduates who return from courses abroad.

Other teaching facilities are the Royal Bhutan Polytechnic and the Royal Technical Institute, both at Kharbandi, north of Phuentsholing, under the direction of the National Technical Training Authority.

Monastic education is important, taking place in *shedras* (Buddhist colleges) and *drubdras* (meditation centres) inside dzongs and goembas.

A particularly interesting form of education is the *rigney* curriculum where modern education and technology are blended with Buddhist values. Rigney is a Choekey (classical Tibetan) term derived from *rig* (science or craft) and *ney* (domain or place), but it is commonly used loosely to refer to the study of Buddhist literature.

Environmental Education

Environmental and nature conservation studies are part of the school curriculum from primary school all the way through to college. The RSPN works to enhance this study through its program of nature clubs.

WWF has been helping the Sherubtse College develop an environmental studies program, and the college conducts environmental workshops and training programs on campus.

ARTS

Bhutanese tradition defines its artistic heritage as *zorig chusum* ('zo' – ability to make, 'rig' – science or craft, 'chusum' – thirteen), the 13 arts and crafts.

All Bhutanese art, dance, drama and music has its roots in the Buddhist religion. Paintings are not done for sale, but for specific purposes. Festivals are not quaint revivals, but are living manifestations of a long tradition and national faith. Almost all representation in art, music and dance is a dramatisation of the struggle between good and evil.

Bhutanese arts and crafts have been undergoing a period of revival in recent years. This is a result of both increased wealth of patrons and also the government's emphasis on preserving and promoting the nation's rich cultural heritage.

The Purpose of Bhutanese Buddhist Art

According to Bhutanese tradition, the arts are concerned with interpreting values rather than describing facts. The artist is trying to transmit in symbols, shapes or signs something that contains a spark of that eternal stream of life or consciousness that abides when material forms decay. An artist's basic aim is to teach, by the symbolic value of their art, the way to the spiritual experience of which their work is the outward and visible sign. The issue of whether Buddhist art is 'beautiful' or not is irrelevant to its intended purpose.

The Artistic Tradition in Bhutan

The development of a high order of Buddhist arts and crafts in Bhutan may be traced to the 15th-century terton Pema Lingpa, who was an accomplished painter, sculptor and architect. The country's artistic tradition received a further boost when, in 1680, under instructions from the Shabdrung (himself an artist), the fourth desi, Gyalse Tenzin Rabgye, opened the School of Bhutanese Arts and Crafts, which is now called the National Institute for Zorig Chusum.

Traditional Bhutanese artistry is maintained through the support of all levels of society. The royal family, nobility and clergy have provided continued zealous patronage. Meanwhile, the common people support the arts because they depend on artisans to provide the wide variety of wooden and metal objects indispensable to typical Bhutanese households and painting both inside and outside of homes.

Bhutanese art has two main characteristics: it is religious and anonymous. The Bhutanese consider commissioning paintings and statues as pious acts, which gain merit for the *jinda* (patron). The name of the jinda is sometimes written on the work so that their pious act may be remembered. Often the artist is a religious man who also gains merit from creating the work. However, the artist's name is almost never mentioned.

Because the iconographical conventions in Bhutanese art are very strict, the first responsibility of the Bhutanese artist is to observe them scrupulously. However, artists can also express their own personality in minor details or scenes.

Paintings and sculptures are executed by monks or laymen who work in special workshops. The disciples of a master do all the preliminary work, while the fine work is executed by the master himself.

The Thirteen Arts & Crafts

Even such seemingly mundane activities as carpentry, blacksmithing and weaving are part of Bhutan's heritage of zorig chusum, and are therefore integral elements of Buddhist artistic tradition.

Painting Drawing and painting is called *lhazo* and encompasses all types of painting, including *thangkas* (religious pictures), wall paintings and decorative paintings. Proficiency in lhazo is basic to all other arts. The geometric proportions and iconography that are essential to Buddhist art are important parts of the school of painting.

Carpentry Woodworking for the construction of dzongs, monasteries, houses and household goods is called *shingzo* (wood art).

Carving The art of carving in wood, slate and stone is *parzo*. Parzo plays an important part in the Tibetan Buddhist tradition because most religious texts are printed from wooden blocks on which monks have laboriously carved a mirror image of the text.

Sculpture Mud work, known as *jinzo*, includes the making of clay statues and ritual objects such as drum stands, *torma* (ritual cakes) and masks. Most large statues are made by forming plaster or mud on a hollow frame and are part of this tradition. Jinzo is understood specifically as the making of statues and ritual objects, but may also be applied to construction works using mortar, plaster and rammed earth.

Casting *Lugzo* applies to two types of casting: sand casting and the lost-wax method. Lugzo craftsmen produce statues, bells and ritual instruments. The term is also used for jewellery and less exotic items such as kitchen goods.

Blacksmithing The *garzo* tradition is the manufacture of iron goods such as swords, knives, chisels, axes, spades, shovels, darts, helmets, chains and plough blades.

The Special Role of Painting

Other than its spectacular architecture, the most visible manifestation of Bhutanese art is painting. Bhutanese tradition defines three forms of painting: thangkas, wall paintings and statues. A painting may depict a deity, a legend or religious story, a meditational object or an array of auspicious symbols, but it is always religious in nature. Despite the religious aspect of the painting, many artists are laymen, not monks.

A monastery may sponsor paintings, but most are commissioned by a lay person, often a noble or member of the royal family, as an act of merit making. The jinda often specifies the central figure, which is usually a favourite deity important to the achievement of certain personal goals. The main figure may be surrounded by other related deities or by prescribed designs that include clouds, flowers, trees, scrolls and geometric borders.

Paintings, in particular the portrayal of human figures, are subject to strict rules of iconography. The proportions and features must be precise, and there is no latitude for artistic licence in these works. The initial layout is constructed with a series of geometrical patterns using straight lines to lay out the proportions of the figure. These proportions are well defined in religious documents called *zuri pata*. In other cases the initial sketch is made with a stencil providing the basic outline of the figures. The outline is transferred to the canvas by patting the stencil with a bag filled with chalk dust.

Paints are traditionally made from earth, minerals and vegetables, though in recent times chemical colours are also used. The material is first reduced into powder and then mixed with water, glue and chalk. The brushes are made from twigs and animal hair. The colours are applied in a particular order laden with symbolic meaning.

Thangkas are painted on canvas that is stretched and lashed to a wooden frame. When the work is completed it is removed from the frame and surrounded by a border of colourful brocade, with wooden sticks at the top and bottom used for hanging. Although some thangkas are hung permanently, most are rolled up and stored until they are exhibited at special events. This applies particularly to the huge *thondrols* that are displayed for a short time in the early morning from the front of dzongs during a tsechu. Thondrols are often classified as paintings because they follow the normal rules of iconography, but they are usually applique.

The inner walls of dzongs and *lhakhangs*, or temples, are usually covered with paintings. In Bhutan most wall murals are painted on a thin layer of cloth applied to the wall using a special paste. Old paintings are treasured because of their historic and artistic value, but this was not always the case in the past. Many old wall paintings were repainted because the act of painting gives merit to both the jinda and the artist.

Over the centuries, Bhutanese style has become more and more ornate, with increasingly lavish use of gold paint and landscape elements treated in the Chinese manner. Many of the paintings are inscribed with the names of the figures represented, which help to date the works.

Many Bhutanese paintings favour a central composition with adjacent figures. Examples of these paintings are found in the monasteries of Taktshang, Tango and Phajoding. Other artists use the entire space and the interest is not focused on one main figure. Sometimes, the paintings illustrate scenes of a famous person's life around a central figure. An example is the illustration of the life of Milarepa in Paro Dzong.

Most statues are finely painted to sharply define the facial features. Many religious statues in lhakhangs, especially the larger statues, are made from clay. In addition to the face, the entire surface of these large figures is painted, often in a gold colour, giving them a bronze aspect. On bronze statues, some of which are quite small, only the face is painted. The amount a statue has been painted helps determine from a distance whether that statue is made of clay or bronze.

Bamboo Work The art of working with cane and bamboo is *tshazoo*. These craftsmen produce bows and arrows, *bangchung* (baskets) to carry food, *zem* and *palang* for storing and carrying *arra* and *chang* (local drinks), *belo* (bamboo hats), *redi* (bamboo mats), *lachu* and *bohm* for storing grains and *balep* (bamboo thatch).

Goldsmithing & Silversmithing The art of working with gold and silver is called *serzo ngulzo*. These craftsmen produce objects ranging from household goods to jewellery to ritual objects. Some of these objects include *koma japtha* (brooches and chains), *thingkhap* (rings), *chaka timi* and *batha* (cases for carrying doma – betel nut), *dung* (ritual trumpets), *dorji* (thunderbolt symbols) and *gau* (Buddhist amulets).

Weaving The entire process of weaving, from preparation of yarn, to dyeing and eventually to the final weaving is called *thagzo*. See the special section 'The Warp & the Weft' in the Eastern Bhutan chapter.

Embroidery The art of working with needle and thread is *tshemzo*. There are two categories of tshemzo. *Tshendrup* is embroidery, and includes traditional boot making. The second is *lhendrup* (applique), the technique of sewing pieces of cloth onto a background to produce a picture. This process is used in thondrols such as the ones displayed at dzongs during tsechus.

Masonry The art of cutting and stacking stone walls is called *dozo*. This term is especially applied to the construction of the huge stone outer walls of dzongs, monasteries and other buildings.

Leather Work The art of working with leather is *kozo*. These craftsmen produce such items as *gayu*, the leather bags for carrying grains, and *shadha*, leather ropes and belts for swords.

Paper-making The art of making paper is *dezo*. The word *de* refers to the daphne plant, from which the traditional paper is made.

Dzoe – Bhutanese Spirit Catcher

Sometimes you will come across a strange construction of twigs, straw and rainbow-coloured thread woven into a spider web shape. You may see one near a building or by a roadside with flower and food offerings. This is a *dzoe* (also known as a *tendo*, pictured here from behind to show its structure), a sort of spirit catcher used to exorcise something evil that has been pestering a household. The malevolent spirits are drawn to the dzoe. After prayers, the dzoe is cast away, often on a trail or road, to send away the evil spirits it has trapped.

Dance

The primary dance form is the *cham* (classical lama dancing) at the tsechu and other festivals. The form of these dances was established by the terton Pema Lingpa in the 15th century and further enhanced by the Shabdrung in the 17th century. All of the dances are religious and symbolise the destruction of evil spirits. Tsechus take place outdoors, in the courtyards of the great dzongs. They celebrate the faith, legends, myths, and history of Bhutan and are important religious and social gatherings. (See the special section 'The Tsechu' in the Facts for the Visitor chapter for more information.)

Folk dances are performed in schools and villages, and also by professional dancers as interludes during the tsechus. The dancers form a line or circle and move in an intricate series of forwards and backwards walking steps accompanied by graceful arm movements. Each song has different dance steps, and, while the songs sound monotonous to the Western ear, they are actually quite varied. Most of the dancers are women who sing the accompanying songs, but men frequently join the line.

Music

Bhutanese popular music, called *rigsar*, is evolving rapidly and more than 100 albums have been produced. Cassette tapes of this music are available at several outlets in Thimphu and in shops in Bumthang and Trashigang.

Rigsar music is an interesting blend of Tibetan and Bhutanese tunes, with influence from popular Hindi film music. The Bhutanese music scene has numerous popular male and female singers. There are also numerous classical and folk songs, some of which are dance oriented, others are religious and still others are purely vocal.

SOCIETY & CONDUCT
Traditional Culture

Although they welcome tourism and modernisation, the Bhutanese still feel that their independence is threatened and that their precious culture may disintegrate. Many of their attitudes towards tourism, politics and the environment are based on the vulnerability they feel as their country expands its contacts with the modern world.

The desire of the Shabdrung Ngawang Namgyal to create and maintain a distinct cultural identity for Bhutan continues today. Bhutanese realise their country can easily be swallowed by either of its huge neighbours. However, rather than feel inferior because of the country's size and insecure geographical position, Bhutan defines its strength in terms of its identity and cultural uniqueness.

Numerous factors threaten this identity, and many Bhutanese feel they are almost an endangered species. You will often hear a Bhutanese person say: 'it is our very survival that is at stake'. Most people sincerely feel that cultural and environmental preservation is the only way to ensure the survival of Bhutan as an independent country.

Bhutan's code of etiquette, *driglam namzha*, describes the correct way to dress, eat, speak, behave and greet elders and high officials.

In accordance with Buddhist tradition, there is a strict taboo on killing in Bhutan. This prohibition applies to the act of killing, but a practising Buddhist may eat meat that is slaughtered by someone else. Hindus and some Tibetans handle the local meat production in Bhutan.

Fishing also violates this precept, and it is not allowed in many streams in Bhutan, though it is possible to obtain a fishing licence for the rivers. You can fish in lakes and some rivers in the countryside, but you are not allowed to fish in towns. There is no commercial fishing in Bhutan; all the fish sold in the market is from India.

Various foreign-sponsored projects have tried to set up small-scale industries in Bhutan and have found that the activities violate Buddhist principals. There are plenty of mulberry trees in the country, and silkworms thrive at altitudes of about 1000m, but pious Bhutanese refuse to throw the cocoons into boiling water as is required for quality silk. Instead, they let the worms chew their way out, which results in a poor grade of silk. Beekeeping projects have limited success because Bhutanese are reluctant to kill the bees in order to extract the honey.

Efforts to control the proliferation of stray dogs in Thimphu and other towns causes conflicts with Bhutanese tradition. There was an outcry when dogs were poisoned, and another when local officials put dogs in jute bags and threw them in the river. There is now a campaign to sterilise dogs in order to reduce the population; sterilised dogs are marked by cutting off their tails.

Personal Names The system of names in Bhutan differs between the north and south of the country. In the north, with the exception of the royal family, there are no family names. Two names are given to children by monks a few weeks after birth. These are traditional names of Tibetan origin and are chosen because of their auspicious influence or religious meaning. Two names are always given, although a few people have three names. It is often impossible to tell the sex of a Bhutanese person based on their name. A few names are given only to boys, and others apply only to girls, but most names may apply to either.

People may be called by both names, or simply by the first name, but it's not correct to use only the second name. It does become complicated, however, because many names, particularly Dorji, are commonly used as both first and second names. For example, Karma Dorji is a government official who helped with this book and Dorji Wangdi is a trekking cook. You would not call Kunzang 'Dorji', and should not call the cook simply 'Wangdi'.

In the south of the country, where there is more Hindu influence, a system resembling family names exists. Brahmans and Newars retain their caste name, such as Sharma or Pradhan, and others retain the name of their ethnic group, such as Rai or Gurung.

Titles & Forms of Address Titles are extremely important. All persons of rank should be addressed by the appropriate title followed by their first or full name. Members of the royal family are addressed as 'Dasho' if they are male, and 'Ashi' if female. A minister has the title 'Lyonpo' (pronounced 'lonpo').

The title Dasho designates those persons who have been honoured by the king with the title and the accompanying red scarf. In common practice, many senior government officials are addressed as Dasho even if they have not received the title, but officially this is incorrect.

You would address a senior monk or teacher with the title 'Lopon' (pronounced 'loeboen') or, if he has been given the title, as Lam. A *trulku* (reincarnate lama) is addressed as 'Rinpoche' and a nun as 'Anim'.

A man is addressed as 'Aap' and a boy as 'Busu'; a woman is addressed as 'Am' and a girl as 'Bum'. If you are calling someone whose name you do not know, you may use 'Ama' for ladies and 'Aapa' for men. In the same situation, girls are 'Bumo' and boys 'Alou'. When Bhutanese talk about a foreigner whose name they don't know, they use the word 'Chilip' or, in eastern Bhutan 'Pilingpa'.

At night, do not shout a person's name, as it's believed this may attract a ghost.

White silk scarves called *kata* are exchanged as customary greetings among ranking officials and are offered to high lamas as a sign of respect, but they are not exchanged as frequently as they are in Tibet and Nepal.

Traditional Dress Bhutan's traditional dress is one of the most distinctive and visible aspects of the country. It is compulsory for all Bhutanese to wear national dress in schools, government offices and formal occasions. Men, women and children wear traditional clothing made from Bhutanese textiles in a variety of colourful patterns.

Gho The men wear a gho, a long robe similar to the Tibetan *chuba*. The Bhutanese hoist the gho to knee length and hold it in place with a woven cloth belt called a *kera*. The kera is wound tightly around the waist, and the large pouch formed above it is traditionally used to carry a bowl, money and the makings of doma. One man suggested that the best part of the day was when he was able to loosen the uncomfortably tight belt.

To be perfectly correct, men should carry a small knife called a *dozum* at the waist. Traditional footwear is knee-high, embroidered leather boots, but these are now worn only at festivals. Most Bhutanese men wear leather shoes or show off with fancy trainers, running shoes or trekking boots.

Ghos come in a wide variety of patterns, though often they have plaid or striped designs reminiscent of Scottish tartans. Flowered patterns are taboo, and solid reds and yellows are avoided because these are colours worn by monks; otherwise patterns have no special significance. Historically, Bhutanese men wore the same thing under their gho that a true Scotsman wears under his kilt, but today it's usually a pair of shorts. In winter it's correct to wear a pair of tights or thermal underwear, but it's more often a pair of jeans or a track suit, which gives the costume a peculiar look that some people liken to a dressing gown. Formality in Thimphu dictates that legs may not be covered until winter has arrived, which is defined as the time that the monks move to Punakha.

Formal occasions, including a visit to the dzong, require a scarf called a *kabney* that identifies a person's rank. The kabney has to be put on correctly so it hangs in exactly the right way. In dzongs, and on formal occasions, a dasho or someone in authority carries a long sword called a *patang*.

Kira Women wear a long floor-length dress called a kira. This is a rectangular piece of brightly coloured cloth that wraps around the body over a Tibetan-style silk blouse called a *wonju*. The kira is fastened at the shoulders with elaborate silver hooks called *koma* and at the waist with a belt that may be of either silver or cloth. Over the top is worn a short, open, jacket-like garment called a *toego*. Women often wear large amounts of jewellery in the Tibetan manner.

The kira may be made from cotton or silk and may have a pattern on one or both sides. For everyday wear, women wear a kira made from striped cloth with a double-sided design, and on more formal occasions they wear a kira with an embellished pattern woven into it. The most expensive kira are *kushutara* (brocade dresses), which are made of hand-spun, hand-woven Bhutanese cotton, embroidered with various colours and designs in raw silk or cotton thread. The Kurtoe region (Lhuentse) is known for its kushutara designs.

When visiting dzongs, women wear a cloth sash called a *rachu* over their left shoulder in the same manner as men wear a kabney.

For guidelines on how to wear traditional Bhutanese dress, see the boxed text

Ceremonial Scarves

Bhutanese men wear a scarf called a kabney as part of the dress protocol on formal occasions and when visiting dzongs and monasteries. The kabney, about 90cm wide and 3m long, is usually made of raw silk with long fringes at the ends. Wearing the kabney is an important part of Bhutanese etiquette, and must be put on in a particular manner so that it drapes in the correct way and can be ceremonially 'unfurled' for the traditional respectful bow to the king, the Je Khenpo or other high officials. It is always worn over the left shoulder and the colour denotes a person's rank. Historically, the kabney is derived from the shawl or shoulder scarf worn by Tibetan monks.

The kabney is not an item of everyday wear, and is usually carried over the arm or on the dashboard of a vehicle until the wearer enters a dzong. Despite its ceremonial importance, the kabney may also be used for lesser purposes such as carrying luggage.

Citizens wear a kabney of unbleached white silk and each level of official wears a different coloured scarf:

- Saffron for the king and Je Khenpo
- Orange for lyonpos
- Blue for members of the Royal Advisory Council
- Red for those with the title Dasho and for senior officials whom the king has recognised
- White with blue stripes for chimis
- White with red stripes on the outside for gups
- Small white cloth scarf with a red border for members of the army

Women wear a coloured shoulder cloth called a rachu. These are smaller than the kabney – about 90cm by 2m. Women use it unfolded to carry children on their backs. For formal occasions it is folded in thirds lengthwise and once to bring the two ends together, forming a narrow scarf that is draped over the left shoulder. A more convenient modern version of the rachu – a small prefolded cloth – is frequently worn by women working in government offices.

The rachu is traditionally woven in silk or raw silk in festive shades of red, maroon or orange, and is embellished at the fringed ends with fine embroidery.

'Traditional Dress' in the Facts for the Visitor chapter.

Hair Style Unlike most women in regions of Tibetan influence, Bhutanese women traditionally wear their hair short, although this tradition is changing, especially in Thimphu.

Traditional Games Bhutan's national sport is *datse* (archery; see the boxed text 'Archery' in the Facts for the Visitor chapter).

Monks are forbidden to participate in archery, so often play a stone-throwing game called *daygo*. A round, flat stone is tossed at a target and the winner is the one that gets the closest.

The Bhutanese version of shot put is called *pungdo*, and is played with large heavy stones.

Khuru is a darts game played on a field about 20m long with small targets similar to those used by archers. The darts are usually home-made from a block of wood, and a nail and some chicken feathers for fins. If a chicken can't be found, bits of plastic make a good substitute. Teams compete with a lot of shouting and arm waving designed to put the thrower off his aim. The game is a favourite of monks and young boys; beware of dangerous flying objects if you are near a khuru target.

Dos & Don'ts

Despite the deep religious sentiment and the pervasiveness of traditional culture, Bhutanese are quite open and liberal. They have a reputation for being the least complicated Asian people to communicate with. There are many complex customs and traditions in Bhutan, but you are not expected to follow all of these.

If you are courteous and respectful of religious sentiment, you are unlikely to cause offence. Using the word *la* at the end of a sentence in either Dzongkha or English is a sign of respect, as in *kuzo zangpo la* (hello).

You should also follow the normal Asian standards of courtesy and behaviour in Bhutan. These include respect for religion and the monarchy, modest dress and no

---

A (Bhutanese) Dog's Life

If merit is to be earned, be good and kind to dogs.
Popular Bhutanese aphorism

Dogs are more than man's best friend in Bhutan and there are several reasons why a Bhutanese dog's life isn't actually so bad.

Unlike Darwinian theory which points to the ape family as the next closest to humans, Bhutanese believe that, from among sentient beings, dogs have the best opportunity to be reborn as humans.

Folklore also refers to a time when the gods were displeased with excessive human greed and decided to withhold the natural bounty of this earth. The dogs are said to have interceded with the gods and pleaded with them to at least leave something for all beings to share. It is said that the food left behind for the dogs is what we survive on today.

Dogs are also said to be helpful in our afterlife: When we're lost in the darkness of the hereafter, dogs are believed to lead us with a light glowing on their tails to a better place.

Many Himalayan Buddhist saints, such as the irrepressible 'divine madman', Drukpa Kunley, had dogs as their closest companions.
Kunzang Dorji

---

public displays of affection. Use the right hand or, better yet, both hands to give or receive an object. Don't use your finger to point, especially at deities or religious objects; use an open hand with the palm up. When waving someone towards you, keep your palm pointing down.

Most lakes are the abode of gods or spirits. Don't swim, wash clothes or throw stones into them.

Visiting Temples Himalayan Buddhism has a generally relaxed approach to religious sites, but you should observe a few important rules if you are invited to enter a lhakhang or goemba. It is customary to remove one's shoes upon entering the important rooms of a temple. You will most likely be escorted by a caretaker monk, and you can follow his example in removing your shoes at the appropriate doorway. Leave cameras, umbrellas and hats outside. Always move in a clockwise direction and do not speak loudly.

Followers of Himalayan Buddhism will prostrate themselves three times before the primary altar and occasionally before secondary shrines to important saints. You may approach the central altar, and in Bhutanese goembas you will often find a cup containing three dice. Bhutanese roll these dice and the monk interprets the auspiciousness of the result. It is customary to leave a small offering of money on the altar. When you make this offering, the monk accompanying you will pour a small amount of holy water, from a sacred vessel called a *bumpa*, into your hand. You should make the gesture of drinking a sip of this water and then spread the rest on your head.

Feet & Face As in all Asian countries, you should never point your feet at someone. If you are sitting on the floor, cross your legs or kneel so that your feet are pointed behind you. If you happen to sleep in a room where there is an altar or statue, ensure your feet do not point towards it.

The Asian concept of keeping face also applies in Bhutan. Try to suggest instead of insist. When things go wrong, as they are certain to do at some stage, be patient while your guide figures out a solution. Remember, Asian people dislike saying 'no'. If your request to visit a certain landmark, order a particular dish in a restaurant or depart at a specified time is met with an obviously lame excuse, this probably means that it is impossible.

Photography A camera is still a curiosity in most of Bhutan, particularly in remote villages, and your camera may draw a curious crowd. See Photography & Video in the Facts for the Visitor chapter for advice on photographing people. Photography is not allowed inside any temples; don't embarrass your guide by asking. If you are attending a festival, do not let your picture taking interfere with the dancers or block the view of the spectators.

Dress Here again, Asian standards of modesty apply. Both men and women should avoid wearing revealing clothing, including short-shorts, halter-neck tops and tank tops. Nudity is completely unacceptable.

Resident expatriates in Thimphu are adamant that visitors should dress up when attending a tsechu or other festival. Bhutanese are too polite to suggest it, and would not openly criticise those who did not dress correctly, but they do appreciate the gesture. Bhutanese are flattered if foreigners wear traditional dress, and are more than happy to help you buy, and put on, a gho or kira – which is not an easy process (see the boxed texts 'Wearing a Kira' and 'Donning a Gho' in the Facts for the Visitor chapter).

If you have an appointment with a government official, correct dress is required. One of the jobs of policemen at the entrance to dzongs is to refuse admission to anyone who is not properly dressed.

Social Occasions If you are invited to a Bhutanese home, it's appropriate to bring a small gift, perhaps a bottle of wine or box of sweets. Social occasions tend to start late and involve extended rounds of drinks before dinner, often with several visitors dropping by for a short time. The evening is quickly concluded once dinner is finished.

Gifts It is customary to bring a gift when you visit a Bhutanese home. If you expect to be invited to a home, you might purchase one of the premium brands of duty-free whiskey or cigarettes before you board your Druk Air flight.

Strange as it may sound, another gift that is appreciated by men is a fancy pair of long argyle socks. Cloth, whether a length of fabric or a ready-made item, is the most traditional gift in Bhutan.

RELIGION
Buddhism is practised throughout the country though, in the south, most Bhutanese people of Nepali and Indian descent are

Hindus. Minority groups practise various forms of ancient animistic religions, including Bon, which predates Himalayan Buddhism.

Monks are held in great respect and play an active part in community life. It is a custom for one son from each family to enter the monastic order at about age 10. The custom is less prevalent today because boys now have more freedom to decide for themselves whether they wish to enter a monastery or not.

Bhutan's official religion is Drukpa Kagyu, a school of tantric Mahayana Buddhism. It is similar to the Buddhism of Tibet, but has unique beliefs and practices. To place Bhutan's religion in the full context of Buddhism, it's necessary to go back nearly 2500 years and trace the points at which the Drukpa Kagyu lineage and its antecedents diverged from other schools of Buddhism.

The Origins of Buddhism

Strictly speaking, Buddhism is not a religion, since it is not centred on a god, but a system of philosophy and a code of morality.

Buddhism was founded in northern India in about 500 BC when Siddhartha Gautama, born a prince, achieved enlightenment. Many schools of Buddhism believe that there were previous Buddhas, and most believe that Gautama Buddha is not expected to be the last 'enlightened one'. Buddhists believe that the achievement of enlightenment should be the goal of every being, and eventually we could all reach Buddhahood.

The Buddha renounced his material life to search for enlightenment but, unlike other prophets, found that starvation did not lead to discovery. Therefore, he developed his rule of the 'middle way' – moderation in everything. The Buddha taught that all life is suffering, but that suffering comes from our sensual desires and the illusion that they are important. Delusion causes us to go through a series of rebirths until such time as the goal is reached and no more rebirths into the world of suffering are necessary. By following the Noble Eightfold Path, these desires will eventually be extinguished and

a state of nirvana, where we are free from all delusions, will be reached.

The agent that takes you through this cycle of births is karma – but this is not simply fate. Karma is a law of cause and effect; your actions in one life determine the role you will play and what you will have to go through in your next life.

The Buddha is known to the Mahayana Buddhists as Sakyamuni. He never wrote down his dharma (teachings), and a schism developed so that today there are two major Buddhist schools.

Theravada Buddhism

The Theravada school, or 'doctrine of the elders', holds that the path to nirvana, the eventual aim of all Buddhists, is an individual pursuit. Practitioners believe that an individual can work towards an end to the endless cycle of rebirths by practising monastic discipline in accordance with the *sutras* (teachings of the Buddha) and meditating on the impermanent nature of reality; the worship of deities is secondary. The Theravada school is followed in Sri Lanka, Myanmar (Burma) and Thailand, and by the Buddhist Newars in the Kathmandu valley.

Mahayana Buddhism

In contrast, the Mahayana, or 'great vehicle', school holds that the combined belief of its followers will eventually be great enough to encompass all of humanity and bear it to salvation. Today, various forms of Mahayana Buddhism are practised in Vietnam, Japan, Nepal and China.

Mahayana Buddhists believe in the existence of holy beings who have sacrificed their own release from suffering in order to aid in the salvation of all living things. Such a person is called a bodhisattva, one who has attained enlightenment but delays entry into nirvana in order to lead others to enlightenment. The bodhisattva remains in the world as a teacher or guru, suffering and toiling for the salvation of all beings. Thus, in the Mahayana tradition, bodhisattvas are worshipped as Buddhas. The Historical Buddha, Sakyamuni, is viewed as one of a succession of Buddhas.

Mahayana Buddhism developed into a more metaphysical form than Theravada Buddhism, with elaborate rituals and symbolism. It emphasises mental development and service to humanity.

Vajrayana Vajrayana Buddhism, the 'diamond vehicle', evolved from Mahayana traditions, probably in India during the 2nd to 4th centuries. Often called Tantric Buddhism, it focuses on existential problems and emphasises the use of meditation under the direction of an initiated teacher as a means to achieve enlightenment. Unlike the pure Mahayana tradition, which attaches most importance to theoretical aspects of Buddhism, the Vajrayana tradition portrays Buddhism as part of the individual. Yogic and meditative methods are used to bring about a complete transformation of the practitioner. Female energies and goddesses are worshipped and demonesses exert a powerful influence.

Vajrayana students must be accepted by a recognised teacher and must undergo a long process of initiation and training (tantra means 'practice'). The emphasis is to understand compassion through a process of meditation. Eventually, the student learns yogic or contemplative practices and uses *mudras* (gestures and postures) and *mantras* (sacred syllables and phrases). Vajrayana Buddhism has a collection of texts known as the *Tantras*, which supplement the initial teachings of the Buddha.

Although Buddhism had been practised in Tibet since the reign of King Songtsen Gampo (AD 618–49), it was not the dominant force in the country until much later. Tibet, according to tradition, was plagued by demons, and King Trisong Detsen (AD 755–97) invited Guru Rinpoche to visit Tibet to try to subdue the negative forces that were interfering with the construction of Samye Monastery. Every night the demons destroyed all the previous day's work. The Guru subdued the demons, not by destroying them, but by bringing them under his control. The converted demons helped to build the monastery, accomplishing more at night than the workers did during the day, thus establishing Tibet's first Buddhist monastery.

Guru Rinpoche used a *dorji* to subdue disruptive demons.

Guru Rinpoche's primary weapon to control the demons was the dorji. This symbol is an important icon, and it is from this that the name Vajrayana evolved (*vajra* is the Sanskrit name for dorji).

This branch of Buddhism is sometimes referred to (incorrectly) in the west as Lama Buddhism or Lamaism. The word lama means 'extraordinary master' and is a title used for the heads of monasteries and monks of superior learning. A more descriptive and accurate name is Himalayan Buddhism.

Himalayan Buddhism is different from Western religious practice. Although it has a strict moral code, including the prohibition of killing, it does not require the layman to undertake sophisticated study. The monks memorise texts and recite them on important occasions. Those laymen who do understand the texts and rituals are respected, but most people don't fathom the intricacies of the liturgy. People gain merit by hearing the texts, and it is not necessary for them to understand the deeper meaning of the recitations.

Similarly, merit may be achieved by spinning a prayer wheel, the inside of which contains thousands, or millions, of prayers written on paper. Contributing to the construction of a goemba, supporting the monastic community, erecting prayer flags and sponsoring the recitation of sacred texts all contribute to one's karma. It is also a merit-making exercise to witness dances and ritual performances by lamas, but no real understanding or active participation is necessary. The Earl of Ronaldshay described Himalayan Buddhism as:

...a perfectly bewildering medley of gods and goddesses, Buddhas and bodhisattvas, guardian deities and canonised saints, ghouls, goblins and demons, deified kings and spirits of every conceivable description, paradises, earths and hells.

Important Figures of Drukpa Kagyu Buddhism

This brief guide to some of the gods and goddesses of the Drukpa Kagyu pantheon may help you to recognise a few of the figures in paintings and as statues in Bhutan's goembas. They are known in Bhutan by their Dzonghka names, but many also have Sanskrit names which are shown in brackets.

Guru Rinpoche (Padmasambhava)

The 'lotus-born' Buddha – an 8th-century missionary and saint who visited Bhutan in AD 746 – is worshipped in Bhutan as the second Buddha and may appear in eight forms or manifestations. Most lhakhangs in Bhutan built after Guru Rinpoche's visit have a statue of the Guru as the central figure.

Jampa (Maitreya)

The Buddha of the Future, he is passing the life of a bodhisattva and will return to earth in human form 4000 years after the disappearance of Sakyamuni. Statues of Jampa are the focal point in most older lhakhangs built before the Guru visited Bhutan. Jampa is easily recognised – he is either standing or seated in a Western style. Statues of all other deities are seated in a cross-legged posture.

Jampelyang (Manjushri)

The 'princely lord of wisdom' – the embodiment of wisdom and knowledge – carries a sword in his right hand to destroy the darkness of ignorance. He is the patron of learning and the arts.

Chenresig (Avalokiteshvara)

He is the 'glorious gentle one', the Bodhisattva of Compassion – one of the four great bodhisattvas and the special guardian of Bhutanese religion – pictured sitting in a lotus position, with the lower two (of four) arms in a gesture of prayer. He also appears with 11 heads and 1000 arms arranged in a circle.

Channa Dorji (Vajrapani)

'Thunderbolt in hand' – the god of power and victory– whose thunderbolt represents power and is a fundamental symbol of Tantric faith; it is called a dorji in Tibetan and vajra in Sanskrit. He is pictured in a wrathful form with an angry face and one leg outstretched.

Himalayan Buddhism

Followers of Himalayan Buddhism believe that our consciousness persists in an unbroken stream from lifetime to lifetime. This mindstream is reborn into a new body under circumstances dictated by the good and bad actions we've accumulated in our current and past lifetimes. Meditation is a method of stabilising our minds so all negative emotions (attachment, anger, and indifference), and thus all suffering, are eliminated. The mind, thus stabilised, is able to consciously choose to be reborn in order to help teach other people how to reach this state.

Great lamas almost always choose to be reborn in order to continue to benefit other beings. People who are recognised as the reincarnation of a previous great teacher are called trulkus. Each time a great Buddhist master dies students or close acquaintances will eventually search out his reincarnation, based on various clues that may have been left by the previous master.

The idea that Buddhist lamas can consciously reincarnate for the benefit of other beings is difficult for non-Buddhists to comprehend. It is worth noting that the great spiritual leaders of Tibet and Bhutan were all identified when they were young children.

Himalayan Buddhism was influenced by the ancient indigenous Bon tradition of Tibet, and a few pockets of Bon remain in the Himalayan regions. Many of the demons and shamanistic traditions of Tibetan Buddhism evolved from its interaction with Bon. These demons, by the way, were very real to the people of Tibet.

Many stories tell of Tibetan saints, or bodhisattvas, subduing these demons and spirits and converting them to Buddhism. These saints had great appeal to ordinary Tibetans, and a shamanistic tradition evolved

Guru Rinpoche
(Padmasambhava)

Jampelyang
(Manjushri)

Jampa
(Maitreya)

Chenresig
(Avalokiteshvara)

Channa Dorji
(Vajrapani)

Sakyamuni, the
Historical Buddha

Milarepa

White Tara

Green Tara

Shabdrung Rinpoche

Important Figures of Drukpa Kagyu Buddhism

Sakyamuni

The 'Historical Buddha' – born in Lumbini in southern Nepal in the 5th century BC, he attained enlightenment under a pipal (Bo) tree in Bihar in India, and his teachings set in motion the Buddhist faith. In Tibetan-style representations he is always pictured sitting cross-legged on a lotus-flower throne.

Milarepa

A great Tibetan magician (1040–1123) and poet of the Kagyu lineage who is believed to have attained the supreme enlightenment of Buddhahood in the course of one life. He travelled extensively throughout the Himalayan border lands and is said to have meditated at Taktshang in Bhutan where he composed a song. Most images of Milarepa picture him smiling and holding his hand to his ear as he sings.

Tara

'The saviouress' has 21 different manifestations or aspects. She symbolises fertility and is believed to be able to fulfil wishes. Statues of Tara usually represent Green Tara, who is associated with night, or White Tara, who is associated with day. (In Bhutan, Tara is also known as Dem.)

Tradition has it that Tara represents the two wives of the Tibetan king Songtsen Gampo. The Nepali wife is Green Tara and the Chinese wife is White Tara. You will be able to recognise statues of White Tara because she has seven eyes, including eyes on her forehead, each palm and the sole of each foot.

Shabdrung Rinpoche

Ngawang Namgyal (1594–1651) is revered in Bhutan as Shabdrung Rinpoche (precious jewel at whose feet one prostrates). He is an important Bhutanese saint and his statue appears in many lhakhangs throughout the country. He is depicted in a seated position and has a long grey beard. It is he who established the tradition of tsechus.

as the popular form of Tibetan Buddhism. While the monks studied texts and followed strict rules, the religious practices of lay people included the worship of favourite saints and calling on sorcerers to solve particular problems such as health, financial difficulty or possession by demons.

Each monastery maintained its own leadership and a number of charismatic teachers became recognised, each with an individual interpretation of certain aspects of the scriptures. This difference in interpretation of the scriptures, combined with the influence of worship of the more popular saints, resulted in the evolution of various lineages or schools within Tibetan Buddhism, each with its distinctive style and traditions.

Nyingma Early Western students of Tibetan Buddhism labelled this the 'red hat' school and assumed it was the earliest form of Tibetan Buddhism because its name, Nyingma, means 'old'. It was the practice of Nyingma Buddhism that Guru Rinpoche introduced to Tibet and Bhutan. Nyingma monasteries never became great seats of power because most of their practitioners were local shaman-like teachers in rural villages. Nyingmapa monks may marry and often work individually in small village lhakhangs and remote cave retreats.

Nyingma tradition places a special emphasis on tertons – Nyingma lamas who were the discoverers of Guru Rinpoche's terma. The terma consisted mostly of sacred texts and teachings, often written in secret languages, as well as statues and ritual objects. The concept of termas is a living tradition, and new termas continue to be revealed to this day.

Gelug Known as the 'yellow hat' school, Gelug is a reformed lineage begun in the

Tashi Tagye

Many homes and temples are decorated with *tashi tagye*, the eight auspicious signs of Himalayan Buddhism. Each has a deep symbolic meaning and represents an object used in religious observances.

Precious Umbrella
The *duk* symbolises the activity of preserving beings from illness and negative forces.

Victory Banner
The *gyeltshen* represents the victory of the Buddhist doctrine over harmful forces.

White Conch
The *dungkar* winds to the right and is a symbol of the deep and melodious sound of the dharma teachings.

Endless Knot
The noose of eternity, *pelgibeu*, represents the mind and the union of wisdom and compassion.

Golden Fish
The *sernga* represents the auspiciousness of all beings in a state of fearlessness without drowning in the ocean of suffering.

Lotus Flower
The *pema* is a symbol of the purification of the body, speech and mind.

Vase of Treasure
The *bumpa* represents long life, wealth and prosperity.

Golden Wheel
The *khorlo* is the precious wheel of the Buddha's doctrine.

14th century. Its founder, Tsong Khapa, studied Sakya, Kadam and Kagyu teachings, and eventually his teachings led to a new tradition of Tibetan Buddhism, which he named *Gelug* (virtuous ones).

Tsong Khapa instigated a system of examinations, of which the highest degree granted was *geshe*. In 1409 he founded Ganden, west of Lhasa, one of Tibet's greatest and most important monasteries. Gelug followers later established several important monasteries in Tibet, including Drepung, Sera and Tashilhunpo. From Tsong Khapa's disciples came the line of the Dalai Lama, who is believed to be the incarnation of Chenresig (known in India as Avalokiteshvara), the embodiment of compassionate bodhisattvahood.

Sakya The Sakya school was named after its principal monastery in Tibet. Its systematically organised teachings are called *lam-dre*. They integrate the precepts of sutra and tantra into a discipline designed to bring about Buddhahood in a single lifetime.

Kadam The patriarch of the Kadam (Bound by Precept) school was Atisha, whose teachings stressed the need for austere monastic discipline and devotion to a teacher before the start of tantric practice. Students observed four fundamental rules: celibacy, abstinence from intoxicants, and prohibition of travel and money handling. The Gelug lineage absorbed the Kadampas in the 15th century.

Kagyu The name Kagyu translates as 'whispered transmission'. It places fundamental emphasis on the oral transmission of esoteric teachings directly from master to pupil. The tradition evolved with the early Indian masters, and its most important teacher was the tantric guru Marpa (AD 1012–93). Among Marpa's disciples was Milarepa, Tibet's greatest poet. Milarepa eschewed the study of classical Tibetan texts and wandered throughout Tibet meditating in high mountain caves and composing songs.

One of Milarepa's disciples was Gampopa, who authored important Kagyu texts and passed his teachings on to several gifted students. These students, in turn, founded the monasteries of Drigung, Taklung and Ralung (from which the first shabdrung, Ngawang Namgyal, came).

The Kagyu system emphasises certain aspects of practical mysticism, including yogic practices of breathing techniques and postures. It is possible to achieve enlightenment within a lifetime, or at the moment of death, by relying on the Six Yogas of Naropa. These are self-produced heat, illusory body, dreams, the experience of light, the intermediate state between death and rebirth and the passing from one existence into another. Following the example of the married priest Marpa, Kagyu tradition does not demand celibacy or association with a religious institution.

There are numerous suborders of Kagyu, including Karmapa, Drikungpa and Drukpa. The Karmapa lineage is one of the important schools in present-day Tibet and Sikkim, and the Drukpa lineage is the preeminent religion of Bhutan.

Bhutan's Drukpa Kagyu Lineage

The Drukpa Kagyu lineage was established by Tsangpa Gyarey Yeshe Dorji at Ralung Monastery in central Tibet, and was brought to Bhutan by Lama Phajo Drukgom Shigpo. Kagyu religious practices rely heavily on tantric tradition and emphasise solitary meditation in the Milarepa style. In the 17th century the Drukpa shabdrung, Ngawang Namgyal, established the school as the de facto official state religion. To this day Drukpa Kagyu remains the state religion and continues to be the dominant Buddhist lineage, though the Nyingma lineage also commands great respect and has a significant following.

Every house has a *choesham* (altar or shrine room). Each altar usually features statues of the three great lamas: Sakyamuni, Guru Rinpoche and Shabdrung Rinpoche. In most homes and temples, devotees place seven bowls filled with water on altars. This simple offering is important because it can be given without greed or attachment. On special occasions monks prepare torma, white and pink sculptures made from *tsampa* (barley flour) and butter, as symbolic offerings to deities. A special shape of torma is associated with each deity.

Protective Deities

Buddhism has numerous important gods and protectors of the faith, but there are also many other deities that have special significance only within a certain region. These local protector or guardian deities (often called guardians of the faith), as well as *yidam* (tutelary deities) may be wrathful manifestations of enlightened beings or may be malevolent beings that were subdued and converted by tantric forces. They are an important element of Bhutan's spiritual beliefs and they occupy a special place in lhakhangs. A locally crafted statue, which is often terrifying or wrathful, of a protective deity is found in a corner or in the *goenkhang* of most of Bhutan's lhakhangs.

The deity Mahakala assisted Shabdrung Ngawang Namgyal all his life and is recognised as the guardian deity of Bhutan. He is also known as Yeshe Goenpo, is often described as the overlord of all the mountain gods and is a Tantric Buddhist form of the Hindu god Shiva. Mahakali (Wisdom Defender) is the female form, also known as Palden Lhamo (Great Black One), the dark blue protector.

Most of Bhutan's valleys have a local protective deity. Statues of Thimphu's protector, Gyenyen Jagpa Melen, appear in Dechenphug Lhakhang near Dechencholeing and in Ney Khang Lhakhang next to the dzong. Among the other regional protective deities are Jichu Drakye in Paro, Chhundu in Haa, Talo Gyalpo Pehar in Punakha, Kaytshugpa in Wangdue Phodrang and, in Bumthang, Keybu Lungtsan and Jowo Ludud Drakpa Gyeltshen. These deities are gods who have not left the world and therefore have not gained enlightenment.

As all Himalayan Buddhists do, Bhutanese devotees prostrate themselves in front of altars and deities, first clasping hands above the head, again at throat level and then at the chest. This is a representation of the mind, speech and body.

LANGUAGE

There are 19 languages spoken in Bhutan. The official language is Dzongkha, which is related to Tibetan, but is sufficiently different that Tibetans cannot understand it. Dzongkha is written in the same script as Tibetan, but the orthography has been made more Bhutanese.

English is the medium of instruction in schools, and most educated people speak it fluently. There are English signboards, books and menus throughout the country. Road signs and government documents are written in both English and Dzongkha. The national newspaper, *Kuensel*, is published in three languages: English, Dzongkha and Nepali. In the monastic schools, Choekey, the classical Tibetan language, is taught.

In eastern Bhutan most people speak Sharchop ('language of the east'), which is utterly different from Dzongkha. In the south, most people speak Nepali. Because many parts of the country are very isolated, there are a number of languages other than Dzongkha and Sharchop. Some are so different that people from different parts of the country can't understand each other. Bumthangkha is a language of the Bumthang region, and most regional minorities have their own language. Among the languages in Bhutan's Tower of Babel are Khengkha from Zhemgang, Kurtoep from Lhuentse, Mangdep from Trongsa and Dzala from Trashi Yangtse.

Nepali and English are the two most widely used lingua francas whenever Bhutanese have a communication problem.

Books

Dzongkha Handbook is a small book published in Bhutan that provides a glossary of English words and phrases with their Dzongkha and Sharchop equivalents.

Dzongkha-English Dictionary by Rinchen Khandu has translations in both Dzongkha script and Roman Dzongkha. All the words are organised by topic, not alphabetically.

Dzongkha by George Van Driem is part of the Languages of the Greater Himalayan Region series produced by Leiden University in the Netherlands ([W] iias.leidenuniv.nl/host/himalaya/dzongkha.html). The set includes a textbook and three instructional CDs.

Facts for the Visitor

HIGHLIGHTS
Anywhere you travel in Bhutan you will find spectacular scenery, deep forests, high Himalayan peaks and a traditional Buddhist culture with amazing architecture and massive *dzongs* that dominate the countryside. Almost everything in Bhutan is different from the rest of Asia, and probably unlike anything you have imagined.

The Countryside
The first thing that strikes a visitor to Bhutan is the great expanse of green, forested hillsides. There is a great variety of trees, vegetation and wildlife as you drive from subtropical forests over high alpine passes and back down to broad valleys with houses that look remarkably like Swiss chalets scattered across the landscape.

Dzongs
Bhutan's extraordinary architecture is best represented by the immense white fortress-monasteries that dominate the major valleys. It's possible to enter the dzongs and get a close view of the impressive artwork and traditional construction techniques. Even at a distance, the dzongs offer a unique and photogenic highlight of the country.

Festivals
There are festivals throughout the year, and crowds of Bhutanese and foreign tourists descend on monasteries and dzongs to witness the ceremonies and lama dances that continue for several days. The *tsechu* festivals are colourful pageants and important social occasions, with all comers dressed in their finest traditional dress.

Trekking
Bhutan offers a true wilderness experience while still retaining the comforts of a traditional Himalayan trek. On Bhutan's trek routes there are no hotels, few villages and even fewer trekkers.

Bhutanese Hospitality
The Bhutanese are extraordinarily friendly and hospitable. In towns almost everyone speaks English, and you will easily make friends during your travels. All Bhutanese you come into contact with, whether a government official, driver, guide or policeman, will treat you with a politeness that is almost embarrassing. Service in hotels, while abundant and enthusiastic, is occasionally amateurish, but the broad smile of the server helps to smooth over any shortcomings.

Textiles
The traditional handloom weaving is so exotic and varied that several museums in the West have permanent exhibitions of Bhutanese textiles. Although it is traditionally used for clothing, you can purchase lengths of the colourful material for use as curtains or bedspreads.

SUGGESTED ITINERARIES
When planning your trip, try to arrange to be in Thimphu on a Saturday or Sunday to see the weekend market. Avoid Paro on Monday, the day that the National Museum is closed. If you value sleep, you would do well to schedule your last night in Bhutan at Paro. Most flights leave in the early morning; if you spend your last night in Thimphu, you must wake up at 4am and drive two hours to the airport.

If you have limited time (or money), you can get a good impression of Bhutan with only a three-night stay in the country, visiting Thimphu and Paro.

For a more comprehensive look at Bhutan, spend a week and add an overnight trip over the mountains to Punakha and Wangdue Phodrang. Schedule an extra day in Paro so you can climb to the point overlooking Taktshang, the famous 'tiger's nest' monastery.

A longer program of nine days will allow you a full day in Bumthang with overnight stops in Paro, Thimphu and Trongsa and short stops in Punakha and Wangdue

Phodrang as you drive through. A night in the Phobjikha valley will give you a chance to see Gangte Goemba and also, during the late autumn or winter, to view the rare and endangered black-necked cranes (see the boxed text 'The Black-Necked Crane' in the Facts about Bhutan chapter).

It takes two weeks to make a trip to the east, visiting Trongsa, Bumthang, Mongar and Trashigang. There is much to see on the way, but it involves a lot of driving. You can drive south to the border town of Phuentsholing and into India to visit Darjeeling, Kalimpong and Sikkim and on to Nepal. You can also drive to the airport in Bagdogra and fly to Delhi or Kolkata (Calcutta).

You'll need to allow at least three days, and preferably at least a week, if you want to trek in Bhutan. The Druk Path trek, which goes from Paro to Thimphu, is a short and relatively simple trek, though it does spend two nights at a high elevation. The Jhomolhari trek offers some of the best high-mountain scenery in Bhutan, but it crosses a high (4800m) pass. An excellent alternative is to do only the first three days of this trek to Jhomolhari base camp, spend a day exploring, then return to Paro via the same route. This avoids the high passes and still provides spectacular mountain views and visits to highland villages and yak pastures.

PLANNING
Bhutan's Tourism Policy

The Royal Government of Bhutan requires that foreign visitors travel with a prepaid and preplanned itinerary through a Bhutanese tour company. If you are used to travelling this way, you will find Bhutan's system convenient, efficient and generally comfortable. You can buy a space on a group tour and have everything arranged for you, or you can arrange a custom-made program directly with a Bhutanese operator.

If you usually travel independently, you have to accept a certain degree of planning and regimentation, but within this framework there are many ways to retain your freedom and avoid most of the drawbacks associated with an organised tour. You can travel alone if you wish, and it's easy to de-sign your own itinerary according to dates that are convenient for you. There are a few areas that are closed to tourists, but generally you have a great deal of freedom, though it's sometimes difficult to change your program once you've finalised the arrangements.

Bhutan is a fascinating and rewarding place, but it has an established set of rules that are not going to change. Unless you are a project volunteer (or related to one), an Indian national or a friend of the royal family, you will probably have to accept the Bhutanese way of travel and make the most of it.

Throughout its history Bhutan has never actively encouraged visitors. There were so few foreign visitors before 1974 that most can be chronicled. When the third king, Jigme Dorji Wangchuck, decided to make Bhutan a part of the international community, his policy was to take a series of small, careful steps, and tourism was not a part of his modernisation program.

As Bhutan slowly began to admit foreign tourists in the mid-1970s, foreign tour operators encouraged the government to place limits on the number of visitors. The Bhutanese, horrified at the prospects of a situation similar to Kathmandu's Freak St developing in Bhutan, wisely took the advice. Though initially controlled by a government monopoly on tourism facilities and a quota of 2000 foreign visitors a year, the numbers are now controlled through a system of high prices that automatically limits the number of tourists and the length of their stay.

The policy has achieved the goal of keeping numbers low. In 2000 only 7559 tourists visited Bhutan – the highest annual count on record. The largest number of tourists came from Japan, America and Germany. Other major nationalities were British, French and Italian.

Bhutan's Department of Tourism (DOT) administers tourism, under the authority of the Ministry of Trade & Industry. Its rules are simple, yet are carefully thought out and strictly enforced. There are few loopholes.

The basic policy is that foreign tourists pay US$200 for each night in Bhutan. This is not a visa fee, it's an all-inclusive rate that covers all your food, accommodation, transport and guide services. A portion of the fee, currently 35%, goes directly to the government as a sort of tourist tax, and the rest goes to the private tour operator that provides the services. See the list of Bhutan's tour operators in the Getting There & Away chapter.

The tourism rules are in keeping with government policies of proceeding slowly in all aspects of development and modernisation. The royalty goes into the treasury and has helped Bhutan to provide free medical care and education for everyone in the country.

While US$200 a day seems excessively high by the standards of a budget traveller, it's actually less than what an international business traveller would expect to pay for an all-inclusive package in any major Asian city. It's also less than room-only accommodation in a quality hotel in Europe or America. See Costs under Money later in this chapter for detailed information.

When to Go

You can plan your trip to coincide with the period of best weather, but no matter when you go there is likely to be rain. The climate is best in autumn, from late September to late November, when skies are generally clear and the high mountain peaks are visible early in the morning from passes and other vantage points. This is the ideal time for trekking and for travelling throughout the country. Late autumn is also the time when the black-necked cranes arrive at their wintering grounds in central and eastern Bhutan.

The winter can be a good time for touring in western Bhutan, but you will need warm clothing. From December to February, there is often snow in the higher regions and occasional snow in Thimphu. The road from Thimphu to Bumthang and the east may be closed because of snow for several days at a time. It would be best not to plan to visit these regions at this time. The days are usually sunny, but it's quite cold once the sun disappears behind the hills at about 4pm. Even the monks of Thimphu move to the warmer climate of Punakha for the winter.

Springtime, from March to May, is recognised as the second-best time to visit Bhutan. Though there are more clouds and rain than in the autumn, the flowers are in bloom and birdlife is abundant. You can get occasional glimpses of the high peaks, but these are not the dramatic unobstructed views possible in autumn.

Summer, from June to August, is the monsoon season. And what a monsoon!

Shangri-La

Many travel brochures describe Bhutan as 'the last Shangri-La.' This is a name invented by James Hilton in the 1930s classic novel *Lost Horizon*. Shangri-La is a secluded Himalayan valley where people never age. The high lama of Hilton's Shangri-La ensured that the valley was well hidden to protect its people and culture from the influences of the modern world and to preserve its traditions and teachings until a time when the world would be free from strife and discord. In the lama's words:

We may expect no mercy, but we may faintly hope for neglect. Here we shall stay with our books and our music and our meditations, conserving the frail elegancies of a dying age, and seeking such wisdom as men will need when their passions are all spent. We have a heritage to cherish and bequeath. Let us take what pleasure we may until that time comes.

The high lama seems to be echoing the traditions established by Shabdrung Ngawang Namgyal, which have been carried into the 21st century. Hilton's story is based on the Tibetan tradition of 'hidden valleys', or *bey-yuls*. It is believed that when wars or calamities threaten humanity, these special places will serve as refuges for the followers of Buddhism.

There are several valleys within Bhutan that are believed to be bey-yuls preserved in a state of timelessness as a repository for the culture of humanity. These include the valley of Haa, Khenpalung in Kurtoe (north of Lhuentse) and Thowada in the north of Bumthang's Tang valley, which was hidden by Guru Rinpoche's consort Yeshe Chhogyel.

During these three months 500mm of rain falls in Thimphu and up to a metre falls in the eastern hills. The mountains are hidden, the valleys are shrouded in clouds, and roads disappear in heavy downpours and floods.

Summer is still a great time to visit Paro, Thimphu and other parts of western Bhutan. The intense green of the rice fields contrasts with the darker greens of the forested hillsides in sunlight that is diffused by monsoon clouds. Meat is in short supply because of the lack of refrigeration, but there are ample fresh fruits and vegetables.

A second factor in choosing a time to visit Bhutan, and one that may override considerations of weather patterns, is the schedule of festivals. These colourful events offer a firsthand glimpse of Bhutanese life and provide an opportunity to see the inside of the great dzongs. It's possible, if you plan dates carefully, to work at least one festival into a tour or trek program. See the boxed text 'Festival Dates' later in this chapter.

The largest festivals – at Paro and Thimphu – take place during the best weather. At this time flights become hopelessly overbooked and prices go up. You stand a better chance of getting the dates you want if you schedule your trip around one of the less popular events.

What Kind of Trip

Although you are required to prebook and prepay for your travel in Bhutan, it is not necessary to join a packaged tour group. Booking onto a tour is, however, the easiest and most hassle-free way to visit the kingdom.

You can also arrange an independent program to do pretty much what you want. You can design your own itinerary and contact an agent in Bhutan to arrange your visa and handle the trip.

Bhutan originally classified tourism into two categories, cultural tours and treks, with a lower rate for trekking. Because tour operators abused the system, there is now a single rate for all travel in Bhutan, whether it is in a hotel or under canvas. The term 'cultural tour' has persisted, and most tour operators still use this term to differentiate hotel trips from trekking.

A Fully Inclusive Package Unless you have a special visa provided as part of your employment contract with an embassy or a nongovernmental organisation (NGO), you must arrange your visa through DOT and use a Bhutanese tour operator to arrange your trip. Out of the US$200 per day that you pay to DOT, less than US$120 makes it way back to the tour operator, which then provides all meals, accommodation, transportation and a guide-escort who will accompany you throughout your visit.

Once you have finalised your itinerary and paid for the tour, no alteration, except cancellation of the entire trip, is normally allowed. This preplanning takes a lot of the spontaneity out of travel in Bhutan, but that's part of the plan. You are not supposed to extend your stay or change your destination. You may, however, be *forced* to change your itinerary because of road closure, flight delays, hotel-booking problems or other factors. Such situations can be quite trying, but usually turn out for the best, and if you take things in your stride, you can have a lot of fun.

Group Travel When you apply for your visa – whether you travel as an individual, as a small group of two or three, or as a larger group organised by an adventure travel company – you become a 'group' in the eyes of DOT.

Your group should arrive, travel and depart together, and no other people are supposed to be added to it. A licensed guide will accompany your group throughout Bhutan and ensure that you get all the transportation, accommodation, meals and sightseeing that you've paid for.

If you are on your own, or in a small group, you can take a few liberties, such as eating in local restaurants, making short side trips or visiting homes. If you are in a larger group, especially if you have joined a group tour, things will be more formalised, and you will probably eat all your meals at your hotel and have hotel-prepared packed lunches when you are on long road journeys.

Trekking If you have the time and ability, the best way to experience Bhutan is to take

Features of Bhutanese Travel

A Complex Buddhist Culture

If you have read the description of the culture and religion of Bhutan, you will probably find the country fascinating. If you have never been to Tibet or any other Himalayan kingdom, and don't have a basic grasp of Mahayana Buddhist architecture and iconography, you may find the culture of Bhutan a bit overpowering. In this case you might consider travelling first to Nepal, Tibet or the Indian Himalaya before undertaking a visit to Bhutan. On the other hand, you will find most Bhutanese knowledgeable about their religion and articulate in explaining some of its less complex aspects.

Restricted Entrance to Temples

The Bhutanese view their temples and monasteries as living institutions and since 1988 have not allowed tourists to enter them without special permission – which is generally reserved for bona fide practising Buddhists.

Monks have considerable influence and resist the intrusion of tourists; they also quietly resist efforts to modernise monastic life. They express concern that a large number of visitors disturbs the sanctity of holy places and may cause the disappearance of temple treasures.

Long Drives on Winding Roads

If you confine yourself to the Paro, Thimphu, Punakha and Wangdue Phodrang circuit, you'll stay in good hotels and road travel will be in chunks of two or three hours. If you travel to eastern Bhutan, be prepared for full-day drives on winding, bumpy, sometimes frightening roads that are only 1½ lanes wide with an estimated 17 curves per kilometre. There are great views from high passes, and the white houses scattered across vast expanses of cultivated valleys provide variety on the lengthy drives. There are, however, many long stretches of wooded hillsides that tend to make drives seem endless.

Despite the wild country that the roads traverse, they are extraordinarily well maintained. Some roads are kept up by Dantak, the Indian Border Roads Task Force. The east-west highway and other roads are handled by a countrywide network called the National Work Force, which employs an army of labourers who live in clusters of buildings alongside the road and perform constant repairs.

You rarely have sight of the great snow peaks of the Bhutan Himalaya because, typically, the views are blocked either by clouds or forested ridges.

Overbooking & Mix-Ups

During the high season in October and November and during festival times, hotels are fully booked, and it is difficult for tour operators to get vacancies. Even if you have confirmation, the hotels may be double- (or even triple-) booked, or an unexpected VIP may arrive and demand the last room. Be prepared to take this in your stride if you come to Bhutan. Tour operators, guides and hotels all do their best to provide everything that you've requested, but it's not always possible. More than once, travellers who have had confirmed hotel bookings have been accommodated in private homes – or in tents. If you view this mix-up as a cultural experience, you can turn it into fun, but if you pout and demand what has been promised, you'll just embarrass everyone – and probably still end up in a tent.

The reservation problem also works in reverse. Everything is arranged in advance, and if you decide you would like to stay an extra day somewhere, this whim will usually cause a major complication.

Flight Delays

Planes cannot operate to or from Paro, the site of Bhutan's only international airport, in bad weather, and Bhutan certainly has its fair share of cloudy and rainy days. Flights are often delayed, not by a matter of hours, but rather by one or several days. Druk Air recommends that you allow 24 hours for any connecting flight, and travel on nonrestricted tickets so that you can easily rebook in case of delays. It also suggests that you carry medicine and toiletries in your carry-on luggage in case the weather is bad in Paro and you have to stay overnight at a transit point.

a trek. Treks can last from three to more than 25 days. Most trekking trails are extremely steep and many treks cross high passes of 4500m or more. In Bhutan most treks offer many days of true wilderness experience that is completely different from typical treks in the Nepal or Indian Himalaya. Not only are there few villages, but only 12% of Bhutan's visitors go trekking. It may be hard to contemplate paying US$200 a day to sleep in a tent, but the Bhutanese trek operators do a good job and you will be well fed and cared for. See the Trekking chapter for details of trekking routes and information about how Bhutan's tour companies organise their treks.

Remaining Independent Historically, tourists to Bhutan have travelled in large organised groups arranged by a travel agency or tour operator and escorted by a leader. Bhutanese tour companies have developed good systems to handle these groups, keeping them in large, quiet hotels away from the noise of towns. Sightseeing is well organised and follows established patterns, with a return to the hotel for lunch, followed by a time for rest.

Though this kind of trip is exactly what many people want, for others it creates a feeling of isolation from the culture and people of the country. If you are alone, or in a small group of two to five, it's possible to break out of this pattern. If you stay in a hotel near the centre of town instead of a resort-type hotel on a hilltop, you can wander into the market rather than confining yourself to the hotel gift shop. You can choose to have meals in one of the many local restaurants, or stop in a bar or food stall for a predinner drink, or stay out late at a pub or disco. You can turn your two half-day sightseeing excursions into one full-day outing by carrying a packed lunch or eating in a local restaurant.

Bhutan has no caste system, and there is no social stigma attached to most jobs. You can enhance your Bhutan experience by socialising with your guide and driver in hotels and restaurants – if you can entice them away from their beloved card games.

If you develop a good rapport with your guide and explain your interests and wishes, you can enhance your cultural experience and see many unusual sights. Many smaller *goembas* (monasteries), palaces and temples mentioned in this book are not on the standard sightseeing programs. Some welcome *small* groups of properly dressed visitors who do not intrude on the surroundings. The Bhutanese are very polite, calm people, and if you too are polite, they will try to accommodate your wishes as much as possible.

Maps

There is a dearth of maps of Bhutan. Bhutan is included in Lonely Planet's comprehensive *India & Bangladesh Road Atlas* at a scale of 1:1,250,000. It features a complete index, glossary and handy distance charts. Berndtson & Berndtson produce a handy plastic-laminated folding map with a road map on one side and maps of Thimphu and Paro on the reverse. Paolo Gondoni's 1:390,000 scale *Bhutan Himalaya* map is published by Himalayan Map House (e maphouse@wlink.com.np), PO Box 3924, Kathmandu, Nepal. Shangri La Maps (e sangrilatwa@mos.com.np), PO Box 8124, Kathmandu, Nepal, also produces a good 1:450,000 scale map.

The Trekking chapter lists details of topographical maps, but most of these maps are not available to the public. The Survey of Bhutan has published a large 1:250,000 map that is a composite of Landsat images overlaid with roads, major towns and district boundaries. It is hard to interpret because the rivers look like ridges, but it's a magic Bhutanese map – if you turn it upside down, everything looks as it should. The survey department also produces several specialised maps that are sold in bookshops. Various sheets show historical places, tourist spots, health centres and farming facilities. Colour maps of Thimphu and Paro valleys with detailed town plans are also available in bookshops and some hotel gift shops.

There is a 1:100,000 map series and an atlas, by the Land Use Planning Section assisted by the Danish agency Danida, which includes a large sheet map of each *dzongkhag* (district) with 200m contour intervals.

Spelling

Dzongkha is written in a script very similar to Tibetan, though the Bhutanese believe theirs is a more elegant version. The Dzongkha Development Commission has established a system of transliteration called Romanised Dzongkha that does not use any accent marks. This has produced several proper names that are quite different from the spellings that appear in older books and maps.

Some of the more confusing changes are:

old names	new names
Chirang	Tsirang
Dewathang	Deothang
Gantey	Gangte
Kula Kangri	Kulha Gangri
Lingshi	Lingzhi
Samchi	Samtse
Shemgang	Zhemgang
Tashi Yangtse	Trashi Yangtse
Tashichho Dzong	Trashi Chhoe Dzong
Tashigang	Trashigang
Tongsa	Trongsa
Wangdi Phodrang	Wangdue Phodrang

Bhutan shares India's fascination for official abbreviations and acronyms, and these are used throughout the book and defined in the Glossary.

What to Bring

The following list will cover your needs for a vehicle-based cultural tour. See the Trekking chapter for additional suggestions on specialised trekking clothing and equipment.

Since you will be travelling in a private vehicle, there is less concern about bulk and weight than if you were schlepping your own luggage on and off various forms of public transport. There is a strictly enforced 20kg weight limit (30kg in business class) on Druk Air. You should hold yourself to this allowance; even if you pay for excess baggage, it still travels stand-by and may be offloaded. Plus, as with all travel, the less you carry, the easier it is to move about and the less there is to misplace.

Clothing Casual clothes are fine, but you would do well to have a set of dress-up clothes (jacket and tie for men, dress or appropriately smart pair of pants for women). Dress clothing is appropriate for visiting government offices, festivals, and for social occasions in Thimphu homes. Bhutan has a small-town atmosphere, and you might easily find yourself in the company of a high government official. If you have scheduled your trip around a festival, you definitely should carry a set of dressy clothing. Bhutanese people dress quite formally, and your dirty jeans won't fit in on such occasions. Remember, this is a country with a national dress code (see Society & Conduct in the Facts about Bhutan chapter for more details).

Even in the summer, it can be cool in Paro and Thimphu, and it's downright cold in winter. Days can be quite warm, especially in the lower regions such as Punakha and Phuentsholing, and you could start off driving in the cold of dawn and be uncomfortably warm by mid-morning. Use a layering system, starting with thermal underwear and adding a shirt, pile jacket and windbreaker or parka as necessary. If you are not trekking, you will need:

- thermal underwear for cold weather (and also for sleeping in when it's cold)
- swimming costume (for the hotel swimming pool in Punakha, the pool in Thimphu's sports complex, communal stone baths and hot springs)
- cotton trousers
- cotton skirt for women
- pile jacket or sweater – even in summer
- down or fibrefill jacket – in winter; not needed in summer
- T-shirts or short-sleeved (not sleeveless) cotton shirts
- sneakers or walking shoes and socks
- sandals or flip flops
- rain jacket – Gore-Tex if you can afford it, otherwise a poncho or nylon jacket
- dress-up clothes for festivals
- sun hat
- warm hat and gloves in winter

Both men and women should avoid wearing shorts in towns. Women will probably feel

Visiting a Dzong

A police officer is stationed at the entrance of each dzong. One of their duties is to ensure that visitors are appropriately dressed. For Bhutanese this means a *gho*, complete with a *kabney* (scarf) and proper footwear (either bare feet or shoes with long socks) for men and a *kira* and *rachu* (shoulder cloth) for women.

The National Commission for Cultural Affairs has established the following guidelines for foreigners when they visit a dzong: men should wear trousers and a shirt with a collar; women should wear a dress or smart trousers. Shorts, caps, hats, T-shirts, sandals, umbrellas, smoking and alcohol are not allowed. If you are visiting a government office in the dzong, more formal attire is appropriate.

most comfortable in a skirt, but it's OK to wear pants, as many Bhutanese women wear them in the evening, especially when visiting a disco.

Toiletries Hotels provide soap and toilet paper, but don't expect a fancy collection of shampoo and cosmetics laid out in the bathroom. In Thimphu and Phuentsholing you can find many international brands of toiletries in small shops and the Tashi supermarkets. In other towns you will find only Indian brands of shampoo, toothpaste, shaving lather and other items. A roll of toilet paper in your luggage is useful if you are doing any extensive road travel.

Tampons are not readily available except in Thimphu and Phuentsholing – bring your own supply. Indian sanitary pads are available in remote towns, but you have to search for them.

You will be outside a lot, and much of the time at altitudes above 2500m where there is plenty of sun and wind. Bring a supply of sunscreen and lip protection; these are not easy to find in Bhutan.

Another item that's hard to find is dental floss. Bring some along to clean out the remains of a meal of tough and stringy Bhutanese chicken or yak meat. The quality of Indian brands of nail clippers, contact lens solution and deodorant is poor. Bring these items along with you.

Essential Extras There are several things that you should carry to make a trip to Bhutan more comfortable. The following items are essential.

Pack a folding umbrella. Rain is possible any time, and is almost certain from May to September.

Bring a water bottle and iodine for water purification (see the boxed text 'Water Purification' later in this chapter). Although you can get mineral water in most places, it comes in plastic bottles that cannot be recycled.

Carry ear plugs. This will help to reduce the noise from the barking dogs that scavenge through the streets at night.

If you are travelling to eastern Bhutan, you will be spending many hours on winding roads; bring a remedy for motion sickness. A small inflatable pillow is a useful addition; it's also good to have during long drives. Insect repellent is useful during spring and summer.

There are occasional electricity cuts throughout the country, so you should always keep a torch (flashlight) beside your bed.

Miscellaneous Items It will be difficult to get your laundry done as you travel because you will often stay only one night at a particular hotel. Bring some laundry soap and a length of clothesline so you can do your own washing. You can buy Indian laundry soap in bars, a more convenient form than powdered or liquid soap (which can get squashed and explode in your luggage). A large flat sink stopper is a useful addition to your personal laundry kit, and a small sewing kit is always handy.

Carry a pair of sunglasses (as protection from high-altitude glare). A Swiss army knife has many uses, such as cutting cheese, bread or fruit, and opening bottles. Pack your knife in your checked baggage to avoid confiscation during airport security checks. Bring a small alarm clock to help you wake up because not all hotel rooms have telephones. All hotels have locks on the door, and theft is rare. A padlock is not necessary in Bhutan, but is useful if your itinerary includes travelling or even transiting in India or Nepal. If you are travelling in winter, you might pack a hot-water bottle to warm up your bed at night.

Most Indian batteries are old-fashioned dry cell batteries. You can easily find large D-cell batteries, and can often find smaller AA cells, but other sizes are rare. If you are using a camera or tape recorder that uses alkaline or other special batteries, you will need to bring your own supply.

You can help keep track of where you are by checking the altitude. A global positioning system (GPS) or altimeter is useful, especially if you're going trekking, and can also help you to find out how close you are to a pass as you traverse Bhutan's roadways. Other toys you might bring are a thermometer and a compass.

RESPONSIBLE TOURISM

The policy of low volume and high prices was created by a concerned, culturally sensitive, well-educated and well-travelled government, one that truly feels that this is the best approach for Bhutan. The sensitive and socially conscious traveller will accept these restrictions.

Don't enter temples and monasteries without permission. There are meditation cells near many monasteries; don't disturb them. When you visit a dzong follow the guidelines in the boxed text 'Visiting a Dzong' and don't try to enter a dzong without your guide.

See the Trekking chapter for information on responsible trekking.

TOURIST OFFICES

The Department of Tourism (DOT; ☎ 02-323251, 323252, fax 02-323695, Ⓦ www .tourism.gov.bt), PO Box 126, Thimphu, has a very limited amount of literature available, but can refer you to tour operators who can assist with arrangements to visit Bhutan. There is no official government tourist office outside Bhutan.

VISAS & DOCUMENTS
Passport

You need a passport to enter Bhutan and its neighbouring countries. You should ensure that it has lots of empty pages for stamps, especially if you are travelling via India or Nepal. If your passport has less than six months of validity left, it is worth getting a new one, because many countries in this region will not issue visas to persons whose passports are about to expire.

Keep your passport safe. No country other than India has the facility for issuing a replacement passport in Bhutan. If you lose your passport, you must travel 'stateless' to another country to get it replaced. You should carry some additional form of identification and a photocopy of your passport to help in the event of such a disaster.

Visas

Most countries issue visas from their embassies abroad and stamp it in your passport, but not Bhutan. The Bhutanese visa process may appear complicated, but is actually quite straightforward once you understand it. Visas are issued only when you arrive in the country, either at Paro airport or (if entering by road) at Phuentsholing. You must apply in advance through a tour operator and receive approval before you travel to Bhutan.

All visas are approved by the Ministry of Foreign Affairs in Thimphu and there is no point in applying for a visa through a Bhutanese embassy abroad. All applications for tourist visas must be initialised by a Bhutanese tour operator. The operator submits the visa application to DOT in Thimphu. It, in turn, checks that you have completely paid for the trip and then issues an approval letter to the tour operator. With this approval in hand, the tour operator then makes a final application to the Ministry of Foreign Affairs, which takes up to a week to process the visa.

It's not necessary to fill in a special visa application form. Just provide the following information to the operator in Bhutan: your name, permanent address, occupation, nationality, date and place of birth, passport number and its date and place of issue and date of expiration. If any item is missing the whole process is delayed. Double-check that the information you send is correct; if there are any discrepancies when you arrive in Bhutan, there'll be further delays and complications in issuing the visa.

When the visa clearance is issued by the Ministry of Foreign Affairs, it sends a visa confirmation number to the tour operator and to Druk Air. Druk Air will not issue your tickets to Paro until it receives this confirmation number and then rechecks the visa information when you check in for the flight.

The actual visa endorsement is stamped in your passport when you arrive at one of the two ports of entry for tourists. When the visa is issued, you need to pay US$20 and present a passport photo with your passport number written on the back. You will then receive a visa for the exact period you have arranged to be in Bhutan. If some unusual event requires that you obtain a visa extension, your tour operator will arrange it.

It's an amazingly efficient system considering all the time, distance and various levels of bureaucracy involved. When you arrive in Bhutan, the visa officer will invariably be able to produce your approval form from the file and the visa will be issued on the spot. It's helpful, however, to have the reference number or even a faxed copy of the visa authority available to aid the immigration officials and Druk Air to find your information quickly.

Visas for Indian Nationals Upon arrival, Indian visitors are issued a 14-day permit, which may be extended in Thimphu. No passport or visa is required, but some form of identification such as a passport, driving licence or voters registration card is necessary. Indians arriving by road at Phuentsholing need five photos: three for the Indian certificate and two for the Bhutanese permit. Those arriving by air need two photos for the arrival permit in Paro.

Visa Extensions A visa extension for a period not exceeding six months costs Nu 510. Since tourist visas are issued for the full period you have arranged to stay in Bhutan, it's unlikely that you would need a visa extension.

Travel Permits
Restricted-Area Permits All of Bhutan outside of the Paro and Thimphu valleys is classified as a restricted area. Tour operators obtain a permit for the places on your itinerary, and this permit is checked and endorsed by the police at immigration checkpoints strategically located at important road junctions. The tour operator must return the permit to the government at the completion of the tour, and it is scrutinised for major deviations from the authorised program.

There are immigration checkpoints in Hongtsho (east of Thimphu), Chhukha (between Thimphu and Phuentsholing), Rinchending (above Phuentsholing), Wangdue Phodrang, Chazam (near Trashigang), Wamrong (between Trashigang and Samdrup Jongkhar), and in Samdrup Jongkhar. All are open from 5am to 9pm daily.

Permits to Enter Temples DOT rules state that visitors are not permitted to visit/enter certain places and religious establishments. This condition precludes entrance to the major *lhakhangs* (temples) and goembas. If you are a practising Buddhist, you may apply for a permit to visit specific dzongs and religious institutions. This is issued by the National Commission for Cultural Affairs, and application should be made in advance through a tour operator. The credibility of your application will be enhanced if you include a letter of reference from a recognised Buddhist organisation in your home country.

In 2001 the rules were changed to allow tourists to visit the courtyards of dzongs and, where feasible, one designated lhakhang in each dzong but only when accompanied by a licensed Bhutanese guide. This provision is subject to certain restrictions, including visiting hours, dress standards and other rules that vary by district. Because dzongs are open to all during the time of a tsechu, you may visit the courtyard, but not the lhakhangs, if your trip coincides with a festival.

Visas for Neighbouring Countries

India Nationals of most countries need a visa to visit India. If you are travelling overland to or from Bhutan via the border post in Phuentsholing you will need an Indian visa.

The government of India strongly prefers that you obtain your Indian visa in the country that issued your passport. It's usually a simple task to get your Indian visa before you leave home, but it's complicated to get one overseas. It is possible to obtain a seven-day transit visa overseas if you have confirmed flights in and out of India and can produce the appropriate tickets. Otherwise, you must pay a fee to the overseas embassy to send a fax to the Indian embassy in your own country and wait up to a week for a reply.

Tourist visas are issued for six months, are multiple entry, and are valid from the date of issue of the visa, not the date you enter India. This means that if you first enter India five months after the visa was issued, it will be valid for one month.

Six-month multiple-entry tourist visas cost A$75 for Australians, UK£30 for Britons, US$65 for Americans, and about €48 for French passport holders.

Nepal Visas for Nepal are available on arrival at Kathmandu airport or at land border crossings, including Kakarbhitta, the road crossing nearest to Bhutan. Normal visas are valid for 60 days. A single-entry visa costs US$30, a double-entry visa costs US$55, and a multiple-entry visa costs US$90. The catch is that the second time you enter Nepal during the same calendar year you have to pay US$50 for a 30-day visa. If you are making a side trip to Bhutan from Kathmandu, get a double-entry visa the first time you arrive in Nepal.

You can obtain a visa for Nepal in advance from embassies abroad or from the Nepali embassy or consulate in the gateway cities of Bangkok, Delhi, Dhaka or Kolkata.

Travel Insurance

A travel insurance policy to cover theft, loss and medical problems is always highly recommended. The cancellation rules for Bhutan are severe and inflexible. Trip cancellation insurance is almost essential.

Most policies will cover costs if you are forced to cancel your trip because of flight cancellation, illness, injury or the death of a close relative. If you have such a problem, travel insurance can help protect you from major losses due to Bhutan's prepayment conditions and hefty cancellation charges.

Some policies specifically exclude 'dangerous activities', and these can include motorcycling and even trekking. Read your policy carefully to be sure it covers ambulance rides or an emergency helicopter airlift out of a remote region, or an emergency flight home. If you have to stretch out you will need two seats and somebody has to pay for them. Many travel insurance policies include repatriation and evacuation through the worldwide network of International SOS Assistance.

You may prefer a policy that pays doctors or hospitals directly rather than you having to pay on the spot and claim later. If you have to claim later make sure you keep all documentation. Some policies ask you to call back (they suggest reversing the charges, an impossibility from Bhutan) to a centre in your home country where an immediate assessment of your problem is made.

It's a good idea to photocopy your policy in case the original is lost. If you are planning to travel for a long time, the insurance may seem very expensive – but if you can't afford it, you certainly won't be able to afford to deal with a medical emergency overseas.

Driving Licence & Permits

Driving is a harrowing experience. Roads are narrow, and trucks roar around hairpin bends, appearing suddenly and forcing oncoming vehicles to the side. Because roads are only about 3.5m wide, passing any oncoming vehicle involves one, or both, moving off the pavement onto the verge.

Since all transportation is provided by tour operators, you normally do not have to concern yourself with driving. If for some reason you are arranging your own transportation, you are still far better off using the services of a hired car or taxi. If you insist on driving in Bhutan, you should obtain a driving licence issued by the Road Safety and Transport Authority. Bhutanese licences are also valid throughout India.

An international driving permit is not valid in Bhutan. An Indian driving licence is valid in Bhutan, and it's possible for Indian nationals to drive in Bhutan, but unless you are an accomplished rally driver or are from a hill station such as Darjeeling and have experience in motoring in the mountains, it's safer with a professional driver.

Vehicle Documents If you drive a vehicle into Bhutan, you can get a 14-day permit at the Phuentsholing border. You will need the help of a tour operator to handle the paperwork. If you are driving a vehicle that is registered overseas, you will need a carnet in order to get through India.

Indian visitors may travel throughout most of Bhutan in their own vehicle, but need a permit from the Road Safety and Transport Authority at the border. Traffic regulations are the same as in India and are strictly enforced.

You can recognise how and where Bhutanese vehicles are registered by their numberplates. 'BP' at the beginning of the plate means private, 'BG' is government, 'BT' is taxi, 'RBA' is the Royal Bhutan Army and 'BHT' is the royal family. The first number indicates where the vehicle is registered: '1' for Thimphu, Punakha and Paro; '2' for Phuentsholing; '3' for Bumthang and Trongsa; and '4' for eastern Bhutan.

Student & Youth Cards

There is a 25% student discount on the US$200 daily tariff for tourists visiting Bhutan. If you are a student aged 25 or under and have applied for the discount, carry your student ID card as proof.

Vaccination Certificates

The only immunisation that is required for Bhutan and neighbouring countries is yellow fever if you are coming from a yellow-fever–infected area (sub-Saharan Africa and parts of South America. A certificate proving you have been vaccinated against yellow fever is unnecessary unless you are travelling directly from an infected area. See the Health section, later, for suggested immunisations.

Copies

Make a photocopy of the important pages of your passport (especially the one with your name and photograph). If you have a visa for India, photocopy this at the same time. Carry the copies separately from your travel documents so that you will have some form of identification in case you lose the passport. It's also a good idea to photocopy your airline ticket and list of the serial numbers of you travellers cheques.

EMBASSIES & CONSULATES

As already mentioned, it is pointless to apply for a Bhutanese visa through a Bhutanese embassy. All tourist visas must be channelled through DOT in Thimphu, and from there through the Ministry of Foreign Affairs.

Bhutanese Embassies

Bhutan has chosen not to have a wide network of resident embassies abroad, largely because of the expense involved.

Bangladesh
Embassy: (☎ 02-882 6863, 882 7160, fax 882 3939) House No F5 (SE), Gulshan Ave, Dhaka 1212

India
Embassy: (☎ 011-6889807, 6889230, fax 687 6710) Chandragupta Marg, Chanakyapuri, New Delhi 100 021

Kuwait
Embassy: (☎ 533 1506, fax 533 8959) PO Box 1510, Safat 13016

Switzerland
Permanent Mission to the UN: (☎ 022-799 0890, fax 799 0899) Palais des Nations, 17–19 Champ d'Avier, CH-1209 Geneva

Thailand
Embassy: (☎ 02-274 4740, fax 274 4743) 375/1 Soi Ratchadanivej, Pracha-Uthit Rd, Samsen Nok, Huay Kwang, Bangkok 10320

USA
Permanent Mission to the UN: (☎ 212-826 1919, fax 326 2998) 2 UN Plaza, 27th floor, New York, NY 10017

Embassies & Consulates in Bhutan

Only three foreign countries have an official presence in Bhutan. Bhutan's relations with other countries are handled through its embassies in Delhi and Dhaka.

Bangladesh
  Embassy: (☎ 02-322539, fax 322629) Thori Lam, Thimphu
India
  Embassy: (☎ 02-322162, fax 323195) India House, Thimphu
  Indian Embassy Liaison Office: (☎ 05-252635, 252992) Phuentsholing. Open 9.30am to 11.30am and 3.30pm to 5pm Monday to Friday.

CUSTOMS

Customs officials are generally lenient with tourists and rarely open baggage. They do, however, carefully check the baggage of returning residents, both Bhutanese and expatriate.

You will receive a baggage declaration form to complete when you arrive in Bhutan. For tourists, the main purpose of this form is to ensure that you re-export anything you bring into the country. List any expensive equipment that you are carrying, such as cameras and portable computers. Customs officials usually want to see the items that you list, then they endorse the form and return it to you. Don't lose it as you must return it when you leave the country.

There are no restrictions on other personal effects, including trekking gear, that you bring into the country. Duty-free allowances are generous, including 2L of liquor and 400 cigarettes. You can utilise these allowances to bring much-appreciated gifts to your tour operator and guide.

Departure formalities are straightforward, but you'll need to produce the form that you completed on arrival and may need to show all of the items listed on it. A lost form means complications and delays. If you lose the form, let your guide know as soon as possible so that special arrangements can be made to avoid any inconvenience.

The export of antiques and wildlife products is prohibited. If you purchase a souvenir that looks old, have your guide clear it as a nonantique item with the Division of Cultural Properties in Thimphu (☎ 02-322284, fax 02-323286). Customs authorities pay special attention to religious statues. It would be prudent to have any such statue cleared, old or not.

MONEY
Currency

The unit of currency is the *ngultrum* (Nu), which is equivalent to one Indian rupee. The ngultrum is further divided into 100 *chetrum*. There are notes of Nu 1, 5, 10, 20, 50, 100 and 500, each depicting a different dzong. There is a handsome Nu 1 coin that depicts the eight auspicious symbols (see the boxed text 'Tashi Tagye' in the Facts about Bhutan chapter). Indian rupees may be used freely anywhere in Bhutan, but ngultrums are not at all welcome in India.

It is OK with the Bhutanese if you bring a reasonable amount of Indian currency into Bhutan, though Indian regulations prohibit currency export.

Exchange Rates

Exchange rates for cash are as follows:

country	unit		Nu
Australia	A$1	=	Nu 23.40
Canada	C$1	=	Nu 28.80
euro zone	€1	=	Nu 41.85
Hong Kong	HK$1	=	Nu 5.80
India	Rs 1	=	Nu 1.00
Japan	¥100	=	Nu 36.65
Singapore	S$1	=	Nu 24.80
Switzerland	Sfr 1	=	Nu 27.40
UK	UK£1	=	Nu 66.50
USA	US$1	=	Nu 47.10

Exchanging Money

Since your trip is fully prepaid, theoretically you could manage in Bhutan without any local money at all, though you'll probably want some to pay for laundry, drinks, souvenirs and tips. You'll also need Nu 300 for airport tax on departure.

The exchange counters at the airport, larger hotels and the banks in Thimphu and Phuentsholing can change all the currencies listed, and sometimes Scandinavian currencies. If you are heading to central and eastern Bhutan, you will do better with more common currencies such as US dollars or pounds sterling.

In smaller towns foreign-currency exchange may be an unusual transaction; be prepared for delays while the person who knows how to do it is found.

If you plan to make a major purchase, for example textiles or art, consider bringing US dollars in cash. Most shops will accept this, and it can save you the hassle of exchanging a large quantity of money in advance and then attempting to change it back if you don't find the exact piece you were looking for.

You may change your unused ngultrums back to foreign currency (though usually only into US dollars) on departure if you can produce your original exchange receipts. Ngultrums are useless outside of Bhutan (except as a curiosity).

Bhutan has two banks, each with branches throughout the country. The Bank of Bhutan, a joint venture between the Bhutanese government and the State Bank of India was established in 1968. The Bhutan National Bank, was established in 1997 and is a public corporation, though the government retains 51% of its shares.

While the Bank of Bhutan still uses an antiquated hand-written ledger system, the Bhutan National Bank is a modernised operation, with a computer system and relationships with major overseas banks, though it has branches only in Thimphu. Phuentsholing and Trashigang.

The Bank of Bhutan's main branches are open 9am to 1pm Monday to Friday and 9am to 11am on Saturday, though the branches in Trongsa, Trashigang and Mongar are open on Sunday and closed Tuesday. It also has a branch in Thimphu that stays open later for the convenience of office workers (and travellers).

The Royal Monetary Authority is the central bank. It issues banknotes and processes interbank transfers, but does not change money or engage in any banking transactions for the public.

Travellers Cheques You can cash travellers cheques at any bank, most hotels and the foreign-exchange counter at the airport. There are bank charges of 1% for cheque encashment. You should carry only well-known brands such as American Express, Visa, Thomas Cook, Citibank or Barclays. Chhundu Travels (☎ 02-322592) in Thimphu can replace lost American Express travellers cheques; there is no replacement facility for any other travellers cheques in Bhutan.

Credit Cards & ATMs You should not count on using a credit card in Bhutan. American Express, Visa and MasterCard are accepted at the government-run Handicrafts Emporium, a few other handicraft shops and some of the larger hotels in Thimphu, but these transactions take extra time. The credit card companies charge high fees and the verification office is only open from 9am to 5pm. This precludes paying your hotel bill at night or when you check out early in the morning. There are no ATMs in the country.

International Transfers You are not likely to be in Bhutan long enough to need to have money transferred to you. If, however, you do need to make an international transfer, check with the Bhutan National Bank for its list of overseas correspondent banks and try to initiate the transaction through one of those.

Black Market There is no black market in Bhutan. The Indian rupee is a convertible currency, and the rate is set by market conditions, not by the Indian government. Subject to some restrictions, Indians and Bhutanese can buy dollars officially to purchase goods from abroad. Therefore, there is not much difference between the market rate and the official rate for the Indian rupee, and thus, the ngultrum.

It's sometimes possible to buy Indian rupees at a slightly better rate in Bangkok or Hong Kong and then bring them to Bhutan, but the small gain is hardly worth the hassle.

Security

Few Bhutanese hotels have safes for guests' valuables. You can use a money belt or a pouch that hangs around your neck to carry money and important documents such as your passport. Theft is rare, although not unheard of in Bhutan, but such protection is essential in adjoining countries.

Costs

Prices and payment procedures are a bit complicated. If you are going through an overseas agent, you can avoid many of the complications, but if you are working directly with a Bhutanese tour operator, you'll spend considerable time sending email and faxes, and may have to learn more than you want to about making international bank transfers.

The daily tariff for tourists visiting in a group of four people or more is US$200 per day (US$165 per day in the low season of December to January and June to August, whether you stay in hotels (a 'cultural tour') or go trekking. To further complicate matters there is a special rate of US$250 per day that will be applied from 2003 for the period that includes the Paro and Thimphu festivals. The rate is calculated according to the number of nights in Bhutan.

To encourage trekkers to make longer treks, DOT allows a 10% discount on days 11 to 20 and 20% from day 21 onwards.

The payment includes all of your accommodation, food, land transport within Bhutan, services of guides and porters, supply of pack animals on treks, and cultural programs as appropriate.

The tour rate applies uniformly irrespective of location or the type of accommodation asked for or provided. This clause means that if you have arranged to stay in a fancy hotel and get bumped, you have no recourse.

Individual tourists and couples are subject to a surcharge, over and above the daily rate. The surcharge may also be applied if a member of a group arrives or departs on a separate flight from the rest of the party. The surcharge is US$40 per night for one person, and US$30 per night per person for a group of two people. Visitors qualifying for any kind of discount still have to pay this small-group surcharge.

Most tour operators expect you to pay separately for all drinks, including liquor, beer, mineral water and bottled soft drinks. You'll also have to pay extra for laundry, riding horses, and cultural splurges such as a Bhutanese hot-stone bath.

Discounts & Special Categories The following categories of visitors are eligible for discounts on the daily rate:

Children Up to the age of five, children are free. Kids from six to 12 accompanied by parents or guardians receive a 50% discount on the daily rates.

Diplomats A 25% discount on the rates applies to diplomats from foreign embassies or missions accredited to Bhutan.

Group Leaders A discount of 50% on the rates is given to one person in a group of 11 to 15 people. A free trip is allowed for one member per group exceeding 15 people.

Students Full-time students 25 years and younger with valid identity cards from their academic institutions are allowed a 25% discount, resulting in a rate of US$150 per night (plus small group surcharges, if applicable). You should deal directly with a Bhutanese tour operator rather than through a travel agency or tour company at home if you plan to utilise this facility.

Travel Agents Tour companies intending to put Bhutan into their programs may apply for a discounted familiarisation tour. It's unlikely that you can manage this arrangement unless you are already a serious player in the travel industry. DOT has an excellent network of connections worldwide and will check your bona fides beforehand. It also requires both a pretrip and a post-trip briefing.

Volunteers & Project Employees If you are working in Bhutan, you are not subject to the normal rules for tourists, and the agency employing you will arrange your visa. Soon after you arrive in Bhutan, you will be enrolled in a cultural-orientation course for new volunteers given by the Royal Institute of Management. Volunteers are allowed two visitors a year; the visitors must be close relatives and are not subject to the tourist tariff.

Special Rules for Indian Nationals
Because of Bhutan's special relationship with India, Indian tourists are categorised differently from other international tourists. Indians do not require a visa and may pay local rates for food, transportation and accommodation. They may travel independently throughout most of Bhutan, though a special permit is required. DOT recommends that Indian visitors use the services of a Bhutanese tour operator to arrange such permits and to expedite hotel and transport bookings.

The initial permit for Indian nationals is for 14 days, and they still need a travel permit to go beyond Paro and Thimphu. Indians may also wander freely into all the border towns of Bhutan, though they must leave by 10pm unless staying in a hotel.

Payment Procedure If you have arranged your trip directly with a tour operator in Bhutan and are not using an overseas agent, you must make payment directly to DOT in Bhutan. This is not a trivial process.

The most straightforward and efficient procedure is to make a US dollar transfer to the account of the Bhutan National Bank at Citibank in New York. Transfers into this account are monitored by DOT and credited to the agent in Bhutan. Transfers should be made to Citibank, 111 Wall St, 19th floor, New York, NY 10043, account of Bhutan National Bank, ABA No 0210-0008-9, account No 36023474, Swift Code Citius 33, Chips Routing No 008. The name of the tour operator should be stated as the 'beneficiary'.

If this procedure is not practical for you, contact the tour operator you have chosen to handle your trip for alternative, but more complicated, bank transfer methods.

Once you make the payment, fax a copy of the deposit details to the tour operator in Bhutan so that it can present this documentation to DOT to start the visa process.

In cases of last-minute bookings or other exceptional circumstances it is possible to pay in travellers cheques (but not cash) upon arrival in Bhutan, but this entails a visit to the DOT office to sign a few documents.

Note that you are paying an agency of the Bhutanese government, not the tour operator directly, therefore you have more protection against default on the part of the tour company.

Cancellation Charges Tour programs booked and subsequently cancelled are subject to cancellation charges. Travel insurance is an extremely worthwhile investment given that you must make full payment up front. The fee depends on how many days before the start of the tour program you cancel:

More than 30 days	No charge
Within 21 days	10%
Within 14 days	15%
Within 7 days	30%
Fewer than 7 days	50%
Without notice	50%

Cost of Delays There is no charge for the number of days of delay in your arrival or departure due to weather conditions, Druk Air problems or road blocks. In cases of delayed departure, tour operators are allowed to charge the actual expenses for accommodation, food, transport and any other services required.

These rules are controlled by requiring tour operators to notify the DOT in writing about any change in the program as a result of delays and to account for any extra services they provide.

Tipping & Bargaining
Tipping is officially discouraged in Bhutan, but it's becoming a common practice and it's OK to do so if you want to reward good service. Servers and hotel staff do appreciate the gesture.

You will usually be accompanied throughout your visit to Bhutan by the same tour guide and probably the same driver. Though it's against the official DOT policy, these people expect a tip at the end of the trip. Many leaders on group tours take up a collection at the conclusion of the trip and hand it over in one packet. With a large group this can be a substantial amount of money and the practice has created high expectations on the part of Bhutanese guides. Obviously an individual traveller cannot tip the same amount as a group of 15 travellers, but this sometimes escapes the mind of the guides. Offer a reasonable reward for good service, but don't feel pressured into excessive tipping.

If you've been trekking, it's appropriate to tip the guide, cook and waiter. Horsemen also expect tips, but this can be minimal if they are the owners of the horses or yaks and are making money by hiring out their animals.

The stakes go up, however, if they have been especially helpful with camp chores and on the trail.

Bargaining is not a Bhutanese tradition, and you won't get very far with your haggling skills here, except with trailside vendors on the hike to Taktshang and in the local handicrafts section of the Thimphu weekend market. Shops, restaurants and hotels all have fixed prices.

Taxes & Refunds

Most hotels and restaurants throughout the country charge government tax at 10% and a 10% service charge. Assuming you are on a normal tourist program, this is absorbed by the tour operator.

The prices listed for hotels and restaurants do not include tax or service charges.

Once you have made a payment to DOT, any refunds for cancellation or delays are made by international bank transfer unless you find yourself willing to accept ngultrums or Indian rupees. The bank transfer does take a long time, therefore you should be certain of your plans before you pay any money.

POST & COMMUNICATIONS
Postal Rates

Airmail postage rates for the first 20g of ordinary (nonpackage) mail are:

destination	letters	postcards
India, Nepal		
& Bangladesh	Nu 4	Nu 3
All other countries	Nu 20	Nu 20

Collecting Bhutanese Stamps

You probably won't strike it rich by buying postage stamps from Bhutan, but they make a colourful addition to any collection. Some items are issued specifically for sale to collectors by an agency in New York, and others are locally produced by the government itself. There is not much demand for Bhutanese stamps, and the value is generally low. However, the number of stamps issued in each series is generally so small that any increase in demand sends prices skyrocketing.

The price of 3D mushroom stamps shot up to US$25 a set when topical collectors of mushroom stamps discovered them and exhausted the supply. The issue of playable record stamps sold out quickly in Bhutan, and only a few thousand were produced because of the expense. These are now worth US$300 a set. Some surcharged provisional issues from the late 1960s fetch US$60 to US$70 at auction and some of the Disney issues are becoming hard to find, with imperforate souvenir sheets selling for US$100 each. Most, however, are available in adequate quantities at a reasonable mark-up over face value. Bhutanese stamps often are auctioned on the Internet through eBay.

Some shops sell older issues and handsome souvenir sheets, but the philatelic counter in the Thimphu post office has the largest selection. For more information on Bhutanese stamps check the Web sites at W www.bhutan .org and www.bhutanpost.com.bt.

Sending Mail

You can send mail from hotels and post offices. The mail service from Bhutan is quite reliable, and no special procedures are necessary. It would be better, however, to avoid sending important letters, money or film through the mail.

If you mail cards or letters from the Thimphu post office, you can buy exotic postage stamps from the philatelic bureau.

Bhutan Post offers both outgoing and incoming Expedited Mail Service (EMS), which is a reliable and fast international mail delivery facility that is cheaper than courier services. It also has a Local Urgent Mail (LUM) service for delivery within Thimphu.

If you have made a purchase and want to send it home, it's best to have the shop make all the arrangements for you. Keep the receipt, and let your guide know what you are doing so they can follow up in case the package does not arrive. Send all parcels by air; sea mail, via Kolkata, takes several months.

DHL (☎ 02-324729, e dhl@druknet.net .bt), on Thori Lam in Thimphu, provides efficient international courier service to and from Bhutan. There are several smaller courier companies that specialise in service to India.

Receiving Mail

The best way to receive mail is to have it sent to the post office box of the Bhutanese tour operator that is handling your trip. Unless you are on a long trek, you will probably not be in Bhutan long enough for a letter to reach you.

Telephone

Telephones were first introduced in Bhutan in 1963. The satellite earth station in Thimphu was installed in 1990 along with a sophisticated international telephone service. Direct dial calls go through quickly and clearly. Domestic telephone service is through a network of microwave links, and most of the country's major towns now have both domestic and international direct dial facilities.

The country code for Bhutan is 975. Local dialling codes are:

Thimphu	☎ 02	Mongar	☎ 04
Paro	☎ 08	Samdrup Jongkhar	☎ 07
Bumthang	☎ 03	Trashigang	☎ 04
Trongsa	☎ 03	Phuentsholing	☎ 05

The international access code is 00. There are numerous public call offices (PCOs) throughout the country from which you can make STD (long-distance) calls within Bhutan or to India at a standard rate of 30% above the normal tariff. Some PCOs also offer international subscriber dialling (ISD) calls overseas. In many PCOs the length of your call is likely to be measured by the proprietor's watch, not by a fancy meter. Most hotels can arrange both local and in-

ternational calls, though none have in-room direct dial facilities.

There is a 10% discount on international telephone rates from 6pm to 9am. Domestic direct-dial calls cost Nu 2 to 8 per minute depending on the time of day. The number for directory enquiry is 140.

Bhutan Telecom also provides satellite phones using the Thuria system, which allows direct dialling from anywhere in the country, even on trek. Some tour operators have these phones and can rent them, though the charges are higher than for normal calls.

Fax

Nearly all hotels and some PCOs have facilities to send and receive faxes. Tour operators in Bhutan now rely on email for most of their communications, but still use fax for documents such as visa authority letters.

Email & Internet Access

Full international Internet service was inaugurated on 2 June 1999, the 25th anniversary of the king's coronation. You can access Druknet (W www.druknet.net.bt), Bhutan's Internet provider, from any telephone in Bhutan by dialling ☎ 100 or ☎ 101. At the time of research Bhutan had not yet joined any of the global Internet roaming agreements, so a local Druknet account was needed to log in. There are Internet cafes in many large towns.

Email & Internet Changes

As this book went to press, all Internet and email addresses in Bhutan were changed. Where once addresses ended with 'com.bt', 'net.bt' or 'gov.bt' these now all end '.bt'.

DIGITAL RESOURCES

The World Wide Web is a rich resource for travellers. You can research your trip, hunt down bargain air fares, book hotels, check on weather conditions or chat with locals and other travellers about the best places to visit (or avoid).

There's no better place to start your Web explorations than the Lonely Planet Web site (W www.lonelyplanet.com). Here you will find succinct summaries on travelling to most places on earth, postcards from other travellers and the Thorn Tree bulletin board, where you can ask questions before you go or dispense advice when you get back. You can also find travel news and updates to many of our most popular guidebooks, and the subWWWay section links you to the most useful travel resources elsewhere on the Web. Visit Destination Bhutan for all the latest news and views.

In addition to the commercial sites of travel agencies, Druk Air (W www.drukair .com.bt) and Bhutan's national newspaper *Kuensel* (W www.kuenselonline.com), there are numerous sites established by people, including many Japanese, with an interest in things Bhutanese.

An interesting travelogue with pictures is at W www.bluepeak.net/bhutan. The World-Wide Web Virtual Library of Bhutan is at W www.bhutan.org. Thinley Namgyal, a Bhutanese student, has created a site on Bhutan at W www.geocities.com/Tokyo/ Island/8111.

The Department of Information Technology is at W www.dit.gov.bt and the Bhutan Planning Commission is at W www.pcs .gov.bt. Try the Bhutanese food site at W members.tripod.com/thinley/recipe/index .html and a Japanese site in English with lots of background information and links at W www.tashidelek.com. The University of California at Berkeley's bibliography of books on Bhutan is at W www.lib.berkeley .edu/SSEAL/SouthAsia/bhutan.html.

BOOKS
There are three bookshops in Thimphu and one in Phuentsholing. Many gift and handicraft shops throughout the country also stock a few books. Most of the books are published in India. These include books on Bhutan and inexpensive Indian editions of English novels and textbooks, but there is a serious lack of variety. If you want a page-turner to while away the time at airports, bring it with you.

As you would expect, the selection of books on Bhutan available in Thimphu is more extensive than anywhere else in the world. Some of the books listed below, particularly the history books, are published in India and are available only in Bhutan and select bookshops in Nepal and India. Most of the books that are still in print can be ordered on the Internet through W www .amazon.com or W www.altbookstore.com. Other excellent sources for books about Bhutan, both current and out of print, are Chessler Books (W www.chesslerbooks .com) and Powells (W www.powells.com) in the US and, in the UK, Himalayan Books (W www.himalayanbooks.co.uk) and Stanfords (W www.stanfords.co.uk).

Pilgrims Book House in Kathmandu (☎ 977-1-424942, fax 424943) also has a good selection. You can write to them at PO Box 3872, Kathmandu, Nepal, or order direct from W www.pilgrimsbooks.com.

Lonely Planet
Lonely Planet's *India* and *North India* guidebooks will help you if you are visiting India before or after visiting Bhutan. Similarly, the *Nepal* guidebook is essential if you are passing through Kathmandu or travelling by road between Nepal and Bhutan.

Travel
Bhutan, Kingdom of the Dragon by Robert Dompnier is a coffee table book by a French photographer who has travelled extensively throughout Bhutan.

Bhutan by Françoise Pommaret has a great deal of cultural background and information about Bhutan's customs and traditions as well as descriptions of many of the important temples and dzongs.

So Close to Heaven, The Vanishing Buddhist Kingdoms of the Himalayas by Barbara Crossette is an excellent account of Bhutan's history and culture. The author is a *New York Times* correspondent who has spent considerable time in Bhutan and other Himalayan regions. Published in 1995, the book discusses some of the current development and political problems facing Bhutan.

Beyond the Sky and the Earth by Jamie Zeppa tells the story of a Canadian teacher who fell in love with Bhutan during her teaching assignment in eastern Bhutan. Jamie offers many anecdotes and explanations of strange Bhutanese traditions as she describes her experiences, many of which you may recognise during your travels.

Dreams of the Peaceful Dragon by Katie Hickman is a traveller's account of a walk across Bhutan in the 1970s, before the road between Bumthang and Mongar was completed. It gives a good picture of trekking in Bhutan.

In The Himalayas by Jeremy Bernstein describes the author's journeys through Nepal, Tibet and Bhutan. The Bhutan chapter is not extensive, but Bernstein makes many interesting comparisons to the conditions and his experiences in Nepal.

Joanna Lumley in the Kingdom of the Thunder Dragon is by Joanna Lumley, the costar of the BBC program *Absolutely Fabulous*. Her grandfather, Lt Col JLR Weir, was a political officer in Sikkim; the book is based on a TV program that traced his trek through the country in 1931.

History & Politics

Of Rainbows and Clouds: The Life of Yab Ugyen Dorji As Told to His Daughter by Yab Ugyen Dorji & Ashi Dorji Wangmo Wangchuck is a fascinating and intimate account of life in Bhutan. It includes an account of the assassination of Shabdrung Jigme Dorji in 1931 and of the royal wedding in 1988. The large-format book is illustrated with many contemporary and historical photographs.

The Raven Crown by the late Michael Aris is the definitive history of Bhutan's monarchy. Aris, who lived in Bhutan with his wife (Ang San Suu Kyi) from 1967 to 1972, is the leading Western authority on Bhutan's history. The book is lavishly illustrated with rare photographs of the early days of Bhutan that help show what a unique civilisation existed in the early 20th century.

Bhutan, the Early History of a Himalayan Kingdom, also by Michael Aris, is the most authoritative history of Bhutan

available in English. It is difficult to get through, largely because of the complex transliteration system of Bhutanese and Tibetan terms that is used in the book.

Sikhim and Bhutan, Twenty-one Years on the North-east Frontier by J Claude White describes White's 1905 expedition to Bhutan to present the insignia of Knight Commander of the Indian Empire to Sir Ugyen Wangchuck. Originally published in 1909, there is an Indian reprint edition available.

Political Missions to Bootan by Ashley Eden contains a pompous Victorian account of the history of Bhutan. Eden disliked the people and their habits intensely, and after reading a few pages, you'll have a better idea of why Eden was treated so badly by the *penlop* (governor) of Trongsa when he arrived in Punakha. The original edition is long out of print, but an Indian reprint was issued in 1972.

Bhutan and the British by Peter Collister is a comprehensive and even-handed account of the interaction between Britain and Bhutan from 1771 to 1987.

Lands of the Thunderbolt by the Earl of Ronaldshay is one of the most readable accounts of a British expedition to Bhutan. The earl's full name was Lawrence John Lumley Dundas, Marquis of Zetland. He was president of the Royal Geographic Society from 1922 to 1925.

Bhutan, A Kingdom in the Himalayas by Narendra Singh is a study of the land, people and government of Bhutan. The author is an Indian lawyer who served as the constitutional advisor to the government of Bhutan in the early 1970s. His description of the history is quite thorough and the appendix includes copies of Bhutan's treaties with Britain and India. This book is out of print; it was published in India and is hard to find.

India and Bhutan: A Study in Frontier Political Relations 1772–1885 by Arbinda Deb is yet another Indian thesis that documents, rather well, the early relations between Bhutan and Britain.

Sources for the History of Bhutan by Michael Aris is a scholarly work that translates several historically important texts.

A Political and Religious History of Bhutan by Dr CT Dorji lists the major personalities in both the religious and political history of the country. The companion volume is *History of Bhutan Based on Buddhism.*

The Jesuit and the Dragon by Howard Solverson is a biography of the late Father William Mackey. It describes his contributions to the establishment of a modern educational system in Bhutan.

Bayonets to Lhasa by Sir Francis Younghusband is a description of the first British expedition to Lhasa. There is an interesting discussion of King Ugyen Wangchuck, who accompanied the expedition when he was still the penlop of Trongsa.

Religion

The Divine Madman by Keith Dowman is a wonderful translation of the poems and works of Lama Drukpa Kunley.

The Treasure Revealer of Bhutan by Padma Tshewang, Khenpo Phuntshok Tashi, Chris Butters & Sigmund K Sætreng is a recent study of Pema Lingpa and the tradition of *tertons* (treasure discoverers).

The Lotus Born, translated by Erik Pema Kunsang, is a complex account of the life of Guru Rinpoche (Padmasambhava). It is a translation of the biography written by his foremost Tibetan disciple, the *dakini* (angel) Yeshi Tshogyal. It's very heavy going.

The Power Places of Central Tibet by Keith Dowman has considerable background on Tibetan saints and lamas, many of whom travelled to Bhutan. More detailed information is available in Dowman's *The Sacred Life of Tibet.*

The Tibetan Book of Living and Dying by Sogyal Rinpoche is a translation of Guru Rinpoche's *Tibetan Book of the Dead.* It's a sophisticated Himalayan Buddhist text, but worth a look if you are especially interested in learning about some of Bhutan's religious foundations.

General

The Hero with a Thousand Eyes by Karma Ura is an historical novel. It is based on the life of Shingkhar Lam, a retainer who served in the court of the second, third and fourth kings of Bhutan. It offers extraordinary insight into social conditions in the early days of the 20th century and the reforms and modernisations introduced by the third king, Jigme Dorji Wangchuck.

Bhutanese Tales of the Yeti by Kunzang Choden describes the Bhutanese beliefs about where and how this creature may live.

The Dragon Country by Nirmala Das was published in 1974 and is out of print, though there are a few copies in Thimphu bookshops. It is an excellent introduction to the history of the country and its dzongs and temples written by the wife of the first Indian representative stationed in Bhutan.

The Ballad of Pemi Tshewang Tashi by Karma Ura is a translation of a Bhutanese folk tale with a lot of cultural and historical background notes.

The Thunder Dragon Kingdom by Steven K Berry is one of the few accounts of a mountaineering expedition to Bhutan. It chronicles a 1986 British attempt on Gangkhar Puensum.

Memoirs of a Mountaineer by F Spencer Chapman chronicles the first ascent of Jhomolhari in 1973 from Phari in Tibet, which he described as the dirtiest town on earth.

Conservation & Environment

Wild Rhododendrons of Bhutan by Rebecca Pradhan is a well-organised guide to the rhododendrons of Bhutan with colour photographs of all 46 species.

Birds of Bhutan by Carol Inskipp, Tim Inskipp & Richard Grimmett is a comprehensive field guide to Bhutan's birds.

An Introduction to Birdwatching in Bhutan by Carol & Tim Inskipp is a small Worldwide Fund for Nature (WWF) publication that provides descriptions and drawings of important species of birds found in Bhutan. It also has an introductory section on basic bird-watching practice.

Birds of Bhutan by Salim Ali, B Biswas & S Dillon Ripley was published by the Zoological Survey of India and is available only in India and Bhutan. It does not have illustrations, but has some good descriptions and an extensive list compiled by the recognised authorities on Himalayan birds.

Trees and Shrubs of Nepal and the Himalayas by Adrian & Jimmie Storrs is the best field book on the forests of Bhutan. It was published in Kathmandu but printed in Thailand, so those are the most likely places to find a copy.

Geology of the Bhutan Himalaya by Augusto Gansser is a large-format book with everything you could possibly want to know about Bhutan's geology.

Bhutan and its Natural Resources is a collection of essays on the environment published by Sherubtse College in Bhutan.

Bhutan: Environment, Culture and Development Strategy by PP Karan is an Indian publication written by an American professor of geography. Based on several years of research in Bhutan, it chronicles major developments in the country up to 1985.

Art & Architecture

Bhutan – Mountain Fortress of the Gods, a large-format book, provides the documentation for a 1998 Bhutanese exhibition in Vienna. Edited by Christian Schicklgruber & Françoise Pommaret, it has extensive illustrations and excellent information.

From the Land of the Thunder Dragon: Textile Arts of Bhutan by Diana K Myers is a detailed study of traditional Bhutanese textiles – their uses, design and weaving methods. Based on an exhibition of textiles from Bhutan at the Peabody Essex Museum in Massachusetts, it has colour photographs of many designs and finished items of clothing.

Traditional Bhutanese Textiles by Barbara Adams is the first published study of Bhutanese textiles. There are numerous colour photos of textiles that she collected from Bhutanese who travelled to Nepal in the late 1970s.

An Introduction to Traditional Architecture of Bhutan is a publication of the Bhutan Department of Works, Housing and Roads. It has chapters on iconography and on the design of dzongs, monasteries, *chortens* and temples. There are detailed descriptions of traditional design and construction methods for houses.

Views of Mediaeval Bhutan by Michael Aris is a coffee-table book that presents the diary and drawings of Samuel Davis, an excellent artist who was a member of George Bogle's 18th-century expedition to Bhutan.

Tibetan Thangka Painting, Methods and Materials by Davis & Janice Jackson is a fascinating guide to how artists lay out the intricate designs of Mahayana Buddhist art.

FILMS

There are a few documentary films about Bhutan, the most recent being the BBC TV special *Joanna Lumley in the Kingdom of the Thunder Dragon*. The Royal Society for Protection of Nature (RSPN) has produced *On Wings of Prayer*, a video about the black-necked cranes, which is available in souvenir shops in Bhutan. Much of the film *Little Buddha* was shot in Bhutan, and Bhutanese boys played the role of the Dalai Lama at various ages in the 1997 movie *Seven Years in Tibet*.

The first feature film produced by a Bhutanese filmmaker was *The Cup* by Khyentse Norbu, which was nominated as best foreign-language film for the 2000 Academy Awards. It chronicles the impact of World Cup soccer fever on the young monks of the Chokling monastery in India. It's an interesting view of life in a Himalayan monastery.

NEWSPAPERS & MAGAZINES

Kuensel is the weekly national newspaper of Bhutan. The name translates as 'enlightenment', and it is available on Saturday morning in English, Dzongkha and Nepali editions. It is well edited, articulate and informative. Each edition contains local news, cultural titbits, a summary of the week's international news, a children's page and numerous government announcements. It is available from bookshops in Thimphu and at many agencies throughout the country.

If you want to stay in touch with current events in Bhutan, you can subscribe to *Kuensel* or visit its Web site at **W** www .kuenselonline.com. A one-year subscription, delivered by airmail, costs US$76 to America, US$66 to Europe, US$56 to Asia, Africa and Australia and US$15 to India, Nepal and Bangladesh. For more detailed information contact Kuensel Corporation (☎ 02-322483, fax 02-322975), GPO Box 204, Thimphu.

Indian newspapers and magazines are available in Phuentsholing and Thimphu. They arrive two to three days after publication. Look for the Indian news magazines *India Today* and the *Illustrated Weekly of India*. A few copies of international news magazines appear in bookshops about 10 days after publication.

RADIO & TV

Bhutan Broadcasting Service is on the air from 4pm to 8pm on the 60MHz band (5030 kHz) and FM 96 Monday to Saturday. On Sunday it broadcasts from 10am to 4pm on the 49MHz band (6035 kHz) and FM 96. Programs are in Dzongkha, English, Nepali and Sharchop. The English news is at 7.15pm Monday to Saturday, and at 3pm on Sunday.

On 2 June 1999, Bhutan became the last country in the world to establish its own television broadcasting station. Bhutan television broadcasts from 8pm to 9pm daily with news in English and Dzongkha, and additional locally produced programming. Cable companies serve Thimphu and other large towns with feeds from satellite broadcasts including the BBC, CNN and a vast array of Hindi channels.

VIDEO SYSTEMS

There is an enormous number of video rental shops throughout the country. All video tapes use the PAL format. Many of the videos are second- or third-generation copies of Hindi song-and-dance epics. There is also a large collection of English films. You won't find videos with sexual content but, surprisingly, some portray extreme violence.

One Bhutanese company has produced an MTV-style music video of Bhutanese popular songs called *Joge Joge* (Let's Go, Let's Go).

PHOTOGRAPHY & VIDEO
Film & Equipment

Bring as much film as you think you will need, and then add several more rolls. You will be unhappy if you run out of film in Bhutan.

A limited supply of colour print film makes its way into Bhutan and is sold in shops throughout the country. The major brand available is Konica ASA 100 colour print film, and it costs about Nu 100, more than it does overseas. Sometimes you can find Kodak and Fuji print film, but if you are shooting transparencies, bring all your film with you, as slide film is not available.

There are colour-printing facilities in Thimphu and Phuentsholing. Kuenphen Colour Lab (☎ 02-324058) on Norzin Lam in Thimphu has an automatic machine. The quality of processing sometimes suffers because the labs don't have enough business to change the chemicals as frequently as they should. Unless you are processing snapshots that you want to give to people in Bhutan, it's best to wait until you get home, or to Bangkok, Kathmandu or Hong Kong, to have your film developed. No lab in Bhutan has facilities to process colour slides.

Fit a UV filter to your lens to cut down ultraviolet light and to protect your lens from scratches. You will probably find a telephoto, or better yet, zoom lens useful for photographing people without having to stick a camera in their faces.

Many of the dzongs and mountain peaks are best photographed at a distance with a long lens. Bear in mind that there will be little or no opportunity for photography inside buildings, therefore you don't need to organise a flash attachment and tripod for that purpose. A polarising filter will help make your mountain pictures more dramatic by increasing the contrast between the sky and the white peaks and clouds. Bring extra batteries, as these are hard to find in Bhutan. If you are going trekking, buy a good camera bag to protect your camera and lens from dust and rain.

For video cameras, make sure you have the necessary charger, plugs and transformer to handle Bhutan's 230V power supply. In Thimphu the Sony shop below the NT Hotel and Jimmy Brothers Stationery near the clock tower sell blank video cartridges, but don't count on finding them elsewhere.

Technical Tips

It has been said that it's impossible to take a poor photograph in Bhutan. Indeed, the landscape, buildings and people are some of the most photogenic in the world. However, there are many cloudy days in Bhutan and it's rare to find bright sunshine except between October and January. You'll also discover that power lines frequently appear in the viewfinder when you set up the perfect shot.

Be careful with exposure settings. The extreme light intensity in the mountains and at higher elevations can overexpose your pictures. Most good photographs are taken during the first or last few hours of the day when the light is softer and shadows more pronounced.

Many areas of Bhutan are forested, and it's cloudy for much of the year. You will need film with a rating of at least 100 ASA for these conditions. If you are using a telephoto lens, you may find ASA 200 or faster film useful.

Properly used, a video camera can give a fascinating record of your holiday. As well as videoing the obvious things – sunsets, spectacular views – remember to record some of the everyday details of life in the country. Often the most interesting things occur when you're actually intent on filming something else. Remember too that, unlike still photography, video 'flows' – so, for example, you can shoot scenes of the winding road from the front window of a vehicle, to give viewers an impression of the landscape that isn't possible with ordinary photos. If your video camera has a stabiliser, you can use it to obtain good footage while travelling on bumpy roads.

Restrictions

Bhutan is generally liberal about photography by tourists. There are a few places with signs prohibiting photography such as the telecom tower above Thimphu. It would also be prudent to refrain from taking pictures of military installations.

There are no restrictions on photographing the outside of dzongs and goembas. Photography is strictly prohibited inside goembas and lhakhangs. There are several reasons for this. One is that tourists in the past have completely disrupted holy places with their picture taking. Another is the fear that photos of treasured statues will become a catalogue of items for art thieves to steal. And thirdly, some early tourists made photographs of religious statues into postcards that were then sold, which is unacceptable to the Bhutanese religious community.

During festivals you may enter the dzong courtyard where the dances take place. This provides an excellent opportunity to photograph the dzongs, people and local colour.

Remember, however, that this is a religious observance and that you should behave accordingly. Use a telephoto lens without a flash. Don't intrude on the dance ground or on the space occupied by local people seated at the edge of the dance area. If you do end up in the front row, remain seated.

There is an extensive set of rules and restrictions, including payment of royalties, for commercial movie making in Bhutan. DOT publishes a booklet that details all these rules.

Photographing People

Bhutanese people are naturally shy but will usually allow you to take a photograph, especially if you ask them first. Many people, especially children, will pose for you, and a smile or joke will help to make the pose a little less formal. Remember that almost everyone understands English, even if they are too embarrassed to try to speak it.

After you take a picture, many people will write down their address so that you may send them a copy. This seems a simple request. Don't take pictures of people unless you are prepared to honour your promise to send a copy (many people leave their best intentions at Paro airport on their way home). Don't photograph a member of the royal family, even if you happen to be at a festival or gathering where they are present.

For video cameras remember to follow the same rules regarding people's sensitivities as for still photography – having a video camera shoved in your face is probably even more annoying and offensive than a still camera. Always ask permission first.

Airport Security

Consider using a lead-lined bag to protect your film from X-ray inspection. There is an X-ray machine for hand luggage at Paro airport and there is stringent X-ray inspection at all airports that are served by Druk Air. Most of these airports will, reluctantly, agree to hand-inspect film, though they will insist that their machines will not damage your film. Be particularly careful departing from Kathmandu where signs on the machines say that they *will* damage unexposed film. If you are worried about X-ray damage, take your film out of the box and canisters and keep it in a separate clear plastic bag so it's obvious what it is.

Avoid placing film in your checked baggage because it may be zapped with powerful X-rays on check-in or before it is delivered to you at your destination.

TIME

Bhutan time is GMT/UTC plus six hours; there is only one time zone throughout the country. The time in Bhutan is 30 minutes later than India, 15 minutes later than Nepal, and one hour earlier than Thailand. When it is noon in Bhutan, standard time is 6am in London, 4pm in Sydney, 1am in New York and 10pm the previous day in San Francisco.

ELECTRICITY
Voltages & Cycles

The voltage in Bhutan is the same as India: 230V, 50 cycles AC. The Chhukha hydroelectric project provides a reliable, well-regulated power supply throughout western Bhutan, though excessive use of electric heaters can cause brownouts on winter nights. If you are planning to use sensitive electronic equipment, you should still be prepared for possible outages and fluctuations, especially power surges. Electricity in the rest of Bhutan is generated by small hydroelectric projects near major towns. Floods and landslides often disrupt the generating stations or the distribution lines. In central and eastern Bhutan there are occasional short and long-term power failures and voltage instability.

Plugs & Sockets

Bhutan uses the standard Indian round-pin sockets. These come in a variety of sizes, and there's no assurance that a particular plug will fit the socket in your hotel. Most European round-pin plugs work, but their pins are usually smaller than the Indian variety, and they fit loosely and provide an unreliable connection. There are plenty of electrical shops in Thimphu that can make up an adapter if you have trouble plugging in an appliance. If you have an appliance that uses Australian plugs, bring a converter.

WEIGHTS & MEASURES

The metric system is used throughout the country. In villages, rice is sometimes measured in a round measure called a *gasekhorlo*. There is a scale called a *sang* that is used for butter and meat.

LAUNDRY

Hotels can do laundry, but few outside of Thimphu have dryers. Outside the capital same-day service is possible, but it depends on the amount of sunshine available. The only dry-cleaning shops are in Thimphu and Phuentsholing. Dry-cleaning will take at least three days, so plan accordingly. Many expats pack up all their clothing and take it with them on a holiday to Bangkok to have it dry-cleaned there.

TOILETS

There are few public toilets except near town vegetable markets and along Norzin Lam in Thimphu. Existing public toilets are of the Asian squat variety and toilet paper is never available, though there may be a container of water to use. Most hotels and guesthouses provide Western toilets and loo paper, though there are some exceptions, particularly in eastern Bhutan.

In older goembas and palaces you may find an old-fashioned Bhutanese toilet. This is a strange hobbyhorse commode built in a little room that extends out from the side of the building, featuring a large square pipe leading straight down into a pit. There's an example of one of these in the Folk Heritage Museum in Thimphu.

HEALTH

Because many people using this book will be trekking, it includes more extensive advice on self-treatment than we would normally provide. If you are not trekking, you can rely on local medical care. There are no private health clinics or physicians in Bhutan, but all district headquarters towns have a hospital, and will accept travellers in need of medical attention. The best facility is the Jigme Dorji Wangchuk National Referral Hospital in Thimphu. It has general physicians and several specialists, labs and operating rooms. Treatment is free, even for tourists. If you are seriously ill or injured you should consider evacuation to the excellent medical facilities in Bangkok.

Bhutan is a relatively uninhabited, naturally beautiful country and this can temporarily lull the visitor into thinking that it is not a developing country. The main health concerns in Bhutan are similar to those in other south Asian destinations: the relatively high risk of acquiring travellers' diarrhoea, a respiratory infection, or a more exotic tropical infection. If you go trekking, there are also risks associated with accidents and altitude sickness. The infectious diseases can interrupt your trip and make you feel miserable, but they are rarely fatal. Falling off trails, or having a rock fall on you as you trek is rare, but can happen.

In most large towns there are shops that sell medicines. Most of the medical supplies mentioned in this section are available in these medicine shops without a prescription.

Predeparture Planning

Immunisations The government of Bhutan does not check vaccination records when you enter the country. However, there are several major diseases that can be prevented, or whose risks can be significantly decreased, by immunisations.

Cholera Although cholera (a severe form of diarrhoea) can be devastating to local populations at times, the risk of acquiring cholera as a traveller is close to zero, and the few cases have been indistinguishable from ordinary travellers' diarrhoea. Therefore cholera vaccine is not necessary to visit Bhutan.

Hepatitis A New vaccines against hepatitis A have made it extremely easy to avoid this disease. A single injection of hepatitis A vaccine offers nearly immediate protection for travel. This single injection protects for several years, but a booster is recommended after one year. These two injections confer life-long protection against hepatitis A.

Hepatitis B The hepatitis B vaccine should be considered for long-term travellers, or expatriates taking up residence abroad. If you anticipate doing medical work, or being sexually active with local people, this vaccine is highly recommended. The regimen for hepatitis B immunisation is a series of three shots over a six month period. A combined hepatitis A and B vaccine (Twinrix) is now available for those who require both immunisations.

Japanese Encephalitis This disease is caused by a virus transmitted by mosquitoes, with a maximum risk during the monsoon and just afterwards. The risk to travellers in Bhutan is unknown, but the location and geography of the lower areas suggest that the risk may be similar to southern Nepal and northern India. Consider vaccination against Japanese encephalitis (JE) if you will be staying a month or more in southern lowland areas from July to December. There is no need to have the JE vaccine in order to visit the main tourist areas of Bhutan.

Polio At the time of research this disease had not been detected in Bhutan in the previous three years. However, nearby India and Nepal were still reporting cases. A polio booster for people who have been previously immunised is recommended before travelling to India or Nepal. If you are travelling directly to Bhutan from Thailand, a polio booster is not needed.

Rabies Modern rabies vaccine is a highly purified substance with high effectiveness and few side effects. The drawback is that it is relatively expensive. Pre-exposure immunisation consists of three shots spaced over one month. These injections prime your immune system against rabies, and if you are bitten by an animal, you need two more shots, three days apart, as a booster. If you don't take the pre-exposure immunisation, and you are bitten by a potentially rabid animal, you will need the full postexposure immunoprophylaxis, which consists of five injections spaced over one month and a single injection of rabies antibodies called human rabies immune globulin (HRIG). HRIG is often very hard to obtain, and is not available in Bhutan. If you were bitten in Bhutan and required HRIG, you would have to fly to either Bangkok or Nepal to obtain this product.

Tetanus & Diphtheria The vast majority of people from Western countries receive these vaccines in childhood. The tetanus and diphtheria germs occur worldwide. You should have a booster if it has been longer than 10 years since your last one. It is especially important to ask for a tetanus booster if you are over 50 years old, as studies have shown that this population is more likely to have let their tetanus boosters lapse.

Tuberculosis (TB) This disease is endemic in Bhutan. However, because infection requires continuous close contact with an infected person, tuberculosis cases are extremely rare among travellers to Bhutan. Those who are concerned about acquiring tuberculosis while travelling should have a skin test before travel; if the test is negative they can be tested after they return to see if they have been exposed to TB. Although a vaccine exists that offers some protection against TB, it gives incomplete protection, and changes the skin test to positive, making it difficult to tell if a person has actually been exposed to TB or not. We do not recommend TB vaccine for travellers to Bhutan.

Typhoid Fever Two typhoid vaccines are available. The capsular polysaccharide typhoid vaccine (Typhim Vi) offers good protection from a single injection, which has very few side effects. There is also an oral typhoid vaccine (Vivotif) that must be taken as a pill every other day for three or four doses. It is slightly less effective than the injectable typhoid vaccine.

Yellow Fever There is no yellow fever in Asia in general, or Bhutan in particular. However, vaccination is a requirement for entry into Bhutan when coming from an infected area.

Malaria Medication Antimalarial drugs do not prevent you from being infected but kill the malaria parasites during a stage in their development and significantly reduce the risk of becoming very ill or dying. Expert advice on medication should be sought, as there are many factors to consider, including the area to be visited, the risk of exposure to malaria-carrying mosquitoes, the side effects of medication, your medical history and whether you are a child or an adult or pregnant.

Health Insurance Make sure that you have adequate health insurance. See Travel Insurance under Visas & Documents earlier in this chapter.

Travel Health Guides If you are planning to be away or travelling in remote areas for a long time, you should consider taking a more detailed health guide. Lonely Planet's *Healthy Travel Asia & India* by Dr Isabelle Young is a handy pocket size and packed with useful information, including pretrip planning, emergency first aid, information about immunisation and advice about what to do if you get sick on the road. Some other health guides are listed below.

Travellers' Health by Dr Richard Dawood is comprehensive, easy to read, authoritative and highly recommended, although it's rather large to lug around.
Travel with Children by Cathy Lanigan includes advice on travel health for younger children.
Where There is No Doctor by David Werner is a very detailed guide intended for someone, such as a Peace Corps worker, going to work in an underdeveloped country.

There are also a number of excellent travel health sites on the Internet. From the Lonely Planet home page there are links at W www.lonelyplanet.com/weblinks/wlprep .htm to the World Health Organization and the US Centers for Disease Control & Prevention.

If you have specific questions while preparing for your trip that are not answered in this chapter, you may find the answer at the Web site of the Kathmandu-based CIWEC Clinic at W www.ciwec-clinic.com. The Web site offers more in-depth discussion of certain health risks, and will provide updates on recent health concerns.

Other Preparations Make sure you're healthy before you start travelling. If you are going on a long trip make sure your teeth are OK. If you wear glasses take a spare pair and your prescription.

If you require a particular medication take an adequate supply, as it may not be available locally. Take part of the packaging showing the generic name, rather than the brand – replacement will be easier. It's a good idea to have a legible prescription or letter from your doctor to show that you legally use the medication to avoid any problem.

Basic Rules

Food Just treating your water carefully will not eliminate the chances of eating harmful bacteria. Lapses in kitchen hygiene, such as the preparation of raw meat on the same counters as other foods, failure to wash kitchen surfaces regularly, and cooks who do not wash their hands after going to the toilet, contribute to the risk of gastrointestinal illness. Vegetables and fruits can also be contaminated from the soil they are grown in, or from handling along the way.

The general rule is to not eat any vegetables that cannot be peeled or freshly cooked unless you are certain of the methods that have been used to soak them. Many restaurants soak their vegetables in an acceptable manner to make them safe, but if you are not sure, don't eat them. Avoid salads.

Meat, because it has to be thoroughly cooked just before eating, is generally safe to eat. Chicken meat is produced locally, while other meats are imported, possibly under unhygienic conditions, eg, travelling long distances in unrefrigerated trucks.

Water Tap water is not safe to drink in Bhutan. Local Bhutanese mineral water is available throughout the country. You can ask your tour company to provide you with bottled water at meals and in your hotel room. If you are trekking, or are concerned about litter caused by used the plastic bottles, an environmentally friendly solution is to carry a water bottle and treat water yourself. See the boxed text for details.

Personal Hygiene Making a point of washing your hands frequently can also help prevent illness. The tiny amounts of water that might cling to dishes and glasses

Water Purification

In Bhutan all water must be viewed as being potentially contaminated. Some urban water may be extremely contaminated while some mountain water may be almost pure, but it is better to disinfect all water before drinking it.

Boiling

All of the stool pathogens (disease producers) are killed by boiling water. Just bringing water to a vigorous boil is sufficient to kill all potential disease-causing organisms, even at high altitude.

Iodine

As an alternative to boiling, chemicals can be added to water to kill the germs. Iodine preparations and chlorine preparations are equally effective in killing the germs, but iodine preparations are more available. There are three practical ways to carry iodine while travelling: as tetraglycine hydroperiodide tablets, Lugol's solution or iodine crystals.

If your main objection to using iodine is the taste, this can be completely eliminated by adding a small quantity of vitamin C (ascorbic acid) after you have waited for the iodine to work. Approximately 50mg of vitamin C when crumbled into a litre of water and shaken for a few seconds will completely neutralise the iodine flavour in the water, making it taste like pure spring water.

Water Filters

Filtering devices for field use have become popular in recent years. No filtering device can guarantee the elimination of viruses that cause diarrhoea or hepatitis, so iodine must also be used in addition to a filter in Bhutan. Some filters incorporate a pentaiodine resin which iodinates the water as it filters it. For the most part, water in Bhutan appears clear and has good taste, so filtering for sediment and taste is not usually necessary. If you plan to use a filter, make sure it has a pore size of 0.2 microns or less.

Don't believe manufacturers' claims that filtering without also adding iodine will eliminate viruses from water.

David Shlim, MD

washed in untreated water are not likely to make you sick, and drying the dishes can eliminate this problem. In general, the likelihood of getting sick is related to the amount of contaminated material you ingest. You should always do your best to avoid known sources of contamination, but don't worry excessively about those areas over which you have no control.

Environmental Hazards

Altitude Sickness Lack of oxygen at high altitudes (over 2500m) affects most people to some extent. The effect may be mild or severe and occurs because less oxygen reaches the muscles and the brain at high altitude, requiring the heart and lungs to compensate by working harder.

For detailed information see the boxed text 'Acclimatisation & Altitude Illness' in the Trekking chapter.

Frostbite This refers to the freezing of extremities, including fingers, toes and nose. Frostbite is only a risk when people are trekking through snow. If your hands or feet become numb, you must stop to warm them up. Once there is numbness, actual freezing can start at any time. Rapid rewarming of the frozen hands or toes is the recommended treatment. Use water at a temperature of 34°C (94°F).

Hypothermia Too much cold can be just as dangerous as too much heat. If you are trekking at high altitudes or simply taking a long bus trip over mountains, particularly at night, be prepared. In Bhutan you should always be prepared for cold, wet or windy conditions even if you're just out walking or hiking.

Motion Sickness Eating lightly before and during a trip will reduce the chances of motion sickness. If you are prone to motion sickness try to find a place that minimises movement – near the centre on buses. Fresh air usually helps; reading and cigarette smoke don't. Commercial motion-sickness preparations, which can cause drowsiness, have to be taken before the trip commences.

Ginger (available in capsule form) and peppermint (including mint-flavoured sweets) offer some relief.

Sunburn In the tropics and at high altitude you can get sunburnt surprisingly quickly, even through cloud. Use sunscreen, a hat and barrier cream for your nose and lips. Protect your eyes with good-quality sunglasses, particularly if you will be near water, sand or snow.

Diarrhoea

Diarrhoea is the most common illness acquired by travellers in Bhutan. Travellers' diarrhoea is simply infectious diarrhoea, acquired while travelling where standards of public health and hygiene are minimal to nonexistent. The organisms that cause diarrhoea are passed in faeces, and are acquired from eating or drinking contaminated food or water. See Basic Rules, earlier, for advice on how to avoid contaminated food and water.

Travellers' diarrhoea is often described in travel books as a mild, self-limiting disorder, for which no specific treatment is required. However, antibiotic treatment for travellers' diarrhoea has been shown to be highly effective at shortening the illness, sometimes ending it within several hours. Since travellers' diarrhoea can vary in intensity from a few loose bowel movements to severe fever, cramps, vomiting and watery diarrhoea, the decision to treat should be based on the severity of illness and the need to carry on with your travel plans. Dehydration is the main danger with any diarrhoea, particularly in children or the elderly, and fluid replacement is the most important thing to remember. The following section discusses when and how to treat your own diarrhoeal illness.

Causes The vast majority of cases of travellers' diarrhoea in Bhutan are caused by some form of bacteria. Bacteria cause 80% to 90% of travellers' diarrhoea. Bacteria are all susceptible to antibiotics, and thus a bacterial diarrhoea can easily be shortened by antibiotic treatment.

There are three other organisms, known as protozoa, that can also cause diarrhoeal disease. The most common protozoan and the cause of giardiasis is *Giardia lamblia*, which accounts for about 12% of diarrhoea cases. Amoebiasis is caused by the protozoan *Entamoeba histolytica*. It accounts for only about 1% of diarrhoea in travellers, although local laboratories tend to over diagnose it. From late spring to midsummer, another protozoan called *Cyclospora* is a significant risk of diarrhoea, but this is outside the main tourist seasons.

Diarrhoea can also be caused by toxins or viruses. The toxins are waste products of certain bacteria that can grow on food and, once ingested, can cause severe intestinal symptoms, such as vomiting and diarrhoea, for six to 12 hours. This is what is known as food poisoning; no infection takes place in the intestine and treatment can only be supportive. Viruses can cause vomiting and diarrhoea, or either alone, but only account for around 5% to 10% of diarrhoea cases in Bhutan. Once again, treatment can only be supportive.

Diagnosis The most common variety of diarrhoea, bacterial diarrhoea, is characterised by the sudden onset of relatively uncomfortable diarrhoea. Protozoal diarrhoea is characterised by the gradual onset of tolerable diarrhoea. Although these two syndromes can overlap to some extent, this is a useful way of distinguishing between the two. 'Sudden onset' means that you can usually recall the precise time of day your illness began. Patients will also report that the diarrhoea and associated symptoms were quite troublesome right from the start. In contrast, protozoal diarrhoea usually begins with just a few loose stools, making people wonder if they are getting sick. The symptoms might be two to five loose stools per day, with mild cramping and urgency as the usual accompanying symptoms. People often wait one to two weeks before seeking treatment, whereas those with bacterial diarrhoea will seek help within one to two days.

Bacterial Diarrhoea This type of diarrhoea is almost always self-limiting, varying from a few hours to over two weeks. Currently, all pathogenic bacteria in Bhutan that can cause diarrhoea are susceptible to a group of antibiotics known as fluoroquinolones. The most commonly used antibiotic is ciprofloxacin. Treatment with a fluoroquinolone can shorten the illness to one day, and side effects are extremely rare.

The treatment doses for bacterial diarrhoea is ciprofloxacin 500mg twice a day for one day. An alternative for people who can't take ciprofloxacin is azithromycin 500mg once a day for two days.

Protozoal Diarrhoea Once Giardia protozoa have been ingested, they begin causing symptoms after one or two weeks (not the day after a suspect meal). Upper abdominal discomfort, 'churning intestines', foul-smelling burps and farts, and on-and-off diarrhoea are the main characteristics of giardiasis. Vomiting is rare.

The best treatment for giardiasis is tinidazole, which is available in Bhutan without prescription. The dose is 2g as a single dose each day for two consecutive days. Side effects of tinidazole include mild nausea, fatigue and a metallic taste in the mouth. Tinidazole cannot be taken with alcohol. An alternative is albenazole (400mg) once a day for seven days. This drug has very few side effects.

A person with **amoebiasis** (infection with *Entamoeba histolytica*) will commonly have several weeks of low-grade diarrhoea, alternating every few days with either normal stool or constipation. Very rarely, a person with this infection will have the symptoms of classic amoebic dysentery: frequent passage of small amounts of bloody, mucoid stool, associated with cramps and painful bowel movements.

E histolytica is treated easily with 2g of tinidazole per day for three consecutive days, followed by 500mg of diloxanide furoate (furamide) three times a day for 10 days. However, diloxanide furoate may not be readily available in Bhutan. This follow-up treatment does not have to be taken immediately after the tinidazole, but should be obtained within two to three weeks of initial treatment.

The Cyclospora organism infects the upper intestine, causing diarrhoea, fatigue and loss of appetite. The untreated illness lasts from two to 12 weeks, averaging six weeks. The risk of cyclospora in Bhutan is unknown, but in neighbouring Nepal, cyclospora is a risk mainly from May to September, which is outside the main trekking seasons, so most trekkers are not at risk. It has been shown to be waterborne; iodine does not kill it but it is easily killed by boiling and can be filtered by most water filters. The treatment for Cyclospora diarrhoea is trimethoprim-sulfamethoxazole (Bactrim DS) taken twice a day for seven days. This is a sulpha drug, and cannot be taken by people allergic to sulpha.

Supportive Care Diarrhoea can result in the loss of a great deal of fluid from the body, and much of the ill feeling associated with diarrhoea (weakness, dizziness) occurs as a result of dehydration. Under all circumstances *fluid replacement* (at least equal to the volume being lost) is the most important thing to remember. Oral rehydration solution (ORS), a mixture of sugars and salt that is easily absorbed by the intestines, is important when vomiting is present, which limits the amount of fluid intake, and for severe diarrhoea. Packets of ORS are sold in pharmacies in Bhutan. Urine output is the best guide to the adequacy of replacement: if you have small amounts of concentrated urine, you need to drink more. The best approach to rehydration is to take frequent small sips of fluid.

Antimotility Drugs Antimotility drugs, such loperamide (Imodium) can be used to control the symptoms of diarrhoea until the self-limited infection runs its course. Use of these drugs may cause distended bowel, increased discomfort and prolonged constipation. If your diarrhoea is severe enough to make you think about an antimotility agent, you should consider treatment with an antibiotic. An antimotility drug should be used when travel is required before the antibiotic can bring the infection under control.

Vomiting When vomiting is associated with bacterial diarrhoea it is a potentially serious problem, since it adds to dehydration and hinders efforts at rehydration. Vomiting almost always occurs at the beginning of bacterial diarrhoea, and usually lasts six to 12 hours. Rarely, vomiting and diarrhoea persist together for four or five days, resulting in individuals who are severely dehydrated.

Vomiting also means you can't take an oral antibiotic to shorten the infection. There are currently no injectable drugs known to shorten the course of bacterial diarrhoea. The only option is to try treatment with an antivomiting drug until the person can take an oral antibiotic, such as ciprofloxacin.

Upper Respiratory Tract Infections
Colds Upper respiratory tract infections always begin as a virus (the common cold). Under normal circumstances the cold should last three to seven days and go away by itself. However, under the stress of travel, and particularly trekking, colds can be complicated by bacterial infection. The viruses break down the defensive barriers in the lining of your nose, throat and lungs, allowing the normal bacteria that are living there to become invasive. This can result in ear infections, sinus infections or bronchitis (chest infection).

Sinus Infection Sinusitis, or sinus infection, is the most common complication of a cold. The sinuses are hollow spaces in the bones of the face that connect to little holes in the back of the nose. Viruses can travel from the nose to the sinuses, causing inflammation, which can allow bacteria to invade. Symptoms of sinusitis include pressure or pain around the sinuses, and thick yellow and green mucus from your nose. Finding small amounts of blood when you blow your nose is also common. As the infection goes on, you may lose your appetite and feel much more tired than usual.

There may be no clear-cut division between your initial cold symptoms and the sinus infection. Any cold that is either not getting better, or getting worse, after seven days should be considered a possible sinus infection, and you should think about taking an appropriate antibiotic. Some of these prolonged infections will eventually clear up on their own, but an antibiotic will make them better within days. A new antibiotic, azithromycin 250mg, has the advantage of once-a-day dosing for five days. A good alternative is cephalexin 500mg four times a day for 10 days (if you are not allergic to penicillin).

Bronchitis & Pneumonia Bronchitis is the second most common complication of a cold. Bronchitis is an infection of the breathing tubes in the lungs. The symptoms are a progressively worse cough, accompanied by the production of greenish or yellowish mucus when you cough. Bronchitis is similar to sinusitis in that there may not be a clear point in time at which your viral cold becomes a bacterial bronchitis. Seven days is long enough to wait before thinking of treating a cough that is not getting any better on its own. The same drugs recommended for sinusitis are good treatment for bronchitis as well, and the two infections often occur at the same time.

A deep cough accompanied by high fever may represent pneumonia (an infection of the lung tissue itself). The same antibiotics can be used, but you may be quite sick with pneumonia and should seek professional medical attention.

Inner-Ear Infection The third common complication of a cold is an inner-ear infection. This type of infection is very common in young children. The infection is uncommon in adults, but seems to be more common in adult travellers and usually begins with a cold followed by the sudden onset of severe ear pain, usually in only one ear. If medical care is not available, you can treat yourself with any of the antibiotics used to treat sinusitis or bronchitis.

Fever

Normal body temperature is usually 37°C (98.6°F). Fever almost always means that you have acquired some kind of infectious

disease. By itself, it does not tell you the cause, but by evaluating the associated symptoms and the travel history, you can often make a good guess, even while trekking in a remote area. Some fever-related illnesses go away without treatment (eg, the flu), while others require treatment (eg, typhoid fever). The purpose of trying to guess the cause of a fever is to determine whether specific treatment will be of benefit, and whether your trek should be abandoned.

Sometimes a fever occurs with only a vague feeling of being unwell, such as headache, fatigue, loss of appetite, or nausea. In the first few days of such an illness it is difficult to determine the cause of the fever. In south Asia, there are six main diseases that account for almost all the presentations of fever with headache and malaise. By taking a careful history and noticing key aspects of the fever and headache, a presumptive diagnosis can often be made. The diseases are as follows:

Viral Syndromes The circumstances of travel bring exposure to many more viruses than one would encounter at home. Influenza viruses can be passed through respiratory droplets, which means they can be inhaled in aeroplanes, buses and crowded restaurants. The disease usually has an abrupt onset of fever, often very high (40°C) on the first day. A headache is often present, and is typically very motion-sensitive, which means it hurts to turn the head suddenly or to step down hard. The illness usually lasts two to four days and goes away without specific treatment. It usually ends abruptly, the fever and headache staying for the duration of the illness. The pointers to a viral infection are the abrupt onset, the characteristic motion-sensitive headache, and the fact that it goes away just about the time that you are getting worried that it might not.

Enteric Fever This fever is an infection with one of two specific bacteria, *Salmonella typhi* (typhoid fever) or *Salmonella paratyphi* (paratyphoid fever). The bacteria are passed in the stools of infected people. The same precautions that one follows to prevent diarrhoea will help to prevent enteric fever. Any of the three typhoid vaccines (see Immunisations earlier) can significantly reduce, but not eliminate, your chances of getting enteric fever. So don't think that because you took a typhoid vaccine that you can't get enteric fever.

The illness begins with the gradual onset of fever, headache and fatigue. For the first few days the fever is often low, and it is hard to tell if you are really getting sick or not. After three or four days, the fever rises to 40°C or more, and fatigue begins to be profound, although some people have milder cases. The headache is typically dull and not motion sensitive. Loss of appetite, nausea, and even vomiting can develop, as well as poor concentration. Overall, after four or five days, the patient feels very weak, moves slowly, and doesn't want to eat. The disease can be distinguished from the viral illnesses by its gradual onset, the dull character of the headache, and the fact that the person is getting worse at a time when the viral patient should be getting better.

The response to treatment is slow but steady, with the fever persisting for another two to five days. You can tell that the treatment is working because the patient starts to feel better, and the height of the fever is a little bit lower each day until it is gone. The infected person is only contagious through his or her stool, and does not need to be isolated from the group. Since the disease produces such profound fatigue and malaise, the person almost always has to abandon their trek.

Hepatitis The general term for inflammation of the liver is hepatitis. There are three main viruses that can cause hepatitis in Bhutan: hepatitis A and hepatitis E are transmitted by contaminated food and drinking water, while hepatitis B is only spread by blood or sexual contact. Hepatitis A can be prevented by vaccination (see Immunisations, earlier). If you get sick with fever, headache and nausea, and you have been immunised against hepatitis A, you can basically rule it out as the cause. Hepatitis E is an illness very similar to hepatitis A, and there is currently no way to immunise against this virus. Very few travellers, however, get hepatitis E.

The incubation period of hepatitis is usually four weeks. If you have travelled for a few months, and have not taken any protection against hepatitis A, then you must consider the diagnosis. Hepatitis A starts with the gradual onset of fever, headache, nausea and loss of appetite. These symptoms go on for four or five days. At this point the urine turns a dark tea colour, and the whites of the eyes appear yellow (this colour change is called jaundice). The fever ends at this point; nausea, fatigue and loss of appetite are now the main symptoms and can go on for two weeks to a month. There is no specific treatment to shorten the illness, and your trip is finished at this point.

There are almost 300 million chronic carriers of hepatitis B in the world. It is spread through contact with infected blood, blood products or body fluids, for example through sexual contact, unsterilised needles and blood transfusions, or contact with blood via small breaks in the skin. Other risk situations include having a shave, tattoo or body piercing with contaminated equipment. The symptoms of hepatitis B may be more severe than type A and the disease can lead to long-term problems such as chronic liver damage, liver cancer or a long-term carrier state.

There are vaccines against hepatitis A and B, but there are currently no vaccines against the other types of hepatitis. Following the basic rules about food and water (hepatitis A and E) and avoiding risk situations (hepatitis B) are important preventative measures.

Malaria This is a serious and potentially fatal disease caused by a protozoan parasite that is transmitted between humans by certain species of mosquito. In Bhutan, malaria transmission is limited to the lowland area adjoining India (the duars, including Phuentsholing) and the low valley of Punakha. Resistance to chloroquine is confirmed. There is no risk of malaria in Paro, Thimphu, or any of the main trekking areas.

Travellers to areas where malaria is a risk must rely on trying to prevent mosquito bites and taking prophylactic medication to try to avoid malaria infections. If you will be spending time in malaria-infected districts, you should consider taking malaria prophylaxis. Three regimens are available: mefloquine (Lariam), doxycycline, and atovaquone/proguanil (Malarone). Your doctor can help you pick the best regimen for you.

There are no reported cases of malaria among travellers to Bhutan, but someone who has travelled to a malaria-risk destination prior to Bhutan might become ill while in Bhutan. The clues to a malaria infection are travel in an endemic area without prophylaxis (or in a *Plasmodium falciparum* area that might be resistant), and the abrupt onset of chills followed by high fever and sweats. The initial bout resolves in several hours, leaving the person feeling remarkably well between episodes of illness. A return bout of the symptoms in one to two days is the clue that malaria might be present. Steady fever can also occasionally be a symptom of malaria, and a blood test might eventually be necessary to make the diagnosis. Only self-treat if you do not have access to medical services.

Travellers are advised to prevent mosquito bites at all times. The main messages are:

- Wear light-coloured clothing.
- Wear long trousers and long-sleeved shirts.
- Use mosquito repellents containing the compound DEET on exposed areas (prolonged overuse of DEET may be harmful, especially to children, but its use is considered preferable to being bitten by disease-transmitting mosquitoes).
- Avoid perfumes or aftershave.
- Use a mosquito net impregnated with mosquito repellent (permethrin) – it may be worth taking your own.
- Consider impregnating clothes with permethrin, which effectively deters mosquitoes and other insects.

Dengue Fever This viral disease is caused by a virus carried by a mosquito that tends to favour urban environments. It is endemic in northern India, particularly during the month of October. The disease is not known to exist in the upper parts of Bhutan. Whether there is a risk of dengue fever in the lowlands is also not known.

The disease has a very predictable incubation period, from three to 10 days. Thus, if the person has not been in an endemic area within the past 10 days, it is not possible that they have the disease. Exposure in transit in Delhi or Bangkok, however, can be a risk factor.

Dengue fever has very typical symptoms, which can allow the diagnosis to be made presumptively in most cases. The onset is very abrupt, with high fever on the first day. A headache is almost always present, centred behind the eyes, and movement of the eyes exacerbates the pain. Muscle aches and backaches are more prominent than in the other diseases discussed here. The nickname for the disease is 'breakbone fever'.

There is no treatment for the disease, but making the diagnosis avoids you starting treatment for some other disease, or panicking. Note that aspirin should be avoided. The fever lasts from three to six days, then goes away suddenly, along with all the other symptoms. Most people feel weak for an additional one to two weeks, but some recover quite quickly.

Other Diseases
Rabies This is a fatal brain infection caused by a virus transmitted by animal bites. All mammals are thought to be capable of carrying and passing on rabies. Dogs are the most common transmitter of the rabies virus to humans, but the virus has been passed by cats, monkeys, cows, horses, raccoons, foxes, bats and skunks among others. Although rodents are generally thought not to become rabid, it is not certain that they cannot transmit rabies. Bhutan is considered to be highly endemic for rabies, mainly in the dog population. If you receive a bite or a scratch from an animal in Bhutan, and the animal is not a closely observable pet, you will need to seek postexposure rabies immunoprophylaxis. You should try to obtain these shots as soon as possible after the incident, but it is not necessary to try to

find a doctor in the middle of the night. See Immunisations, earlier, for details of rabies treatment.

Conjunctivitis This is a bacterial or viral infection of the pink lining around the eye (the conjunctivae). Signs of conjunctivitis include a slightly swollen eye with increased redness in the pink areas, and occasionally some redness in the white part of the eye. Usually there is some sticky material around the eye that you can wash away in the morning. Although it can be painful, it is more of a nuisance than anything else. Antibiotic eye drops can clear up bacterial infections within a day or so. Viral infections will clear themselves in a few days as well. Most of the infections seem to be bacterial, so using antibiotic eye drops makes sense. The infection almost always starts in one eye, but can spread to the other eye. Use the drops frequently on the first day, every two to three hours. As the infection improves, you can use the drops less often, and then stop as soon as the eye seems normal (usually two to three days).

If the eye is severely painful, or the white part of the eye is very red, or your vision is impaired, seek medical help from an eye specialist. There are a few eye conditions that travellers occasionally get that require specialised diagnosis and treatment, such as uveitis, or herpes-virus infections of the cornea.

Gastritis This is a painful irritation of the stomach lining, which can occasionally be incapacitating. If you develop a consistent pattern of burning upper-abdominal pain while trekking, you can treat it either with antacid pills or liquid, which soak up the acid in your stomach, or more effectively, with an acid-blocking medication which stops the stomach from making acid. The two most commonly used acid-blocking medications are ranitidine and omeprazole. If you have any history of ulcer or gastritis, carry some of these medicines with you in case your symptoms are stirred up by the combination of new organisms, stress and diet.

Skin Diseases Skin problems are common in travellers. Travellers generally are bothered by one of four major problems: allergic reactions, bacterial skin infections, fungal infections and skin mites (scabies).

A generalised rash due to an allergic reaction consists of raised red spots in a variety of locations, often symmetrical on both sides of the body. You can also get slightly raised flat red lesions called urticaria (hives) that come and go relatively rapidly over a period of time. These rashes are usually caused by a new medicine, a new vaccine, or a new food. However, in many instances, it is impossible to figure out just what triggered the rash. Travellers are often taking new medications for the first time and may discover that they have an allergy to one of these new drugs. In general, a rash scattered over most of the body is due to something taken internally, and not to something that you touched with your skin. The rash can be treated with antihistamines in mild cases, or corticosteroids in more severe cases.

A painful, red swelling that worsens is probably a bacterial skin infection. Staphylococcal infections that cause boils are common. If the boil is tense and painful, it may need to be opened and drained by a physician. Antibiotics are necessary to get rid of the infection. Cephalexin (if you are not allergic to penicillin) or azithromycin are the best choices of an antibiotic.

A round red patch, clearing in the centre and advancing at its edges, is usually a fungus and can be treated with an antifungal cream. These lesions can also occur in the groin and in the armpits. They are not painful, and do not cause swelling of the skin around the lesion.

Small, very itchy red spots, usually seen in clusters or in small straight lines, suggest an infestation with a tiny skin mite, causing a disease called 'scabies'. This is relatively common in travellers, and is treated by a skin cream rubbed onto the whole body and left on for one day.

HIV & AIDS Infection with the human immunodeficiency virus (HIV) may lead to acquired immune deficiency syndrome

(AIDS), which is a fatal disease. HIV is a major problem in many countries. Any exposure to blood, blood products or body fluids may put the individual at risk. The disease is often transmitted through sexual contact or dirty needles – vaccinations, acupuncture, tattooing and body piercing can be potentially as dangerous as intravenous drug use.

AIDS can also be spread by infected needles and by blood transfusion. Insist on brand-new disposable needles and syringes for injections. These can be purchased from local pharmacies. Blood screening for AIDS has been introduced in most Asian countries, but can't always be done in an emergency.

Sexually Transmitted Infections (STIs)
HIV/AIDS and hepatitis B can be transmitted through sexual contact. Other STIs include gonorrhoea, herpes and syphilis; sores, blisters or rashes around the genitals and discharges or pain when urinating are common symptoms. In some STIs, such as wart virus or chlamydia, symptoms may be less marked or not observed at all, especially in women. Chlamydia infection can cause infertility in men and women before any symptoms have been noticed. Syphilis symptoms eventually disappear completely but the disease continues and can cause severe problems in later years. While abstinence from sexual contact is the only 100% effective prevention, using condoms is also effective. The treatment of gonorrhoea and syphilis is with antibiotics. The different sexually transmitted infections each require specific antibiotics.

Women's Health
Gynaecological Problems Antibiotic use, synthetic underwear, sweating and contraceptive pills can lead to fungal vaginal infections, especially when travelling in hot climates. Thrush or vaginal candidiasis is characterised by a rash, itch and discharge. The risk of developing thrush while trekking is large enough that all women should carry with them an appropriate treatment. Nystatin, miconazole or clotrimazole pessaries are the usual treatment. A new oral

medication, taken as a single dose, is also available. Some people use a more traditional remedy involving vinegar or lemon juice douches, or yogurt. If the symptoms don't clear up promptly you should try to see a doctor if you can.

Sexually transmitted infections are a major cause of vaginal problems. Symptoms include a smelly discharge, painful intercourse and sometimes a burning sensation when urinating. Medical attention should be sought and male sexual partners must also be treated. For more details see Sexually Transmitted Infections, earlier. Besides abstinence, the best thing is to practise safe sex using condoms.

Amenorrhoea Some women travellers note that their periods stop for a while, or become irregular. This may be associated somehow with the stress of travel. Your periods will return to normal after a while. Pregnancy is the other main reason that travellers might stop having periods, so be sure to check for this possibility if you have been sexually active.

Urinary Tract Infection The urinary tract is usually free from bacteria. In women, the short tube from the bladder to the outside (the urethra) can allow bacteria to invade from the vagina. An infection called cystitis (inflammation of the bladder) can result. The symptoms are burning on urination and having to urinate frequently and urgently. Blood can sometimes be seen in the urine. There is usually no fever unless the infection has spread to the kidneys. Sexual activity with a new partner, or with an old partner who has been away for a while, can trigger an infection, probably from the trauma of sexual intercourse. Symptoms of cystitis should be treated with an antibiotic because a simple infection can spread to the kidneys, causing a more severe illness. The best choice of antibiotic is either norfloxacin (400mg) or ciprofloxacin (500mg), taken twice a day for three days.

Pregnancy Although not much is known about the possible adverse effects of altitude on a developing foetus, many authorities recommend not travelling above 4000m while pregnant. In addition to altitude, there is the constant risk of getting ill, and not being free to take most medications to relieve either the symptoms or the disease. There's no evidence that travel increases the risk of miscarriage, but one in five pregnancies ends in miscarriage in any case, sometimes accompanied by profound bleeding that might require emergency treatment and could put you at risk of requiring a blood transfusion.

Most vaccinations can be given safely during pregnancy, but the actual effects of all immunisations during pregnancy are not known.

There are many examples of successful travel while pregnant. But since the outcome of pregnancy is always in doubt, you should be careful about exposures to altitude, infectious diseases, or trauma while pregnant.

Medical Kit Check List

Following is a list of items you should consider including in your medical kit – consult your pharmacist for brands available in your country.

- ☐ **Aspirin or paracetamol (acetaminophen in the USA)** – for pain or fever
- ☐ **Antihistamine** – for allergies, eg, hay fever; to ease the itch from insect bites or stings; and to prevent motion sickness
- ☐ **Cold and flu tablets, throat lozenges and nasal decongestant**
- ☐ **Multivitamins** – consider for long trips, when dietary vitamin intake may be inadequate
- ☐ **Antibiotics** – consider including these if you're travelling well off the beaten track; see your doctor, as they must be prescribed, and carry the prescription with you
- ☐ **Loperamide or diphenoxylate** – 'blockers' for diarrhoea
- ☐ **Prochlorperazine or metaclopramide** – for nausea and vomiting
- ☐ **Rehydration mixture** – to prevent dehydration, which may occur, for example, during bouts of diarrhoea; particularly important when travelling with children
- ☐ **Insect repellent, sunscreen, lip balm and eye drops**
- ☐ **Calamine lotion, sting relief spray or aloe vera** – to ease irritation from sunburn and insect bites or stings
- ☐ **Antifungal cream or powder** – for fungal skin infections and thrush
- ☐ **Antiseptic (such as povidone-iodine)** – for cuts and grazes
- ☐ **Bandages, Band-Aids (plasters) and other wound dressings**
- ☐ **Water purification tablets or iodine**
- ☐ **Scissors, tweezers and a thermometer** – note that mercury thermometers are prohibited by airlines

WOMEN TRAVELLERS
Attitudes Towards Women

Bhutan prides itself on its lack of a class system and an absence of sexual discrimination. Bhutanese women have the same rights as men, including rights to education, voting and holding positions in government.

The family system is basically matriarchal, with the daughters inheriting the family estate. Upon marriage the husband moves into the wife's house and becomes part of her family. Women are free to decide whom to marry and either the husband or wife has the right to initiate a divorce – which is a frequent occurrence in Bhutan. Many 'marriages' are quite informal and society does not look down on a divorcee or unwed mother. In such cases the father is required to pay 20% of his salary as support until the child reaches the age of 18.

Bhutanese women are proud of their position in society. Many women own shops and run family businesses while their husbands work in government offices. Several large travel agencies are run by women. Rural women are active in farming and the growing of cash crops and their sale in the market.

There are a few women in high government positions, but not many. Until the 1960s, women had limited educational opportunities; the problem today is more a lack of educated women than discrimination. Women in government compete equally with men according to their own capability, not on any system of quotas.

In spite of the generally liberated position of women, a few ancient discriminatory traditions still exist. Tradition has it that women are not allowed to touch an archer's bow, and it is believed that it decreases performance if an archer sleeps with a woman the night before a contest.

In most temples there is a room called the *goenkhang* that contains statues of warlords and protective deities that women must not view. Women are not allowed to sleep in dzongs or enter rooms where weapons are stored.

Promiscuity on the part of Bhutanese males is accepted and common, but women are expected to remain faithful to a single partner.

Safety Precautions

Women, both foreign and Bhutanese, are not subject to harassment and do not need to take any special precautions. Bhutanese are more likely to help a woman in distress than a man.

Young men have a reasonably liberated attitude towards their relations with women. There are several opportunities for misunderstanding if you don't make your intentions clear from the very outset. Female travellers should be aware that romantic liaisons between tourists and Bhutanese guides are quite common. You might also be invited to a 'party' at the home of a Bhutanese male, and discover too late that you are the only guest.

Organisations

The only women's organisation in the country is the National Women's Association of Bhutan (NWAB; ☎ 02-322910), established in 1981 and now headed by Dasho Dawa Dem, one of the few women who have received the honorific title of Dasho from the king.

NWAB operates and manages many projects for rural women, including nonformal education, credit schemes, training centres and sales outlets for handicraft production. NWAB has also been active in the installation of fuel-efficient smokeless stoves in rural homes.

GAY & LESBIAN TRAVELLERS

Like most Asians, the Bhutanese believe that what one does in private is strictly a personal matter, and they would prefer not to discuss such issues. Public displays of affection are not appreciated and everyone, regardless of orientation, should exercise discretion.

DISABLED TRAVELLERS

A cultural tour in Bhutan is a challenge for a traveller with physical disabilities, but is possible with some planning. The Bhutanese are eager to help, and one could arrange a strong companion to assist with moving about and getting in and out of vehicles. The roads are rough and sidewalks, where they exist, often have holes and sometimes steps. Hotels and public buildings do not have wheelchair access, and there are no toilets designed to accommodate wheelchairs.

For further general information there is a Web site for and by disabled travellers at Ⓦ http://www.travelhealth.com/disab.htm.

SENIOR TRAVELLERS

Because of the high cost of Bhutanese travel many visitors are seniors travelling in organised groups. Hotels, guides and tour operators are all familiar with the needs of seniors and treat them with the traditional respect that the Bhutanese have for their elders. The primary precaution one should take is to have an ample supply of any special medicines, since these probably will not be available in Bhutan. There is no advantage to carrying any sort of senior identification in Bhutan.

TRAVEL WITH CHILDREN

As there are discounts for children travelling in Bhutan, it needn't break the bank if you bring kids along. They may become bored, however, with long, monotonous drives, few hotels with TV and little other 'entertainment' available. On the other hand, they will be immediately accepted by local kids and their families, and they could make many new friends. Lonely Planet's *Travel with Children* by Cathy Lanigan has lots of useful advice and suggestions. Peter Steele's book *Two and Two Halves in Bhutan* describes the joys of travelling with children here.

USEFUL ORGANISATIONS

Thimphu's Centre for Bhutan Studies (☎ 02-321005, fax 321001, Ⓦ www.bhutanstudies .com), PO Box 1111, is a government-sponsored organisation that, among other activities, publishes the *Journal of Bhutan Studies*.

The Association of Bhutanese Tour Operators (ABTO; ☎ 02-322862, fax 325286, Ⓔ abto@druknet.net.bt), PO Box 938, Thimphu, is the professional society of Bhutan's tour operators. It lobbies the government for improvements in tourism rules and facilities, and assists with promotional activities.

See also the Facts about Bhutan chapter for contact information for conservation organisations.

DANGERS & ANNOYANCES

Fortunately, travel in Bhutan is still largely immune to the major banes of travel in Asia – theft and begging. It does, however, have some irritations of its own.

Altitude

The maximum elevation that you can reach on a Bhutanese road (3140m in the west and 3750m in the east) is lower than that which causes altitude problems for most people. There are rare individuals who can suffer from altitude problems even at elevations as low as Thimphu (2320m); if you have had previous altitude problems at these elevations avoid travelling to Bhutan.

Most treks go to extremely high elevations. If you are planning a trek, you should follow the advice about acclimatisation in the Trekking chapter.

Winding Roads & Breakdowns

If you venture east of Thimphu, you will spend hours driving on rough, winding roads. Even those who have never been car-sick before can get squeamish with the constant bouncing and motion, especially in the back seat of a van or bus. Vehicles do break down, no matter how well maintained they are, and there is no emergency road service. It's unlikely, but not impossible, for you to be forced to spend a night sleeping in a vehicle at the side of the road, or hitch a ride in a crowded bus to the next town.

Dogs

Those same cute dogs that wag their tails for you during the day turn into barking monsters at night. Don't forget to bring the earplugs recommended earlier. There is little danger of dog bites, but if you are going trekking, be wary of big dogs if you enter what looks like someone's front yard.

Weather

You are close to nature in Bhutan, and often this proximity affects your travel schedule, especially Druk Air flights. Even on a cultural tour you will be windblown in towns such as Paro, Wangdue Phodrang and Jakar. Clouds often obscure the mountain views that you made such an effort to see. Rain can turn trails and paths into a sea of mud, and flights are often delayed by bad weather. Leeches inhabit the lower valleys, and can be a real irritation in the monsoon season. A rainstorm can turn small streams into torrents, moving huge boulders and smashing bridges.

Hotel Service

Food in hotels and restaurants can sometimes take a frustratingly long time to prepare, but there is no hint of this when you order. Be patient, or choose a meal from the buffet. Just when you are used to everyone speaking fluent English, you will ask someone for something and they will nod knowingly even though they haven't the faintest idea what you are talking about. You will then receive something totally unexpected, or – more likely – nothing at all, because they were too embarrassed to ask you to repeat your request.

EMERGENCIES

The numbers for emergency services are the same throughout the country. For an ambulance call ☎ 112. The police number is ☎ 113, and the fire department is on ☎ 110.

BUSINESS HOURS

Government offices open at 9am and close at 5pm in the summer and 4pm in the winter, Monday to Friday. Banks are open from 9am to 3pm Monday to Friday and 9am till noon Saturday. Shops are usually open from 8am until 8pm or 9pm. In Phuentsholing, shops are open on Saturday and Sunday, but closed Tuesday. Half the shops in Thimphu are closed Tuesday and the other half are closed Wednesday. In other towns, most shops are open every day. Some restaurants in Thimphu stay open as late as 10pm, but many close earlier. Bars and discos stay open till the early morning on Wednesday, Friday and Saturday.

The idea of appointments is relatively new in Bhutan. Unless you're meeting a very high-level official, you may be given a vague meeting time – usually anytime during the morning (or afternoon). When you arrive the person may be out or in another meeting. Be patient and wait, or come back later.

PUBLIC HOLIDAYS & SPECIAL EVENTS

Bhutan's national day is 17 December, the date of the establishment of the monarchy in 1907. Other important holidays are the king's birthday on 11 November and Coronation Day on 2 June. The Black-Necked Crane Festival in Phobjikha is always held on 12 November, the day after the king's birthday.

The New Year is called Losar, and is celebrated according to the highly complicated Bhutanese calendar. Losar usually falls between mid-January and mid-March. To complicate matters further, there are different

Festival Dates

The following are the festival dates according to the Bhutanese calendar and the corresponding dates for 2002. Dates for later years can vary by two weeks or more, especially if they are adjusted to conform to auspicious dates. Before you schedule a trip around a specific festival, check with a tour operator for the correct dates for the year in which you plan to travel.

festival	Bhutanese month	days	place	2002 dates	2003 dates
Punakha Domchen	1	5–9	Punakha	17–21 Feb	8–12 Mar
Chorten Kora	1	13–15	Tashi Yangtse	27 Feb–1 Mar	18 Mar & 1 Apr
Gom Kora	2	8–10	Tashi Yangtse	22–24 Mar	10–12 Apr
Chhukha tsechu	2	8–10	Chukha	22–24 Mar	10–12 Apr
Paro tsechu	2	11–15	Paro	24–28 Mar	12–16 Apr
Ura Yakchoe	3	13–15	Bumthang	23–27 Apr	11–16 May
Nimalung tsechu	5	8–10	Bumthang	18–20 June	7–9 July
Kurjey tsechu	5	10	Bumthang	20 June	9 July
Wangdue tsechu	8	8–10	Wangdue Phodrang	14–16 Sept	3–5 Oct
Thimphu tsechu	8	10–12	Thimphu	16–18 Sept	5–7 Oct
Tamshing Phala Choepa	8	9–11	Bumthang	15–17 Sept	4–6 Oct
Thangbi Mani	8	14–16	Bumthang	20–22 Sept	9–11 Oct
Jambey Lhakhang Drup	9	15–18	Bumthang	21–24 Oct	8–12 Nov
Prakhar tsechu	9	15–18	Bumthang	21–24 Oct	9–12 Nov
Ngang Lhakhang Shey	10	15–17	Bumthang	19–21 Nov	8–10 Dec
Mongar tsechu*	10	7–10	Mongar	11–14 Nov	30 Nov – 3 Dec
Trashigang tsechu*	10	8–11	Trashigang	12–15 Nov	1–4 Dec
Lhuentse tsechu	10	9–11	Lhuentse	13–15 Dec	1–3 Jan (2004)
Trongsa tsechu*	11	9–11	Trongsa	13–15 Dec	1–3 Jan (2004)

* The first day is *Cham Ju*. *Cham* means 'dance' and *ju* means 'ending'; it is the last day of the rehearsal and the dances are performed without masks.

dates for the New Year in various parts of the country.

On an auspicious day near the end of the monsoon season the people celebrate Blessed Rainy Day. This is the day when *khandroms* (celestial beings) shower blessings on the earth in the form of rain to wash away bad luck. People wash their hair and shower to help wash off evil and sins.

On the first day of the fourth month the Thimphu *rabdey* (district monk body) moves to Punakha. The procession includes the Je Khenpo (the Chief Abbot of Bhutan), the four *lopons* (senior monks) and the entire monk body. The Khamsum Zilnoen, a sacred image of the Shabdrung, and other relics are also moved with the monks. Local people line up outside the dzong to get blessed with the image and relics. The rabdey returns to Thimphu on the first day of the 10th month.

Bhutanese Calendar

The Bhutanese calendar is based on the Tibetan calendar, which evolved from the Chinese. In the 17th century the Bhutanese scholar Pema Karpo developed a new way of computing the days of the week. This caused a divergence between the Tibetan and Bhutanese calendars, and dates do not agree between the two systems.

In the Bhutanese system, months have 30 days, with the full moon on the 15th. The eighth, 15th and 30th days of the month are auspicious. The fourth is also auspicious: Buddha first preached his religious principles on the fourth day of the sixth month.

Years are named according to the Tibetan system of five elements and 12 animals, producing a 60-year cycle. For example, the year 1998 is Earth-Tiger year, and 1974, the year of King Jigme Singye Wangchuck's coronation, is the Wood-Tiger year.

The calendar operates according to a very flexible system that allows bad days to be avoided. Astrologers sometimes add a day if it's going to be an auspicious one or lose a day if it's not. They can even change months. In some years, for example, there

[Continued on page 116]

Years in Bhutanese Sexagenary Cycle

Year	Name	Year	Name	Year	Name
1952	Water-Dragon	1972	Water-Mouse	1992	Water-Monkey
1953	Water-Serpent	1973	Water-Ox	1993	Water-Hen
1954	Wood-Horse	1974	Wood-Tiger	1994	Wood-Dog
1955	Wood-Sheep	1975	Wood-Hare	1995	Wood-Pig
1955	Wood-Sheep	1975	Wood-Hare	1995	Wood-Pig
1956	Fire-Monkey	1976	Fire-Dragon	1996	Fire-Mouse
1957	Fire-Hen	1977	Fire-Serpent	1997	Fire-Ox
1958	Earth-Dog	1978	Earth-Horse	1998	Earth-Tiger
1959	Earth-Pig	1979	Earth-Sheep	1999	Earth-Hare
1960	Iron-Mouse	1980	Iron-Monkey	2000	Iron-Dragon
1961	Iron-Ox	1981	Iron-Hen	2001	Iron-Serpent
1962	Water-Tiger	1982	Water-Dog	2002	Water-Horse
1963	Water-Hare	1983	Water-Pig	2003	Water-Sheep
1964	Wood-Dragon	1984	Wood-Mouse	2004	Wood-Monkey
1965	Wood-Serpent	1985	Wood-Ox	2005	Wood-Hen
1966	Fire-Horse	1986	Fire-Tiger	2006	Fire-Dog
1967	Fire-Sheep	1987	Fire-Hare	2007	Fire-Pig
1968	Earth-Monkey	1988	Earth-Dragon	2008	Earth-Mouse
1969	Earth-Hen	1989	Earth-Serpent	2009	Earth-Ox
1970	Iron-Dog	1990	Iron-Horse	2010	Iron-Tiger
1971	Iron-Pig	1991	Iron-Sheep	2011	Iron-Hare

THE TSECHU

Most *dzongs* and many monasteries have an annual festival, the largest of which is the *tsechu*. This is a series of dances in honour of Guru Rinpoche. The biography of the Guru is highlighted by a 12-episode dance drama. The dates and the duration of the festivals vary from one district to another, but they always take place on or around the 10th day of the month in the Bhutanese calendar.

The dances are performed by monks as well as lay people. Many of the dances were established by Shabdrung Ngawang Namgyal or by Pema Lingpa. The dancers take on the aspects of wrathful and compassionate deities, heroes, demons and animals. The dances, known as *cham*, bring blessings upon the onlookers, instruct them in the dharma (Buddhist teachings), protect them from misfortune, and exorcise evil influences. The tsechu is a religious festival and people believe they gain merit by attending it. Deities are invoked during the dances; through their power and benediction, misfortunes may be annihilated, luck increased and wishes realised. The tsechu is also a yearly social gathering where the people rejoice together, dressed in their finest clothing and jewellery.

During the dances, *atsaras* (clowns) mimic the dancers and perform comic routines wearing masks with long, red noses. The name is a corruption of the Sanskrit *acharya* (master). While entertaining the onlookers, atsaras also help to keep order and they harass both tourists and local people for money. Take it as a good-natured game; the money goes to the monks and if you contribute you may even receive a blessing from the wooden phallus they carry. During the intervals between the masked dances, elegantly dressed women sing and perform traditional dances.

During many tsechus a large *thangka* (religious picture) is unfurled before sunrise from the building overlooking the dance area. Large thangkas of this sort are called *thondrols*, and are usually embroidered rather than painted. Thondrol literally means 'liberation on sight', and it is believed that one's sins are washed away simply by viewing one of these large relics. When the thondrol is rolled up again, old people chant to ensure that they will see it again the following year.

During some tsechus a small fair is erected outside the dzong or *goemba*. Some of the stalls offer various kinds of gambling for astonishingly high stakes. Watch for fortune tellers with *Tashi-go-mang*, miniature, multistorey temples with tiny doors that open to reveal statues of deities.

The sequence of dances at the Thimphu tsechu follows. Most dances are the same at other tsechus, but the sequence varies. For a more learned treatise on the dances, including words to songs and details of the various steps, look in a Bhutanese bookshop for a copy of *The Origin and Description of Bhutanese Mask Dances* by Dasho Sithel Dorji, the former dance master of the Royal Academy of Performing Arts.

Inset: The dance of the Black Hat magicians during Gantey tsechu (Photo by Nicholas Reuss)

Day One
The Dance of the Four Stags (Shazam Cham) This dance
shows how Guru Rinpoche subdued the God of the Wind, who created much unhappiness in this world, and rode the stag that was the god's mount. The dancers in the role of the stags wear yellow knee-length skirts and horned deer masks.

Dance of the Three Kinds of Ging (Pelage Gingsum) This long
dance is a visual representation of Zangto Pelri, the heavenly paradise of Guru Rinpoche, as seen by Pema Lingpa. The dances show how *ging* (beings that are emanations of Guru Rinpoche) subdue the *jungpo nyulema* (demons that are creating obstacles to religion).

Although the demons are fleeing throughout the three worlds, the *jug ging,* with sticks and animal masks, can find the demons thanks to their foreknowledge. The jug ging catch them with the hook of compassion, beat them with the stick of wisdom and tie them with the noose of compassion.

The lords of the cremation grounds bring a box that contains the minds and the bodies of these demons. Then the *dri ging*, with swords and terrifying masks, purify the atmosphere of the evil deeds that were caused by the demons. After the demons have been vanquished, the *nga ging*, with drums, dance with happiness.

Dance of the Heroes (Pacham) When Pema Lingpa arrived at
Zangto Pelri he saw Guru Rinpoche sitting among his assistants in the centre of a limitless mandala that was made of lines of rainbow beams.

The purpose of this dance is to lead the believers of the human world into the presence of Guru Rinpoche. The dancers wear yellow skirts and golden crowns but do not wear masks. They carry a *dri-lbu* (small bell) and a *damaru* (small drum).

Dance of the Stag & the Hounds (Shawa Shachi) This dance
represents the conversion to Buddhism of the hunter Gonpo Dorji by the saint Milarepa. It is performed like a play in two parts. The first part takes place on day one of Thimphu tsechu, and the second part is on day two. The first part is quite comical: The hunter's servant appears and jokes with the clowns. The hunter then appears, crowned with leaves, carrying a bow and arrows and accompanied by his two dogs. The servant jokes very irreverently with his master, who, before going hunting, must perform some good-luck rituals. A priest is called and he performs the rituals in ways contrary to the Buddhist tradition, while the atsaras and the servant go on with their jokes.

Dance with the Guitar (Dranyeo Cham) This cheerful dance
celebrates the diffusion of the Drukpa lineage in Bhutan by Shabdrung Ngawang Namgyal. The dancers carry swords and each is dressed in a circular headdress, felt boots and heavy woollen clothes – a long black skirt, yellow shirt and brown coat. One dancer carries a guitar called a *dranyen.*

Day Two

Black Hat Dance (Shana Cham) The dancers assume the appearance of yogis who have the power to kill and recreate life. It is believed that the gestures of the dancers' hands are transformed into *mudras* (sacred mystic gestures), and their feet, which pound the earth, form a mandala. The dancers first build a mandala and then cut the demons into pieces. Thus they take possession of the earth in order to protect it and they dance the special thunderbolt step to impress their power on it.

Because of the importance of this ritual, the Shabdrung himself used to perform it. It is also a ground purification rite performed for the construction of dzongs, temples and *chortens*. Its aim is to conciliate the malevolent beings of the ground in order to take possession of the site.

The dancers wear brocade dresses, wide-brimmed black hats, and black aprons with an image representing the protective deities whose images are kept in the *goenkhang*, the chapel devoted to them.

Dance of the 21 Black Hats with Drums (Shaa Nga Cham)

In honour of the victory of religion over the enemies, the black hats beat the great drums of Buddhism. The sound of the drums represents the religion itself, which cannot be represented in any other way because it has no visible form. The dancers wear large black hats, felt boots and a long, colourful, brocade dress.

Kyecham This accompanying dance has performers carrying swords and wearing knee-length yellow skirts, bare feet and animal masks.

Dance of the Noblemen & the Ladies (Pholey Molay)

This dance depicts events in the life of King Norzang. It is a comical and very crude play rather than a dance.

The characters are two princes, two princesses, an old couple and the atsaras. The princes go to war and leave the princesses in the care of the old couple. As soon as they depart the atsaras frolic with the princesses and corrupt the old woman, who is also misbehaving. When the princes return, they are scandalised by this behaviour and cut off the noses of the princesses and the old lady as punishment. A doctor is then called to put the nose of the old woman back, but she smells so much that the doctor has to use a stick because he does not want to approach her. Finally the princes marry the princesses and everybody is reconciled.

Dance of the Drums from Drametse (Drametse Nga Cham)

The learned lama Kuenga Gyeltshen, son of Pema Lingpa, had a vision of Guru Rinpoche and his paradise Zangto Pelri during his meditation. The attendants of the Guru were transformed into 100 kinds of peaceful and terrifying deities. The deities each took in their left hand a big drum and in their right hand a drumstick and performed a dance. Kuenga Gyeltshen went to Drametse Goemba and established the tradition of this dance, which depicts his vision. The players hold big drums and wear animal masks and knee-length yellow skirts.

NICHOLAS REUSS

The riot of colour belies the name of the Black Hat Dance.

STAN ARMINGTON

The dance of the black-necked crane is specific to the Phobjikha area, the cranes' winter home.

STAN ARMINGTON

NICHOLAS REUSS

IZZET KERIBAR

Tsechus are inclusive events: Monks and lay people are both performers in and spectators of the colourful festivities.

STAN ARMINGTON

NICHOLAS REUSS

STAN ARMINGTON

Tsechus are performed in the courtyards of *dzongs* and *goembas*; dancers embody human, animal and spiritual life, taking on the aspects of wrathful and compassionate deities, demons and animals.

STAN ARMINGTON

Women perform a traditional dance during an interlude in the religious festivities at Paro tsechu.

JULIA WILKINSON

Festival-goers browse the stalls selling gifts and decorations.

Dance of the Stag & the Hounds (Shawo Shachi) This is the conclusion of the dances staged on day one and is more serious and religious than the other dances. Milarepa appears wearing a long, white dress and a white hat, and holding a pilgrim's staff. He holds his right hand near his ear and sings in a soft voice. The dogs, the stag and the hunter arrive and Milarepa converts them with his song. The conversion is symbolised by a rope that the dogs and the hunter have to jump.

Day Three

Dance of the Lords of the Cremation Grounds (Durdag) This dance was composed by Shabdrung Ngawang Namgyal. The dancers represent the protectors of the religion, who live in the eight cremation grounds on the external edges of the symbolic Mt Sumeru. They wear short, white skirts, white boots and white skull masks.

Dance of the Terrifying Deities (Tungam) This dance is performed with the aim of delivering beings by showing them Zangto Pelri. This dramatic dance has a very deep symbolic meaning, namely that a sacrificial murder is performed. First the dancers representing the gods try to enclose the bad spirits in a circle and in a box. Once this is done, Guru Rinpoche, in the form of Dorji Drakpo (Fierce Thunderbolt), kills them with a *phorbu* (ritual dagger). He thus saves the world from them and delivers them into salvation at the same time. The dancers' costumes are beautiful brocade dresses, boots and terrifying masks.

Dance of the Rakshas & the Judgement of the Dead (Raksha Mangcham) This dance is based on the *Bardo Thoedrol* (Book of the Dead), a text hidden by Guru Rinpoche and rediscovered by Karma Lingpa in the 14th century. This is one of the most important dances of the tsechu and is watched carefully by many old people in preparation for their own death.

When all beings die, they wander in the *bardo* (intermediate state) waiting to be led by the love of the Buddhas into the pure fields where no suffering exists. However, the Buddhas assume both peaceful and terrifying forms. Those who didn't follow Buddhist doctrine during their lives do not recognise the Buddhas in their terrifying form, they are frightened and cannot be led into paradise.

Shinje Chhogyel, Lord of Death, estimates the value of the 'white' and 'black' deeds during the judgement. Also present are the White God and Black Demon who live with every being from birth, and all the *rakshas* (helpers of Shinje) who emanate under numerous forms. These include: the ox-headed justice minister; the wild hog–headed helper who takes account of the black and white deeds; the khyung-headed bird, who holds a small sword to cut the root of the three poisons (ignorance, envy, anger) and a big hammer to destroy the rocky mountains of sins; the lion-headed helper who holds a lasso representing love and an iron chain representing compassion; the fierce, bear-headed helper who holds the magical noose binding the means and wisdom together and a saw to cut selfishness; the serpent-headed helper who holds a mirror reflecting all actions; and the monkey-headed helper who weighs them on a scale. The rakshas separate the black actions from the white actions of all beings. The frightening judgement cannot be avoided by the damned beings. But after enduring certain sufferings, their sins are washed away and they are purified.

The dance is like a play and lasts over two hours. First is the long dance of all the rakshas. Then Shinje himself appears, symbolised by a huge puppet holding a mirror. The White God and the Black Demon enter with him. The judgement begins. The Black Demon and his helpers perform a dance. The sinner, dressed in black and wearing a red hat, is frightened and tries to escape but is recaptured at each attempt. From his basket a freshly severed cow's head is taken, implying that the sinner was responsible for killing it. As the judge weighs up the sinner's actions the White God sings of the merits of the man and the Black Demon expounds his sins. Finally a strip of black cloth, symbolising the road to hell, is spread and the sinner is sent to hell.

After a general dance everyone sits again. Another man arrives, clad in white and holding a prayer flag and a ceremonial scarf. The scene is re-enacted and at its conclusion a strip of white cloth, symbolising the road to heaven, is deployed. Fairies elaborately dressed in brocade and bone ornaments come to fetch him. At the last moment, the Black Demon, furious at having lost a being, tries to grasp the virtuous man but the White God protects him.

Day Four

Dance of Tamshing in Bumthang (Bumthang Ter Cham) On
the occasion of the consecration of the Tamshing Goemba in Bumthang, Pema Lingpa had a dream and created this dance to depict what he saw. When this miraculously discovered dance is performed, all the earth demons in the country are appeased and the Gods rejoice. The dancers perform in white, peaceful-looking masks and knee-length yellow skirts, and they carry a little bell and drum.

Dance of the Lords of the Cremation Grounds (Durdag)
This is the same dance as that performed on day three.

Dance of Ging & Tsholing (Ging dang Tsholing) On the occasion of the consecration of the Samye Monastery in Tibet, Guru Rinpoche initiated this dance to show the people Zangto Pelri. When the ging and *tsholing* perform this miraculous dance, they demonstrate their magical powers in order to discourage the demons.

The ging wear orange skirts that hang like a skin and terrifying black-and-orange masks with a flag on top, and each holds a big drum. They represent the assembly of heroes, deities and *khandroms* (celestial beings), as well as various male and female terrifying deities. On the outside dance, the tsholing, who represent the protectors of religion, wear long, colourful dresses and terrifying masks.

The dance is a ceremony of purification for the arrival of Guru Rinpoche. People whistle to chase away bad spirits and the ging hit everybody on the head with their drumsticks to chase impurity out of their bodies. After having destroyed the evil spirits (symbolised by an effigy in a black box), the tsholing are chased away by the ging who then stay alone to beat their drums and perform a victory dance.

Dance of the Eight Manifestations of Guru Rinpoche (Guru Tshengay)

The eight different forms of Guru Rinpoche are represented in this dance. Guru Rinpoche is with his two consorts, Mandarava (on the right) and Yeshe Chhogyel (on the left).

This dance is a play and a dance at the same time, and people revere the manifestations of Guru Rinpoche during the dance. Guru Dorji Drakpo enters first, dressed in a colourful brocade dress and wearing a terrifying red mask.

The eight manifestations enter as follows: **Tshokye Dorji**, wearing a brocade dress and a peaceful-looking blue-green mask and carrying a small thunderbolt; **Loden Chogsey**, wearing a red brocade dress and a peaceful white mask and carrying a small drum and a bowl; **Pema Jugney**, wearing a red-and-yellow monk's dress, white mask and tall red hat; **Guru Rinpoche** himself, under a canopy, wearing a golden mask, and with khandroms as attendants, symbolised by small children wearing white masks; **Shakya Senge**, wearing a red-and-yellow monk's dress and a Buddha-like mask with blue hair and carrying a bowl; **Padma Gyalpo**, wearing a red brocade dress and orange-bearded mask with white tufts of hair and carrying a small drum and a mirror; **Nyima Yoezer**, wearing a golden brocade dress and yellow-bearded mask with blue tufts of hair and carrying a trident; and **Sengye Dradrok**, wearing a blue brocade dress and terrifying blue mask and followed by a retinue, who also wear frightening blue masks.

Guru Rinpoche is followed by Shakya Senge. The other manifestations dance turn by turn as people rush to be blessed by Guru Rinpoche. When each manifestation finishes his dance, he joins the others sitting with the Guru.

Sixteen fairies then appear and they sing and perform two dances in front of the Guru and his manifestations. They dance first holding drums, and then holding small bells and small drums. After these dances, everybody goes out in a long procession. The dancers wear brocade dresses and carved-bone ornaments.

Religious Song (Chhoeshey)

This dance is performed to commemorate the opening of the gateway to the pilgrimage site of Tsari, in eastern Tibet, by Tsangpa Jarey, founder of the Drukpa school. The dancers' costumes are similar to those worn during day one's guitar dance.

Courtesy of the Royal Government of Bhutan

[Continued from page 109]

may be no October because it has been deemed an inauspicious month, or there may be two Augusts because that happens to be a good month.

Bhutanese include the nine months in the womb in the calculation of their age. Everyone considers themselves a year older on Losar, New Year's day, and thus people can be nearly two years younger than they say they are.

ACTIVITIES

There are lots of things to do in Bhutan after you have had your fill of dzongs and temples. Tour operators are developing new activities in an effort to convince visitors to stay longer, and some of these offer some unusual opportunities.

Bhutan's only aquatic sports centre is the covered swimming pool in Thimphu. You might find an Indian-made bicycle for rent in the flats of Phuentsholing, but they are not available in any other towns. Mountain biking is being introduced in a limited way.

There are many possible day hikes, particularly in Thimphu, Paro and Bumthang. These are described in the related sections. For serious treks ranging from three to 25 days, see the Trekking chapter. Mountaineering in Bhutan has been prohibited since 1994. Horse riding is available in Paro and on some treks, but remember the Bhutanese adage: It is not a horse that cannot carry a man uphill, and it is not a man that cannot walk downhill.

Fishing is possible in many lakes and a few rivers, though it is frowned upon by many Bhutanese. A licence is required, and fishing is prohibited in many rivers, including the Mo Chhu in Punakha. Yangphel Adventure Travel is promoting fly-fishing and encourages a 'catch and release' approach.

Wildlife viewing is generally confined to Royal Manas National Park in the south, currently off-limits because of the dangers posed by separatist groups in India.

For details of companies offering activity-based tours in Bhutan, see the Getting There & Away chapter.

Rafting & Kayaking

DOT is promoting rafting as a way to give tourists access to beautiful undeveloped areas of Bhutan without unduly affecting the local population. Though rafting in Bhutan is in its infancy, those who have scouted the rivers feel that it has the potential for some of the best rafting on earth.

From small alpine runs like the Paro Chhu to the big water Puna Tsang Chhu, the white water of Bhutan is as diverse as its topography. Since 1997 small groups of paddlers have been exploring 14 rivers and over 22 different runs that vary from class II (beginner with moderate rapids) to class V (expert only).

There are two superb day trips on the Pho Chhu and the Mo Chhu. The trip on the Pho Chhu combines a hike up the side of the river through forest and farmland to the put-in at Samdinka. The raft trip has a couple of class III rapids and ends in a bang with the 'Wrathful Buddha' rapid next to the Punakha Dzong.

The second trip, a very easy scenic float on the Mo Chhu, is suitable for all abilities and is a good introduction for the novice. The run starts about 6km above the Punakha Dzong at the Khamsum Yuelley Namgyal Chorten. As the river meanders through the wide valley you float past one of the queen's winter residences, the king's weekend retreat and some beautiful farmland before taking out just below the dzong.

The fees for river rafting are the same as cultural tours and trekking, though there are extra charges for hiring equipment. Presently only one Bhutanese operator, Lotus Adventures, has trained river guides and equipment for river running in Bhutan (see the list of Bhutanese tour operators in the Getting There & Away chapter).

Mountain Biking

Mountain biking is a new sport in Bhutan, but is gaining popularity with both Bhutanese and expats, who have recently organised the Bhutan Mountain Biking Club (☎ 02-321905, Ⓦ www.bhutanmtb .com). Some adventure travel companies have organised trips that allow bikers to

Rivers for Rafting & Kayaking

river (chhu)	location	river section	km	grade	recommendation
Paro	Paro	Mitsi Zam	10	III & IV	kayaking
Paro	Paro	lower Paro Chhu	7	III with one class IV	kayaking
Upper Wang	Chhuzom	Chhuzom to Tam Chhu	4	IV & V	kayaking
Lower Wang	Tam Chhu	Tam Chhu	4	Class III	rafting & kayaking
Pho	Punakha	upper Pho Chhu	7	III & IV	rafting & kayaking
Pho	Punakha	lower Pho Chhu	7	III	rafting & kayaking
Mo	Punakha	upper Mo Chhu	3	IV & V	kayaking
Mo	Punakha	Sonam's put-in	5	III & IV	rafting & kayaking
Mo	Punakha	lower Mo Chhu	6	I & II	rafting & kayaking
Dang	Wangdue Phodrang	upper Dang Chhu	3	IV & V	kayaking
Dang	Wangdue Phodrang	middle Dang Chhu	5	IV & V	rafting with an experienced team & kayaking
Dang	Wangdue Phodrang	lower Dang Chhu	5	III	rafting & kayaking
Mangde	Trongsa	Ema Datsi Canyon	7	III & IV at medium flow	kayaking
Bumthang	Bumthang	Thankabi	5	II & III	rafting & kayaking
Tang	Bumthang	Mesithang Tang	10	III	kayaking
Kuri	Lhuentse	upper run	14	IV & V	kayaking
Kuri	Lhuentse	middle run	20	IV with a couple of V	kayaking
Kuri	Lhuentse	lower run	10	III	rafting & kayaking
Puna Tsang	Tsirang	Wakley Tar	15	III & IV	rafting & kayaking

bring their own cycles and travel throughout Bhutan accompanied by a 'sag wagon' for support. Long journeys are difficult because there's a lot of uphill peddling and approaching vehicles roar around corners, not expecting cyclists. Local cycling excursions in the Paro, Thimphu and Bumthang valleys offer a safer and less strenuous mountain-biking experience.

Golf

There's an international-standard golf course in Thimphu and there are small courses in Haa and Deothang. The Thimphu course is used mainly by Bhutanese and expatriates, though a few Japanese tourists play there both for the experience and because it's very inexpensive compared with green fees in Japan. For details see the Activities section of the Thimphu chapter.

COURSES

There are no formal courses offered in Bhutan but your tour operator may be able to arrange programs to meet your particular interest. Given sufficient notice, the Dzongkha Development Commission can arrange brief courses and lectures on language and music.

The Royal Institute of Management and the Royal Civil Service Commission team up twice a year to provide a two-week orientation course on Bhutanese religion and culture for international volunteers working in Bhutan.

WWF (☎ 02-323528, fax 02-323518) and RSPN (☎ 02-326130) can arrange lectures and discussion groups on wildlife and environmental issues.

By prior arrangement, the Folk Heritage Museum (☎ 02-327133) can provide courses in Bhutanese cooking and paper making.

WORK

Bhutan is selective about the type of projects it wants in the country and disdains indiscriminate assistance. Each donor or charitable agency is limited to specified projects or activities, and is allowed only a certain number of volunteers. The opportunities for volunteer work in Bhutan are therefore limited. Since 1980, only 1000 volunteers from various organisations have served in Bhutan, and in 2001 there were 58 working in the country.

Volunteer Work

If you want to do volunteer work in Bhutan, the following agencies may be able to help. Americans will find it difficult to get a position, because the US Peace Corps does not have a Bhutan program.

The United Nations has numerous programs in Bhutan, all coordinated through the United Nations Development Programme (UNDP). Among the agencies are the United Nations Children's Fund (Unicef), United Nations Capital Development Fund (UNCDF), United Nations Volunteers (UNV) and the United Nations Educational, Scientific, and Cultural Organization (Unesco).

Two other agencies are: Australian Volunteers International (☎ 03-9279 1788, fax 03-9419 4248, W www.ozvol.org.au), PO Box 350, Fitzroy, Vic 3065, Australia; and the Coordinating Committee for International Voluntary Service (CCIVS; ☎ 01 45 68 49 36, W www.unesco.org/ccivs/), c/o Unesco House, 1 rue Miollis, 75732 Paris, France.

Other agencies that operate programs in Bhutan include the European Community, Save the Children, ACB (Austrian), SNV (Dutch), VSA (New Zealand), JOCV and JICA (Japan), Danida (Danish), GTZ (German) and Helvetas (Swiss).

ACCOMMODATION

Tour operators are supposed to book you into DOT-approved hotels. Since you pay the same rate whether you stay in a noisy local guesthouse or in the best place in town, it makes sense to ask for the top of the line when you make your travel arrangements. During the high season, particularly at tsechu time, you may not get the hotel you have asked for, and you may even be accommodated in a hotel that caters primarily to Indian and Bhutanese travellers. Still, these can be comfortable, though the toilet facilities may not be what you're used to, and may be noisy.

The prices in this book are for standard rooms at normal foreign-tourist rates and do not include 10% tax or service charges.

Hotels

There is a variety of hotels in Bhutan, ranging from simple huts that cater to Bhutanese yak herders to Paro's fancy Olathang Hotel, which was built for royal guests. At the time of research there were no international chain hotels and not much imported hotel equipment. What you get is a Bhutanese version of what they think Western tourists expect. In most cases, the facilities and service are pretty good, but still only about the standards of India and Nepal 10 years ago. This may all change when luxury resorts planned by the Aman Group, Four Seasons and Oberoi become operational.

All rooms in the DOT-approved hotels in Thimphu, Paro and Phuentsholing have electricity, telephone, private bathroom and (at certain times of day) hot water. Every hotel has a restaurant that serves buffet meals when a group is in residence and a la carte dining at other times. Bars, when they exist, are usually just a few stools in a corner of the dining room. Several hotels advertise that they have IDD, but this simply means that the phones connect to the front desk and the hotel operator will then dial the international number.

There's a strange system when you discuss hotel rates, because Indians and project people can book a hotel directly (without a Bhutanese travel agent). All the hotels publish their room rates and many have various standards of rooms, including normal and deluxe rooms, as well as suites, though the difference between these facilities in most hotels is minimal. When you book a trip, you may specify which hotel you wish, but unless you are particularly charming to the agent, you'll probably get a standard room. If you want fancy accommodation or a single room, you may be asked to pay for this in addition to the standard tourist fee. If you are travelling off season you can often pay less; if it's tsechu time, you will probably pay more. Some hotels also have a lower rate for Indian tourists.

In Bhutan, as in many parts of the Indian subcontinent, the word 'hotel' is often used to identify a place to eat. Many small establishments in Bhutan that have signs saying 'hotel' are, in fact, restaurants and have no accommodation available.

No matter how simple the accommodation is, the room is likely to be elegantly decorated in Bhutanese style, and at first glance you may think you are being shown into a monastery, not a hotel room. Lavish use of wood for floors and panelling is the norm. Bedspreads and curtains are often made of colourful handloom material, the bedside table is of brightly painted carved wood and the wall paintings can range from mediocre to exquisite.

It's *cold* at night in Bhutan and there is no central heating. In Thimphu and Paro there are small electric heaters, and in Bumthang many hotel rooms are heated by a wood stove called a *bukhari*, which often has a pile of rocks on the top to retain the heat. All hotels provide sheets, blankets or quilts, and a pillow. Unless you are trekking, you won't need to carry bedding or a sleeping bag, but in the winter you may find yourself wearing all your clothing to bed. Hotel pillows tend to be extra firm.

Many of the older hotels, especially those run by the Bhutan Tourism Corporation Limited (BTCL), have old-fashioned British Raj-style metal teapots that burn your fingers – use a napkin when you pick them up. In several hotels the hot and cold water taps are mislabelled; check both taps before you give up and wash with cold water. In many hotels the water heaters, including those of most solar heating systems, are placed far from the rooms. You may have to run the water for a long time before hot water reaches you. If there is an electric water heater (called a geyser) in the room, turn it on as soon as you check in.

The water flasks in hotel rooms are not always filled, and there is no assurance that the water they contain is boiled. (For details on purifying water see the boxed text 'Water Purification' earlier in this chapter.)

Reservations Unfortunately a confirmed hotel reservation does not always guarantee a booking in hotels as small as those in Bhutan. A large tour group can exert a powerful influence, and you may discover that there is an extended negotiation taking place between your guide and the desk clerk when you check in. Don't worry; *something* will be arranged.

Many hotels are owned and operated by tour companies. When space is tight, you might get bumped in favour of clients on a tour arranged by the company owning the hotel. The biggest chain of hotels is operated by BTCL; in many towns theirs are the only facilities approved by DOT.

Hot-Stone Baths Some hotels have a traditional Bhutanese hot-stone bath. This is said to have health benefits in addition to its cleansing properties. The bathtub is either a wooden structure or simply a hole dug into the ground. A fire is built nearby to heat large stones, which are eventually rolled down a metal chute into the tub. A wooden grill inside the tub separates you from the red-hot rocks as they splash and sizzle into the water. It's an amusing experience, and one bather commented that she came out only a little bit dirtier than when she went in.

It takes time to heat the rocks – typically two hours or more. Hotels charge extra for this luxury. At the Tigers Nest Resort in Paro, the rate is Nu 800 for one person, Nu 600 per person if there are two of you and Nu 300 per person for four.

FOOD

Since travel in Bhutan is an all-inclusive package, you can expect to eat most of your meals in your hotel dining room. Most hotels cater to groups and have developed the habit of providing buffet-style meals. Even if you are alone and the only guest in a hotel, you may find a minibuffet set up just for you. There is usually a continental dish, and sometimes an Indian, Chinese or Bhutanese dish. There is almost always rice, either white or the local red variety, and dal (lentil soup). If you are in a small group, or have booked your tour directly, you can specify that you want to order from the menu, though sometimes the buffet meals offer a wider selection. Most experienced Bhutan travellers recommend that you stick to Bhutanese or Indian food rather than Western fare.

Drinks, including mineral water, are usually charged as extras, and payment is collected at the end of the meal or the following morning when you check out of the hotel.

On long drives or hikes you will not return to your hotel for lunch, and most tour operators arrange packed lunches from the hotel. These tend to be an uninspired collection of sandwiches, boiled potatoes, eggs, fruit and inevitably a small carton of mango juice. Consider a visit to a bakery for some bread or rolls and perhaps buy some Indian tinned cheese or biscuits to make your picnic more interesting.

The other way to liven up lunch is to forego the packed lunch and eat in a local roadside restaurant. There are some quite good restaurants at strategic spots along the east-west road and also between Thimphu and Phuentsholing. Once you go east of Bumthang the choice becomes more limited and the food is much more Bhutanese, but as long as you stick to cooked food that is served hot, it should be safe to eat.

The food in hotels is often the best in town, but if you want to sample local restaurants, your guide can arrange it so that the tour operator pays for your restaurant meals. Restaurant food in Bhutan is not particularly special, and beware of local dishes with chillies. If you are ordering from a menu, don't be surprised if two-thirds of the offerings are not available. In eastern Bhutan you may find that there is no meat, bread or other key item of food available in the whole town.

Meat is frequently dry and stringy. There are no slaughterhouses, and only a few cold storage facilities. Beef and fish come from India, often travelling long distances in unrefrigerated trucks. Don't eat beef during the monsoon season, and be very wary of pork at any time. During the summer you are usually limited to chicken, or a vegetarian diet. Yak meat is sometimes available, but only in the winter. You will rarely find mutton or lamb served in Bhutan.

One dish that is frequently available is *dal bhat* (rice and lentils), the traditional mainstay of Nepali meals. Hotel and trekking cooks make some excellent nonspicy dishes, such as *kewa datse* (potatoes with cheese sauce) and *shamu datse* (mushrooms with cheese sauce).

Local Food

All large towns have restaurants, but in smaller villages there is often no public eating facility at all. In small restaurants in remote villages the fare is likely to be the national dish, *ema datse* (chillies and cheese), and meat of questionable vintage. If the food appears unappetising, you can always settle for tea and biscuits or a bowl of instant noodles.

Traditional Bhutanese food always features spicy red or green chillies. Ema datse comprises large green (very hot) chillies, prepared as a vegetable, not as a seasoning, in a cheese sauce. The second-most popular dish is *phak sha laphu* (stewed pork with radish). Other typical dishes, always served with chillies, are *no sha huentseu* (stewed beef with spinach), *phak sha phin tshoem* (pork with rice noodles) and *bja sha maroo* (chicken in garlic and butter sauce).

Pork fat is a popular dish in the wilds because of its high energy content. Western visitors find it almost inedible because it is usually quite stale or is just fat with lumps of hairy skin attached – no meat.

Several Tibetan-style dishes are common in Bhutan. Small steamed dumplings called *momos* may be filled with meat or cheese. Fried cheese momos are a speciality of several Thimphu restaurants. Another Tibetan dish is *thukpa* (noodles), which may be fried or served in soup. Both of these are available in many small restaurants and are good to order when you want a quick meal. Village people also eat *tsampa*, the Tibetan-style dish of roasted-barley flour mixed with salt and yak-butter tea and kneaded into a paste.

Although there is plenty of white rice, the Bhutanese prefer a locally produced red variety, which has a slightly nutty flavour. At high altitudes where rice is not available, wheat and buckwheat are the staples. *Zow* is rice that is boiled and then fried. It's sometimes mixed with sugar and butter and is commonly carried in a *bangchung* (covered basket). In Bumthang *khule* (buckwheat pancakes) and *puta* (buckwheat noodles) replace rice as the foundation of many meals. A common snack food in the east is *gesasip*, corn (maize) that has been fried and beaten.

Be careful of Bhutanese chillies. If you bite into a bunch of hot chillies, a few mouthfuls of plain rice will often help ease the pain. A spoonful of sugar seems to absorb some of the fiery oil.

Vegetarian

There is a good variety of vegetarian food available, although much of it is made using chillies as the primary vegetable. Unusual ingredients such as nettles, ferns, orchids, asparagus, taro and mushrooms appear in traditional Bhutanese vegetarian dishes.

Even if you are a keen carnivore, you might temporarily go vegetarian during the monsoon season because of the lack of reliable refrigeration for meat.

Doma

One of the great Bhutanese vices is chewing *doma*, also known by its Indian name, *paan*.

The centrepiece is a hard nut that is chewed as a digestive. Though the nut is called betel nut, it is actually from the *Areca catechu* palm. Indians use dried nuts for their paan, but the Bhutanese prefer the nuts fresh.

The nut is mixed with lime powder (the ash, not the fruit) and the whole collection is rolled up in a heart-shaped betel leaf and chewed slowly. It's a bittersweet, mildly intoxicating concoction and it stains the mouth bright red. When the remains are spat out, they leave a characteristic crimson stain on the pavement.

There is an array of accoutrements associated with chewing doma that many men carry in the pouch of their gho. The ingredients are carried in ornate boxes and there are special knives designed to slice the nuts.

Worryingly, studies in India and the US have found a direct link between the consumption of paan and submucous fibrosis (SMF), a painful disease of the mouth for which there is no cure. Sufferers of SMF are 400 times more likely to contract oral cancer than nonsufferers. Trying doma occasionally may not cause any harm, but don't make a habit of it. The government is trying to convince people not to chew doma but the great incidence of stained teeth you'll see in Bhutan indicates a singular lack of success.

DRINKS
Nonalcoholic Drinks
Tea & Coffee Invariably coffee is instant Nescafé. Often you will simply be presented with a cup of hot water, a jar of instant coffee and a spoon. Tea may be served in a pot, but more often it appears as a cup filled with hot water, with a tea bag on the saucer.

Sweet tea is called *ngad-ja* in Dzongkha. Bhutanese frequently drink *sud-ja*, Tibetan-style tea with salt and butter, which is more like soup than tea. Try it.

Water Don't drink water from a tap or flask anywhere in Bhutan. The only exception is the tap water at the Swiss Guest House in Bumthang, which has its own safety-tested spring. The flasks in hotel rooms are sometimes filled with untreated water.

Ideally, you should always drink water that has been boiled to kill the various germs in it, but few restaurants boil the drinking water they serve. Confine yourself to hot drinks or mineral water, or treat the water yourself using iodine (see the boxed text 'Water Purification' earlier in this chapter). Water filters do not protect against some water-borne diseases, most importantly hepatitis. Most restaurants will give you hot water to drink if you ask for it.

Mineral Water Bottles of locally bottled 'mineral water' are available throughout Bhutan, though in the east the supply may be limited to Indian brands. It's usually safe, though many brands of Indian 'mineral water' are simply tap water that has been 'purified' by passing it through a filter and ultraviolet light system.

Soft Drinks Indian brands of soft drinks are available throughout Bhutan. Pepsi is the most easily available, thanks to an aggressive marketing and distribution system to support its bottling plant in Phuentsholing. You can usually find colas, lemon drinks and soda water.

Excellent Bhutanese apple juice is served in hotels and restaurants. Large tins of Druk-brand orange, mango, tomato and pineapple juice are available, but outside of hotels, you might have to buy the whole tin. Small cartons of sweet mango juice are available throughout the country.

Alcoholic Drinks
The only beer brewed in Bhutan is Red Panda, an unfiltered brew bottled in Bumthang. It's not to everyone's liking, though the new *Weissbier* (wheat beer) gets good reviews. Throughout the country there's an ample supply of imported canned beer – Tiger from Singapore or Indian beer, which comes in large (650mL) bottles. The most popular brands are Black Label, Golden Eagle and Dansberg from Sikkim. If you want a cheap high, try one of the brands with 8% alcohol content: Hit, Volcano, Black Knight or 10,000. Beer is inexpensive thanks to a strange loophole in the taxation system. In

shops a 650mL bottle of Black Label costs Nu 27. Prices are higher, of course, in bars and hotels. At high altitudes such as Thimphu, alcohol has a more potent effect.

Army welfare projects have a monopoly on Bhutanese alcohol production. There are several brands of whiskey, including Special Courier, Black Mountain Whiskey (better known as 'BMW'), Royal Supreme and Changta, the cheapest. The better brands compare favourably with good Scotch whiskey. There are two local rums: XXX Bhutan Rum is the stronger, and Dragon Deluxe the next. There are also the local Crystal and Pacham gins. Most hotels also have a stock of international brands.

There is a good supply of wine available at the duty-free shop in Thimphu. Still, it is likely to be expensive and disappointing.

The most common local brew is *bang chhang*, a warm beer-like drink made from wheat. The favourite hard drinks are *arra*, a spirit distilled from rice, and *sinchhang*, which is made from millet, wheat or rice. *Chhang kuy* is a soupy drink made from fermented rice; it is usually regarded as 'a woman's drink'.

Throughout the country alcohol may not be served before 1pm. Tuesday is a 'dry day' and in most towns hotels and restaurants don't serve alcohol on this day.

SMOKING
The sale of tobacco is banned in 18 of Bhutan's 20 districts. Though smoking is discouraged, many people do, and you can smoke in the tobacco-free districts except in dzongs, goembas, hospitals and any restaurants or shops that have 'no smoking' signs.

ENTERTAINMENT
The bar scene comprises mostly of tiny shops with a few tables and a supply of beer and local spirits. If you poke your head into any small establishment that is advertised as a bar, you will probably be welcomed. In towns virtually everyone speaks English and it's easy, and often rewarding, to strike up a conversation.

Many bars are also *carom* parlours. Carom is a game played on a board like a small pool table with a pocket in each corner. Instead of stroking balls, the players flick checkers into the pockets. Carom is a highly competitive game, usually played with beer or money as the stakes. Cards are another common diversion; the most common card game is a very complicated one called 'marriage'.

Saturday is disco night, and well-heeled Bhutanese of all ages frequent the few establishments in Thimphu and Paro that have loud music and dancing.

There are only five cinemas in Bhutan – two in Phuentsholing and one in Thimphu. The others are in Samtse (which is an unlikely destination for tourists) and the last is a rudimentary facility with wooden benches in Samdrup Jongkhar. All show very long Hindi films with extravagant sets and rampant singing and dancing. Thimphu's cinema shows one old English film daily. Cinema tickets are at a premium, with long queues of punters, pushing and crowding.

SPECTATOR SPORTS
Football
Football tournaments are held most summer evenings in large towns. The season continues through October and matches are held

Archery

Since time immemorial Bhutanese have been passionate about their national sport of *datse* (archery). Nearly all villages in the kingdom boast an archery range and each dzong has a space set aside nearby for a *bha cho* (field of target).

Competitions are a riot of colour and excitement, with two teams in traditional dress shooting at small wooden targets placed 140m apart (Olympic standard is 50m). The distance is so great that team members gather dangerously close to the target to yell back how good the archer's aim was. This is often accompanied by howls, chanting, encouragement and jokes. Members of the opposing team may shout back how terrible the archer's aim is and make ribald remarks. When an arrow hits the target, team-mates perform a celebratory slow-motion dance and sing the praises of the shooter, who tucks a coloured scarf into his belt.

For major tournaments each team brings its own cheerleading section of girls decked out in their finest clothes. They perform dances in between play, and during the shooting they do brief routines and shout lewd and disparaging comments about the opposing archer's parentage or sexual prowess.

Tradition has it that women are not allowed to touch an archer's bow, and it is believed to decrease performance if an archer sleeps with a woman the night before a contest.

The traditional Bhutanese archery equipment is a long bamboo bow. Most archers nowadays use a state-of-the-art carbonite Hoyt brand bow with a complicated-looking pulley system that releases the arrows with tremendous speed.

The use of imported equipment hasn't diluted the rich traditions of the game, although Bhutanese archers are now encouraged to train for the Olympics. International coaches who have trained Bhutan's Olympic archers have been impressed with the natural talent and think that, with expert coaching, Bhutan could possibly win an Olympic medal one day. The national newspaper, *Kuensel*, urges young archers, including women, 'It is time to shoot beyond participation'.

The Bhutan National Archery Federation organises two national archery tournaments a year, one with traditional bamboo bows and one open to archers using modern imported equipment. The traditional bow tournament takes place in Dechencholeing in May.

Archery matches are among the most picturesque and colourful events you'll find here and well worth a visit. There are formal competitions on many weekends, and archers practise most afternoons and weekends when there is no competition. It's easy to find a session to watch.

even in the heaviest downpours. During the national school tournament in August, Thimphu's Changlimithang Stadium is crammed with spectators as teams battle it out to the cheers of hordes of schoolgirls.

SHOPPING

Bhutan boasts a variety of handicrafts. Until recently, nothing in Bhutan was made especially for sale to tourists and it was possible to find high-quality arts and crafts almost everywhere. Now there is a fair amount of tourist schlock on offer; one of the worst places for this is alongside the trail to Taktshang Goemba. A few creative souvenir items, such as Dragon Kingdom T-shirts, coin purses shaped like *bangchung* (round covered bamboo baskets) and mini *atsara* (clown) masks available.

There are many handicraft shops in Thimphu and Paro, and most hotels have a shop selling Bhutanese crafts. As you shop, remember that it is illegal (and immoral) to export antiques. Don't get carried away. Try to visualise how an ethnic Bhutanese mask or ritual object will look in your living room at home.

Some of the crafts sold in Bhutan are actually made in Nepal or India; if in doubt, ask. Most shopkeepers will be honest with you, and your guide can probably offer some independent advice. There does not seem to be a racket of shops paying commissions, and you can rely on your guide for an objective opinion.

Thangkas

Thangkas are Buddhist paintings, usually on canvas. Traditionally, they are mounted on a background of brocade and hung by a stick sewn across the top. You can also buy an unmounted painting and roll it up to take home. If you buy an expensive one and don't want it damaged in your luggage, stop at a hardware shop and get a short length of plastic pipe to protect it.

Prices vary tremendously, with small paintings made by students selling for Nu 300 to 500 and large mounted thangkas starting at Nu 30,000. The price depends on size, quality of work and detail. One

excellent place to buy paintings is the National Institute for Zorig Chusum in Thimphu (for an example of its craft see the boxed text 'Important Figures of Drukpa Kagyu Buddhism' in the Facts about Bhutan chapter). The money you pay here goes to the students to help support their training. You can be confident that any painting you buy in Bhutan was made by a local artist.

Textiles

Hand-woven cotton fabric is the most traditional and useful item you can buy in Bhutan. The quality is almost always good, but the price will vary depending on the intricacy of the design and whether any expensive imported silk was used in the weaving. Hand-woven fabric is sold in 'loom lengths' that are 30cm to 45cm wide and 2.5m to 3m long. Bhutanese sew three of these lengths together to make the traditional dress of gho and kira. You can find handmade cloth in handicraft shops or in the Khaling handloom project in eastern Bhutan, but it may be more fun to search in ordinary fabric shops.

Indian machine-made cloth, in a variety of Bhutanese designs, is also sold at a price far lower than handmade cloth.

Hand-woven woollen cloth is also available. *Yathras* are lengths of rough woollen cloth that can be sewn together to make sweaters, scarves or blankets. A length costs Nu 800 to 3000, depending on the tightness of the weave and whether wool or cotton threads were used for the weft. The best place to shop for yathras is in Zungney in Bumthang's Chhume valley.

Other Items

Brass statues and Buddhist ritual items, such as bells, cymbals, trumpets and *dorjis* (stylised thunderbolts) are available from specialist shops, and you can also find ritual items at the north end of the weekend market in Thimphu.

Jewellery and other silver items are best purchased from a reputable shop or from the artisans themselves. Much of the low-priced silverwork sold in Bhutan is actually made in Nepal from white metal.

Traditional Dress

Donning a Gho

The *gho*, when first put on, should reach almost to the ground. Fold the sleeves of the *tego* (shirt) back to form cuffs. Tuck the right front panel into the left and bring the left panel over to the right. Grasp the gho at the sides and fold towards the back. Gather the material at your waist until the hemline is above the knee (the king wears his below the knee).

The gho is secured with a narrow woven belt called a *kera*, which forms a pouch. You need shoes and knee-high socks to complete the outfit. Pants are worn under the gho in winter and tucked into the long socks.

Donning a Kira

The *kira* is first draped around the back under the right arm. Wrap it around the front and fasten on your left shoulder with a *koma* (silver hook). Fold it left to right across your front and then right to left. The remaining cloth is gathered under the left arm and wrapped around the back to the right shoulder, and fastened with a second koma. A kera is wrapped around the waist to form a pouch.

The *kaymeto* (widthways border) is always worn at the back.

A *toego* (jacket) is often worn with the kira, and the sleeves of the *wonju* (blouse) can be folded back over the toego to form cuffs.

If you have lots of space in your luggage, you can choose from a variety of carved wooden pieces. Useful items such as picture frames and furniture are available, as are wooden masks similar to those used in the tsechu dances. Prices vary considerably, and shipping can be a problem (see Sending Mail under Post & Communications earlier in this chapter). Wooden bowls, either plain or lined with silver, are a speciality of eastern Bhutan.

Bamboo work is available in most of the handicraft shops and sometimes at roadside stalls. The round bangchung baskets, which some people have nicknamed 'Bhutanese Tupperware', can easily be stuffed into a bag or suitcase. The large baskets called *zhim* that are fastened on horses to carry gear on treks are hard to find, but a smaller version is available in many shops. Another unusual item is the large bamboo pipes covered with weaving that are used for carrying local liquor.

Handmade paper is available in large sheets and sometimes is packaged into handy packets of letter-writing size. Several local artists sell their paintings in small art galleries in Thimphu and sometimes in hotel shops.

Carpet manufacturing is a recent innovation in Bhutan; traditionally most carpets in Bhutan were imported from Tibet or Nepal. There is a large factory in Phuentsholing and a small carpet workshop in the Phobjikha valley. Carpets are available in most handicraft shops, and a limited supply is on hand at the workshop behind the Phuntsho Chholing Guest House in Phobjikha.

Some of Bhutan's minority groups wear peculiar-looking hats, which make curious gifts for your friends at home. If you look carefully, you can find bamboo hats from Laya, Brokpa yak-hair 'spider' hats and conical bamboo Bumthang hats in shops throughout Bhutan.

Traditional Bhutanese songs can be haunting, if monotonous. The popular songs are an interesting combination of Bhutanese, Tibetan and Indian influences. You can find recordings of both classical and popular Bhutanese songs in most towns. The cassette tapes are not high quality, but for Nu 65 to 80 provide a lingering reminder of the spirit of Bhutan. Locally produced CDs cost Nu 250. There's also a CD titled *Zangto Pelri* that showcases the musicians of the Royal Academy of Performing Arts.

Getting There & Away

There are only two entry points to Bhutan open to foreigners. Most travellers arrive by air at Bhutan's only international airport in Paro. The alternative is to travel through the Indian state of West Bengal and enter Bhutan by road at Phuentsholing on the southern border of Bhutan. At the time of research, it was no longer possible for foreigners to travel via Samdrup Jongkhar in the east of the country. In any event, unless you are an Indian national, you are required to fly in one direction using Druk Air, the national carrier.

AIR
Druk Air

Bhutan has one airport and one airline. Druk Air operates two 72-seat BAe 146-100 four-engine jet aircraft. These planes are now obsolete and the airline is upgrading its fleet, although there are only a few aircraft types that can operate on a runway that is as short and high as Paro's. When you board a Druk Air flight you may discover that you are on an Airbus A-319 or other aircraft carrying 100 or more passengers.

The schedule changes by season, but normally there are two flights per week from New Delhi (via Kathmandu) and four flights a week from Bangkok via Dhaka or Kolkata (Calcutta), depending on the day of the week. To allow for extra visitors to the Thimphu *tsechu* in October and the Paro tsechu in April, the airline provides extra flights.

Reconfirm your Druk Air flight with your tour operator a few weeks before departure to ensure that the schedule has not changed, and also check the flight time the day before your departure. Druk Air is quite good about announcing schedule changes at least a week in advance in *Kuensel*, the national newspaper. Check in early for Druk Air flights as they occasionally depart before the scheduled time, especially if the weather starts to change for the worse. Flights are often delayed because of weather and Druk Air recommends that you travel on non-restricted tickets and allow at least 24-hours

Warning

The information in this chapter is particularly vulnerable to change: Prices for international travel are volatile, routes are introduced and cancelled, schedules change, special deals come and go, and rules and visa requirements are amended. You should check directly with the airline or a travel agency to make sure you understand how a fare (and ticket you may buy) works and be aware of the security requirements for international travel.

The upshot of this is that you should get opinions, quotes and advice from as many airlines and travel agencies as possible before you part with your hard-earned cash. The details given in this chapter should be regarded as pointers and are not a substitute for your own careful, up-to-date research.

As this book went to press, all Internet and email addresses in Bhutan were changed. Where once addresses ended with 'com.bt', 'net.bt' or 'gov.bt' these now all end '.bt'.

transit time with your connecting flight in order to minimise the complications of delays. When flights cannot land in Paro there is no charge for the unscheduled tour of Bagdogra, near Siliguri, or Kolkata. Druk Air flights are all nonsmoking.

Schedules vary between summer and winter. In summer, flights depart earlier, while it is still cool. High temperatures reduce engine power, so in hot weather the aircraft can't carry as much weight and passengers must be offloaded. That's why the check-in staff ask all passengers to step on the scales – with their hand luggage – to be weighed for all flights out of Bhutan. Between mid-February and mid-May, high afternoon winds in the Paro valley make landing difficult, and schedules are rearranged so that all flights arrive in Paro before noon.

Druk Air is not allowed to issue tickets to Paro for foreign visitors until they receive a 'visa clearance' from the Ministry of Foreign Affairs in Thimphu. When the visa is authorised, the information is entered into the computer record for your reservation even though the actual visa will not be issued until you arrive at Paro airport.

Druk Air will issue your ticket once it receives this number. For this reason, it's difficult to get tickets for Paro flights issued along with your other international air tickets.

Because Druk Air has no interline agreements with other carriers, your ticket to Paro will be separate from your other international tickets. This means you cannot check your baggage all the way through to Paro via a connecting flight. You will need to reclaim your baggage and recheck it at the Druk Air counter. Similarly, when you depart from Bhutan, you can only check baggage as far as you are travelling with Druk Air, not all the way through to your final destination.

Paro Airport

All landings and takeoffs in Paro are by visual flight rules (VFR), which means the pilot must be able to see the runway before landing, and the surrounding hills before takeoff. No flights can be operated at night or in poor visibility. When Paro valley is clouded-in, flights are delayed, sometimes for a few days. The record is three days waiting for weather to clear. When this happens, your tour program will have to be changed and everything rebooked. The upside of such a delay is that you can probably put some spontaneity into your schedule in Bhutan and make a few modifications as you go, depending on what you find interesting.

In 1999 the old terminal building was replaced with a large modern building that looks more like a dzong than an airport terminal.

The Flight from Kathmandu to Paro

The Druk Air flight from Kathmandu to Paro provides the most dramatic view of Himalayan scenery of any scheduled flight. (Get a window seat on the left if you can.) After the plane climbs out of the Kathmandu valley a continual chain of peaks appears just off the left wing. The captain usually points out Everest (a black pyramid), Makalu (a grey chair-shaped peak) and Kanchenjunga (a huge massif), but if you have trekked in Nepal and are familiar with the mountains you can pick out many more. The elusive Shishapangma (8013m) is visible inside Tibet. Other easily recognisable peaks are Gauri Shankar (7185m), with its notch shape, Cho Oyu (8153m), Nuptse (7906m), with its long ridge, Lhotse (8501m) and Chhamlang (7319m). With a sharp eye, you can even spot Lukla airstrip and the town of Namche Bazaar at the foot of Khumbila (5761m) in Nepal.

When you pass Kanchenjunga, look for the dome-shaped peak on the western skyline. That is Jannu (7710m), which some French climbers have described as a 'peak of terror'; the Nepalis have renamed it Khumbakarna. Once past Kanchenjunga, the peaks are more distant. This is the Sikkim Himalaya; the major peaks, from west to east, are Chomoyummo (6829m), Pauhunri (7125m) and Shudu Tsenpa (7032m).

As the plane approaches Paro you may be able to spot the beautiful snow peak of Jhomolhari (7314m) and the grey ridge-shaped peak of Jichu Drakye (6989m). The plane then descends, often through clouds, into the wooded valleys of Bhutan.

The captain may announce that you are about to see the mountains closer than you have ever seen them before. He's not joking. Depending on the approach pattern that day, you may drop into the Paro valley and weave through the hills, with *goembas* and prayer flags on the hillsides above. If you are on the left side of the plane, look for Taktshang Goemba and Paro Dzong as you descend towards the airport, before using almost the entire 1830m of the runway to stop. On other occasions, you may overfly the airport, then bank, skim over a few tree-covered ridges and the roofs of houses, and make a gut-wrenching plunge into the valley before turning for the final approach to the runway.

On Arrival The first task when you arrive is to queue at the visa fee counter where the clerk will miraculously find your visa clearance paper and collect the US$20 visa fee. You then proceed to the immigration desk where the officer will find another copy of your visa approval, and issue the visa. It is useful to have a photocopy of the visa clearance, or at least the visa number, to expedite the process. It's then like any normal airport arrival. You get your passport stamped, change money, and clear customs.

Buying Tickets

Druk-Air Fares Because there is no competition with other airlines for flights to Paro, Druk Air fares are expensive. There are no discounts or student fares except for citizens of Bhutan. The Druk Air rules say that if fares are increased after the ticket is issued, they may collect the difference when you check in. Recently a US$5 per sector insurance surcharge was levied on all tickets and is collected at the airport. One-way fares to Paro in US dollars are:

from	economy (US$)	business (US$)
Bangkok	360	440
Delhi	315	380
Dhaka	190	230
Kathmandu	190	230
Kolkata	190	230

Druk Air Offices & Agents Druk Air's head office (☎ 08-271856, 271860, fax 271861, W www.drukair.com.bt) is in Paro, just below the dzong. Travel agents in Thimphu have to travel to Paro to make reservations or issue tickets for visitors. This, predictably, causes delays in confirming and issuing tickets.

Overseas offices include:

Bangladesh
Druk Air Corporation (☎ 02-891 1066, fax 891 3038) Room No 3237, Central Block, 2nd floor, Zia International Airport, Dhaka
Mams Travels & Tours (☎ 02-887 969, 886 896, fax 888 439, e mams@bdmail.net) 33 Gulshan Avenue Rd No 45, Gulshan-2, Dhaka 1212

India
Druk Air Corporation (☎ 033-2402419, ☎ airport 569976, fax 2470050) 51 Tivoli Court, 1A Ballygunge Circular Rd, Kolkata
Druk Air Corporation Ltd (☎ 011-5653207, 5652011, ext 2238) Indira Gandhi International Airport, Terminal Bldg, New Delhi
Unique Air Travels (☎ 033-2474333) G2, Circular Centre, 222 AJC Bose Rd, Kolkata 700017

Nepal
Malla Treks (☎ 01-410089, fax 423143, e drukair@mallatreks.com) Lekhnath Marg, PO Box 5227, Kathmandu

Thailand
Druk Air Corporation (☎ 02-535 1960, fax 535 3661, e drukair@loxinfo.co.th) Room 3237, Central Block, Bangkok International Airport
Oriole Travels & Tours (☎ 02-237 9201, fax 2379200, e oriole@samart.co.th) 5th floor Skulthai Suriwong Tower, 141 Suriwong Rd, Bangkok 10500

Thai International can issue tickets on Druk Air; the Bangkok offices know how to do this, but most of the overseas offices are not familiar with the procedures. Once your Bhutanese agent has confirmed the flight and the visa authority has been issued, allow another week for the reservation information to make its way to Thai International's computers. You'll probably still have to communicate several times with your agent in Thimphu to get Druk Air to send a confirmation message to Thai.

Many overseas agents that arrange groups to Bhutan have the tickets issued in Kathmandu, Bangkok or Delhi. A local representative waits at the Druk Air counter to deliver the tickets and check you in for your flight. If you have booked directly with a Bhutanese tour operator, you can send payment for the air fare directly to the agent in Thimphu as a separate bank transfer, not as part of the payment for the tour. The agent can then issue the Paro ticket and mail or courier it to you.

Connecting to Druk Air You will need to buy a ticket to and from the place where you will connect to Druk Air. Bangkok is the best place to connect if you are coming from North America, Australia or Asia. Delhi is the best place to connect if you are coming from Europe or the Middle East. A connection via Kathmandu will give you a taste of the Himalaya and of Tibetan Buddhism before you fly to Bhutan. Other connections via Kolkata or Dhaka are possible, but these are off the routes of direct flights for major airlines, and few discounted air fares are available to these places.

Tickets to Gateway Cities With a bit of research – ringing around travel agencies, especially those that specialise in India and Thailand, checking Internet sites, perusing the travel ads in newspapers – you can often get yourself a good travel deal. Start early as some of the cheapest tickets need to be bought well in advance and popular flights can sell out.

Full-time students and people under 26 years (under 30 in some countries) have access to better deals than other travellers. You have to show a document proving your date of birth or a valid International Student Identity Card (ISIC) when buying your ticket and boarding the plane.

Generally, there is nothing to be gained by buying a ticket direct from the airline. Discounted tickets are released to selected travel agencies and specialist discount agencies, and these are usually the cheapest deals.

One exception to this rule is the expanding number of 'no-frills' carriers, which mostly sell only direct to travellers. Unlike the 'full-service' airlines, no-frills carriers often make one-way tickets available at around half the return fare, meaning that it is easy to put together an open-jaw ticket when you fly to one place but leave from another.

The other exception is booking on the Internet. Many airlines offer some excellent fares to Web surfers. They may sell seats by auction or simply cut prices to reflect the reduced cost of electronic selling.

Many travel agencies around the world have Web sites, which can make the Internet a quick and easy way to compare prices. There is also an increasing number of on-line agents that operate only on the Internet.

Online ticket sales work well if you are doing a simple one-way or return trip on specified dates. However, online superfast fare generators are no substitute for a travel agent who knows all about special deals, has strategies for avoiding layovers and can offer advice on everything from which airline has the best vegetarian food to the best travel insurance to bundle with your ticket.

You may find the cheapest flights are advertised by obscure agencies. Most such firms are honest and solvent, but there are some rogue fly-by-night outfits around. Paying by credit card generally offers protection, as most card issuers provide refunds if you can prove you didn't get what you paid for. Similar protection can be obtained by buying a ticket from a bonded agency, such as one covered by the Air Travel Organisers' Licensing (ATOL) scheme in the UK (more details are available at **W** www.atol.org.uk). Agencies that accept only cash should hand over the tickets straight away and not tell you to 'come back tomorrow'. After you've made a booking or paid your deposit, call the airline and confirm that the booking was made. It's generally not advisable to send money (even cheques) through the post unless the agent is very well established – some travellers have reported being ripped off by fly-by-night mail-order ticket agents.

If you purchase a ticket and later want to make changes to your route or get a refund, you need to contact the original travel agency. Airlines issue refunds only to the purchaser of a ticket – usually the travel agency that bought the ticket on your behalf. Many travellers change their routes halfway through their trips, so think carefully before you buy a ticket which is not easily refunded.

Round-the-World Tickets & Circle Pacific Fares Round-the-world (RTW) tickets can get you to both Delhi and Bangkok, but you still have to purchase an extra ticket to Paro. RTW tickets are often real bargains, and can work out even cheaper than an ordinary return ticket. Prices start at about UK£800, A$2299 or US$1300 and are subject to numerous restrictions.

Circle Pacific tickets use a combination of airlines to circle the Pacific – combining Australia, New Zealand, North America and Asia. There are advance purchase restrictions and limits to how many stopovers you can take. Circle Pacific tickets are likely to be around 15% cheaper than RTW tickets.

Travellers with Special Needs

If they're warned early enough, airlines can often make special arrangements for travellers, such as wheelchair assistance at airports or vegetarian meals on the flight. Children under two years travel for 10% of the standard fare (or free on some airlines) as long as they don't occupy a seat. They don't get a baggage allowance. 'Skycots', baby food and nappies should be provided by the airline if requested in advance. Children aged between two and 12 can usually occupy a seat for around two-thirds of the full fare, and do get a baggage allowance.

Airports and airlines can sometimes be surprisingly helpful, but they do need advance warning. Most international airports will provide escorts from check-in desk to plane where needed, and there should be ramps, lifts, accessible toilets and reachable phones. Unfortunately, none of these facilities exist at Paro airport but, with advance notice, a tour operator could arrange for someone to assist with special arrangements.

The disability-friendly Web site W www .everybody.co.uk has an airline directory that provides information on the facilities offered by various airlines.

Departure Tax

The airport tax on departure from Paro is Nu 300, which must be paid in Bhutanese or Indian currency. Other departure taxes in the region are:

Bangkok	Baht 500
Delhi	IRs 150 to SAARC countries*
	IRs 750 to other destinations
Dhaka	Taka 300
Kathmandu	NRs 660 to SAARC countries*
	NRs 1100 to other destinations
Kolkata	IRs 150

*SAARC – South Asian Association for Regional Cooperation

The USA

Discount travel agencies in the USA are known as consolidators (although you won't see a sign on the door saying 'Consolidator'). San Francisco is the ticket consolidator capital of America, although some good deals can be found in Los Angeles, New York and other big cities.

Council Travel, America's largest student travel organisation, has around 60 offices in the USA. Call it for the office nearest you (☎ 800-226 8624) or visit its Web site at W www.counciltravel.com. STA Travel (☎ 800-777 0112) has offices in Boston, Chicago, Miami, New York, Philadelphia, San Francisco and other major cities. Call the toll-free 800 number for office locations or visit its Web site at W www.statravel.com.

Ticket Planet is a leading ticket consolidator in the USA and is recommended. Visit its Web site at W www.ticketplanet.com.

The best connections from the US west coast to Bhutan are via Bangkok. The fares are also the cheapest, starting at US$800 return. From the east coast you can also travel to Bangkok from around US$1100 or you can find a return ticket to Delhi from around US$1350. The cheapest one-way tickets will be around US$865. An alternative way of getting to Delhi from New York is to fly to London and buy a cheap fare from there.

Two companies that specialise in flights to Thailand and India are Himalayan Treasures and Travel (☎ 800-223 1813, 510-222 5307, e govindsh@himtrek.com) and Ticket Planet (W www.ticketplanet.com).

Canada

Canadian consolidators' air fares tend to be about 10% higher than those sold in the USA.

Travel CUTS (☎ 800-667 2887) is Canada's national student travel agency and has offices in all major cities. Its Web address is W www.travelcuts.com.

Australia

Advance-purchase return fares from the east coast of Australia to Delhi are A$1350 to A$1800 depending on the season. Fares are slightly cheaper from Darwin and Perth.

Tickets from Australia to London or other European capitals with a Bangkok or Delhi stopover range from A$960 to A$1400 one way and A$1499 to A$2150 return, again depending on the season.

Two well-known agencies for cheap fares are STA Travel and Flight Centre. STA Travel (☎ 03-9349 2411) has an office at 222 Faraday St, Carlton, in Melbourne, and offices in all major cities and on many university campuses. Call ☎ 131 776 Australiawide for the location of your nearest branch or visit its Web site at W www.statravel.com.au. Flight Centre (☎ 131 600 Australia-wide) has a central office at 82 Elizabeth St, Sydney, and there are dozens of offices throughout Australia. Its Web address is W www.flightcentre.com.au.

Quite a few travel offices specialise in discount air tickets. Some travel agencies, particularly smaller ones, advertise cheap air fares in the travel sections of weekend newspapers.

New Zealand

Advance-purchase return fares from New Zealand to India and Thailand start at NZ$1200 to Bangkok and NZ$1800 to Delhi.

Flight Centre (☎ 09-309 6171) has a large central office in Auckland at National Bank Towers (on the corner of Queen and Darby Sts) and many branches throughout the country. STA Travel (☎ 09-309 0458) has its main office at 10 High St, Auckland, and has other offices in Auckland as well as in Hamilton, Palmerston North, Wellington, Christchurch and Dunedin. The Web address is W www.statravel.co.nz.

The UK

From London to Delhi, fares start at around UK£220/370 one way/return. The cheapest fares are usually with Middle Eastern or Eastern European airlines. Thai International always seems to have competitive fares to Bangkok despite its high standards.

Various excursion fares are available from London to both India and Thailand, but you can get better prices through London's many cheap-ticket specialists.

Discount air travel is big business in London. Advertisements for many travel agencies appear in the travel pages of the weekend broadsheet newspapers, in *Time Out*, the *Evening Standard* and in the free magazine *TNT*.

For students or travellers under 26 years, popular travel agencies in the UK include STA Travel (☎ 020-7361 6262, W www.statravel.co.uk), which has an office at 86 Old Brompton Rd, London SW7, and branches across the country. This agency sells tickets to all travellers but caters especially to young people and students.

Continental Europe

From Europe, travellers will need to get to Delhi or Mumbai (Bombay) where they can connect with flights up to Bhutan. Although London is the best for good fare deals, most major European cities have fairly competitive deals. Fares start from around €680 from Paris, €750 from Frankfurt and €730 from Copenhagen.

Asia

Bangkok has replaced Hong Kong as the discount-ticket capital of the region. Its bucket shops are at least as unreliable as those of other cities. Ask the advice of other travellers before buying a ticket. STA, which is reliable, has branches in Hong Kong, Tokyo, Singapore, Bangkok and Kuala Lumpur.

Africa

There are plenty of flights between East Africa and Mumbai due to the large Indian population in Kenya. From Mumbai you can make your way to Delhi or Kathmandu to connect to Paro. Typical fares from Nairobi to Mumbai are around US$653 return with either Ethiopian Airlines, Kenya Airways, Air India or Pakistan International Airlines (PIA; via Karachi).

LAND

Unless you are an Indian national, the Department of Tourism rules require that you either enter or exit Bhutan on a Druk Air flight. This limits the options for road travel.

The best way to plan a trip via road is to start in Kathmandu and travel one direction by air and the other by land, perhaps visiting Darjeeling and Sikkim en route. You could also enter Bhutan by road and then exit by air to Kolkata or Bangkok, for example.

Border Crossings

The two border crossings from India into Bhutan that are permitted to foreigners are at Phuentsholing, on the border with the Indian state of West Bengal, and at Samdrup Jongkhar, on the border with the state of Assam. At the time of research, foreigners could only use the Phuentsholing border crossing.

India

To/From Phuentsholing If you are travelling to or from Bhutan by land, all roads lead through Siliguri, the major transport hub in north-east India. Here you have the option of a train or bus connection to Kolkata or Delhi, a road trip to Nepal, or a flight from nearby Bagdogra to Delhi or Kolkata. From Siliguri you can also travel on to Sikkim or the hill stations of Darjeeling and Kalimpong.

The easiest way to travel the 169km between Phuentsholing and Siliguri is to arrange for your Bhutan tour operator to provide a vehicle. There are also taxis and shared hire cars available in both Phuentsholing and Siliguri. If you are given a choice, opt for the less crowded route via the 'coronation bridge' to Mainaguri, then on to Hasimara, Jaigaon and finally Phuentsholing.

Several Bhutanese transport companies operate a direct bus service twice a day between Siliguri and Phuentsholing; buses leave at 8am and 2pm and cost IRs 55 for the 3½-hour journey. In Siliguri the booking office is on Tenzing Norgay Rd (also known as Hill Cart Rd), opposite the Shree Punjab Hotel. You can also find Bhutanese taxis (yellow-roofed minivans with numberplates beginning with 'BT') looking for a return fare; you can sometimes buy a seat for IRs 150, but usually you will have to charter the whole taxi for about IRs 650. Indian bus companies also operate services between Siliguri and Jaigaon on the Indian side of the Bhutanese border.

The gate between Phuentsholing and Jaigaon closes at 9pm for vehicles, but people can cross on foot until 10pm. In 2001 Phuentsholing was declared a 'free zone', a facility that allows foreigners to enter the town from India and spend a night without paying the US$200-per-day tourist fee.

Foreigners Don't forget to get your passport stamped when leaving India. The Indian immigration office, open 24 hours, is in a compound on the east side of the main road in the centre of Jaigaon, next door to the Hotel Kasturi and about 400m south of the Bhutan entrance gate. (There is a plan to relocate the office to a better spot.) If your transport has already deposited you in Bhutan, you can simply walk back across the border to complete the paperwork.

To obtain a Bhutanese visa, foreigners need to present their passport, two photos and a US$20 fee to the visa officer in the *drungkhag* (subdistrict) office near the east end of town. The visa is issued here, but the arrival details will be stamped in your passport when you pass the immigration checkpoint at Rinchending, 5km away.

Foreigners may cross back and forth across the border during the day but are required to leave by 10pm unless staying in a hotel – a useful facility in case you neglected to complete Indian departure formalities before you crossed into Bhutan.

Indian Nationals At the time of reserach Indian nationals needed a total of five photos, to fill in two copies of a form and present two photographs and photocopies of an identification document such as a driving licence or voter card to the office of the Indian embassy in Phuentsholing (☎ 05-252635, 252992), near the post office. The office is open 9.30am to 11.30am and 3.30pm to 5pm Monday to Friday. You then receive a request form to be presented to the Rinchending immigration officer along with three photographs. On weekends and holidays when the office is closed, Indian nationals who have either a voter registration card or a passport may go directly to the entry station in Rinchending.

Indian nationals may wander freely into Phuentsholing during the day, but are required to leave by 10pm unless staying in a hotel.

To/From Delhi & Kolkata The nearest main-line Indian train station to Phuentsholing is in New Jalpaiguri. From there, it's a 12-hour rail journey to Kolkata and a 33-hour trip to Delhi. You can travel by road direct to New Jalpaiguri from Phuentsholing or drive to Siliguri where you can connect to a local train to New Jalpaiguri.

From Siliguri it's easy to arrange a share-taxi or bus to Darjeeling, 77km away, or to Gangtok in Sikkim, 114km away. If you are travelling to Sikkim, arrange a permit in Siliguri at the Sikkim Tourism office.

To/From Samdrup Jongkhar Until September 2001 foreign tourists were allowed to depart Bhutan at Samdrup Jongkhar, but this has been temporarily stopped. Indian nationals may, however, enter via Samdrup Jongkhar. Check with Bhutanese or Indian authorities on the current status of Assamese separatist groups before you decide to travel by land through Assam.

The primary reason you would want to exit this way is to avoid the long drive back over the mountains to Thimphu after visiting eastern Bhutan. The easiest connection from Samdrup Jongkhar is to fly to Kolkata from Guwahati airport in Assam. It is an 80km, 2½-hour drive from the Bhutanese border to Guwahati, on the south bank of the Brahmaputra River. It is then a further 20km from Guwahati to the airport. One-way air fares from Guwahati are US$70 to Kolkata, US$220 to Delhi and US$43 to Bagdogra.

The alternative is a 400km drive through the Indian duars to Siliguri. On this route you could visit Kaziranga National Park, famous for its rhino population, 233km east of Guwahati.

Nepal

Panitanki, in northern West Bengal, is opposite the eastern Nepal border town of Kakarbhitta. A long bridge separates the two towns across the Mechi River. Bhutanese tour operators can pick you up or drop you at Panitanki or you can arrange for them to take you to Bharatpur or Biratnagar to catch a flight to Kathmandu.

Panitanki is only one hour (35km) from Siliguri (India). Buses run regularly on this route (IRs 10) and taxis are easy to arrange (IRs 250). A cycle-rickshaw across the border to Kakarbhitta costs IRs 10. Buses depart Kakarbhitta daily at 5pm for Kathmandu (17 hours, NRs 350), a long rough drive via Narayanghat, Mugling and the Trisuli River valley. See Lonely Planet's *Nepal* for details of what to see and do along this route.

A better option is to take a one-hour bus or taxi ride from Kakarbhitta to Bhadrapur and take a domestic flight to Kathmandu. There is a larger airport at Biratnagar, a four-hour drive from the border. Fares to Kathmandu are US$99 from Bhadrapur and US$77 from Biratnagar. Several airlines have offices in both towns, but airlines come and go and schedules change frequently. Jhapa Travels Agency (☎ 977-23-29006) in Kakarbhitta may be able to book a flight.

INTERNATIONAL TOUR OPERATORS

There are a few travel agencies and adventure travel companies that specialise in Bhutan, but most operate their Bhutan trips only as part of a series of programs. In addition to removing the hassle of faxing Thimphu and transferring money, they will also arrange your tickets on Druk Air.

Most group tours to Bhutan fly to Paro together, often collecting their tickets at the check-in counter in Bangkok, Delhi or Kathmandu. The agent should also be able to either recommend a group flight or arrange air transportation, hopefully at a reasonable rate, on flights that they have prebooked to the connecting point for the flight on to Paro.

Many adventure travel companies organise treks in Bhutan in addition to cultural tours. Their group treks are escorted by a leader, though some can also organise private trips.

Australia

Peregrine Adventures (☎ 03-9663 8611, fax 9663 8618, W www.peregrine.net.au) 258 Lonsdale St, Melbourne, Vic 3000

World Expeditions (☎ 02-9279 0188, fax 9279 0566, W www.worldexpeditions.com.au) 3rd floor, 441 Kent St, Sydney, NSW 2000

The USA & Canada

Above the Clouds (☎ 802-482 4848, fax 482 5011, W www.abovecouds.com) PO Box 388, Hinesburg, VT 05461

Adventure Center (☎ 800-227 8747, fax 654 4200, W www.adventure-center.com) 1311 63rd St, Suite 200, Emeryville, CA 94608

Asian Pacific Adventures (☎ 818-886-5190, 800-825 1680, W www.asianpacificadventures .com) 9010 Reseda Blvd, Suite #227, Northridge, CA 91324

Bhutan Travel (☎ 800-950 9908, 516-378 3805, fax 868 1601, W www.bhutantravel .com) PO Box 757, Baldwin, NY 11510

Far Fung Places (☎ 415-386 8306, fax 386 8104, W www.farfungplaces.com) 1914 Fell St, San Francisco, CA 94117

Geographic Expeditions (☎ 415-922 0448, fax 346 5535, W www.geoex.com) 2627 Lombard St, San Francisco, CA 94123

Himalayan Travel (☎ 800-225 2380, fax 203-797 8077, W www.himalayantravelinc.com) 8 Berkshire Place, Danbury, CT 06810

Ibex Expeditions (☎ 541-345 1289, fax 343 9002, W www.trekibex.com) 2657 West 28th Ave, Eugene, OR 97405

Journeys International (☎ 313-665 4407, fax 665 2945, W www.journeys-intl.com) 4011 Jackson Rd, Ann Arbor, MI 48103

Mountain Travel Sobek (☎ 510-527 8100, fax 525 7710, W www.mtsobek.com) 6420 Fairmount Ave, El Cerrito, CA 94530

Reach for the Sky Adventure (☎ 954-327 1594, W www.rftsadventure.com) 4328 SW 49 Court, Ft Lauderdale, FL 33314

Wilderness Travel (☎ 510-558 2488, fax 548 0347, W www.wildernesstravel.com) 1102 Ninth St, Berkeley CA 94710

The UK

Abercombie & Kent (☎ 020-7730 9600, W www.abercrombiekent.co.uk) Sloane Square House, Holbein Place, London SW1W 8NS

Exodus Travels (☎ 020-8675 5550, W www .exodus.co.uk) 9 Weir Rd, Balham, London SW12 0LT

Explore Worldwide (☎ 01252-344161, fax 760001, W www.explore.co.uk) 1 Frederick St, Aldershot, Hants GU11 1LQ

Himalayan Kingdoms (☎ 01453-844400, fax 844422, W www.himalayankingdoms.com) Old Crown House, 18 Market St, Wotton-under-Edge, Gloucester, GL12 7AE

KE Adventure Travel (☎ 017687-73966, fax 74693, W www.keadventure.com) 32 Lake Road, Keswick, Cumbria CA12 5DQ

Steppes East Ltd (☎ 01285-651010, fax 885888, W www.steppeseast.co.uk) The Travel House, 51 Castle St, Cirencester, Gloucester, GL7 1QD

Wexas International (☎ 020-7589 3315, fax 7589 8418, W www.travelleronline.com) 45 Brompton Rd, Knightsbridge, London SW3 1DE

World Expeditions (☎ 020-8870 2600, fax 8870 2615, W www.worldexpedition.co .uk) 3 Northfields Prospect, Putney Bridge Rd, London SW18 1PE

Continental Europe

Dav Berg-und-Skischule (☎ 089-651 0720, fax 651 07272) Am Perlacher Forst 186, D-81545 München

Explorator (☎ 01-53 45 85 85, fax 42 60 80 00, e explorator@explo.com) 16 Rue de la Banque, 75002 Paris, France

Hauser Exkursionen (☎ 089-235 0060, fax 291 3714, W www.hauser-exkursionen.at) Marienstrasse-17, D-80331 München

Horizons Nouveaux (☎ 027-771 7171, fax 771 7175, W www.horizonsnouveaux.com) Centre de l'Etoile, Case postale 196, 1936 Verbier, Switzerland

Rotas do Vento (☎ 01-364 9852, fax 364 9843, W www.rotasdovento.pt) R Lusiadas 5 4-K, PO Box 3010, 1300 Lisboa, Portugal

Terres d'Aventure (☎ 0825 857 800, W www .terdav.com) 6 rue Saint Victor, 75005 Paris, France

Thailand

Oriole Travel & Tours (☎ 02-237 9201, fax 237 9200, e oriole@samart.co.th) Skulthai Surawong Tower, 141 Surawong Rd, Bangkrak, Bangkok 10500

Specialised Tours

Motorcycle trips can be arranged through Himalayan Road Runners (☎ 908-236 8970, fax 236 8972, W www.ridehigh.com), PO Box 1402, Waitsfield, VT 05673, USA.

The only overseas company specialising in river trips in Bhutan is Excellent Adventures (☎ 828-488 6785, 888-900 9091,

W www.excellent-adventures.net), 5013 Needmore Rd, Bryson City, NC 28713, USA.

A total of 616 species of birds have been recorded in Bhutan. The following companies specialise in tours accompanied by an ornithologist:

Limosa Holidays (☎ 01263-578143, fax 579251, **e** limosaholidays@compuserve.com) Suffield House, Northrepps, Norfolk NR27 0LZ, UK

Peregrine Holidays (☎ 01865-559988, fax 512583, **W** www.peregrineholidays.co.uk) 41 South Parade, Summertown, Oxford OX2 7JP, UK

Sunbird (☎ 01767-682969, fax 692481, **W** www.sunbird.demon.co.uk) PO Box 76, Sandy, Bedfordshire SG19 1DF, UK

Wings (☎ 888-293 6443, 520-320 9868, fax 320 9373, **W** www.wingsbirds.com) 1643 N Alvernon, Suite 105, Tucson, AZ 85712, USA

BHUTAN-BASED TOUR OPERATORS

If you do want to use a Bhutanese operator, it is easy to make your own arrangements through one of the following operators.

When tourism was privatised in 1991, the state-run Bhutan Tourism Corporation was disbanded. Many of the ex-employees used their expertise to set up their own operations, and there are now more than 90 licensed tour companies. They range from one-person operations to large and professional organisations such as Etho Metho Tours and Treks and Bhutan Tourism Corporation Limited, which have fleets of vehicles and, in some places, their own hotel facilities.

The following list includes the largest and most reliable companies. For a complete list see the Department of Tourism Web site at **W** www.tourism.gov.bt.

Bae-Yul Excursions (☎ 02-324335, fax 323728, **W** baeyul.tripod.com) PO Box 437, Thimphu

Bhutan Dorji Holidays (☎ 02-322747, fax 325174, **W** www.bhutan-dorji.com) PO Box 550, Thimphu

Bhutan Holidays (☎ 02-322692, fax 323248, **W** www.bhutanholidays.com) PO Box 522, Thimphu

Bhutan Kaze Tours (☎ 02-326623, fax 323178, **e** wings@druknet.net.bt)

Bhutan Mandala Tours and Treks (☎ 02-323676, fax 323675, **e** mandala@druknet .net.bt) PO Box 397, Thimphu

Bhutan Tourism Corporation Limited (BTCL; ☎ 02-324045, 22647, fax 323292, **W** www.kingdomofbhutan.com) PO Box 159, Thimphu

Bhutan Travel Bureau (☎ 02-321749, fax 325100, **W** www.btb.com.bt) PO Box 959, Thimphu

Bhutan Travel Service (☎ 02-325785, fax 325786, **W** www.bhutantravel.com.bt) PO Box 919, Thimphu

Chhundu Travels and Tours (☎ 02-322592, 323586, fax 322645, **W** www.chhundu.com.bt) PO Box 149, Thimphu

Discovery Bhutan (☎ 02-322457, fax 322530, **W** www.discoverybhutan.com) PO Box 825, Thimphu

Dragon Trekkers and Tours (☎ 02-323599, fax 323314) PO Box 452, Thimphu

Etho Metho Tours and Treks (☎ 02-323162, fax 322884, **W** www.ethometho.com) PO Box 360, Thimphu

Gangri Tours and Trekking (☎ 02-323556, fax 323322, **W** www.gangri.com) PO Box 607, Thimphu

International Treks and Tours (☎ 02-329100, fax 323675, **W** www.intrekasia.com /bhutan.htm) Lango, Paro

Jamphel Tours (☎/fax 02-321111, **e** jamphel@ druknet.net.bt)

Lhomen Tours and Trekking (☎ 02-324148, fax 323243, 23108, **W** www.lhomen.com.bt) PO Box 341, Thimphu

Lingkor Tours (☎ 02-323417, fax 323402, **W** www.bhutan-tours.com) PO Box 202, Thimphu

Lotus Adventures (☎ 02-322191, fax 325678, **e** equbhu@druknet.net.bt) PO Box 706, Thimphu

Namsey Adventures (☎ 02-325616, fax 324297) PO Box 549, Thimphu

Passage to Himalayas (☎ 02-321726, fax 321727, **e** lekid@druknet.net.bt)

Rabsel Tours and Treks (☎ 02-324165, fax 324918, **W** www.rabsel.com.bt) PO Box 535, Thimphu

Rainbow Tours (☎ 02-323270, fax 322960, **e** rainbow@druknet.net.bt)

Rinchen Tours and Treks (☎ 02-324552, fax 323767) PO Box 550, Thimphu

Sakten Tours and Treks (☎ 02-323899, fax 323545, **W** www.bootan.com) PO Box 532, Thimphu

Shangrila Bhutan Tours (☎ 02-324012, fax 324410, Ⓦ www.shangrilabhutan.com) PO Box 541, Thimphu

Snow Leopard (☎ 02-321822, fax 325684, Ⓦ www.snowleopardtreks.com) PO Box 953, Thimphu

Tashi Tours and Travels (☎ 02-323361, fax 323666, Ⓦ bhutantashitours.com) PO Box 423, Thimphu

Thunder Dragon Treks (☎ 02-321999, fax 321963, Ⓔ thunder@druknet.net.bt) PO Box 303, Thimphu

White Tara Tours (☎ 02-322446, fax 325305, Ⓔ wtara@druknet.net.bt)

Windhorse Tours (☎ 02-326026, fax 326025, Ⓔ windhor@druknet.net.bt) PO Box 1021, Thimphu

Yangphel Adventure Travel (☎ 02-323293, fax 322897, Ⓦ www.yangphel.com) PO Box 236, Thimphu

Yeti Tours and Trekking (☎ 02-323941, fax 323508, Ⓦ www.bhutanyeti.com) PO Box 456, Thimphu

Yod-Sel Tours (☎ 02-323912, fax 323589, Ⓦ www.yodsel.com) PO Box 574, Thimphu

Yu Druk Tours and Travels (☎ 02-323461, fax 322116, Ⓦ www.yudruk.com) PO Box 140, Thimphu

All operators in Bhutan are subject to government regulations that specify services, standards and rates. You are quite safe no matter which company you choose,

though the large companies do have more clout to obtain reservations in hotels and on Druk Air.

In addition to Etho Metho and BTCL, the largest operators are Yangphel, Gangri and International Treks and Tours.

There are both advantages and disadvantages in dealing with the largest companies. One Bhutanese hotelier suggested that the next 10 largest companies would be large enough to handle overseas queries, but still small enough that the owner would pay personal attention to your program. The operators in this category are Bhutan Kaze, Bhutan Mandala, Chhundu, Rainbow, Sakten, Tashi, Thunder Dragon, Windhorse, Yodsel and Yu Druk.

Chhundu is renowned for its high-quality personal service, and it's responsible for looking after many VIP clients. Other companies known for their personal attention and quality service are Lhomen, Namsey, Yu Druk and Bhutan Travel Bureau. Bhutan Kaze and Bhutan Mandala specialise in service to Japanese clients.

If you are planning to go trekking, you might consider one of the companies that specialises in this area. The biggest operators of treks are Yangphel, International, Yu Druk, Lhomen, Tashi and Namsey.

Getting Around

Because Bhutan has no domestic air service, doesn't yet possess any helicopters, and does not have a centimetre of railway track, the only way to see the country is either by foot or by road.

There is one main road: the National Highway, a 3.5m-wide stretch of tarmac that winds its way up and down mountains, across clattering bridges, along the side of rock cliffs, and over high mountain passes. Rivers, mudflows and rockfalls present continual hazards, especially when it rains. The road can easily become blocked due to snow or landslides and can take anywhere from an hour to several days to clear. Take plenty of reading material.

Unless you want to walk, the only way to travel between towns in the south of Bhutan is via India. This is impractical for foreigners since the only road entry point that foreigners are allowed to use is Phuentsholing.

If you are travelling on a tourist visa, the cost of all transport is included in the price of your trip and you'll have a vehicle available for both short- and long-distance travel. You'll only have to rely on public transport if you are an Indian national or if you are working with a project and don't have your own vehicle.

BUS

Public buses are crowded and rattly, and Bhutan's winding roads make them doubly uncomfortable. The government's Bhutan Post Express, Dawa Travels and other companies operate Indian minibuses. So many passengers suffer from motion sickness that long-distance buses have earned the nickname 'vomit comets'. Some private operators, including Leksol Bus Service, use more comfortable Toyota Coasters at about double the normal fare. In eastern Bhutan you might arrive at the bus stop to discover that your bus is actually a truck with seats in the back.

There are three or four buses a day between Thimphu and the major centres of Phuentsholing, Paro and Punakha. Fares

and schedules are all monitored by the Road Safety and Transport Authority.

Tour operators use Japanese-made buses, minivans and cars, depending on the size of the group. These vehicles can take you almost anywhere in the country, but for trips to central and eastern Bhutan during winter (December to February) or the monsoon (June to September) a 4WD vehicle is an advantage, and often a necessity.

CAR, JEEP & MOTORCYCLE

There are taxis in Phuentsholing and Thimphu, but they are expensive. It is usually cheaper to hire a vehicle with a driver. If you don't already have one at your disposal, the best way to hire a car is through a tour company (see the Getting There & Away chapter).

Most two-wheelers are Indian scooters that are used in towns and also for long-distance journeys across mountain passes. It's unlikely that you'll find one for rent. Himalayan Roadrunners (W www.ridehigh .com) operates motorcycle tours in Bhutan,

Bailey Bridges

Many of Bhutan's rivers are spanned by clattering girder bridges known as Bailey bridges. These are structures composed of rectangular panels about 3m long that are pinned together to produce spans of up to 64m. This type of bridge is named after its inventor, Sir Donald Coleman Bailey (1901–85), a British engineer. Bailey bridges were used extensively in Bhutan during and after WWII and many early bridges still survive today.

Bailey bridges are an excellent means of spanning Bhutan's rivers because they are easily transported along the country's narrow roads. They are also very easy to assemble, and do not require any specialised design.

but they are hair-raising adventures because it's necessary to dodge lots of oncoming trucks.

Road Rules

Traffic keeps to the left, and is much more orderly than in most other south Asian countries. Speeds are low in towns and on rural roads; you will be lucky to average more than 30km/h on the hairpin bends of roads in the hills.

As is the case throughout Asia, it is important that the police establish who was at fault in any traffic accident. This means that the police must arrive and make the decision before any of the vehicles can be moved, even if the vehicles are blocking a narrow road. A relatively minor fender-bender can block the road for hours while everyone waits patiently for the police to arrive from the nearest town.

BICYCLE

Some travellers have ridden mountain bikes in Bhutan, and the Department of Tourism (DOT) is interested in promoting this kind of travel. As with travelling by motorcycle, it can be frightening to turn a sharp curve and find yourself in the path of a large, oncoming truck. It doesn't take a cycling expert to work out that roads without much traffic make for better biking territory. Good routes include the upper parts of the Paro and Thimphu valleys. For a wild ride, get dropped off at the top of the Cheli La, above Paro, and ride 35km nonstop downhill. See Mountain Biking under Activities in the Facts for the Visitor chapter.

You might find a clunky Indian bike for rent in the flats of Phuentsholing, but there are no bikes for rent in Thimphu. Traffic rules prohibit bicycle riding on the streets of both Thimphu and Paro.

HITCHING

Most people pay for a ride, either in a bus or cab or back of a truck. But bus services are limited, especially in the east, and it's not unusual to see someone flagging down a vehicle asking for a ride. If you have paid for a vehicle, you will only need to hitch if that vehicle has broken down and you are stranded on a mountain road. Hitching is never entirely safe in any country in the world, and we don't recommend it, but if you do have to hitch because of a breakdown, Bhutan is about as safe a place as you could find.

LOCAL TRANSPORT
Taxi

Taxis have meters, but drivers rarely use them. For long-distance trips they operate on a flat rate that is rarely open to negotiation.

You should expect to pay Nu 30 to 50 for a local trip within Thimphu, Nu 500 for a full day and Nu 1000 from Thimphu to Phuentsholing. If you are travelling between Thimphu and Phuentsholing, look for a taxi that is from the place to which you want to go (vehicles with BT-2 numberplates are from Phuentsholing and those with BT-1 numberplates are from Thimphu or Paro) – you may be able to negotiate a lower price.

Thimphu

☎ 02 • pop 46,000 • elevation 2320m

There were *goembas* and a small population in the Thimphu valley even before the time of the Shabdrung, but Thimphu didn't really exist as a town until it became the capital of Bhutan in 1961. The first vehicles appeared in Thimphu in 1962 and the town remained very rural until the late 1970s. The population has grown dramatically since 1990, and is now estimated to be 46,000.

It is often said that Thimphu is the only world capital without traffic lights. One was installed several years ago, but the residents complained that it was impersonal and ugly and it was removed within days. Traffic continues to be directed by policemen stationed at two traffic circles, one at the north end and another near the south end of Norzin Lam, Thimphu's wide, tree-lined main street. They keep Thimphu's traffic flowing throughout the day using elegant, exaggerated gestures. They disappear at night and leave drivers to sort things out for themselves.

Given Thimphu's elevation, don't be surprised if you become short of breath or have trouble sleeping your first few nights here.

ORIENTATION

Thimphu lies in a wooded valley, sprawling up a hillside on the west bank of the Wang Chhu. Several north-south streets run through the town, and numerous smaller streets weave their way uphill to government offices and the posh suburb of Motithang above the town.

In the central district, numerous lanes and alleys lead off the north-south streets to provide access to the new shopping centres as well as shops, bars and small restaurants.

The new expressway from Chhuzom passes below Simtokha Dzong and enters Thimphu from the south. At the western end of Lungten Zampa, the bridge that leads across the Wang Chhu, a road climbs to a petrol station, which demarcates the southern end of the central business district. The road leading north is Norzin Lam, Thimphu's

Highlights

- Visit Trashi Chhoe Dzong, built as the symbol of the capital.
- Take in the spectacular view of Thimphu valley from the telecom tower.
- Explore the shops along Norzin Lam and in Thimphu's new shopping centres.
- Take a day walk up to either Tango Goemba or Cheri Goemba.
- Stay up late and sample Bhutanese nightlife in Thimphu's friendly discos and bars.

❗ All Bhutanese Internet and email addresses have changed, see page 86.

main street, which leads through the town centre past the two traffic circles. At the northern traffic circle Desi Lam leads to government offices, the golf course and Trashi Chhoe Dzong. North of the *dzong* is the large India House compound.

Doebum Lam leads south from the northern traffic circle, making a loop above and to the west of the central business district and passing the Ministry of Trade and Industry and the large swimming pool in the sports complex before reaching the National Memorial Chorten. Here you have a choice of three roads: Zogchen Lam winds its way downhill to the foot of Norzin Lam; Chorten Lam loops back to the southern traffic circle, and Gongphel Lam leads south past the hospital and motor workshops, then loops back north, passing under the bridge to become Chhogyel Lam.

Most shops and hotels are centred on Thimphu's main intersection at the southern traffic circle, although, at the time of research, some were moving into the new shopping complexes, especially the large Zangto Pelri Shopping complex. Shops are numbered, but in no apparent sequence. The renovated clock tower square is blocked to traffic and has a seating area for open-air

THIMPHU

THIMPHU

PLACES TO STAY
16 Motithang Hotel
31 Rabten Apartments
37 Pine Wood Hotel

PLACES TO EAT
25 Golf Course Restaurant

OTHER
1 Dechen Phodrang
2 Indian Embassy
3 Centre for Bhutan Studies
4 Wangditse Goemba
5 Cremation Ground
6 Ney Khang Lhakhang
7 Trashi Chhoe Dzong
8 SAARC Building
9 Royal Banquet Hall
10 Government Offices
11 Drubthob Goemba
12 Telecom Tower
13 Mini-Zoo
14 Youth Centre
15 Kuengachholing State
   Guest House
17 Petrol Station
18 National Institute of
   Traditional Medicine
19 Survey Department
20 Folk Heritage Museum
21 National Institute for
   Zorig Chusum
22 Sangay Traditional Arts
   & Crafts
23 National Library
24 Choki Handicrafts
26 High Court

27 Satellite Station;
   Druknet Office
28 Dzongkha Development
   Commission
29 National Commission for
   Cultural Affairs
30 DHL Office
32 Bangladesh Embassy
33 Changangkha Lhakhang
34 RSPN Office
35 Jigme Dorji Wangchuck
   National Referral Hospital
36 Kuensel
38 Gagyel Lhundrup
   Weaving Centre
39 Vertical Bhutan's
   'The Nose' Climbing Face

To Samtenling
Palace

Chhu

Wang Chhu

Dechen Lam

Dechhu

Samtenling

Belpina

Langjo

Zilungkha

Sangaygang

Motithang

Gaden Lam

Chhophel Lam

Memi Lam

Thori Lam

Chhubar

Thori Lam

Deki
Lam

Norzin Lam

Doebum Lam

Desi Lam

Chhophel Lam

Wang Chhu

Golf
Course

Chhu

Rabten Lam

Lhuendrup
Lam

Khanchoe
Lam

See Thimphu City Map p144

Menkhang Lam

Gongphel Lam

**Samar
Dzingkha**

To Simtokha
& Eastern Bhutan

Ring Rd

Expressway
To Chhuzom

0   0.5   1km
0   0.25   0.5mi

events. North of the traffic circle are shops, the Bank of Bhutan, the cinema and the government handicraft emporium. Changlimithang Stadium and a few shops and hotels are on Chang Lam, between Norzin Lam and the river.

Maps
The Department of Survey & Land Records publishes a colour map of Thimphu that is available in bookshops and in most hotel handicraft shops. This map shows all the ministries and other government offices, which are spread throughout Thimphu. A similar map of Thimphu city is reproduced on the reverse side of the Bhutan road map published by Berndtson & Berndtson.

It's hard to get lost in Thimphu; the town really has only one main street, and local people are amazed that a tourist might need a map. Though all streets have names and are well marked by signposts, most Bhutanese do not bother with the street name and give directions by referring to well-known shops and landmarks. To add to the confusion, many of the street names on signposts differ from those on the survey department map.

INFORMATION
Shops are open from 8am or 9am until 8pm or 9pm, depending on the owners. Shops to the west of Norzin Lam are closed on Tuesday and those on the east side are closed on Wednesday. Government offices shut for the weekend and travel agencies close on Sunday.

There are three petrol stations; with its Bhutanese architecture, the one at the south end of town is a minor tourist attraction.

Thimphu has undergone a lot of recent development but still retains its charm because buildings are not allowed to exceed a certain height and must be designed in traditional Bhutanese style with roofs painted either red or green. A new town plan is being implemented to improve the infrastructure of roads, electricity, water and sewage. This has resulted in a considerable amount of construction work, particularly at the southern end of town, as the Ring Road and expressway near completion.

Tourist Offices
The Department of Tourism (DOT; ☎ 323 251, fax 323695, Ⓦ www.tourism.gov.bt) is next to the Ministry of Trade and Industry and can provide advice and assistance in the event of a problem with your tour company.

Money
Most hotels can change money at the normal government rates, although they usually have a limited supply of cash on hand. The computerised office of Bhutan National Bank (☎ 322767), in the same building as the main post office, is open 9am to 3pm Monday to Friday and 9am to 11am Saturday. Money changing is relatively straightforward although you may be led into a back office and invited to relax in a chair while the staff do the paperwork.

The Bank of Bhutan's (☎ 322266) main branch on Norzin Lam is open 9am to 1pm Monday to Friday and 9am to 11am Saturday. It tends to be busy, but its smaller city branch on Wogzin Lam is only two blocks away and is open noon to 4pm Wednesday to Saturday and noon to 2pm Monday.

Credit Cards A few places advertise that they accept AmEx and Visa cards, but card transactions are unusual enough that you may have to wait for the one person in the shop who does know how to write up the charge slip.

If you're planning to use a credit card to pay a bill in a hotel, settle the bill between 9am and 5pm, while the authorisation office is open.

Post
The main post office (☎ 322381) is a well-organised facility. Many hotels and shops sell stamps. Unlike many Asian countries, it is safe to simply drop cards and letters into post boxes here. Because there is no systematic system of house numbers, most incoming mail is delivered to post office boxes.

Telephone & Fax
Thimphu's area code is 02. Directory inquiries is ☎ 140 for Bhutan and ☎ 116 for international numbers. Many public call

offices (PCOs) have direct international dialling. Trunk calls may be booked through the operator on ☎ 117 for international numbers, ☎ 119 for domestic numbers and ☎ 118 for calls to India.

Email & Internet Access

Info Tech Solutions (☎ 326474, e its@ druknet.net.bt), Thimphu's largest Internet cafe, is on the first floor of Jojo's One Stop Shop. It's open 9am to 8pm Monday to Saturday. Other smaller Internet facilities are Atsara Business Centre (☎ 325276, e atsara@visto.com) in the City Centre Complex building, Cyber Café (☎ 326936) upstairs next to Lhanam's restaurant, and MG Cyberpoint (☎ 324664, e cyberpoint@ druknet.net.bt) on the first floor of Dragon Shopping Complex. All charge a standard Nu 3 per minute.

Several hotels have a rudimentary business centre with Internet access; most charge Nu 5 per minute.

Travel Agencies & Airline Offices

Travel agency offices are spread throughout the town, but many are near the clock tower and the cinema. Since it is likely that you will already be in the hands of a travel agency by the time you reach Thimphu, and it's almost impossible to change agencies in the middle of a trip, there's not much point in chasing down other agencies, unless you want to plan a return trip to Bhutan with a different company.

The office of Druk Air (☎ 322215, 322825, fax 322775) is west of the northern traffic circle. The Thimphu office only deals with tickets for Bhutanese passengers. Reservations and tickets for foreigners have to be made through the head office in Paro. It's far more efficient to buy your ticket and reconfirm reservations with a tour operator than to make arrangements directly with the airline.

No other airlines have offices in Bhutan. Most tour operators can arrange reservations and tickets for international connecting flights, but tickets are issued through their associates abroad. Bhutan Travel Bureau (☎ 324241, 324092, fax 325100), on Desi Lam, and Tashi Tours and Travel (☎ 323027,

323361, fax 323666, e tasitour@druknet .net.bt), on Wogzin Lam, have airline computers and can confirm flights immediately. Other agencies specialising in international ticketing are Takin Travels (☎ 326600, fax 323124, e takin@druknet.net.bt), Atlas Travel (☎ 325581, fax 315582) and World Travel Services (☎ 321866, fax 321867).

Bookshops

All three of Thimphu's bookshops carry *Kuensel*, Indian newspapers and periodicals and a selection of books on Bhutan, Tibet and Buddhism. You can also find children's books, textbooks and English novels to read if your flights are delayed. Prices are quite reasonable, especially for Indian editions which are cheaper than overseas editions.

DSB Books (☎ 323123, fax 325575, e dsb@druknet.net.bt) is on the ground floor of Jojo's shopping complex, and Pekhang Bookshop (☎ 323094) is in the same building as Luger Cinema. Megah Books (☎ 321063) at the southern end of Norzin Lam has a smaller selection of books and also sells prayer flags and Buddhist ritual objects.

Libraries

The small Thimphu public library (☎ 322 814) at the northern end of Norzin Lam is open 12.30pm to 5.30pm Monday to Friday and 9am to 1pm Saturday. It has a collection of paperback novels and a few reference books. For books about Bhutan, the National Library near the Folk Heritage Museum may be a better resource, though the selection of books in English is small.

Laundry

Most hotels offer laundry services, but none have in-house dry-cleaning facilities. Dry-cleaning takes two days at Kelly Dry Cleaners (☎ 326434), next to the Luger Cinema. The larger hotels have clothes dryers and provide same-day service. When the weather is bad smaller hotels may return your laundry damp, or even the following day. If you are on a tight travel schedule, ask about the drying facilities before you hand in your laundry.

Toilets
There are a few public toilets scattered along Norzin Lam; the charge is Nu 2.

Medical Services
The Jigme Dorji Wangchuck National Referral Hospital (☎ 322496, 322497) in Thimphu is the best in Bhutan. The India Bhutan Friendship Hospital (☎ 322485), on Chorten Lam, is an alternative.

Because medical services are free to Bhutanese citizens, there are only a few shops selling medical supplies. City Pharmacy (☎ 321382) is on Wogzin Lam, upstairs in the back of the City Centre Complex, and Norling Medical is on Norzin Lam, opposite the Hotel Tandin.

Emergency
For an ambulance call ☎ 112. The Thimphu police number is ☎ 113. The fire department is on ☎ 110.

Dangers & Annoyances
There's almost nothing in Thimphu to cause concern. Dogs roam at night and bark across town at each other, but earplugs solve that problem quite easily. Beware of steep steps and open drains on the sidewalk along the west side of Norzin Lam. Be careful crossing roads and don't trust cars to stop when you are in a pedestrian crosswalk (when they are visible after their annual repainting, that is).

WALKING TOUR
The best way to see Thimphu is to wander along the main street, turning into lanes and following your nose to see where it leads you. It's impossible to get lost; if you get confused in the maze of streets, just head downhill and you will soon come across something you recognise.

For a slightly more strenuous excursion, start at the southern traffic circle and walk uphill along Chorten Lam to the National Memorial Chorten, then turn north along Doebum Lam for a short distance. The second road to the left is Rabten Lam, which leads uphill until it passes below Changangkha Lhakhang, perched on a ridge like a fortress. Climb to the courtyard for a view, then follow your instincts. Either head straight downhill back to the town centre, or continue north for a while before turning east and walking downhill. Any of these roads will take you past houses and tiny shops and restaurants as you make your way back to Thimphu's main street, Norzin Lam.

TRASHI CHHOE DZONG
In 1216 Lama Gyalwa Lhanangpa built Dho-Ngen Dzong (Blue Stone Dzong) on the hill above Thimphu where Dechen Phodrang now stands. A few years later Lama Phajo Drukgom Shigpo, who brought the Drukpa Kagyu lineage to Bhutan, took over Dohon Dzong. In 1641 the Shabdrung acquired the dzong from the descendants of Lama Phajo and renamed it Trashi Chhoe Dzong (Fortress of the Glorious Religion). He arranged to house both monks and civil officials in the dzong, but it was soon found to be too small for both. The Shabdrung then built another dzong, known as the lower dzong, for the civil officials and used the original building for the monks. The 13th Druk Desi, Chhogyel Sherab Wangchuck (1744–63), later enlarged Trashi Chhoe Dzong so that it could again accommodate both civil officials and monks.

The original dzong was destroyed by fire in 1771 and was abandoned in favour of the lower dzong, which was expanded. That dzong itself suffered a fire in 1866 and twice since then. The five-storey *utse* (central tower) was damaged in the 1897 earthquake and rebuilt in 1902.

When he moved the capital to Thimphu in 1962, King Jigme Dorji Wangchuck began a five-year project to completely renovate and enlarge the dzong. The royal architect performed the repairs without touching the utse, Lhakhang Sarpa or any other of its chapels at the centre. Other than these structures, the entire dzong was rebuilt in traditional fashion, without nails or written plans.

The dzong housed the original National Assembly and now houses the secretariat, the throne room and offices of the king and the ministries of home affairs and finance. The northern portion is the summer residence of the *dratshang* (central monk body).

THIMPHU

THIMPHU CITY

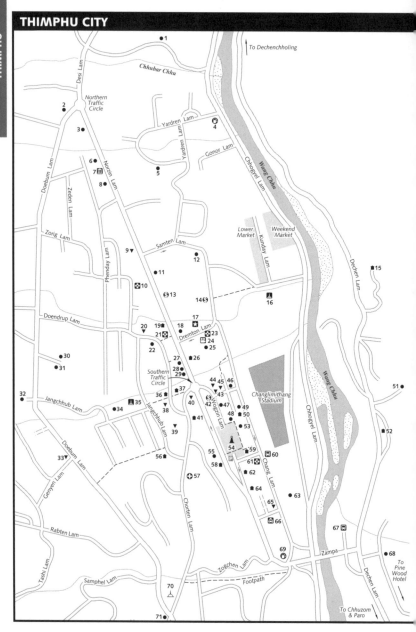

```
0        100        200m
0        100        200yd
```

The outer structure is two storeys high with three-storey towers at the four corners projecting out over the walls. The outer walls are built of trimmed and fitted granite blocks, unlike other dzongs, which were made of roughly dressed stones. Similarly, the *dochey* (courtyard) is paved with rectangular stone slabs, in contrast to other dzongs, which use only rough, irregularly shaped stones as paving.

Unlike most other dzongs, Trashi Chhoe has two main entrances. One leads to the administrative section at the south, and another at the north leads to the monastic quarter where the dances of the annual *tsechu* festival are performed (see the special section 'The Tsechu' for more details). The dzong's Sangay Tsokhorsum Thondrol depicts the Buddha Sakyamuni and his two disciples.

Below the dzong is an excellent example of a traditional **cantilever bridge**. To the south of the dzong is a set of low buildings that houses additional administrative offices. West of the dzong is the small tower of **Ney Khang Lhakhang**, which houses a statue of Sakyamuni flanked by the protective deity Gyenyen Jagpa Melen and Dorje Daktshen, the female guardian deity of Phajoding.

NATIONAL LIBRARY

West of the golf course is the National Library (☎ 322885, *Pedzoe Lam; open 9.30am-1pm & 2pm-5pm Mon-Fri)*. It was established in 1967 to preserve many ancient Dzongkha and Tibetan texts.

The traditional books are kept on the upper floor. These books are Tibetan-style, printed or written on long strips of handmade paper stacked between pieces of wood and wrapped in silken cloth. In another section are some wooden blocks that are used for printing books and prayer flags. The library has a branch at Kuenga Rabten palace south of Trongsa in central Bhutan.

There is a collection of English-language books and a small collection of modern academic texts on the ground floor. Most of these are about Buddhism and Himalayan history. There are also a few travel books about India and Tibet. There is a collection of bound volumes of *Kuensel* in all three

THIMPHU

languages and another collection that includes many of the reports produced by various agencies that have undertaken development or research projects. There is a small collection of books about Bhutan on a shelf behind the checkout desk.

Sometimes you will see people circumambulating the National Library building and chanting mantras. This is because the building houses many holy books. An altar on the ground floor, with statues of Bhutan's most important historic figures, Shabdrung Ngawang Namgyal, Pema Lingpa and Guru Rinpoche, also contributes to the building's sacred importance.

NATIONAL INSTITUTE FOR ZORIG CHUSUM

The National Institute for Zorig Chusum (☎ 322302, e izc@druknet.net.bt, Pedzoe Lam; open 9am-5pm Mon-Sat) is commonly known as 'the painting school'. It operates under the auspices of the National Technical Training Institute and offers a six-year course that provides instruction in many of Bhutan's traditional arts to students from throughout the country whose aptitude is more artistic than academic. The images of the Buddhist deities in the boxed text 'Important Figures of Drukpa Kagyu Buddhism' in the Facts about Bhutan chapter were painted by senior students of the school.

Most tour operators include a visit to the school in their sightseeing program, though large groups of visitors disrupt the classes. The students follow a comprehensive course that starts with drawing and progresses through painting, woodcarving, embroidery and statue-making.

If you want to purchase art by the students, see Shopping later in this chapter.

SAARC BUILDING

The large traditional Bhutanese-style building across the river from Trashi Chhoe Dzong was built in the early 1990s to provide a venue for a meeting of the heads of state and government from the South Asia Association for Regional Co-operation (SAARC). The meeting was never held in Bhutan and the structure now houses the planning and for-

The Four Friends

One of Bhutan's favourite fables is that of the four friends. In Dzongkha the name of the story is *Thuenpa puen shi* (Cooperation, relation, four) and it illustrates the concept of teamwork. You will see paintings illustrating this story on homes and shops throughout the country.

The story tells how the elephant, monkey, peacock and rabbit combined forces to obtain a continual supply of fruit. The peacock found a seed and planted it, the rabbit watered it, the monkey fertilised it and the elephant guarded it. When the fruit was ripe the tree was so high that they could not reach the top. The four animals made a tower by climbing on one another's backs, and plucked the fruit from the high branches.

SCHOOL OF ARTS & CRAFTS, THIMPHU

eign ministries. The National Assembly was relocated to this building in 1993. Nearby is the Royal Banquet Hall.

NATIONAL MEMORIAL CHORTEN

This large Tibetan-style *chorten* was built in 1974 to honour the memory of the third king, Jigme Dorji Wangchuck. There are numerous religious paintings and complex tantric statues inside reflecting both peaceful and wrathful aspects of Buddhist deities.

The memorial chorten is one of the most visible religious structures in Thimphu, and for many people it is the focus of their daily worship. Throughout the day people circumambulate the chorten and pray at a small shrine inside the gate.

FOLK HERITAGE MUSEUM

A three-storey rammed mud and timber building houses the Folk Heritage Museum *(Phelchey sToenkhym;* ☎ *327133, Pedzoe Lam; admission Nu 25 for SAARC nationals, Nu 150 others; open 10am-4.30pm Tues-Fri, 10.30am-1pm Sat, 11.30am-3.30pm Sun).* The house has been turned into a replica of a traditional farmhouse as it would have been equipped about a century ago. A tour of this almost-living museum will give you a glimpse into the way most Bhutanese lived then, and how many rural people still live today. Bring a torch (flashlight) as some of the rooms are quite dimly lit.

NATIONAL INSTITUTE OF TRADITIONAL MEDICINE

Established in 1988, one of the more interesting facilities in Thimphu is the National Institute of Traditional Medicine *(☎ 324647, Serzhong Lam; open 9am-3pm Mon-Fri, 9am-1pm Sat).* The European Union (EU)

[Continued on page 156]

Traditional Medicine

The Himalayan Buddhist system of medicine is called *So-ba Rig-pa* and is practised in many countries today. Because it originally developed in ancient Tibet, it is commonly known as Tibetan medicine.

It is believed that at the beginning of time, the art of healing was a prerogative of the gods. It wasn't until Kashiraja Dewadas, an ancient Indian king, went to heaven to learn medicine that medicine could be offered to humans as a means to fight suffering. He taught the principles and the practice of healing, and this knowledge was spread as part of early Buddhist sacred writings. Some of the fundamental beliefs of this system are the basis of Buddhism itself.

When Buddhism was first brought to Tibet in the seventh century, some of these medicinal texts were translated into Tibetan and the rulers became interested in the subject. From that time, So-ba Rig-pa was considered a single system of medicine, although some differences are found in the different lineages based on the discovery of *terma*, which occasionally include medicinal teachings.

When Shabdrung Ngawang Namgyal came to Bhutan, his minister of religion, Tenzin Drukey, an esteemed physician, spread the teaching of So-ba Rig-pa. Though the basic texts are the same, the Bhutanese tradition of So-ba Rig-pa has developed independently from its Tibetan origins. Today, the Himalayan Buddhist tradition is the most common type of medicine practised in Bhutan. It has been recognised by the government as the official medical tradition of the country and has been included in the national health system since 1967.

Therapeutic Practices Several forms of treatment are applied in traditional medicine. Hundreds of medicinal plants, minerals and animal parts form the basic drugs used by the practitioners. These ingredients are processed and mixed in different combinations to make about 300 medicines in the form of pills, tablets, syrups, powders and lotions. Other treatments include dietary and behavioural advice.

There are also so-called surgical procedures that include *gtar* (blood letting), *bsregs* (cauterisation by herbal compounds), *gser bcos* (acupuncture by a golden needle), *tshug* (cauterisation with instruments of different materials), *dugs* (applying heat or cold to parts of the body), *byugs-pa* (medicated oil massage), *sman-chu* (stone-heated bath), *tsha-chu* (bath at a hot spring) and *lum* (vapour treatment).

Diagnostic Techniques The decision about what kind of treatment to use for a particular condition is made by the physician mainly through the reading of the pulses. In modern medicine, pulse reading is only used to detect anomalies of the heart and of the circulatory system. Using the So-ba Rig-pa method, it is possible to detect diseases of any organ through the pulses. The eyes, tongue and urine are also examined for signs that will help with the diagnosis, and sometimes the physician will record the patient's medical history.

ARCHITECTURE

Bhutanese architecture is one of the most striking features of the country. Each type of building subscribes to a similar style, however, there are many variations and very few structures are of the same design.

Some styles and building methods are unique to the region and others are particular to Bhutan itself.

Houses

The style of Bhutanese houses varies depending on the location and, more particularly, elevation. Thatched bamboo houses predominate in the south of the country. At high altitudes, most homes are simple stone structures or even yak-hair tents. Although the design varies from place to place, homes in the inner-Himalayan zone are built in a Bhutanese style oddly reminiscent of Swiss chalets.

A typical Bhutanese house is two storeys high and has an attic. In rural areas the ground floor is always used as a cattle barn and the upper floor as the living quarters. In most houses, one elaborately decorated room called a *choesum* serves as a chapel.

The foundation is made from stones placed in a trench and built up to a height of about 50cm above the ground. In central and eastern Bhutan the walls are usually made of stone. In the west the walls are 80cm to 100cm thick and are made of compacted mud, which provides an extremely strong and durable structure. To build these walls, a wooden frame is constructed and filled with damp mud. The mud is compacted by being pounded with wooden poles to which a flat ram is attached. When the wall reaches the top of the frame, the frame is shifted upwards and the process begins again. This method of construction is known for producing very rigid walls.

The pounders are usually teams of women, who sing and dance as they beat the walls. Although Bhutanese women are usually shy and modest with outsiders, they traditionally loosen their inhibitions and exchange ribald comments with men as they perform the pounding, which can take several weeks for a large house. Once the mud wall is finished, it is either left in its natural colour or is whitewashed.

On the lower floor, an opening for a door, and perhaps some windows, is left in the mud wall that forms the front of the house, which traditionally faces south. The upper floor is supported by wooden beams that fit into holes in the mud wall. Central columns are used to support the beams, because it is difficult to find a single piece of timber to span the entire width of the house. The earthen walls for the upper floor form only the back of the house and the back half of the two side exterior walls. The front portion of the living area is always built of timber, which is sometimes elaborately decorated, with large divided windows facing south. The wooden portion of the house extends out over the front and side mud or stone walls.

Inset: Chimi Lhakhang, Metshina
(Photo by
Stan Armington)

Following tradition, and also structurally logical, the windows on the lower floor are small; larger windows are built on upper floors. In older houses the windows are sliding wooden panels, not glass. Above all, windows in Bhutan comprise a cut-out of a curved trefoil motif, called a *horzhing*. In Bhutan there are often several explanations for everything, and this motif is said to be either of Persian influence or simply a practical design which allows a person to look out of the window while the smoke blows out through the opening above their head.

Often an elaborate wooden cornice is built along the top of the wall directly under the roof of the house. Traditional roofs are pitched and covered with wooden shingles. Often the roofs leak because the pitch is insufficient or the shingles have been badly prepared. During heavy rainstorms the rainwater runs slowly down the roof, percolating through the shingle cover at the joints, or is blown up under the shingles by the high winds. Shingles need to be replaced frequently and many people now choose corrugated sheet metal for their roofs. A feature missing in all Bhutanese architecture is a gutter – expect to get wet when you enter or leave a house during a rainstorm.

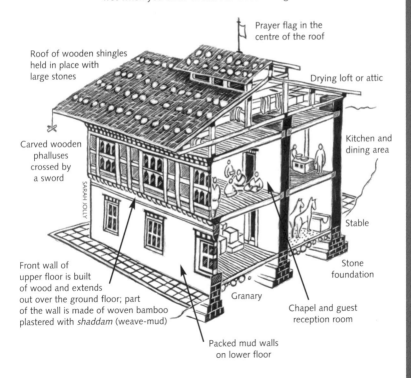

Prayer flag in the centre of the roof

Roof of wooden shingles held in place with large stones

Drying loft or attic

Carved wooden phalluses crossed by a sword

Kitchen and dining area

SARAH JOLLY

Stable

Front wall of upper floor is built of wood and extends out over the ground floor; part of the wall is made of woven bamboo plastered with *shaddam* (weave-mud)

Stone foundation

Granary

Chapel and guest reception room

Packed mud walls on lower floor

The internal walls, and often parts of the external walls, are built with a timber frame that is filled in with woven bamboo and plastered with mud. This construction is called *shaddam* (weave-mud).

The heavy wooden doors are made from several planks held firmly together using a tongue-and-groove technique. This technique is used to fit together all the woodwork, and not a single nail is used in a traditional structure. The door hinge is a pair of wooden pegs that fit into round holes above and below the door frame.

A large space is left below the roof. This serves as an attic and a place for storing hay or for drying animal skins and chillies. In winter the hay helps insulate the house. Sometimes woven bamboo mats are placed around the attic, but often it is simply left uncovered.

The stairways to the upper floor and attic are ladders made by carving steps into a whole tree trunk. If you find yourself climbing one of these ladders, reach around behind the right edge and you may find a groove cut there to serve as a handrail.

After a house is built, the all-important decoration begins. Wooden surfaces are painted with various designs, each with a special significance. Swastikas, floral patterns representing the lotus, cloud whirls and the *tashi tagye* (eight auspicious symbols) are the most common (see the boxed text 'Tashi Tagye' in the Facts about Bhutan chapter). Beside the front door are larger paintings, often of mythical animals such as the *garuda*, or large red phalluses. The phallus is not a fertility symbol; it is believed to ward off evil. Many houses are decorated with carved wooden phalluses, often crossed by a sword, which are hung at the four corners or over the door. A prayer flag called a *goendhar* is erected on the centre of the roof of all Buddhist homes.

Dzongs

Bhutan's *dzongs* are perhaps the most visibly striking architectural aspect of the kingdom. They are outstanding examples of grand design and construction. These huge white citadels dominate the major towns and serve as the administrative headquarters of all 20 of the country's *dzongkhags* (districts) and the focus of secular and religious authority in each. As well as the large, active district dzongs, there are a few dzongs that have been destroyed or abandoned, or are now used for other purposes, such as Simtokha Dzong, south of Thimphu, and Dobji Dzong, south of Chhuzom. Not all dzongs are ancient monuments; for example, a new dzong was built in Trashi Yangtse in eastern Bhutan in 1998.

The word 'dzong' is of Tibetan origin and translates as 'fortress'. Tibetan dzongs were large castle-like structures perched on hilltops overlooking broad river valleys. The dzongs were both military fortresses and administrative centres. Often the entire population of the valley sought refuge in the dzong during a war.

Because dzongs were usually placed on ridges, a tunnel was often constructed to the nearest water supply so that those in the dzong could survive a long siege. Many dzongs had a *ta dzong* (watch-tower), which was either part of the building, as in Jakar Dzong, or a separate structure, as in Paro and Trongsa Dzongs. This structure was also used as an ammunition store and dungeon. Many dzongs were accessed by cantilever bridges as an additional protective measure. Most dzongs have inward-sloping walls, an architectural feature known as battered walls, which make the building look even larger than it is. They usually have only one massive door, which leads into a small passage that makes two right-angle turns before it enters the main courtyard. This is a design feature to keep invaders from storming the dzong.

During the time of Shabdrung Ngawang Nyamgal (1594–1651), the dzongs served their primary function as fortresses well and each was the stronghold of a *penlop* (regional governor). Many of the feuds and battles for control during the 17th to 20th centuries were waged by penlops whose troops attacked neighbouring dzongs. The key to success in these battles was to capture the dzong of the opposing penlop, thereby gaining control of that district.

Bhutan's dzongs were built of stone or pounded mud and a considerable amount of timber, including wooden shingle roofs. This, combined with the large number of butter lamps used in temples, has caused fires in almost all dzongs. Most of Bhutan's dzongs suffered severe damage during the 1897 earthquake and were repaired or rebuilt in their original style. All important dzongs have been (or are being) rebuilt using ancient construction methods, though in many places corrugated-iron roofs have replaced the traditional wooden shingles.

Each dzong has unique details, but all follow the same general design principles. Dzong architects don't prepare any plans or drawings. They rely only on a mental concept of what is to be built. This tradition continues to the present day; the reconstruction of Thimphu's Trashi Chhoe Dzong in 1966 was carried out without any blueprints or sketches. The Bhutanese proclaim proudly that no nails are used even to construct dzongs.

Most dzongs are divided into two wings: one containing temples and monks' quarters and one for government offices. The monastic wing of many dzongs actually serves as a monastery, with the resident monk body called a *rabdey*. In early days, most dzongs had a rabdey, but today only the dzongs of Thimphu, Punakha, Paro, Mongar, Trongsa, Jakar and Trashigang serve as monasteries. The Dratshang (central monk body) maintains monastic schools in the dzongs of Punakha, Trongsa and Paro. Punakha Dzong is the seat of the chief abbot, His Holiness the Je Khenpo.

The main courtyard of the dzong is the *dochey*, which is paved with large flagstones. Along the outer walls of the dzong are several storeys of rooms and galleries overlooking the paved courtyard; these rooms are the monks' quarters and classrooms. Because the monastic wing of the dzong is separated from the secular wing, many dzongs have two docheys, the second being surrounded by administrative offices.

The central structure of the dzong is a tower-like building called the *utse*. In most dzongs, the utse has a series of chapels, one on each floor. On the ground floor of the utse is the *lhakhang*.

Entry to dzongs is through a single gate controlled by a policeman who restricts entry and enforces dzong protocol. Bhutanese are required to wear formal dress (*gho* for men and *kira* for women) and scarf (*kabney* and *rachu*) at all times within the dzong.

According to tradition, no woman can be in a dzong between sunset and sunrise. This tradition has only been broken once, when the former Indian prime minister, Indira Gandhi, stayed in Trashi Chhoe Dzong, in Thimphu, after receiving special permission from the Je Khenpo.

Goembas & Lhakhangs

Bhutan has an enormous number of religious buildings. According to the National Commission for Cultural Affairs there are 2002 such buildings – 437 are owned by the state in the custody of the dratshang and another 127 are in the care of reincarnate lamas. In addition, there are another 870 village lhakhangs and an estimated 568 that are privately owned. Each was designed for a different purpose to suit the wishes of the founders, architects or sponsors.

In Dzongkha, a monastery is called a *goemba*, and the word is pronounced quite differently from the corresponding Tibetan word, *gompa*. A primary reason for selecting the location of a monastery is to have a remote location where the monks can find peace and solitude. This is particularly evident in Bhutan where goembas are built atop rocky crags or on remote hillsides.

Several goembas in Bhutan were built at sacred caves that had previously been places of meditation. Taktshang in Paro and Kurjey in Bumthang are two famous examples that were built around caves where Guru Rinpoche is believed to have meditated for extended periods.

All Bhutanese goembas are different, but they all possess certain common features. They are self-contained communities, with a central lhakhang and separate quarters for sleeping. The lhakhang is at the centre of a dochey, similar to that of the dzongs. The dochey is used as a dancing area by the monks during festivals.

On all religious buildings in Bhutan, and on dzongs too, a painted red band called a *khemar* runs just below the roof. One or more circular brass plates or mirrors representing the *nima* (sun) are often placed on the khemar. The golden deer above a goemba are symbols of the deer park at Varanasi where the Buddha did his earliest teachings.

The term lhakhang is a bit confusing, because it may be used to refer to both the building itself and to the room inside the building that is the primary chapel. Furthermore, some goembas have several lhakhangs within the central building.

RICHARD I'ANSON

RICHARD I'ANSON

RICHARD I'ANSON

STAN ARMINGTON

Embodying unique design and adaptable engineering, many *dzongs*, such as Jakar Dzong (top) and Trongsa Dzong (bottom), hug the contours of Bhutan's dramatic landscape. Elaborate paintwork and carved figures (centre) ornament houses and religious buildings alike.

Receptacles for religious offerings, *chortens* can be found throughout Bhutan. You'll encounter multiple variations on the three primary styles – Nepali, Tibetan and Bhutanese.

Traditional architectural styles found in houses (top right & centre) and also in the Ugyen Chholing (top left) have been replicated in the recently completed terminal building at Paro airport (bottom).

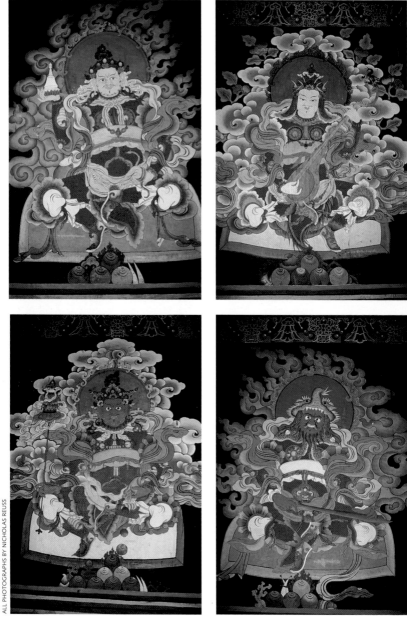

The guardians of the four directions: Chenmizang, the red king of the west (top left); Yulkhorsung, the white king of the east (top right); Namthose, the gold king of the north (bottom left); and Phagchepo, the blue king of the south (bottom right).

Guardians of the Four Directions

Paintings or statues of the guardians, or kings, of the four directions, pictured opposite, appear on the *gorikha* (veranda) to guard the entrance to most lhakhangs. The guardians have an origin in ancient Mongol tradition, and each one holds a different object. They are warriors who guard the world against demons and earthly threats.

Chenmizang, the red king of the west, holds a chorten and a snake, and is the lord of the *nagas* (serpents).

Yulkhorsung, the white king of the east, plays the lute and is the lord of celestial musicians.

Namthose, the gold king of the north, holds a mongoose and a banner of victory. He is a god of wealth and prosperity.

Phagchepo, the blue king of the south, holds a sword in his right hand.

A typical lhakhang has a cupola and a gilded ball-shaped ornament, called a *serto*, on the roof. Most have a paved path around the circumference of the building. On the outside wall are racks of prayer wheels, which monks and devotees spin as they circumambulate the building.

The entrance to the lhakhang is through a raised veranda called a *gorikha*, which is covered with murals, usually depicting the guardians of the four directions or a wheel of life. Entry is via a large painted wooden door that is often protected by a heavy cloth or yak-hair curtain. The door opens to a *tshokhang* (assembly hall), also called a *dukhang* or *kunre*. The hall is usually so large that it has rows of pillars to hold up the roof, and on its walls are paintings that describe the life of Buddha.

At the far end of the tshokhang is an elaborately decorated altar *(choesham)* that can be part of the main room or else be housed in a separate room or lhakhang. The two-tiered choesham, with its large gilded statue, is a focal point of the lhakhang, and depending on when and why the lhakhang was built, the statue may be of Sakyamuni, Guru Rinpoche or another figure. Jampa is the central figure in many lhakhangs built before Guru Rinpoche's visits to Bhutan, particularly those attributed to Songtsen Gampo. The central statue is usually flanked by two smaller figures, sometimes the consorts of Guru Rinpoche, and other deities related to the central image. (See the boxed text 'Important Figures of Drukpa Kagyu Buddhism' in the Facts about Bhutan chapter for the names of key deities.)

On the upper level of the choesham are *torma* (ritual cake) and various objects used in worship, such as a *dorji*, conch shells, trumpets made of thigh-bone, small drums and bells. On the lower tier are butter lamps and offerings of rice, flowers, water and money. Frequently a silk parasol hangs over the altar. Often just a single butter lamp burns on the altar, unlike temples in Tibet where there may be hundreds of lamps burning. On auspicious occasions in Bhutan, however, 108 or even 1000 butter lamps are lit. To prevent fires, arrays of butter lamps are often burned in a separate small building.

In most lhakhangs, often on the upper floor, is a room called a *goenkhang*, which is devoted to the protective and terrifying deities (see the boxed text 'Protective Deities' in the Facts about Bhutan chapter). The statues in these rooms are usually covered except when rituals are performed. Weapons are stored in this room and may include old muskets, armour, and round shields made from rhinoceros hide. Teams of archers sometimes sleep in a goenkhang before a major match, but women are never allowed to enter and the monks are reluctant to allow entry to any visitors.

Another way that lhakhangs in Bhutan differ from those in Tibet is that they feature a pair of elephant tusks alongside the altar to symbolise good. Buddhists revere the elephant because when the Buddha was born, his mother had a vision of a white elephant.

If the lhakhang is in a monastery, then opposite the altar, facing the central image, is a throne upon which the abbot, or *khenpo*, sits during ceremonies. Between the khenpo's throne and the altar are rows of cushions on which monks sit during prayers and ceremonies.

Chortens

A chorten is literally a receptacle for offerings, and in Bhutan all chortens contain religious relics. The classical chorten shape is based on the ancient Indian form of a stupa. Each of the chorten's five architectural elements has a symbolic meaning. The square or rectangular base symbolises earth. The hemispherical dome symbolises water. The conical or pyramidal spire symbolises fire (the spire has 13 step-like segments that symbolise the 13 steps leading to Buddhahood). On top is a crescent moon and a sun, symbolising air, and a vertical spike symbolising ether or the sacred light of the Buddha. Inside is placed a carved wooden pole called a *sokshing*, which is the life-spirit of the chorten.

Some chortens, such as the National Memorial Chorten in Thimphu, are built in memory of an individual. Others commemorate the visit of a saint or contain sacred books or the bodies of saints or great lamas. Bhutan has three basic styles of chorten, usually characterised as Bhutanese, Tibetan and Nepali.

The Nepali-style chorten is based on the classical stupa. On Nepali chortens the four sides of the tower are painted with a pair of eyes, the all-seeing eyes of Buddha. What appears to be a nose is actually the Sanskrit character for the number one, symbolising the absoluteness of Buddha. The prototypes for the Nepali chortens in Bhutan are Swayambhunath and Bodhnath in Kathmandu. The large Chorten Kora in Trashi Yangtse and Chendebji Chorten near Trongsar are two examples of the Nepali style of chorten.

The Tibetan-style chorten has a shape similar to the stupa, but the rounded part flares outward instead of being a dome shape. Thimphu's National Memorial Chorten is an excellent example of this style.

SARAH JOLLY

The Bhutanese design comprises a square stone pillar with a khemar near the top. The exact origin of this style is not known, but is believed to be a reduced form of the classical stupa, with only the pinnacle and square base. Some Bhutanese chortens have a ball and crescent representing the moon and sun on top.

Several other types of chorten are also found in Bhutan. The *khonying* (two legs) is an archway that forms a gate over a trail. Travellers earn merit by passing through the structure, which is decorated with interior wall paintings and a mandala on the roof. The *mani chukor* is shaped like a Bhutanese chorten but is hollow and contains a large prayer wheel. It is built over or near a stream so that the water turns a wooden turbine below the structure, which then turns the prayer wheel.

Another structure common in Bhutan is the *mani* wall. As its name implies, this is a wall with carved mani stones placed in it. Bhutanese mani walls are usually quite short, but long mani walls can be found in Bumthang.

Always walk to the left of a chorten or mani wall.

THIMPHU

[Continued from page 147]

provides funding for this project, which prepares and dispenses traditional herbal and other medicines. There is an impressive, large laboratory and production facility that ensures the quality of the products, the components of which may include plants, minerals, animal parts, precious metals and gems.

The production of medicines is directed entirely towards the needs of the Bhutanese, though there is a plan to eventually export traditional medicines. There is a day-care facility and clinic where doctors diagnose patients and prescribe appropriate traditional medicines or treatments. Tour operators can arrange visits to the institute. There is a small museum and *gift shop* where you can purchase Tsheringma, a safflower-based herbal tea that is produced here.

The institute also researches the use of medicinal herbs and plants and has a trial plot on the premises. It has field units that collect medicinal plants from far away places such as Lingzhi in western Bhutan, where a number of important medicinal species grow in abundance.

THIMPHU CITY

Indian workers and Bhutanese young people gather along Norzin Lam and the square in front of the Luger Cinema. Many of Thimphu's shops are within easy walking distance.

Weekend Market

The weekend market is in a permanent set of stalls north of Changlimithang Stadium. Vendors from throughout the region arrive on Friday afternoon and remain until Sunday night. It's an interesting place to visit, where village people jostle with well-heeled Thimphu residents for the best – and cheapest – vegetables and foodstuffs. This is the only time that fresh produce is easily available and the shopping is enhanced by the opportunity to catch up on the week's gossip.

Depending on the season you may find potatoes, onions, numerous varieties of chillies, red and white rice, buckwheat, flour, cauliflowers, cabbages, lettuces, eggplants, asparagus, peas, squash, yams, several kinds of mushrooms and ferns, strange spices and herbs. Fruits come from local orchards and from the south of the country. You will find oranges, apples, pineapples, bananas, mangoes, apricots, peaches and plums. If you wander off into one corner of the market, you'll find an odoriferous collection of dried fish, beef and balls of *datse* (homemade soft cheese that is used to make sauces). During the winter you can even pick up a leg of yak (with the hoof still attached).

At the northern end of the market is a collection of stalls called 'the indigenous goods and handicrafts section'. Here you will find locally produced goods, including religious objects, cloth, baskets and strange hats from various minority groups. They are more than happy to sell these to tourists, but it's mostly intended for local consumption. If you shop here, you may find a Bhutanese housewife or a monk from a nearby monastery to advise you on the quality of your purchase. Bargaining is very much in order here.

National Textile Museum

Thimphu's National Textile Museum (☎ 321516, Norzin Lam; admission Nu 25 for SAARC nationals, Nu 150 others; open 9am-5pm Tues-Fri, 1pm-4pm Sat, 10am-3pm Sun), which opened in June 2001, is worth a leisurely visit to get to know the living national art of weaving. Changing exhibitions introduce the major weaving techniques, styles of local dress and textiles made by women and men. The small *shop* features work from the renowned weaving centres in Lhuentse Dzongkhag, the ancestral home of the royal family in northeastern Bhutan. Each item is labelled with the name of the weaver, at prices ranging from Nu 1600 to 25,000.

Royal Academy of Performing Arts

The home of the Royal Dance Troupe is the Royal Academy of Performing Arts (☎ 322569, Chumachu; open 8.45am-4.30pm Mon-Fri). It provides formal training for masked dancers and also works to preserve Bhutan's folk-dancing heritage.

Unless there's a practice session on there's little to see here. The professional dancers from this school perform several of the dances at the Thimphu tsechu. With advance notice they will provide a one-hour performance for visitors.

Zangto Pelri Lhakhang
This private chapel, built in the 1990s by Dasho Aku Tongmi, a musician who composed Bhutan's national anthem, is south of the weekend market. It's beside the older **Yigja Dungkhar Lhakhang** and is a replica of Guru Rinpoche's celestial abode. It is Bhutan's tallest *lhakhang* and houses many large statues, including a 4m-high image of Guru Rinpoche.

Changlimithang Stadium
The national stadium occupies the site of the 1885 battle that helped establish the political supremacy of Ugyen Wangchuck, Bhutan's first king. It is now the site of the national archery ground, a large football stadium and parade ground, basketball, tennis and squash courts, as well as the headquarters of the Bhutan Olympic committee. It's always worth checking what event is taking place when you are in town.

Voluntary Artists Studio Thimphu
The Voluntary Artists Studio Thimphu *(VAST; ☎ 325664, Chang Lam)* is hidden away on the top floor above the Handicrafts Bhutan shop. It's a busy place with after-school and weekend classes in drawing and painting for young artists. The goal of the studio is to use Bhutanese artistic values to create both traditional and contemporary works. There's a small library and coffee shop where budding artists are encouraged to congregate. Art by the students is sold in the Art Shop Gallery in the clock tower square.

MOTITHANG
Motithang is a maze of roads that switchback up the steep hillside above the town. Many of Thimphu's well-to-do families live here in homes that blend into the surrounding pine forests.

At the top of Motithang is the original Motithang Hotel, which was built to accommodate visitors to the coronation of King Jigme Singye Wangchuck in 1974. Along with the Olathang Hotel in Paro, it was one of the first hotels in the country. Tour groups stayed here until the mid-1990s when it became too expensive to maintain and was turned into a youth centre. The Druk Path Trek from Paro ends here.

High on the hillside south of the youth centre is the Kuengachholing State Guest House, where high government officials and visiting heads of state stay.

Telecom Tower
There's a wonderful view of Thimphu valley from the hillside below the telecommunications tower (elevation 2685m), high above the town at the end of a road that branches off from the approach to the youth centre. The complex also houses the broadcasting studios of Bhutan Television. Don't photograph the telecommunications installation, but the valley is worth a few snaps. The area is known as Sangaygang and it becomes a lover's lane late at night.

Mini-Zoo
A short distance up the road to the telecom tower is a trail leading to a large fenced area that was originally established as a mini-zoo. The king decided that such a facility was not in keeping with Bhutan's environmental and religious convictions, and it was disbanded some time ago. The animals were released into the wild but the takins were so tame (some people say they are simply stupid) that they wandered around the streets of Thimphu looking for food, and the only solution was to put them back into captivity. It's worthwhile taking the time to see these strange, quite ugly animals. The best time to see them is early morning when they gather near the fence to feed. It's a five-minute walk from the road to a viewing area where you can take advantage of a few holes in the fence to take photographs. (For more about this curious creature see the boxed text 'The Takin – Bhutan's National Animal' in the Facts about Bhutan chapter.)

THIMPHU

Changangkha Lhakhang

Changangkha Lhakhang is an old fortress-like temple and monastic school perched on a ridge above Thimphu, south-east of Motithang. It was established in the 12th century on a site chosen by Lama Phajo Drukgom Shigpo, who came from Ralung in Tibet. The central statue is Chenresig in an 11-headed manifestation, and the books in the temple are larger in size than usual Tibetan texts. There is an excellent view of Thimphu from the courtyard.

DRUBTHOB GOEMBA

After you drive down the road from the telecom tower, you will find yourself on Gaden Lam, the road that runs high above the golf course. There are some great views of the town, and of Trashi Chhoe Dzong, and above you can see Drubthob Goemba, which now houses the Zilukha nunnery.

DECHEN PHODRANG

At the end of Gaden Lam is Dechen Phodrang, the site of Thimphu's original Trashi Chhoe Dzong. Since 1971 it has housed the state monastic school, and a long procession of monks often travels between here and the dzong. A team of 15 teachers provides an eight-year course to more than 450 students. The 12th-century paintings in the goemba's Guru Lhakhang are being restored by a United Nations Educational, Scientific, and Cultural Organization (Unesco) project. The upper floor features a large figure of Shabdrung Ngawang Namgyal as well as the *goenkhang* (chapel devoted to protective and terrifying deities). The central figure in the downstairs chapel is the Buddha Sakyamuni.

ACTIVITIES

It hardly seems worth spending US$200 a day to swim, play tennis or go to a cinema, but these activities are available if you want them.

There are two tennis courts, squash courts and a basketball court at the north end of the Changlimithang Stadium.

Golf

The **Royal Thimphu Golf Club** (☎ *325429, Chhophel Lam; green fees US$25 per day*)

has a nine-hole course beautifully situated above Trashi Chhoe Dzong. Indian Brigadier General TV Jaganathan, posted in Bhutan between 1968 and 1973, got permission from King Jigme Dorji Wangchuck to construct a few holes. The king later granted permission to expand the course to nine holes, recognising that it would provide a green area to preserve the beauty of Trashi Chhoe Dzong. The course was formally inaugurated in 1971 as the Thimphu Golf Club and was renovated in 1992 as part of a Japanese project.

Japanese visitors find the club's prices reasonable, even considering the tourist rate, compared to playing golf in Japan.

You can hire a set of clubs for US$15, and you can buy lost balls from kids who retrieve them from the course and sell them for Nu 20 to 50. Caddies are available, but since they are mostly schoolboys, they are not on site until late afternoon. You don't need to make an appointment to play, but weekends are busy, and you may have to wait to tee off.

Rock Climbing

Bhutan's only rock-climbing club, **Vertical Bhutan**, gathers most weekends to climb on The Nose, a rock face high above the south-west part of Thimphu. There are several prepared routes with names such as 'Wedding Present' and 'Reach and Preach'. Contact the club by email at [e] verticalbhutan@ hotmail.com or call the club secretary, Dilu Giri, on ☎ 322966 for the climbing schedule.

Swimming

You can swim in the pool at Thimphu's **Sports Complex** (☎ *322064, Doebum Lam; 1-hr swim Nu 70; open 4pm-8pm Mon-Fri, 1pm-6pm Sat & Sun Mar-Dec*). There is also a basketball court and gym. The facility is busy and noisy in the afternoon when school children take tae kwon do classes.

Mountain Biking

The **Bhutan Mountain Biking Club** (☎ *321 905,* [w] *www.bhutanmtb.com*) organises rides and has a few bikes for hire. Bike riding is not permitted within the Thimphu city limits, but the club can arrange to have the bike transported to the start of the ride.

PLACES TO STAY

If you are on a normal tourist visa, you will probably be booked into one of the top-end hotels unless you have scheduled your trip in the autumn during the Thimphu tsechu. All hotels charge 10% tax and 10% service on the rates shown.

All hotels are completely full at tsechu time, and you may find yourself in a smaller guesthouse, a private home, or even a tent. If you end up as a house guest, you will certainly have a chance to make new friends, and will have found the perfect recipient for the bottle of duty-free liquor you bought en route to Paro.

If you are an Indian national or are working in Bhutan on a project, you may want to choose a more moderate hotel. The mid-range hotels listed here are not as fancy as the tourist hotels, but they're all quite adequate, though they can be noisy once the dogs start howling. Many of the smaller hotels make no distinction between double or single occupancy and simply charge by the room.

Places to Stay – Top End

Druk Hotel (☎ 322966, fax 322677, *Wogzin Lam,* [e] *drukhotel@druknet.net.bt*) Singles/doubles/suites Nu 1800/2300/5000. This 53-room hotel is considered by many to be the best in Thimphu. It is in the centre of town and boasts, a bar, a restaurant noted for its Indian food, a hair salon and a health club with a gym, sauna and steam bath. All rooms have heaters and cable television.

Motithang Hotel (☎ 322435, *Thori Lam*) Singles/doubles Nu 1020/1290. This Bhutan Tourism Corporation Limited (BTCL) property was previously known as the Zangto Pelri. It is in the Motithang area, quite a distance above the business district, and has 15 large wood-panelled rooms.

Riverview Hotel (☎ 323497, fax 323496, *Dechen Lam*) Singles/doubles Nu 1500/1800. This is a large concrete structure in pseudo-Bhutanese style above the east bank of the Wang Chhu. All 50 of the well-appointed rooms have a phone and a balcony with a view of the town.

There's a restaurant, business centre, conference room and gift shop. It usually hosts a disco on Saturday nights and special occasions. Both Riverview and Motithang are inconvenient if you want to wander around town.

Jumolhari Hotel (☎ 322747, fax 324412, [e] *dorji@druknet.net.bt, Wogzin Lam*) Singles/doubles Nu 1150/1350. This hotel has been extensively renovated and has now regained its position as one of Thimphu's better hotels. Just south of the clock tower, it has 27 rooms with televisions. There's a good restaurant with continental, Indian, Chinese and Bhutanese dishes.

Wangchuk Hotel (☎ 323532, fax 326232, [e] *htlwchuk@druknet.net.bt, Chang Lam*) Singles/doubles Nu 1050/1250. This hotel overlooks the stadium and is a favourite of many project staff and expatriates. You may find an interesting collection of knowledgeable Bhutan hands in the dining room. The 20 wood-panelled rooms have carpets and television.

Hotel Taktsang (☎ 322102, fax 323284, *Chorten Lam*) Singles/doubles Nu 1100/1300. Opposite the Swiss Bakery, the rooms at the 34-room Taktsang offer a fascinating view over the centre of the town. The restaurant has one of the most extensive menus in town although, like all the others, the food suffers from a lack of ingredients.

Yeedzin Guest House (☎ 325702, fax 324995, [e] *yeedzin@druknet.net.bt, Jangchhub Lam*) Singles/doubles Nu 550/800. This pleasant 16-room establishment overlooks central Thimphu. For long-staying guests there are three deluxe suites, each with a kitchen. The hotel restaurant serves continental, Chinese and Bhutanese food (Prince Charles ate here); you can sit at tables or on Bhutanese-style benches.

Pine Wood Hotel (☎ 325924, fax 325507, [e] *pinewood@druknet.net.bt, Lungten Zampa*) Singles/doubles Nu 1200/1500. The Pine Wood Hotel is on a hill high above the eastern end of Lungten Zampa. All the nine rooms and suites are of a different size and design. To stay in a suite here, as Richard Gere did, you would probably have to pay a surcharge to the tour operator.

Hotel Pedling (☎ *325714, fax 323592,* [e] *pedling@druknet.net.bt, Chang Lam)* Singles/doubles Nu 1300/1700. The well-run Pedling has 39 double rooms with television and direct dial phones. It has a good restaurant and a business centre.

Jambayang Resort (☎ *322349, fax 323669,* [e] *jambayangs@druknet.net.bt, Dechen Lam)* Singles/doubles Nu 1200/1500, apartments per month Nu 15,000. Above the Riverview is the Jambayang Resort with four rooms and four apartments with kitchens. Many Bhutanese recommend the restaurant at this hotel.

Places to Stay – Mid-Range

Hotel 89 (☎ *322931, Chorten Lam)* Rooms Nu 550. This centrally located 20-room hotel is a favourite with Indian tourists. It also has one of the most consistently good and popular restaurants in Thimphu.

Druk Sherig Guest House (☎ *323911, fax 322714, Wogzin Lam)* Singles/doubles Nu 550/750. This 12-room hotel is often used by Worldwide Fund for Nature (WWF) guests and expatriates. Breakfast is served in the small restaurant on the top floor, but other meals have to be specially arranged in advance.

NT Hotel (☎ *323458, fax 323692, Norzin Lam)* Rooms Nu 300-400. Previously known as Kelwang, this seven-room hotel is above the restaurant of the same name. The hotel reception desk is at the restaurant cashier counter.

Rabten Apartments (☎ *323587,* [e] *rabten@druknet.net.bt, Thori Lam)* Apartments per month Nu 16,000. Long-term guests can rent one of the seven apartments. The restaurant specialises in Bhutanese food, but call ahead for a reservation.

Places to Stay – Budget

Hotel Tandin (☎ *322380, Norzin Lam)* Singles/doubles Nu 350/450. The Tandin is in the centre of the city, near the cinema.

Hotel Norling (☎ *322997, Norzin Lam)* Singles/doubles Nu 150/275. The 24 rooms of the Norling are small with basic facilities.

Hotel Yoedzer (☎ *324007, fax 325927, Wogzin Lam)* Singles/doubles Nu 450/550.

This 22-room hotel is in the City Centre complex. The restaurant has a tandoori oven, which offers a change from the standard fare.

Hotel Tak-Seng-Chhung-Druk (☎ *321 509, Norzin Lam)* Singles/doubles Nu 200/300. This is on the second floor of a shopping complex, as yet unnamed at the time of research. All rooms have private bathroom and television.

PLACES TO EAT

There are plenty of restaurants in Thimphu, but it's hardly a gourmet paradise. You can escape the tourist buffets that hotels provide, but all restaurants produce pretty much the same dishes.

Menus tend to be a fantasy of what the hotel would like to serve, and don't necessarily reflect what is actually in the kitchen. Ask what meat is available before you set your heart on a beef or pork dish. There are few cold-storage facilities in town. Except in the dead of winter the only meat that is usually available is chicken. Bhutanese food is available in most restaurants, but beware of the hot chillies that are an essential ingredient in many dishes.

In most restaurants you can expect to pay about Nu 100 for a complete meal that might include rice, dal (lentil soup), vegetables, *ema datse* (chillies and cheese) and a meat curry. In larger hotels prices may go up to Nu 200. In smaller snack places you can eat noodles or *momos* (steamed or fried dumplings) for Nu 30 to 50. Most hotels and restaurants add 10% tax and 10% service charge (usually identified as such on the bill).

Hotel Restaurants

The most reliable restaurants for health, variety and consistent quality are in hotels. When there are groups in residence, most hotels have a buffet at Nu 250 to 330, but it's usually possible to also order from the a la carte menu.

Hotel Tandin has friendly staff and serves excellent Indian and good Chinese food. It caters to a largely Indian clientele and does not serve beef. Other good places for Indian food are the *NT Hotel* and *Jumolhari Hotel*.

Symbolising a fusion of the spiritual and the secular, *dzongs* function as both monasteries and district administrative centres. Taktshang Goemba, or monastery (top left), Trashi Chhoe Dzong (top right & bottom) and Paro Dzong (centre) are excellent examples of Bhutan's dramatic monastic architecture.

STAN ARMINGTON

STAN ARMINGTON

ALISON WRIGHT

Spread along the valley floor (bottom left), Thimpu – a city without a single traffic light but with the human face of traffic police (bottom right) – is the centre of national life. Crowds regularly turn out to support football at Thimphu's Changlimithang Stadium (top).

The *Druk Hotel* has an Indian chef and offers a business lunch for Nu 75.

Other good hotel restaurants are the *Wangchuk Hotel Restaurant*, the *Hotel Pedling Restaurant* and, for a view of the Thimphu valley, the *Jambayang Resort*. The specialities in the *Hotel 89* restaurant are fried cheese momos, Indian tandoori food and, in season, yak steaks at Nu 150. Drinks are accompanied by a complimentary plate of the best chips (french fries) in Bhutan.

Rabten Apartments has a restaurant that specialises in Bhutanese food, which is served Bhutanese style with benches and tables arranged around the walls. The restaurant usually caters to groups and you must book in advance.

Other Restaurants

Plums Café (☎ *324307, Chorten Lam*) Open 11am-9.30pm Mon-Sat. It's a bit hard to find the entrance to Plums. There is a small sign above a door facing north on Chorten Lam that leads upstairs to the restaurant, which has tablecloths, cloth napkins and a buffet table that swings into action for groups. It offers a small range of continental food, including a chicken sizzler plate, and an extensive menu of both Chinese and Bhutanese dishes. Plums provides catering services for functions in many private homes.

Lhanam's Restaurant (☎ *321556, Chorten Lam*) Open 8am-9pm daily. This is upstairs in the back of the same building as Plums. It's a good place for coffee or a quick lunch of curry or momos, and is packed with Bhutanese office workers.

Swiss Bakery (☎ *322259, Chorten Lam*) Open 8am-7pm Wed-Mon. On a hill above the southern traffic circle, this was Bhutan's first attempt at a fast-food joint. It was opened in 1970 by Tenzing Dorji, one of the first expatriates to come to Bhutan. It serves great cheese omelettes or you can order from a display of plastic-wrapped sandwiches and hamburgers. At the far end of the counter is a selection of rum balls, cakes, pastries, 'moon rocks' and potato crisps. Despite its rustic appearance, it's a

high-tech operation; hamburgers are microwaved and there are several electronic gadgets, including an electronic lock on the toilet door and a fancy phone system. It's a favourite lunch spot for expatriates and Bhutanese office workers, and can become quite crowded during the traditional 1pm to 2pm lunch hour.

Benez Restaurant (☎ *325180, Chang Lam*) This is a small restaurant (only six tables) in the centre of town with a tiny bar in the back that is popular with locals. It tends to be livelier than other restaurants in Thimphu. In addition to the usual Thimphu fare, it serves pork spareribs and chicken sizzlers for Nu 105.

Jichu Drakey Bakery (☎ *322980, Doebum Lam*) Open 7am-12pm & 1.30pm-7.30pm daily. For excellent takeaway cakes, pies and pastries, walk up the hill to this large bakery. Most items are Nu 10, including cream rolls, eclairs and tarts. It also produces apple pie, strudel and several varieties of bread. The owner learned his trade as an apprentice pastry chef in Austria.

Blue Poppy (☎ *322003, Doebum Lam*) Open 9am-10pm daily. Upstairs, next to the Swiss Bakery, the Blue Poppy serves the usual menu of Indian, Chinese and Bhutanese food. The United Nations Development Programme (UNDP) staff gather here after work on Fridays for a social hour.

Mid Point (☎ *321269, Wogzin Lam*) Open 10am-10pm daily. This is a favourite restaurant of many Bhutanese and has a few tables in a garden outside – a rarity in Thimphu.

S.N.S. (☎ *326177, Chang Lam*) Open 9am-10pm daily. Conveniently located next to All Stars Disco, S.N.S. is a busy place on disco nights and is the only restaurant in town where you might get a late-night snack. It has good momos as well as the only Japanese food in town.

Jojo's Food Court (☎ *325756, Chang Lam*) Dishes Nu 30-45. Open 11am-7pm Thu-Tues. Bhutan's second fast-food centre serves a tasty selection of curry and rice, momos, hamburgers, hot dogs, pies and cakes. There's a separate coffee shop with cakes and pastries. It's on the south end of the third floor of Jojo's shopping complex.

Zhidey Restaurant (☎ 325196, Norzin Lam). You'll have to look carefully to find this small restaurant along the line of shops, but some expats claim that it's the best Bhutanese food in town. There is no menu, but the owner will be happy to make suggestions.

Hasty Tasty (☎ 323329, Wogzin Lam) provides quick snacks such as momos and noodles.

Central Cafe (☎ 326557, Dremton Lam) is a bright place with large windows on the second floor of Centrepoint Complex. It's a popular lunch spot with Bhutanese.

Other small restaurants are *Seasons Restaurant* in the Namsay Shopping Complex. It's a brightly lit place that serves soup, salad and sandwiches and the best pizza in town at Nu 150 to 220.

The *Golf Course Restaurant (☎ 327231, Chhophel Lam)* in the clubhouse at the Royal Thimphu Golf Course has a bar and restaurant. It's open 8.30am to 7pm Tuesday to Sunday and on a warm day it's a good place to have lunch.

ENTERTAINMENT

Entertainment is sparse in Thimphu unless it's tsechu time. There are occasional concerts and video shows at the sports complex, and these are all well advertised by posters and in *Kuensel*.

Cultural Programs

If you are in a group of more than four, your tour operator can arrange a dance performance at the *Royal Academy of Performing Arts*. A more relaxed atmosphere prevails at *Tashi Nencha Music Studio (☎ 322804)* near the Zangto Pelri Lhakhang. The studio can provide a Bhutanese meal and an evening of classical and folk music around a bonfire.

Mila Restaurant (☎ 322175, Norzin Lam), in the five-storey Dragon Shopping Complex, features singers and a Dzongkha comedian most nights. There is a largely local audience and the performers, both amateur and professional, sing traditional Bhutanese songs. There is a Nu 50 cover charge from 6pm to 8pm; after that members of the audience can request songs at Nu 100 each.

Cinema

The *Luger Cinema* in the centre of town screens Hindi and Bhutanese movies, as well as the occasional ancient English movie. It's a crowded, uncomfortable facility and the ticket window is inside a metal cage designed to keep the queue orderly.

Nightclubs

All Stars Disco (Chang Lam) Admission Nu 300. Open 9pm-2am Wed, Fri & Sat. All Stars is upstairs in a shopping centre complex and becomes lively from about 11pm until closing time. On some Saturdays the *disco* in the Riverview Hotel is open.

Dzomsa Café & Club (☎ 324869, Chang Lam) Party nights Wed & Sat. Though primarily a disco, Dzomsa is also open for lunch with momos, noodles and other inexpensive meals.

Pubs & Bars

There are numerous small bars throughout the town. Most bars are closed on Tuesday, the national 'dry day'.

Om Bar (☎ 326344, Ⓦ www.changkhang .com) Open from 5pm. This is Thimphu's largest bar. On the second floor of Jojo's shopping complex, it's a quiet gathering spot early in the evening and becomes busy with a diverse collection of locals and expats after 10pm on disco nights.

Locals gather at the small bar at *Benez Restaurant*, though Danish expats take over on Friday nights. For culture shock, visit the modernistic bar, complete with karaoke on Friday, in the *Hotel Druk*.

SPECTATOR SPORTS
Archery

Archers practise at the target field at the south end of Changlimithang Stadium on most mornings. Tournaments are scheduled on many weekends. (See the boxed text 'Archery' in the Facts for the Visitor chapter for more details.)

Football

The national football tournament takes place in August at Changlingmethang Stadium, with teams from schools throughout the country competing. At major matches the Royal Bhutan Army band provides the half-time entertainment.

SHOPPING

Most shops in Thimphu contain a hodge-podge selection of items. Many shops advertise themselves as 'general' shops, and even a tiny shop may sell such diverse items as light bulbs, stationery, farm implements, shampoo, computer disks and canned fish. To provide even more variety, shops may sell drinks by the glass and their sign may read 'shop cum bar' or the all-encompassing 'general cum bar shop'.

Many of the items on sale are made in India, but there are lots of interesting Bhutanese products, especially textiles, baskets, jewellery, incense, books and religious items. Thimphu is especially known for the fine metal work that local artisans produce.

You can buy imported liquor, wine and other items at the large **Duty Free Shop** (☎ 322167, Norzin Lam) in Thimphu, but you have to pay the full price, including duty, unless you're a diplomat or a senior government official.

Traditional Arts

There is a small **shop** at the National Institute for Zorig Chusum that sells works by senior students, including *thangkas* at prices from Nu 18,000 to 24,000. To purchase other works by students visit **Sangay Traditional Arts & Crafts** (☎ 327419), upstairs in a building on the road below the school.

Behind the school, a narrow lane leads through a garden to a small house where a traditional craftsman makes drums and Tibetan violins. If the artisan is home, and you have space in your luggage for a large fragile object, the drums and violins make an unusual and interesting souvenir.

Handicrafts

Tshering Dolkar (☎ 323324, Norzin Lam) Tshering's shop is near the southern traffic circle and has high-quality handicrafts, carpets, jewellery and textiles.

Handicrafts Emporium (☎ 322810, Norzin Lam) Open 9am-1pm & 2pm-5pm Mon-Sun. Be sure to visit the upper floor, as it's not obvious that it's part of the sales area. This is a large government-run emporium with fixed prices.

Handicrafts Bhutan (☎ 324469, fax 324470, Chang Lam) Opposite the stadium, this small shop has quality goods at reasonable prices.

Bhutan Arts & Crafts Centre (☎ 323861, Doebum Lam) Opposite the Swiss Bakery, this shop has a large supply of Indian goods in addition to Bhutanese handicrafts.

Druktrin Rural Handicrafts (☎ 324500, fax 326232, Chang Lam) On the third floor above the Sakten Health Club, this shop offers great variety and has a small museum with antique jewellery and textiles.

Choki Handicrafts (☎ 324728, fax 323731, Pedzoe Lam) Near the National Institute for Zorig Chusum, this establishment manufactures and sells high-quality masks, thangkas, paintings and painted lama tables called *choektse*. It accepts American Express cards.

Don't neglect the handicraft section at the **weekend market** and also look in the **Druk Shopping Complex** on the lower floors of the Hotel Tandin and the new **Zangto Pelri Shopping Complex** west of Norzin Lam.

Archery

Yangphel Archery Shop (☎ 323323, fax 322897, Chorten Lam) Catering to the large community of Bhutanese archers, it's rare to find a foreigner here. It specialises in American-made Hoyt brand bows that range in price from Nu 6000 for a fibreglass version to Nu 30,000 for the top-of-the-line carbonite variety. The bows can be set for pulls of 35lb to 80lb. Arrows are the steel-tipped Easton brand, which sell for Nu 280 to 500. It's a relatively expensive sport.

The archery shop sponsors several tournaments with prestigious prizes such as free bows and trips to Bangkok.

Music

Cassette tapes and CDs of Hindi and Bhutanese songs are available for Nu 65 to 80 in many shops including **Norling Tshongkhang** on Norzin Lam.

THIMPHU

Jewellery
Norling Handicrafts (☎ *323577, fax 321196, Norzin Lam*) has one of the largest selections of jewellery in Thimphu and is a reliable dealer in semiprecious stones.

Gho & Kira
If you want to try wearing Bhutanese dress, there are many shops to choose from in Thimphu. Many of the shops along the west side of Norzin Lam north of Tshering Dolkar handicrafts shop and inside the Druk Shopping Complex across the street have ready-made *gho* and *kira* in a variety of patterns and qualities, including children's sizes.

A handmade cotton kira costs from Nu 4000 to 22,000, and a silk kira sells for Nu 35,000 to 60,000 or more. A gho costs about Nu 2000 if it's made from machine-woven cloth and Nu 4000 to 6000 for hand-woven cotton cloth. A silk gho can cost from Nu 20,000 to 60,000.

Gagyel Lhundrup Weaving Centre (☎ *327534, Changzamtok*) in the industrial estate at the south end of Thimphu produces hand-woven textiles on site and has a selection of cloth and ready-made garments for sale. As most Bhutanese weavers work at home, this is one of the few places where you can watch weavers at work.

Trekking Equipment
If you are missing a piece of gear for your trek, try *DD Tshongkhang* (☎ *325797, Norzin Lam*) opposite the cinema. There are also a few shops around town that sell Bangladeshi-made fleece jackets, hats and pants at bargain prices.

Postage Stamps
Philatelic Bureau (☎ *322296, Dremton Lam*) Bhutan Post occupies the northern half of a large building on Dremton Lam, a back road north of the cinema. The Philatelic Bureau here has a counter near the front door and sells stamps and souvenir sheets of exotic Bhutanese stamps. For more choice visit the small shop on the ground floor of the Tandin Hotel, which has a good selection of postcards and unusual stamps.

Contemporary Paintings & Handmade Paper
There are two paper makers across the river above the Riverview Hotel. *Jungshi Handmade Paper Factory* (*Dechen Lam*) produces paper as well as cards, envelopes, calendars and other items made from traditional Bhutanese paper. *Mangala Paper House* (☎ *322898, Dechen Lam*) produces high-quality paper in unusual designs. A short but rough gravel road leads from the Jungshi factory to here.

Art Shop Gallery (☎ *325664, Wogzin Lam*) near the clock tower has Bhutanese paper, handicrafts and paintings, and the *Yudruk Gallery* (☎ *321905, Chorten Lam*), below the Blue Poppy restaurant, sells framed watercolours of dzongs and lhakhangs.

GETTING THERE & AWAY
To/From Paro Airport
You can book a taxi at the tea stall outside Paro airport at a fixed rate of Nu 800 to Thimphu. It is 53km from the airport to Thimphu; the journey takes less than two hours.

If your tour operator has not arranged transport for your departing flight, the most reliable way is to have your hotel arrange a vehicle. Arrange your transportation well in advance. If you have an early-morning flight from Paro (and most are), you'll either have to spend the night in Paro or get up early to make the long drive to the airport.

Druk Air closes the counter an hour before flight time and won't reopen it if you're late. Allowing a safety net of two hours for the drive from Thimphu to the airport, you will need to depart at 4am for a 7am departure. Sensible people spend the night before the flight in Paro.

To/From Phuentsholing
This journey took up to 10 days before the road was completed in 1962. It now takes six hours. See the Western Bhutan chapter for details of the drive.

GETTING AROUND
If you are on a normal tourist visa, you will have a car, driver and guide available

throughout your stay in Bhutan, and you'll have little trouble getting around. Most shops and points of interest are within easy walking distance of Thimphu's major hotels; it's easy to pop out for a drink or a round of shopping on foot.

Bus
A public bus service operates throughout Thimphu between 7.30am and 7.30pm from a starting point at the parking area on Chang Lam. Fares are Nu 1 to 7 depending on the distance. In addition to several city routes, the buses also operate to Dechenchoeling in the north and Simtokha and Babesa to the south.

At the bus station below the east end of the bridge at the southern end of town you can find crowded buses to Phuentsholing and other destinations throughout the country.

Taxi
Most of the taxis are Indian Maruti-brand minivans with meters that the drivers rarely use. The taxi stand is on Chang Lam, although you can flag down an empty taxi in the street. Taxi drivers have a habit of charging foreigners, including Indians, as much as they can – one of Bhutan's few flagrant rip-offs. You should be able to hire a taxi for the whole day for about Nu 300, and local trips should cost between Nu 30 and 60 in a shared taxi.

Around Thimphu

NORTH OF THIMPHU
As you travel up the east side of the Wang Chhu, north of Lungten Zampa and past the Riverview Hotel, you'll eventually pass the SAARC building, which overlooks the dzong. On the opposite side of the river you may catch a glimpse of Samtenling Palace, the cottage that is the king's residence. A short distance north is the suburb of Taba where the Forestry Institute has its offices.

The large Dechencholing Palace is some distance north of the dzong. It was built in 1952 and is the official residence of the queen mother. North of the palace is the Royal Body Guard (RBG) facility.

Dechenphu Lhakhang
Dechenphu Lhakhang is a 2km drive on a rocky road up a side valley from a turn-off near Dechencholeing, then a short climb up a stone staircase to an elevation of about 2660m. The imposing tall red goenkhang is dedicated to the powerful deity Gyenyen and is said to be able to supply armour and weapons for an endless number of soldiers. Unesco financed a project to restore many of the paintings in the adjoining goemba.

Pangri Zampa
North of Dechencholeing and east of Dechenphu Lhakhang is Pangri Zampa, two imposing white buildings in a grove of giant cypress trees. Shabdrung Ngawang Namgyal lived here after he arrived in 1616 because this temple appeared in the vision that directed him from Tibet to Bhutan. A well-respected astrologer now lives on the upper storey.

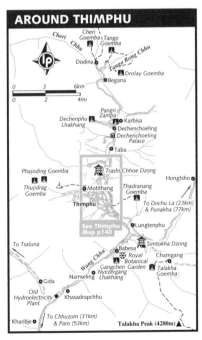

AROUND THIMPHU

Tango Goemba

Continuing up the valley the road crosses to the east side of the Wang Chhu at Begana, near a training facility operated by the electricity department. A few kilometres beyond this, 12km from Thimphu, a road leads east and climbs a short distance to a parking lot. The trail to Tango Goemba is a climb of 280m and takes about half an hour if you follow the steeper shortcut, or about an hour if you take the longer, more gradual trail.

Lama Gyalwa Lhanampa founded the goemba in the 12th century. The present building was built in the 15th century by the 'divine madman', Lama Drukpa Kunley (see the boxed text 'The Divine Madman' in the Western Bhutan chapter). In 1616 Shabdrung Ngawang Namgyal visited Tango Goemba and meditated in a cave nearby. His meditations helped ensure the defeat of an invading Tibetan army. The head lama, a descendent of Lama Drukpa Kunley, presented the goemba to the Shabdrung, who carved a sandalwood statue of Chenresig, which he installed in the monastery.

The picturesque three-storey tower and several surrounding buildings were built in the 18th century by the eighth *desi* (secular ruler), Druk Rabgye. The Shabdrung Jigme Chhogyel added the golden roof in the 19th century. Tango is the residence of an important young *trulku* (reincarnate lama) who is recognised as the seventh reincarnation of the highly respected fourth desi, Gyalse Tenzin Rabgye, whose previous incarnation passed away in 1830.

There are no restaurants or shops nearby. If you plan a full-day excursion to either Tango Goemba or Cheri Goemba, bring a water bottle and a packed lunch.

Cheri Goemba

A short distance beyond the turn-off to Tango Goemba the road ends at Dodina (elevation 2600m). A walk of about 1½ hours leads to Cheri Goemba (Cheri Dorji Dhen). The trail starts by crossing a lovely covered bridge that spans the Wang Chhu, then climbs steeply to the monastery. Shabdrung Ngawang Namgyal, built this goemba in 1620 and established the first monk body

here. A silver chorten inside the goemba holds the ashes of the Shabdrung's father.

SOUTH OF THIMPHU

A road leads uphill from Babesa to the **Royal Botanical Garden** at Serbithang, which was inaugurated in 1999 and has a collection of 500 species of plants. It's a favourite picnic spot of Thimphu residents and has an information centre that sells seedlings and medicines from the medicinal-plants project.

South of Babesa a steep gravel road leads 1.3km uphill to the **Gangchen Nyezergang Lhakhang**, an ancient lhakhang that was rebuilt and reconsecrated in 2001 under the sponsorship of Lyonpo Jigme Thinley.

Simtokha

Simtokha is about 5km south of Thimphu on the old road to Paro and Phuentsholing. The junction with the road to eastern Bhutan is just before Simtokha.

In the valley below the road are the EU-funded plant-and-soil-protection project, the National Mushroom Centre and the large, red-roofed Royal Institute of Management.

Simtokha Dzong Officially known as Sangak Zabdhon Phodrang (Palace of the Profound Meaning of Secret Mantras), Simtokha Dzong was built in 1629 by Shabdrung Ngawang Namgyal. It is often said to be the first dzong built in Bhutan. In fact, there were dzongs in Bhutan as early as 1153, but this is the first dzong built by the Shabdrung, is the oldest dzong that has survived as a complete structure, and is the first structure to incorporate both monastic and administrative facilities. It is the home of the Institute for Language and Culture Studies; the students are both monks and lay people.

The site is said to have been chosen to guard over a demon that had vanished into the rock nearby, hence the name Simtokha, from *simmo* (demoness) and *do* (stone). Conveniently, the site is also an excellent location from which to protect the Thimphu valley and the valley leading to the Dochu La and eastern Bhutan. The dzong is about 60m square and the only gate is on the south side.

The utse is three storeys high and behind the usual prayer wheels around the outside there is a line of more than 300 fine slate carvings with painted faces depicting saints and philosophers. The large central figure in the central lhakhang is of Sakyamuni; he is flanked by images of eight Bodhisattvas: Jampelyang, Channa Dorji, Chenresig, Jampa, and the less familiar Sai Hingpo (Shritigarva), Dupa Nampasel, Namkhe Hingpo (Akash Garva) and Kuentu Zangpo. The paintings inside this lhakhang are said to be some of the oldest and most beautiful in Bhutan. One of the lhakhangs, Gen Khang, may be visited only by the lamas. In the west lhakhang chapel are paintings of Chenresig, green and white Taras and an early painting of Shabdrung Ngawang Namgyal, which was restored and cleaned in 1995. Large paintings of mandalas and the guardians of the four directions adorn the *gorikha* (veranda).

During its construction Simtokha Dzong was attacked by a coalition of Tibetans and five Bhutanese lamas who were opposed to the Shabdrung's rule. The attack was repelled and the leader of the coalition, Palden Lama, was killed. In 1630 the Tibetans again attacked and took control of the dzong. The Shabdrung regained control when the main building caught fire and the roof collapsed, killing the invaders. Descriptions of the original Simtokha Dzong were provided by the two Portuguese Jesuit priests who visited here in 1629 on their way to Tibet.

Expansion and restoration of the dzong was performed by the third Druk Desi, Mingyur Tenpa, in the 1670s after Tibetan invaders attacked it in 1630. It has been enlarged and restored many times since.

DAY WALKS
In addition to the walks to Tango Goemba and Cheri Goemba (described earlier), there are good walks to monasteries and lookout points near Thimphu. You cannot go into the monasteries, but most are architecturally interesting and command good views of the valley. The Royal Society for Protection of Nature (RSPN) has published *Mild and Mad Day Hikes Around Thimphu* by Piet

van der Poel & Rogier Gruys, with details of 27 hikes as well as numerous alternatives and side trips. As the title suggests, the hikes range from easy walks to the 25km Thimphu to Paro 'Punishment Trail.' It is important to remember that many of these hikes pass meditation cells near monasteries. Don't shout, disturb them or knock on the door to ask for directions. You can download a preview of the book from W www.bhutan-trails.org.

Walks to Nearby Goembas
Talakha Goemba The 15th-century Talakha Goemba (3080m) offers spectacular views of the Bhutan Himalaya and Thimphu valley. It used to be possible to walk here from Simtokha Dzong, but many of the apple orchards along the route have been fenced in, making this walk impossible. You can drive here on a rough road that turns quite muddy when it's wet, or better yet, drive part way and then set out on foot. From the small goemba you can make a strenuous six- to nine-hour hike up to the 4280m Talakha peak.

Drolay Goemba It's a two- to three-hour round trip from the parking lot below Tango Goemba to Drolay Goemba at 3400m. The walk offers amazing views of the Thimphu valley and you can combine it with a walk to Tango Goemba.

Lungchuzekha Goemba The best easy walk in the area is a three- to four-hour round trip from Dochu La to Lungchuzekha Goemba. It affords excellent views of the Bhutan Himalaya and you can return via the same route or descend to Trashigang Goemba and Hongtsho.

Phajoding Goemba It is a 5km walk uphill from the youth centre in Motithang to Phajoding Goemba (3640m), a large monastic complex with 10 lhakhangs and 15 monastic residences, many of them used for extended meditation retreats. It was founded in the 13th century by Togden Pajo, a yogi from Tibet, who was searching for a place of meditation. Most of the buildings were constructed in 1748 through the efforts of Shakya Rinchen, the ninth Je Khenpo, whose image is the central figure in the main Khangzang Lhakhang here. The monastic school is housed in the Jampa Lhakhang and offers a more secluded environment than the Dechen Phodrang School in Thimphu.

From Phajoding you can ascend another 300m to **Thujidrag Goemba**. This is the last day of the Druk Path Trek in reverse. See the Trekking chapter for details of the walk.

Thadranang Goemba Another strenuous two-hour uphill hike leads to Thadranang Goemba (3270m). Start at the Yangchenphug High School and climb steeply up the ridge through a blue-pine forest.

Trashigang Goemba It's two hours from the hillside below Hongtsho to Trashigang

Goemba (3200m). This goemba was built in 1786 by the 12th Je Khenpo. It is an important meditation centre, and there are numerous small houses for pilgrims near the goemba. In addition to about 16 monks, there are a few *anims* (nuns). Inside the lhakhang there are statues of several Je Khenpos who meditated here.

Wangditse Goemba A one-hour walk uphill from the telecom tower takes you to Wangditse Goemba, which was founded in 1750 by the attendants of Bhutan's eighth desi, Druk Rabgye, and was renovated in 2001. The lhakhang houses the statues of the guardian deities Yeshey Goenpo (Mahakala), Palden Lhamo (Mahakali) and Tsheringma (the goddess of longevity). See the boxed text 'Protective Deities' in the Facts about Bhutan chapter for more details.

Western Bhutan

Whether you arrive by air at Paro or by road at Phuentsholing, your first impression of Bhutan is one of stepping into a world that you thought existed only in storybooks or your imagination. Western Bhutan is the heartland of the Drukpa people, and here you are confronted with the largest, oldest and most spectacular *dzongs* in the kingdom. You will soon realise you are well off the beaten path of world tourism and far away from whichever culture you call home.

The rugged Black Mountain range forms a barrier that separates western Bhutan from the rest of the country.

There are three major river systems in western Bhutan: the Torsa Chhu in the south-west, the Wang Chhu in the west and the Puna Tsang Chhu to the east. The Wang Chhu and Puna Tsang Chhu are separated by a range of hills that extends from the Tibetan border in the north to the Indian border in the south. The only road across this range traverses the Dochu La at an elevation of 3140m, between Thimphu and Punakha.

Two major rivers join to form the Wang Chhu, each with its own large and long valley. The Paro valley extends from Jhomolhari on the Tibetan border all the way to Chhuzom, the confluence of the Paro Chhu and Wang Chhu. A side valley leads to the Tremo La, the 5000m pass that was once an important trade route to Tibet and was also the route of several Tibetan invasions. The Haa Chhu flows from the head of the steep, isolated Haa valley to join the Wang Chhu as it flows through a deep gorge below Chapcha.

The Puna Tsang Chhu is formed by the joining of the Pho Chhu and the much larger Mo Chhu at Punakha. The river then flows south, passing below Wangdue Phodrang and exiting Bhutan at the small border town of Kalikhola.

The Torsa Chhu cuts across the far south-west of the country, flowing from

Highlights

- Visit the spectacular *dzongs* of Paro, Wangdue Phodrang and Punakha.

- Admire the mountain views on an early morning drive to Dochu La, or drive west of Paro to catch a glimpse of Jhomolhari, Bhutan's most sacred mountain.

- Immerse yourself in Bhutanese culture and history, encapsulated in Paro's National Museum.

- Visit the remote Phobjikha valley to see the black-necked cranes.

! All Bhutanese Internet and email addresses have changed, see page 86.

Tibet into Bhutan, forming a valley south of Haa, then flowing out of Bhutan near Phuentsholing.

History

The history of western Bhutan is reflected in the history of Bhutan as a whole. Punakha was the capital of a unified Bhutan from the 17th to the 19th century. The seat of government was later moved to Paro, which became the commercial, cultural and political centre of the country. Before the construction of roads, most of Bhutan's trade came through Paro, either from Tibet via the Tremo La or from the south via Haa and the Cheli La.

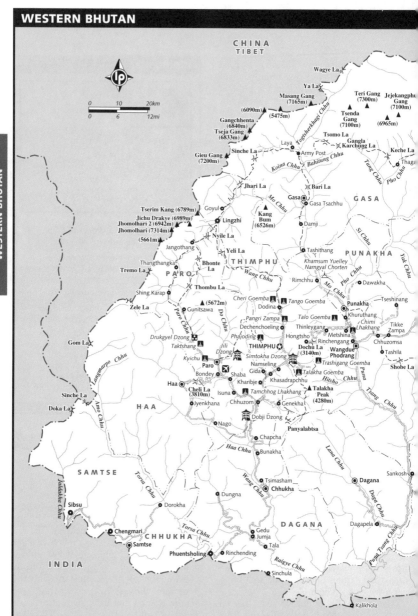

Paro Dzongkhag

Willow trees line many of the roads, contrasting with the bright green of the rice terraces and the brilliant white of the dzongs and temples to give the valley a fresh look and pleasant atmosphere. The broad Paro valley is excellent agricultural land and the people of Paro are better off than many elsewhere in Bhutan. One indication of their affluence is the preponderance of metal roofs throughout the valley, which have replaced the traditional wooden shingles.

There is quite a large Japanese-assisted agricultural project in the valley. One of its aims was to line much of the area between the airport and Paro town with an embankment that protects the valley from flooding and damage by the Paro Chhu. Another was the construction of an unpaved road along the upper portion of the valley, designed to allow farmers to move tractors into their fields. Among the important crops here, in addition to both red and white rice, are apples, strawberries and asparagus.

A high ridge separates the Paro valley from the Haa valley to the south. A road crosses this ridge via the 3810m Cheli La. To the north of Paro a gravel road follows another valley formed by the Do Chhu. On the eastern side of the Do Chhu valley, a series of high ridges separates Paro from the Thimphu valley. The Druk Path trek follows these ridges, crossing a 4200m pass before descending to Thimphu.

Several other treks begin in or near Paro. The Jhomolhari, Laya-Gasa and Snowman treks all lead west from Drukgyel Dzong to Jhomolhari base camp and then wind their way through Lingzhi and beyond (see the Trekking chapter for details).

PARO
☎ 08

The town of Paro (2280m) lies in the centre of the valley on the banks of the Paro Chhu and is a short distance north-west of Paro Dzong.

Orientation

The town centre, built in 1985, is aligned along a wide street about 500m long that parallels the river in a roughly north-west to south-east direction. The road from Chhuzom and the airport enters the town from the south, then makes a left turn at a T-junction into the main street near the archery ground.

Central Paro is littered with shops and video stalls as well as eating and drinking places of varying standards. There's a grass area that forms a town square. Around the square are more shops and a few hotels, handicraft shops and restaurants. Many of the shops have doors at the back; a strange ladder system provides access through the front window. At the south-east end of the square is the large white Chhoeten Lhakhang and behind it is the Sunday market. The petrol station, bus station and police post mark the western limits of the town proper. If you follow the main street south-east instead of turning south towards the airport, you'll reach the archery ground, Ugyen Pelri Palace, the head office of Druk Air and the covered bridge to the massive structure of Paro Dzong. An unusual local regulation prohibits bicycle riding within Paro town.

Downstream from the dzong is a large complex housing the National Institute of Education, one of two teacher-training institutes in the country. The other is in Samtse, in the south-west of Bhutan.

Information

Money The Bank of Bhutan (☎ 271230), underneath the Sonam Trophel Restaurant, is open 9am to 1pm Monday to Friday and 9am to 11am Saturday.

Post & Communications Paro's post office is on a corner near the petrol station. There are several shops offering services as public call offices (PCOs).

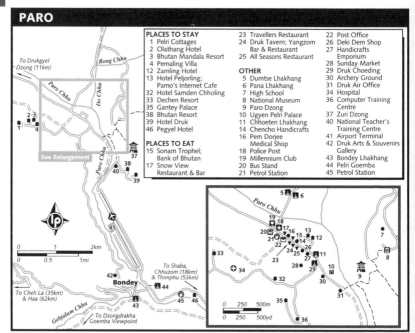

PARO

PLACES TO STAY
1 Pelri Cottages
2 Olathang Hotel
3 Bhutan Mandala Resort
4 Pemaling Villa
12 Zamling Hotel
13 Hotel Peljorling;
   Pamo's Internet Cafe
32 Hotel Samden Chholing
33 Dechen Resort
35 Gantey Palace
38 Bhutan Resort
39 Hotel Druk
46 Pegyel Hotel

PLACES TO EAT
15 Sonam Trophel;
   Bank of Bhutan
17 Snow View
   Restaurant & Bar

23 Travellers Restaurant
24 Druk Tavern; Yangzom
   Bar & Restaurant
25 All Seasons Restaurant

OTHER
5 Dumtse Lhakhang
6 Pana Lhakhang
7 High School
8 National Museum
9 Paro Dzong
10 Ugyen Pelri Palace
11 Chhoeten Lhakhang
14 Chencho Handicrafts
16 Pem Dorjee
   Medical Shop
18 Police Post
19 Millennium Club
20 Bus Stand
21 Petrol Station

22 Post Office
26 Deki Dem Shop
27 Handicrafts
   Emporium
28 Sunday Market
29 Druk Choeding
30 Archery Ground
31 Druk Air Office
34 Hospital
36 Computer Training
   Centre
37 Zuri Dzong
40 National Teacher's
   Training Centre
41 Airport Terminal
42 Druk Arts & Souvenirs
   Gallery
43 Bondey Lhakhang
44 Pelri Goemba
45 Petrol Station

For Internet access, Computer Training Centre (☎ 02-271954, ⓔ khandu@druknet .net.bt), near the turn-off to Gangte Palace Hotel, charges Nu 4 per minute. Pamo's Internet Cafe (☎ 02-271365, ⓔ langado@ druknet.net.bt), in the Hotel Peljorling on the town square, charges Nu 3 per minute and serves snacks, including hamburgers for Nu 40.

Medical Services Paro's large hospital (☎ 271571) is on a hill to the west of town, and will accept visitors in cases of emergency. The Pem Dorjee Medical Store on the main street stocks basic medical supplies.

Paro Dzong

The Paro Dzong is one of Bhutan's most impressive and well-known dzongs, and the finest example of Bhutanese architecture you'll see. The inward-sloping walls form a massive structure that towers over the town and is visible as a great white monolith from vantage points throughout the valley.

The dzong's correct name, Rinchen Pung Dzong, means 'fortress on a heap of jewels'. This is usually contracted to Rinpung Dzong. In 1644 Shabdrung Ngawang Namgyal ordered the construction of the dzong on the foundation of a monastery built by Guru Rinpoche. One of Bhutan's strongest and most important fortresses, it was used on numerous occasions to defend the Paro valley from invasions by Tibet. John Claude White reported that in 1905 there were old catapults for throwing great stones stored in the rafters of the dzong's veranda.

The dzong survived the 1897 earthquake and caught fire only once, in 1907. The fire severely damaged the dzong, and it was rebuilt the following year. Large statues of Sakyamuni, Guru Rinpoche and Shabdrung Ngawang Namgyal were installed during the reconstruction. The dzong was formerly the meeting hall for the National Assembly and now houses a monastic school and district government offices.

The dzong is built on a steep hillside, and the courtyard of the administrative section is 6m higher than the courtyard of the monastic portion. Though a bridge leads to the foot of the dzong, the only entrance is from the hillside on the north wall. A road climbs the hill to the dzong's entrance, which leads into the *dochey* (courtyard) on the 3rd storey. The *utse* (central tower) inside the dochey is five storeys tall and was built in the time of the first *penlop* (regional governor, literally 'lord-teacher') of Paro in 1649. There are two *lhakhangs* (temples) on the utse's top storey which have excellent wood carvings on the beams. To the east of the utse is another small lhakhang dedicated to Chuchizhey, an 11-headed manifestation of Chenresig.

A stairway leads down to the monastic quarter, which houses about 200 monks. In the south-east corner is the *kunre*, which is where the monks eat their communal meals. Numerous paintings adorn the walls in front of this structure, including an unusual Bhutanese mystic spiral interpretation of a *mandala* (cosmic diagram). On the opposite side of the monastic dochey is the large *dukhang* (assembly hall). The paintings on the porch of this building depict the life of Milarepa.

Outside the dzong, to the north-east of the entrance, are the archery competition field and a stone-paved area where the dancers perform the Paro tsechu (a *tsechu* is a series of dances in honour of Guru Rinpoche) each spring. A *thondrol* (huge *thangka*) more than 18m square is unfurled early in the morning on the final day of the tsechu. It depicts Guru Rinpoche as the central figure. It was commissioned in the 18th century by the eighth *desi* (secular ruler of Bhutan, also known as *druk desi*), Chhogyel Sherab Wangchuck, and survived the 1907 fire.

Scenes from the 1995 film *Little Buddha* were filmed in Paro Dzong. You may recall that at the end of this film three incarnations of the same bodhisattva were discovered, a phenomenon similar to the body, speech and mind incarnations of both Shabdrung Ngawang Namgyal and Pema Lingpa.

West of the dzong, a traditional wooden covered bridge called **Nyamai Zam** spans the Paro Chhu. This is a reconstruction of the original bridge, which was washed away in a flood in 1969. Earlier versions of this bridge were removed in time of war to protect the dzong. You can walk from the parking area near Ugyen Pelri Palace across the bridge to the outside walls of the dzong. The most famous pictures of Paro Dzong are taken from the west bank of the river, just downstream from the bridge.

National Museum

At the top of the hill above Paro Dzong is an old structure that was renovated in 1968 to house the National Museum, also known as Ta Dzong (*☎ 271257; admission Nu 25; open 9am-4pm Tues-Sat, 11am-4pm Sun, closed Mon & national holidays*). This unusual round building is said to be in the shape of a conch shell; it was completed in 1656 and was originally the *ta dzong* (watchtower) of Paro Dzong. There is a specific route to follow through the entire building that ensures that you walk clockwise around important images. Cameras are not allowed inside the museum. The museum is a local, as well as a tourist, attraction. When you visit you may be accompanied by Bhutanese from remote villages or groups of school children on an outing.

The museum is managed by the National Commission for Cultural Affairs (NCCA), which has rearranged the exhibitions with help from Unesco and other sources. There are six floors of galleries, each with a special emphasis.

Among the exhibits is a spectacular collection of thangkas, both ancient and modern. Of particular importance are thangkas depicting Shabdrung Ngawang Namgyal, the first Je Khenpo (Chief Abbot of Bhutan) and the first druk desi. Other thangkas portray all of Bhutan's important saints and teachers.

There is a display of Bhutan's extensive philatelic collection on the top floor. At the end of the gallery a doorway leads to the **Tshogshing Lhakhang**, the Temple of the Tree of Wisdom, which was built between 1965 and 1968.

The centrepiece of this temple is a complex four-sided carving depicting the history of Buddhism and its propagation. On one side are Sakyamuni and the great teacher Atisha, representing the Sakya school. On the next is Gelug, a disciple of the Dalai Lama, and Dagpo Lhaje, representing the Gelug lineage. Another side represents the Nyingma lineage, with Guru Rinpoche as the centrepiece, and on the final side is Drukpa Kagyu with figures of Vajra Dhara, Marpa, Milarepa and the Indian teachers Naropa and Tilopa.

Remove your shoes before entering the temple and walk clockwise around the room.

Other galleries include ancient bronze and stone objects, an exquisite collection of bronze statues and a display of ancient weapons and shields, many captured during various Tibetan invasions. There are stuffed animals, old and new household objects, jewellery and decorative arts on the lower floors.

There is said to be an underground tunnel that leads from the watchtower to the water supply below. You can walk down a path from the museum to the dzong and back to the town, enjoying good views of the valley and of Ugyen Pelri Palace.

Ugyen Pelri Palace

Ugyen Pelri Palace is in a secluded wooded compound on the south side of the river just west of the dzong. This palace was built by the Paro penlop, Tshering Penjor, in the early 1900s and is now a residence of the queen mother. It is designed after Guru Rinpoche's celestial paradise, Zangto Pelri, and is one of the most beautiful examples of Bhutanese architecture.

On the road beside Ugyen Pelri Palace are five square *chortens* that were built in memory of the first king, Ugyen Wangchuck. Monks will remind you if you forget to walk to the left of these chortens.

Chhoeten Lhakhang

Chhoeten Lhakhang, a large Bhutanese-style chorten, is south of the town square. The caretaker may allow you to visit the upstairs chapel.

Druk Choeding

Also known as Tshongdoe Naktshang, Druk Choeding is the town temple. It was built in 1525 by Ngawang Chhogyel

(1465–1540), one of the prince-abbots of Ralung in Tibet and an ancestor of the Shabdrung Ngawang Namgyal.

Dumtse Lhakhang

To the west of the road is Dumtse Lhakhang, a chorten-like temple that is closed to tourists. This unusual building was built in 1433 by the iron bridge builder Thangtong Gyalpo (see the boxed text 'The Iron Bridge Builder' later in this chapter). It has three floors representing hell, earth and heaven and the paintings inside are said to be some of the best in Bhutan.

Beyond Dumtse Lhakhang, to the east of the road, the tiny **Pana Lhakhang** is quite old and is believed to have been built in the seventh century.

Places to Stay

Paro is one of the most scenic valleys in Bhutan, and many hotels offer panoramic views. Most of the hotels were built before the town was developed, therefore all of Paro's best accommodation is in resort-style hotels throughout the valley, not in the town itself. All hotels charge 10% tax and 10% service on the rates given, and most increase their rates significantly during the time of the Paro Tsechu in the spring. Many hotels stage dance performances around a campfire when there are enough guests to warrant it.

Top End *Hotel Druk (☎ 271386, 271458, fax 271513)* Singles/doubles Nu 1800/2300. This 52-room hotel is part of the Druk Hotel chain. It's built in the style of a dzong and dominates the top of a hillock to the east of the airport. It has the requisite bar, restaurant and gift shop and a conference hall that is sometimes used by Indian groups. The health club has a hot-stone bath and sauna.

Olathang Hotel (☎ 271304, 271305, fax 271454, e ohotel@druknet.net.bt) Singles/doubles Nu 1625/2000, cottages Nu 2125/2500. This Bhutan Tourism Corporation Limited (BTCL) establishment is on the opposite side of the valley. It is a cavernous dzong-like stone structure with a stuffed tiger and yak guarding the entrance to the conference hall. In the main building there are 24 rooms and

six suites with elaborate Victorian furniture. The Olathang was built in 1974 for guests invited to the coronation of the present king and has abundant Bhutan decor. For comfortable facilities in a traditional setting, ask to stay in one of the 22 well-appointed wooden cottages. Each cottage has a television, phone, electric heater and a balcony overlooking the Paro valley.

Kichu Resort (☎ 271468, fax 271466, e intkichu@druknet.net.bt) Singles/doubles Nu 1500/2000, deluxe singles/doubles Nu 1875/2500. About 3km up the valley from Paro town is this collection of stone buildings on the banks of Paro Chhu. The central building houses a restaurant, bar, gift shop and conference hall. This hotel is popular with Indian tourists as well as Bhutanese and expats from Thimphu looking for a weekend getaway. It's owned by International Trekkers, which also operates the Kichu Resort in Wangdue Phodrang.

Tigers Nest Resort (Eye of the Tiger; ☎ 271310, fax 271640) Singles/doubles Nu 750/850. Just past the turn-off to Taktshang, this resort offers a view of the reconstructed Taktshang Goemba (see Around Paro, later) and, on clear days, the snowcapped peak of Jhomolhari. It has 15 rooms, all with private facilities, in four cottages. It also has a hot-stone bath, which costs extra.

Bhutan Resort (☎ 271609, 271989, fax 271728, e lama@druknet.net.bt) Singles/doubles Nu 1800/2000. This hotel, a short distance below Hotel Druk, is a new collection of 10 cottages, each containing two double rooms. Each room overlooks Paro valley and has a television and phone.

Bhutan Mandala Resort (☎ 271997) Singles/doubles Nu 1000/1500. A steep paved road winds its way up to Paro's newest hotel, a 12-room facility below the Olathang Hotel. Each room has a balcony, and the dining room offers a great view of the valley. There's an Internet facility and the owners are making an effort to provide a home stay–style experience.

Mid-Range *Dechen Resort (☎/fax 271392, e dchncot@druknet.net.bt)* Singles/doubles Nu 1300/1700. This 15-room hotel, in a secluded area below the road, is a favourite with expats. Each room has a phone and television and the Indian food in the restaurant is the best in Bhutan. There is a good view of the dzong and the lower part of the valley.

Gantey Palace *(☎ 271301, 271452)* Singles/doubles Nu 1300/1500. With 19 double rooms, Gantey Palace is housed in a 19th-century, traditional palace-style building that was once the residence of the penlop of Paro. The rooms are comfortable, although not as exotic as the rest of the building, but you can get a more traditional flavour by spurning the shower and arranging for a hot-stone bath. The hotel is on a low hill overlooking the town and was renovated in 1997. Outside the gate is the small Gangten Lhakhang.

Pemaling Villa *(☎ 271473)* Singles/doubles Nu 700/1112. With eight double rooms overlooking the valley, this smaller facility closes in the monsoon season; if you're planning to stay here, call ahead to book.

Pegyel Hotel *(☎ 271472)* Singles/doubles Nu 1200/1500. With 15 double rooms, this hotel is in a rural setting among rice fields in Shaba, 9km from Paro town.

Hotel Samden Chholing *(☎ 271449, fax 271826)* Singles/doubles Nu 1200/1400. Opened in 1999, the 14-room Samden Chholing is the closest hotel to town. You can follow your hot-stone bath with drinks or dinner on a terrace overlooking Paro.

Pelri Cottages *(☎ 271683)* Singles/doubles Nu 1400/1600. A recent addition to Paro's hotel scene, Pelri has 18 rooms in a group of cement tin-roofed buildings on a hill above the Olathang Hotel.

Budget There are several small hotels that cater to Bhutanese near the town square, including the ***Hotel Welcome*** *(☎ 271845)*, ***Hotel Rinpung*** *(☎ 271709)* and ***Hotel Yangzom*** *(☎271366)*. There are lots of barking dogs in Paro; expect to pay Nu 250/350 for singles/doubles in a noisy room in any of these places.

Hotel Peljorling *(☎ 271365)* Singles/doubles Nu 700/800. Operated by the same group as the Peljorling in Phuentsholing, this three-room hotel and restaurant is in the centre of town.

Zamling Hotel *(☎ 271302)* Singles/doubles 250/400. There are only five rooms here, all with private bathroom.

Places to Eat

In addition to the hotels, Paro has some good restaurants and bars. The ***Sonam Trophel*** *(☎ 271287)*, upstairs over the Bank of Bhutan, has excellent food and is popular with Japanese volunteers working in Paro. *Momos* (dumplings) are a speciality at Nu 25 to 40 and it advertises that it doesn't use *aji na moto* (MSG).

If you've just arrived on Druk Air and want lunch before driving to Thimphu try the ***Druk Tavern*** *(☎ 271821)*, which caters to tourist groups with well-prepared food, including a fixed lunch for Nu 230.

Downstairs is the ***Yangzom Bar & Restaurant*** *(☎ 272016)*, a clean restaurant patronised mostly by locals. Two other good restaurants that are both upstairs over shops along the main street, are ***Travellers Restaurant*** *(☎ 271896)* and ***All Seasons Restaurant*** *(☎ 271665)*.

The restaurant in the ***Zamling Hotel*** offers basic rice and curry. At the western end of town, near the petrol station, is the ***Jachung Milk Bakery*** (*jachung* means 'garuda'), where you can load up on bread and pastries.

The ***Snow View Restaurant & Bar*** at the north end of town offers fried chillies and other Bhutanese versions of fast food and is a favourite eating spot for the monks from the dzong.

For a real taste of Bhutan, arrange to have a meal at ***Maikha-Nemjo*** *(☎ 02-323949, 08-271704, **e** deki_y@hotmail.com)*, a rural house in rice fields west of Paro. You will need to book ahead for lunch (Nu 200) or dinner (Nu 300), served farmhouse style on wooden plates.

Entertainment

The local entertainment scene in Paro centres around the ***Millennium Club*** *(☎ 271934)*, west of the Paro Chhu bridge. The disco is open 10pm onwards only on Saturday. There's also a health club with a locally built sauna and steam room.

STAN ARMINGTON

IZZET KERIBAR

If arriving by land from India, your first view of Bhutan will be framed by the ornate gateway into the border town of Phuentsholing; if arriving by air, rice fields will border your road trip between Paro airport and Thimphu.

The strategically situated Punakha Dzong is the winter residence of the Dratshang, the central monk body

Due to the efforts of the local administrator, the main street of Wangdue Phodrang is spotlessly clean

With its distinctive yellow roof, Gangte Goemba sits amid chalet-style houses above Phobjikha valley.

Shopping

Shops in Paro are open every day. There are numerous handicraft shops throughout the valley. *Chencho Handicrafts (☎ 271633)* is on the corner of the town square and the government-run *Handicrafts Emporium (☎ 271211)* open 9am to 6pm daily, is on the main street. Further down the street is *Deki Dem Shop*, marked by a row of colourful prayer wheels, where prayer flags, incense and other religious items are sold. *Gyelt-shen Tailor Shop* has a selection of mounted thangkas and other Buddhist accoutrements. *Druk Arts & Souvenirs Gallery (☎ 271232)* is in Woochu, near the Bondey bridge.

Getting There & Away

Paro airport is 7km from Paro town and 53km from Thimphu. If you have not arranged for a vehicle to meet your flight, you can book a taxi at the tea stall outside the airport. The cost is Nu 300 to Paro or Nu 800 to Thimphu.

AROUND PARO
West of Paro

Though the valley extends west all the way to the peaks on the Tibetan border, the road only goes as far as Drukgyel Dzong, 11km beyond Paro. The road leads north-west out of town past the Sonam Pelkhil sawmill, then turns in a westerly direction, following quite close to the river. The route is lined with willow trees and there are rice fields and many houses to the south of the road.

Kyichu Lhakhang A short distance south of the road is Kyichu Lhakhang. This temple is said to have been built in 659 by King Songtsen Gampo of Tibet. It holds down the left foot of an ogress whose body is so large that it covers Bhutan and most of eastern Tibet (see the boxed text).

The original building was rebuilt after a fire with a large statue of Sakyamuni as the central figure. Additional buildings were constructed in 1839 by the penlop of Paro and the 25th Je Khenpo. A large statue of Chenresig with 11 heads and 1000 hands was added at that time, as well as a golden roof.

The queen mother, Ashi Kesang, sponsored the construction of a new temple in 1968. This lhakhang contains a 5m-high statue of Guru Rinpoche and another of Tara, who represents one of the wives of King Songtsen Gampo. There is also a statue of the iron bridge builder Thangtong Gyalpo (see the boxed text 'The Iron Bridge Builder' later in this chapter), and another of Dilgo Khyentse Rinpoche, a

WESTERN BHUTAN

The Ogress in Tibet

The Tibetan king Songtsen Gampo married the Chinese princess Wencheng in 641. A part of her dowry was a statue called Jowo, which was an Indian image of the Buddha, Sakyamuni, as a small boy. As the statue was being transported through Lhasa, it became stuck in the mud and could not be moved. The princess divined that the problem was being caused by a huge supine ogress (also referred to as a demoness) lying on her back with her navel in the place where Lhasa's cathedral, the Jokhang, now stands.

In 659 the king decided to build 108 temples in a single day to pin the ogress to the earth forever and, at the same time, convert the Tibetan people to Buddhism. The head of the ogress was to the east, and her legs were to the west, so temples were constructed at the shoulders and hips, which corresponded to the four districts of central Tibet. The knees and elbows of the demoness were in the provinces, which were also duly pinned and the people converted. The arms and legs lay in the borderlands of Tibet, and several temples were built in Bhutan to pin down the left leg.

The best known of these temples are Kyichu Lhakhang in Paro, which holds the left foot, and Jampa Lhakhang in Bumthang, which pins the left knee. Other lesser-known temples were also built throughout Tibet and Bhutan. Many of these have been destroyed, but it is believed that, among others, Konchogsum Lhakhang in Bumthang, Khaine Lhakhang south of Lhuentse, and two temples in Haa may have been part of this ambitious project.

revered Nyingma Buddhist master who passed away in 1992.

On a side road is **Drongja Goemba**, where Dilgo Khyentse Rinpoche was cremated, and a royal guesthouse. The unpaved Japanese-funded road that traverses the edge of the valley ends here. High on the hill on the opposite side of the valley, Tsacho Chuko monastery is visible; below it is a small private *goemba*.

Taktshang Goemba Taktshang is the most famous of Bhutan's monasteries, perched on the side of a cliff 900m above the floor of Paro valley, where the only sounds are the murmurs of wind and water and the chanting of monks. The name means 'tiger's nest'; the Guru is said to have flown to the site of the monastery on the back of a tigress. He then meditated in a cave here for three months.

On 19 April 1998 a fire destroyed the main structure of Taktshang and all its contents. It had already suffered a previous fire and was repaired in 1951. Reconstruction

started on an auspicious day in April 2000 and authentic replicas of the original structures have been built.

The site has long been recognised as a holy place. It was visited by Shabdrung Ngawang Namgyal in 1646 and pilgrims from all over Bhutan come here. Milarepa is also said to have meditated here, while Thangtong Gyalpo revealed a *terma* (treasure text) at Taktshang. The primary lhakhang was built in 1692 around the Dubkhang (also called the Pelphug), the holy cave in which Guru Rinpoche meditated, by the penlop of Paro, Gees Tenzi Rabgye. There are several other buildings in the complex. **Phorbu Lhakhang** contains a *phorbu*, the three-bladed ritual dagger used to stab demons. Above the main temple complex is **Ugyen Tshemo Lhakhang**, and higher still is another goemba, named **Zangto Pelri** after Guru Rinpoche's heavenly abode.

The Hike to Taktshang The monastery itself is closed to tourists except by special

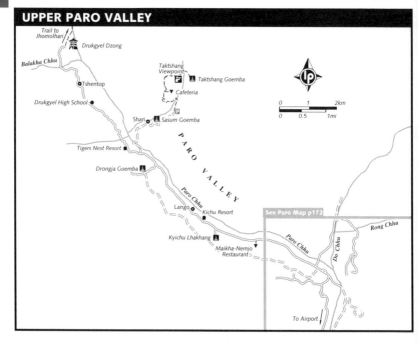

UPPER PARO VALLEY

Trail to Jhomolhari

Drukgyel Dzong

Balakha Chhu

Tshentop

Drukgyel High School

Taktshang Viewpoint

Taktshang Goemba

Cafeteria

Shari

Sasum Goemba

Tigers Nest Resort

Drongja Goemba

PARO VALLEY

Paro Chhu

Lango

Kichu Resort

See Paro Map p172

Rong Chhu

Kyichu Lhakhang

Maikha-Nemjo Restaurant

Paro Chhu

Do Chhu

To Airport

0   1   2km
0   0.5   1mi

permit. However, the one-hour walk to the viewpoint where there is a small wooden teahouse, improbably named a cafeteria, provides a close-up view of the monastery. Allow about 1½ hours for the round trip, including a rest stop at the viewpoint. This hike is a major part of any tourist itinerary and is very worthwhile for the spectacular view and historical interest. It's also a good warm-up hike if you are going trekking.

A new road that was built to aid the reconstruction climbs 3km to a new trailhead at 2600m elevation. To get to the viewpoint, follow the unpaved road that begins 8km north of Paro. The road descends to the Paro Chhu, crosses on a bridge at 2385m and switchbacks uphill through blue pine forests past the settlement of **Shari** and the small **Sasum Goemba**. The drive continues past the construction site and the foot of a cableway to a large parking area.

From the parking area the trail climbs through blue pines, then switchbacks steeply up the ridge. Wear a hat; there is little shade once you leave the trees, and the sun is intense. If you have just flown into Paro, walk slowly because the elevation is above 2600m and you are likely to become breathless because of the altitude. Once you reach the ridge there are excellent views across the valley. The village to the south-west is Drukgyel; you can see the large school below the village and the army camp above it. After a climb of about one hour and a gain of 300m from the parking lot you will reach a small chorten and some prayer flags on the ridge. Be watchful here as the trail crosses an archery ground. It's then a short, level walk to the cafeteria at 2940m, which consists of a few buildings with wood-shingle roofs. You can sit in front of the building and admire the monastery as you drink the tea that your guide will arrange. The cafeteria also serves full meals; if you arrange your schedule accordingly, you can have breakfast or lunch here.

Most visitors return downhill from this viewpoint, making the downhill trip in about half an hour. The trail to Taktshang itself continues up from the chorten on the ridge. If you have time and are feeling fit,

continue for another 45 minutes uphill through the trees, bearing right at all obvious trail junctions. This will bring you to a spectacular lookout at 3140m that is at about the same level as the monastery. From this vantage point Taktshang looks like it is growing out of the rocks. It seems almost close enough to touch, but it's on the far side of a deep chasm, about 150m away. If you descend past the police checkpoint you will reach a second viewpoint where a cable crosses the deep chasm in front of the monastery. The cable is used to carry heavy goods and construction material across the chasm, because the trail between here and the goemba is very narrow and exposed. You can continue on the narrow trail to the entrance to the goemba, but if you don't have a permit to visit Taktshang this is as far as you should go.

Drukgyel Village Beyond Taktshang, 11km from Paro, is the farming village of Drukgyel. Below the road is the large Drukgyel High School, which was built as part of a British aid project. Above the road is a Royal Bhutan Army (RBA) facility.

Beyond Drukgyel village there are army training camps scattered in the bushes and pine forests. Further on are the houses of Tshentop village, which is inhabited by people from the valley of Haa.

Drukgyel Dzong At the end of the road, 14km from Paro, stand the ruins of Drukgyel Dzong. This dzong was built in 1649 by Shabdrung Ngawang Namgyal in a location chosen for its control of the route to Tibet. The dzong was named 'Druk' (Bhutan) 'gyel' (victory) to commemorate the victory of Bhutan over Tibetan invaders in 1644. One of the features of the dzong was a false entrance that was designed to lure invaders into an enclosed courtyard. This is said to have worked successfully during the second attack by Tibetan invaders in 1648.

The dzong sits at the point where the trail from Tibet via the Tremo La enters the Paro valley. Once the Tibetan invasions ceased, this became a major trade route between Bhutan and the Tibetan town of Phari. A

WESTERN BHUTAN

small amount of informal trade continues to the present day. On a clear day there is a spectacular view of **Jhomolhari** from the area near the dzong.

Drukgyel Dzong was featured on the cover of the US *National Geographic* magazine when an article was published about Bhutan by John Claude White in 1914. The building was used as an administrative centre until 1951, when a fire caused by a butter lamp destroyed it.

Now the dzong is in ruins and is closed to all visitors. There have been a few attempts at renovation, but all that has been accomplished is the installation of some props to keep the roof of the five-storey main structure from collapsing. You can walk up a short path into the front courtyard of the dzong. On the way up you can see the remains of the large towers and the tunnel that was used to obtain water from the stream below during a long siege.

North of Paro

Passing Dumtse Lhakhang, the wide bridge built by the Japanese in 1995 leads to the Do Chhu valley. A paved road leads uphill to the junior high school, the entrance to the dzong and the National Museum.

South-East of Paro

The road that leads south-east from Paro is the main exit from the valley and leads to the confluence at Chhuzom, 24km from Paro and 18km from Bondey.

Paro to Bondey Just south of Paro is the settlement of Taju, which has a bank and telephone exchange. The road passes above the airport and then past **Kahangkhu Lhakhang** to Bondey, which straddles the Paro Chhu to the east of the airport.

Beyond the intersection of the road to Cheli La and Haa in Bondey is the 400-year-old **Bondey Lhakhang**. On the north side of the Paro Chhu one road leads west to the airport and another follows the valley south-west to Chhuzom. Above the north side of the bridge is the small Pelri Goemba and in the village is an unusual round chorten-shaped temple.

A bumpy, unpaved road leads west from Bondey to some houses and fields and the small, recently constructed Changchi Lhakhang. A walk or drive up this road affords a view of **Dzongdrakha Goemba**, four sets of buildings and a large white chorten hanging on the side of a cliff.

Cheli La The 35km drive to Cheli La makes an interesting road excursion and is an excellent jumping-off point for day walks. From the pass at 3810m there are views of Jhomolhari as well as down to the Haa valley. One of Bhutan's designated treks is a walk from Bondey to Cheli La, a 1500m elevation gain, followed by a trek downhill to Drukgyel Dzong.

PARO TO THIMPHU

The journey from Paro to Thimphu is 53km long. The road traverses rice fields, then climbs high above the river, providing a great view of Paro airport far below. It then descends to Bondey and crosses the Paro Chhu near the entrance to the airport.

Bondey to Chhuzom
18km • ½ hour

If you're coming from the airport you'll first reach the settlement of Bondey, where there are some lovely old traditional Bhutanese houses.

About 3km from Bondey is **Shaba**, a small settlement with an army camp. At Isuna, 12km from Bondey, the road crosses a bridge to the south bank of the Paro Chhu. There are a few houses here and Drag Karpo, a place where Guru Rinpoche meditated, clings to the rocks above.

After a stretch of uninhabited country the road passes **Tamchhog Lhakhang** on the opposite side of the river. This is a private temple owned by the descendants of Thangtong Gyalpo of Tibet, who was responsible for building numerous iron bridges throughout Bhutan. The red soil around the temple contains low-grade ore that once supplied the raw material for iron works.

Chhuzom, better known as 'the Confluence' is at the juncture of the Paro Chhu and the Wang Chhu (*chhu* means 'river', *zom*

The Iron Bridge Builder

Thangtong Gyalpo (1385–1464) was a wonder-working Tibetan saint who is believed to have originated the use of heavy iron chains in the construction of suspension bridges and who built 108 bridges throughout Tibet and Bhutan.

He was also known as Lama Chazampa (the Iron Bridge Lama). In 1433 he came to Bhutan in search of iron ore and built eight bridges in places as far removed as Paro and Trashigang. His only surviving bridge is believed to be at Duksum on the road to Trashi Yangtse in eastern Bhutan, and his most famous one crossed the Yarlung Tsangpo at Chaksam, 50km south-west of Lhasa in Tibet.

He also cast images of Buddhist saints and built the chorten-shaped Dumtse Lhakhang in Paro. His descendants still maintain Tamchhog Goemba Lhakhang at the eastern end of the Paro valley. Among his other achievements was the composition of many occupational songs, still sung today by people as they thresh wheat or pound the mud for house construction.

He was an important *terton* of the Nyingma lineage and attained the title Drubthob (Great Magician). Statues of Thangtong Gyalpo depict him as a stocky shirtless figure with a beard, curly hair and a topknot.

SARAH JOLLY

WESTERN BHUTAN

means 'to join'). Sometimes this confluence is considered a union of a mother and father river, similar to that of the Pho Chhu and Mo Chhu at Punakha. The Paro Chhu represents the father, and is sometimes called the 'Pho Chhu', and the Wang Chhu is the 'Mo Chhu', or mother river.

Because Bhutanese tradition regards such a joining of rivers as inauspicious, there are **three chortens** here to ward away the evil spells of the area. Each chorten is in a different style – Bhutanese, Tibetan and Nepali.

Chhuzom is also a major road junction. One road leads along the west bank of the Wang Chhu, climbing 79km to Haa. Another road leads south along the eastern bank of the Wang Chhu and travels 141km to the border town of Phuentsholing. The third road leads north up the east bank of the Wang Chhu.

A checkpoint here keeps track of vehicle movements. Dantak, the Indian road construction organisation, operates a simple coffee shop next to the checkpoint. People from nearby villages often sit by the side of the road south of the checkpoint selling vegetables, apples and dried cheese.

Chhuzom to Thimphu
31km • 1 hour

The countryside is almost barren and you may wonder about the stories of Bhutan's extensive forest cover as you drive through this area. Foresters believe that this valley, as well as the lower part of the Paro valley, were never forested because of the lack of ground water on these slopes. They cite the absence of landslides as evidence of this. Despite this, you can see the afforestation efforts on the lower hillsides.

At 1km past Chhuzom there is a rough, unpaved side road that leads to Geynikha and the start of the Dagala trek. The road passes **Kharibje**, a village in a valley on the opposite side of the river. This village is inhabited by *bja-wap* (goldsmiths) who make jewellery and brass trumpets, as well as butter lamps and other items used in goembas. A small bridge across the Wang Chhu provides road access to the village.

Khasadrapchhu is a small settlement with a few shops and restaurants. On the opposite side of the river is the hydro plant that served Thimphu before the large Chhukha hydroelectric project came on line in 1988. The road up the side valley to the west follows the Bemang Rong Chhu to a marble factory, a leprosy hospital, and eventually Tsaluna village.

At several places along the road you will see what look like ancient ruins. These are the remains of houses that either burned down or were abandoned. It is considered unlucky to move into the house of a family whose members have died out or a house that has been abandoned, therefore there are numerous derelict houses scattered around the country. The packed mud walls are so tough that they survive for years after the rest of the structure has disappeared.

The valley widens near the small village of Namseling. Below the road are extensive rice paddies. Rice is planted in mid-June and harvested in October. Terraces are barren during the winter. Above the road are numerous apple orchards. Much of the fruit is exported, particularly to Bangladesh. In the autumn people sell apples and mushrooms from informal stalls at the side of the road.

The new 'expressway' to Thimphu drops off the road towards the valley floor and travels past rice terraces on the east side of the river. The large ponds by the riverside are part of Thimphu's sewage treatment plant, which was funded by Danida, the Danish development agency. The project uses a microbiological system to treat urban waste from Thimphu so that no polluted water flows to communities downstream.

After passing below the army helipad at Lungtenphug the road crosses the river and enters Thimphu from the south, passing the industrial area and climbing to the petrol station at the south end of the town centre.

The Old Road Via Simtokha The old road is longer and provides access to Simtokha, the highway to eastern Bhutan and the south-eastern part of Thimphu. After rounding a sharp bend, the road passes large statues of the guardians of the east and north and enters the suburb of Babesa.

Just beyond the headquarters of the Dantak construction project the road rounds a corner and enters **Simtokha** (see Around Thimphu in the Thimphu chapter), then crosses a bridge and turns a switchback. As the road climbs, you can look back and see **Simtokha Dzong** on the hill to the south. Vehicles detour around a large prayer wheel in the middle of the road, then go under a road overpass at the junction of the road that leads to Punakha and the east of the country.

Soon you can see Thimphu, and at the suburb of Lungtenphug you arrive at the outskirts of the town. The RBA headquarters is above the road and there is a suburban housing development below. The road passes the bus station, crosses Lungten Zampa over the Wang Chhu and enters the city from the south.

Punakha Dzongkhag

THIMPHU TO PUNAKHA

The 76km, 2¾-hour drive from Thimphu to Punakha, on the National Highway via Dochu La, leads from the cold of Thimphu to the hot, almost tropical country of the Punakha valley.

Thimphu to Dochu La
23km • ¾ hour

From Thimphu the road goes south to Simtokha (2250m). The route to the east leaves the road to Paro and Phuentsholing and loops back over itself to become the east-west National Highway, which was constructed in 1984. About a kilometre past the turn-off there is a good view of Simtokha Dzong (see Around Thimphu in the Thimphu chapter). The route climbs past the forestry research station at Yusupang, then through apple orchards and forests of blue pine. On a hill above the road is **Hongtsho Goemba** and some monks' meditation cells.

Ngawang Chhogyel founded this goemba in the 15th century; he was a cousin of Lama Drukpa Kunley and also founded Druk Choeding in Paro. At the village of Hongtsho (2890m) there is an immigration checkpoint that controls all access to eastern Bhutan. You must have a restricted-area travel permit to proceed; this is arranged as a matter of course by all tour operators.

High on a ridge across the valley to the south is **Trashigang Goemba**, which is described in Around Thimphu in the Thimphu chapter.

The road climbs to **Dochu La** (3140m), marked by a large array of prayer flags and a chorten. On a clear day the pass offers a panoramic view of the Bhutan Himalaya. Such days are rare in Bhutan. You will have the best chance of a view in the early morning between October and February.

On the hill above the pass is the *Dochu La Cafeteria* (☎ 02-329011). It offers an early-morning breakfast at Nu 120 and a set lunch for Nu 230. There's also a gift shop selling paintings, old and new weavings, masks and other souvenirs. Each item is labelled with a very stiff price quoted in US dollars – in some cases hundreds of dollars. The cafeteria proprietor also makes embroidered thangkas, including some large thondrols for tsechus. Sometimes smaller versions are for sale here.

There is a powerful binocular telescope in the cafeteria. This was a gift from the Kyoto University Alpine Club after members made the first ascent of Masang Gang (7165m) in 1985. A photograph on the wall above the telescope has the peaks labelled (with different spellings and elevations from those shown here). From west to east they are:

Kang Bum	6526m
Gangchhenta	6840m
Masang Gang	7165m
Tsenda Gang	7100m
Teri Gang	7300m
Jejekangphu Gang	7100m
Zongophu Gang (Table Mountain)	7100m
Gangkhar Puensum	7541m

However, the photo was taken from a spot higher on the hillside and you cannot see Kang Bum from the cafeteria. Gangkhar

Puensum is the highest peak that is completely inside Bhutan; Kulha Gangri (7554m) is higher, but it is on the border with Tibet. Using the telescope, it's also possible to see the distinctive shape of Gasa Dzong, a small white speck almost 50km to the north.

The area near the pass is believed to be inhabited by numerous spirits, including a cannibal demoness. Lama Drukpa Kunley, the 'divine madman', built Chimi Lhakhang (see Metshina to Punakha, later) to subdue these spirits and demons.

Dochu La to Metshina
42km • 1½ hours

The vegetation changes dramatically at the pass from oak, maple and blue pine to a moist mountain forest of rhododendron, alder, cypress, hemlock and fir. There is also a large growth of daphne, a bush that is harvested for making traditional paper. The large white chorten a few kilometres below the pass was built because of the high incidence of accidents on this stretch of road. It's a long, winding descent past Lumitsawa to **Thinleygang** (1860m), where the vegetation becomes more tropical with chir pine, cactus, oranges and bamboo. The road then passes a chorten that flows with holy water that is said to have its source in a lake far above. Along the winding route are several Bhutanese roadside versions of *mani* walls. Instead of being carved as is traditional in the hills, mantras are painted on rocks and cliffs. Some invoke the traditional *'om mani peme hum'* ('hail to the jewel in the lotus') and others display the Guru Rinpoche mantra, *'om ah hum vajra Guru Pema siddhi hum'*, a sacred chant.

High on the opposite hill is **Dalay Goemba**, which was founded by the Shabdrung and is affiliated with the Nalanda University in India. High on the ridge to the west of Dalay is **Talo Goemba**.

Below Mendigang is the small *Dechen Hill Resort* (☎ 02-322204), where singles/doubles cost Nu 1050/1400. It's a steep 15-minute drive on an unpaved road up to a grove of rhododendrons, orchids and chir pines. Here you'll find a pleasant collection of cottages with 18 rooms with private toilet, but for a bath you have to rely on the hot-stone bath in a small building above. Advance reservations are required.

The road continues its descent, looping in and out of a side valley, to a road junction at **Metshina**. This is a small bazaar where the road to Punakha branches off from the National Highway. The small *Passang Restaurant cum Samol Bar* offers snacks and drinks, but not real meals. If you are continuing to Wangdue Phodrang, stay on the main road.

Metshina to Punakha
11km • ½ hour

The road to Punakha makes a switchback down past a collection of shops and houses at **Sopsokha**. After descending to the banks of the small Tabe Rong Chhu, the road follows it downstream before crossing a clattering bridge and climbing over a ridge into the valley of the Punak Chhu. The road drops

to the river and then follows it upstream. Watch for black great cormorants sitting on rocks beside the river looking for fish.

Seven kilometres from Lobesa is the new town of Khuruthang. All the shops in Punakha were moved to this collection of three-storey structures in 1999. There are several restaurants and hotels and a vegetable market on Saturday. The large complex west of Khuruthang is a junior high school. It's then 3km to the high school and an excellent view of Punakha Dzong at 1250m. A kilometre past the high school is the footbridge leading across the Mo Chhu to the dzong.

Chimi Lhakhang On a hillock in the centre of the valley below Metshina is Chimi Lhakhang, built by Lama Drukpa Kunley in 1499. He subdued the demoness of the Dochu La with his 'magic thunderbolt of

The Divine Madman

Lama Drukpa Kunley (1455–1529) is one of Bhutan's favourite saints. He was born in Tibet, was trained at Ralung Monastery and was a contemporary and a disciple of Pema Lingpa. He travelled throughout Bhutan and Tibet as a *neljorpa* (yogi) using songs, humour and outrageous behaviour to dramatise his teachings. He felt that the stiffness of the clergy and social conventions were keeping people from learning the true Buddhist teachings. His teaching was through conduct that was shocking, insulting or obscene.

His outrageous actions and sexual antics were a deliberate method of provoking people to discard their preconceptions. He is also credited with having created Bhutan's strange animal, the takin, by combining the body of a cow with the head of a goat. On one occasion when he received a blessing thread to hang around his neck, he wound it around his penis instead, saying he hoped it would bring him luck with many more ladies.

He spoke the following verse on one occasion when he met Pema Lingpa:

> I, the madman from Kyishodruk,
> Wander around from place to place;
> I believe in lamas when it suits me,
> I practise the Dharma in my own way.
> I choose any qualities, they are all illusions,
> Any gods, they are all the Emptiness of the Mind.
> I use fair and foul words for Mantras; it's all the same,
> My meditation practice is girls and wine;
> I do whatever I feel like, strolling around in the Void,
> Last time, I saw you with the Bumthang trulku;
> With my great karmic background, I could approach.
> Indeed it was auspicious, to meet you on my pilgrim's round!

His sexual exploits are legendary, and the flying phalluses that you see painted on houses and hanging from rooftops are his.

wisdom'. A wooden effigy of the lama's thunderbolt is preserved in the lhakhang, and childless women go to the temple to receive a *wang* (blessing) from the saint.

It's a 20-minute walk across fields from the road at Sopsokha to the temple. The trail leads across rice fields to the tiny settlement of Pana, which means 'field'. It then follows a tiny stream downhill to **Yoaka** (which means 'in the drain') and across more fields before making a short climb to Chimi Lhakhang. During the wet season, this is an especially muddy and slippery walk.

There are a few monks at the temple, which is surrounded by a row of prayer wheels and some very beautiful slate carvings. No permit is required for entrance to the temple, so you may visit and see the statues of the lama and his dog Sachi, as well as statues of the Shabdrung, Sakyamuni and Chenresig. Make a small offering and you will be rewarded with a blessing from the lama's wooden phallus and his iron archery set. The small chorten on the altar is said to have been crafted by Drukpa Kunley himself.

PUNAKHA & KHURUTHANG
☎ 02

The low altitude of the Punakha valley allows two rice crops a year, and oranges and bananas are in abundance.

Orientation & Information
All of Punakha's shops and facilities are in the new town of Khuruthang. The area opposite the dzong has only private homes and the hospital. The Mo Chhu (Mother River) and Pho Chhu (Father River) join here to form the Punak Chhu. In the south of Bhutan this river is known as the Sankosh.

Punakha Dzong
History Punakha Dzong was the second of Bhutan's dzongs. For many years, until the time of the second king, it served as the seat of the government. The construction of Punakha Dzong was foretold by Guru Rinpoche, who predicted that '...a person named Namgyal will arrive at a hill that looks like an elephant'. The Shabdrung

visited Punakha and chose the tip of the trunk of the sleeping elephant at the confluence of the Mo Chhu and Pho Chhu as the place to build a dzong. It's not obvious, but with a bit of imagination you may be able to visualise the hill as an elephant.

There was a smaller building here called Dzong Chug (Small Dzong), which housed a statue of the Buddha. It is said that the Shabdrung ordered the architect, Zowe Palep, to sleep in front of the statue. While Palep was sleeping, the Shabdrung took him in his dreams to Zangto Pelri and showed him the palace of Guru Rinpoche. From his vision, the architect conceived the design for the new dzong, which, in keeping with tradition, was never committed to paper.

Construction began in 1637 and was completed the following year. It was named Pungthang Dechen Phodrang (Palace of Great Happiness). Later embellishments included the construction of a chapel to commemorate the victory over the Tibetans in 1639. The war material captured during the battle is preserved in the dzong.

The Shabdrung established a monk body here with 600 monks that were brought from Cheri Goemba in the upper Thimphu valley. Punakha is still the winter residence of the Dratsheng (Central Monk Body). The dzong was the seat of government when Punakha was capital, and the third king convened the new National Assembly here in 1952.

Punakha Dzong is 180m long and 72m wide and the utse is six storeys high. The gold dome on the utse was built in 1676 by the *dzongpen* (lord of the dzong), Gyaltsen Tenzin Rabgye. Cantilever bridges across the Mo Chhu and the Pho Chhu were constructed between 1720 and 1730. They have both been destroyed, however, and the Mo Chhu is now spanned by a cable suspension bridge that stands next to the remains of the original cantilever bridge.

There were fires in the dzong in 1750 and 1798. During the reconstruction after the second fire, several new temples were added. Lama Lhakhang was built to house a statue of Shabdrung Ngawang Namgyal. Also added were Genkhang Chhenpo (the temple of Mahakali and Mahakala) and

Nange Tseum (receptacles for the relics of the saints). Many of the dzong's features were added between 1744 and 1763 during the reign of the 13th desi, Sherab Wangchuk. He was also responsible for the gold statues of the Buddha, Guru Rinpoche and the Shabdrung that are in the main assembly hall. Another item he donated was the thondrol named Chenmo, a large thangka depicting the Shabdrung that is exhibited to the public once a year during the tsechu festival. A brass roof for the dzong was a gift of the seventh Dalai Lama, Kelzang Gyatso.

There was another fire, which was believed to have been deliberate, in 1802. There were further fires in 1831 and 1849, then the dzong suffered more damage in the severe 1897 earthquake. A glacial lake burst on the Pho Chhu in 1960 and again in 1994, causing damage to the dzong that has since been repaired. Outside the dzong is a memorial to the 23 people killed in that flood.

The latest fire, in 1986, damaged the residence of the Je Khenpo in the south-west corner of the dzong. It is now being repaired using traditional methods. The workshop of the craftspeople performing the repairs is to the south of the dzong. A visit to this workshop provides an interesting insight into the techniques of traditional crafts making. The Je Khenpo's residence is now in the northeast corner of the dzong.

Visiting the Dzong In addition to its strategic position, the dzong has several features to protect it against invasion. The steep wooden stairs at the front are designed to be pulled up, and there is a heavy wooden door that is still closed at night. The dzong is unique because it has three docheys instead of the usual two. The front gate leads first to the northern courtyard, which houses the administrative functions. The second courtyard is in the monastic quarter and the utse is here. In this courtyard are two halls, one of which was used when Ugyen Wangchuck, later the first king, was presented with the Order of Knight Commander of the Indian Empire by John Claude White in 1905.

In the southernmost courtyard is the temple where the remains of the terton, Pema Lingpa, and Shabdrung Ngawang Namgyal are preserved. The Shabdrung died in Punakha Dzong, and his body is still preserved in **Machey Lhakhang** (*machey* means 'sacred embalmed body'), which was rebuilt in 1995. The casket is sealed and may not be opened. Two lamas, Machin Zimpon and Machin Simpon, are assigned to look after the room where the casket is kept. Other than these lamas, only the king and the Je Khenpo may enter this room. Both come to take blessings before they take up their offices.

At the south end is the **'hundred-pillar' congregation hall**, which actually has only 54 pillars. The paintings in this hall, which was commissioned by the second druk desi, are exceptional. The structure is still being

The Punakha Tsechu

The Punakha tsechu is unusual because of the recreation of the battle scene in which the Shabdrung tricked the Tibetan invaders. In 1639 a Tibetan army invaded Bhutan to seize Bhutan's most precious relic, the Rangjung Kharsapani, a self-created image of Chenresig. The Shabdrung concocted an elaborate ceremony in which he pretended to throw the relic into the Mo Chhu and the disappointed Tibetans withdrew.

On the final day of the 11-day Punakha Domchoe the thondrol, which features an image of the Shabdrung, is displayed. Later a group of 136 people dressed in battle garb perform a dance, then shout and whistle as they descend the front stairs of the dzong. Next, a procession of monks led by the Je Khenpo proceeds to the river to the accompaniment of cymbals, drums and trumpets. At the river the Je Khenpo throws a handful of oranges representing the Rangjung Kharsapani into the river. This is both a recreation of the Shabdrung's trick and also an offering to the *luu*, the sub-surface spirits in the river. The singing and cheering warriors then carry their generals back into the dzong as firecrackers explode around them.

restored, with massive new statues of Sakya-muni and other deities, and gold panels on the pillars.

Another temple, **Nag Yul Bum**, is closely associated with the Je Khenpo. Inside the dzong is a set of the 108 volumes of the Kanjur, the holy book of the Drukpa Kagyu lineage, written in gold. Bhutan's most treasured possession is the Rangjung Kharsapani, a self-created image of Chen-resig that is kept in the Tse Lhakhang in the utse of the Punakha Dzong. It was brought to Bhutan by the Shabdrung, who described the image as a treasure as vast as the sky.

Beyond the dzong is the cremation ground, which is marked by a large chorten.

The Upper Punakha Valley

The road up the west side of Mo Chhu val-ley passes Puntsho Pelri Palace and many farms and homes of Bhutan's nobility. In Yambesa, 7km from Punakha, is the huge **Khamsum Yuelley Namgyal Chorten**, perched high on a hill on the opposite bank of the river. The chorten, which took eight years to build, was consecrated during a three-day ceremony in December 1999. The three-level chorten is topped by a dome and a stack of 12 circular rings, then an umbrella, the sun, moon and finally a jewelled pinnacle. A road leads from a viewpoint down to a parking lot by the river, where a bridge leads across to pro-vide access to a footpath up to the chorten. This is also a put-in spot for rafting and kayaking on the Mo Chhu.

Beyond the chorten the road is unpaved and leads 11km to Tashithang where the unfinished road to Gasa begins. The road is expected to reach Damji, a half-day walk from Gasa, by 2003. Tashithang is the jumping-off point for treks to Gasa and the hot springs below it; it's also the ending point of the Laya-Gasa trek (see the Trekking chapter for details).

Places to Stay

The accommodation in Punakha is limited. The Zangto Pelri Hotel is the best hotel east of the Dochu La and rooms are in great demand by tour operators.

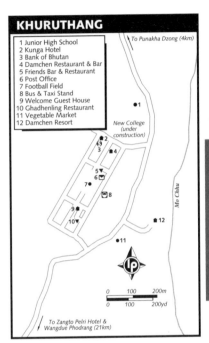

KHURUTHANG

1 Junior High School
2 Kunga Hotel
3 Bank of Bhutan
4 Damchen Restaurant & Bar
5 Friends Bar & Restaurant
6 Post Office
7 Football Field
8 Bus & Taxi Stand
9 Welcome Guest House
10 Ghadhenling Restaurant
11 Vegetable Market
12 Damchen Resort

To Punakha Dzong (4km)

New College (under construction)

Mo Chhu

0   100   200m
0   100   200yd

To Zangto Pelri Hotel & Wangdue Phodrang (21km)

WESTERN BHUTAN

Zangto Pelri Hotel (☎ 584178, fax 584203) Singles/doubles in main building Nu 1000/1320, in cottages Nu 1200/1440. Named after the paradise of Guru Rin-poche, this hotel is 8km south of Punakha on a hill above Punakha valley. There are 18 rooms in the central building, and several cottages offering additional facilities, mak-ing a total of 45 rooms. There are televi-sions in all rooms and there is a swimming pool on the grounds below the hotel. If you stay here, get up very early and drive 6km up the paved road to Laptshaka (1900m) for a beautiful view of the mountains.

Meri Puensum Resort (☎ 584195, fax 584236, **e** mpuensum@druknet.net.bt) Singles/doubles Nu 800/1000. This new hotel (built in 1999) has five rooms in the central building and 12 rooms in structures that hug the steep hillside overlooking the rice terraces of the Punakha valley.

Damchen Resort (☎ 584353, fax 584354) Singles/doubles Nu 1100/1320. On the banks of the Punak Chhu, below Khuruthang, the five-room Damchen resort offers a different atmosphere from other hotels in Bhutan. You can even disco in the underground Damchen Blue River Club on weekend nights.

In Khuruthang there are smaller guest houses including *Welcome Guest House* (☎ 584106) with singles/doubles at Nu 250/400 and *Kunga Hotel* (☎ 584128), which has four rooms with private bathroom at Nu 550 and three rooms with shared facilities at Nu 300. The *Damchen Restaurant & Bar* (☎ 584353) is a 20-room hotel with singles/doubles at Nu 1100/1320.

Above the road department complex in Lobesa, *Y.T. Hotel* (☎ 02-481324, fax 481527, e hotelyt@druknet.net.bt) has 12 double rooms for Nu 1100 and three single rooms for Nu 850. A feature of this family-run establishment is the traditional design of the comfortable sitting room and there are great views of the valley.

Places to Eat
There are several small restaurants in Khuruthang. The *Welcome Guest House* has a menu, but at *Kunga Hotel*, *Ghadhenling Restaurant* (☎ 584299) and *Friends Bar & Restaurant* (☎ 584138) you order food by asking the owner what's available, which might be momos, rice and dal (lentils), or *thukpa* (noodles).

Wangdue Phodrang Dzongkhag

Legends relate that the Shabdrung Ngawang Namgyal met a small boy named Wangdi playing in the sand on the banks of the Punak Chhu and was moved to name the new dzong Wangdi – later Wangdue – Phodrang (Wangdi's Palace).

PUNAKHA TO WANGDUE PHODRANG
It's 21km from Punakha to Wangdue Phodrang. Follow the road back to Metshina and drive a kilometre to Lobesa.

After passing below the large campus of the Natural Resources Training Institute, the road traverses high along the south bank of the Punak Chhu as the valley widens, with rice terraces below and forests above. The long buildings on the hill opposite are the barracks of the army training centre.

Soon the dramatic **Wangdue Phodrang Dzong** comes into view, draped along the end of a ridge above the river. The cacti that cover the hillside below the dzong were planted long ago to discourage invaders from climbing the steep slope.

There is a police and immigration checkpoint before the bridge across the Punak Chhu. A road leads from the bridge to the Basochhu hydroelectric project and the southern region of Tsirang. Tourists are discouraged from visiting this area because of the lack of suitable accommodation and the security problems in the south (see Problems in the South under History in the Facts about Bhutan chapter).

The original bridge over the Punak Chhu is said to have been built in 1685. Old photos show a wooden cantilever structure with massive turrets. Floods washed it away in 1968, and now a two-lane Swiss-engineered bridge spans the river downstream of the remains of the original structure.

As the road climbs you can look back to **Rinchengang** on the opposite side of the river. Many of the people who live in this compact village work as stone masons, and the services of Rinchengang's craftsmen are sought after for the construction of dzongs and lhakhangs. Believed to be one of the oldest villages in Bhutan, the closely spaced houses are all made from mud bricks. Development bypassed the community until the early 1990s when electricity, water and schools were introduced.

The road passes the vegetable market and the turn-off to the high school and agricultural research station in Bajo, then it's a short climb to the entrance to the army training centre and the bazaar.

WANGDUE PHODRANG
The old spelling of this town was Wangdi Phodrang, and it is still known colloquially

as Wangdi. Because it is on an exposed promontory overlooking the river, Wangdi is usually windy and dusty, particularly in the afternoon.

Many houses in town have roofs made from slate that was mined at slate mines in Tashi Chholing and Tseshinang, on the hills above Wangdi.

The town is spotlessly clean thanks to the district *dzongdag* (administrator), Pem Dorji, who is strict about cleanliness and makes periodic inspections. He was previously posted in Bumthang, and the result of his efforts may still be seen in Jakar town.

Orientation & Information

The road loops around a large paved parking lot that also serves as the bus station and petrol station. The bazaar is lined with a row of 87 whitewashed wooden shops and small restaurants.

The town's only hotel and the dzong are down a side road to the south-west of the bazaar. Nearby is the 17th-century **Radak Naktshang**, the town temple, which is dedicated to an ancient warlord. The main statue is of Sakyamuni, and there is also a statue of a mermaid who lived in the river and was an obstacle to the construction of this building.

At the north-eastern end of town are the bank and junior high school. The main vegetable market and high school are far below the bazaar on a side road. A large army training centre sprawls on the hill to the north of the town.

The post office is in a compound behind the bazaar, and the telephone exchange is on the road to the dzong. Many shops in the bazaar offer telephone services.

Wangdue Phodrang Dzong

Wangdue Phodrang Dzong was founded by the Shabdrung in 1638. It sits atop a high ridge between the Punak Chhu and the Dang Chhu. It is obvious that the site was selected for its commanding view of the valleys below. Legend relates another reason for choosing this spot: As people searched for a site for the dzong, four ravens were seen flying away in four directions. This was considered an auspicious

sign, representing the spreading of religion to the four points of the compass.

Wangdi is important in the history of Bhutan because in the early days it was the country's secondary capital. After Trongsa Dzong was established in 1644 the penlop of Wangdue Phodrang became the third most powerful ruler, after the penlops of Paro and Trongsa. The dzong's position gave the penlop control of the routes to Trongsa, Punakha, Dagana and Thimphu. Its complex shape actually consists of three separate narrow structures that follow the contours of the hill. There is only one

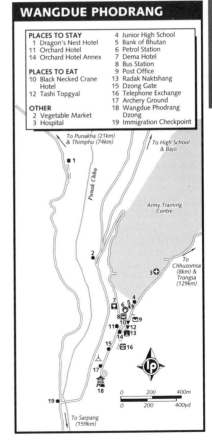

WANGDUE PHODRANG

PLACES TO STAY	4 Junior High School
1 Dragon's Nest Hotel	5 Bank of Bhutan
11 Orchard Hotel	6 Petrol Station
14 Orchard Hotel Annex	7 Dema Hotel
	8 Bus Station
PLACES TO EAT	9 Post Office
10 Black Necked Crane	13 Radak Naktshang
Hotel	15 Dzong Gate
12 Tashi Topgyal	16 Telephone Exchange
	17 Archery Ground
OTHER	18 Wangdue Phodrang
2 Vegetable Market	Dzong
3 Hospital	19 Immigration Checkpoint

WESTERN BHUTAN

entrance, a large door flanked by huge prayer wheels, which is reached by a road that leads downhill from the bazaar.

The administrative portion surrounds a large flagstone-paved dochey at the north end of the dzong. The utse divides the two portions of the dzong. The Guru Tshengye Thondrol, depicting Guru Rinpoche, is unfurled from it each year in the early hours of the final day of the autumn tsechu festival. Inside the main prayer hall at the far south of the dzong are statues of Sakyamuni, Guru Rinpoche and Shabdrung Ngawang Namgyal. As in most temples, the walls are covered with paintings depicting the lives of the Buddha. The dzong was repaired after a fire in 1837 and again after it was severely damaged in the 1897 earthquake.

Places to Stay
There's not a lot of demand for hotel rooms in Wangdi. Many travellers just make a day trip to see the dzong or else stay in Punakha and drive straight through to Gangte, Trongsa or Bumthang. At tsechu time in autumn, however, the town is packed and rooms are at a premium.

Orchard Hotel (☎ 481297) Rooms Nu 500-750. Just below the bazaar on the road to the dzong, this hotel has a restaurant and three rooms – the more expensive – in the main building. The six cheaper rooms with shared bath are in a separate facility, the annexe, on the opposite side of the road and have a flat rate whether used as a single or double. The hotel operates a *restaurant* in a tent during the Wangdi tsechu.

Dragon's Nest Hotel (☎ 481367, fax 481272, e dorji@druknet.net.bt) Singles/doubles Nu 1200/1500. This hotel is on the west side of the river 4km below Wangdi. It has 17 rooms (some with television) with balconies overlooking the river and a small Internet cafe next to the restaurant. The water heater is some distance away from the rooms. Be patient and let the water run for a while before you give up and wash with cold water.

Kichu Resort (☎ 481319, fax 481360) Singles/doubles Nu 1400/1800. In Chhuzomsa, 8km east of the town, this hotel has

22 well-appointed rooms overlooking the Dang Chhu. The restaurant serves only vegetarian food and prepares it in tasteful, interesting ways. If you're staying here during warm weather, bring some insect repellent to protect against the vicious sand flies that thrive along the river.

Places to Eat & Drink
The *Black Necked Crane Hotel* is a good place for lunch; try their Nepali-style *dal bhat* (rice and lentils). The restaurant in the *Orchard Hotel* also serves good food. There are numerous small restaurants where you can get a quick meal of noodles or momos. The *Tashi Topgyal* is run by a friendly family and the *Dema Hotel* has overstuffed chairs and a sofa so you can relax with a beer and watch the world pass by the front window.

WANGDUE PHODRANG TO PELE LA
61km • 1¾ hours
Pele La crosses the Black Mountains, the boundary between western and central Bhutan. From Pele La the road drops to Trongsa (see the Central Bhutan chapter). The road to the Phobjikha valley, known for its winter population of black-necked cranes, leads south from a junction west of Pele La.

Leaving Wangdue Phodrang, the road passes the hospital and the turn-off to the army camp, then traverses the valley, high above the Dang Chhu. There are no settlements along the road itself, but there are several villages on the hills both above and on the opposite side of the river from the road. Unlike the dense forests between Thimphu and Punakha, the hillsides here are relatively bare, with only grass and small bushes covering the slopes. The large building far below the road, alongside the river, is a jail.

By the time the road reaches **Chhuzomsa** at the confluence of the Pe Chhu and the Dang Chhu, 8km from Wangdi, it is level with the river. There are a few shops here and the Kichu Resort is below the road on the banks of the river.

Just beyond Chhuzomsa is a ropeway that climbs 1340m in 6km to Tashila. The ropeway is primarily used to carry goods up to the village and to bring logs back down the hill, but it makes two special trips daily to carry people. Passengers sit in an open wooden box and dangle high above the trees for 45 minutes (if there is no break-down) to the top. The price is Nu 60 for lo-cals and Nu 250 for tourists, who are only allowed to ride in cases of emergency. The Gangte trek passes the top of the ropeway, and some tired trekkers declare an emer-gency and ride down from Tashila.

At **Tikke Zampa**, 4km past Chhuzomsa, the road crosses to the south bank of the Dang Chhu and begins a long climb to Pele La, past rice terraces and a few houses scat-tered on the hillside. The valley gets steeper as the road ascends along the edge of the valley, following a spectacular, and occa-sionally frightening, route. In many places the way for the road has been blasted out of the side of the cliff and the road hangs high above the deep forests of the valley below.

It's a long 27km stretch to **Nobding** (2640m), a small village on the hillside. A short distance above is the ***Gaden Tashid-ing Restaurant***, which offers the best food and toilet facilities on this drive. It's an-other 7km to Dungdung Nyelsa, a cold, damp place in deep forests where there are a few basic local-style restaurants. In spring the hillside is covered with red, white and pink rhododendron blossoms. The route bears right on a new road that was com-pleted in 2001 to replace a long loop through Zelela that was subject to frequent landslides and often closed by snow. It climbs steeply up the hillside for 5km to a turn-off at Lawala where a gravel road leads 6km to Gangte Goemba and the Phobjikha valley. From Lawala it's 3km through forests to the top of **Pele La** (3420m), which is marked by a chorten and an array of prayer flags. On a clear day (which is rare in these parts) there is a view of Jhomolhari (7314m), Jichu Drakye (6989m) and Kang Bum (6526m) to the west from the road, but there are no mountain views from the pass. A side road leads uphill from the pass to a logging area. Pele La marks the western border of Black Mountains National Park and the gateway to central Bhutan.

PHOBJIKHA VALLEY

Phobjikha is a glacial valley on the western slopes of the Black Mountains. The valley is a designated conservation area and bor-ders the Black Mountains National Park. Because of the large flock of black-necked cranes that winters here, it is one of the most important wildlife preserves in the country. In addition to the cranes there are also muntjaks (barking deer), wild boars, sambars, Himalayan black bears, leopards and red foxes in the valley and surrounding hills. The Nakey Chhu drains the valley, flowing south-west and into the lower reaches of the Punak Chhu.

Some people refer to this entire region as Gangte after the goemba that sits on a ridge above the valley.

Gangte Goemba

Gangte Goemba overlooks the large green expanse of the Phobjikha valley. The exten-sive complex consists of the goemba itself and several other buildings, which include monks' quarters, meditation centres, schools and a small hotel. In front of the yellow-roofed goemba is a Tibetan-style chorten with a wooden roof.

During a visit to the Phobjikha valley, Pema Lingpa prophesied that a goemba named *gang-teng* (hill top) would be built on this site and that his teachings would be spread from there. A temple was founded here in 1613 by Gyalse Pema Thinley, the grandson and reincarnation of the mind of Pema Lingpa, and the goemba was built by Tenzing Legpai Dhendup, the second rein-carnation. The current abbot, Kunzang Pema Namgyal, is the ninth reincarnation.

It is a Nyingma goemba and is affiliated with other Nyingma goembas in Bhutan in-cluding Tamshing in Bumthang, the home of Pema Lingpa (see the boxed text 'Terton Pema Lingpa' in the Central Bhutan chap-ter). The *tshokhang* (prayer hall) is built in the Tibetan style with eight great pillars and is one of the largest in Bhutan. On the top floor are statues of the eight manifestations of Guru Rinpoche and several smaller lhakhangs. The structure is surrounded with images of saints and disciples of Guru

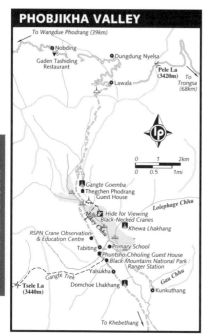

PHOBJIKHA VALLEY

To Wangdue Phodrang (39km)

Nobding

Gaden Tashiding
Restaurant

Dungdung Nyelsa

Pele La
(3420m)   To
            Trongsa
Lawala   (68km)

0   1   2km
0   0.5   1mi

Gangte Goemba
Thegchen Phodrang
Guest House

Hide for Viewing
Black-Necked Cranes   Lolephage Chhu

RSPN Crane Observation   Khewa Lhakhang
& Education Centre

Tabiting   Primary School

Phuntsho Chholing Guest House
Black Mountains National Park
Ranger Station

Gangte Trek   Yalsukha   Gau Chhu

Tsele La   Domchoe Lhakhang   Kunkuthang
(3440m)

To Khebethang

WESTERN BHUTAN

mini–hydro plants in this sparsely populated valley. The valley is snowbound during the height of the winter and many
people, including the monks, shift to winter
residences in Wangdue Phodrang during
December and January.

The road from Gangte Goemba descends
to the valley floor, then traverses the edge of
the valley past fields and scattered houses.
The extensive fields of potatoes that are the
region's primary cash crop enhance the rich
green of the valley. Gangte potatoes are one
of Bhutan's important exports to India.

Your first stop should be the Royal Society for Protection of Nature (RSPN) **Crane
Observation & Education Centre**. It's open
7am to 7pm Monday to Friday and has informative displays about the cranes and the
valley environment. You can use the centre's powerful telescopes to observe the
cranes feeding nearby. Further on is the
small settlement of **Tabiting**, where there is
a primary school and a few shops. The road
becomes a 4WD track as it continues another 6km past Yalsukha village and Domchoe Lhakhang to a footbridge. It's then a
one-hour walk to Khebethang.

The centre of the valley is wetland and is
the winter residence of a flock of 200 to 300
rare and endangered **black-necked cranes**
(see the boxed text 'The Black-Necked
Crane' in the Facts about Bhutan chapter)
that migrate from Tibet to Bhutan in late autumn, typically between the 23rd and 26th
of October. The Bhutanese have great respect for these magnificent birds, and songs
about the cranes are popular among village
folk. In mid-February, the cranes circle
Gangte Goemba and fly back across the
Himalaya to their summer homes in Tibet.
One of the most popular folk songs of the
people of Phobjikha laments the time when
the cranes leave the valley.

You can view the roosting place of the
cranes from a wooden hide. There are two
trails: One starts before the bridge where
the road reaches the valley floor, and the
other is about 1km beyond and leads south
from the road. It's about a 15-minute walk
to the hide on a trail that crosses the swamp
on rough wooden slabs. Either get up before

Rinpoche carved on slates and also numerous small prayer wheels.

A *shedra* (Buddhist college) was built in
1986 with government funds and offers a
nine-year course in Buddhist studies. The
long white building on the hill to the north
of the goemba is Kuenzang Chholing, a
drubdey (retreat and meditation centre for
monks) that was started in 1990 by the Je
Khenpo. The normal period of meditation is
three years, three months and three (sometimes seven) days, during which time the
monks remain inside and eat food that is
passed in to them by another monk.

Much of the woodwork inside the 450-
year-old goemba is infested with beetles,
and a major renovation project is under way
to replace most of the wood and restore
both the interior and exterior.

Around Phobjikha Valley

There are no telephones, and the only electricity is either solar-powered or from

dawn to watch them depart or else hike to the hide at dusk when all the birds in the valley congregate for the night. In either case, be sure to bring binoculars, a torch (flashlight) to help you find your way and extra warm clothing. The RSPN urges you stay in the hide and not to approach the roosting place.

RSPN sponsors the Black-Necked Crane Festival on 12 November, the day following the king's birthday. It's primarily an effort to instil conservation values into the people of Phobjikha, but tourists are welcome to watch the festivities, most of which are folk dances staged by school children.

Behind the Phuntsho Chholing Guest House is the small **Norsang Carpet Factory**. Established in 1992 by a local woman, Dorji Wangmo, it has a small hall housing eight weavers who produce about 90 carpets a year. Most of the carpets are bed-sized and sell for Nu 3000 to 3500; the weavers also produce smaller carpets for use on the seats of chairs or cars. One of their specialities is nontraditional designs such as 'Tintin in Bhutan' and carpets depicting the Bhutanese flag or local landmarks.

Places to Stay
Phuntsho Chholing Guest House, at the far end of the valley, is a very large Bhutanese-style house that was converted to a hotel in 1994. It has lovely polished wood floors and shared toilet facilities. It has 10 rooms at Nu 200/400 for singles/doubles; each has wall paintings that are characteristic of well-to-do homes, and there is a chapel on the 2nd floor. The hotel is run by a friendly family, and a stay provides a good opportunity to experience firsthand the traditional architecture and rural life of Bhutan. Most tour guides arrange a 'cultural show', which features the weavers from the carpet factory dancing and singing folk songs in the hotel dining room. It usually doesn't have a supply of drinks, but you can pick up a bottle of local spirits at one of the very rustic shops-cum-bars just down the road.

Thegchen Phodrang Guest House is on the ridge above the valley, opposite the

Gangte Goemba. Singles/doubles cost Nu 700/800. It's a concrete structure, which makes it quite cold. All eight rooms have a private bathroom. The dining-cum-sitting room has big overstuffed chairs, which look strangely out of place in the rustic setting.

Getting There & Away
The road to Phobjikha diverges from the main road at Lawala. It's then a 3km drive on a gravel road that climbs through forests to a pass at 3360m, where you may encounter a few stray yaks. There are also barking deer and serows in this area. The lichen hanging down from the trees is *usnea*, commonly called 'old man's beard'. The road descends into the picturesque Phobjikha valley, passing scattered houses until it reaches the turn-off to Gangte Goemba. From the goemba junction, the road switchbacks steeply down to the green expanse of the valley floor.

Gasa Dzongkhag

Gasa is in the far north of the country. Previously a subdistrict of Punakha, it was upgraded to a dzongkhag in 1993.

GASA
The village of Gasa is north of Punakha and the only way to get here is on foot. There is a road from Punakha to the southern border of the district at Tashithang, but the final 18km is not yet complete. The Laya-Gasa and Gasa Hot Spring treks pass through this region (see the Trekking chapter).

Trashi Thongmoen Dzong
The Trashi Thongmoen Dzong in Gasa lies on the old trade route to Tibet. The Shabdrung built it in 1646 after his victories over the Tibetans. Originally called Drukgyel (Victorious) Dzong, it saw a lot of activity when defending the country against Tibetan invasions in the 17th and 18th centuries. It lay in ruins after being destroyed by fire, but has been renovated and now serves as the dzongkhag administrative headquarters.

LAYA

Laya is a large, isolated region in the far north-west of the Gasa district. The roughly 800 people of this area are from a group called the Layap, who have their own language, customs and distinct dress. Laya language is similar to Dzongkha, but if people speak fast, Dzongkha speakers cannot understand them. The Layap language uses a very respectful form of speech.

The women keep their hair long and wear peculiar conical bamboo hats with a bamboo spike at the top, held on by a beaded band that reaches to the back of the head. They dress in a black woollen jacket with silver trim and a long woollen skirt with a few stripes in natural earth colours like orange and brown. They wear lots of silver jewellery on their backs; on many women this display includes an array of teaspoons.

Spread out over a hillside near the Tibetan border, Laya is one of the highest villages in the country at 3700m. The peak of the daunting **Tsenda Gang** (7100m) towers over the village. The villagers raise turnips and mustard and produce one wheat or barley crop a year before the region is snowed in for the winter.

This is Bhutan's primary yak-breeding area; during the summer, people move to the high pastures and live in black tents woven from yak hair.

The village women are easily encouraged to stage an evening 'cultural show', which consists of Bhutanese circle dancing accompanied by traditional Bhutanese and Layap songs.

Women often offer to sell their bamboo hats for Nu 150 or so. It's fine to buy these because they are made locally from native materials, but don't buy ones with beads as these are often family heirlooms and, once sold, cannot be replaced except with cheap plastic beads. Layap women also sometimes come around to trekking camps selling jewellery; most of this is made in Nepal. Unless you particularly want to contribute to the Laya economy you'll probably get less value than what you pay for.

Shabdrung Ngawang Namgyal passed through Laya and in a small meadow below the village is a chorten with the footprints of the Shabdrung and his horse.

The region is believed to be a *bey-yul* (hidden land) protected by an ancient gate that leads to Laya village. The Layaps perform a ceremony each year in honour of the protective forces that turned all the stones and trees around the gate into soldiers to repel Tibetan invaders.

Getting There & Away

Without a helicopter, the only way to get to Laya and Gasa is to trek. The Laya-Gasa and the Snowman treks pass through Laya village (see the Trekking chapter).

LINGZHI

Lingzhi is actually a *drungkhag* (subdistrict) within Thimphu Dzongkhag, but is discussed in this chapter because it's closer to Laya and Gasa than to Thimphu.

It is in the far north-western corner of the country and may be visited on either the Jhomolhari or Laya-Gasa treks. It is a very isolated region and, from whatever direction you approach it, it's necessary to cross a pass more than 4500m high to reach it. There are several settlements near Lingzhi Dzong at an elevation of about 4000m.

The Lingzhi region has a wide variety of herbs, many of which have medicinal value. The National Institute of Traditional Medicine in Thimphu has a large herb collecting and drying project here. Because of the high elevation, the only other major crop that grows well is barley.

The Lingzhi La at the head of the valley was a trade route between Punakha and the Tibetan town of Gyantse and was also used by Tibetan armies during various attacks on Bhutan.

Yugyel Dzong

The third druk desi, Mingyur Tenpa, who ruled from 1667 to 1680, built the dzong in Lingzhi. It is on a hill about 200m above Lingzhi village and is quite close to the Tibetan border. The dzong was destroyed in the 1897 earthquake, but was rebuilt in the 1950s to serve as an administrative headquarters.

It is quite small, with a few offices along the outside wall and a two-storey utse in the centre. Some years ago the basement was used as a jail to house murderers and temple robbers, but the facilities were quite primitive and the dzong is no longer used for this purpose. There are only a few monks that stay in the dzong.

Getting There & Away
The only way to reach Lingzhi is to trek for several days over high passes (see the Trekking chapter for details).

Chhukha Dzongkhag

The Chhukha district in the south extends from Chhuzom to the Indian border. Phuentsholing, the primary land crossing to Bhutan, is here. This is the home of the large Chhukha and Tala hydroelectric projects that produce electricity for all of western Bhutan, with enough surplus to export to India.

THIMPHU TO PHUENTSHOLING
The trip by car from Thimphu to Phuentsholing takes about six hours to cover 172km. The route follows the first road in Bhutan, which was built in 1962 by Dantak, the Indian border-roads organisation.

The first stage of the trip is from Thimphu to Chhuzom (31km, one hour). See Paro to Thimphu earlier in this chapter for a description of this route (as travelled in the opposite direction, ie, from Chhuzom to Thimphu).

Chhuzom to Chapcha
23km • ¾ hour
The road follows the Wang Chhu south from Chhuzom, passing beneath **Dobji Dzong**, which sits atop a promontory high above the river. You can see the road to Haa climbing on the opposite side of the Wang Chhu valley. Staying near the banks of the river, the road passes the settlement of Hebji Damchu (2020m). About 4km further is the tiny *Hotel Damchu*, which has a huge

parking lot but almost no business. Here the road starts climbing away from the river, making several switchbacks as it makes its way out of the valley.

Finally the road crests a ridge and passes the **Chapcha Bjha** (Chapcha Rocks), a vertical rock face to the left, and an equally vertical drop to the right of the road. Cross the Chapcha La to reach the Dantak road-construction camp at Chapcha (2450m). After you pass the village, look back and uphill for a view of the small **Chapcha Dzong**.

Chapcha to Chhukha
34km • 1 hour
There are farms and houses scattered on the hillside beyond the Dantak camp; on a cliff far above is Thadra Ney Lhakhang, built into the side of a rock face. The road switchbacks steeply down to a large bridge that the engineers named Tachhong Zam (most excellent high bridge). It then climbs the side of a steep forested slope to Bunakha (2270m), where the *Bunakha Cafeteria* (☎ 08-478216) caters to travellers. The restaurant looks like a country-style log cabin and has an extensive menu (though not everything is available) and also clean restrooms. The valley is quite picturesque, with big Bhutanese-style houses below the road and across the valley.

From Bunakha the road traverses to a petrol station and the goemba of Chhukha Rabdi. There is a large monk body here, which performs the Chhukha tsechu each April. A few kilometres further, in **Tsimasham** (formerly Chimakothi) at 2210m, is the *Karma Hotel* (☎ 08-478221), which has food and, across the road, basic rooms for Nu 150. A side road leads 2km uphill from here to Tshilakha and the offices of the Chukkha project and further on another leads to the Tashigyatsel Police Academy.

The road switchbacks down to the Chhukha hydroelectric project. Several side roads lead down to the dam site and the intake structures that divert the river into seven tunnels bored though the hill. The road descends further to the entrance to the powerhouse and the buildings that once housed construction workers. The complex

WESTERN BHUTAN

has been converted into the Wangchhu high school. The dark cement building alongside the road is the **Deki Hotel & Bar**, a very basic fast-food restaurant.

Chhukha to Gedu
38km • 1 hour

Beyond the restaurant there is an immigration checkpoint and the Theg Chen Zam (Strong High Bridge), which takes the road to the west side of the Wang Chhu. This is the mid-point between Thimphu and Phuentsholing.

The road climbs to a lookout where a sign advertises a 'bird's-eye view' of the Chhukha project. The turbines are inside the hillside, but you can see the transformers and the transmission station. Beside the distribution station are the ruins of **Chhukha Dzong**. Beyond the lookout is the first of several roads leading to the new 1020MW Tala hydroelectric project. This road leads 8.5km to the intake structure where water is diverted into a 22km-long tunnel.

The rest of the climb is over the ridge that separates the Wang Chhu valley from the Torsa Chhu drainage. The road passes Wangkha (which Dantak labels Honka), a road-construction camp, and a large Tala project facility, then climbs to a chorten that is a memorial to an important official who died here in a road accident. There's a short bridge over what's left of Toktokachhu Falls (also known as Takti Chhu) after a flood brought down a collection of huge boulders. A spectacular high waterfall is also visible to the east on the opposite side of the Wang Chhu valley. Atop the next ridge at 2020m is a Dantak canteen that specialises in *dosas* (paper-thin pancakes made from lentil flour). It also has public toilets. Beyond a second road to the Tala project is another road crew camp at Makaibari (Cornfield), then Asinabari (Field of Hailstones) and the small settlement of Chasilakha (*la kha* means 'grazing field').

Another climb leads to **Gedu**, a fair-sized village with several small restaurants near the road. The Gedu Wood Factory operated here from 1990 until 1996. The government closed the factory because of the environmental damage that the tree harvesting caused. The offices of the plywood factory have been converted into the administrative facility for the Tala project. The best bet for a meal is the **Lhamu Restaurant & Bar** (☎ 05-272332) next to the petrol station at the south end of town.

Beyond Gedu a road leads downhill to Mirching and the power station and will eventually be completed all the way to join the Phuentsholing road just north of Rinchending.

Gedu to Rinchending
41km • 1¼ hours

A short distance on from Gedu is a chorten that marks Jumja village at 2050m. A dairy facility here produces *datse* (Bhutanese cheese) and butter from milk produced in nearby villages. The road makes a sharp bend and crosses the huge Jumja slide that often slips away during the monsoon, closing the road. Passing the Kinga Chholing Lhakhang in the village of Kamji, the road turns a corner and starts winding its way down to the plains.

At Sorchen there is a road-construction camp to house the workers who continually repair damage from the huge landslides that frequently close the road. A diversion was built in 2001 that avoids the area most prone to problems, but the road is still under constant attack from the elements. From the bottom of the slide area it's a 12km drive past an industrial area and army camp to the checkpoint at Rinchending.

Rinchending to Phuentsholing
5km • 10 minutes

Rinchending is the immigration checkpoint where your passport is stamped and your departure from (or arrival in) Bhutan is recorded. Below Rinchending is the town of Kharbandi and Bhutan's two technical schools: the Royal Technical Institute and the Bhutan Polytechnic Institute. Below the technical school is the grand, queen mother's winter residence and the small **Kharbandi Goemba**. There are a few resident monks and tourists are allowed to visit the lhakhang. The temple was built in 1967 and houses large statues of Sakyamuni, Shabdrung Ngawang Namgyal and Guru Rinpoche. On the grounds are examples of eight different styles of Tibetan chortens. Below Kharbandi the road switchbacks down to Phuentsholing, which sprawls from the hills onto the edge of the plains.

PHUENTSHOLING
☎ 05

The road from Thimphu enters Phuentsholing from the east, passing the archery ground and post office, then makes a turn onto the main street with the often-photographed

Bhutanese-style entrance gate. If you are coming from India, you will travel north through the crowded Indian bazaar of Jaigaon. At the top end of town the road turns east and passes through the gate where you will notice an instantaneous change in the degree of cleanliness and organisation.

To the north of the town a stream, the Dhoti Chhu, flows west to join the Torsa Chhu, which in its upper reaches is known as the Amo Chhu and has its headwaters in Tibet's Chumbi Valley. In 1999 monsoon floods caused the Dhoti Chhu to jump its banks and submerge much of the town. An

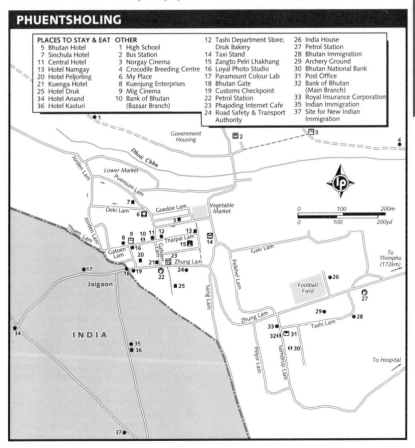

extensive embankment system now protects against a repeat performance. Several hours' walk away, on the opposite side of the Torsa Chhu, is the home of the minority group known as the Doya.

Orientation

The main road through town runs in an east-west direction. From the Bhutan gate it passes the Hotel Druk and bus station on the south side and several smaller hotels on the north side. About 200m from the gate it reaches a roundabout. The road to the left leads to an industrial and residential area. The road to Thimphu turns right and climbs a hill to the post office, banks and government offices, then starts immediately climbing towards the capital, 172km away.

The bazaar, called the upper market, is dominated by a park and the Zangto Pelri Lhakhang. Surrounding the park are shops, the large Tashi department store complex and the Namgay Hotel. To the west of the park is Tharpai Lam with a cinema, many shops and small restaurants. At the east end of Tharpai Lam is Thuen Lam; one side of this street is in Bhutan, the other in India.

Information

Arrival Formalities See India under Land in the Getting There & Away chapter for information about visa and other formalities upon arrival in Phuentsholing for foreigners and Indian nationals. In 2001 Phuentsholing was declared a 'free zone', a facility that allows foreigners to enter the town from India and spend a night without paying the daily tourist fee of US$200.

Money The Bank of Bhutan (☎ 521123) main branch is open 9am to 1pm Monday to Friday and 9am to 11am Saturday. The bazaar branch has exactly the same hours but is open on Sunday and closed on Tuesday.

Post & Communications The post office is next to the headquarters of the Bank of Bhutan and the Royal Insurance Corporation on a hill above the town. There are numerous PCOs, and several have automated billing systems.

Phajoding Internet Cafe (☎ 254070, e pic@druknet.net.bt, Zhung Lam), opposite the Hotel Druk, charges Nu 2 per minute.

Photography If you need passport photos quickly get them from Loyal Photo Studio on Gatoen Lam in Phuentsholing or Paramount Colour Lab in Jaigaon. Both charge Nu 30 for four black-and-white instant photos.

Bookshops Kuenjung Enterprises (☎ 252 771) has paperback novels, children's books, Indian newspapers and a few books about Bhutan.

Things to See

The **Zangto Pelri Lhakhang** is a replica of Guru Rinpoche's celestial paradise. The statues in the temple are the eight manifestations of Guru Rinpoche. On the upper floor is a statue of Chenresig and on the top is an image of the saint Amitabha.

If you run out of things to do in Phuentsholing you can visit the sleepy collection of marsh mugger and gharial crocodiles at the **Crocodile Breeding Centre**.

Places to Stay & Eat

All of the following hotels have rooms with attached toilets. Hotel Druk has air-con and the other hotels have ceiling fans, though some do have one or two air-con rooms.

Unless you are adventurous and want to sample ethnic fare in small stalls, stick to the restaurants in the *Druk*, *Namgay*, *Peljorling*, *Kuenga* or *Sinchula* hotels.

The *Druk Bakery* in the Tashi department store has an excellent selection of biscuits, pastries and cakes.

Phuentsholing *Hotel Druk (☎ 252426, 252427, fax 252929, e h-druk@druknet.net .bt, Zhung Lam)* Singles/doubles Nu 1200/ 1600. This hotel is in a secluded spot near the Bhutan gate and has 35 rooms with phone and television. There's a well-managed bar, and the restaurant serves good Indian food.

Hotel Namgay (☎ 252374, fax 254147, Tharpai Lam) Singles/doubles Nu 485/585. Overlooking the lhakhang, the Namgay has 16 rooms with phone and television.

Sinchula Hotel (☎ 252589, fax 252155, Puensum Lam) Singles/doubles Nu 350/450. This older hotel has 15 rooms and a rooftop terrace bar that looks out on the surrounding hills.

Central Hotel (☎ 252172, Cnr Tharpai & Gatoen Lams) Singles/doubles Nu 450/675. Situated in the town centre, this hotel is popular with Indian tourists.

Kuenga Hotel (☎ 252293, Gatoen Lam) Singles/doubles Nu 280/390. With 16 rooms, all with TV, the Kuenga has a busy restaurant that's popular with locals.

Hotel Peljorling (☎ 252833, Zhung Lam) Singles/doubles Nu 350/450. The flagship of Bhutan's second hotel chain, the Peljorling has basic rooms and a busy restaurant and bar with good food.

Bhutan Hotel (☎ 252576) Singles/doubles Nu 140/180. The 23-room Bhutan Hotel is in the middle of the bazaar and caters to a mostly Bhutanese clientele.

Throughout the town there are many smaller hotels with rooms in the Nu 100 to 200 range that cater to Bhutanese students and travellers and to Indian workers.

Jaigaon The best places to stay in Jaigaon are the *Hotel Anand (☎ 03566-63783)* with singles/doubles at INRs 250/375 and the *Hotel Kasturi (☎ 03566-63036)* next to the immigration checkpoint with singles/doubles at INRs 250/450.

Entertainment
If you like Hindi movies, you are in luck. The *Mig Cinema* in the centre of town and the *Norgay Cinema* near the Dhoti Chhu at the north end of town offer several three-hour screenings daily.

For a drink, the favourite local gathering places are the garden of the *Hotel Peljorling* and the funky bar at the *Bhutan Hotel*. A new bar and disco, *My Place*, has opened in the basement of the Gechu shopping mall. It has a large-screen television for sports events.

Getting There & Away
Jaigaon is a large, nondescript Indian village opposite Phuentsholing. You can make road connections from Jaigaon or Phuentsholing

to the airport in Bagdogra or the train station in Siliguri, both in West Bengal (169km, about six hours). There are also convenient connections to the Nepali border at Kakarbhitta or the Indian hill stations of Kalimpong, Gangtok and Darjeeling. Bhutanese vehicles may travel freely in India, and a Bhutanese tour operator can easily arrange a vehicle to any of these destinations.

Haa Dzongkhag

The Haa valley runs north-east to south-west and lies south of the Paro valley. One road into Haa diverges from the Phuentsholing-Thimphu road at Chhuzom and travels south, high above the Wang Chhu, before turning into the Haa valley. Another road reaches Haa from Paro, crossing the Cheli La. It is the ancestral home of the Dorji family, to which the queen mother, Ashi Kesang Wangchuck, belongs. Many people from Haa move to Samtse in winter.

There's not a lot to see in Haa, first opened to tourists in 2001, but it's a picturesque remote valley that is ideal for mountain biking and hiking, and the Association of Bhutanese Tour Operators (ABTO) is scouting new trekking routes here. It is a large fertile valley and the staple crops are wheat, potatoes, barley and millet. People also raise yaks here; Thimphu people believe that yak meat from Haa is superior. Though there is easy access to Tibet from Haa, it was never a major trade route because of the remoteness of the valley.

CHHUZOM TO HAA
It's 79km from the road junction at Chhuzom (2090m) to Haa town. The road climbs gently out of the Wang Chhu valley, traversing in and out of side valleys above **Dobji Dzong**, which overlooks the valley below. Near the few houses of Tshongkha is a road leading to a radio tower and a trail leading uphill to Phundup Pedma Yowzing Goemba.

Beyond Mendegang the road enters a huge side valley, passing below the village of Susuna and traversing again past a school before turning into the Haa valley, staying high above the Haa Chhu.

Passing the large village of Gayshina the road reaches two small restaurants at Rangshingang, 42km from Chhuzom at an elevation of 2660m. It's another 5km to Bietakha, then 4km to Nago. After a long stretch of forest the road reaches the large village and school at Jyenkana. Two kilometres beyond is Karnag, then it's a 7km drive to a bridge over the Haa Chhu and the outskirts of Haa town at 2670m.

Much of the town is occupied by the Indian Military Training Team (IMTRAT) camp (complete with a golf course that has sand 'greens') and a Bhutanese army training camp. The Haa monk body is housed in Haa Trasang at the entrance to town, not in the dzong, which is on the edge of the Indian installation.

The road crosses back to the north bank of the river and passes the road to Cheli La, then the high school, bank and bazaar, where there are a few basic shops and eating places.

Beyond the bazaar the road crosses back to the river's south bank and passes several small settlements as it heads up the valley. The large village in the side valley to the north is Talung; Yangthang Goemba is on the eastern ridge of the side valley.

Chhundu Lhakhang, one of several dedicated to the protective deity of Haa, is a five-minute walk below Gayekha at 2930m. Chhundu did not get along very well with his neighbours. He was banished to Haa by the Shabdrung after an altercation with Gyenyen, Thimphu's protector. He also had a quarrel with Jichu Drakye of Paro and the Paro guardian stole all of Haa's water – and that's why there is no rice grown in Haa.

The road ends at Damthang, 15km from Haa town, but it would be prudent to turn around before you reach the gates of the large Bhutanese army installation here.

HAA TO CHELI LA

It's 26 km from Haa to Cheli La. There's no habitation on the route as the road switchbacks through a forest of blue pine, fir and oak. At about 3400m the road traverses through alpine country towards the pass. Many fir trees here were killed by bark beetles, and the only way to prevent the spread

of these pests was to burn the trees. At Cheli La a sign says the elevation is 3988m, but it's really 3810m. It's then a 35km drive down to the junction with the Paro road in Bondey.

Haa Dzong

Wangchulo Dzong in Haa is one of Bhutan's newest, built in 1915 to replace a smaller structure. It is a large square structure with battered (inward-sloping) walls.

Southern Dzongkhags

TSIRANG DZONGKHAG

This district (previously spelt 'Chirang') is in the south of the country, but is separated from the southern border by Sarpang Dzongkhag.

The major town is **Damphu**, reached by a road leading south from Wangdue Phodrang. The road passes through Sankosh, said to be the hottest place in the country, then continues south-east from Damphu to the border town of Sarpang.

DAGANA DZONGKHAG

This dzongkhag was previously known as Daga. The administrative headquarters is in **Dagana** and the region is noted for farming and cattle production. It is said that the people of 17th-century Dagana were lawless and out of control, and Shabdrung Ngawang Namgyal sent Donyer Druk Namgyal with soldiers to conquer them. Druk Namgyal built the dzong in 1655 and gave it the name Daga Trashi Yangtse Dzong.

SAMTSE DZONGKHAG

Samtse (previously spelt 'Samchi') is in the far south-west and is closed to tourists. Access is from India, though a road is under construction from Phuentsholing. The Teachers' Training College is here, as is the factory that produces Druk-brand tinned fruit and jams.

Early British expeditions used a route through Samtse to travel to the centre of Bhutan. From Darjeeling they crossed over the hills of Samtse to Haa, then over the Cheli La to Paro.

Central Bhutan

There is a great variety of people, architecture and scenery in central Bhutan. Because it is difficult to get here, the countryside and hotels are less crowded than in Thimphu, Paro and Punakha. Until the 1970s the only way to reach this part of Bhutan was on foot or atop a sure-footed horse. Across the 3420m-high Pele La is the large, fertile Mangde Chhu valley, which is protected by the great Trongsa Dzong. A short drive over the mountains from Trongsa leads to the four valleys of Bumthang, Bhutan's cultural heartland where the landscape is dotted with palaces, ancient temples and monasteries.

Bordered on the west by the Black Mountains – a range of hills that extends roughly north-south across the country – and on the east by a chain of near-vertical hills, central Bhutan is drained by two major rivers. To the west, the Mangde Chhu flows from the peaks of the Himalaya through a narrow gorge to Trongsa. As the river flows south the valley widens and becomes a collection of fertile rice terraces. To the east, the Bumthang Chhu drains four culturally rich valleys before joining the Mangde Chhu. In the south the Royal Manas National Park protects a region of tropical vegetation and jungle wildlife.

History
Central Bhutan is believed to be the first part of Bhutan to have been inhabited, with evidence of prehistoric settlements in the Ura valley of Bumthang and the southern region of Khyeng. These and many other valleys were separate principalities ruled by independent kings. One of the most important of these kings was the 8th-century Indian Sindhu Raja of Bumthang, who was eventually converted to Buddhism by Guru Rinpoche. Bumthang continued to be a separate kingdom, ruled from Jakar, until the time of Shabdrung Ngawang Namgyal in the 17th century.

During the rule of the first *desi* (secular ruler), Tenzin Drugyey, all of eastern Bhutan came under the control of the Drukpa gov-

Highlights

Choskhor
Valley p213
Jakar p209
Trongsa p205

INDIA

- See the sprawling Trongsa Dzong, one of the most picturesque examples of Bhutanese architecture.

- Explore Bumthang, the cultural heartland of Bhutan and home to some of the kingdom's most precious and ancient Buddhist sites.

- Visit Chendebji Chorten, smaller, but patterned after, Swayambhunath in Kathmandu.

- Walk to the hundred-year-old Ugyen Chholing Palace, now home to a museum in the Tang Valley.

! All Bhutanese Internet and email addresses have changed, see page 86.

ernment in Punakha. Chhogyel Mingyur Tenpa unified central and eastern Bhutan into eight provinces known as Shachho Khorlo Tsegay. He was then promoted to Trongsa *penlop* (governor).

Because of Trongsa Dzong's strategic position, the penlop exerted great influence over the entire country. It was from Trongsa that Jigme Namgyal, father of the first king, rose to power.

Bumthang retained its political importance during the rule of the first and second kings, both of whom had their principal residence at Wangdichholing Palace in Jakar.

Trongsa Dzongkhag

WANGDUE PHODRANG TO TRONGSA

It takes almost four hours to drive the 129km between the windswept town of Wangdi (Wangdue Phodrang's colloquial name) not far from Thimphu in western Bhutan, and Trongsa right in the middle of the country. The route crosses the Black Mountains via Pele La (3420m) before entering the broad, heavily cultivated Mangde Chhu valley.

Wangdue Phodrang to Pele La

61km • 1¾ hours

See the Western Bhutan chapter for details of this drive.

Near Pele La much of the hillside is covered with a strange dwarf bamboo called *cham*. This bamboo never gets large enough to harvest for any useful purpose, but when it is small, it is a favourite food of yaks and horses. The area near Pele La is the best place in Bhutan to see yaks from the road. Be alert, though, as these great shaggy beasts are skittish and likely to run off into the forest when your vehicle approaches.

Yaks

Westerners tend to oversimplify the many manifestations of the yak into this single word, yet it is only the full-blooded, long-haired bull of the species *Bos grunniens* that truly has the name yak. In Bhutan the name is pronounced 'yuck' and females of the species are called *jim*. Females are prized for their butterfat-rich milk, used to make butter and cheese.

Large, ponderous and clumsy looking, yaks have the ability to move very quickly when startled. They are used as pack animals for seasonal migration to alpine pastures in Laya and other high regions of western Bhutan. If you are trekking with yaks, give them a wide berth, and don't put anything fragile in your luggage. If an animal becomes alarmed, it charges up a hill and your baggage falls off and gets trampled as the yak bucks and snorts while its keeper tries to regain control.

Though some yaks are crossbred with local cows, there are many purebred yaks in Bhutan – massive animals with thick furry coats and impressive sharp horns.

SARAH JOLLY

There is no view from the pass, but on a clear day you can see Jhomolhari, Jichu Drakye and Kang Bum from the road as you approach the pass.

Pele La to Chendebji
27km • 1 hour
From Pele La the road drops through more dwarf bamboo and patches of fir trees, finally emerging into the abundant evergreen forests of the Longte valley. The first village on the east side of the pass is Kgebji. The village high in the valley, far from the road, is Longte. Here people raise sheep and yaks.

Lower down into the valley the vegetation changes to broadleaf species and bamboo. The road passes opposite **Rukubji** village with its big school and *goemba* at the end of a huge alluvial fan believed to be the body of a giant snake. The houses in this village are all clustered closely together, an unusual layout for Bhutan. Surrounding the village are extensive fields of mustard, potatoes, barley and wheat.

The groups of small white houses along the road are quarters for road maintenance crews. Road workers are housed throughout Bhutan near those parts of the road that require frequent repair.

The road enters a side valley and drops to **Sephu** (2610m), which is beside the bridge that spans the Nikka Chhu. This is the ending point of the 23-day Snowman trek that starts from Paro and passes through the remote Lunana district (see the Trekking chapter). It's worth a brief stop here to examine the bamboo mats and baskets that villagers sell in shops alongside the road. The larger baskets, called *zhim*, are tied to horses' pack saddles to transport goods. ***Tsering's Restaurant cum Bar*** beside the bridge offers breakfast or, throughout the day, *momos* (dumplings) and tea. It also has a clean toilet.

The road follows the Nikka Chhu to two chortens that mark the river's confluence with the Nyala Chhu. It is then a gentle, winding descent through rhododendrons, blue pines, spruces, oaks and dwarf bamboo to the village of **Chendebji** on the opposite side of the Nikka Chhu. This was a night halt for mule caravans travelling from Trongsa during the reign of the second king.

Two kilometres beyond Chendebji village is **Chendebji Chorten**, a large white structure beside a stream at 2430m. The chorten is patterned after Swayambhunath in Kathmandu and was built in the 19th century by Lama Shida, from Tibet, to cover the remains of an evil spirit that was killed at this spot. The proper name of this structure is Chorten Charo Kasho; it is the westernmost monument in a 'chorten path' that was the route of early Buddhist missionaries. The easternmost monument in this path is Chorten Kora in Trashi Yangtse. The Bhutanese-style chorten nearby was constructed in 1982.

Chendebji to Trongsa
41km • 1¼ hours

From the chorten the road continues down the valley through a forest of hemlocks. After passing a few farms and crossing a side stream it climbs again to a ridge, passing above the village of Tangsibji. The valley widens and the road turns a corner into the broad Mangde Chhu valley. After the road weaves in and out of a few side valleys there is a view of Trongsa and its huge, sprawling white *dzong*, with its distinctive yellow roof. The dzong is perched at the end of a ridge and seems to hang in space at the head of the valley.

On the opposite side of the Mangde Chhu you can see the road that heads south to Zhemgang and Gelephu near the Indian border.

The shrubs along this part of the road are edgeworthia, which is used to make paper, and the brown monkeys you will probably see are rhesus macaques. Pass the settlement of Tashiling to another lookout. There is a small chorten here and an excellent view of the dzong, which looks almost close enough to touch even though it's still 14km away.

To reach Trongsa, you switchback into the upper reaches of the Mangde Chhu valley, cross the river on a Bailey bridge, and then climb again above the north bank of the river to finally reach Trongsa.

TRONGSA
☎ 03 • elevation 2180m

Trongsa is smack in the middle of the country, separated from both the east and the west by mountain passes. The town had a large influx of immigrants from Tibet in the late 1950s and early 1960s, and Bhutanese of Tibetan descent run most shops here. The Tibetans are so well assimilated into Bhutanese society that there is almost no indication of Tibetan flavour in the town.

Orientation & Information
As the road enters the town a turn-off leads uphill to the tourist lodge and the high school. The main road stays level, traverses above the dzong and makes a switchback after it crosses a stream. East of the stream is the vegetable market; above the road is the small **Thruepang Palace** where the third king, Jigme Dorji Wangchuck, was born in 1928.

The road climbs to a cluster of shops and hotels that form the bazaar. A traffic circle marks the junction of the road that leads south to Gelephu. This road, completed in 1972, goes downhill from the traffic circle, passing several hotels and shops, then travels about a kilometre to the town's only petrol pump and another 244km to Gelephu. A short walk down this road will provide good views of the dzong.

The road towards the east goes uphill from the traffic circle. A short walk on this road leads to a steep, narrow path that will take you to the watchtower.

There is no formal bus stand in Trongsa. The few buses that ply this route drive to the traffic circle and blow their horns early in the morning to wake up passengers.

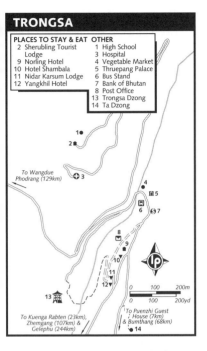

TRONGSA

PLACES TO STAY & EAT	OTHER
2 Sherubling Tourist Lodge	1 High School
9 Norling Hotel	3 Hospital
10 Hotel Shambala	4 Vegetable Market
11 Nidar Karsum Lodge	5 Thruepang Palace
12 Yangkhil Hotel	6 Bus Stand
	7 Bank of Bhutan
	8 Post Office
	13 Trongsa Dzong
	14 Ta Dzong

To Wangdue Phodrang (129km)

To Kuenga Rabten (23km), Zhemgang (107km) & Gelephu (244km)

To Puenzhi Guest House (7km) & Bumthang (68km)

The Bank of Bhutan (☎ 521123) is open 9am to 1pm Sunday to Monday and Wednesday to Friday and 9am to 11am Saturday.

Trongsa Dzong

This is the most impressive dzong in the kingdom, and can be seen from a great distance in its strategic position high above the Mangde Chhu. It has been described as being perched so high on a mountain that the clouds float below it. It is one of the most aesthetic and magnificent works of traditional Bhutanese architecture. The dzong is a rambling collection of buildings that trails down the ridge, and it has a remarkable succession of street-like corridors, wide stone stairs and beautiful stone courtyards.

The dzong was built in its present form in 1644 by Chhogyel Mingyur Tenpa, the official who was sent by the Shabdrung to unify eastern Bhutan, and enlarged at the end of the 17th century by the desi, Tenzin Rabgye. Its official name is Chhoekhor Raptentse Dzong, and it is also known by its short name of Choetse Dzong.

The southernmost part of the dzong, Chorten Lhakhang, was built in 1543, before the current surrounding structure was built. The dzong was severely damaged in the 1897 earthquake and repairs were carried out by the penlop of Trongsa, Jigme Namgyal, father of Bhutan's first king. Most of the existing decoration, including a 6m-tall statue of the Buddha, was designed during the rule of the first king, Ugyen Wangchuck. The audience hall is still preserved as it was during his reign. There is a painting of the court as it was then, and other paintings of the guardians of the four directions and the deity Phurba in the main hall. There is also a 17th-century mural depicting Swayambhunath in Nepal and another with a pictorial map of Lhasa.

The dzong's location gave it great power over this part of the country. The only mule and foot trail between eastern and western Bhutan leads straight through Trongsa and it used to run through the dzong itself. Before the construction of the road, this gave the Trongsa penlop complete control over all east-west travel in the country. There are 25 separate *lhakhangs* in the dzong and extensive wood carvings that make it the most elaborately decorated dzong after Trashi Chhoe in Thimphu.

Trongsa Dzong is the ancestral home of Bhutan's royal family. The first two hereditary kings ruled from this dzong, and it is still a tradition that the crown prince first serves as Trongsa penlop before acceding to the throne. The monastic body shifts to Trongsa for the winter and to Bumthang in the summer, just as they do between Thimphu and Punakha. Major renovation work is under way to repair cracks in the exterior walls and several buildings are being dismantled and rebuilt.

Ta Dzong

There are three watchtowers on the hill to the east of the dzong, and it's worth making the short climb for the view and to take a brief look at the ta dzong.

CENTRAL BHUTAN

How Trongsa Got its Name

Trongsa Dzong has a rich history dating back to the 16th century. The first construction on the site of the dzong was carried out by Lam Ngagi Wangchuk, son of Ngawang Chhojey, who established Pangri Zampa in Thimphu. He came to Trongsa in 1541 and lived in the village of Yueli, which is a few kilometres above the dzong.

One night while meditating at Yueli, he observed a light burning on a ridge below. This was an auspicious omen and he went down to the light and saw the footprints of the horse of Palden Lhamo, Bhutan's guardian deity. Realising that this was a sacred abode of Palden Lhamo, he built a *tshamkhang* (small meditation quarter) and meditated there.

Lam Ngagi Wangchuk attracted many disciples who built other tshamkhangs and temples nearby. The people of Yueli, observing that the place now began to look like a new village, called the area Trong-sar (the people of Yueli pronounce *dong*, or village, as *trong*, hence Dong-sar or Trong-sar, meaning 'new village').

A chapel inside the tower is dedicated to the 19th-century penlop of Trongsa, Jigme Namgyal. In another small chapel upstairs, there is an interesting representation of a palace, with small statues of horses, yaks and elephants. Two British soldiers are said to have been kept in the dungeon here for several months during the Duar War.

Places to Stay & Eat

Sherubling Tourist Lodge (☎ 521116, fax 521107) Singles/doubles Nu 600/750, single/double cottages Nu 845/1105. Run by the Bhutan Tourism Corporation Limited (BTCL), this lodge has five rooms in the main building and another nine rooms in adjoining cottages. It has a good view of Trongsa Dzong and the Mangde Chhu valley. A set lunch costs Nu 200 and dinner Nu 240.

Norling Hotel (☎ 521171, fax 521178) Singles/doubles Nu 950/1050. This 10-room hotel occupies a cement building in the centre of town. The food in the dining room is quite good.

Puenzhi Guest House (☎ 521197) Singles/doubles Nu 800/1000. A 4km drive above the town leads to this new 22-room facility occupying several cottages on the steep slope below the main building. This hotel offers the best aerial view of the Trongsa Dzong and there are no dogs to keep you awake. Steep footpaths lead down to the town and the Ta Dzong.

Yangkhil Hotel (☎ 521126) and *Nidar Karsum Lodge* (☎ 521126) are on a short spur off the main road at the southern end of town. Both are small, friendly places with simple rooms upstairs and Tibetan-style restaurants downstairs. Like the nearby *Hotel Shambala* (☎ 521135), neither place has a menu. Wander into the kitchen and ask what is available. Expect to pay about Nu 60 for a meal of rice, curry and vegetables and Nu 30 for a plate of momos.

AROUND TRONGSA
Kuenga Rabten

The winter palace of the second king, Jigme Wangchuck, is 23km (one hour) south of Trongsa. It's an interesting drive, passing Takse Goemba and a large expanse of rice terraces in the lower Mangde Chhu valley. The palace is under the care of the National Commission for Cultural Affairs, and you don't need a permit to enter. It's a good afternoon side trip from Trongsa and gives an intimate insight into life in the early days of Bhutan's monarchy.

The first storey was used to store food; the second was the residence of royal attendants and the army; and the third housed the royal quarters and the king's private chapel. Part of this floor has been converted into a library and many books from the National Library are stored here. On the top floor is Sangye Lhakhang, with statues of Sakyamuni, the Shabdrung and Guru Rinpoche. Nearby is a large nunnery and further down the valley is Eundu Chholing, the winter palace of the first king, Ugyen Wangchuck.

Bumthang Dzongkhag

The Bumthang region encompasses four major valleys: Choskhor, Tang, Ura and Chhume. Because the dzongs and the most important temples are in the large Choskhor valley, it is commonly referred to as the Bumthang valley.

There are two versions of the origin of the name Bumthang. The valley is supposed to be shaped like a *bumpa*, the vessel that contains holy water and is usually found on the altar of a lhakhang. *Thang* means 'field' or 'flat place'. The less respectful translation relates to the particularly beautiful women who live here – *bum* means 'girl'.

Many great kings and ministers have graced these valleys,
And many are the magnificent monasteries there.

From an ancient text

Day Hikes
There are many opportunities for hikes in the Bumthang region, most involving visits to remote goembas (see Choskhor Valley section, following). If you are on a tourist visa, you will have a vehicle at your disposal, and can arrange for the driver to take you to the start of the walk and then collect you from a different spot at the end. You can walk the 17km to Thankabi Goemba from Kurjey Lhakhang and have a vehicle pick you up. It's a full-day excursion if you want to continue up the valley from Thankabi to Ngang Lhakhang.

You can also walk from Lamey Goemba over the ridge to Tharpaling Goemba at 3500m in the Chhume valley and then hike down to the road at Domkhar where you can meet your vehicle. Many walks begin or end in the Tang valley, hiking from the Swiss Guest House to Petsheling Goemba and over the ridge to Kunzangdrak Goemba.

TRONGSA TO JAKAR
It takes 2½ hours to cover the 68km from Trongsa to Bumthang. It's one of the easier and more interesting drives in Bhutan because it passes numerous villages and goembas in the Chhume valley.

Trongsa to Yotong La
28km • 1 hour
The road switchbacks up the ridge above Trongsa, climbing steeply for 7km past the Puenzhi Guest House to a viewpoint where you can look down on the town and dzong. It's then a long climb past the small **Dorjun Goemba** to the head of a valley. Finally the road traverses across the top of the valley to a Tibetan chorten and array of prayer flags atop Yotong La (3425m).

Yotong La to Zungney
24km • 1 hour
The descent from the pass is through firs, then blue pines and bamboo. The road enters the upper part of the **Chhume valley**, marked by the small roadside Chuchi Lhakhang at **Gaytsa**. On a hill to the north of Gaytsa is **Buli Lhakhang**, built by Tukse Chhoying, the son of Dorje Lingpa (1346–1405). On the ground floor is Jowo Lhakhang and on the upper floor is Sangay Lhakhang. A few black-necked cranes winter in the fields to the north-east of the village.

To the east of Gaytsa are the remains of Samtenling Goemba on a forested knoll. The red roofs of **Tharpaling Goemba** are visible above the trees on a cliff to the north-east. Nyingma philosopher and saint Longchen Rabjampa (1308–64) founded Tharpaling. It has several temples, and houses about 100 monks. It's possible to visit the goemba by driving 9km up a rough road from Gaytsa or by trekking over the hill from Jakar. Above Tharpaling, at about 3800m, is the large white complex of **Choedrak Goemba**. Pema Lingpa revealed several *terma* near these monasteries.

From Gaytsa the road follows the Gaytsa Chhu gently down the valley for 2km to Domkhar. A dirt road leads uphill to the south of this village for about 500m to **Domkhar Trashi Chholing**, the summer palace of the second king. It was completed in 1937 and is a replica of Kuenga Rabten, which is south of Trongsa. It served for several years as the residence of the grand queen mother, and is now under the care of the *rabdey* (monk body) of Trongsa Dzong. The large building to the south of Domkhar Trashi Chholing is a monastic school built in 1968 by the previous reincarnation of the Karmapa, the head of the Karmapa lineage, but it is not currently in use.

Beyond Domkhar village is the settlement of **Chhume** with several shops and two large schools alongside more than 500m of straight road, perhaps the longest stretch of its kind in the hills of Bhutan. Speed bumps have been strategically placed to ensure that your driver does not take advantage of this to make up time.

The people of this valley have traditionally been sheep herders. The Australian government is helping to upgrade the quality and quantity of the wool produced here. If you are interested in this project, you can visit the Bhutan Australian Sheep and Wool Development project offices west of Zungney.

On the outskirts of **Zungney** (2750m) is the 1.5MW Chhume mini–hydro plant, which supplies electricity to Trongsa and Bumthang.

Stop at the two shops at the eastern end of Zungney village to watch the weavers. The

Yathra

Hand-spun, hand-woven wool strips with patterns specific to the Bumthang region are called yathras. They mostly have geometric designs, sometimes with a border. Three strips may be joined to produce a blanket or bed-cover called a *charkep*. In earlier days yathras were often used as shawls or raincoats to protect against the winter cold of Bumthang. Yathras were once made from wool from Tibet; nowadays some of the wool is imported from New Zealand and some wool is used from the recently introduced sheep-breeding projects in Bumthang.

Since Bhutan does not have the carpet weaving tradition of Tibet, yathra pieces have often served the same function as Tibetan rugs. Today yathras are fashioned into *toegos*, the short jackets that women often wear over the *kira* in cold weather.

speciality here is yathra, distinctive strips of woven woollen fabric in numerous colours and patterns. You can buy single strips of cloth or woollen jackets and blankets. **Zungney Lhakhang** is the small building to the west of the first yathra shop.

Zungney to Jakar
16km • ½ hour

East of Zungney, **Prakhar Goemba** is visible on a promontory on the opposite side of the river. It's a 10-minute walk to the three-storey goemba, which was built by Dawa Gyaltshen, a son of Pema Lingpa, one of the most important figures in Bhutanese history (see the boxed text 'Terton Pema Lingpa' later in this chapter). On the ground floor is a statue of Sakyamuni crafted by artists from Nepal. On the middle floor are statues of Guru Tshengay, the eight manifestations of Guru Rinpoche and the top floor contains nine small chortens and some paintings that are as old as the goemba. The Prakhar *tsechu* is held in autumn in the courtyard of a nearby newer building.

A 30-minute walk uphill from Prakhar leads to **Nimalung**, a Nyingma goemba that was founded in 1935 by Dorling Trulku. It now houses more than 100 monks who study here in the *shedra*. The small lhakhang contains an important statue of Tara as well as statues of Chenresig, Sakyamuni and Guru Rinpoche. A large *thondrol* with the eight manifestations of Guru Rinpoche was donated to the monastery in 1994 and is displayed at the close of the Nimalung tsechu.

The road follows the valley down past the apple orchards of Mangar and into blue pine forests. It's a short climb to Kiki La, a crest at 2860m marked by a chorten and many prayer flags. Once over the side ridge, the road descends into the Choskhor valley towards the Bumthang Chhu.

JAKAR
☎ 03 • elevation 2580m

Near the foot of the Choskhor valley, Jakar is the major trading centre of the region. This will probably be your base if you visit the valley as most of the hotels and services

STAN ARMINGTON

JULIA WILKINSON

ivers, or *chhus*, score the country with deep valleys: Wangdue Phodrang Dzong stands sentry over ang Chhu in central Bhutan (top) and many rivers, such as Bumthang Chhu, are spanned by /ooden cantilever bridges (bottom).

RICHARD I'ANSON

JULIA WILKINSON

RICHARD I'ANSON

Images and instruments of devotion draw together artistic and religious practices. Prayer wheels (top left & bottom) focus the mind and symbols such as the kalacakra (top right) and the lotus detail in the wheel (bottom) signal one's belief system.

are found here. The rest of the valley is covered under the separate heading 'Choskhor Valley' later in this chapter.

There is a strong wind from the south every afternoon, which makes Jakar extremely cold during the evenings. You will need to dress warmly.

Orientation & Information

The road from Trongsa enters Jakar from the south, passing a football field that is also an army helipad. A traffic circle and the 14th-century **Jakar Lhakhang** mark the centre of the town. A wide main street leads east from the traffic circle to a bridge over the Bumthang Chhu. Just before you cross the bridge to leave the town, a small chorten marks the spot where a Tibetan general's head was buried after the defeat of a 17th-century Tibetan invasion force.

There are many shops and a few restaurants lining the main street and, as in Trongsa, many are run by people of Tibetan descent. Some Chinese goods have been brought over the high passes from Tibet and are for sale here.

There is a T-junction at the eastern end of the bridge; the northbound road leads to the

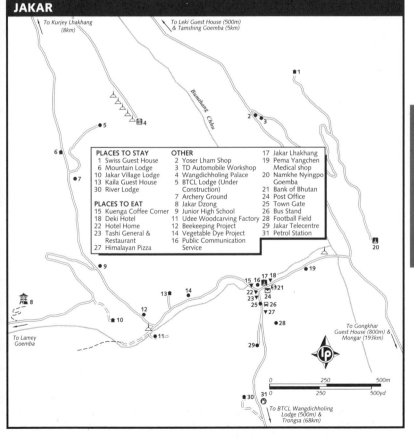

JAKAR

To Kurjey Lhakhang (8km)

To Leki Guest House (500m) & Tamshing Goemba (5km)

Bumthang Chhu

CENTRAL BHUTAN

PLACES TO STAY
1 Swiss Guest House
6 Mountain Lodge
10 Jakar Village Lodge
13 Kaila Guest House
30 River Lodge

PLACES TO EAT
15 Kuenga Coffee Corner
18 Deki Hotel
22 Hotel Home
23 Tashi General & Restaurant
27 Himalayan Pizza

OTHER
2 Yoser Lham Shop
3 TD Automobile Workshop
4 Wangdichholing Palace
5 BTCL Lodge (Under Construction)
7 Archery Ground
8 Jakar Dzong
9 Junior High School
11 Udee Woodcarving Factory
12 Beekeeping Project
14 Vegetable Dye Project
16 Public Communication Service

17 Jakar Lhakhang
19 Pema Yangchen Medical shop
20 Namkhe Nyingpo Goemba
21 Bank of Bhutan
24 Post Office
25 Town Gate
26 Bus Stand
28 Football Field
29 Jakar Telecentre
31 Petrol Station

To Lamey Goemba

To Gongkhar Guest House (800m) & Mongar (193km)

0   250   500m
0   250   500yd

To BTCL Wangdichholing Lodge (500m) & Trongsa (68km)

Swiss Guest House and temples on the eastern side of the Bumthang Chhu. The southbound road is the route to Mongar and eastern Bhutan. On the hill above the east side of the bridge is the **Namkhe Nyingpo Goemba**. This Nyingma monastery was founded in the 1970s and has more than 300 monks in residence. The new prayer hall has massive statues of Guru Rinpoche, Chenresig and Sakyamuni.

Turning left from the traffic circle, a road leads up the west side of the valley. It makes a short climb past the Kaila Guest House to an intersection at the top of the town. A dirt road leads south to Udee Woodcarving Factory and another unpaved road leads west to the Public Works Department camp. The paved road leads north past a bee-keeping project, the junior high school and the road to the dzong, then continues past the hospital up the western side of the valley to Kurjey Lhakhang.

If you are having car trouble, you're in luck. The large TD Automobile Workshop (☎ 631106) on the east side of the road at the turn-off to the Swiss Guest House is one of the better repair facilities in the country.

Jakar is a compact town and most facilities are within a very short walking distance of the traffic circle. There are several public call offices (PCOs) throughout the town. Medical supplies are available from the Pema Yangchen Medical Shop on the main street.

Money The Bank of Bhutan (☎ 631123) in the centre of Jakar is open 9am to 1pm Monday to Friday and 9am to 11am Saturday.

Email & Internet Access The Jakar Telecentre on a hill at the south end of town has Internet and email facilities available for Nu 3 per minute. It is open 9am to 5pm Monday to Friday and 9am to 1pm Saturday. The small Public Communication Service (☎ 631250) is next to the Jakar Lhakhang and charges Nu 5 per minute.

Jakar Dzong

According to legend, when the lamas assembled in about 1549 to select a site for a monastery, a big white bird rose suddenly in the air and settled on a spur of a hill. This was interpreted as an important omen, and the hill was chosen as the site for a monastery and for Jakar Dzong, which roughly translates as 'castle of the white bird'.

Jakar Dzong is in a picturesque location overlooking the Choskhor valley. The current structure was built in 1667 and is said to be the largest dzong in Bhutan, with a circumference of more than 1500m. Its official name is Yuelay Namgyal Dzong, in honour of the victory over the troops of Tibetan ruler Phuntsho Namgyal. The *utse* (central tower) is about 50m tall and is located on the outside wall, so there is no way to circumambulate it other than by walking around the entire dzong. A covered passage leads from the dzong to a nearby spring – a feature that ensured water could be obtained in the event of a long siege. The dzong was damaged once by fire, and was again s everely damaged by the 1897 earthquake.

The paintings inside the dzong's lhakhang feature Channa Dorje and the life of Milarepa. Compared to other dzongs, there are relatively few wood carvings here; most of the timber is decorated with paintings.

The entrance to the dzong leads into a very narrow courtyard surrounded by administrative offices. The utse is on the east side of the courtyard, and beyond that is the monks' quarters and the district court. The rabdey from Trongsa moves here in summer; there is only a small group of caretaker monks during the winter. When the monks arrive, they perform a ceremony commemorating the defeat of the Tibetan invaders from Lhobrak in 1644. At the west end of the dzong is a slightly larger courtyard surrounded by administrative offices.

The road to the dzong starts near the junior high school and climbs westwards to a parking lot. The final approach to the dzong is made on foot along a stone-paved path. Even if the dzong is closed it's a worthwhile climb because there is a good view of Choskhor valley from the front courtyard. The road continues past the dzong to the high school and Lamey Goemba.

Wangdichholing Palace

The extensive palace of Wangdichholing was built in 1857 on the site of a battle camp of the penlop of Trongsa, Jigme Namgyal. It was the first palace in Bhutan that was not designed as a fortress. Namgyal's son, King Ugyen Wangchuck, chose it as his principal residence. It was used throughout his reign and also during the reign of the second king. The entire court moved from Wangdichholing to Kuenga Rabten each winter in a procession that took three days. Wangdichholing was the early home of the third king, who moved the court to Punakha in 1952.

Wangdichholing was inherited by Ashi Choeki Wangchuck, an aunt of the present king, but is no longer used and is not open to the public. The only inhabitants of the palace are a few caretakers who maintain Jigme Namgyal's chapel atop the utse. It is reached by turning south on a road that passes behind the eastern side of the hospital. There are five giant water-driven prayer wheels inside square chortens as you approach the gates of the palace.

Lamey Goemba

High on a hill sits Lamey Goemba, a large palace and monastery built in the 1800s as a residence for King Ugyen Wangchuck. Its design is in the palace style of the time, and is similar to Wangdichholing. It is now being used by the Integrated Forest Development Project. There is a large elaborately decorated courtyard that is being renovated and restored. There are a few houses nearby. A trail leads from Lamey Goemba over the hill to Tharpaling Goemba in the Chhume valley.

Vegetable Dye Project

An interesting vegetable dye project (☎ 631 121) east of the Kaila Guest House is supported by Ideas International, an Australian NGO, with additional assistance from a Bangladesh NGO. The project is producing traditional vegetable dyes to use in the production of cotton thread and a raw silk. Some of the plants used to produce various colours are indigo (blue), turmeric (yellow), onion skin (off-white), oak bark (brown), walnut shell (blackish-brown), fern (light yellow), peach bark (cream colour), madder (light red), walnut bark (dark brown and grey) and rhododendron bark (yellow).

Places to Stay

All of Bumthang's guesthouses follow a similar design with the dining room in a separate building and, except for the BTCL lodge, all are family run. Most guesthouses have *bukharis* (wood stoves) to heat the rooms. If you're cold, ask the room attendants to light the stove – they start it with a dollop of kerosene. The efficient bukharis heat the room quickly, but don't burn for very long.

River Lodge (☎ 631287) Singles/doubles Nu 800/950. This converted farmhouse above the road has nine rooms with attached toilets and another five rooms with shared facilities. The lodge has helpful management and a small library and hot-stone bath.

Swiss Guest House (☎ 631145, fax 631278) Singles Nu 450-650, doubles Nu 750-1500. This place is in a pleasant setting perched on a hill 60m above the valley floor and surrounded by an apple orchard. The original hotel has 13 rooms; these are the cheaper rooms and all but one share toilet facilities. Nine new rooms in an adjoining building are more expensive and have private bathrooms. The hotel is decorated with lovely carvings and varnished pine panelling throughout. The water supply is from a rock spring; this is probably the only place in south Asia that advertises that you can safely drink the tap water. Each of the two buildings has its own private dining room heated by a bukhari in the winter.

Jakar Village Lodge (☎ 631242, fax 631377, ⓔ gaseyjvl@druknet.net.bt) Singles/ doubles 800/1000. Said to have the best food in Bumthang, this 16-room hotel situated below the dzong is run by an ex-*dzongdag* (district administrator) who will regale you with stories as you sample his assortment of teas in the hotel lounge.

Kaila Guest House (☎ 631219, fax 631227) Singles/doubles Nu 500/750. This is the closest hotel to Jakar and is frequented by Bhutanese and expatriates. It has 12 rooms that open onto the parking lot like a motel, and a busy dining room with good food. The

CENTRAL BHUTAN

owner is an accommodating host and was the cook at the Swiss Guest House for many years before opening his own establishment.

Mountain Lodge (☎ 631255, fax 631275) Singles/doubles Nu 950/1100. The lodge has 22 wood-panelled rooms in a large two-storey building overlooking Wangdich-holing Palace.

Leki Guest House (☎ 631434) Singles/doubles Nu 850/950. Leki has 10 rooms with shared bathroom in a three-storey house, 10 rooms with private bathroom in cottages and a highly decorated dining room with a friendly atmosphere. The rooms have electric heaters instead of bukharis.

Yangphel Pilgrims Lodge (☎ 631191, fax 631176) Singles/doubles Nu 700/1008. Near Jampa Lhakhang, Yangphel is a 10-room guesthouse in traditional style with a large hot-stone bath facility.

Gongkhar Guest House (☎ 631288, fax 631345) Singles/doubles Nu 850/1000. This excellent hotel has 10 rooms with bukharis and abundant hot water. There's a good view of the dzong and food is good with lots of variety.

BTCL Wangdichholing Lodge (☎ 631107, fax 631138) Singles/doubles Nu 800/1000. The very old Wangdichholing Lodge, which served travellers for many years, has been torn down and the BTCL is building a new facility in the same location. In the mean-while, it operates a new 10-room facility on a hill south of town.

Places to Eat & Drink

There are plenty of small bars and local restaurants along Jakar's main street, but they only offer snacks and *thukpa* (noodle soup). The small *Deki Hotel*, next to the Jakar Lhakhang, usually has a pot of the local fast food, momos, steaming away in the kitchen. Across the road the *Hotel Home* (☎ 631406) and the clean *Tashi General & Restaurant* (☎ 631280) serve good local fare.

There are a few places to try if you're craving Western-style food. With prior notice the *Swiss Guest House* can produce Swiss specialities such as *roesti* (crispy, fried, shredded potatoes), fondue (Nu 560 for four people) and *racklette* (a melted cheese dish; Nu 600 for 4 people). *Himalayan Pizza* (☎ 631437), at the south end of town, produces good pizza at Nu 28 a slice as well as spaghetti. You may have to use sign language; there is no menu and the owner speaks fluent Swiss-German but no English. *Kuenga Coffee Corner* (☎ 631357) in the Udee Shopping Complex next to the Jakar Lhakhang has espresso coffee.

Shopping

As in most towns in Bhutan, the shops in Jakar contain a hodgepodge of goods. A typical shop may sell shoes, pens, nails, candy, soap, toy cars, locally made baskets, dried fish and prayer flags. A shop on the corner south of the traffic circle advertises: 'Fulfil your wishes with all kinds of Bhutanese traditional gift items'. It sells a few baskets and strips of yathra as well as chillies, potatoes and stationery.

One item in good supply in Jakar is *chugo*, dried cheese. Unless you want to break your teeth, let a piece soften for a long time in your mouth before you bite into it.

Udee Woodcarving Factory employs a few woodcarvers who turn out traditional lama tables and painted carvings.

Swiss Farm is a development project overseen by Fritz Maurer, one of the first Swiss to work in Bhutan. The project has introduced brewing, farming machinery and fuel-efficient, smokeless wood stoves to the valley. The milk from large Jersey cattle is used in Bhutan's only commercial cheese factory. The outlets selling its produce are alongside the road near the junction of the road to the Swiss Guest House. The *Yoser Lham Shop* (☎ 631193) here sells cheese, apple juice, brandy and apple wine. It has soft Gouda cheese at Nu 150 per kg and hard Emmenthal at Nu 138. This cheese is made for eating off the block, unlike the soft Bhutanese *ema*, which is used only in sauces. Red Panda beer is brewed here. Look for their new beer, *Weissbier*.

CHOSKHOR VALLEY

To most people the Choskhor valley *is* Bumthang and the Choskhor valley is often called the Bumthang valley or just simply Bumthang.

It is too high to grow rice here. Instead, large fields of buckwheat cover the valley, and so buckwheat noodles and pancakes are a Bumthang speciality. The Bumthang Chhu is famous for its large stock of trout, and despite the Buddhist reluctance to take life, fish do mysteriously appear on dinner plates, especially at Kaila Guest House in Jakar.

Western Side of the Valley

The road that leads up the western side of the valley reaches many of the most inter-

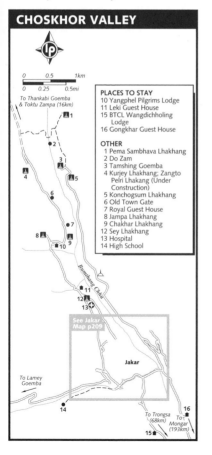

CHOSKHOR VALLEY

```
0      0.5      1km
0    0.25    0.5mi
```

To Thankabi Goemba
& Toktu Zampa (16km)

To Lamey
Goemba

Jakar

See Jakar
Map p209

To Trongsa
(68km)

To
Mongar
(193km)

PLACES TO STAY
10 Yangphel Pilgrims Lodge
11 Leki Guest House
15 BTCL Wangdichholing Lodge
16 Gongkhar Guest House

OTHER
1 Pema Sambhava Lhakhang
2 Do Zam
3 Tamshing Goemba
4 Kurjey Lhakhang; Zangto Pelri Lhakang (Under Construction)
5 Konchogsum Lhakhang
6 Old Town Gate
7 Royal Guest House
8 Jampa Lhakhang
9 Chakhar Lhakhang
12 Sey Lhakhang
13 Hospital
14 High School

esting features of Bumthang. Most of the temples on this side of the valley are connected in one way or another with the visit of Guru Rinpoche to Bumthang in 746.

Sey Lhakhang Beyond the hospital north of Jakar is Sey (Gold) Lhakhang, also known as Lhodrak Seykhar Dratshang. This is a monastic school, established in 1963, and has about 25 monks studying at any one time. The central figure in the lhakhang is Marpa Lotsawa, a great teacher of the Kagyu lineage. The goemba is open to visitors.

Jampa Lhakhang This temple is up a short side road about 1.5km past Sey Lhakhang. It is believed to have been built in the year 659, on the same day as Kyichu Lhakhang in Paro built by the Tibetan king Songtsen Gampo (see the boxed text 'The Ogress of Tibet' in the Western Bhutan chapter). The central figure in the lhakhang is Jampa, the Buddha of the Future. The statue is protected by an iron chain mail that was made by Pema Lingpa.

The temple was visited by Guru Rinpoche during his visit to Bumthang and was renovated by the Sindhu Raja after the Guru restored his life force. It has been repaired several times, and a golden roof built over time by various penlops of Trongsa. When Ugyen Wangchuck was penlop, he added the temple of **Dus-Kyi-khorlo**, which is within the enclosed compound on the northern side of the *dochey* (inner courtyard).

Chimi Dorji, the administrator of Jakar Dzong, added another temple here, **Guru Lhakhang**, on the south side of the dochey. In the centre of the courtyard is a chorten in memory of Lama Pentsen Khenpo, spiritual adviser to the first and second Bhutanese kings. There are two large stone chortens behind the temple; one is in memory of the second king's younger brother, Gongsar Dorji.

The pile of carved mani stones in the parking lot in front of the goemba is called a *thos* and represents the guardians of the four directions. Tourists are allowed to enter the courtyard, passing four large prayer wheels in front and two more inside. The building in the centre of the courtyard has a thousand butter lamps.

Inside the primary chapel are three stone steps representing ages. The first signifies the past, the age of the Historical Buddha, Sakyamuni. This step has descended into the ground and is covered with a wooden plank. The next age is the present, and its step is level with the floor. The top step represents a new age. It is believed that when the step representing the present age sinks to ground level, the gods will become like humans and the world as it is now will end.

It is said that under the lhakhang there is a lake in which Guru Rinpoche hid several terma. Look up into an alcove above the front door to see a statue of the Guru. He sat in this alcove and meditated, leaving behind a footprint.

Each October one of the most spectacular festivals in Bhutan, the **Jampa Lhakhang Drup**, is staged here. On one evening, after the lama dances, the monastery is lit by a fire dance to bless infertile women so that they may bear children.

Chakhar Lhakhang Beside the main road, a short distance beyond Jampa Lhakhang, is Chakhar (Iron Castle) Lhakhang. Although it is easy to mistake it for a house and drive right by, this is an interesting temple and is worth a short visit. It is the site of the palace of the Indian king Sendha Gyab, better known as the Sindhu Raja, who first invited Guru Rinpoche to Bumthang. The original palace was made of iron, hence the name Chakhar, and was said to have been nine storeys high, holding within it all the treasures of the world.

The current building was built in the 14th century by the saint Dorji Lingpa and its correct name is Dechen Phodrang. The main statue inside the lhakhang is of Guru Rinpoche, and there are numerous masks that are used for a small festival that takes place here in the autumn.

Kurjey Lhakhang This lhakhang is named after the body print of Guru Rinpoche, which is preserved in a cave inside the oldest of the three buildings that make up the temple complex. It is at the end of the paved road, 7km from Chakhar Lhakhang, at an elevation of 2640m.

As you enter the complex, the monks' quarters are on the left. There are three large lhakhangs against a hillside on the right. The first temple is the oldest and was built in 1652 by Mingyur Tenpa when he was penlop of Trongsa. Protruding below the roof is a figure of a white lion with a *garuda* above it, which represents the famous struggle between Guru Rinpoche (appearing as the garuda) and the local demon, Shelging Karpo (as the white lion) – see the boxed text 'The Story of Kurjey Lhakhang'. At the entrance to the lower-floor sanctuary is a small crawl-through rock passage; Bhutanese believe that in crawling through a narrow tunnel like this you will leave your sins behind. The lower-floor sanctuary has statues of the past, present and future Buddhas, while the far wall has paintings of gods who represent riches and wealth.

The upper-floor sanctuary is the holiest at the complex, and has an image of Shelging Karpo inside the door. There are a thousand small statues of Guru Rinpoche neatly lined up along the same wall, plus three larger statues. The main statue in this sanctuary is again of Guru Rinpoche, flanked by his eight manifestations. Hidden behind this image is the meditation cave where he left his body imprint. The far wall has paintings of Guru Rinpoche, his manifestations, his 25 disciples and various other figures connected with the Guru. The big cypress tree behind the lhakhang is said to have grown from the Guru's walking stick.

Ugyen Wangchuck, the first king of Bhutan, built the second temple, Sampa Lhundrup Lhakhang, in 1900, when he was still penlop of Trongsa. On the entrance porch of the temple are paintings of the guardians of the four directions and of various local deities who were converted to Buddhism by Guru Rinpoche at the same time as Shelging Karpo. The white ghostlike figure on the white horse is Shelging Karpo. Inside the temple is a statue of Guru Rinpoche, this one 10m high, flanked again by his eight manifestations. A smaller image of the Guru sits against the opposite wall.

The third building in the complex is an elaborate three-storey lhakhang built by the queen mother, Ashi Kesang Wangchuck, in 1984 under the guidance of Dilgo Khyentse Rinpoche. She also had the courtyard in front of the three temples paved with stones and built a wall with 108 chortens around the whole complex. On the porch in front of the temple is a large wheel of life depicting various hells and heavens. At the bottom you can see a man being judged, to decide to which place he will be sent. There's a beautiful mystic spiral mandala on the opposite wall and paintings of the guardians of the four directions in the hallway. The inside is elaborately decorated, and contains huge statues of wrathful deities, including Palchen Heruka and life-size statues of the Shabdrung and the fourth desi, Gyalse Tenzin Rabgye.

Two gigantic *lhadhars* (prayer flags) and a chorten dominate the centre of the courtyard. These mark the cremation sites of the first three kings of Bhutan.

The **Kurjey tsechu** is held in June and includes a masked dance that dramatises Guru Rinpoche's defeat of Shelging Karpo. A large *thangka*, called Guru Tshengye Thondrol, depicting the eight manifestations of Guru Rinpoche, is unfurled in the early morning before the dances, which are performed by the monks from Trongsa.

The new Zangto Pelri Lhakhang is under construction a short distance south of the Kurjey Lhakhang compound.

Thankabi Goemba The yellow-roofed Thankabi Goemba was founded in 1470 by Shamar Rinpoche and, after a dispute, was taken over by Pema Lingpa. It's a 17km drive north of Kurjey Lhakhang on an unpaved

The Story of Kurjey Lhakhang

In 746 the saint Padmasambhava (Guru Rinpoche) made his first visit to Bhutan. Sendha Gyab, an Indian, established himself as the king of Bumthang, with the title Sindhu Raja. He was feuding with Naochhe (Big Nose), a rival Indian king in the south of Bhutan. Naochhe killed the Sindhu Raja's son and 16 of his attendants. The raja was so distraught that he desecrated the abode of the chief Bumthang deity, Shelging Karpo, who then angrily took revenge by turning the skies black and stealing the king's life force, bringing him near to death.

One of the king's secretaries invited the tantric master Padmasambhava to Bumthang to use his supernatural powers to save the Sindhu Raja. The Guru came to Bumthang and meditated, leaving a *jey* (imprint) of his *kur* (body) in the rock, hence the temple's name. Guru Rinpoche was to be married to the king's daughter, Tashi Khuedon. He sent her to fetch water in a golden ewer. While she was away the Guru transformed into all eight of his manifestations and, together, they started to dance in the field by the temple. Every local deity appeared to watch this spectacle, except the stony-faced Shelging Karpo who stayed hidden away in his rocky hideout above the present temple.

Guru Rinpoche was not to be set back by this rejection, and when the princess returned he changed her into five separate princesses, each clutching a golden ewer. The sunlight flashing off these ewers finally attracted Shelging Karpo, but before he ventured out to see what was going on he first transformed himself into a white lion. On seeing the creature appear the Guru changed into a *garuda*, flew up and grabbed the lion and told Shelging Karpo in no uncertain terms to behave himself. He thus recovered Sendha Gyab's life force, and for good measure converted both the rival kings to Buddhism, restoring the country to peace.

Shelging Karpo agreed to become a protective deity of Buddhism; to seal the agreement the Guru planted his staff in the ground at the temple where its cypress tree descendants continue to grow. Furthermore, Guru Rinpoche made the king, Sendha Gyab, and his enemy from the south make peace; a stone pillar at Nabji in the Black Mountains marks the spot where the agreement was made.

road to Toktu Zampa where you leave the road, cross a stream on a small suspension bridge and walk 20 minutes past fields of buckwheat to Thankabi Goemba. This is the same route as the beginning of the Bumthang cultural trek (see the Trekking chapter).

Ngang Lhakhang Several hours walk up the Bumthang Chhu from Thankabi Goemba is the small region known as **Ngang-yul** (Swan Land). It's a climb of about 100m

above the valley to Ngang Lhakhang, the Swan Temple. The site was visited by Guru Rinpoche, but the present temple was built in the 15th century by Lama Namkha Samdrup, a contemporary of Pema Lingpa.

Despite the rustic and decrepit exterior, the interior contains numerous statues and paintings that were restored in the 1930s and again in 1971. The primary statue is of Guru Rinpoche, flanked by his two consorts, Yeshe Chhogyel from Tibet and

---

Terton Pema Lingpa

Pema Lingpa (1450–1521) was one of the five great tertons of Nyingma Buddhism, and the most important terton in Bhutan. The texts and artefacts he found, the dances he composed and the art he produced are important parts of Bhutan's heritage.

He was born in the hamlet of Drangchel in Bumthang's Tang valley. As a boy he learned the craft of blacksmithing from his grandfather. It's said that some of the frying pans and knives that he made are still in existence. At age 25 he had a dream in which a monk gave him a scroll in a fairy script that instructed him to take five companions and go to a point at the foot of the Tang valley where he would find a treasure.

His First Terma

On the night of the full moon he collected his younger brothers and went to a point where the river forms a large pool that looks like a lake, but here he could see no-one. After a while, standing on a large rock, he saw a temple with many doors, only one of which was open. He plunged naked into the lake and entered a large cave where there was a throne upon which sat a life-sized statue of Lord Buddha and many large boxes. An old woman with one eye handed him one of the chests and he suddenly found himself standing on the rock at the side of the lake holding the treasure.

He and his brothers excitedly took the chest back to their father, who suggested that Pema Lingpa go to a monastery and pray and try to decipher the text. He eventually managed to translate the scroll. This was a huge project, because in the fairy script one word stands for 1000 words and each

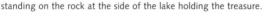

Mandarava from India. There is a painting of the Shabdrung on the wall opposite the altar and a picture of Guru Rinpoche with the lotus and the swans.

A three-day festival, the **Ngangbi tsechu**, is held here each December with masked dances in honour of the founder.

The upper chapel is a *goenkhang*, with statues of Chenresig, Jampa and Yeshe Goenpo (Mahakala). The masks for the tsechu are stored along the rafters here.

Eastern Side of the Valley

The best way to visit the eastern side of the Choskhor valley is to walk north from Kurjey Lhakhang then follow a path east to cross a footbridge, then uphill to a trail on the opposite side. Downstream of the bridge you can see a natural formation named **Do Zam**. This is the remains of a stone bridge that was built by a goddess who was trying to meet Guru Rinpoche, but the bridge was destroyed by a demon.

Terton Pema Lingpa

has a deeper meaning. Later, assisted by the khandroms, he used the text as a basis for teachings. His residence at the time was in Kunzangling, which is on a cliff above the Tang valley and is now the site of the Kunzangdrak Goemba.

The Burning Lake

Pema Lingpa's second discovery was the most famous. In the original terma there were instructions to return to the lake and collect more treasure. When Pema Lingpa went back to the lake, many people gathered to watch the event and the sceptical penlop of the district accused him of trickery. Under great pressure to prove himself, Pema Lingpa took a lighted lamp and proclaimed: 'If I am a genuine revealer of your treasures, then may I return with it now, with my lamp still burning; if I am some devil, then may I perish in the water.' He jumped into the lake, was gone long enough that the sceptics thought they were proven right, and then suddenly he emerged back on the rock with the lamp still burning and holding a statue and a treasure chest. The lake became known as Membartsho, or Burning Lake (see the Membartsho section in the Tang Valley section of this chapter).

More Treasures & Visions

During Pema Lingpa's life he found a total of 34 statues, scrolls and sacred relics in Bhutan and as far away as Samye in Tibet. Many of the statues and relics he discovered are preserved in lhakhangs throughout Bhutan.

In his visions, Pema Lingpa often visited Zangto Pelri, Guru Rinpoche's celestial paradise. During these visions he observed the dances of the khandroms and *yidam* (tutelary deities). He taught three of these dances, called *pa-cham*, to his disciples, and several of these are still performed as part of the tsechu.

Pema Lingpa built Tamshing Goemba in Bumthang in 1518. He also built Kunzangdrak Goemba in Bumthang. After his death he was reincarnated in three forms, consisting of *ku* (body), *sung* (speech) and *thug* (mind).

Through his six sons, one daughter and numerous reincarnations, Pema Lingpa left behind a legacy that still influences much of Bhutan. His most important son, Dawa Gyeltshen, was born in 1499 and settled in Chhume, one of Bumthang's valleys. Another of his sons, Pema Thinley, was a reincarnation of Pema Lingpa himself. This incarnation founded the Gangte Goemba in the Phobjikha valley, and the Gangte Trulku lineage continues, with Kuenzang Pema Namgyal, born in 1955, as the ninth reincarnation.

Another of his sons, Kuenga Wangpo, born 1505, settled in Lhuentse (known then as Kurtoe). His great-grandsons founded Dungkhar Dzong, north of Lhuentse Dzong. The royal family of Bhutan, the Wangchuck dynasty, is descended from this line.

Follow the east-bank trail south to a small (30kW) hydroelectric plant and on to Tamshing Goemba. The walk takes about 30 minutes; you can send your vehicle back through Jakar to meet you on the opposite side. If you want some exercise, walk the 5km from Tamshing Goemba back to Jakar, or save a kilometre of walking and have your vehicle pick you up at the Yoser Lham Shop at the Swiss Farm. There are good views from Tamshing back across the river to Kurjey Lhakhang.

As you travel back down this side of the valley you will pass a square white chorten with a Sanskrit inscription. On a nearby rock there are marks said to be made by the claws of a garuda.

The major influence in the temples on this side of the valley was Pema Lingpa, the great terton of the 16th century.

Tamshing Goemba This goemba (also known as Tamshing Lhendup Chholing, literally 'Temple of the Good Message') is at the northern end of the road, 5km from Jakar. It was established in 1501 by Pema Lingpa and is the most important Nyingma goemba in the kingdom. Pema Lingpa built the structure himself, with the help of *khandroms* (female celestial beings) who made many of the statues. On the inner walls are what are believed to be original unrestored images that were painted by Pema Lingpa, though recent research has uncovered even older paintings beneath them.

In the outer courtyard are monks' quarters. The entrance to the lhakhang is via an inner courtyard, or dochey. On the east side of the dochey is the small **Dunkur Lhakhang**, built in 1914. The main lhakhang has an unusual design with the key chapel in the centre of the assembly hall, almost like a separate building. In the front part of the hall are three thrones for the three incarnations (body, mind and speech) of Pema Lingpa. During important ceremonies the reincarnations sit here, although a statue may be substituted if one of the incarnations is not present.

The upper floor forms a balcony around the assembly hall. Pema Lingpa was a short man and it is said that he built the low ceiling of the balcony to his exact height. Around the outside are 100,000 old paintings of Sakyamuni. In the upper chapel is a statue of Tshepamey, the Buddha of Long Life, and a large collection of masks that are used for lama dances. On the walls are paintings of Guru Rinpoche's eight manifestations, four on each side.

In the inner sanctuary the primary statue is of Guru Rinpoche. On his right is Jampa (Maitreya, the Buddha of the Future) and on the guru's left is Sakyamuni. The statue here of Guru Rinpoche is particularly important because it was sculpted by the khandroms. The statue's eyes are looking upward, following the angels in their flight; another unique aspect of the statue is that the Guru is not wearing shoes. Above the altar are two crocodiles and a garuda. On the walls are paintings of the eight manifestations of Guru Rinpoche, four on each side.

A small statue of Pema Lingpa occupies a glass case in front of the upper chapel. On the lower floor is a suit of chain-mail armour made by Pema Lingpa. It weighs about 25kg and it is an auspicious act to carry it around the goemba three times.

Konchogsum Lhakhang A short distance below Tamshing is a small rural-looking temple – the source of many interesting stories. It was renovated in 1995 and looks quite new, but it is in fact very old, probably dating back to the 6th or 7th century. The current structure, however, dates from the 15th century, when Pema Lingpa restored it.

There is a pedestal in the courtyard upon which a large and ancient bell used to sit. It is said that when this bell was rung, it could be heard all the way to Lhasa in Tibet. A 17th-century Tibetan army tried to steal the bell, but the weight was too great and they dropped it, which cracked the bell. It is said to comprise 10% gold, 20% silver, 50% bronze and 20% tin. After a period on display in the National Museum in Paro it is now back inside the lhakhang.

It was on the hillside behind this goemba, and also in the lake said to be beneath the lhakhang, that Pema Lingpa revealed terma.

The small statues of the three Buddhas (past, present and future) in the sanctuary are said to have flown here straight from Khaine Lhakhang in Kurtoe. Hence the name of this lhakhang is Konchogsum – *konchog* (divine being), *sum* (three).

The central figure in the lhakhang is Vairocana (also known as Namnang, the Dhyani Buddha of vast space). On Vairocana's left is Chenresig, and to the right is Guru Rinpoche. Other statues are Pema Lingpa and Longchempa, a great Nyingma scholar, on the far right.

Pema Sambhava Lhakhang At the end of the road, a short climb above the valley floor leads to the small Pema Sambhava Lhakhang. The original lhakhang was built in 1490 by Pema Lingpa around the cave where Guru Rinpoche meditated and assumed his manifestation of Padmasambhava. It was expanded by Jigme Namgyal, the father of the first king, and restored in the early 1970s.

TANG VALLEY

Tang is the most remote of Bumthang's valleys. As it is higher than Choskhor and the soil not as rich. There's not much agriculture here, although the valley, through which runs the Tang Chhu, turns bright pink with buckwheat flowers in October. The people of this valley raise sheep and, at higher elevations, yaks.

From Jakar it is a 10km drive past the Dechenpelrithang sheep farm to an unpaved road that leads north up the Tang valley. The Tang road climbs past the trail to Membartsho, then passes Drangchel, Pema Lingpa's birthplace. There is a small chorten here, but no longer a village. The road climbs high above the river, passing Gemtshong, a picturesque village and lhakhang perched on a ridge at 2760m. After a short descent to the river it's 3km to a school at **Mesithang** and to Tang Rimochen Lhakhang. The road becomes rougher as it approaches Kizum, 20km from the road junction. The road continues further, to Gamling and on to a sheep breeding project at Wobtang, but it gets rougher the further it goes.

The Bumthang cultural trek ends nearby; depending on arrangements made, trekkers either walk or drive back down the valley.

Membartsho

It's a five-minute walk from the parking spot alongside the road to Membartsho (Burning Lake), which is actually a wide place in the Tang Chhu.

Pema Lingpa found several of Guru Rinpoche's terma here. A wooden bridge crosses the river and is a good vantage point to look down into the lake. Perhaps you can spot the temple that is said to exist in the lake's depths. The importance of the site is indicated by the extensive array of prayer flags and the small clay offerings called *tsha-tsha* in rock niches.

There is a large rock with a carving of Pema Lingpa and his two sons. Under the carved rock is a cave that virtuous people can crawl through, no matter how big they are. Beware: it's quite small, and very dusty.

Kunzangdrak Goemba

A two-hour walk above Drangchel leads to one of the most important sites related to the Pema Lingpa. He began construction of the goemba in 1488, and many of his most important sacred relics are kept here, one of which is a gilded stone bearing his footprint.

One of the four buildings was Pema Lingpa's house. Another, the Khandroma Lhakhang, is spectacularly situated against a vertical rock face, which was made possible by the help of the khandroms during its construction. Holy water seeps from the rock face above the building.

Tang Rimochen Lhakhang

Tang Rimochen Lhakhang marks a sacred place where Guru Rinpoche meditated. A rock in front of the lhakhang has a body-print of the Guru and two khandroms. The name 'Tag Rimochen' (an impression of tiger's stripes) is derived from the tiger stripes that appear on a rock cliff behind the building. Footprints of Guru Rinpoche and his consorts can be seen below the lhakhang where there are also two huge rocks representing the male and female *jachung* (garudas).

CENTRAL BHUTAN

Ugyen Chholing Palace

From either Gamling or Kizum it's a 45-minute climb to this 16th-century palace, originally built by Deb Tsokye Dorje, a descendant of Dorje Lingpa. The present structures, including the lhakhang, servants' quarters and a massive residential building, are more recent, having been rebuilt after their collapse in the 1897 earthquake.

The family that owns Ugyen Chholing has turned the complex into a museum to preserve its legacy and provide a place for religious studies, research and solitude. It is an interesting and well-executed facility that provides a worthwhile full-day outing from Jakar. Permanent exhibits in the main building are captioned with extensive, informative descriptions of the lifestyle and artworks of a Bhutanese noble family. The complex is supported through the Ugyen Chholing Trust, which charges Nu 100 admission.

The *Ugyen Chholing Guest House* (☎ 03-631221) in the palace grounds has four rooms at Nu 300 and two larger rooms at Nu 800 per night. Proceeds go to the trust.

Thowada Goemba

Thowada Goemba clings to the highest rocks above the north end of the Tang valley. It is said to have been founded by Mandarava, the Indian mystic consort of Guru Rinpoche, and the Guru is believed to have meditated here. The goemba was built by Dorji Lingpa. It is carved into the rock and has balconies overlooking the valley. There are numerous small meditation caves on the hillside above.

The region is said to have been sealed as a *bey-yul* (hidden valley) by Guru Rinpoche's consort Yeshe Chhogyel.

URA VALLEY

South-east of Jakar, Ura is the highest of Bumthang's valleys and is believed by some to have been the home of the earliest inhabitants of Bhutan.

Jakar to Ura
48km • 1½ hours

The road crosses the bridge to the east of Jakar, then travels south along the east bank of the Bumthang Chhu. It climbs and winds around a ridge and heads east past the National Sheep Breeding Centre. Pass the turn-off to Tang valley and Membartsho and cross a bridge over the Tang Chhu. The road starts climbing from here past a few small villages and blue pine forests. As the road climbs, you can look back at excellent views up the Choskhor and Chhume valleys.

The few houses that make up **Tangsibi** are 24km from Jakar. There are large fields of potatoes on both sides of the road. The road climbs to 3420m, where there is a monument with a cross in memory of a Indian road supervisor who died here in a 1985 road accident.

The road reaches a false summit from where you'll glimpse the top of Gangkhar Puensum. It finally crosses the **Shertang La** (3590m), marked with a yellow marker and small mani wall. Just before the pass there is a view of the Gangkhar Puensum (7541m) to the north-west.

It's then a long descent into the Ura valley to the village of Ura, which lies in the valley below the road.

Ura Village

Ura (elevation 3100m) is quite a large village. The lhakhang dominates the town and is reached by turning off the road to Mongar on a short unpaved road that leads off the main road east of the village. A 50kW hydroelectric plant provides power for the village.

There are about 40 closely packed houses along cobblestone streets, giving the town a medieval atmosphere. The Geyden Lhakhang dominates the village.

A traditional addition to the clothing of Ura women is a sheepskin shawl that serves as both a blanket and a cushion.

Places to Stay & Eat Situated alongside the road, *Hotel Zambala* (☎ 03-635003) has a few rooms for rent in an adjoining farmhouse and can provide basic meals. A new 10-room facility is under construction.

Shingkhar Guest House is a traditional house 9km up a gravel road in Shingkhar village (elevation 3400m). Rooms cost Nu 700 and meals are available.

URA VILLAGE, YESTERDAY & TODAY

The arresting beauty – most striking in the summer – of this blessed valley contrasts with the meagreness of its land. In earlier times, nothing was plentiful in winter except radishes buried under the straw in the attic with their bundled dried leaves. Hens scratched deep into the soil for food and animals foraged hungrily on the dry and cold slopes. In the evening, people huddled around the fire, the men patching clothes and repairing tools and the women spinning wool in the flickering light of resin wood. While the children inched closer to the fire, the old people, almost bandaged with quilts, murmured mantras from dark corners of the house.

Subsistence farming, which involved each family doing a little of everything, was the main drive of the village. Every household had a few domestic animals, tended by the children who also collected fire-wood during the day.

At the start of the village day, juniper or spruce smoke billowed above every house while, inside, children recited the alphabet. Early risers chatted on the streets on their way to fetch water from ponds and springs before these could become contaminated by animals. Then they would leave to work in the fields.

Inset & below: Crowds come out to see the king when he visits Ura village.

KUENSEL NEWSPAPER, BHUTAN

People worked in poor soil with backbreaking effort to raise wheat, buckwheat and vegetables. The preparation of *amg li ri* (fallow land) by breaking the frosty sods and burning them through the winter was particularly hard, but it served to increase the temperature of the soil and allow the decomposition of vegetative materials. The figure of a wizened woman or man threshing a clump of pale yellow sod in the chilly wind was an all-too-familiar sight.

Yet even after this grim effort, food shortages were not unknown. Borrowing flour, salt or chillies was part of a dependable relationship among the villagers. Otherwise, locally grown foods were supplemented with chillies, maize, millet and rice, exchanged with people in subtropical areas for butter and textiles woven by the women.

Most houses had three floors: the lowest for domestic animals; the middle for the family's living and sleeping quarters; and the top for the family shrine and to accommodate for lamas and guests. Beliefs and faith ruled people as much as law and custom. People turned to lamas to be cured of illness and to parents and local worthies for guidance. Death was not always prevented by rituals, which were the remedies of first choice. But the bereaved took solace in knowing that the best that could have been attempted was done.

For more than a generation, a few enlightened lamas and respected elders provided remarkable leadership for the village. With a moral stature that set them above the others, they together possessed a strength of leadership that allowed them to keep peace and order, never betraying the motto that within a village achievements are collective and misfortune should be shared. No outsider got a hint of unsavoury disputes in the village because they were able to contain controversy, and no difference was referred to an external authority. The alluring myth of a civilised village with people of temperate nature spread far and wide; it was widely believed that the people of Ura were more human and sensible than most.

The village was ruled from the fortress of Jakar where lived the district governor and his small staff – authorities held in both fear and respect. People went to the fortress to receive instructions on which temple, fortress, bridge or mule track they had to repair and maintain, and where official consignments had to be transported. Taxes were heavy and the obligatory contribution of labour was all too frequent.

Most people were small in stature, perhaps because of carrying loads on their backs during childhood, eating mediocre food and suffering parasitic infections. Tattered and patched clothes, readily repaired with needle and thread stuck to the collar, were common. But once a year these were put away during the village festival when the whole population gorged on delicacies and drinks and came out in their raw-silk dresses. During the festival, youth awakened to sexuality during riotous moments of celebration late at night. Around the ramparts of the temple, the venue of the festival, the young flirted and teased, sang and danced, and found love and friendship, with dawn breaking before anyone found sleep.

In winter, many villagers migrated to warmer, subtropical places where they camped in rice terraces in imitation of their ancestors' lifestyle of transhumance. Every few years, some would go to the border towns of India to get a stock of soaps, salt, pots and clothes. People did not marry outsiders nor did they settle far away. Messages, written or verbal, were sent with travellers passing through the village. An average villager lived and died within the horizon of a few surrounding districts.

That is how life was some 25 years ago. That things would change so much over this period was inconceivable to anybody in my village at that time. Most of my friends thought the future would be like the past and saw no reason to continue their studies. They dropped out of the village school, which had difficulty in getting enough students to keep going. Now, with parents realising that education leads to jobs and financial success, enrolment has jumped to more than 80%. In Bhutan, both education and medical care are free.

Many new amenities have come to the village. There is a referral hospital in the next valley and a basic health unit in the village, from where contraceptives are available and fearful AIDS posters are displayed. A few shops have sprung up next to the village. Electricity from a mini-hydroelectric plant provides lighting. Stoves that emit less smoke have been installed, and there is a piped water tap near every house.

Now a motor road passes right around the village and the transporting of goods on back or in caravans is very rare. The valley has a phone line from which it is even possible to call Europe. Many villagers have been on pilgrimages to India, and some have travelled further abroad by air. Tourists – no longer a curiosity – pass by in increasing hordes, encouraging the villagers to suspect that people elsewhere are very rich and life is more enjoyable in the lands from which tourists come. The villagers, like tourists, increasingly wear imported fabrics. Fewer woven textiles are seen. Much-wanted articles such as video recorders, radios, Swiss boots and refrigerators have come within some families' reach. A few even own trucks and Toyotas, although they come with mortgages.

Farming systems have changed. Brown Swiss breeding bulls are kept in the village livestock centre for raising the crossbred cattle that can be seen grazing on clover and alfalfa pastures around the village, and halfinger stallions are kept at the centre, too. Merino sheep from Australia have also been introduced. People no longer keep their livestock in their houses – they are penned outside the perimeter of the village. Less buckwheat and wheat is cultivated because farmers can buy imported rice out of a wage income or profits from potato sales, their main cash crop. Yet it is harder for them to protect their crops effectively from the wild boars that have increased with the expanding forest. Thanks to stringent environmental policies, the forest around the village is growing rapidly, but at the same time, the village's open grazing area is shrinking.

A block-development committee consisting of elected members meets regularly to consider issues of general interest. There are also special committees concerned with the temple, its calendar rituals and festivals, the school and the mini-hydroelectric project. But there are some entanglements that cannot be resolved by any committee. Recently, an ugly squabble broke out, tying everyone in knots. The venality of the villagers, rarely seen earlier, seems to have been triggered by cunning manipulation.

Although the village birth rate has increased, the number of people actually living in the village has decreased. Many people leave to get jobs or join the government service. Others marry outside the village. The village then has no real meaning in their lives, nor they in its. They may come to visit, but more as sentimental guests than as villagers.

An acute labour shortage has left a large portion of the fields lying fallow year after year. To make up for this, a few people have bought power tillers that now can be heard shattering the silence of the mountains. The government provides agricultural machinery at a huge subsidy and preferential credit, but not every field is flat enough for machines. The ploughman won't disappear overnight. A pair of draft animals can be grunting under a yoke in the field next to the roaring power tiller.

Despite astounding progress, some younger people expect more amenities to come in the next stage of development and are anticipating an easier future. The older villagers think that enough has been provided and, now that everybody is comfortably above hardship and the subsistence level, the next preoccupation of the village should be culture and faith. However, ambitious and materialistic youth think that the leaders live in the twilight of the past.

The village was honoured by a visit by His Majesty in the autumn of 1997. The people listened with folded hands to His Majesty, who is revered as a bodhisattva, as he gave precious advice to the students and explained his larger vision for the country. In the 28 years of his rule, Ura has gone from a marginal community in a harsh environment to a prosperous valley.

Karma Ura

Karma Ura is the author of the historical novel *The Hero with the Thousand Eyes* and he heads the Centre for Bhutan Studies.

Southern Dzongkhags

Two dzongkhags lie on the southern border of central Bhutan. Unfortunately, tourists are not permitted to travel in these regions because of the threat posed by separatist groups that have moved across the border from Assam. Years ago it was possible to trek here and to visit what is now Royal Manas National Park. If the region reopens, it offers a unique nature experience in an area of extreme biodiversity.

ZHEMGANG DZONGKHAG

Zhemgang, along with neighbouring Mongar, was once a collection of tiny principalities, collectively known as Khyeng, absorbed into Bhutan in the 17th century.

Panbang, near the Indian border, is known for its round baskets called *bangchung*.

A two-day walk from Zhemgang town leads to **Nabji**. Here a stone pillar commemorates the settlement of the dispute between the Sindhu Raja and Naochhe that was mediated by Guru Rinpoche. (See the boxed text 'The Story of Kurjey Lhakhang' earlier in this chapter.)

SARPANG DZONGKHAG

Sarpang is on the southern border, and a large part of the district is protected within the Royal Manas National Park. **Kalikhola** is a border town that has no road connection with the rest of Bhutan. Travel to and from Kalikhola involves passing through Indian territory. It is in the far western part of Sarpang Dzongkhag.

Gelephu
☎ 06

The large border town of Gelephu is the gateway to the south and to the Manas area. There are a few hotels here, including the ***Dragon Guest House*** *(☎ 251252)*, ***Hotel Peagadly*** *(☎ 251079)*, ***Hotel Lhaden*** *(☎ 251101)* and ***Hotel Tashi Paykhel*** *(☎ 251143)*.

Royal Manas National Park

There are simple lodges at Kanamakra, Rabang and Panbang, and, if the area is reopened, a tented camp can be established at Pantang. A 25km road leads from Gelephu to Kanamakra at the south-western corner of the park. There is also a road from Tingtibi on the Trongsa-Gelephu road. This 40km road passes along the northern boundary of the park from Gomphu to Panbang village.

CENTRAL BHUTAN

Eastern Bhutan

Even though it is the most densely populated region, eastern Bhutan remains the kingdom's hinterland. Roads reach the major towns, but there are numerous remote and isolated valleys hidden among the hills, some of which are home to minority ethnic groups comprising less than 1000 people.

The dominant language here is Sharchop (language of the east), although there are many local languages and dialects. Sharchop is different enough from Dzongkha that people from eastern and western Bhutan usually have to use English or Nepali to communicate. If you visit a particularly remote village your guide may have to resort to sign language.

The sale of tobacco is banned in all the *dzongkhags* of eastern Bhutan. There are efforts to limit alcohol consumption, but this is so engrained in the culture of the east that they have not been very successful. Don't become overly concerned if you see someone sleeping it off by the side of the road.

Eastern Bhutanese are also great fans of chillies, and both Lhuentse and Trashigang are known for their excellent large green chillies.

The hills are extremely steep in the east and much of the land is inaccessible. Because of the slash-and-burn system of shifting cultivation called *tseri*, the forest cover at lower elevations is less extensive than in other parts of Bhutan; there are large fields of corn and, at lower elevations, rice.

The general quality of hotels, food and service in eastern Bhutan is far lower than it is in Thimphu and Paro. Don't venture into this part of the kingdom unless you have a sense of humour, are prepared for a few rough spots and are able to take the lack of hot water and Western toilets in your stride.

Eastern Bhutan is separated from the rest of the country by a large and extremely steep chain of hills that runs from the Tibetan border almost to the Indian border. The road from Bumthang crosses these hills via Thrumshing La (3750m). Other than

Highlights

- Visit Trashigang, one of the most attractive and lively towns in Bhutan.

- Follow the dramatic cliff-hugging road over Thrumshing La.

- Visit the picturesque Lhuentse Dzong in the remote and ancient region of Kurtoe.

- Visit the Institute for Zorig Chusum in remote Trashi Yangtse, where some of Bhutan's highest quality handicrafts are produced.

! **All Bhutanese Internet and email addresses have changed, see page 86.**

trails, this one road is the region's only link to the rest of the country. If the road is closed because of snow or landslides, the only way to reach Thimphu by road is to travel via India, but few Bhutanese now opt for this route because of security problems in India caused by Assamese separatist groups.

The Manas river system, Bhutan's largest river and a major tributary of the Brahmaputra, drains most of eastern Bhutan. Two tributaries of the Manas extend through the region and form a large system of relatively low valleys. The headwaters of the Kuri Chhu are in Tibet; it crosses into Bhutan at only 1200m elevation before it passes below Lhuentse. Below Mongar it is tapped by the large Kuri Chhu hydroelectric project before it joins the Drangme Chhu to become the Manas. One fork of the Drangme Chhu rises to the east of Bhutan, in the Indian state of Arunachal Pradesh. The other major fork, the Kutong Chhu, drains the Trashi Yangtse valley, then flows south and joins the Indian branch and flows below Trashigang before turning south-west to join the Kuri Chhu. Just before it exits Bhutan, the Manas is joined by the Mangde Chhu, which drains Trongsa and most of central Bhutan.

History

In ancient times eastern Bhutan was a collection of separate petty states, each ruled by a king. The region was an important trade route between India and Tibet. Goods flowed via Bhutan through what is now Singye Dzong in the Lhuentse district to the Tibetan town of Lhobrak.

The most important figure in this region's history was Chhogyel Mingyur Tenpa. When he was *penlop* (governor) of Trongsa he led his armies to eastern Bhutan to quell revolts in Bumthang, Lhuentse, Trashigang, Mongar and Zhemgang. His efforts were responsible for bringing eastern Bhutan under the rule of the *desi* (secular ruler of Bhutan) and went a long way towards the ultimate unification of the country. Mingyur Tenpa built the Trongsa Dzong and was responsible for the construction of most of the *dzongs* in eastern, as well as central, Bhutan. In 1668 he was enthroned as the third desi and ruled until 1680.

Mongar Dzongkhag

The Mongar district is the northern portion of the ancient region of Khyeng. Shongar Dzong, Mongar's original dzong, is in ruins, and the new dzong in Mongar town is not as architecturally spectacular as others in the region. Drametse Goemba, in the eastern part of the district, is an important Nyingma monastery, but it's difficult to get to.

JAKAR TO MONGAR

It takes about seven hours to cover the 193km between Jakar and Mongar, crossing

two passes and traversing several wild roads that cling to the hillsides. It is one of the most spectacular drives in the country, descending 3200m in a distance of 84km.

For a description of the road between Jakar and Ura see Ura Valley in the Central Bhutan chapter.

Ura to Thrumshing La
36km • 1¼ hours

Beyond the office of the Thrumshing La National Park and the 50kW Japanese-funded hydroelectric plant, the road crosses the small Lirgang Chhu on a large bridge called Liri Zam. It climbs and winds in and out of side valleys covered in dwarf bamboo and crosses a ridge that is labelled Wangthang La on some maps. It then drops into another valley, crosses a stream and starts climbing again past a road workers' camp and a small local-style restaurant.

The forest is mostly fir with an undergrowth of several varieties of rhododendron, including some with large red and pink flowers and others with small yellow blossoms. Because the soil is very sandy, the road is unstable and has left a large scar on the hillside. If you are lucky enough to travel on a clear day, watch for a view of Gangkhar Puensum (7541m) as you approach the pass. A *mani* wall and prayer flags adorn the pass and a sign proclaims: 'You are at highest point'. This is **Thrumshing La** (3750m), 85km from Jakar, and the border of Mongar Dzongkhag; you are now officially in eastern Bhutan.

Thrumshing La to Sengor
22km • 1 hour

The eastern side of the pass is much rockier; the road switchbacks down through a fir forest past a road sign that says 'Life is a journey, complete it'. At about 3000m, 20km from the pass, the route emerges from the trees and enters the pastures of the Sengor valley. There is a settlement at **Sengor** of a few houses near the road, although the main part of the village, about 20 houses, is in the centre of the valley, a few hundred metres away. If you're carrying a picnic lunch and have not already eaten it, this is

EASTERN BHUTAN

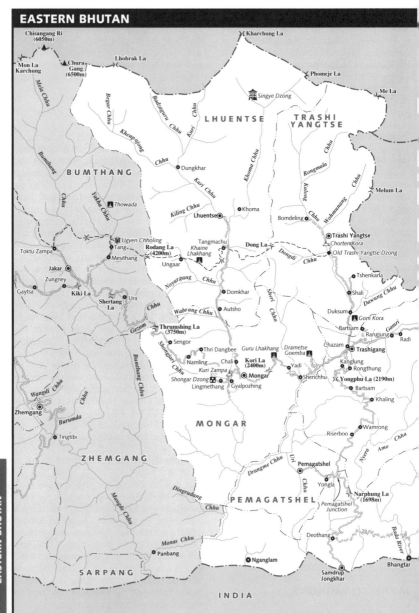

an excellent place to do so – there is no good place to stop for the next two hours. A sign in Dzongkha adorns the rustic **Kuenphen Hotel** (☎ 03-635002) where you can get a simple local-style meal. A large road construction contingent here keeps the pass open. The large fancy building below the road is a project office that has been converted into an outreach clinic and school.

Sengor to Kuri Zampa
62km • 1¾ hours

The next stretch of road is the wildest in Bhutan. Five kilometres beyond the Sengor valley the road begins a steep descent into the Kuri Chhu valley, clinging to the side of a rock cliff with numerous streams and waterfalls leaping out onto the road. It's often foggy and cloudy on this side of the pass, making it difficult to see what's below – which is fortunate, because more often than not, it's nothing.

There are several *chortens* here – erected as memorials to the almost 300 Indian and Nepali contract labourers who were killed during the construction of this portion of the road. As you drive along the narrow way that was hacked into the side of a vertical cliff, you may wonder if you will soon join them. There are no settlements here except for a camp at **Namling**, 22km from Sengor, where a crew works frantically to protect the road from tumbling down the mountainside.

About 17km from Namling, after a long descent that traverses the side of a cliff, the road reaches safer ground. At Thri Dangbee it emerges into the upper part of a large side valley of the Kuri Chhu, a land of bamboo, ferns and leeches. You pass extensive cornfields and descend to the valley floor on a road that winds around like a pretzel. Rice terraces appear and the vegetation becomes much more tropical. Near the foot of the valley, where the elevation is quite low, tropical fruits such as mango and pineapple flourish.

Atop a hill on the opposite side of the river, near the kilometre marker 123, is a view of the ruins of **Shongar Dzong**. There's not much to see – just some stone walls almost hidden by trees on the top of a hillock. This is believed to have been one of

EASTERN BHUTAN

Essential Oil

The Essential Oils Development Project markets lemongrass oil to overseas buyers and finances distillation units for villagers in eastern Bhutan. The grass grows in abundance throughout the region and the collection and distillation process provides additional revenue for several thousand families whose only other source of income is herding or farming.

Lemongrass is currently the only commercially processed plant and most of the produce is sold to Germany. There are plans to expand into the production of wintergreen, artemisia, silver fir, juniper, rhododendron and pine oils.

the earliest and largest dzongs, perhaps built as early as 1100. Like Trongsa, Shongar was powerful because the dzong was ideally situated to control movements between eastern and western Bhutan. It was destroyed by fire in 1899 and a new dzong was built in Mongar town. You can hike to the dzong on a rough trail that also offers views of a variety of birdlife.

A few kilometres further, in **Lingmethang** (650m), there is an animal husbandry farm where Jersey cows, which are known for the large quantity of high-fat-content milk that they produce, are raised. It's not much of a village, there's only a large Public Works Department (PWD) station, some small rough wooden shops, a pig farm and a big sawmill.

The road turns north at a chorten that marks the junction of the main Kuri Chhu valley. After dropping to Kuri Zampa at 570m it crosses a Bailey bridge with lots of prayer flags hanging from it – a total descent of 3200m from the pass. On the east side of the bridge is a large chorten that is patterned after Bodhnath in Nepal; it is said to contain relics from the original Shongar Dzong. Beside the bridge is a factory that extracts oil from lemongrass.

A secondary road leads downstream 4km to the new town of **Gyalpozhing** and another 3km to the 60MW Kuri Chhu power project. Gyalpozhing consists of two large schools and housing for students and teachers. The government plans to build an entire town similar to Khuruthang here, including restaurants, hotels and a resort. Included in the plan is a 64km-long road down the Kuri Chhu valley to the Indian border.

Kuri Zampa to Mongar
25km • ¾ hour

The road to Mongar climbs through chir pine forests up the eastern side of the Kuri Chhu valley. A side road leads to the old Mongar hydroelectric plant, which has become redundant now that the Kuri Chhu project is operating.

To the north you can see the road to Lhuentse traversing the side of the valley. This road leaves the Mongar road at Gangola, 12km before Mongar, and travels 65km to Lhuentse (see Mongar to Lhuentse under Lhuentse Dzongkhag later in this chapter).

The Mongar road climbs through cornfields towards a cluster of houses on top of the hill. A final switchback leads into Mongar.

MONGAR
☎ 04 • elevation 1600m

Most towns in the west of Bhutan are in valleys. In eastern Bhutan most towns, including Mongar, are on the tops of hills or ridges. A row of large eucalyptus trees protects the town from the wind.

There is little of real interest to see in Mongar, but many people spend a night here before continuing to Trashigang. It takes about 11 hours to drive from Jakar to Trashigang. This often means driving at night, which is pointless in such interesting countryside.

Orientation

Mongar was redesigned in 1997 when a bypass road was constructed and a large part of the bazaar razed and rebuilt. At the western end of the town is the petrol pump and a turnoff to the bypass, which travels below the vegetable market and a collection of new shops and houses. The old road leads to the town centre where two hotels sit in a tiny cul-de-sac off the main street. The dzong is on a ridge above the town.

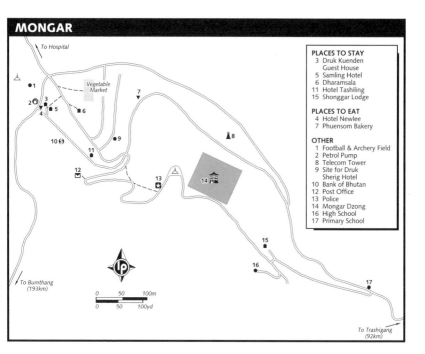

MONGAR

PLACES TO STAY
3 Druk Kuenden
Guest House
5 Samling Hotel
6 Dharamsala
11 Hotel Tashiling
15 Shonggar Lodge

PLACES TO EAT
4 Hotel Newlee
7 Phuensom Bakery

OTHER
1 Football & Archery Field
2 Petrol Pump
8 Telecom Tower
9 Site for Druk
Sherig Hotel
10 Bank of Bhutan
12 Post Office
13 Police
14 Mongar Dzong
16 High School
17 Primary School

Information

The Bank of Bhutan (☎ 641123) branch in Mongar is open 9am to 1pm Sunday and Monday and Wednesday to Friday and 9am to 11am Saturday.

The post office is up the hill to the south of the bazaar, on the road to the dzong. There is a public telephone booth in the bazaar next to the Samling Hotel.

The hospital in Mongar (☎ 641112) north of town is a regional referral hospital.

Mongar Dzong

The present Mongar Dzong was rebuilt in 1953 and is unusual because it has two entrances. It is two storeys high with the *utse* (central tower) in the centre of the courtyard. The dzong was established here in 1930 to replace the original Shongar Dzong, although the utse dates from an earlier time. There are 50 to 60 monks in the dzong, many of them young boys aged eight to 10 years old.

The images in the *lhakhang* are of the Buddha of Long Life, Tshepamey, as well as Guru Rinpoche and the Shabdrung.

Places to Stay

Mongar is in desperate need of good accommodation after the venerable *Shongar Lodge* was turned into a government guesthouse (for which travellers can obtain permission to stay). There are three hotels planned: one by the people who run the Druk Sherig Guest House in Thimphu, one by Bhutan Tourism Corporation Limited (BTCL) and another by the Druk Kuenden group.

Druk Kuenden Guest House (☎ 641127) You will find this in the cul-de-sac at the end of the bazaar overlooking the football field. It's a cement building with four guest rooms; only one has an attached toilet.

Samling Hotel (☎ 641111, fax 641265) Rooms with shared bathroom Nu 250, rooms with private bathroom Nu 350. This

EASTERN BHUTAN

hotel has eight rooms and is opposite the Druk Kuenden Guest House.

There are numerous small local-style hotels here because the Trashigang-Thimphu bus stops in Mongar on the first night of its three-day journey. Among these smaller and more basic hotels catering to bus passengers is *Hotel Tashiling* (☎ 641207) in the bazaar. As a last resort there is always the *Dharamsala*, a simple pilgrims resthouse.

Places to Eat

Both the *Druk Kuenden Guest House* and the *Samling Hotel* provide basic meals, as does the nearby *Hotel Newlee* (☎ 621240). The *Phuensom Bakery* (☎ 641143) is the place to load up on bread for the following day's picnic lunch. Eat early; the entire town closes by 8pm.

AROUND MONGAR
Drametse Goemba

Although it's in Mongar dzongkhag, Drametse is accessible only from far eastern Bhutan. From Mongar it's 93km to Sherichhu and another 12km from Sherichhu to the Drametse turnoff. It's then a 19km, 1¼-hour drive north to Drametse, a *goemba* and small village at 2100m. The road is steep (climbing 1350m), unpaved and very rough. In the rainy season there's a lot of mud; at that time the road is suitable only for 4WD vehicles.

There are about 60 *gomchens* (married Nyingma monks) here. The monastery was founded in 1511 by the great-granddaughter of Pema Lingpa, Ani Chhoeten Zangmo, and her husband, Yeshe Gyalpo, in a place she named Drametse, which means 'the peak where there is no enemy'.

Prayer Flags

Prayer flags are ubiquitous in Bhutan, found fluttering on mountain passes, ridges, mountain meadows, rooftops, dzong and temple courtyards and in front of houses.

The prayer flags are in five colours – blue, green, red, yellow and white – symbolising the elements of water, wood, fire, earth and iron, respectively. They also stand for the five *dhyani* or meditation Buddhas; the five wisdoms; the five directions; and the five mental attributes or emotions.

They may all look similar, but prayer flags have several important variations. Some prayer flags are hung from strings near holy places, but traditional Bhutanese prayer flags are long strips of printed cloth mounted on vertical poles. The text for the flag is carved into wooden blocks and then printed on the cloth in repeating patterns. Each of the four varieties of prayer flag has a specific function, but they all serve the same basic purpose – to invoke the blessings and protection from the deities for conscious beings, living or dead.

Goendhar

The smallest prayer flags, *goendhars*, are those mounted on the rooftops of Buddhist homes. These white banners have small blue, green, red and yellow ribbons attached to their edges. They invoke the blessings and patronage of Yeshe Goenpo, the main protective deity of the country, to ensure the family's welfare and prosperity. A purification ceremony is performed and the goendhar is erected once a house has been completed. Each year, during a special ceremony celebrated by Bhutanese families honouring their personal local deities, a new banner is unfurled.

Lungdhar

The *lungdhar* (wind flag) is erected on hillsides or ridges for a number of purposes. It invokes various gods according to the needs, be they mundane or spiritual, of the person for whom it flutters. It could be for good luck, protection from an illness, the achievement of a personal goal, or the acquisition of wisdom. These flags are printed with the Wind Horse or Lungta, which carries a wish-fulfilling jewel on its back.

Inside the outer wall of the goemba is a large flagstone-paved *dochey* (courtyard) and a three-storey lhakhang. The pictures in the front of the lhakhang were painted in the 1950s and repainted in 1982. Drametse's three-day festival is in the middle of the ninth Bhutanese month, September-October (see the boxed text 'Future Festival Dates' in the Facts for the Visitor chapter). Visitors may go into the courtyard between 6am and 7pm, but not inside the lhakhang. The *thondrol* that is unfurled at the Drametse tsechu in November has an image of Pema Lingpa as the central figure.

This is wonderful potato-growing country. In the autumn there are huge piles of potatoes waiting for trucks to carry them down to the market for eventual sale in India and Bangladesh. There are some very basic food stalls in the village. There is also a Renewable Natural Resources extension office south of the monastery. In the distance to the south-east you can see the college at Kanglung.

Lhuentse Dzongkhag

Lhuentse is an isolated district although there are many sizeable villages in the hills throughout the region. It is very rural; in the whole district there are fewer than five vehicles, including the ambulance, and there is not a single petrol station.

Formerly known as Kurtoe, the region is the ancestral home of Bhutan's royal family. Although geographically in the east, it was culturally identified with central Bhutan,

Prayer Flags

The name and age of the person is printed on the flag along with the text pertaining to the exact need. Astrological charts are used to determine the direction, colour and location of the flag, and a consecration ceremony is performed when it is erected.

Manidhar

The *manidhar* is erected on behalf of a deceased person, and features prayers to the Bodhisattva of Compassion, Chenresig. When a family member dies, such flags are commissioned to cleanse the sins of the deceased. The *mani* prayer banner takes its name from the mantra *'om mani peme hum'* ('hail to the jewel in the lotus'), which is the special sacred mantra of Chenresig. These prayer flags are generally erected in batches of 108 and invoke Chenresig's blessing and immeasurable compassion for the deceased.

Both the lungdhar and the manidhar flags are placed at strategic high points from which a river can be seen. In this way, the belief is that the prayers will waft with the wind to the river, and be carried by the river on its long and winding journey.

Lhadhar

The largest flag in the country is the *lhadhar* (god flag). These huge flags can be seen outside dzongs and other important places and represent victory over the forces of evil. There is normally no text on these flags; they are like a giant version of the goendhar. The only difference, apart from size, is at the top, where the lhadhar is capped by a colourful silk parasol. You must be formally dressed in traditional Bhutanese attire for Bhutanese and in appropriate dress for foreigners to enter any place where a lhadhar stands.

The Pole

At the top of the pole is a *redi*, a wood carving of a traditional knife. It is joined to the flagpole by a *khorlo*, a wooden wheel. The redi represents the god of wisdom, Jampelyang, and the khorlo represents the lotus, which is associated with the birth of Guru Rinpoche.

Kunzang Dorji

EASTERN BHUTAN

and the high route over Rodang La was a major trade route until the road to Mongar was completed.

Many Lhuentse women are weavers, but it is usually necessary for you to ask from house to house to find textiles for sale. Khoma is especially famous as the home of the special weaving known as *kushutara* (brocade).

MONGAR TO LHUENTSE

Lhuentse is 63km from the turnoff at Gangola, and 76km (three hours) from Mongar on a road that was inaugurated in 1980. There are some rough spots, but the road is well maintained and it's a relatively comfortable drive if there have not been any recent landslides.

Mongar to Autsho
38km • 1¼ hours

It is 12km down the hill from Mongar to the junction of the Lhuentse road at Gangola (1110m). The Lhuentse road winds around the hill to Chali then to the few houses of Palangphu. Here it begins a descent through a large slide area towards the Kuri Chhu and two shops that make up the village of **Rewan**. Passing a large Tibetan-style chorten that is surrounded by 108 smaller chortens, the road reaches the extensive cornfields and roadside shops of Autsho (920m). Near the river you may be able to spot rhesus monkeys playing on stones and black cormorants looking for fish.

Autsho to Tangmachu
26km • 1 hour

The road passes beneath some towering cliffs en route to Phowan. Beyond the village there's a stretch where the route was blasted out of the side of a cliff. The road switchbacks 100m above the river to the roadside settlement of Gorgan opposite the large valley of the Noyurgang Chhu, which enters from the west. Near this part of the road, in Umling, are said to be the remains of an ancient underground stone castle built by Bangtsho Gyalpo in about 1500 BC.

After a while the Kuri Chhu valley begins to widen. Beyond a large white chorten the road crosses to the west bank of the river on a suspension bridge made out of Bailey trusses at 1150m. Tangmachu is a large collection of settlements that lies in a bowl-shaped side valley above the road. Oranges grow at the foot of the valley and the hillside is planted with red and white rice, millet and corn. A rough unpaved road leads 10km up through the valley to the isolated Tangmachu high school on a ridge 600m above.

Tangmachu to Lhuentse
13km • ½ hour

The road traverses the foot of the Tangmachu valley for about 6km, passing a road construction camp and a hydrology station at Sumpa. Rounding a corner there's a view of Lhuentse Dzong, which dominates the head of the valley. A small suspension bridge leads across the river here, providing access to the trail to **Khoma** and Singye Dzong. It's a two-hour hike to Khoma.

A short distance on the valley narrows and the road begins climbing towards the town. As the road passes the hospital there is an excellent view of the dzong perched dramatically atop a bluff.

LHUENTSE

There is little to see and do in Lhuentse, but the dzong is one of the most picturesque in Bhutan. There are a few shops and food stalls along the road as it enters the town. The road terminates at a parking lot in front of the dzong; nearby is the telecommunications office and the Bank of Bhutan. Adjoining the parking lot are quarters for government officials working in Lhuentse who have been posted to this remote area where housing is scarce.

Lhuentse Dzong

Lhuentse Rinchentse Phodrang Dzong, as it is correctly known, sits high on a rocky outcrop overlooking the Kuri Chhu valley. There are near-vertical drops on all sides of the dzong; the entrance is reached by a flagstone-paved path that switchbacks up the hill from the parking lot on the south-east side. It leads into the administrative portion of the dzong; the utse and monastic sector are at the north end on a slightly higher level.

Although Pema Lingpa's son Kuenga Wangpo established a small goemba on this site early in the 16th century, the dzong itself was built by the Trongsa penlop Mingyur Tenpa in 1654. It has been renovated several times and numerous lhakhangs have been added. It now houses a body of more than 100 monks.

Places to Stay & Eat

Royal Guest House (☎ 04-545109) You will find Lhuentse's only hotel on a hill 100m above the town. It has three rooms in the main building and three more in cabins below. You need permission from the dzongkhag administration to stay here.

From the garden of the guesthouse is an excellent view of the dzong and the snow peaks at the head of the Kuri Chhu valley. The peak at the head of the valley to the north-west of the guesthouse is Sheri Nyung.

If you arrive here without a packed lunch, order some *momos* (dumplings) or noodles at the very basic *Shangrila Hotel (☎ 04-545123)*, which is below the road opposite the dzong. The dining area is on the lower floor; the upper floor is a video parlour.

AROUND LHUENTSE
Dungkhar

An unpaved road that will eventually reach Dungkhar begins near the hospital. The first phase of 10km is partially complete. From the end of the road it's still a full-day ride to the small village of Dungkhar, named because the ridge upon which it sits is shaped like a conch *(dungkhar)*. Kuenga Wangpo settled here, and it is through him that Bhutan's royal family, the Wangchucks, trace their ancestry to the Kurtoe region. Jigme Namgyal, father of the first king, was born here in 1825 and left home when he was 15 to eventually become Trongsa penlop and the 51st desi. Special permission is required to visit Dungkhar, although this may change when the 37km-long road is completed. The Jigme Namgyal Naktshang and the 16th-century Dungkhar Naktshang are above the village. (A *naktshang* is a

temple dedicated to a warlord or protective deity.) Guru Rinpoche meditated in a cave overlooking Dungkhar, and Pema Lingpa visited the area many times and built Goeshog Pang Lhakhang near the river below the village.

Singye Dzong

Singye Dzong is on the old trade route from Bhutan to Lhobrak in Tibet. Guru Rinpoche meditated here and it's an important pilgrimage place for Bhutanese. The trek takes three days in each direction, but is off-limits to tourists. Yeshe Chhogyel, the consort of Guru Rinpoche who concealed many *terma* here, founded the goemba.

Trashigang Dzongkhag

Trashigang is the heart of eastern Bhutan and was once the centre of important trade with Tibet. There are several goembas and villages that make a visit worthwhile, but a lot of driving is required to reach this remote region.

MONGAR TO TRASHIGANG

The Mongar to Trashigang stretch is easier and shorter than the journey from Jakar to Mongar, but it still requires about 3½ hours to cover the 92km between the two towns. The road crosses one low pass, then follows a river valley before making a final climb to Trashigang.

Mongar to Kori La
17km • ½ hour

Leaving Mongar, the road climbs past fields of corn to the power substation and *shedra* (Buddhist college) at Kilikhar, then through rhododendron and blue-pine forests to the few houses in the scattered settlement of Naling. Soon the road is clinging to the side of a cliff, passing through a deep forest of rhododendrons and orchids.

About 3km past a forest nursery is Kori La (2400m), where there is an array of prayer flags and a small mani wall. The forest surrounding the pass is under a management plan regulating the harvest of trees and bamboo.

Kori La to Yadi
21km • 1 hour

The road drops from the pass into the upper reaches of the extensive Manas Chhu drainage, switchbacking down through broadleaf forests to Naktshang where **Guru Lhakhang**, a small private goemba, sits beside the road at 1890m. Above the road are several small buildings used by monks as retreat and meditation centres.

The road continues its descent through fields of corn and mustard past the road crew camp at Ningala, finally reaching the substantial village of **Yadi** (1480m). There are a few shops here, and the ***Sherub Hotel*** offers basic food and accommodation.

Below Yadi a dirt road leads 10km to Shershong and, for Bhutanese pilgrims, a two-day walk to **Aja Ney**. The 'A' of Aja is a sacred letter and 'ja' means 'one hundred'. Guru Rinpoche placed one hundred letter A's on rocks here, and for devotees it's like a treasure hunt: The more you see the more merit you gain. Those without sin usually find the most.

Yadi to Chazam
45km • 1½ hours

Beyond Yadi a long stretch of prayer flags lines the road; below are numerous switchbacks, nicknamed the **Yadi Loops**, that lead down through a forest of chir pine, dropping 350m in 10km. There is a good viewpoint where you can see the road weaving down the hill; pictures taken from here often appear in books and brochures to show how circuitous Bhutan's roads are. The unpaved road that heads west before the loops begin leads to the village of Chaskhar and a 20kW hydroelectric plant. In Pakhadang, at the foot of the steepest part of the loops, is a stream and the remains of a lemongrass distillation plant.

After more switchbacks, the road finally crosses a steel bridge into the nondescript bazaar of **Sherichhu** (600m). There are a few tea shops, a road construction camp and a small rosin and turpentine factory in a

grove of eucalyptus trees. Climb out of the Sherichhu valley to a chorten and cross a ridge to meet the large Drangme Chhu, which flows from the eastern border of Bhutan and is a major tributary of the Manas Chhu. The road doesn't climb much but traverses grassy hillsides and winds in and out of side valleys. There are a few rice terraces below.

At Thugdari, 12km from Sherichhu, is a side road to Drametse Goemba, the biggest and most important monastery in eastern Bhutan (see Around Mongar earlier in this chapter).

From several points along the road above the Drangme Chhu, it's possible to see Trashigang Dzong high above the south bank of the river. Much of the hillside beside the road is made up of loose alluvial deposits. Boulders embedded in the sand often break loose during rainstorms and fall onto the road, causing delays while road crews scramble to remove them.

After passing a PWD camp at Rolong, the road reaches a new 90m-long bridge at **Chazam** (710m). This place was named after the original chain-link bridge here, said to have been built by the Tibetan bridge builder Thangtong Gyalpo (see the boxed text 'The Iron Bridge Builder' in the Western Bhutan chapter) in the 15th century (*cha* means 'iron', *zam* means 'bridge'). The large building that formed the abutment of the old bridge has been partially restored and can be seen a short distance upstream of the new bridge; the chain is on display in the courtyard of Trashigang Dzong. There are toilets on the opposite side of the bridge.

An unpaved side road leads steeply uphill from Chazam to Gangthung and Yangnyer. The complex that is visible a short distance up this road is a jail.

Chazam to Trashigang
9km • ¼ hour

On the north side of the bridge is an immigration checkpoint where police inspect your travel permit. The road north from here follows the Kulong Chhu valley and then climbs to Trashi Yangtse (see the Trashi Yangtse Dzongkhag section later in this chapter).

The road switchbacks up through cornfields towards Trashigang, passing a turn-off that leads down to the small settlement of Chenary and the old Trashigang hydro-electric plant. There's also the Druk Seed Corporation here that produces seeds for subtropical fruit. The nursery grows olives, pomegranates, passion fruit, almonds, figs, citruses and mangoes.

At the top of the hill is a collection of motor workshops and a road junction. The road to southern Bhutan leads to the right. The left fork leads to Trashigang, 3km away. Go round a bend where there's a good view of Trashigang Dzong, then follow the road into Trashigang, which is well hidden in a wooded valley.

TRASHIGANG
☎ 04 • elevation 1070m

Trashigang is a reasonably large town with lots to explore; it is a good base for excursions to Trashi Yangtse, Khaling, Radi, Phongme and elsewhere in eastern Bhutan.

The accommodation here is pretty basic, but there is a variety of restaurants and, among the town's 21 bars, at least one amusing place to drink. Not many tourists make it to Trashigang, but there used to be many Canadian teachers working here and the people of Trashigang are used to Westerners.

Orientation
Trashigang is at the foot of a steep wooded valley with the tiny Mithidang Chhu running through it. The road enters the town from the north and just as you enter there's a cobbler shop, almost next door to which is the tiny shop of Deepak, the only barber in the hills of eastern Bhutan. The road crosses the stream on a substantial bridge near a chorten. A side road leads downhill from the chorten past a collection of shops, bars and small restaurants, then through trees and bougainvillaea past a chorten to the dzong.

On the right of the main road, opposite the large telecommunications tower, is a central plaza and parking area. A large prayer wheel sits in the centre of the square. The pedestal on the covered structure, holding the prayer wheel, is a favourite sleeping place for villagers waiting for buses. People turn this wheel day and night, with a bell signalling each revolution. Surrounding the parking area are several hotels and restaurants, a bakery and the main liquor outlet.

An unpaved road leads downhill from the centre of Trashigang to Rangjung and then to Radi and Phongme. This road begins just as the main road leaves the town and starts to emerge from the valley.

From the bazaar the road climbs the hill, turning two long switchbacks, to a dogleg around the Royal Guest House. The junior high school and post office are on the right and a short distance beyond the road forks at the hospital. The left fork leads to Kelling Lodge, a short distance downhill. The road makes a large loop through a residential area and eventually returns back to the hospital.

Information
The town boasts two banks. The Bank of Bhutan (☎ 521294) is next to the bridge and is open 9am to 1pm Sunday and Monday and Wednesday to Friday, and 9am to 11am Saturday. The Bhutan National Bank (☎ 521129) is in the town square and is open 9am to 1pm Monday to Friday and 9am to 11am Saturday.

The post office is above the town, near the high school. There are numerous public call offices (PCOs) in the bazaar.

The only *Kuensel* agency in town is the small Kuenphen Medical Store. The newspaper arrives here each week on Tuesday or Wednesday.

For medical supplies, the Kuenphen Medical Store (☎ 521175) is on the road leading to Radi. A large new hospital is under construction but until it's complete this may not be the best choice for long-term treatment; however, it will accept tourists.

Trashigang Dzong
The dzong is on a high promontory that overlooks the confluence of the Drangme Chhu and the Gamri Chhu. It was built in 1667 by Mingyur Tenpa, Bhutan's third desi. The entire eastern region was governed from this dzong from the late 17th century until the beginning of the 20th

EASTERN BHUTAN

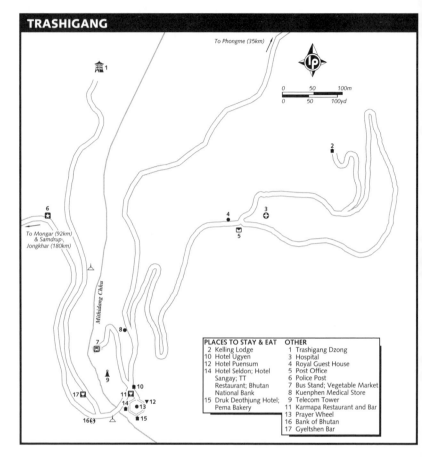

TRASHIGANG

To Phongme (35km)

To Mongar (92km)
& Samdrup
Jongkhar (180km)

Mithidang Chhu

PLACES TO STAY & EAT	OTHER
2 Kelling Lodge	1 Trashigang Dzong
10 Hotel Ugyen	3 Hospital
12 Hotel Puensum	4 Royal Guest House
14 Hotel Seldon; Hotel	5 Post Office
Sangay; TT	6 Police Post
Restaurant; Bhutan	7 Bus Stand; Vegetable Market
National Bank	8 Kuenphen Medical Store
15 Druk Deothjung Hotel;	9 Telecom Tower
Pema Bakery	11 Karmapa Restaurant and Bar
	13 Prayer Wheel
	16 Bank of Bhutan
	17 Gyeltshen Bar

century. It was destroyed by fire and rebuilt in only three years.

This dzong is different in that both the administrative and monastic sectors face onto a single dochey. On the *gorikha* (veranda) are paintings of the kings, or guardians, of the four directions. Inside the lhakhang is a statue of the deity Gasin-re or Yama, the wrathful aspect of Chenresig. He is a protector of the faith, the god of death and the king of law. He is the one that weighs good and evil at the end of a person's life. Many lama dances are performed in Trashigang to appease Yama. This particular dance is not included in the festival

schedule, but if one happens when you are in town, you will be welcomed.

There is a length of chain from the old Chazam iron bridge lying atop a wall in the outer courtyard of the dzong.

Places to Stay & Eat

Trahingang has a dearth of good hotels. The old **Kelling Lodge** (☎ 521145), once the town's best accommodation, has been turned into a government guesthouse (for which travellers can obtain permission to stay).

Druk Deothjung Hotel (☎ 521214, fax 521269) Singles/doubles Nu 650/800. This

EASTERN BHUTAN

12-room hotel near the prayer wheel is now the best in town.

Hotel Ugyen (☎ 521140) Singles/doubles Nu 80/150. Formerly the Sonam Wangchuck, this place is very much a second choice. It has 15 rooms that are similar in standard to a trekking lodge in Nepal.

Meals are less expensive in eastern Bhutan and you can find momos for Nu 25 and rice, dal (lentil soup) and curry for Nu 35. As in most of Bhutan, in Trashigang the word hotel becomes confused with restaurant.

The **Hotel Puensum** (☎ 521137) is a wood-panelled restaurant above a shop selling rice cookers and thermos flasks. It used to be a favourite of Canadian volunteers, but now provides only local fare and you need to order meals well in advance. The **Hotel Seldon** (☎ 521140) and **Hotel Sangay** (☎ 521226) are restaurants that share a common building. There are some rooms for rent upstairs, but they tend to be noisy because of the continual ringing of the bell on the prayer wheel in the town square.

The **Druk Deothjung Hotel** has the best food in town and has a small garden with tables outside. Next door the **Pema Bakery** (☎ 04-52196) produces rolls, bread and pastries. For a quick meal of rice, *ema datse* and meat try the busy **TT Restaurant** (☎ 04-521184), downstairs in the back of the Hotel Seldon.

Entertainment
There are plenty of small restaurants in the town that serve drinks. You must drink quickly, though, as the entire town closes promptly at 8pm.

Gyeltshen Bar (☎ 521149) is open daily. The sign simply says 'bar' and has a picture of a cowboy on one side and a local artist's peculiar adaptation of Donald Duck on the other. The owner, Tandin Chhenzom, is a hospitable hostess, and the bar is a popular gathering place. Alternatively, try the **Karmapa Restaurant and Bar** on the town square.

Villagers come to town on holy days, which occur on the first, 10th and 15th of the Bhutanese month. They sell the goods that they have produced and buy manufactured goods to take home, then sample the local *arra* (alcoholic spirits).

Getting There & Away
The local jeep drivers say that if you leave Trashigang at 3.30am you can reach Thimphu at 8.30pm, a total of 17 hours of gruelling driving later.

TRASHIGANG TO KHALING
If you're interested in textiles, an interesting day trip is to drive for a few hours to visit the weaving centre at Khaling.

Trashigang to Kanglung
22km • ¾ hour
Three kilometres from Trashigang bazaar the southern road turns off the Mongar road and climbs past the petrol station.

Climbing around a ridge and heading south the road passes the settlement of **Pam**. There are few houses near the road, but there is an extensive settlement and a lhakhang on the hillside above. The narrow unpaved road that leads uphill from here goes to Rangshikhar Goemba.

Descend into a side valley, cross a stream on a clattering steel bridge and climb through rice terraces to the prosperous farming community of **Rongthung**, 17km from Trashigang. The road then climbs to a ridge and enters Kanglung (1870m), where you can see the clock tower and extensive campus of the college below.

Father William Mackey, a Jesuit priest, was instrumental in setting up **Sherubtse College**, Bhutan's only college. It was first a junior high school, then became a high school and is now a college. India aided the construction of the school in 1964 as part of the construction of the road from Trashigang to the Indian border.

Outside the college gate are several small restaurants including **Hotel N.P.**, an Indian snack bar that serves espresso, and **Pala's** (Father's) (☎ 04-535117), a student hangout. Note that no alcohol or tobacco is sold here in Kanglung.

[Continued on page 242]

EASTERN BHUTAN

THE WARP & THE WEFT

Hand-loomed fabrics have been integral to Bhutanese culture for centuries and remain the country's most distinctive art form. Everyday articles such as clothing, sturdy wrappers for bundled goods and covers for cushions are still often stitched from colourful cloth woven at home. Taxes, too, were once paid in cloth, each region contributing its own speciality: woollen cloth came from the colder valleys; silk cloth from the temperate east; and cotton- and bast-fibre cloths from the tropical south. Cloth taxes generally took the form of simply decorated, unstitched lengths from the loom and were collected at a nearby *dzong*. Over the course of the year, the authorities would distribute the loom lengths, for example, as annual 'payments' to monastic and civil officials and to monasteries. Recipients would in turn stitch the yards of cloth into useful forms – sitting mats for monks, altar coverings, the backing of religious pictures and for clothing.

Bhutanese weaving appears to have flourished particularly since the mid-to-late 19th century, a period of political stability during which the nobility kept weavers at their estates throughout central Bhutan. These retainers, who owed labour to the local lord as a form of tax, were free from the pressures of producing for the general marketplace. Instead they wove for the noble household's needs, working as and when they felt inspired. Their finest work is known as 'heart weaving' – the most exquisite silks, woollens or cottons, usually made into traditional garments – characterised by brilliant individuality and careful finish. These weavings are treasured even now as family heirlooms. The tradition of weaving for a patron or by commission continues in many parts of Bhutan today.

Until the 1970s the few textiles to leave Bhutan were gifts from the royal family or high officials to prominent visitors. Many of these found their way to the storerooms of British and North American museums, but an interesting collection is on permanent exhibition at a small museum in Neuchatel, Switzerland. The first comprehensive exhibition of Bhutanese textiles was organised at the Peabody Essex Museum in Massachusetts in 1994 and was accompanied by the well-illustrated publication, *From the Land of the Thunder Dragon: Textile Arts of Bhutan*.

Gender & Social Context

Weaving is closely associated with women, and is the only one of Bhutan's 13 traditional arts and crafts that is dominated by women. While imported fabrics which are easier to care for and much less expensive are popular for everyday wear, especially in towns, a woman is still expected to weave or design the clothing that her family wears on special occasions. Annual *tsechus* (festivals) throughout the country and important weddings in Thimphu are events where everyone wears their best clothing – and where woman look keenly at new designs that others are wearing. Preferences in colours and patterns change every year and so new garments are a must to stay in fashion.

A family's wealth is still associated with the fine fabrics tucked away in trunks, and these may be sold when money is needed. Likewise, on

Inset: Bhutan's textiles are intricately designed and highly prized. (Photo by: Jeff Cantarutti)

JEFF CANTARUTTI

STAN ARMINGTON

In a country where everyone wears the national dress and wealth is associated with fine weavings, the age-old skills inherent in creating lengths of colourful fabric are highly regarded.

NICHOLAS REUSS

TONY WHEELER

NICHOLAS REUSS

The most elaborate patterns of this art form resemble *kushu*, or embroidery. New designs and colour combinations are adapted from existing styles, demonstrating the vitality of Bhutan's textile tradition

occasions such as weddings and promotions, it is still customary to present a set of cloth panels from the loom, the number and quality of which reflect the social relationship between the giver and the recipient. While giving an envelope with money is common on such occasions, it would be bad form indeed to give a gift of cash alone. So while hand-loomed textiles remain essential to Bhutanese culture, it follows that weaving skills are still valued when a man seeks a wife.

While women dominate in this art, men do contribute to it. They are known especially for assembling luxury textiles for the court, household shrines, temples and monasteries. While there are a few men that weave (and their work is very highly prized), generally men cut, stitch and embroider applique seat covers, religious images and altar accessories. Skilled laymen and monks still produce decorative tents and *thondrols* (huge religious embroideries) similar to the one displayed at the annual Paro tsechu.

Technique & Production

Bhutan's weavers specialise in working additional decorative warps and wefts into the 'ground' of a fabric. Using one's fingers or a slender pick (made from a porcupine quill or of brass), the weaver creates intricate patterns, which, to an untutored eye, look much like embroidery work. The designs are drawn from an extensive traditional repertoire but are modified, reinterpreted and combined according to each weaver's imagination. The most elaborate weavings are usually for the traditional *kira* and *gho*, and these garments may take up to a year to weave in silk.

One of the best-known styles of weaving comes from the ancestral home region of the royal family, Lhuentse in the north-east. Weavers here specialise in decorating kira, bags and other textiles with elaborate patterns that resemble embroidery. The famous *kushuthara kira* – featuring red and blue, and multicoloured silk patterning on a white ground – originated here. Other parts of eastern Bhutan are renowned for distinctively striped garments woven from wild silk. The local names of the five colour combinations indicate that these designs are indigenous and very old.

Another sought-after fabric is *yathra*, a striped woollen cloth from the Bumthang region. Lengths of this colourful yardage are stitched into blankets, cloaks and cushion covers, and nowadays, into car-seat covers.

Most weaving in Bhutan is done on a simple back-strap loom, similar to looms found throughout South-East Asia and Tibet. The loom is easily transported and is ideal for setting up in a warm kitchen, on the porch of a house or beside a tent. The horizontal frame loom seen throughout central Bhutan was imported from Tibet in the mid-20th century.

Locally produced cotton, silk, wool and nettle or hemp fibres have been used alongside imported Chinese silk, Tibetan wool and Indian cotton for centuries. And while bright powder dyes from India were available to the nobility by the early 1900s, their use didn't become widespread in Bhutan until the 1950s and 1960s. Today vegetable-dyed woollen cloth can be found in Jakar, but most locally dyed yarns are tinted with a mix of natural and chemical dyes.

Diana Myer

[Continued from page 239]

The small **Zangto Pelri Goemba**, built in 1978, is on the opposite side of the road. Beyond the college are a junior high school and numerous dormitories and student hostels, and further on is an assortment of shops that is the town proper. The region near Kanglung is quite heavily populated. If you look across the valley from Kanglung you can see Drametse Goemba.

Kanglung to Khaling
32km • 1 hour

The road climbs through fields of corn and potatoes and past an agricultural project, then makes a switchback around a line of eight chortens. Above the road is the Yonphula army camp and further on is Yongphu Goemba. Hidden on a ridge above the road is Yonphula, Bhutan's second airstrip. There are hopes that this small airstrip will soon be served by domestic flights, which would make eastern Bhutan much more accessible. The hopes are unlikely to be fulfilled because clouds frequently obscure the approach, which would make flights quite unreliable.

The road crosses Yongphu La (2190m) and swoops along the top of the Bartsam valley, cuts across a ridge into another valley, then winds down again. A short climb leads the road over yet another ridge marked by chortens. It then descends to **Gumchu**, a collection of road workers' shacks and one Bhutanese-style house. Below, in a pretty valley, are several traditional houses surrounded by large, lush meadows.

Rounding a corner, the road enters Khaling, spread out in a large valley high above the Drangme Chhu. Several shops and small restaurants line the main street. Above the town is a narrow, unpaved road that leads downhill into the centre of the valley towards the elementary school and a school for the disabled.

In the centre of the valley below Khaling is the National Institute for the Disabled. This is a very well-organised institution that tries to assimilate students from all over Bhutan who are blind or otherwise handicapped into the local educational system by providing special resources and training. One of their accomplishments is the development of a Dzongkha version of Braille. The school was originally set up by missionaries 20 years ago and has been run by the government since 1987.

Three kilometres beyond Khaling is the **National Handloom Development Project** (☎ 04-58112; open 10am-5pm Mon-Fri), operated by the National Women's Association of Bhutan (NWAB). It contracts out weaving and provides cotton yarn on credit to villagers, who then return the finished product to be sold here or in Thimphu. It has samples of about 300 designs, although it doesn't have fabric from every design in stock. It will, however, take orders, and you can ask your guide to ensure that the order eventually gets delivered.

There are samples of the natural dyes that are used and there is a small display showing the various parts of plants that are used to produce each colour. Photography of the workshops and of the design samples is strictly prohibited. Prices for a length of woven cloth vary from Nu 950 up to Nu 12,000. Most of the cotton is Indian, imported from Kolkata. NWAB has produced a book, *Bhutanese Weaving, A Source of Inspiration*, by Alet Kapma & Wouter Ton.

FAR EASTERN BHUTAN

A paved road heads downhill from Trashigang and travels up the valley of the Gamri Chhu to Rangjung, then continues as an unpaved track to Radi and Phongme.

There is a daily bus that plies this route, but it's a converted truck, which provides a very bumpy and dusty ride.

Trashigang to Rangjung
16km • 3/4 hour

The road descends from Trashigang, weaving in and out of side valleys to the banks of the Gamri Chhu at 820m. A side road crosses the river here and leads 19km uphill to the town and goemba at Bartsam. The Rangjung road stays on the south side of the river, passing a large Tibetan-style chorten and the village of Lungtenzampa. After traversing fields for 6km it crosses the small Kharti Chhu and makes a short climb to **Rangjung** at 1120m. Beyond the high school an elaborate chorten dominates the centre of the town, surrounded by shops and small eateries. Above the town is the **Rangjung Wodsel Chholing Monastery**, a large Nyingma goemba founded in 1990 by Garub Rinpoche. The monastery has a small *guesthouse (☎ 04-561146)* that is occasionally booked by tourists.

Rangjung to Radi
8km • ½ hour

The road continues east, climbing through large rice terraces and fields of corn to Radi (1570m). There is a single shop, but nowhere to eat in Radi, which has a primary school and a cluster of houses above and below the road.

For an unusual outing, hike downhill for about 30 minutes from the Yeshe Lhundup shop west of Radi to the small village of **Tzangkhar**. Most of the women here are weavers who specialise in fabrics made from *bura* (raw silk), and it's fun to walk from house to house to see the results. Enough cloth to make a *gho* or *kira* costs about Nu 30,000 for a flower design and about Nu 10,000 for a plainer pattern. It's a climb of about 130m back to the road.

Radi to Phongme
9km • ½ hour

Beyond Radi the road climbs through forests interspersed with barren hillsides, passing above the Thekcho Kunzang Chhoeten nunnery. There is a tiny shop at the end of the road in **Phongme** (1840m).

On the hill above is Phongme Lhakhang, which is about 150 years old. It has no resident monks; the caretakers are elderly women. The central statue is of Chenresig with 1000 arms and 11 heads; Sakyamuni is to the right. Many elaborate masks used in the small Phongme tsechu are stored on the rafters of the goemba's lower chapel. The upstairs chapel has rough statues of Sakyamuni, the Shabdrung and Guru Rinpoche, and a wall painting depicting the life of Milarepa.

From Phongme a trail leads east to the minority villages of **Merak** and **Sakteng**, which are inhabited by seminomadic tribesmen called Brokpa. Tourists were permitted to make this three-day trek in the past, but since 1995 the route has been closed to foreigners out of concern for the unique culture of the people living there. Tall Brokpa men often come into Phongme and Trashigang to trade. You can recognise them by their sheepskin and yak-hair clothing and unusual yak-hair hats called *shamo*, which have hanging spider-like legs that act as rainspouts.

Trashi Yangtse Dzongkhag

Previously a *drungkhag* (subdistrict) of Trashigang, Trashi Yangtse became a fully fledged dzongkhag in 1993. It borders the Indian state of Arunachal Pradesh, and there is some cross-border trade. The old trade route between east and west Bhutan used to go through Trashi Yangtse, over the mountains to Lhuentse and then over Rodang La (4200m) to Bumthang. This route is difficult and became neglected when the road from Trashigang to Bumthang via Mongar was completed. The district lies at the headwaters of the Kulong Chhu, and was earlier known as Kulong.

TRASHIGANG TO TRASHI YANGTSE

The drive from Trashigang to Trashi Yangtse is 53km and takes about one hour 45 minutes, but allow extra time to visit Gom Kora on the way. If you don't have time to drive all the way to Chorten Kora, do make the effort to make the short trip to Gom Kora.

To get from Trashigang to Chazam (9km, 15 minutes), follow the switchbacks down to the bridge at Chazam. From Chazam, the road is level as it winds its way through sparse clumps of chir pine above the west bank of the Drangme Chhu to Gom Kora (13km, 30 minutes).

Gom Kora

Gom Kora is a small temple to the east of the road 13km north of Chazam. Its correct name is Gomphu Kora. *Gomphu* is a sacred meditation site of Guru Rinpoche and *kora* means 'circumambulation'. The Guru meditated here and left a body impression on a rock, similar to that in Kurjey Lhakhang in Bumthang.

The central figure in the goemba is Guru Rinpoche. To his left are Chenresig in his 1000-armed aspect and the protective angel of Guru Rinpoche. To the far right is a *jang-shu*, a special kind of small chorten that is found only inside monasteries and dzongs. The paintings on the walls of the goemba are believed to be from the 15th century.

On a shelf under the statue of Guru Rinpoche are numerous sacred objects that either miraculously appeared here or were brought by the Guru himself. The largest item is a dragon's egg, which is a very heavy, perfectly shaped, stone-like egg. There is also a hoof of Guru Rinpoche's horse and the footprint of a *khandroma* (female celestial being).

The old thondrol is stored here for safe-keeping. It's unique because it is a painted, not appliqued, thondrol. Gom Kora has a new thondrol, which is displayed at the Gom Kora tsechu in spring. This festival is different from most other tsechus. People circumambulate the goemba and sacred rock throughout the night and *Kuensel* suggests that the evening's activities result in many marriages.

Behind the goemba is a large black rock with many fantastic aspects. As Guru Rinpoche was meditating in a small cave near the bottom of the rock, a demon in the shape of a cobra appeared from the side of the river. The Guru, alarmed, stood up quickly and left the impression of his pointed hat at the top of the cave. The Guru then made an agreement with the demon to stay away until the end of his meditation. The contract was sealed with thumb prints, which are still visible on the rock.

A small sin-testing passageway leads from the cave to an exit below the rock. Only virtuous people can get through this passage. Visitors are welcome to try but you'll get dirty. There are two sharp bends along the way – one successful participant reported that you must move like a snake to get through the cave. There is a narrow crevice on the side of the rock in which water flows down on certain holy days.

Gom Kora to Trashi Yangtse
28km • 1¼ hours

Two kilometres from Gom Kora is the substantial village of **Duksum** (860m). There are many shops and small eating places here because it's the roadhead for many large villages higher in the valley, the largest of which is Tongmijangsa. Many of the shops in Duksum sell particularly colourful patterned cloth that is woven by the women of the village using back-strap looms.

Behind the village is an old, abandoned **iron chain-link bridge**. Despite its neglected condition, this bridge is of some historical importance. It is believed that this is the last surviving bridge of those built by Thangtong Gyalpo (see the boxed text 'The Iron Bridge Builder' in the Western Bhutan chapter) in the 15th century. Nine wrought-iron chains form the platform and hand rails. The bridge houses are a mess, but if you enter carefully, you can see how the chains were securely held in place through several walls.

The road turns north-west and follows the Kulong Chhu valley towards Trashi Yangtse. The eastern fork of the river flows from India and is known as the Dawung Chhu.

Climbing high above the Kulong Chhu, the road passes the intersection of a paved road that leads 9km to a junior high school in the town of **Tshenkarla**. Above the school are the ruins of Tshenkarla dzong. The dzong was built in the first half of the 9th century by Tsangma, who was the eldest son of Tibetan king Trisong Detsen. Tsangma was banished from Tibet and established himself in eastern Bhutan. The old name of this town is Rangthang Woong.

Beyond the small settlement of Shali are many farms and houses, but the habitation soon disappears as the valley becomes steeper and less suitable for cultivation. After traversing along a rocky cliff, a house-like building appears on a promontory where a side stream, the Dongdi Chhu, joins the valley. This is the original Trashi Yangtse Dzong built by Pema Lingpa and now houses a small monastery.

TRASHI YANGTSE

Old maps and road signs place Trashi Yangtse at the site of the old dzong, but the real town has always been near Chorten Kora, 3km to the north. The old dzong is very small and is in a particularly inconvenient location; in 1996 a new dzong was built above Chorten Kora. Everyone now calls this area Trashi Yangtse.

Orientation

It takes 10 minutes to visit the entire town. The road enters from the south near the large Chorten Kora. North of the chorten is a bazaar area with a few shops. A tall, elaborately decorated Bhutanese-style chorten sits beside a small stream spanned by a concrete bridge, and doubles as the town's vegetable market. The road reaches a dead end 100m beyond and below the impressive headquarters of the Bomdeling Wildlife Sanctuary.

Paved roads lead from the town centre to the east. One goes to the new dzong, on a ridge 130m above the town and onto the high school. Another goes to the junior high school and a third leads to the Institute for Zorig Chusum.

Institute for Zorig Chusum

The Trashi Yangtse Institute for Zorig Chusum (☎ 04-781141, fax 781149) was opened in June 1997 in the buildings that used to be the subdistrict headquarters. The curriculum reflects Bhutan's efforts to provide opportunities for vocational training for those who, for one reason or another, do not continue in the system of higher education. The school strives to produce technically proficient craftspeople, while providing them with a basic educational foundation. The mornings are spent studying both spoken and written Dzongkha and English. After lunch the students learn crafts. The course lasts six years and includes all of the Zorig Chusum (13 arts and crafts). You can visit the school and watch the students at work. You can also purchase crafts made here from the shop on the premises (see Shopping, later).

Trashi Yangtse Dzong

The dzong in Trashi Yangtse was inaugurated in 1997 and is high on the side of a ridge overlooking the valley. It's not as architecturally stunning as other dzongs and, being new, has little historical significance.

Places to Stay & Eat

If you have connections, you might be able to stay in the *Dzongkhag Guest House* (☎ 04-781148), which is on the road to the dzong. The alternative is the *Sonam Chhoden Hotel* (☎ 04-781152), which has six simple rooms at Nu 120/160 for singles/doubles. There are two tables in the restaurant and you can get a simple meal here, but don't insult the owner – he's the school's tae kwan do instructor. He also has a plan to turn the old office of the Bomdeling project into a nine-room hotel. It's also possible to camp near Chorten Kora.

Shopping

The town is known for the excellent wooden cups and bowls made here using water-driven and treadle lathes. You can find them on sale in small shops and local restaurants and at the Institute for Zorig Chusum or in the Tenzing Jamtsho shop, which doubles as the bus station. Covered bowls made from giant avocado trees cost about Nu 900 and large ones are Nu 8000 and up. The best cups are made from burls of maple trees; a small one costs between Nu 5000 and 8000.

Trashi Yangtse is also a centre of paper making. They use the *tsasho* technique with a bamboo frame, which produces a distinctive pattern on the paper.

AROUND TRASHI YANGTSE
Chorten Kora

Chorten Kora is large, but not nearly as large as the stupa of Bodhnath, after which it was patterned. A small goemba has been built next to it and several rows of prayer flags flutter in the wind in the cornfields at its front. It was constructed in 1740 by

Lama Ngawang Loday, who had three purposes for the construction of this chorten.

The first purpose was as a religious monument in memory of his late uncle, Jungshu Phesan. Secondly, the people of this valley were very religious and wanted to go to Nepal to see the Bodhnath stupa. The lama went to Nepal himself and brought back a model of Bodhnath carved in a radish. He had it copied here so that people could visit this place instead of making the trip to Nepal. The reason that Chorten Kora is not an exact copy of Bodhnath is because the radish shrank during the trip and distorted the carving. The third purpose of the chorten was to subdue the many evils and devils that were here in those days. The 13th Je Khenpo (Chief Abbot of Bhutan) consecrated the site.

During the second month of the lunar calendar there is a kora here, whereby people gain merit by walking around the chorten. It is celebrated on two separate days, 15 days apart. The first day is for the people from the community behind the hill in Arunachal Pradesh, India. It is said that during the construction of this stupa an eight-year-old girl from Arunachal Pradesh sacrificed her life by entering the stupa. In her memory, one day is granted as the kora for her people. The second kora is for the Bhutanese, who come from all over eastern Bhutan.

Bomdeling

Bomdeling is a two- to three-hour walk north of Chorten Kora. It is the roosting place of a flock of black-necked cranes (see the boxed text 'The Black-Necked Crane' in the Facts about Bhutan chapter). The flock, smaller than that in Phobjikha, returns here year after year.

Samdrup Jongkhar Dzongkhag

There is almost nothing of interest to the traveller in south-eastern Bhutan, and the Home Ministry closed Samdrup Jongkhar as well as the Indian border crossing to foreign tourists, but not Indian nationals, in September 2001.

TRASHIGANG TO SAMDRUP JONGKHAR

It's a 180km drive from Trashigang to Samdrup Jongkhar on a winding road; the trip takes at least six hours. See Trashigang to Khaling, earlier, for details of the drive from Trashigang to Khaling.

Khaling to Wamrong
27km • ¾ hour

Beyond Khaling the road traverses above scattered houses and cornfields. Leaving the cultivation and settlements behind, it climbs to the head of a rhododendron-filled valley, crossing a ridge at 2350m. There's a short descent through lots of loose rock, then another climb to a pass at 2430m.

Descending, the route passes a side road that leads east to Thrimshing, then a small private goemba that overlooks the valley and the town of **Wamrong** (2130m). The local style *Dechen Wangdi* (☎ 04-571103) and *Yeshey Dorji* (☎ 04-571119) hotels can provide tea, biscuits and maybe a plate of rice. There is an immigration checkpoint below the town.

Wamrong to Pemagatshel Junction
20km • ¾ hour

The road here descends from the village, passes the junior high school and makes its way down to **Riserboo** and a hospital that is Norwegian funded. There is a good view down the valley as the road stays fairly level, traversing in and out of side valleys past the hamlet of Moshi. Cross several ridges and a stretch of road blasted out of the side of a cliff. Eventually descend to two shops that comprise the settlement of Tshelingkhor at the road junction to Pemagatshel.

Pemagatshel Junction to Deothang
55km • 1¾ hours

The road descends into the upper part of the Bada River valley, passing a Shiva temple built into a cliff at the side of the road.

From the small village of **Narphung** the road climbs again to the Narphung La at 1698m. It follows a ridge that leads to the east, crossing from one side to the other and climbs to 1920m before beginning the final descent to the plains.

The road weaves down, reaching the PWD camp at **Morong** at an elevation of about 1600m. The workers here are probably responsible for the corny Indian-style homilies on road signs here: 'speed thrills but kills' and 'no hurry, no worry'.

The Choekey Gyantso Institute for Advanced Buddhist Philosophy marks the outskirts of **Deothang** at 850m. The town's old name town was Dewangiri, and it was the site of a major battle between the Bhutanese and the British in 1865. The town is dominated by a large Royal Bhutan Army (RBA) camp. A road winds its way east from Deothang to Bhangtar, another border town.

Deothang to Samdrup Jongkhar
18km • ½ hour

At a curve in the road there is finally a view of the plains. Drop to a stream and follow it along the valley bottom past Chhoden Chemical Industries, which manufactures cement, carbide and ferro-silicon. In the jungle, well before Samdrup Jongkhar, is the police and immigration checkpoint. You must have a valid permit in order to be allowed into the town and these are not issued to foreigners.

SAMDRUP JONGKHAR

The road enters the town from the north, passing the Hifi Guest House and a road that leads west to the dzong. The road crosses a bridge then turns south into the town itself. There are several hotels and many shops on this street and another parallel street to the west. If you go straight instead of turning south, you will pass the town's only petrol station and then cross the border to the Indian town of Darranga.

Places to Stay & Eat

The *Hifi Guest House* (☎ 07-251455) is in a tree-shaded compound at the north end of town. Other hotels are in the town centre. The *Peljorling Hotel* (☎ 07-251094) is the largest with singles/doubles at Nu 700/800. It's an Indian-style establishment with a bar on the ground floor and the *Chopstix Restaurant* upstairs. The *Hotel Shambala* (☎ 07-251222), south of the Peljorling, also has a very Indian atmosphere.

Pemagatshel Dzongkhag

The name Pemagatshel means 'blissful land of the lotus'. This rural dzongkhag in the south-eastern part of the country is Bhutan's smallest district. Its headquarters, **Pemagatshel**, is reached via a side road that leads off the Samdrup Jongkhar to Trashigang road.

NWAB operates a weaving centre here where about 40 women are trained annually in traditional weaving techniques and product design.

Yongla Goemba is a few kilometres above the dzong in Pemagatshel. It is one of the holiest shrines in eastern Bhutan.

The goemba was founded in the 18th century by Kheydup Jigme Kuenduel, who was advised by the great *terton* Rigzin Jigme Lingpa to establish a monastery on a mountain that looked like a *phurba* (three-bladed ritual dagger) and overlooked the vast plains of India. Later the goemba was used as a base for religious ceremonies by Trongsa penlop Jigme Namgyal during the great Duar War with the British in 1865.

EASTERN BHUTAN

Trekking

Towns, *dzongs* and temples are one aspect of Bhutan, but the majority of the country is deep forests with a scattering of tiny settlements and high grazing lands. A trek provides the best opportunity to experience the real heart of Bhutan and to get a unique insight into the rural culture of the kingdom through contact with people in remote villages and the staff accompanying you.

Many places feel so remote that you can imagine you are the first person ever to visit. As you sit contemplating this, read about the invading armies or royal processions that preceded you decades – or centuries – ago and you will be amazed at what these people accomplished.

WHAT IS A TREK?

Government rules dictate that all treks must be arranged as camping trips. This also happens to be the only practical solution because there are no lodges or hotels in the hills and few villages in the high country visited by most treks.

A Bhutanese crew treks with you to set up camp, cook and serve meals. You carry a backpack with only a water bottle, camera and jacket. The rules specify that a licensed guide accompany all trekkers, but there is still a very limited number of guides who are seasoned trekking guides. The Department of Tourism (DOT) operates a guide training and registration program to try to overcome this shortage, but you may still find that you have more camping experience than your guide.

Treks in Bhutan do not rely on porters. Instead, all your personal gear, plus tents, kitchen and food, is carried by packhorses or, at higher elevations, yaks. There are so few villages and facilities along trek routes that the people driving the pack animals carry their own food and tents and camp each night alongside you.

You will sleep in a two-person tent with foam pads placed on the floor as a mattress. All your gear goes into the tent with you at night. Having a tent gives you a reasonably

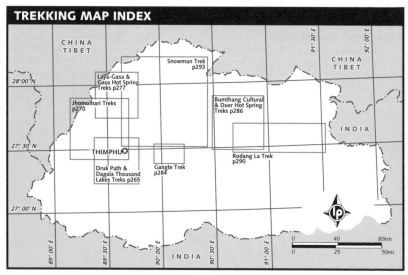

TREKKING MAP INDEX

CHINA
TIBET

Snowman Trek
p293

Laya-Gasa &
Gasa Hot Spring
Treks p277

28°00' N

Jhomolhari Treks
p270

Bumthang Cultural
& Duer Hot Spring
Treks p286

CHINA
TIBET

INDIA

27° 30' N

THIMPHU

Druk Path &
Dagala Thousand
Lakes Treks p265

Gangte Trek
p284

Rodang La Trek
p290

27° 00' N

89° 00' E   89° 30' E   90° 00' E   90° 30' E   91° 00' E   91° 30' E   92° 00' E

INDIA

0   40   80km
0   25   50mi

private place and you have the freedom to go to bed when you choose. Because there are also tents for the Bhutanese guides and the packers, you do not need to camp near villages and can trek comfortably to remote regions and high altitudes.

For information on trekking companies abroad and on Bhutanese tour companies, see the Getting There & Away chapter.

A Trek is...

A Wilderness Experience Most of Bhutan's landscape is covered with forests, and nowhere is this more obvious than on a trek. All treks climb up and down hills, passing through various vegetation zones with a great variety of trees. As there is a lot of wildlife in the hills of Bhutan, and most treks are in protected areas, there is a chance, albeit small, of seeing wildlife in its native habitat.

Once you step off the road to start the trek you are in true wilderness much of the time. Although there are established trails, there are no planes flying overhead, no roads and very few villages; instead there are views of snowcapped peaks and forested hillsides stretching to eternity.

Long A short trek in Bhutan is three or four days in duration, an average trek is a week, but a trek of 25 days or more is possible. Every day your walk leads you one day further into the hills and you will have to walk that same distance to get back to a road. Make proper preparations before you start so that three days into the trek you

---

Differences Between Treks in Nepal & Bhutan

People used to trekking in Nepal will find that conditions are generally similar in Bhutan. The differences that do exist are mostly due to geography. The hillsides in Bhutan tend toward the near-vertical. This means there are fewer farms, villages and reasonable camp sites.

Because geographical considerations make the distance between camp sites greater than the average distance between camps in Nepal, trekking days tend to be longer. Side-hill climbing on steep slopes also means that you do more up-and-down climbing to get around vertical cliffs, avalanche tracks and side canyons. The trails are generally good but, through centuries of use, in many places they have been worn down to paths of scattered rounded rocks or just plain mud.

You may not see other trekkers on the trail but, because camp sites are designated, you are likely to share your camp spot with other parties on the popular Jhomolhari and Laya-Gasa treks. On other treks you probably won't see another group at all. Generally speaking, the trekkers are older than those trekking in Nepal. This, I assume, is because older, settled people are better able to afford the high cost of travel in Bhutan. In some camp sites there are huts that can serve as kitchens for your crew, or used as dining rooms, but most of the time meals are served in a dining tent. There are no Nepal-style teahouses or trekkers' lodges in Bhutan.

In my experience, trekkers' meals in Bhutan compare well with restaurant meals. If you are used to Nepal's two-hour-plus lunch breaks, you'll learn to adjust to a much shorter midday stop here. In Nepal, the crew takes time to cook a hot meal while the members nap. In Bhutan, they bring along a hot dish in an insulated container (with other goodies) for what amounts to a glorified trail lunch. The crew, incidentally, tends to be much smaller than crews in Nepal. Three or four people do the work of five to seven or more. Maybe one reason for this is that there are fewer security problems in Bhutan and thus no need for extra people to guard the camp.

In most places in Nepal, the local people have become accustomed to trekkers but in Bhutan you are still a curiosity. People stare at you with open, friendly faces or greet you warmly as you pass – even come up to you and shake your hand. You become used to kids running to greet you, shouting: 'Bye-bye'. Some have not learned that it is a no-no to ask for pens. Others startle you by bowing low and bidding 'Good morning, sir'.

Robert Peirce

don't find that you are ill-equipped, exhausted or unable to cope with the thought of walking all that distance back.

Physically Demanding A Bhutan trek is physically demanding because of its length and the almost unbelievable changes in elevation. If you add all the climbing in the 14-day Laya-Gasa trek, for example, it is more than 6800m of elevation gain and loss during many steep ascents and descents. On most treks, the daily gain is less than 500m in about 18km, although 1000m ascents are possible on some days. You can always take plenty of time during the day to cover this distance; the physical exertion, although quite strenuous at times, is not sustained. You can take time for rest, but the trek days in Bhutan are long, requiring seven to nine hours of walking and you do have to keep moving to get to camp before dark.

Many of the climbs and descents are on rocky trails. Bhutan is amazingly rocky and on many routes the trail traverses long stretches of round river rocks. It requires some agility to hop between these. The trail is often extremely muddy, sometimes requiring a diversion to keep your feet dry. It can be a tricky balancing act on stones and bits of wood to get across stretches that have been ground into sloppy mud by the hooves of passing horses, yaks and cattle.

Many of the treks are on old trade routes that fell into disuse once a road was built. Some trails, especially in eastern Bhutan, have had little or no maintenance for 20 or 30 years. It's always possible to encounter snow, especially on high passes.

Probably the only physical problem that may make a trek impossible is a history of knee problems on descents. Throughout the Himalaya the descents are long, steep and unrelenting. There is hardly a level stretch of trail in the entire Himalayan region. If you are an experienced walker and often hike 20km to 25km a day with a backpack, a trek should prove no difficulty. You will be pleasantly surprised at how easy the hiking can be if you carry only a light backpack and do not have to worry about setting up a camp, finding water and preparing meals.

Previous experience in hiking and living outdoors is, however, helpful as you plan your trek. The first night of a two-week trek is too late to discover that you do not like to sleep in a sleeping bag.

Another unpleasant aspect of a trek in Bhutan is attacks by leeches during the rainy season. Leeches are rare during the normal trekking seasons, but if you want to see alpine flowers you need to come during July and August when the rain and leeches make life more difficult.

Not a Climbing Trip A Bhutan trek will not allow you to fulfil any Himalayan mountaineering ambitions. Bhutan's regulations prohibit climbing any peak higher than 6000m because of local concerns for the sanctity of the mountain peaks, which are revered as the home of deities.

WHEN TO TREK

There are a tremendous number of factors that can influence your plans for a trek in Bhutan, but the most important consideration is weather. Most trekkers come in autumn; spring is the second most popular season.

Winter snow and summer rain limit the ideal trekking season in Bhutan to two brief periods. Late September to mid-November is generally recognised as the best time for trekking and the March to April period is the next best time. No matter when you trek you will have rain at some time.

The high tourist season is during the period of best weather in autumn. Flights and hotels are fully booked and you will probably meet other trekkers on the popular routes.

During autumn, nights are cold in the mountains, but the bright sun makes for pleasant daytime temperatures – in the high 20s, falling to 5°C at night, between 1000m and 3500m. At higher altitudes, temperatures range from about 20°C down to minus 10°C. Mornings are usually clear with clouds building up after 1pm, but they typically disappear at night to reveal spectacular starry skies. Most high passes are snowbound from late November until around February and in some years the snow does not disappear until April or May.

Schedule Changes

Despite all the preplanning and the complicated advance arrangements, there are still numerous factors that can upset a trek schedule. Rain and mud can make the trail slippery and the camping miserable. Snow can block trails, horses can fail to appear on schedule or the horse drivers may consider the trail too dangerous for their animals. These things happen more frequently than you might imagine. There is little recourse when the trek cannot proceed and you should always be prepared for possible disappointment.

Late March to mid-May affords warmer weather and blooming rhododendrons, but there is a higher chance of rain or snow if you trek during this time. There will be long periods of constant rain during a trek between May and August. Alpine wildflowers are in bloom during August and September, but the mud is deep and there are no mountain views. The ardent botanist (or the insane) might select July and August for a trek.

GUIDES & CAMP STAFF

A small but efficient number of trek staff will accompany you. If you are trekking with a small group, the guide and cook will team up to handle the logistics. With a large group, the team will include a 'trek organiser' who will see that the loads are packed, tents set up and pack animals loaded on time. English names, not Dzongkha, are used for the various job titles. In addition to the cook and guide, there will be one or more 'waiters' who serve food and handle the kitchen chores.

PACK ANIMALS

There is a well-organised system for arranging pack animals in Bhutan. Contractors at the starting point of each trek arrange for horses to carry the loads. The animals' owners accompany the trek to arrange the loads and see that they get where they are supposed to each day. The ancient *dolam* system in Bhutan allocates specific grazing grounds to each village. For this reason,

pack animals are not allowed to cross *dzongkhag* (district) boundaries. Messages are sent ahead so that replacement animals are, hopefully, waiting at the boundary. At higher elevations, yaks carry the loads.

Food, tents and camp gear are packed in large, rectangular, covered baskets called *zhim*, which are then lashed to a wooden pack saddle. Trekkers' duffel bags are usually placed inside a jute sack for protection and then tied onto the animals. The process of saddling and loading the animals in the morning is a slow and tedious chore.

You won't have much to do with your pack animals, except at camp, but you will probably pass them, and other pack animals, along the trail. Just stand off to the side to let horses pass, but with yaks you must get as far as possible off to the side because they are much more skittish and won't pass if you are close to them. Yaks can be dangerous, especially their sharp horns. Stand on the uphill side of the trail so you don't get pushed off as the animals pass.

TREKKING FOOD

You can rely entirely on the camp meals and not carry any food with you to Bhutan. You might carry a small supply of chocolate bars or trail mix for snacks, and possibly a few packets of seasoning to liven up soups, but it's not really necessary. The trekking company sends along an extensive assortment of supplies for the cook to work with, so you don't need to worry about food. Your cook can look after any special dietary requirements if given notice.

Because there is almost no fresh food available on trek routes, the entire food supply must be carried from the start of the trek. As you begin the trek, fresh vegetables and meat are available and camp meals tend to be even better than those available in Thimphu. On a longer trek, the fresh food goes off after the first week or so and you are largely reduced to tinned food.

Meals usually include a rice dish, a potato dish or, frequently, both. The cook prepares meals over stoves fuelled by bottled gas, and most Bhutanese trekking cooks are adept at producing a reasonable variety of Western and Asian dishes. They often add interesting Bhutanese touches, such as cheese sauces, but know to avoid hot chillies unless you specifically request them.

The midday meal is often a packed lunch, carried by the cook, and may consist of fried rice or noodles, boiled potatoes or chapattis. It is normally accompanied by tea from a large flask. Sometimes the cook loads a lunch horse with a gas cylinder and a basket of food and produces a hot lunch on the trail, but this is infrequent because on most trekking days there is not a good place to cook and eat at the right time.

CLOTHING & EQUIPMENT

There is no trekking gear available in Bhutan; you must bring all your equipment with you. Everything on the Personal Equipment Check List opposite is useful, and most of it necessary, on a long trek. All of this gear (except perhaps the sleeping bag) will pack into a duffel bag weighing less than 15kg.

Some gear will not be necessary on your trek. You might be lucky enough to trek during a rare warm spell and never need a down jacket. It might be so cold and rainy that you never wear short pants. These are, however, unusual situations, and it is still important to be prepared for extremes.

Make a special effort to reduce the weight of the baggage you bring on the trek. Each pack animal carries 30kg and it is expected that one animal will carry the luggage of two trekkers. Hence, any baggage over 15kg is a complication.

What is Provided

The trek operator will provide two-person tents with foam mattresses, as well as eating utensils and kitchen equipment. Government rules specify that the trek operator should also provide a first-aid kit and a pressure bag (Portable Altitude Chamber) for high-altitude treks, but you should still carry your own supply of basic medical needs.

Most trek operators expect you to bring your own sleeping bag. There are no sleeping bags available for rent in Bhutan.

General Trekking Clothing

Down- or Fibre-Filled Jacket You should bring a good jacket on a trek. Most ski jackets are not warm enough and most so-called expedition parkas are too heavy and bulky. Down clothing has the advantage of being light and compressible. It will stuff into a small space when packed, yet bulk up when worn.

Your down jacket can serve many functions on the trek. It will become a pillow at night and on long car trips and can also protect fragile items in your backpack or duffel bag. If you are extremely cold, wear your down jacket to bed inside your sleeping bag. You don't wear down gear for walking as it rarely gets that cold, even at 5000m.

Artificial-fibre jackets (filled with Polargard, Thinsulate or Fibrefill) are a good substitute for down and much cheaper.

Jumper or Pile Jacket Two light layers of clothing are better than a single heavy layer, and one or two light jumpers (sweaters), shirts or polypropylene layers are superior to a heavy jacket.

Pile jackets made of polyester fleece come in a variety of styles and thicknesses. They are light, warm (even when wet) and easy to clean. If possible, buy a jacket that uses fleece made from recycled plastic bottles.

Hiking Shorts or Skirt Most treks are at altitudes where it is cool, even during the day, so most people are comfortable in long pants. Pants, however, pull at the knees and are hot, so some prefer shorts. Either 'cutoffs' or hiking shorts with big pockets are fine, but only for men. Skimpy track shorts are culturally unacceptable throughout Bhutan.

Women should wear a skirt, perhaps over a pair of shorts. Many women who have worn skirts on treks are enthusiastic about them. The most obvious reason is the ease in relieving yourself along the trail. There are long stretches where there is little chance to drop out of sight, and a skirt solves the problem. A wrap-around skirt is easy to put on and take off in a tent. Long 'granny' skirts are not practical because you will be walking through mud.

Personal Equipment Check List

FOR ALL TREKS
Clothing
- ☐ down- or fibre-filled jacket
- ☐ jumper or pile jacket
- ☐ hiking shorts (for men) or skirt
- ☐ waterproof jacket, poncho or umbrella
- ☐ hiking pants
- ☐ T-shirts or blouses
- ☐ long-sleeved shirt
- ☐ underwear
- ☐ sun hat
- ☐ swimwear (optional)

Footwear
- ☐ trekking or running shoes
- ☐ camp shoes or thongs
- ☐ socks (polypropylene)

Other Equipment
- ☐ backpack
- ☐ sleeping bag
- ☐ water bottle
- ☐ torch (flashlight), batteries & bulbs

Miscellaneous Items
- ☐ toiletries & toilet paper
- ☐ cigarette lighter
- ☐ small knife
- ☐ sunscreen (SPF 15+)
- ☐ towel
- ☐ laundry soap
- ☐ medical & first-aid kit
- ☐ premoistened towelettes
- ☐ sewing kit
- ☐ bandanna

Photographic Equipment
- ☐ camera & lenses
- ☐ lens cleaning equipment
- ☐ film (about 20 rolls)

FOR TREKS GOING ABOVE 4000M
Clothing
- ☐ insulated pants
- ☐ nylon windbreaker
- ☐ nylon wind pants
- ☐ long underwear
- ☐ woollen hat or balaclava
- ☐ gloves
- ☐ gaiters

Footwear
- ☐ mountain trekking boots
- ☐ socks (wool)
- ☐ socks (light cotton) to wear under wool socks
- ☐ down booties (optional)

Miscellaneous Items
- ☐ goggles or sunglasses
- ☐ sunscreen for lips
- ☐ binoculars
- ☐ books
- ☐ duffel bag with a padlock, a few stuff sacks and lots of plastic bags
- ☐ another duffel bag or suitcase to leave your city clothes in

Rain Gear It is almost certain to rain at some time during your trek. The condensation inside a waterproof jacket can make you even wetter than standing out in the rain. Gore-Tex jackets are supposed to keep you dry by allowing the jacket to breathe, but in Bhutan you'll sweat a lot on the steep hills and the jackets don't always work as advertised.

One way to keep dry while hiking in the rain is to use a poncho – a large, often hooded, tarp with a hole in the centre for your head. An inexpensive plastic poncho is often as good as more expensive coated nylon gear.

Another way of keeping dry is an umbrella. This is an excellent substitute for a poncho (except on windy days) and can serve as a sunshade, a walking stick, an emergency toilet shelter and a dog deterrent.

Hiking Pants Almost any long pants will do. Many women wear tights under their skirt in order to stay both warm and culturally inoffensive.

T-shirts or Blouses You'll spend a lot of time walking in short sleeves – what the equipment catalogues call the first layer.

Cotton garments are fine, but if you can afford (and find) a synthetic T-shirt, you will be much more comfortable. You will perspire excessively, and a polypropylene shirt (with brand names such as Capilene and Thermax) wicks the moisture away from your skin. This means that when you put your rucksack on after a rest stop your back is not cold and damp.

Sun Hat Obviously, a hat with a wide brim affords greatest protection. Fix a strap to the hat that fits under your chin so it does not blow away in a wind gust.

Swimwear The only reasonable places to bathe on a trek are in hot springs. Skinny dipping is taboo if you are more than 10 years old. Bring along swimwear or use shorts or a skirt when you go into the hot spring.

High-Altitude Clothing

Insulated Pants Some kind of insulated pants are a real asset on a trek that goes above 4000m. You can bring pile pants, ski warm-up pants or down pants and put them on over your hiking pants or under a skirt when you stop. You can also wear them to bed for extra warmth when the nights become particularly cold.

Often you will arrive at your camp at 3pm and will not dine until 6pm or 7pm. Unless you choose to do some exploring, there will be several hours of sitting around before dinner. In cold weather, insulated pants make these times much more comfortable.

Nylon Windbreaker Strong winds are rare in the places visited by most treks, but a windbreaker is helpful in light wind, light rain and drizzle, when a poncho is really not necessary. If you already have a waterproof jacket as your 'outer layer', you don't need another shell garment. Your windbreaker should breathe, otherwise perspiration cannot evaporate and you will become soaked. A windbreaker is more in the line of emergency gear. If there is a strong wind, you must have it, otherwise you will probably not use it. If you can afford it, or spend a lot

of time in the outdoors, a Gore-Tex parka is a good investment.

Nylon Wind Pants If you prefer to hike in shorts wear a pair of wind pants over your shorts or under your skirt in the morning, then remove them to hike in lighter gear during the day. Most wind pants have special cuffs that allow you to remove them without taking off your shoes.

You can substitute ski warm-up pants, or even cotton jogging pants, for both wind pants and down-filled pants. The cost will be lower and there is hardly any sacrifice in versatility or comfort.

Long Underwear Long johns are useful. A complete set makes a good, warm pair of pyjamas and is also useful during late-night emergency trips outside your tent. Unless the weather is especially horrible, you will not need them to walk in during the day. You can bring only the bottoms and use a woollen shirt for a pyjama top. Cotton underwear is OK, although wool or polyester is much warmer.

Woollen Hat or Balaclava A balaclava is ideal because it can serve as a warm hat or you can roll it down to cover most of your face and neck. You may even need to wear it to bed on cold nights. Because much of your body heat is lost through your head, a warm hat helps keep your entire body warm.

Gloves Warm ski gloves are suitable for a trek. You might also consider taking along a pair of woollen mittens, in case your gloves get wet.

Gaiters There is an enormous amount of mud on Bhutan's trails, and a pair of high gaiters is a must to help keep your boots and socks clean and dry.

Footwear

Trekking or Running Shoes Proper footwear is the most important item. Your choice will depend on the length of the trek and the terrain. Tennis or running shoes are good, even for long treks, provided you won't be walking in snow.

There are numerous brands of lightweight trekking shoes that have stiffer lug soles and are available in both low- and high-top models. High-top shoes provide ankle protection, but low-cut shoes are cooler to walk in. Most trekking shoes are made of a leather and nylon combination and many have Gore-Tex waterproofing, but they are expensive, ranging from US$60 to US$100.

Mountain Trekking Boots Wherever there is snow (likely anywhere above 4000m), proper waterproof boots can become an absolute necessity. Since animals are carrying all your gear, you have the luxury of carrying two sets of shoes and swapping them from time to time.

Camp Shoes Tennis shoes are comfortable to change into for the evening. They can also serve as trail shoes in an emergency.

Socks Nylon-wool blend socks are fine, but polypropylene hiking socks (which cost astronomical prices) are the best. Several manufacturers, including Thorlo, Wigwam and Patagonia, make several varieties of hiking socks designed to prevent blisters by wicking moisture away from your feet. Bring more socks than you think you will need because it's sometimes difficult to wash clothes on a trek in Bhutan.

Down Booties Many people consider these excess baggage, but they are great to have and weigh little. If they have a thick sole, preferably with ensolite insulation, they can serve as camp shoes at high elevations. They're also good for midnight trips outside in the cold.

Other Equipment
Backpack A backpack should have a light internal frame to stiffen the bag and a padded waistband to keep it from bouncing around and to take some weight off your shoulders. There are many advantages to keeping your pack small. It will prevent you from trying to carry too much during the day, is handy to carry on a plane and will fit easily inside your tent at night.

Sleeping Bag Buy the best sleeping bag you can afford, and be sure it is large enough. It is quite cold from November to March, even in the lowlands, so a warm sleeping bag is a very worthwhile investment.

Water Bottle By day your bottle provides the only completely safe source of cold drinking water. If you use iodine, fill your water bottle from streams, add the iodine and have cold, safe water 30 minutes later.

Torch (Flashlight) Almost any torch will do, although many people prefer a headlamp – which is particularly useful for reading or when finding a toilet. Spare batteries are almost impossible to find during a trek, so bring a supply with you. Larger batteries perform better in the cold than small penlight cells, but they are heavier.

Duffel Bag You will need a strong duffel bag in which to pack your gear. Several companies make good duffel bags with a zip along the side for easy entry. This is not an item to economise on; get a bag that is durable and has a strong zip. A duffel 35cm in diameter and about 75cm long is large enough to carry your gear and will usually meet the weight limit of pack animals – typically 15kg.

Your duffel bag will sit on the back of a horse or yak all day; when it rains, it will get wet. Pack it in a way that important items stay dry during rainstorms.

Use a small padlock that will fit through the zip pull and fasten to a ring sewn to the bag. The lock will protect the contents from pilferage during the flight to and from Bhutan and will help protect the contents on your trek.

Extra Duffel Bag or Suitcase When starting a trek, you will leave your city clothes and other items in the storeroom of your hotel or travel agent. Bring a small suitcase or extra duffel bag with a lock for this purpose.

Stuff Bags It is unlikely that you will be able to find a completely waterproof duffel bag or backpack. Using coated nylon stuff bags helps you to separate your gear and provides additional protection in case of rain. You can also use plastic garbage bags, but these are much more fragile. A plastic bag inside each stuff sack is a good bet during the rainy season. Given the high likelihood of rain in Bhutan, it would not be unreasonable to pack your gear in a waterproof river bag.

Sunglasses or Goggles The sun reflects brilliantly off snow, making good goggles or sunglasses with side protection essential. At high altitude they are so essential you should have an extra pair in case of breakage or loss. A pair of regular sunglasses can serve as a spare if you rig a side shield. The lenses should be as dark as possible. At 5000m, the sun is intense and ultraviolet rays can severely damage unprotected eyes. Store your goggles in a metal case as, even in your backpack, it is easy to crush them.

Sunscreen During April and May and at high altitude throughout the year, sunburn can be severe. Use a protective sunscreen; those with sensitive skin will need a total sunscreen such as zinc oxide cream. Snow glare at high altitude is a real hazard; you'll need a good sunscreen, not just suntan lotion.

To protect your lips at high altitude you need a total sunscreen such as Dermatone or Labiosan.

Camera A trek is long and your gear will be subjected to heat, dust, blowing sand and moisture. Carry lens caps, lens tissue and a brush to clean the camera and lenses as frequently as possible.

Three lenses – wide angle (28mm or 35mm), standard (50mm or 55mm) and telephoto (135mm or 200mm) – are useful but heavy. Since you will probably carry them in your backpack day after day, you may want to limit your selection. If you must make a choice, you will find a telephoto (or zoom) lens is more useful than a wide angle, because it will allow close-up pictures of wildlife, mountains and portraits of shy people. A polarising filter is a useful accessory. Insure your camera equipment.

Additional Items If there are two people travelling, divide a lot of this material to save weight and bulk.

Bars of Indian laundry soap are available in Bhutan. This avoids an explosion of liquid or powdered soap in your luggage.

Premoistened towelettes are great for a last-minute hand wash before dinner. You can avoid many stomach problems by washing frequently. If you bring a supply of these, check the way they are packaged. Buy them in a plastic container and avoid leaving a trail of foil packets in your wake.

A pair of scissors on your pocketknife is useful. Also bring a sewing kit and some safety pins – lots of uses.

Put all your medicines and toiletries in plastic bottles with screw-on lids.

Bring a cigarette lighter or matches so you can burn your used toilet paper. You might also bring a small trowel to dig a toilet hole when you get caught on the trail with no toilet nearby.

Carry with you at all times items to deal with blisters. It's important to treat blisters as soon as you discover them.

MAPS

The entire country has been mapped by the Survey of India at 1:50,000. These maps are restricted and difficult to obtain – large-scale topographic maps are secret documents in India. There is a related series of topo maps produced by the Survey of Bhutan, but these are also restricted. The US Army Map Service produced a set of now-outdated maps in the 1950s (Series U502 at 1:250,000, sheets NG45-4 and NH46-1) based on the Survey of India maps. The topography is extremely inaccurate and they, too, are difficult to obtain. Another series is the 1:200,000 Russian Military Topographic set which takes 10 sheets to cover Bhutan, but its text is in Russian.

In cooperation with an Austrian project, DOT produced large-scale contour maps of the Jhomolhari and Dagala Thousand Lakes treks based on the Survey of Bhutan series. These are the best (although not entirely accurate) trekking references available and can be purchased from the DOT office in Thimphu for Nu 300 each.

ron chain bridges date from the 15th century.

Busy Mongar bazaar, high above the valley floor

he design of Chorten Kora in Trashi Yangtse was brought back from Bodhnath (Nepal) carved in a radish.

JULIA WILKINSON

RICHARD I'ANSON

IZZET KERIBAR

JULIA WILKINSON

Prayer is an important part of daily life. Flags 'recite' the prayers written on them as they flutter in the wind; wheels are filled with written prayers that are 'said' each time the wheel is turned.

TREKS IN THIS BOOK

In this chapter, 12 of the 13 officially permitted trekking routes in Bhutan are described. The other trek, the two-day Cheli La trek, is described briefly in the Paro section of the Western Bhutan chapter. Other trekking routes may be possible with prior negotiation between tour operators and DOT, but the major treks offer everything that a trekker could want, including what is described as the world's most difficult trek. Numerous variations are possible, even within the prescribed itineraries. Most of the routes can be trekked in the reverse direction, although this sometimes causes logistical problems because horses are not always available at the standard trek end points.

Discussions are under way to open several more trekking routes, including the Royal trek from Bumthang to Trongsa, and several routes in the newly opened Haa district. Treks to Gangkhar Puensum base camp may become officially permitted, which would allow the reopening of the extension of the Snowman trek from Thanza to Gangkhar Puensum base camp and on to join the Duer Hot Spring trek.

Route Descriptions

The trek descriptions in this book provide a general explanation of the lie of the land and cultural background, but are not self-guiding trail descriptions. Although some treks follow old trade routes, local people don't use many of them today. Because there is usually no-one around to ask for directions, you need to stay reasonably close to the guide or horsemen to ensure you are on the correct path.

Daily Stages The route descriptions are separated into daily stages. This helps to make them readable and gives a quick estimate of the number of days required for each trek. The stages are those defined by DOT as designated camp sites, and the rules state that you must camp at these places. This doesn't usually create any hardship because in most cases the designated sites are the only spots with water and a space flat enough for making a camp.

Be sure you have the itinerary, including rest days, worked out in advance. Messages are sent ahead to arrange pack animals. If you don't meet them on the specified day, they might not wait for you.

As you discuss the following day's trek with your guide and horsemen, be particularly careful to ensure that everyone agrees on the place you will camp for the night. More than once the horsemen have set off for a camping place beyond the destination the trekkers expected.

Some Bhutanese trekking staff have a very relaxed approach to schedules and late morning starts are common. Because many daily stages are quite long, this can result in late arrivals to camp, sometimes after dark. Always carry a torch in your backpack.

Times & Distances The route descriptions list approximate walking times. These are estimates based on personal experience and information produced by DOT. Any moderately fit trekker can accomplish the suggested daily stages in a single day. The times and daily stages are 'tourist times' and offer a leisurely, comfortable trek with plenty of time for rest, sightseeing or just viewing the mountains. Bhutanese horsemen and over-enthusiastic trekkers can reduce these times to less than those shown here.

The distances shown are those published by DOT. They are estimates and have not been determined by any accurate method of measurement.

Rest Days The route descriptions are based on a reasonable number of days needed to complete the trek. You will enjoy the trek more if you add the occasional day for rest, acclimatisation or exploration – even at the cost of an extra US$200.

Maps in this Chapter

The maps included in this chapter are based on the best available maps of each region. To make them legible, only those villages and landmarks mentioned in the route descriptions are shown on the maps. The maps show elevations for peaks and passes only – other elevations, including for each camp, are given in the route descriptions. Trails and roads follow the general direction indicated on the maps, but maps this size obviously cannot show small switchbacks and twists in the trail.

Instead of contour lines, the maps depict ridge lines. This is the line of the highest point on a ridge. If the trail crosses one of these lines, you will walk uphill. If the trail leads from a ridge line to a river, you must walk downhill.

Altitude Measurements

The elevations given in the route descriptions are composites, based on measurements with an altimeter or GPS and the best available maps. There is no definitive list of the elevations or names of peaks and passes in Bhutan, and various maps and publications differ significantly. In most cases the peak elevations are those defined in the mountain database produced by the Alpine Club in Britain. All other elevations are rounded to the nearest 10m.

Place Names & Terminology

Bhutan is a maze of valleys and rivers that wind around in unexpected turns. It is, therefore, difficult to always define in which compass direction a river is flowing at a particular spot. Instead of referring to the north or south bank of rivers, the slightly technical term of 'river right' or 'river left' has been used in the route descriptions. This refers to the right or left side of the river as you face downstream, which is not necessarily the direction you are walking. In the route descriptions, right and left in reference to a river always refers to river right or river left.

The route descriptions list many mountains and places that do not correlate with names in other descriptions of the same route or with names on maps. The variance occurs because most maps were made before the Dzongkha Development Commission produced its guidelines for Romanised Dzongkha. An effort has been made in this book to use the new standards for all place names throughout Bhutan.

Many streams and landmarks remain nameless in the trail descriptions. Most trekking routes go through sparsely populated country, where there is less formality about place names. Although some places have official, historically accurate names, many camping places are in meadows or yak pastures. Local herders, or perhaps trekking guides, made up names for some of these places and these now appear on official maps. Numerous small streams, valleys and other landmarks do not have any names at all or, if they do have local names, there is usually nobody living nearby to ask.

In some places there is a facility that the Bhutanese call a 'community hall'. This is a stone building that the staff can use for cooking and shelter and may be available for trekkers to use as a dining room.

Route Finding

It isn't easy to get totally lost in the hills, but it has happened to some trekkers, and there are very few people around who can help you find the correct trail. If you are on a major trekking route, the trail is usually well defined and there is only one route, although there may be a few confusing short cuts. Watch for the lug-sole footprints of other trekkers or for arrows carved into the trail and marked on rocks by guides with trekking parties. You can also use the hoofprints and dung of your pack animals to confirm that you are on the correct trail. If you find yourself descending a long way when the trail should be going up, if the trail vanishes, or if you suddenly find yourself alone ahead of the rest of your party, *stop and wait for the other trekkers and guides to catch up*. If you noticed a trail junction some distance back, retrace your steps to try to find where you went wrong.

RESPONSIBLE TREKKING

Bhutan's trekking rules require that your staff carry a supply of fuel for cooking. Until 1996, the use of wood was allowed. The horsemen and yak drivers sometimes violate the code and cook their own meals over wood. Although theoretically prohibited, it's a hard rule to enforce.

Considerations for Responsible Trekking

Trekking places great pressure on wilderness areas and you must take special care when trekking to help preserve the ecology and beauty of Bhutan. The following tips are common sense, but they are also mandated by the government, and you, or your guide, could be fined for not observing them.

Rubbish

• Carry out all your rubbish. If you've carried it in you can carry it out. Don't overlook those easily forgotten items, such as silver paper, cigarette butts and plastic wrappers. Empty packaging weighs very little and should be stored in a dedicated rubbish bag. Make an effort to carry out rubbish left by others.

• Minimise the waste you must carry out by reducing packaging and taking no more than you will need. If you can't buy in bulk, unpack small packages and combine their contents in one container before your trek. Take reuseable containers or stuff sacks.

• Sanitary napkins, tampons and condoms should also be carried out despite the inconvenience. They burn and decompose poorly.

Human Waste Disposal

• Contamination of water sources by human faeces can lead to the transmission of hepatitis, typhoid and intestinal parasites. It can cause severe health risks not only to members of your party, but also to local residents and wildlife. A toilet tent will be set up at each camp; please use it.

• Where there is no toilet tent, bury your waste. Dig a small hole 15cm deep and at least 100m from any watercourse. Consider carrying a lightweight trowel for this purpose. Cover the waste with soil and a rock. Use toilet paper sparingly and burn it or bury it with the waste. In snow, dig down to the soil otherwise your waste will be exposed when the snow melts.

Washing

• Don't use detergents or toothpaste in or near watercourses, even if they are biodegradable. For personal washing, use biodegradable soap and a basin at least 50m away from any watercourse. Widely disperse the waste water to allow the soil to filter it fully before it finally makes it back to the watercourse.

Erosion

• Hillsides and mountain slopes, especially at high altitude, are prone to erosion. It is important to stick to existing tracks and avoid short cuts that bypass a switchback. If you blaze a new trail straight down a slope it will turn into a watercourse with the next heavy rainfall and eventually cause soil loss and deep scarring.

• If a well-used track passes through a mud patch, walk through the mud: Walking around the edge of the patch will increase the size of the patch.

• Avoid removing the plant life that keeps the topsoil in place.

Wildlife Conservation

• Don't assume animals found in huts to be nonindigenous vermin and attempt to exterminate them. In wild places they are likely to be protected native animals.

• Discourage the presence of wildlife in camp by not leaving food scraps behind.

• Do not disturb or feed wildlife or do anything to destroy their natural habitat.

Cultural Conservation

• Respect the culture and traditions of local people, whether they are villagers, your camp staff or your horse drivers.

• Do not give candy, money, medicines or gifts to local people, particularly children, as this encourages begging.

• Do not buy local household items or religious artefacts from villagers.

Fires

Camp fires are prohibited and you should decline the offer if your staff suggest one. Bring enough warm clothing and you won't need to stand around a fire. It's a dilemma if the packers build a fire, or if one appears as part of a 'cultural show' in a village. Don't get too upset, however; as long as they burn dead wood the impact is minimal.

Trash Fires Burning garbage can be offensive to deities, especially within sight

Acclimatisation & Altitude Sickness

Most treks in Bhutan reach altitudes that bring about symptoms of altitude sickness in many people. Be sure you understand the dangers and symptoms of altitude sickness before you begin a trek. So far there has been only one reported death from altitude sickness in Bhutan. The following information will help prevent you becoming a victim of this life-threatening illness.

Our bodies have the ability to adjust to higher altitudes if given enough time. Altitude sickness occurs as the result of failure to adapt to a higher altitude, because the rate of ascent has been too rapid. Fluid leaks from blood vessels and eventually collects where it can do the most harm: in the lungs and brain. When fluid collects in the brain, you develop a headache, loss of appetite, nausea and sometimes vomiting, a syndrome that is called acute mountain sickness (AMS). You become increasingly tired and want to lie down and do nothing. As the sickness progresses, you develop a problem with your balance and coordination (ataxia). At this point, the sickness is called high-altitude cerebral oedema (HACE). Eventually, you lie down and slip into coma; death is inevitable if you are not transported to a lower altitude.

If the fluid leaks into the lungs, you become breathless more easily while walking and eventually more breathless at rest. A cough begins, initially dry and irritative, but progressing to the production of pink, frothy sputum in its most severe form. You ultimately drown in this fluid if you don't descend. This syndrome is referred to as high-altitude pulmonary oedema (HAPE). HAPE and HACE can occur singly or in combination.

Since individual susceptibility to altitude sickness varies widely and most people don't have prior experience with prolonged stays at high altitude, it is impossible to design itineraries that will completely prevent altitude-sickness symptoms in all people. Therefore, some people will get altitude sickness, even on reasonable itineraries. The important thing is to react appropriately if symptoms do occur. To prevent altitude sickness follow these rules:

Rule One

Learn to recognise the early symptoms of mountain sickness. Early symptoms of altitude illness include headache, loss of appetite, nausea and fatigue. Once you are familiar with these symptoms, you must be willing to admit you have them. Trekkers tend to be very goal-oriented and ambition can lead people to deny their symptoms. If you feel ill at altitude and you are not sure of the reason, assume it is AMS and respond accordingly. Guessing wrong can have serious consequences.

Rule Two

Never ascend to sleep at a new altitude if you have *any* symptoms of AMS. Once you recognise that you have the early symptoms of AMS, it is imperative that you do not do this. Virtually all fatalities from altitude sickness occur in people who persist in ascending despite symptoms that should have been recognised as AMS. You may find yourself in a situation where it is necessary to ascend in order to descend – for example, when crossing a pass. If your symptoms are still mild and you feel certain you can get over the pass to a lower height by the end of the day, this may be all right. But it is a decision that requires some mountaineering judgement. However, if you climb to a higher altitude and spend the night, even the mildest symptom of AMS will become worse. This rule is the single most important point to prevent deaths from altitude sickness.

of a sacred mountain such as Jhomolhari to the west. Be aware of this cultural issue and try to arrange for trash to be packed out with you if trekking, burned safely or disposed of in a way that does not cause offence.

What You Can Do to Help

Try to follow the guidelines in the boxed text. If your trek staff are not digging the toilet pits deep enough, or not filling them in properly, the time to solve that problem is on the spot. It does no good to go home and

Acclimatisation & Altitude Sickness

Rule Three

Descend immediately if your symptoms persist or are getting worse while resting at the same altitude. Once the cycle of AMS symptoms starts to get progressively worse, it will not improve without descent. Most of the time it is necessary to get below the height at which the symptoms began; in any case you must descend until you feel that the symptoms are starting to get better. Once they begin to improve, you can generally continue to rest at that altitude until recovery is complete.

The two most important symptoms are breathlessness at rest (HAPE) or inability to walk a straight line (HACE). Anyone displaying these symptoms has developed HAPE or HACE, and should descend immediately, regardless of the time of day.

Once you have recovered completely from altitude sickness by descending, you have the option of reascending slowly, watching for relapse. Many people will have had enough by then, but determined people can try to return to altitude if they have completely recovered from all their symptoms.

Drug Treatment of AMS

In addition to the advice about descent above, there are other treatment options available. Descent will always bring improvement and, in serious cases, should not be delayed to try some other form of therapy. However, the use of certain drugs, or a pressure chamber, can buy time and facilitate later descent.

Drug treatments should never be used to avoid descent or to enable further ascent.

Acetazolamide (Diamox) Diamox can prevent AMS symptoms if taken prior to ascent, and can more rapidly improve the symptoms of AMS if taken after they have begun. Most treks in Bhutan are associated with gradual ascents that would not routinely require the use of Diamox. Severe symptoms of HAPE or HACE can still occur despite taking Diamox. Diamox prevents or improves AMS by increasing the breathing rate, mimicking the breathing of someone who is a good acclimatiser. Thus, if you feel better on Diamox, you actually are better; Diamox does not mask the symptoms of AMS.

The usual dose is 125mg (half a tablet) every 12 hours as needed. Mild tingling of hands and feet is common after taking Diamox and is not an indication to stop its use. Diamox is a diuretic, so increased urine output can be expected. People with a known allergy to sulphur drugs should not take Diamox.

Dexamethasone (Decadron) This potent steroid drug improves the symptoms of HACE by helping to stop the leak of fluid from vessels, but it does not improve acclimatisation. It is an important drug to carry for emergency use, but should never be taken prophylactically to prevent AMS. People with severe headache and loss of balance can be improved enough to avoid a night descent, or convert them from a stretcher case to being able to walk. Do not be tempted to continue ascending while still taking the drug. Either descend or remain at the same elevation until you no longer need the drug.

The dose is 4mg every six hours, whether given orally or by injection.

Nifedipine A drug ordinarily used to treat heart problems and high blood pressure, nifedipine has been shown to reduce pressure in the main artery in the lungs, dramatically improving severe HAPE. For this reason, nifedipine should be included in trekking first-aid kits. The initial dose is 10mg to 20mg every eight hours. Treatment with nifedipine should be accompanied by immediate descent.

David Shlim, MD

write a letter complaining about something that could have been easily solved by some simple assistance and instructions from you.

HEALTH & SAFETY

For general advice on medical issues not specifically related to trekking see Health in the Facts for the Visitor chapter.

Trekking in Bhutan involves multiple long ascents and descents. This can prove physically tiring, especially as the altitude increases. The best training is to walk up and, in particular, down hills as much as possible. If you have a busy life, with little access to hiking on weekends, you should train with exercise machines (such as 'Stairmasters'), ride a bicycle or jog. Trekking puts most of the strain on the quadriceps muscles in the front of the thigh. If you have no hills to train on, try putting a pack on your back to increase the strength training associated with walking or jogging. Take stairs whenever possible in preference to a lift (elevator).

People over 45 often worry about altitude and potential heart problems. There is no evidence that altitude is likely to bring on previously undiagnosed heart disease. If you are able to exercise to your maximum at sea level, you should not have an increased risk of heart attack while trekking at altitude. However, if you have known heart disease and your exercise is already limited by symptoms at low altitude, you may have trouble at altitude. If you have a history of heart disease, you should consult a doctor who has some knowledge of high altitude before committing yourself to a trek.

Common Ailments

Trekkers' Knee If your legs have not been gradually accustomed to walking uphill and downhill through training, there is a chance that you will develop some degree of knee soreness after a long descent. The pain generally comes from mild trauma repeated thousands of times on the descent. The two areas most affected are the outer side of the knee and the area under the kneecap. You may experience difficulty walking and have to rest for a few days before continuing.

Anti-inflammatory pills are helpful, as are ski poles or a walking stick. The pain can take several weeks to go away completely, but there are no long-term consequences.

Blisters The repeated rubbing of the skin against a hard surface (the inside of your shoe or boot) can cause blisters. The superficial surface of the skin eventually gets lifted off its base and fluid collects in the resulting bubble. Blisters can usually be avoided by conscientious attention to your feet as you hike. You should immediately investigate any sore spot on your foot and put some form of additional protection over the area that is being rubbed. There are many commercial products that protect your feet from blisters. Moleskin is the most popular item, but adhesive tape can also work well. Newer products, utilising soft gels, have recently been added to the mix. Using a thin inner sock inside a thicker sock can provide a sliding layer that reduces the friction on the foot. Try not to begin a trek in brand-new shoes or boots.

Blisters are not infected when they first form, but after the bubble breaks bacterial infection can develop. Wash the area and keep it clean. If swelling and redness develop, you will need to take oral antibiotics.

Snow Blindness This is a temporary, painful condition resulting from sunburn of the clear surface of the eye (the cornea). It comes from heavy exposure to ultraviolet radiation, almost exclusively in situations where someone is walking on snow without sunglasses. If you are in a party of trekkers attempting to cross a high pass covered with snow, try to make sure everyone has something to protect their eyes, even if it means using pieces of cardboard with narrow slits cut in them.

The treatment is simply to try to relieve the pain. Cold cloths held against the outside of the eyelids can bring relief. Antibiotic eye drops are not necessary and anaesthetic drops should be avoided as they slow the healing and make the eyes vulnerable to other injuries. The cornea will be completely repaired within a few days and there are no long-term consequences.

Overview of Treks

trek	start	finish	No. of days	maximum elevation (m)	standard
Druk Path	Paro Ta Dzong	Motithang	6	4210	medium
Dagala Thousand Lakes	Geynikha Primary School	Chamgang	6	4720	medium
Jhomolhari	Drukgyel Dzong	Dodina	9	4930	medium-hard
Jhomolhari 2	Drukgyel Dzong	Drukgyel Dzong	8	4520	medium
Laya-Gasa	Drukgyel Dzong	Tashithang	14	5005	medium-hard
Gasa Hot Spring	Tashithang	Tashithang	5	2430	easy
Gangte	Phobjikha	Tikke Zampa	3	3480	easy
Bumthang cultural	Toktu Zampa	Mesithang	3	3360	easy-medium
Duer Hot Spring	Duer	Duer	8	4700	medium-hard
Rodang La	Toktu Zampa	Trashi Yangtse	10	4160	medium-hard
Snowman	Drukgyel Dzong	Sephu	25	5320	hard
Samtengang winter	Punakha	Chhuzomsa	4	1500	easy

Rescue

If you find yourself ill or injured in the mountains, don't panic. If someone falls, take some time to assess the situation: Suspected broken bones may only be bruises, and a dazed person may wake up and be quite all right in an hour or two. In most areas of Bhutan, some kind of animal, either horses or yaks, will be available to help transport a sick or injured trekker.

Sometimes either the seriousness of the injuries or the urgency of getting care will make land evacuation impractical. If this is the case, then the only alternative is to request a helicopter rescue flight. Fortunately, this is a reasonably straightforward process, but once you ask for a helicopter, you cannot cancel it later and you will be charged for the service. Prices start at US$1500 and can go much higher, especially if weather conditions are bad and the chopper has to make two or three attempts to rescue you.

Rescue helicopters are Indian units from the air-force base in Hasimara or the army facility at Bagdogra airport. If there is need for an evacuation during a trek, the guide will send a message to the appropriate tour operator. The tour operator contacts DOT to request a rescue helicopter, DOT forwards the request to the Royal Bhutan Army and it, in turn, requests the Indian Army to send a chopper. It's a well-organised and efficient chain of communication and a helicopter is usually dispatched within a day.

DRUK PATH TREK

The Trek at a Glance

Duration 6 days
Max Elevation 4210m
Standard Medium
Season February to June, September to December
Start Paro Ta Dzong
Finish Motithang
Access Towns Paro, Thimphu
Summary One of the most scenic and popular treks in Bhutan, following a wilderness trail past several remote lakes. Although it is a short trek, it still goes to a high altitude, making it moderately strenuous.

The Druk Path trek has two possible starting points. Yours will depend on what arrangements have been made with the horse owners. The traditional start is in Dambji, near a gravel pit on the eastern side of the Do Chhu at 2300m. Most groups opt to save 140m of climbing, starting at a

Druk Path Trek

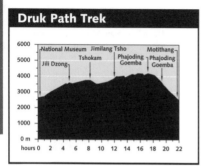

trailhead outside the gate of the National Museum at 2470m.

The trek is usually possible from late February to June and from September to December, although snow sometimes closes the route in late autumn and early spring. Days are normally warm, but nights can be very cold and you should be prepared for snow in winter. Avoid the monsoon season of July and August.

It is possible to shorten the trek to four days, but you must be able to walk for more than eight hours a day. With the shorter schedule you would camp at Jili La, Jimilang Tsho and Phajoding, arriving in Motithang on the morning of the fourth day. Some agents modify the Druk Path trek into a four-day trek in the reverse direction, starting at the youth centre in Motithang and finishing by hiking down from Jimilang Tsho to the roadhead at Tsaluna in the Bemang Rong Chhu valley. If you're a masochist you can even race through the trek in a single day. An old punishment for Bhutanese soldiers was a forced one-day march along this route from Thimphu to Paro.

Day 1: National Museum to Jili Dzong
10km • 4–5 hours • 1090m ascent
The first day is a long climb as you gain more than 1000m of elevation. The trek follows a gravel road past a few farms for about 30 minutes and then climbs steeply up a ridge on the first of many short cuts that avoid road switchbacks, passing Kuenga Lhakhang at 2640m. A further climb past

cultivated fields leads back to the road and another 30 minutes of walking through blue pine forest takes you to a big stone house at **Damchena** (2880m), where the road ends.

The wide trail climbs through blue pine and fir forest to a *mani* wall in a clearing known as Damche Gom at 3020m. It's then a long, but not steep, climb through forests to a meadow at 3260m where it's possible to *camp*. It is better to keep climbing for another hour to a *camping place* in a large pasture just before **Jili La**, marked by a cairn at 3560m.

If you are in a small group you can cross the pass and drop to an excellent *camping place* in a meadow below Jili Dzong at 3480m.

Day 2: Jili Dzong to Jangchhu Lakha
10km • 3–4 hours • 310m ascent, 50m descent
This is a short day, which allows time to visit **Jili Dzong**, atop a promontory at 3570m. If the weather is clear, there is an excellent view of Paro town and the upper Paro valley far below, with Jhomolhari and other snow-capped peaks in the distance.

Jili Dzong was the residence of Ngawang Chhogyel (1465–1540), the cousin of Lama Drukpa Kunley. The large *lhakhang* (temple) contains an impressive statue of Sakyamuni almost 4m high. Once in a state of disrepair, the walls of the lhakhang have now been replastered and await new paintings. One wonders what kinds of mischief the young monks must have perpetrated to warrant banishment to such a high and isolated monastery.

From the dzong the route begins a long ridge walk, first climbing on the west side of the ridge in a rhododendron forest to a saddle at 3550m, then descending through a forest of trees ravaged by bark beetles. Climb again and traverse around the west side of a cone-shaped hill to a meadow. There are views of Jhomolhari and other snow peaks, and you are likely to see or hear some monal pheasants during the day. Cross to the east side of the ridge and make a long traverse through rhododendrons and cedars to Jangchhu Lakha, a pasture at 3760m. There is another good *camping spot* 10 minutes beyond at Tshokam, a yak herder camp at 3770m. There is a primitive wooden tub here in case you want to organise a hot-stone bath.

Day 3: Jangchhu Lakha to Jimilang Tsho
11km • 4 hours • 230m descent, 330m ascent

Beyond Tshokam there is a choice of trails. The high trail follows the ridge, making many ups and downs, and is said to be long

and difficult – about two hours longer than the normal route. From the ridge there are good views of Jhomolhari and 6989m Jichu Drakye, the peak representing the protective deity of Paro.

The normal route descends from Tshokam through forests to the foot of a valley and crosses the upper part of the Bemang Rong Chhu, here only a stream, at 3540m. Trek upstream past a yak pasture called Langrithang. The trail is difficult to see as it traverses muddy bogs, but eventually becomes more distinct as it follows the east side of the stream (river left) to a small

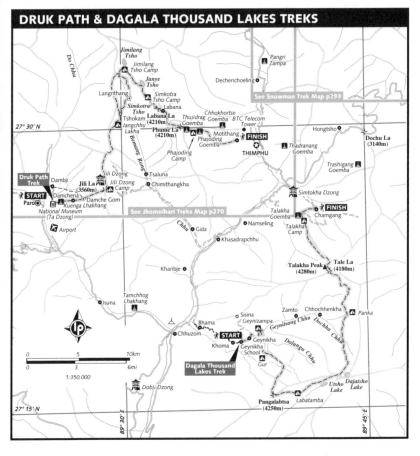

DRUK PATH & DAGALA THOUSAND LAKES TREKS

bridge at 3670m. A short distance above the bridge the high route rejoins after a descent from the ridge. The trail then climbs through forest and finally makes a steep ascent through large rocks and dwarf rhododendrons to a crest, then traverses a short distance to Jimilang Tsho, an isolated lake at 3870m. There is a pleasant *camping place* at the far end of the lake.

Jimilang Tsho means 'Sand Ox Lake', and was named for a bull that emerged from the lake and joined the cattle of a family that uses the area as a summer grazing ground. The lake is also known for its giant trout, which were introduced in the 1970s.

It is possible to cut the trek short by descending towards the south-east through a forest of blue pine to the road at Tsaluna, but the route is not obvious and crosses the river several times. This route passes Tsalu Ney, a 14th-century lhakhang on the site of a cave where Guru Rinpoche meditated.

Day 4: Jimilang Tsho to Simkotra Tsho
11km • 4 hours • 820m ascent, 400m descent

The trail climbs from the lower end of the lake to a ridge at 4010m, makes a traverse along the side of the ridge, then descends to a single stone shelter. Climb to another ridge, then make several ups and downs to a crest at 4050m overlooking Janye Tsho. Descend to a yak herders' camp near the lake and walk along the shore at 3950m before climbing to a ridge at 4150m and descending to some stone ruins and a *camp spot* at 4110m overlooking Simkotra Tsho.

Be sure you have agreement on where to camp on this day. The horse drivers often push to continue over the next pass to a better camp and grazing land at Labana.

Day 5: Simkotra Tsho to Phajoding
10km • 3–4 hours • 130m ascent, 680m descent

It's another long climb past several false summits, then a long rocky traverse to a group of cairns atop Labana La at 4210m. The trail descends gently and traverses above a broad valley to another crest at 4210m. There are views of Dochu La and Jhomolhari along this stretch of trail.

Below Labana La, a side trail descends through rocks to a *camping place* at 4110m near a stone hut beside an almost-dry lake at Labana.

Pass a rough stone wall and soon come to some prayer flags on a hill above the trail that mark a seldom-used sky burial site. Another long traverse leads to a crest at 4120m, then the trail drops and crosses a final ridge at **Phume La** (4080m). Weather permitting, there are views of Gangkhar Puensum and other Himalayan peaks here. Below sprawls the entire Thimphu valley. A trail leads north-east and then descends steeply towards Phajoding. An alternative trail leads south-east and descends steeply to **Thujidrag Goemba**, a meditation centre that hangs on the side of a precipitous rock face at 3950m.

Another steep descent on a maze of eroded trails through juniper and rhododendron bushes leads to a *camp site* above Phajoding at 3750m. Numerous meditation centres and lhakhangs are scattered across the hillside. The large buildings of Phajoding Goemba are a short distance below the camp site. See the Walks to Nearby Monasteries section at the end of the Thimphu chapter for details of Phajoding Goemba.

Day 6: Phajoding to Motithang
4–5km • 2½ hours • 1130m descent

This day's trek is all downhill through forest. Descend to the main monastery building at 3640m and start down on a wide trail, passing a Bhutanese *chorten* at 3440m. Just below the chorten there is a trail junction. The trail leading straight goes to Chhokhortse Goemba and the BTC telecom tower, offering an alternative way to end this trek.

The normal route turns right and descends towards Motithang. There are numerous short cuts, but they all eventually lead to the same place. Pass another chorten at 3070m and descend steeply to a stream, crossing it at 2820m. Climb to a rough road and follow it down, skirting around the wooden buildings of the royal bodyguard camp and on to the Motithang youth centre at 2520m.

DAGALA THOUSAND LAKES TREK

The Trek at a Glance

Duration 6 days
Max Elevation 4720m
Standard Medium
Season April, September to October
Start Geynikha Primary School
Finish Chamgang
Access Town Thimphu
Summary A short trek, near Thimphu, to a large number of lovely, high-altitude lakes (far fewer, however, than the name suggests).

This trek is not difficult and most trekking days are short but there are some long, steep climbs. It is not a popular route, and you will probably encounter no other trekkers.

It's a 29km drive from Thimphu to the junction of a rough, unpaved road leading to the starting point. It's a long walk, therefore it's best to arrange a 4WD vehicle to drive 8km up the steep, rough road to a BHU at Khoma, high above the Geynitsang Chhu at 2850m. It's another 1km to the small Geynikha primary school where the horses usually wait to meet groups.

The best way to arrange this trek is to drive to the starting point after lunch and then make the short descent to the first camp in the late afternoon.

The recommended times for this trek are April and late September through October. Snow in the high country can block the route and make it necessary to retrace your steps to the starting point.

Day 1: Geynikha to Geynizampa
2km • 1 hour • 150m descent

Start walking along the road, which soon turns uphill towards a Geologic Survey of India mining site in Sisina, high on the hillside above. Leave the road and follow the trail that leads straight and level for about 500m to a chorten overlooking the fields of Geynikha (2950m). Make your way through the village and head for the ruins of a house on the ridge to the north-east. The route then descends to a small stream, the Chhokosen Chhu, and follows it down to a chorten and an excellent *camping place* in a forest of blue pines alongside the Geynitsang Chhu at 2800m. There are two villages, Zamto and Chhochhenkha, further up the valley, which are the destination for a day hike described in the Royal Society for the Protection of Nature *Mild and Mad Hikes* book. You can download a preview of the book from W www.bhutan-trails.org.

Day 2: Geynizampa to Gur
5km • 4 hours • 550m ascent, 60m descent

Crossing a suspension bridge, the trail turns south along the east side of the Geynitsang Chhu (river left) to a side stream, the Dolungu Chhu. Cross the stream on a log bridge and start uphill on an eroded trail through a forest of oaks. The trail is used only by yak herders, woodcutters and a handful of trekkers, but it was once a major trading route between Thimphu and Dagana, headquarters of Dagana Dzongkhag, south of Wangdue Phodrang. This accounts for the walls, well-crafted stone staircases and other developments along portions of the route.

A long climb leads to an outstanding lookout point at 3220m. The climb becomes gentler as it ascends towards the top of the ridge where it makes a hairpin turn at 3350m. Be careful here; the trail to the *camp site* is an inconspicuous path that leads south through the forest to Gur, some yak pastures in the trees at 3290m.

Day 3: Gur to Labatamba
12km • 5 hours • 1040m ascent, 110m descent

After climbing back from the camp to the main trail the route continues gently up the ridge on a wide track. A long, stiff climb through blue pines leads to a rocky outcrop where the vegetation changes to spruces, dead firs and larches. The trail traverses into a side valley, crosses a stream at 3870m and begins a long, gentle climb through scattered birches and rhododendrons towards the pass, weaving in and out of side valleys and crossing several tiny streams. At **Pangalabtsa**, a pass marked by cairns at 4250m, there is a spectacular view of the whole Dagala range. This is now yak country and there are numerous herders' camps scattered across the broad Labatamba valley. Descend from the pass to the first herders' hut at 4170m and traverse around the head of a small valley to the main valley floor. Climb beside a stream to a *camp* at 4300m near Utsho Tsho, where there are said to be plenty of golden trout. The high-altitude area near the lakes is a mass of alpine wildflowers in September.

You should schedule an extra day here to walk to the numerous lakes in the vicinity and perhaps do some trout fishing.

Day 4: Labatamba to Panka
8km • 6–7 hours • 260m ascent, 520m descent

There are two possible routes and the pack animals will take the lower one. The trekking route is not well marked, and is more of a cross-country traverse. It climbs along the western side of the lake Dajatsho to a saddle at 4520m, where there are good mountain views. If you want a better view, you could scramble to the top of a 4720m peak to the east. From the pass the trail descends past several herders' camps, then drops to the Dochha Chhu, rejoining the trail at about 4200m. Follow the trail as it climbs over three ridges and descends to Panka at 4000m. Because there is a water problem here during spring, it may be necessary to descend to an alternative *camp* 20 minutes below.

Day 5: Panka to Talakha
8km • 6–7 hours • 180m ascent, 1100m descent

The route leads north to a crest at 4100m where several trails lead off in different directions. The trail to Talakha climbs steeply up a slate slope to the ruins of a house. It's then a long traverse to Tale La at 4180m. From here there is a view of the Dagala range and of Thimphu, far to the north. It is then a long descent through bamboo forests to the goemba at Talakha (3080m).

Day 6: Talakha to Chamgang
6km • 3 hours • 440m descent

There is a steep, eroded trail that leads to Simtokha, but there are numerous fences surrounding apple orchards along the way and there is no longer a direct route.

You can arrange to have vehicles pick you up at Talakha, but it's a long, rough, muddy road suitable only for 4WDs. It's best to walk the three hours down the road, with a few short cuts where trails avoid switchbacks, to Chamgang at 2640m.

JHOMOLHARI TREK

The Trek at a Glance

Duration 9 days
Max Elevation 4930m
Standard Medium-hard
Season April to June, September to November
Start Drukgyel Dzong
Finish Dodina
Access Towns Paro, Thimphu
Summary Bhutan's most popular trek offers spectacular views of the 7314m-high Jhomolhari from a high camp at Jangothang.

The first three days of this trek follow the Paro Chhu valley to Jangothang, climbing gently, but continually, with a few short, steep climbs over side ridges. It then crosses a high pass and visits the remote village of Lingzhi, then crosses another pass before making its way towards Thimphu. The last four days of the trek cover a lot of distance and require many hours of walking. The trek also affords an excellent opportunity to see yaks.

There are two versions of this trek and DOT counts them as two separate treks. About 40% of Bhutan's trekkers follow one of the Jhomolhari trek routes, but this represents fewer than 25 groups a year.

The trek is possible from April to early June and September to November, but the best chance of favourable conditions is April or October. Days are normally warm, but nights can be very cold, especially above Jangothang. There is a lot of mud on this trek and it can be pretty miserable in the rain. Snow usually closes the high passes in mid- to late November and they don't reopen until April.

Day 1: Drukgyel Dzong to Sharna Zampa

17km • 4–6 hours • 360m ascent, 80m descent

The trek starts from Drukgyel Dzong at 2580m with a short downhill walk on a wide trail. After descending about 80m, you reach the river where a primitive hot-stone bath has been carved into the bank. Look back and see how well positioned the dzong was to keep watch over this valley.

A short distance upriver is the small settlement of Chang Zampa, where there's an outreach clinic and a little shop. A bridge *(zam)* crosses to river left here. Don't cross it: The trek stays on the south bank (river right). The fields on this side of the river are planted with potatoes and wheat; on the opposite side of the river, it's red rice.

Thirty minutes of walking takes you to the settlement of Mitshi Zampa. Here the route crosses to the left bank of the clear, fast-flowing Paro Chhu via a new Swiss-built suspension bridge at 2540m.

The trail climbs very gently, traversing through well-maintained rice terraces and fields of millet. It's a well-worn trail with lots of round stones and irrigation water running down it. A short walk through a forest of blue pine leads to a small stream and a white chorten. Beyond is **Sangatung**, a pleasant farmhouse surrounded by fields.

The route now enters an area of apple orchards and blue pine and fir forests and the trail is littered with rocks sticking out of the mud. On some parts of the trail, logs have been placed in washboard fashion. In other places it's necessary to leap from rock to rock to keep your feet dry. If you are lucky, your guide will lead you along a less muddy alternative route that cuts across fields, following a telephone line. Don't cross the cantilever bridge that leads to the south; stay on river left, climbing gently to Chobiso, a single house at 2800m.

Soon the valley widens and you reach the army post of **Gunitsawa** at 2810m. There is also a primary school and a shop here. This is the last stop before Tibet; all army personnel and civilians are required to report to the checkpoint. The trek permit that your tour operator arranged will be checked and endorsed here; wait for your guide so the registration formalities can be completed. The large dormitory-style buildings across the river are quarters for enlisted men and their families.

Below the shop at Gunitsawa the trail crosses the Paro Chhu to river right on a wooden cantilever bridge at 2790m. It then climbs to several *camping places* in meadows surrounded by trees at 2850m. On the opposite side of the river you can see a helicopter pad and archery field.

Day 2: Sharna Zampa to Thangthangka

22km • 7–8 hours • 770m ascent, 10m descent

This is a long, hard day with lots of short ups and downs of 10m to 20m. It's made

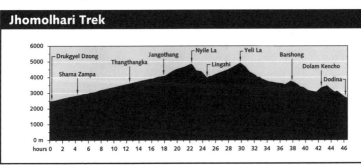

Jhomolhari Trek

more strenuous because of all the rock hopping necessary to avoid mud holes.

The trail continues its gradual climb alongside the Paro Chhu through conifers and rhododendrons. In places it is quite close to the river; if the water is high you might have to scramble over a few small hills to get around it. About 15 minutes beyond Sharna Zampa are the remnants of an old bridge with a house and a chorten on the other side. At this point the route enters Jigme Dorji National Park.

The trail makes a continuous, but gentle, climb on a rocky trail through oaks, rhodo-dendrons and ferns, crossing several small streams. About two hours from camp is **Shing Karap**, a stone house and a clearing at 3110m. This is where most guides choose to serve lunch. Some distance beyond is the route to Tremo La, which is the stone-paved trail leading off to the left. This is the old invasion and trade route from Phari Dzong in Tibet. Don't take this inviting-looking trail: several trekkers have done so in the past and made a long, exhausting side trip to nowhere. Immediately after the trail junction is a wooden bridge over a substantial side stream.

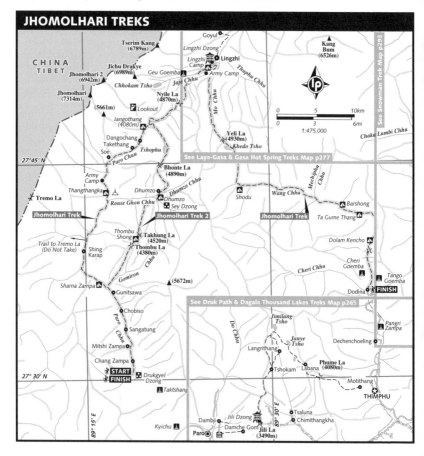

Climb a short set of switchbacks over a little ridge, then descend and cross the Paro Chhu to river left on a wooden cantilever bridge at 3230m. The route up this side of the river goes up and down on a rocky trail through forests of birch and firs. There are numerous short climbs and descents, and one small slide area to cross. There is not much elevation gain, but the continual little ups and downs (plus a 300m elevation gain) add up to a fair amount of uphill. Among the tree species along this part of the trail are blue pine, maple and larch.

After about three hours of trekking there's a bridge back to river right of the Paro Chhu at 3560m. The trail climbs to a place where you can see a white chorten on the opposite side of the river. There is a bridge here that leads back across the river, but don't cross it. That trail leads up the Ronse Ghon Chhu towards the ruins of Sey Dzong and intersects Day 6 of the Jhomolhari trek 2.

Follow the trail on river right as it turns a corner where there is a good view of Jhomolhari. Climb over a small ridge as the Paro Chhu makes a noticeable bend. Fifteen minutes from the bridge is a lovely meadow with Jhomolhari looming at the head of the valley. This is **Thangthangka** (3610m). There is a small stone shelter and a Bhutanese-style house in a cedar grove at the edge of the meadow.

Day 3: Thangthangka to Jangothang

19km • 5–6 hours • 480m ascent

This is not a long day, but there is a significant elevation gain at high altitude, and you will be worn out when you reach camp. Jhomolhari was probably covered with clouds when you arrived last night, but you'll get a good view if you get up early.

As you climb beyond the camp, Jhomolhari disappears behind a ridge. Less than an hour from camp, at 3730m, is an army post with rough stone barracks housing personnel from both the Bhutan army and the Indian Military Training Team. It's depressing to see the number of trees that have been carelessly felled to keep the post going.

The trail crosses a wooden bridge over a fast-flowing stream a short distance beyond the army post. The hillside on the opposite side of the Paro Chhu is a near-vertical rock face with a few trees clinging to it. Along this stretch the trail can be extremely muddy; there are lots of big stones you can use to rock hop around mud holes. At 3770m, about one hour from camp, the trail turns sharply right at a whitewashed mani wall.

A short climb leads to a small chorten on a ridge. You are now entering yak country and you will see these huge beasts lumbering across the hillsides and lazing in meadows alongside the trail. One of the products made from yak milk is dried cheese called *chugo*. The cheese is sold strung on a necklace of white blocks.

There are two trails, an upper and a lower route. Both contour up the valley from the chorten and end up near the river bank, following the bottom of the valley as it makes a sharp bend to the right. Parts of the hillside are covered with larches, which turn a light yellow in autumn. Above the trail is the village of **Soe**. You cannot see it until you are beyond and above it, but you may meet people herding yaks near the river.

One hour beyond Soe is the settlement of **Takethang**, a cluster of stone houses on a plateau at 3940m. The villagers grow barley and a large succulent plant called *kashaykoni* that is fed to the yaks during winter.

The trail follows straight across the plateau, high above the river. It then crosses a little stream on a bridge made of big stones laid on logs. On the opposite side are a white chorten, an outreach clinic and the few houses of **Dangochang**. The people of this village raise yaks and a few sheep, and some households grow potatoes, turnips and radishes. This area is snowbound from mid-November until the end of March; one resident said the snow can be so deep they have to pee out of the second-floor windows, but this sounds like another Bhutanese myth.

It is slow going uphill beside a side stream to the *camp* at **Jangothang** (4080m) and a spectacular view of Jhomolhari. The ruins of a small fortress sit atop a rock in the middle of the side valley that leads north-west to Jhomolhari. A chain of snow peaks forms the eastern side of the Paro Chhu valley and it's often possible to spot blue sheep on the lower slopes.

There's a community hall with a kitchen and several large flat spots for camping. This is a popular trek route and Jangothang is one of the most spectacular camping places in the entire Himalaya. You are unlikely to have the camp to yourself.

The guidelines for pack animals require that you now exchange your horses for yaks from Soe or horses from Dangochang. Don't be alarmed when your loads get dumped at the camp and the animals disappear down the valley, leaving you alone with a mountain of baggage. The replacement pack animals *will* show up on schedule when you are ready to leave.

Day 4: Acclimatisation Day & Exploration of Jangothang

If going on to Lingzhi, you should spend a day here for acclimatisation. If you are returning to Drukgyel Dzong on the Jhomolhari trek 2, a day in Jangothang is the highlight of the trek; the views don't get any better than here. There are lots of day hikes you can make and a day here is very well spent.

There are four major possibilities for day hikes. The first, and best, is a three- to four-hour excursion up the ridge to the north of the camp. There's no trail, but it's a broad open slope and you can just scramble up it. The ridge is endless, but after an hour or so of climbing there is a good view of Jichu Drakye, although the upper part of the ridge blocks the view of Jhomolhari unless you continue to the highest ridge at 4750m. You are likely to encounter grazing yaks, and occasionally blue sheep, on the upper slopes.

A second alternative, which can be combined with the walk up the ridge, is to trek up the main valley towards the last house, then continue up the valley towards Jichu Drakye. You will see much of this country if you trek over Nyile La to Lingzhi.

A third hike is to go up towards the head of the valley in the direction of Jhomolhari. There is a very rough overgrown trail that cuts across moraines and through brush that

leads to the foot of the mountain. You can't get very far, but there are good views in the upper part of the valley.

The last alternative is a fishing expedition to Tshophu, a high-altitude lake. High on the opposite side of the river to the east is a bowl with a lake that has a good supply of spotted trout. To get to the lake, follow the trail north to the last settlement in the valley (as described in Day 5 of the Jhomolhari trek 2). It takes about one hour to get to the top of the ridge and then another 30 minutes following a stream to the lake.

Typical fishing gear is a tin can with some line and a spinner. A fishing licence costs Nu 15 per day for Bhutanese, more for foreigners, but the game warden doesn't come by this lake very often. The desire for variety in meals often outweighs Buddhist sentiment and you may discover that one of your staff has gone on a fishing expedition and produced fresh fish for dinner.

Day 5: Jangothang to Lingzhi
18km • 6–7 hours • 840m ascent, 870m descent

If you are having problems with the altitude at Jangothang, don't go on to Lingzhi.

Ten minutes beyond the camp are three stone houses inhabited by park rangers and a few elderly people. This is the last settlement in the valley and it's an extremely isolated place. Near the houses the trail turns a corner and there's a spectacular view of Jichu Drakye.

Descend and cross a log bridge at 4160m to the left bank of the Paro Chhu, then start up a steep traverse that heads back downstream. The trail crests at the foot of a large side valley and follows the valley eastwards. Jichu Drakye towers above the Paro Chhu valley and soon the top of Jhomolhari appears over the ridge above the camp at Jangothang. The snow peak in the middle is a secondary summit of Jhomolhari.

At 4470m the trail traverses under the big rocks that were visible from the camp, leads to the left and enters a large east-west glacial valley with numerous moraines. The trees have been left far below; there are a few small gentians, but otherwise it's just grass, tundra and small juniper bushes. You may spot blue sheep on the hillside above and see fat marmots darting into their burrows.

There is a false summit with a cairn at 4680m. As the trail approaches the ridge you can see Jichu Drakye to the north-west. After a very short downhill stretch the trail climbs further up a moraine and offers spectacular views of the sharp ridge that juts from Jichu Drakye. You can see the prayer flags on the pass far above.

The final pull is up a scree slope to **Nyile La** (4870m), about four hours from the camp. If you're ambitious you can climb the ridge to the north-west and go even higher. On one side of the ridge you can see the peaks of Jhomolhari 2 and Jichu Drakye; on the other side is Tserim Kang (6789m).

As Nyile La is frequently very windy, you probably won't stay long on the pass. The descent is through more scree along the side of the hill. This makes it awkward and uncomfortable to walk because the trail slopes outward as it traverses the side of the hill.

It's a long descent to a stream on the valley floor at 4450m. There is some vegetation here, mostly grass, juniper and cotoneaster. This is an excellent place to stop for lunch.

The trail now travels north, contouring along the side of the hill high above the valley floor. The opposite hillside is completely covered with rhododendrons. It is a long traverse on a good trail with a couple of little ups, but mostly down and level. Eventually you can see an army camp near the river below; Lingzhi Dzong is visible on the top of a ridge in the distance.

It's a long walk in and out of side valleys to a lookout at 4360m, then the trail descends steeply into the large Jaje Chhu valley. There are a lot of switchbacks on the rocky trail as it makes its way down through heavy stands of rhododendron and birch to a yak pasture on the valley floor. Jichu Drakye and Tserim Kang tower over the head of the valley and there are some remarkable examples of moraines on their lower slopes. Much of the rest of the trek is an outstanding lesson in geography, with several good examples of both terminal and lateral moraines.

The *camp* is at Chha Shi Thang near a large stone community hall (4010m) used by both Bhutanese travellers and trekking groups. Perched on a cliff on the north side of the valley is the small Geu Goemba, but it's not visible from the trail.

If you take a spare day at Lingzhi, you can make an excursion to Chhokam Tsho at 4340m near the base camp of Jichu Drakye. During the hike you may encounter blue sheep and musk deer. If you are continuing to Thimphu, schedule a rest day here. Lingzhi is worth visiting, and it's useful to rest up for the following strenuous trek day.

Day 6: Lingzhi to Shodu
22km • 8–9 hours • 940m ascent, 920m descent

Start early because this day is long and tiring. Climb towards a small white chorten on a ridge above the camp, then turn south up the deep Mo Chhu valley. The trail stays on the west side of the largely treeless valley, climbing steadily and crossing numerous side streams, most without bridges. About three hours from camp the trail crosses the Mo Chhu. There is no bridge and the river has broken into many small channels, presenting an interesting route-finding exercise, jumping among hummocks of grass and slippery rocks.

The trail climbs steeply up the side of the main valley and crosses into a large side valley, climbing above a stream. It then makes an impressive climb up the headwall, switchbacking through rocks to a large cairn atop **Yeli La** at 4930m. Try to avoid walking with the pack animals because the trail is carved into a rock cliff near the pass and is quite narrow. From the pass, on a clear day, you can see Jhomolhari, Gangchhenta and Tserim Kang.

It's a steep descent into a hanging valley, passing a small lake at 4830m. The trail follows the outflow from the lake, descending into another huge valley and another, larger lake, Khedo Tsho, at 4720m. Watch for blue sheep grazing alongside the lake. The trail then crosses the upper reaches of the Jaradinthang Chhu and descends along the valley, following the river southwards

TREKKING

for a very long distance, crossing several side streams. After crossing back to the east bank on a log bridge at 4340m, the trail reaches a chorten at 4150m where it turns eastwards into the upper Wang Chhu valley. Descending and crossing to the south bank (river right) of the Wang Chhu on a log bridge, the trail traverses a narrow, sandy slope to a *camping place* at **Shodu** (4080m), just at the tree line.

Day 7: Shodu to Barshong
16km • 5–6 hours • 250m ascent, 670m descent

Upon leaving Shodu the trail crosses to river left and passes an abandoned army camp and a small alternative *camp site*. The trail traverses under steep yellow cliffs with a few meditation caves carved into them. It is believed that the Shabdrung spent some time in these caves. Descending on a steep stone staircase, the trail reaches the river, crossing it on a log bridge at 3870m. For the next three hours the trail crosses the river five more times, slopping through muddy cypress forests on the south slope and hugging the steep canyon walls and crossing large side streams on the north slope, eventually ending up on the north bank (river left) at 3580m.

The route climbs gradually for one hour to Barshong, where there is a dilapidated community hall and the ruins of a small dzong. The designated *camp* is below the ruins at 3710m, but it is in a swampy meadow and most groups elect to continue to a better camp by the river, about 1½ hours beyond (see the following paragraph).

Day 8: Barshong to Dolam Kencho
15km • 4–6 hours • 290m ascent, 640m descent

The trail descends gently through a dense forest of rhododendron, birch and conifers, then drops steeply on a rocky trail to meet the Wang Chhu. Thirty minutes of walking through a larch forest leads to a clearing known as Ta Gume Thang (Waiting for Horses) at 3370m. Most groups *camp* here or 15 minutes further on at Dom Shisa (Where the Bear Died) instead of Barshong.

Stay on river left, climbing over ridges and descending to side streams. The route then makes a steep climb to 3340m. After traversing for about 30 minutes in rhododendron forests, a trail leads off to the right. This descends to Dolam Kencho, a pleasant *camp* in a large meadow at 3320m. If your group has elected to continue on to Dodina, stay on the left-hand trail, bypassing Dolam Kencho, and climb to a crest at 3430m.

Day 9: Dolam Kencho to Dodina
8km • 3–4 hours • 500m ascent, 930m descent

From the camp the trail climbs back to the trail, reaching a crest with a cairn at 3430m. The trail descends to a stream at 3060m, then climbs again to a pass at 3120m. Another short descent and climb through bamboo forest leads to a rocky stream bed, which the trail follows down to the remains of a logging road along the Wang Chhu at 2720m. It is then a 15-minute walk south along a rocky route to the roadhead at Dodina (2640m), opposite the bridge that leads to Cheri Goemba.

JHOMOLHARI TREK 2

The Trek at a Glance

Duration 8 days
Max Elevation 4520m
Standard Medium
Season April to June, September to November
Start/Finish Drukgyel Dzong
Access Town Paro
Summary The shorter and easier version of the main Jhomolhari trek goes to the Jhomolhari base camp at Jangothang, returning either via the same route or by an alternative trail.

If you want to avoid high altitude it's best to return from Jangothang to Drukgyel Dzong by the same route. The trek described here is an alternative route that is less strenuous than the classic Jhomolhari trek, but still reaches an elevation that could cause altitude problems.

Jhomolhari Trek 2

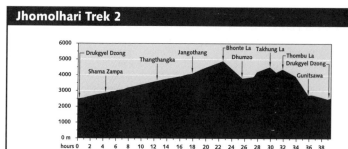

Days 1–4: Drukgyel Dzong to Jangothang
Follow days 1–4 of the main Jhomolhari trek (see pages 268–72).

Day 5: Jangothang to Dhumzo
16km • 6–7 hours • 810m ascent, 1090m descent
The trail leads north to the last settlement in the valley and drops to the Paro Chhu, crossing it on a wooden bridge. Switchback up the side of the hill to a large cirque and the lake of Tshophu (4380m), which is inhabited by a flock of ruddy shelducks. Stay on the eastern side of the lake, passing a second lake as the trail climbs across a scree slope to a crest. Descend into a hidden valley and climb steeply to **Bhonte La** at 4890m.

From the pass the route descends a scree slope, then winds down a ridge with a lot of crisscrossing yak trails. It finally switchbacks down to the Dhumzo Chhu. Trek downstream below the few houses of Dhumzo to a bridge, cross to the south side of the river and continue a short distance to a *camp* at 3800m.

Day 6: Dhumzo to Thombu Shong
11km • 4–5 hours • 720m ascent, 340m descent
The trail climbs 100m over a ridge, then drops to another stream. Crossing that stream, the trail heads up the hillside, dropping into a small side valley before emerging onto a ridge. Here the route turns south, ascending past a few huts to **Takhung La** (4520m). A short descent leads to Thombu Shong (4180m) with three yak herders' huts.

Day 7: Thombu Shong to Sharna Zampa
13km • 4–5 hours • 200m ascent, 1650m descent
Climb out of the valley to **Thombu La** at 4380m, then drop gradually to about 4000m. The trail then makes a steep descent, switchbacking down the ridge, finally reaching the helipad at Gunitsawa (2730m). *Camp* here or cross the river and go upstream to camp at Sharna Zampa, the same place as Day 1.

Day 8: Sharna Zampa to Drukgyel Dzong
17km • 4–6 hours • 80m ascent, 360m descent
Follow Day 1 of the Jhomolhari trek in reverse to Drukgyel Dzong (see page 269).

LAYA-GASA TREK

The Trek at a Glance

Duration 14 days
Max Elevation 5005m
Standard Medium-hard
Season April to June, September to November
Start Drukgyel Dzong
Finish Tashithang
Access Towns Paro, Punakha
Accommodation Camping
Summary This trek is an extension of the Jhomolhari trek. It offers diverse flora and fauna, as well as a good opportunity to spot blue sheep.

This trek begins in the Paro valley and follows the same route as the Jhomolhari trek as far as Lingzhi, then heads north into the high country. Snow can close the high passes, but they are generally open from April to June and mid-September to mid-November. The best trekking month in the Laya region is April.

The trek will introduce you to the unusual culture of the Layap people and offers a stop at a natural hot spring in Gasa. If you are lucky, you may also see takins and Bhutan's national flower, the blue poppy.

Days 1–5: Drukgyel Dzong to Lingzhi

Follow Days 1–5 of the Jhomolhari trek (see pages 269–73).

Day 6: Lingzhi to Chebisa

10km • 5–6 hours • 280m ascent, 410m descent

Cross the stream below the camp on a wooden bridge and climb up the opposite side to a chorten below Lingzhi Dzong. In the valley to the east is a cluster of wood-shingled houses that is one part of Lingzhi village and houses a medicinal plant collection centre. If you look back at Tserim Kang you can see a very distinct rock pinnacle sticking up at the end of the east ridge.

There is a direct route that stays level along the side of the hill, but you can take a short diversion and climb to **Lingzhi Dzong**, which sits at 4220m atop a ridge that separates the main valley from a side valley.

The name of Lingzhi's small dzong is Yugyel Dzong; it was built in the 17th century and played a role in controlling travel over Lingzhi La between Bhutan and Tibet. See the Western Bhutan chapter for more information. From the dzong you can walk down the ridge and rejoin the lower trail.

The largest part of Lingzhi village is hidden in a valley formed by the ridge upon which the dzong was built. There are fields of wheat and barley in the upper part of the side valley. The trail crosses the lower part, where there are a few houses and a post office (with a telephone) at 4080m.

After a look around the village, you walk out of town on a level trail. It's a pleasant walk on a good trail along a hillside covered in flowers and junipers. Far to the north you can see Jhari La and some of the sharp hills you must cross to get to Laya.

The trail traverses high above the river, which flows in a valley so steep that there are very few houses. The path descends to cross a small stream, then continues along the side of the valley, climbing gently. This area is known for its many plants of medicinal value and the entire hillside looks like a colourful herb garden.

About one hour from Lingzhi the trail reaches a cairn and prayer flags on a ridge at 4140m. The route turns into another side valley and makes a long gradual descent to the pleasant settlement of **Goyul** (3870m). In this compact village the stone houses are clustered together, unusual in Bhutan. Surrounding the village are large fields of barley.

Goyul is at the side of a stream with dramatic rock walls towering above. Leaving Goyul, the trail climbs then traverses for an

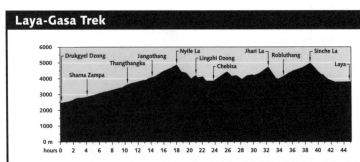

Laya-Gasa Trek

hour to a chorten that overlooks another side valley. A short descent leads into the spectacular Chebisa valley, with a frozen waterfall at its head. The *camp site* is on a meadow opposite Chebisa village (3880m). Upstream of the camp is the twin village of Chobiso.

Day 7: Chebisa to Shomuthang
17km • 6–7 hours • 890m ascent, 540m descent

The route climbs the ridge behind Chebisa, passing a few houses above the main part of the village, then makes a long, steep climb up a featureless slope. There are several large herds of blue sheep living in the rocks above, which you are sure to spot. Also watch for bearded vultures and Himalayan griffons flying overhead. At about 4410m the trail levels out and traverses to Gogu La (4440m). It's not really a pass; it just crosses a ridge that leads off the top of the hill. From the ridge the trail descends into a side valley through a deep forest of rhododendrons.

It's a long descent to a stream at 4170m, then the trail climbs again over a small ridge through a cedar forest, passing several places where the hillside has been burned. The trail crests the ridge at 4210m, then

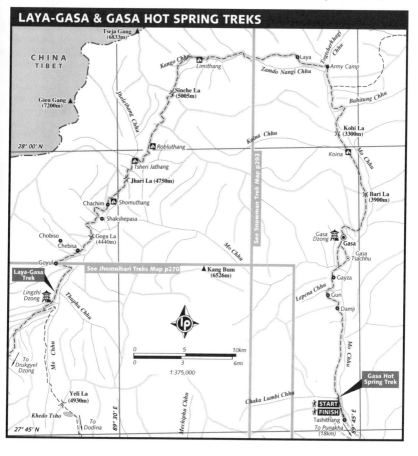

LAYA-GASA & GASA HOT SPRING TREKS

descends on a muddy path into the main Jholethang Chhu valley in a deep forest of fir and birch. There's a little climb past some yak herders' huts and then over the side of the valley and down to **Shakshepasa** (3980m) and a helipad, marked by a big H.

At the bottom there's a marsh and a fairly messy stream crossing with many little channels to jump across on hummocks of moss, muddy earth and rocks. On the opposite side is a good spot for lunch.

There are yak herders' huts downstream, but otherwise the valley is uninhabited. The trail now goes quite steeply up the northern side of the valley. At about 4200m it levels and heads into a side valley, passing a couple of yak herders' huts and traversing high above the valley floor on river right to Chachim, a yak pasture at 4260m.

The *camp* is in a cluster of brush beside a stream at the bottom of the valley. There is a path that leads directly to the camp from Chachim, but it's a steep, rough trail with a lot of bushwhacking. A longer, but better, route follows a larger trail that contours up the side of the valley past the camp. You can then drop down a side trail to Shomuthang (4220m).

This deserted spot is not a particularly good camp site but you get a head start on tomorrow's pass. If you're travelling in the opposite direction, you should camp down by the river at Shakshepasa.

Day 8: Shomuthang to Robluthang
18km • 6–7 hours • 700m ascent, 760m descent

The trail climbs from the camp up the valley, starting on river right, crossing to river left and then crossing back again at 4360m. The white flowers are edelweiss and the snow peak visible to the south-east is Kang Bum (6526m).

The trail climbs out of the valley through pretty desolate country to **Jhari La** (4750m), about two hours from camp. There are four cairns and some prayer flags here. In the distance to the north-east you can see Sinche La, the next obstacle on the route to Laya. The big snow peak to the north is 6840m

Gangchhenta (Great Tiger Mountain; *ta* means tiger). Tserim Kang and the top of Jhomolhari are visible if the weather is clear.

On the north side of the pass the trail switchbacks down to a little stream at 4490m, then becomes a rough, rocky route through rhododendrons on the stream's left. Soon the vegetation changes to big rhododendrons, birches and firs and there are lots of slippery loose rocks on the trail. There is a pleasant lunch spot at the bottom beside a log bridge and stream at 4050m.

Follow the stream gently downhill through bushes on river left as it makes its way to the main valley. It's a gradual descent to a meadow by the Jholethang Chhu at 3990m. Hopefully the bridge that was not there at the time of research will have been rebuilt by the time you read this. If not, there is a small log bridge about 1km upstream, or you may be able to hitch a ride on one of your pack animals. It's also possible to wade the river, but it's cold and the river is quite fast and deep. A yak trail leads west up the valley towards Tibet.

The *camp* by the river is called **Tsheri Jathang**. Herds of takin migrate to this valley in summer and remain for about four months. Takins are very disturbed by the presence of other animals. The valley has been declared a special takin sanctuary, and yak herders have agreed not to graze their animals in the valley when the takins are here.

The trail climbs steeply on the northern side to a crest at about 4150m. It then traverses into a side valley past a tiny lake. There are good *camping places* in a rocky meadow named Robluthang at 4160m.

Day 9: Robluthang to Limithang
19km • 6–7 hours • 850m ascent, 870m descent

This is a long, hard day, crossing Sinche La, the last and highest pass on the trek.

Over the hill above the camp is a little stone house where a Laya woman lives. She'll be happy to sell you trinkets if you are in the mood for shopping; she is also the person responsible for the local *arra* (spirit) your guide was drinking last night. The trail

climbs through the remnants of a burned forest and up the hillside through some boggy
patches. It follows a set of steep switchbacks
to a shelf at 4390m, then turns into another
large glacial side valley. From here the pass
looks a long way away – and it is.

Follow a stream for a while, crossing to
river right on an icy log bridge at 4470m,
then climb onto a moraine and traverse past
lots of marmot holes. You may be able to
spot blue sheep high on the slopes to the
north before the trail crosses back to stream
left. Another climb through rocks leads to
the foot of the pass at 4720m.

It's a tough climb from here to the pass
because the high altitude will slow you considerably. Passing a false summit with a
cairn, the trail levels out a little before
reaching some rock cairns and prayer flags
on **Sinche La** (5005m), about five hours
from camp. The snow-covered peak of
Gangchhenta fills the horizon to the north.

The descent is on a rough, rocky trail that
follows a moraine into another glacial valley. Small rocks on the path keep sliding out
and threatening to twist your ankle. Eventually you arrive at the Kango Chhu, a
stream below a terminal moraine that forms
the end of another valley to the west.

Cross the Kango Chhu to river left on a
small log bridge at 4470m. A short distance
beyond the stream crossing is a yak pasture
and *camping spot* next to a huge rock. It's
best to continue to Limithang to camp; follow the valley northwards, staying high as
the stream falls away below you.

The valley from Gangchhenta enters
from the north-west and provides more
lessons in glaciology. There is a huge terminal moraine and a glacial lake at the foot
of the valley. You can see classic examples
of lateral moraines where the glacier has
pushed rocks up on both sides of the valley.

Beyond an uninhabited stone house the
trail starts a steep descent to the valley floor.
It switchbacks down with the terminal
moraine looming above, crossing the Kango
Chhu on a bridge at 4260m. After a short
climb through rhododendrons the trail levels
out on a plateau above the Zamdo Nangi
Chhu. It's then a short walk on a good trail

through a cedar forest interspersed with small
meadows to Limithang (4140m), a lovely
camp site in a big meadow by the river. The
peak of Gangchhenta towers over the camp
site, even though it's quite a distance away.

Day 10: Limithang to Laya
**10km • 4–5 hours • 60m ascent,
340m descent**
After 20 minutes of walking, the trail crosses
to river left and enters a deep cedar forest,
crossing many little, muddy side streams.
After a while there is a stone herders' hut
with a sod roof; here the vegetation changes
to fir trees draped with lichen.

Cross a large stream that flows in from
the north and make a steep rocky descent
down the side of the valley to the river at
3800m, then cross to river right on a
wooden cantilever bridge. A short distance
later, cross back and make a stiff climb.

It's a long walk through the heavily
wooded, uninhabited valley. Descend, then
cross a waterfall that flows across the trail,
then traverse with many small ups and
downs. Near a point where you can see a
single house on a ridge top to the east, there
is an inconspicuous trail junction. It's not
important which trail you choose: The
upper trail leads to the top of Laya, and the
other leads to the lower part of the village.

If you take the upper trail you will cross
a ridge and see the stone houses and wheat
fields of Laya laid out below you with some
abandoned houses and a *goemba* above.

Gangchhenta dominates the skyline to
the west of the village and from some
places you can get a glimpse of **Masang
Gang** (7165m). In the village centre is a
community school, hospital, archery field
and the first shop since the Paro valley. You
can *camp* in the fields below the school at
3840m. See the Western Bhutan chapter for
a description of Laya and the strange conical bamboo hats worn by Laya women.

Day 11: Laya to Koina
**19km • 6–7 hours • 260m ascent,
1070m descent**
Layaps are not noted for their reliability and
punctuality, and the horses may arrive late.

Below the village, the trail drops back to the river. The trail exits the village through a *khonying* (arch chorten), then passes another chorten at Taje-kha as it descends on a muddy trail to a stream. There are a few houses near the trail, but it's mostly deep forest all the way to the river.

There is an alternative *camping place* on a plateau at 3590m, next to the large Togtsherkhagi Chhu, which flows in from the north-east. Cross the river on a wooden bridge and climb to the stone buildings of the **army camp** on the opposite side. At the army post is a wireless station and a checkpoint where the guide registers the names of the trekkers; you'll have to wait here until the formalities are completed. The peak of Masang Gang is barely visible at the head of the side valley.

The route now follows the Mo Chhu downstream all the way to Tashithang. Beyond the army camp the trail goes uphill, crossing a few streams and making little ups and downs. About 30 minutes from the army post is an inconspicuous trail junction at 3340m. The route for the Snowman trek leads uphill from here on a tiny path. The route to Gasa keeps going downstream on a muddy trail. After a while it turns a corner into a side valley, goes a short distance up the valley and crosses the Bahitung Chhu at 3290m. This is the traditional lunch spot for this day.

The trail travels alongside the Mo Chhu to an overhanging rock that forms a cave, then crosses to river right at 3240m on a cantilever bridge. The canyon closes in and the trail must now make several major

climbs over side ridges as it makes its way downstream. Beyond another cave formed by a large overhanging rock the first long, steep climb starts, cresting at the top of a ridge at 3390m. It's a 150m descent to a clear side stream, then the trail wanders up and down near the river as it runs fast through some big cascades in a gorge. After some more ups and downs through bamboo about 100m above the river there is another serious climb to the Kohi Lapcha at 3300m.

The muddy trail stays high for about 30 minutes until it reaches a stone staircase, where it turns into a side valley, traversing for a bit, then dropping to the large Koina Chhu. Welcome to Koina (3050m), a bamboo bog in the forest by the bridge. There is a single stone house with some muddy *camping places* scattered around. Because of the deep black mud you must wade through and the damp, soft ground upon which you must pitch your tent, this is the worst camp on the whole trek and perhaps the most unpleasant camp in the Himalaya. There is talk of developing an alternative camping place nearby.

Day 12: Koina to Gasa
14km • 6–7 hours • 900m ascent, 1710m descent

You may think that because you are headed downstream the climbs on this trek are finished, but there's another major ascent ahead to get over Bari La.

Cross the bridge at Koina and start up the hill. Parts of the trail are so muddy that logs have been placed to form little bridges. There are also places where the trail follows the side of a ridge and you walk gingerly across logs that dangle out into space. The muddy trail keeps going through a deep forest of fir, in and out of side valleys, for almost three hours to **Bari La** (3900m). There's a small rock cairn and a few prayer flags at the pass, then it's a reasonably level walk to another chorten. There are few good places to stop along this part of the trail, so lunch will probably be an impromptu event.

The route starts down again, sometimes steeply, through a bamboo forest to a stream. At 3080m it rounds a corner where you can

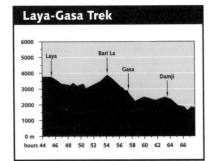

Laya-Gasa Trek

finally see Gasa Dzong on the opposite side of a large wooded side valley. The trail descends past an old chorten, then crosses a ridge into a big side valley below Gasa. It drops and crosses a large stream at 2780m, then traverses along the side of the valley to four chortens on the ridge at 2810m.

The chortens mark the southern boundary of Gasa village (2770m). The trail traverses above the soccer and archery ground, past several small teashops, then intersects Gasa's main street, a stone-paved path that leads uphill to the dzong, school and a Basic Health Unit (BHU). Trek downhill to the bazaar, which consists of about nine shops and a police checkpoint. The police post checks permits, providing a perfect excuse to stop for a soft drink or beer at one of the shops.

You can *camp* in a field near the town, or continue downhill for 1½ hours to the *tsachhu* (hot spring). Many trek itineraries schedule an extra day to laze around in the hot springs – a useful activity after the last two days of strenuous mud walking. See Day 2 of the Gasa Hot Spring trek for details of the springs. If it is raining, the remainder of this trek is perfect country in which to meet leeches.

Day 13: Gasa to Damji
18km • 5–6 hours • 470m ascent, 280m descent

Follow the trail generally south, passing a few houses and mani walls, as it descends to the primary branch of the Mo Chhu, which has flowed through the mountains from Lingzhi to join the other branch of the Mo Chhu that flows from Gasa. Look back for a good view of the dzong, sitting on top of the hill. Be careful as you follow this trail: Near a chorten there is a fork where a second trail leads steeply downhill to the hot spring. The trail towards Damji goes straight here.

After a long descent, cross the river at 2360m on a cable suspension bridge high above the water. The trail starts climbing immediately on the opposite side. At 2510m there's a picnic table at a lookout, from where you can see down to the hot spring and back to a large part of yesterday's trail, although it's all in the forest. Gasa Dzong

with its distinctive rounded front wall is visible, glued to the valley wall and seeming to float in space.

There's a crest at 2330m where the trail turns south along the Mo Chhu (and from here downstream there is only one river known as the Mo Chhu) and then goes up and down on the side of the valley, high above the river. It descends through bamboo to a little stream, then starts climbing back again to a meadow at 2530m. Gasa Dzong and the snow peaks towards Laya are still visible.

The trail stays high, crossing a meadow and descending a little to the small village of Gayza at 2500m. The trail then drops into a deep subtropical ravine filled with trees and ferns, crossing the Lepena Chhu on a spectacular suspension bridge high above a narrow wooded gorge at 2300m.

The trail climbs to another crest and traverses around the top of a side valley to the four houses of Gun at 2400m, then drops again and climbs back up to a chorten. Then it's a short walk to the large village of Damji (2430m), which lies in a huge side valley with an amphitheatre of rice terraces. Pass the school and traverse to the southern end of the village where there is a large cluster of houses and a little chorten at 2380m. A road from Tashithang to Damji is planned for completion in 2003.

Day 14: Damji to Tashithang
16km • 5 hours • 250m ascent, 870m descent

Until the road from Tashithang to Damji is complete you'll have to walk, meeting the road at whatever point the construction has been completed.

Trek past a few more houses and many fields as the trail climbs to a chorten at the southern end of Damji village. The trail begins a long descent to the river, first winding down gently in the jungle past a few streams, then switchbacking steeply down on a rocky trail in the shadow of a huge rock. After a long descent you will cross a wooden bridge over a side stream at 1960m. There is an alternative *camp site* here near the banks of the river, about one hour below Damji.

The trail now follows the Mo Chhu downstream through forests where you may encounter rhesus monkeys and takins alongside the river. You'll have to stick close to your guide as he inquires where the route joins the road. At some point you'll climb from the river to the unfinished road. If you're lucky, vehicles will be waiting there to take you to Punakha, otherwise you will walk down to Tashithang at 1840m. It's then an 18km (one-hour) drive to Punakha Dzong; it's a good road, but the first 5km is unpaved.

GASA HOT SPRING TREK

The Trek at a Glance

Duration 5 days
Max Elevation 2430m
Standard Easy
Season February to March,
October to December
Start/Finish Tashithang
Access Town Punakha
Summary This trek is the last part of the Laya-Gasa trek in reverse. The hot springs are fun, but there is a lot of climbing to get there.

Being at a reasonably low elevation, this trek is possible from February to March and October to December. There are lots of leeches in the lower part of the trek, which make it particularly unpleasant during the rainy season.

Day 1: Tashithang to Damji
16km • 5–6 hours • 870m ascent, 250m descent
Follow Day 14 of the Laya-Gasa trek in reverse, driving as far as possible from Tashithang, dropping to the trail and climbing steeply to the terraced rice fields of Damji (2430m).

Day 2: Damji to Gasa Tsachhu
16km • 4–5 hours • 470m descent
Follow Day 13 of the Laya-Gasa trek in reverse along the side of the valley, then drop to the large stream below Gasa. A trail leads north from here, following the stream

directly to the hot spring at 2240m. The Jigme Dorji National Park administers the hot-spring complex and offers various kinds of accommodation in a grove of large birch trees. There are some houses that can be rented, a few buildings that can be used as kitchens, a dormitory and numerous good *camping places*. It is a pleasant place to spend a day.

The hot springs are by the bank of the stream, below the hotel complex. There are five cement pools and a shower room, with more under construction. The water temperature is 40°C, which is comfortably warm, but not scalding.

You may encounter women selling souvenirs; it's mostly Tibetan-style jewellery made in Nepal.

Day 3: A day at Gasa Tsachhu
You can laze around in the hot springs or take a packed lunch and climb about two hours to Gasa village and the dzong.

Days 4–5: Gasa Tsachhu to Tashithang
Follow Days 13–14 of the Laya-Gasa trek and drive back to Punakha or Thimphu (see page 281–82).

GANGTE TREK

The Trek at a Glance

Duration 3 days
Max Elevation 3480m
Standard Easy
Season March to May, September to November
Start Phobjikha
Finish Tikke Zampa
Access Towns Phobjikha, Wangdue Phodrang
Summary A short trek at relatively low elevations, visiting several remote villages and monasteries.

This trek is recommended from March to May and September to November, although it's usually possible to trek here throughout winter. It is especially beautiful in April, when rhododendrons are in bloom.

Gangte Trek

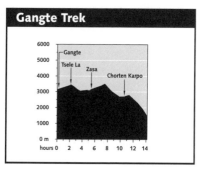

Day 1: Phobjikha to Zasa
15km • 6–7 hours • 610m ascent,
410m descent

The trek starts near the village of Tabiting, a short distance up the road from the Phuntsho Chholing Guest House, just before the Black Mountain National Park warden's office at 2890m. Follow a wide trail uphill from the road beside a stream that climbs above a fenced-in potato field. Climb through a sparse forest of blue pine to Kelwag, a large meadow of scrub bamboo at 3120m. The climb becomes steeper as it switchbacks up a ridge to a few prayer flags at 3370m. It's then a gentle ascent through pines and rhododendrons to **Tsele La** at 3430m.

From the pass the trail descends through scrub bamboo into the huge Kangkha Chhu valley and traverses above a single wooden house at Tsele Pang (3280m). Descend further into a forest of cypress, juniper, rhododendron and daphne to the small village of Tserina at 3120m. There is a trail junction here; if you are in a large group, follow the lower trail to the *camping place* at Dzomdu Gyakha. The upper route to Gogona crosses two small streams and, after a few minutes, reaches the extensive sheep pastures and potato fields of Gankakha at 3030m. It's then a long traverse through forests to a few houses at Gogona (3090m).

Gogona Lhakhang is dominated by statues of Chenresig, Atisha and several manifestations of Guru Rinpoche. The walls are covered with elaborate paintings and on the *gorikha* (porch) is a painting of Lama Drukpa Kunley. Most of the *gomchens*

(married monks) from Gogona travel to Thimphu for winter.

Camping is not allowed at the monastery, therefore it's necessary to trek around the ridge to a large side valley and the pretty village of Dangchu (3040m). The women here weave blankets and speak a different dialect called Bjop-kha (language of the nomads). The usual *camping place* is near the head of the grassy valley beside a small stream in a yak pasture known as Zasa (3130m). This is a small camping place; larger groups usually camp below in the valley at Dzomdu Gyakha.

Day 2: Zasa to Chorten Karpo
16km • 5–7 hours • 450m ascent,
860m descent

An inconspicuous trail leads up the large meadow above Zasa, eventually entering forests on the north-west corner. Climb into a forest of fir, oak, spruce, dwarf rhododendron, miniature azaleas, cypress and juniper. A large area of this forest was burned by a fire that was probably caused by lightning. Much of the undergrowth is daphne, the plant used for hand-made paper, which may be identified by its sweet-smelling whitish-cream-coloured flowers. Climb for about two hours to a crest at 3360m, then another 30 minutes to **Shobe La**, a forested ridge marked by a rock cairn at 3480m. A rocky trail leads down through a forest of cypress, juniper and rhododendron to a clearing at 3270m that offers a good lunch spot.

Descend further on a rocky trail to join a rough forest road at 2970m. The trek from here to the Tashila ropeway strays on and off this road, which is used by tractors to transport the timber harvested in this region. Follow the road across a stream, then through an oak forest, following a few trails that provide short cuts to avoid long loops in the road, eventually arriving at Dolando, an isolated sawmill and several wooden houses at 2790m. The road makes a small detour around a rock that is said to be the remains of a demon. If you look closely you may be able to see the marks left when Guru Rinpoche beat the demon with his stick.

Follow the road alongside a stream, crossing to river right at 2730m, and continue to

TREKKING

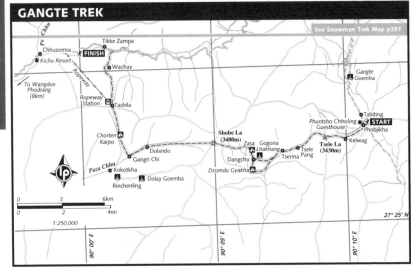

GANGTE TREK

another sawmill at the edge of the broad Karte Thang valley near Gangri Chi village at 2670m. Below is the village of **Kokotkha**, with about 60 rustic houses. The large Kokotkha valley to the south-west is being considered as a site for a domestic airport to serve Wangdue Phodrang and Punakha.

Atop a ridge to the south-west is the large new Rinchenling monastery. It's about a 15-minute walk. High above to the south is Dolay Goemba. The trek route turns north here and follows the small Paza Chhu, then climbs over a ridge on a narrow trail, re-crosses the road and climbs gently to four chortens in a forest of blue pines at 2680m. The Nepali chorten is in honour of a Je Khenpo, a rich merchant from Kokotkha; next is a *kani* (arch-like chorten) with its middle filled in; and the southernmost chorten was built by a Kokotkha flour merchant.

Day 3: Chorten Karpo to Tikke Zampa
12km • 4–5 hours • 120m ascent, 1340m descent

The trail climbs from the camp site to join a forest road at 2720m. It's then an easy walk to the top of the ridge at 2800m. You can take

a trail that cuts across the top of the ridge, but it's more interesting to continue a few minutes to the top of the Tashila ropeway and watch rice and building supplies coming up and logs going down. Depending on the current rules, you may be able to get a ride down the 6km cable and save yourself a knee-cracking descent, but note the warning: 'The passenger who travels by Tashila ropeway will be at their own risk'. For more about the ropeway see the Wangdue Phodrang to Pele La section of the Western Bhutan chapter.

The walk down is through a beautiful forest, with the undergrowth changing from rhododendrons and magnolias to ferns and dwarf bamboo. Experts claim that this stretch of trail is one of the finest bird-watching areas in Bhutan. Among the birds found here are laughing thrushes, shrikes, magpies and woodpeckers.

There's a trail junction at 2250m. Take the right-hand fork and keep descending until you reach the houses and fields of Wachay at about 1880m. You may need to rely on a guide to traverse a few back yards as the trail plunges down past steep terraced wheat fields to two shops at 1460m on the road about 300m east of Tikke Zampa.

BUMTHANG CULTURAL TREK

The Trek at a Glance

Duration 3 days
Max Elevation 3360m
Standard Easy-medium
Season March to May, September to November
Start Toktu Zampa
Finish Mesithang
Access Town Jakar
Summary This trek is so named because the opportunities to visit villages and lhakhangs are greater than on most other treks in Bhutan.

Although it is a short trek, the Bumthang trek is strenuous, featuring a 500m climb to Phephe La. This trek is usually possible from March to May and again from September to November. The start of the trek is a 3km drive up the unpaved road from Kurjey Lhakhang to Toktu Zampa at 2540m. With luck, the packhorses will be waiting and you can start walking with a minimum of delay.

Day 1: Toktu Zampa to Ngang Lhakhang
12km • 4–5 hours • 170m ascent

It's two minutes down to a suspension bridge over a clear stream, the Duer Chhu. A carved Buddha on the rock beyond the bridge is protected by a little shrine. The trail is level as it follows the right bank of the Bumthang Chhu upstream through buckwheat fields to a government animal husbandry office. It's then a short distance to Thankabi Goemba with its distinctive yellow roof and the small village of Thankabi. See the brief description of this goemba in the Central Bhutan chapter.

The trail follows a broad ledge above the river past a 70m-long painted mani wall and a khonying with a mandala painted on the roof inside. Just beyond the arched chorten is a trail junction. The trail to Ngang Lhakhang crosses the river on a suspension bridge and traverses through pleasant meadows and forests of blue pine and scrub bamboo.

Follow the left bank of the Bumthang Chhu (known locally as the Choskhor Chhu) to a small cluster of houses and turn uphill to a small, old Tibetan-style chorten surrounded by prayer flags. The trail then makes a short, steep climb to a settlement of old-looking houses at 2800m. There are two water-driven prayer wheels; the water comes down an interesting sluiceway of carved wooden pipes. This is Ngang Lhakhang, the Swan Temple. See the description of this interesting temple in the Bumthang section of the Central Bhutan chapter.

Alternative Route The camp at Ngang Lhakhang is small, and many guides prefer to camp at Damphay, near the Bumthang Chhu. This adds less than 30 minutes to the next day's walk, so it does not upset the trek schedule much. To get to Damphay, do not cross the large suspension bridge; stay on Bumthang Chhu's right bank. Follow the trail upstream through meadows to a second suspension bridge before Sangsangma village.

Across that bridge you'll find a good *camp* next to a line of prayer flags in a meadow below a small cluster of houses. You can tell this is a popular camping place because the village women sell *yathra* (strips of woven woollen cloth) and trinkets at prices higher than in Thimphu.

This village is an excellent place to try the local Bumthang buckwheat delicacies of *khule* (pancakes) and *putta* (noodles). Wild boar are common in the area and bears will sometimes startle both locals and trekkers.

Day 2: Ngang Lhakhang to Tahung
16km • 6 hours • 750m ascent, 670m descent

The day's walk starts out across meadows, with a view of the valley below and several small hamlets in the hills. Fifteen minutes beyond Ngang Lhakhang the trail forks and you take the lower, smaller, more level path that leads to the right through a muddy area with rocks. There is a lot of dwarf bamboo and several little streams to cross.

The trail cuts across the top of some fields, goes over a small hill and down to a

TREKKING

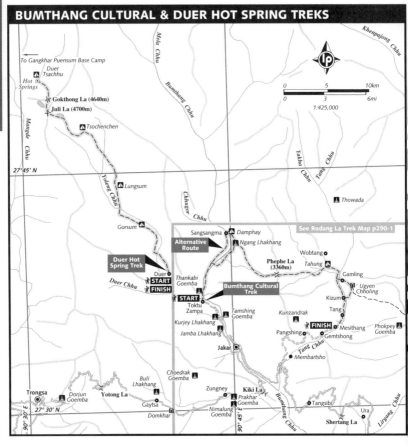

BUMTHANG CULTURAL & DUER HOT SPRING TREKS

To Gangkhar Puensum Base Camp

Mela Chhu

Khenpajong Chhu

Duer Tsachhu
Hot Springs

Gokthong La (4640m)
Juli La (4700m)

Bumthang Chhu

0   5   10km
0   3   6mi
1:425,000

Tsochenchen

Mangde Chhu

27°45′ N

Yoten Chhu

Lungsum

Yakha Chhu

Tang Chhu

Thowada

Gorsum

Chhugor Chhu

Sangsangma   Damphay

See Rodang La Trek Map p290-1

Alternative Route

Ngang Lhakhang

Wobtang

Duer Hot Spring Trek

Phephe La (3360m)   Tahung

Gamling

Duer   Thankabi Goemba

Duer Chhu   START   FINISH

Bumthang Cultural Trek

Ugyen Chholing

Kizum

START

Toktu Zampa   Tamshing Goemba

Kunzandrak   Tang

Kurjey Lhakhang

FINISH   Mesithang   Phokpey Goemba

Jamba Lhakhang   Pangshing   Gemtshong

Jakar

Membartsho

Choedrak Goemba

Buli Lhakhang

Zungney   Kiki La

Trongsa   Dorjun Goemba   Yotong La

Prakhar Goemba

Tangsibi

Gaytsa

Nimalung Goemba

Ura

27°30′ N

Domkhar

Shertang La

Lirgang Chhu

stream. Soon you will be convinced that this cannot be the correct trail and you are hopelessly lost. Don't worry; stick with your guide or the horsemen because it is a narrow, indistinct trail through forests.

After crossing a stream the trail starts climbing, crossing back and forth across the stream on a series of slippery logs and stones. Birches, sycamores, dwarf bamboo and lots of real bamboo form a cold, sunless forest. Spanish moss drapes from the ancient trees, giving an eerie feel to the steep climb.

Finally, the stream disappears and the climb continues through a rhododendron

forest in a dry gully to a rock cairn and a little stone shrine stuffed with offerings of branches and a few ngultrum notes. Tattered prayer flags stretch across the path atop **Phephe La** (3360m). There is no view from the pass; it is a forested ridge with big birch and fir trees.

There is more deep forest on the opposite side; the trail leads down to a stream at 3200m, then into a side valley covered in dwarf bamboo, passing a small mani wall and a khonying chorten. Much of the walk is delightful, breaking out of the forest into broad meadows full of grazing yaks and cows.

It continues through ploughed fields and wide meadows and then into a broad valley, surrounded by rounded, treeless hills. Near a herders' hut the trail becomes indistinct as it crosses a meadow. To stay on track, just aim for the trees on the right side of the meadow.

The route keeps going downhill. As it approaches the bottom of the valley, there are several side trails that lead to pastures and buckwheat fields. Take the most prominent trail, which leads downhill to a large stream and a substantial wooden bridge at 2790m.

There are several alternative *camping places* in this valley. Be sure you are with someone who knows where you are headed at this point. The most likely camp is uphill, behind the village of Tahung. There are other camping places on the flats beside the stream to the east of the village. There is a third possible camp on the banks of the Tang Chhu near Gamling, a large, wealthy village noted for its yathra weaving, about 45 minutes downstream.

Day 3: Tahung to Mesithang
16km • 5–6 hours • 230m descent

Behind Tahung is the Australian-assisted Wobtang sheep development project. A rough road suitable only for tractors follows the right bank of the Tang Chhu from the project all the way down the valley to Tang village. The road improves between Tang and the National Highway below Membartsho. The trekking route leads downstream in meadows next to the river, sometimes on the road and sometimes on a footpath. It crosses the stream you have been following on a road bridge and turns a corner into the main valley of the Tang Chhu at 2640m.

You can head straight back down the road from here to Mesithang, which is 2km south of Kizum and 20km from the junction of the paved road near Membartsho. Vehicles will come to Mesithang to meet you. Alternatively, an interesting side trip leads to Ugyen Chholing, a 45-minute climb from suspension bridge across the Tang Chhu near Gamling.

To follow the side trip, walk downstream from Gamling, crossing a stream and following the trail around a farmyard. Soon it starts climbing onto a ridge, reaching four chortens and several large houses at 2760m. Ugyen Chholing is on the top of the hill to the right. There is more information about the Ugyen Chholing Palace in the Tang Valley section of the Central Bhutan chapter.

DUER HOT SPRING TREK

The Trek at a Glance

Duration 8 days
Max Elevation 4700m
Standard Medium-hard
Season March to April, September to November
Start/Finish Duer
Access Town Jakar
Summary This trek is the old expedition route to Gangkhar Puensum.

With special permission, it might be possible to extend this trek to the base camp of Gangkhar Puensum itself, although this is a rough, difficult route. It is also possible to vary either the upward or return route to travel via the Mangde Chhu valley to meet a gravel road that leads west from Trongsa.

Snow covers the route during winter so the trek is considered open from March to April and from September to early November. Its starting point, Duer village, is one hour (5km) of rough driving from Toktu Zampa. This trek includes a visit to a tsachhu.

Day 1: Duer to Gorsum
18km • 6–7 hours • 380m ascent

The route follows the valley of the Yoleng Chhu, which is famous for trout, up to Gorsum at 3120m.

Day 2: Gorsum to Lungsum
12km • 5 hours • 40m ascent

The route is through a forest of cypress, juniper, spruce, hemlock and maple. The trail is muddy and climbs gradually to the *camp site* at 3160m.

Day 3: Lungsum to Tsochenchen
15km • 6–7 hours • 620m ascent

Trek through more forest to the *camp* above the tree line at 3780m.

Day 4: Tsochenchen to Duer Tsachhu

18km • 8–9 hours • 1340m ascent, 1530m descent

The day starts with a long climb to a small lake and on to Juli La (4700m), a rocky saddle with a few prayer flags and a good view of the surrounding mountains. After crossing the pass the trail descends to a lake at 4220m, then climbs again to Gokthong La (4640m). The path then switchbacks steeply down through jungle to a *camp* near the Duer hot springs at 3590m. Along this part of the trail it may be possible to see musk deer, Himalayan bears and herds of blue sheep.

Day 5: A Day at Duer Tsachhu

Take a rest day to relax in the tsachhu. There are several wooden tubs set into the ground inside a rough wooden shelter.

Day 6: Duer Tsachhu to Tsochenchen

18km • 6 hours • 1530m ascent, 1340m descent

Return via the same route to Tsochenchen.

Day 7: Tsochenchen to Gorsum

27km • 9 hours • 660m descent

Follow the route back down the valley.

Day 8: Gorsum to Duer

18km • 6 hours • 380m descent

Return to the road.

RODANG LA TREK

The Trek at a Glance

Duration 10 days
Max Elevation 4160m
Standard Medium-hard
Season October to November
Start Toktu Zampa
Finish Trashi Yangtse
Access Town Jakar
Summary This trek across eastern Bhutan is tough and involves a tremendously long, steep descent. The logistics are complicated and horses are often difficult to obtain for the final four days of the trek.

Although it was an important trade route before the National Highway was built, few people travel this path any more. Most trekkers combine this route with the Bumthang cultural trek, starting at Toktu Zampa. Alternatively, you can start the trek by driving up the Tang valley to Mesithang or on to Tang village itself, saving two days of walking.

Rodang La is subject to closure because of snow; this trek is best planned in October and early November as well as late spring.

The trek crosses the road near Lhuentse, which breaks up the continuity of the experience, but offers a chance to visit the remote dzong.

Days 1–2: Toktu Zampa to Ugyen Chholing

Follow Days 1–3 of the Bumthang cultural trek to Ugyen Chholing, at an elevation of 2760m (see pages 285–87).

Day 3: Ugyen Chholing to Phokpey

17km • 5–6 hours • 920m ascent

The long climb to Rodang La takes two days. Above Ugyen Chholing the trail is rutted with the hoof prints of cattle. If it's wet, this is a very muddy, miserable, slippery climb. The trail levels out at about 2900m and meets a stream. At about 3000m the cow trails end and it becomes a small footpath through muddy fields and dwarf bamboo.

At 3400m the trail crosses a meadow with more dwarf bamboo. This is a meadow, and not a forest, because of a fire that burned a large part of the hillside. High on the opposite hill you can see the recently built Phokpey Goemba. Climb through the meadow and traverse through forest to another steep, high meadow, finally turning a corner into a side valley. The opposite side is all big firs.

The trail leads up a draw towards the head of the valley and the *camp* in a meadow at 3680m. This is a summer pasture and there is the frame for a house that herders cover with a plastic sheet to use as a shelter. The meadow is surrounded by forest and the ground is dotted with tiny blue

ekking in Bhutan is a necessarily well-orchestrated activity as you'll encounter few villages en route op right & centre). What you will experience is the snow-capped splendour of Himalayan peaks ch as Jhomolhari (top left) and Tserim Kang (bottom).

Trekking the Bhutan Himalaya calls for resolve and physical endurance, but your efforts will be abundantly rewarded with spectacular views, such as that of Jhomolhari saturated in evening light.

TREKKING

alpine flowers. Once the sun goes down, the temperature plummets.

Day 4: Phokpey to Pemi
20km • 6–7 hours • 480m ascent, 1160m descent

The trail goes through a small notch and onto another ridge at 3700m. It traverses the east side of the ridge, passing big rhododendrons with large leaves that curl up in the cold. Soon you will see the pass up ahead. After a long traverse at 3770m, the trail begins the final climb to the pass up big stone slabs and a steep stone staircase. **Rodang La** (4160m) is about a two-hour climb from camp. There's a small stone chorten here.

Once across the pass it's a steep descent of nearly 2500m to the valley floor. The descent starts on some rough rocks and an unbelievably long and steep stone staircase that was built when this was the trade route between eastern and western Bhutan. This is the same near-vertical slope that the road descends on the eastern side of Thrumshing La, which is only 20km to the south.

You can see the trail far below, snaking down the ridge to the east. This is a tough route for horses, and it is said that even the king walked downhill here.

Part of the route is along a vertical face and the trail is on wooden galleries fastened into the side of the cliff. There are a few small meadows as the trail winds its way down on a complex route through a region where sightings of ghosts and yetis have been reported. Leaving the rhododendrons and conifers, it makes a gentle descent through a forest of broad-leafed species along a ridge to the east to a big meadow called Pemi at about 3000m. After a short walk through some dwarf bamboo you reach the ruins of a house and a *camp site* at 2950m. This is not an ideal camping place because the water is 15 minutes down the side of a hill; go easy on the washing here. The ruined stone building was the grain storehouse during the time of the first and second kings, when royal parties travelled regularly between Bumthang and Kurtoe.

Day 5: Pemi to Khaine Lhakhang
21km • 7–8 hours • 350m ascent, 1340m descent

From Pemi the trail tumbles into the valley of the Noyurgang Chhu. The route leads from the camp through dwarf bamboo, then heads down a damp, rock-filled gully with lots of leaves, moss and wet rocks to pick your way through.

At about 2600m the vegetation changes to ferns and more tropical species and there is a long level stretch through the mud. It then goes down steeply again, working its way out towards the end of a side ridge and a meadow called Sang Sangbe (2300m), where a ghost is said to live. High on the hillside on the opposite side of the valley is Yamalung Goemba, hidden behind a bunch of very tall trees planted in a circle. The trail drops off the side of the ridge to a bridge over a stream at 1700m. The village of **Ungaar** is on a ridge above the stream and downstream is another small village named Zhobi. It's then a short walk across rice fields in the bottom of the valley to a suspension bridge over the Noyurgang Chhu at 1660m.

Cross to river left and start climbing away from the bridge through ferns and tropical jungle to the village of **Bulay** (1800m). The trail passes above the rice terraces of the village, turns a corner and

Khaine Lhakhang

Some people believe that the remote Khaine Lhakhang is one of the 108 temples built by King Songtsen Gampo in AD 659. Three small statues from here are said to have flown of their own accord to Konchogsum Lhakhang in Bumthang, which is said to have been built at the same time.

The primary statue is a 2.5m-high Sakyamuni figure. A statue of Karmapa is on his right and Shabdrung Rinpoche is above him on the left. There are also smaller statues of Milarepa and Guru Rinpoche. The main protective deity is a ferocious god named Taxan, who is depicted riding on a horse. A two-day festival is celebrated here in mid-November.

TREKKING

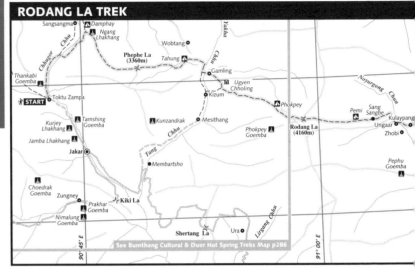

RODANG LA TREK

Sangsangma ● ▲ Damphay
▲ Ngang Lhakhang
Chhugor Chhu
Yakha Chhu
Wobtang ●
Phephe La (3360m)
Tahung ▲
Thankabi Goemba ▲
Gamling ●
Ugyen Chholing
▲ START ● Toktu Zampa
Kizum ●
Noyurgong Chhu
Tamshing Goemba ▲
Kunzandrak ▲ ● Mesithang
Phokpey ●
Pemi ▲ Sang Sangbe
Kulaypang ●
Kurjey Lhakhang ▲
Phokpey Goemba
Rodang La (4160m)
Ungaar ●
Zhobi ●
Jamba Lhakhang ▲
Tang Chhu
Jakar ◉
● Membartsho
Pephu Goemba ▲
Choedrak Goemba ▲
Zungney
Prakhar Goemba ▲
Kiki La
Nimalung Goemba ▲
Shertang La
Ura ●
Lirgang Chhu
See Bumthang Cultural & Duer Hot Spring Treks Map p286
90° 45' E
91° 00' E

climbs up a little draw. The valley below is covered with rice and little temporary shelters used by planters.

The trail makes a long climb as it heads along the valley, traversing in and out of several side valleys and passing numerous villages. **Kulaypang** (1930m) is a few rough houses and some cornfields. There's an inviting-looking trail that goes down and cuts across the next ridge but the correct trail goes up.

The trail passes below the settlement of **Gomda** (2040m). The language spoken in these villages is Kurtepa, which Dzongkha speakers cannot understand. After passing a chorten, the trail drops to cross a stream at 2000m, then climbs again to a mani wall at 2020m. Then it's a level walk past cornfields to the few houses of Gongdra and a Tibetan-style chorten.

Beyond Chanteme, a spread-out village with extensive cornfields, the trail crosses a stream and makes a climb to **Khaine Lhakhang**. Follow the cement irrigation canal for a while and then climb onto a little ridge where the temple sits at 2010m. There are two tall cedars by the monastery and fields of soya beans surrounding it.

You can see a goemba and a village at the eastern end of the ridge on the opposite side of the river. Pephu Goemba is high above and the town below is Songme.

Day 6: Khaine Lhakhang to Tangmachu
18km ● 6–7 hours ● 520m ascent, 810m descent

The trail goes down to a stream and back up to a BHU and community school in Gorsam. It then goes in and out of more side valleys and climbs to 2130m. It's level for about 15 minutes and then starts climbing gently through trees. You can see a glimpse of the road at the bottom of the Kuri Chhu valley.

The Tibetan-style Umling Mani at 2180m is at the corner between the Noyurgang Chhu and the Kuri Chhu valleys. It was built by a lama from Tibet and marks the boundary between the two *gewogs* (administrative blocks). Here the route turns north up the Kuri Chhu.

The next stretch of trail traverses through four large side valleys, descending to a stream and climbing to the next ridge. The trail emerges from the first valley at Gumbar Gang (2120m). After a long, almost

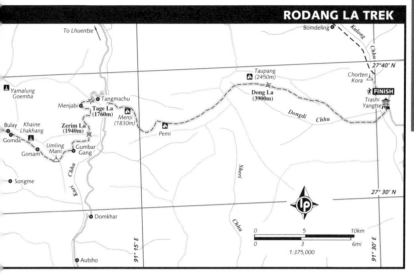

RODANG LA TREK

To Lhuentse

Bömdeling

Kulong Chhu

27° 40' N

Taupang
(2450m)

Chorten
Kora

Yamalung
Goemba

Menjabi
Tangmachu
Tage La
(1760m)
Menji
(1830m)

Dong La
(3900m)

FINISH
Trashi
Yangtse

Dongdi Chhu

Bulay
Gomda
Khaine
Lhakhang
Zerim La
(1940m)

Pemi

Umling
Mani
Gorsam
Gumbar
Gang

Songme

Sheri
Chhu

27° 30' N

Domkhar

Kuri Chhu

Chhu

0   5   10km
0   3   6mi
1:375,000

91° 15' E

91° 30' E

level, stretch the trail goes down and then up again to a chorten on Zerim La (1940m).

The route contours down to the head of a valley at 1840m, where there is a little chorten and a prayer wheel, then immediately starts climbing back through chir pines to 1890m. It then traverses grassy slopes in the main valley to another ridge and several herders' huts.

There's one more big side valley to traverse. Descend to a mani wall and pass the fields and houses of Menjabi, a pretty village with large, white Bhutanese houses. Cross the stream at 1540m, then start a long, hot climb on a grassy slope dotted with chir pines to some chortens and a mani wall on **Tage La** (1760m). South-east of the pass is the Tangmachu High School, where 400 students study on the top of this windswept ridge. It may be possible to *camp* near the school or, better yet, have vehicles waiting to drive you down to the valley.

It's 8km down the dirt road to the paved road, and 13km from the road junction to Lhuentse. The best way to arrange the logistics here is to arrange for a vehicle to meet you at Tangmachu, take you to Lhuentse to see the impressive dzong and then drop you off at the bottom of the hill to finish the last stage of the trek. The vehicle can then drive on to Trashi Yangtse to pick you up four days later.

Day 7: Tangmachu to Menji
16km • 4–5 hours • 690m ascent, 620m descent

From the bridge (1140m) below Tangmachu, the trek starts gradually up through rice terraces and cornfields to Chusa. It then becomes a steep haul up a treeless slope, although the path is beautifully scented with wild mint, lemon grass and artemisia. *Camp* is at 1830m, above Menji village, beside the Darchu Pang Lhakhang. The lhakhang's well-kept garden is full of flowers – marigolds, geraniums, dahlias and nasturtiums – and has a vegetable patch of Indian tomatoes and huge cucumbers. There are banana trees, too, and dozens of long-tailed birds in the trees.

Day 8: Menji to Pemi
20km • 3–4 hours • 620m ascent

Continue uphill through the thick, humid forest packed with a dense foliage of ferns and creepers and a constant whistle of cicadas.

The trail is narrow, steep and rutted. Climb steadily for two hours to a ridge-top meadow, then plunge back into the forest to reach some herders' huts at Pemi (2450m) on a narrow ridge-top clearing with a view to a forested gorge and mountains. There's not a village or house in view, although Menji villagers use this area as a summer pasture. Much of the trail for the next two days has fallen into disuse and is narrow and slippery.

Day 9: Pemi to Taupang
21km • 7–8 hours • 1450m ascent, 1450m descent

The trail stays in damp, cold forest, with occasional summer pastures with bamboo herders' shelters. The climb goes on and on, but the area is a botanist's delight, with shrubs of every kind, pungent with a sweet fermented smell, thick with humus. The next stretch of trail traverses nine passes, nicknamed the Nine Sisters, the highest of which is Dong La. Cross several ridges to **Dong La** (3900m), where there are good mountain views and a few prayer flags on a pile of rocks.

Cross the remaining ridges, each adorned with prayer flags, and descend steeply through thick evergreen forests on a trail strewn with rocks, logs and slippery leaves to a ridge-top meadow called Lisipang. The last part of the trek starts easily enough, turning right and down through a pasture at Yesupang, but then becomes increasingly rocky and muddy as it nears the Dongdi Chhu. There's no bridge, so you either rock-hop across or, if you're lucky, find a tree trunk balanced on rocks.

The path on the other side of the river is even muddier and rockier; parts of it are layered with a makeshift washboard-style log path. It's more like jungle than forest here, with ferns and creepers above and the river roaring nearby. The *camp* is at Taupang (2450m), a clearing in the forest with a cowherds' wooden shelter.

Day 10: Taupang to Trashi Yangtse
24km • 8–9 hours • 720m descent

The path through the forest beside the river is damp and muddy. You will encounter huge ferns, red-berried palms and occasional leeches. The forest is alive with birds and monkeys. Two hours of sloshing through mud or springing from stone to log to stone brings you to the village of Shakshing, a cluster of houses on the hillside, surrounded by corn and millet fields, banana trees and grazing cows.

The trail stays on the ridge on the northern side of the valley, passing above the village of Tongshing. It then descends past some swampy areas and crosses to the southern bank of the Dongdi Chhu on a large bridge. The small, old Trashi Yangtse dzong suddenly appears at the end of the valley on a hill top above the river. The trail crosses back to the north side of the river below the dzong on an old covered cantilever bridge. Finally cross the Kulong Chhu at 1730m and climb up to the road to meet your vehicles, or walk 3km into Chorten Kora.

SNOWMAN TREK

The Trek at a Glance

Duration 25 days
Max Elevation 5320m
Standard Hard
Season September to October
Start Drukgyel Dzong
Finish Sephu
Access Town Paro

Summary The Snowman trek travels to the remote Lunana district and is said to be one of the most difficult treks in the world. Fewer than half the people who attempt this trek actually finish it, either because of problems with altitude or heavy snowfall on the high passes.

The combination of distance, altitude, remoteness and weather makes this a tough journey, and with the 1997 change in regulations that increased trekking fees to US$200 a night, it has seen a sharp decline in the number of trekkers who attempt it. Even though there are reduced rates for long treks, few people can afford a 24-day trek for US$4280.

If you plan to trek this route double-check your emergency evacuation insur-

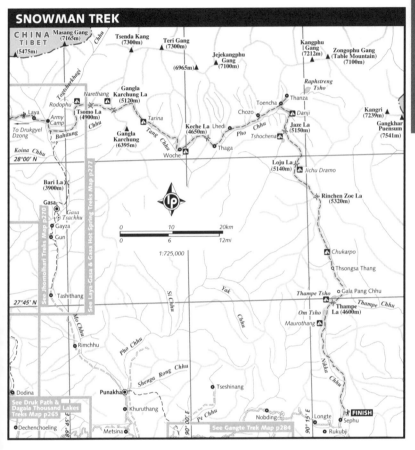

SNOWMAN TREK

CHINA
TIBET

Masang Gang
(7165m)

(5475m)

Tsenda Kang
(7300m)

Teri Gang
(7300m)

Jejekangphu
Gang
(7100m)

Kangphu
Gang
(7212m)

Zongophu Gang
(Table Mountain)
(7100m)

(6965m)

Raphstreng
Tsho

Gangla
Karchung La
(5120m)

Narethang

Rodophu

Laya

Tsomo La
(4900m)

Army
Camp

To Drukgyel
Dzong

Bahitung

Gangla
Karchung
(6395m)

Tarina

Toencha

Thanza

Chozo

Danji

Keche La
(4650m)

Lhedi

Woche

Thaga

Pho Chhu

Tshochena

Jaze La
(5150m)

Kangri
(7239m)

Gangkhar
Puensum
(7541m)

Koina Chhu
28°00' N

Loju La
(5140m)

Jichu Dramo

Bari La
(3900m)

Gasa

Gasa
Tsachhu

Gayza

Gun

Rinchen Zoe La
(5320m)

0   10   20km
0   6   12mi

1:725,000

Chukarpo

Thsongsa Thang

Tashithang
27°45' N

Thampe Tsho

Gala Pang Chhu

Thampe
La (4600m)

Thampe Chhu

Om Tsho

Maurothang

Rimchhu

Punakha

Tseshinang

Dodina

Khuruthang

Nobding

Longte

Sephu

FINISH

Dechencheoling

Metsina

Rukubji

To Drukgyel Dzong
Bahitung

Togbhrabgi

Tang Chhu

Si Chhu

Yak

Chhu

Nikka Chhu

Mo Chhu

Pho Chhu

Shenga Rong Chhu

Pe Chhu

89°45' E

90°00' E

90°15' E

See Jhomolhari Treks Map p270

See Laya-Gasa & Gasa Hot Spring Treks Map p272

See Druk Path &
Dagala Thousand Lakes
Treks Map p265

See Gangte Trek Map p284

ance (see Travel Insurance in the Facts for the Visitor chapter). If you get into Lunana and snow blocks the passes, the only way out is by helicopter, an expensive way to finish an already expensive trek. Another obstacle that often hampers this trek is bridges in remote regions that get washed away.

The Snowman trek is frequently closed because of snow, and is impossible during winter. The season for this trek is generally considered to be from late September to mid-October. Don't plan a summer trek; this is a miserable place to be during the monsoon.

This classic trek follows the Jhomolhari and Laya-Gasa treks to Laya. Many walking days can be saved by starting in Tashithang and trekking north up the Mo Chhu, following the Laya-Gasa trek in reverse.

Days 1–5: Drukgyel Dzong to Lingzhi

Follow Days 1–5 of the Jhomolhari trek (see pages 269–73).

Days 6–10: Lingzhi to Laya

Follow Days 6–10 of Laya-Gasa trek, Drukgyel Dzong to Lingzhi (see pages 276–79).

Day 11: A Rest & Acclimatisation Day in Laya

If you have trekked from Drukgyel Dzong you should spend a day recuperating from the trek to Laya and preparing for the rest of this rigorous trek. If you've trekked from Tashithang, you should also walk up to Laya to acclimatise. The army post below Laya has a radio; you will need to send a runner back here with a message in an emergency.

Day 12: Laya to Rodophu
19km • 6–8 hours • 1030m ascent, 70m descent

The trek leads gradually downhill to the Lunana trail junction, then climbs steeply for 30 to 40 minutes to a hilltop with good views over the Mo Chhu and the Rhodo Chhu. Much of the forest cover here was burned a few years ago. The rough trail continues to climb gradually up the Rhodo Chhu valley, first through mixed conifers, then through rhododendron shrubs above the tree line. At the top of a large rock slide there is an excellent view of the broad glacial valley and a massive glacier on Tsenda Kang (7100m), towering overhead. The *camp site* is just beyond a wooden bridge across the Rhodo Chhu at 4160m.

If you have time in the afternoon, or have come from Tashithang and are taking an acclimatisation day here, you have a choice of several short hikes. A small trail leads up the valley for about 2km to a small knoll with excellent views of the valley and surrounding mountains. You could continue further to the base of the glacier. Another option is to follow a small trail that starts about 500m upstream from the camp and switchbacks up the hill to the north, ending in a small yak pasture with a hut at 4500m.

Day 13: Rodophu to Narethang
17km • 5–6 hours • 720m ascent

The path crosses the wooden bridge and follows the river for about 20 minutes through rhododendron shrubs before turning right up the hill. Climb steadily to a high open valley at 4600m then more gradually through meadows to Tsomo La (4900m), which offers good views towards the Tibetan border and Jhomolhari. The route then crosses a generally flat, barren plateau at about 5000m with yak trails crisscrossing everywhere. Hopefully you'll have a knowledgeable guide and won't get lost. The *camp* is at Narethang (4900m), below the 6395m peak of Gangla Karchung.

Day 14: Narethang to Tarina
18km • 5–6 hours • 270m ascent, 1200m descent

From the camp it takes about one hour to climb to the 5120m **Gangla Karchung La**. The mountain views from the pass are excellent with Kang Bum (6526m) in the distance to the west and the rugged peaks of Tsenda Kang, Teri Gang (7300m) and Jejekangphu Gang (7100m) on the northern horizon.

From the pass the path descends along a large moraine to the edge of a near-vertical wall. The views from the edge of the wall are breathtaking – among the best along the

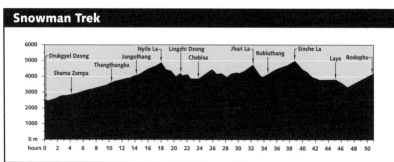

Snowman Trek

entire trek. A massive glacier descends from Teri Kang to a deep turquoise lake at its foot, 1km below you. The glacial lake to the left burst through its dam in the early 1960s, causing widespread damage downstream, and partially destroying Punakha Dzong.

Now the path becomes very steep (almost vertical in places) as it descends into the valley. In the lower half of the descent it passes through thick rhododendron shrubs and trees. When wet, this stretch can be rather nasty, with lots of roots and slippery mud.

At the bottom of the large, U-shaped valley the trail turns right, following the Tang Chhu downstream. There are several good *camp sites* along the river, both before and after the trail crosses the river.

Day 15: Tarina to Woche

17km • 6–7 hours • 275m ascent, 330m descent

The walk leads through conifer forest down the Tang Chhu on river left passing some impressive waterfalls cascading down both sides of the valley. The trail climbs gently out of the valley past several huge landslides and eventually climbs steeply to the north-east into the high side valley of Woche. Woche is a small settlement of five houses at 3940m and is the first village in the Lunana region.

Looking up the valley you can see the following day's route to Lhedi. There have been reports of theft of hiking equipment or clothing here, so you should keep all your gear safely inside your tent.

Day 16: Woche to Lhedi

17km • 6–7 hours • 980m ascent, 950m descent

The path to Lhedi begins below the camp and climbs the Woche valley, crossing a stream and climbing over a moraine before descending to a wooden bridge across the Woche Chhu. It then climbs up a wide trail past an extremely clear lake to **Keche La** (4650m). From the pass there are excellent views of the surrounding mountains, including Jejekangphu Gang's triple peak, the source of the Woche Chhu.

The route descends steeply into the Pho Chhu valley, the heart of the Lunana district. In the small village of **Thaga** (4050m) the farmers grow buckwheat, potatoes, turnips, and radishes. From Thaga the path drops towards the Pho Chhu, then turns north-east again towards Lhedi, which is visible in the distance above the river.

In 1994 a moraine holding back a large glacial lake north of Thanza burst, hurling millions of litres of water down the Pho Chhu. The resulting flash flood caused considerable damage, which is still visible along this stretch of trail.

Passing a few scattered settlements and crossing below a waterfall on a wooden bridge, the trail descends to the banks of the Pho Chhu. Continue along the river bed until you reach Lhedi at 3700m.

Lhedi is a district headquarters with a school, BHU and wireless station, but there is no shop here (or anywhere else in the Lunana district). Everything is carried in by yak trains across 5000m passes. Strong winds

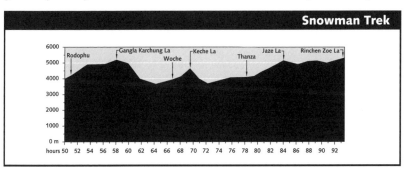

blow up the valley in the late afternoon, making it bitterly cold in autumn and winter.

Day 17: Lhedi to Thanza
17km • 7–8 hours • 400m ascent

The trail follows the north bank of the Pho Chhu past several small farms. In clear weather there are excellent views of **Table Mountain** (7100m) to the north and Tangse Gang across the river. Floods have destroyed parts of the trail so a temporary path winds its way among massive boulders in the river bed, crossing small, rickety bridges across several channels of the river. Around lunch time the trail passes the small village of Chozo at 4090m. The village has a small dzong, which is still in use.

If you are pressed for time, you can gain a day or two by stopping here and taking a direct trail to Tshochena, but most trekkers continue to Thanza (4100m), a couple of hours further up the valley. The first part of the trail to Thanza leads through lush yak pastures on the wide river flats, but soon the grass gives way to a large expanse of fine glacial sand. Protect your camera; if it is windy the sand will enter any little opening.

Eventually the trail leaves the river bed and climbs a bluff overlooking the villages of Thanza, straight ahead, and Toencha, on the other bank of the river. Table Mountain forms an immense, 3000m-high wall of snow and ice only a few kilometres behind Thanza. Most groups *camp* in Toencha (4150m), but there are places to camp in Thanza as well.

Day 18: A Rest Day in Thanza

Most groups schedule a rest day here. This is as far as the yak drivers from Laya go. It takes time to round up enough yaks for the rest of the trek and you may get a rest day even if you have not scheduled one. This provides a good opportunity to explore the villages and glacial lakes up the valley. The closest lake, Raphstreng Tsho, is 100m deep and caused the 1994 flood. A large crew of Indian workers dug a channel through the moraine to prevent a recurrence, but there are several more glacial lakes in the area that could burst through their moraines at any time.

Day 19: Thanza to Danji
8km • 3–4 hours • 80m ascent

If your party is very fit, you can do the hike to Tshochena in one day, but it's a long, hard walk at high altitude and it's better to split it into two half days.

The route climbs from Toencha to a large boulder on the hill south of the village. From the boulder there are excellent views of Thanza, Toencha, Chozo and the surrounding mountains. The path then turns east up a side valley. After a couple of hours of relatively flat and easy walking, the trail enters a yak meadow with some herders' huts. This is an excellent *camping spot*; there are often blue sheep on the hills above, and they have been known to walk into camp.

If you stop here, there is ample opportunity to explore the area. A few hundred metres up the valley, a small trail climbs the ridge to the left, leading to a higher valley behind. The top of the ridge offers excellent views of the surrounding mountainscape.

Day 20: Danji to Tshochena
12km • 5–6 hours • 490m ascent, 240m descent

There is a trail junction near the camp site at Danji. The trail up the valley leads to Gangkhar Puensum base camp and to Bumthang. The path to the end of the trek crosses the creek and leads up a rocky side valley. It is a long climb across several false summits to **Jaze La** at 5150m, which offers spectacular mountain views in all directions. From the pass, the path descends between snow-covered peaks and passes a string of small lakes. The *camp site* is near the shore of Tshochena lake at 4970m. This is the first of two nights of camping above 4900m.

Day 21: Tshochena to Jichu Dramo
14km • 4–5 hours • 230m ascent, 140m descent

The trail follows the shore of the blue-green lake before climbing to a ridge at 5100m. On top you are surrounded by a 360-degree panorama of snowy peaks, while, far below, the Pho Chhu descends towards Punakha. Below the ridge, the road and microwave tower at Dochu La are just visible in the distance.

The path makes several ups and downs over small rounded hills, but because of the altitude, walking can be slow. The trail descends past a glacial lake before climbing up to Loju La at 5140m. Many trails wander around high-altitude yak pastures in this region, and it's easy to go astray. The correct path will lead you across a small saddle at 5100m into a wide glacial valley. The trail descends gradually to the *camp site* at Jichu Dramo (5050m), a small pasture on the east side of the valley.

Day 22: Jichu Dramo to Chukarpo
18km • 5–6 hours • 320m ascent, 730m descent

After leaving camp the trail climbs through a moraine to Rinchen Zoe La (5320m), which divides the Pho Chhu and Mangde Chhu drainages. The pass is surrounded by breathtaking mountain scenery. **Rinchen Zoe peak** (5650m) towers above the pass to the west and major Himalayan mountains stretch along the northern horizon. To the east the western flank of Gangkhar Puensum is visible above the closer ranges, while the Thampe Chhu valley stretches below you to the south.

From the pass the trail descends into a broad, marshy valley with a string of lakes. The trail generally follows the left (east) side of the valley, which narrows the lower you go. Eventually the trail descends steeply down the face of a moraine to a yak pasture in the upper reaches of the Thampe Chhu. There are trails on both sides of the river, but you should cross to the west bank (river right) here, as there is no bridge further down. The vegetation gradually begins to thicken, first to rhododendron and juniper shrubs and eventually to trees of both species, the first real trees since Lhedi. After a couple of hours you reach the *camp site* at Chukarpo (4600m), or you can continue to a better site at Thsongsa Thang (4400m), one hour further down the trail.

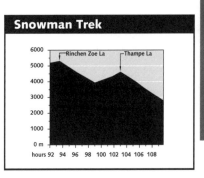

Snowman Trek

Day 23: Chukarpo to Thampe Tsho
18km • 5–6 hours • 400m ascent, 640m descent

The trail continues to descend along the right bank of the river until it reaches a yak pasture at Gala Pang Chhu (4010m). You might be lucky enough to spot some takins on the hills across the river. From this point, the path begins to climb quite steeply through junipers and silver firs towards Thampe Tsho. The path generally follows a stream to the beautiful, clear, turquoise lake, set in a bowl and surrounded by steep mountain walls. The *camp site* is at the far end of the lake at 4300m.

Day 24: Thampe Tsho to Maurothang
14km • 5 hours • 280m ascent, 1020m descent

From the camp the trail climbs steeply to **Thampe La** at 4600m. Along the way you may see blue sheep high on the slopes above the trail.

The path descends to Om Tsho, sacred because Pema Lingpa found a number of *terma* here. The path then skirts the northwestern shore of the lake before crossing its outlet, marked by a string of prayer flags. From here the path drops steeply past a waterfall to a smaller lake, about 100m lower.

From the second lake, the path descends steeply to the headwaters of the Nikka Chhu. It's so steep that yaks are reluctant to come down this stretch. The drainage of

TREKKING

the second lake also forms a waterfall, which can only be seen once you have descended almost to the bottom. The path levels out, following the left bank of the Nikka Chhu. After approximately 2km, it reaches a large open glade near the confluence of a major tributary coming from the east. A wooden bridge crosses the Nikka Chhu to river right, then a broad path follows through mixed forest to Maurothang (3610m), a large clearing on the banks of the river beside a few yak herders' huts.

Day 25: Maurothang to Sephu
18km • 5–6 hours • 990m descent

If horses are not available at Maurothang, the guide will probably send someone ahead to arrange for them further down. Yaks cannot walk all the way to the road because of the low altitude and the many cows in the area.

A well-used trail continues down the west side of the Nikka Chhu for about 30 minutes before crossing to the east bank into a mixed deciduous and bamboo forest, then descends gradually through forests interspersed with pastures. Eventually it emerges into a large grassy area, overlooking the road and the village of Sephu. The path becomes somewhat confusing at this point, as there are many trails. Look for a large trail about 20m to 30m above the river and you'll soon pass a large suspension bridge over the Nikka Chhu, which you shouldn't cross. Soon the trail turns into a narrow tractor road that emerges onto the main road next to the Nikka Chhu bridge at 2600m. There are several stores and a small restaurant near the bridge.

SAMTENGANG WINTER TREK

The Trek at a Glance

Duration 4 days
Max Elevation 1500m
Standard Easy
Season April, September to October

Start Punakha
Finish Chhuzomsa
Access Town Punakha
Summary A low-altitude trek south-east of Punakha. Low elevation makes this trek possible throughout the winter, but miserable when it's hot. This route sees few trekkers.

Day 1: Punakha to Limukha
12km • 4 hours • 880m ascent

Cross the footbridge over the Pho Chhu from Punakha Dzong and walk to Shengana. The trek begins with a gradual climb through a forest of chir pine to Limukha.

Day 2: Limukha to Chhungsakha
14km • 5 hours • 430m descent

The trail descends through rhododendron and oak forests to Chhungsakha.

Day 3: Chhungsakha to Samtengang
13km • 5 hours • 650m ascent, 270m descent

Trek down to the Pe Chhu, crossing it at 1420m, then climb through the village of Sha to Samtengang.

Day 4: Samtengang to Chhuzomsa
15km • 5–6 hours • 730m descent

The trail leads steeply downhill on a treeless slope to the roadhead at Chhuzomsa.

Language

The official language of Bhutan is Dzongkha. While Dzongkha uses the same 'Ucen script as Tibetan – and the two languages are closely related – Dzongkha is sufficiently different that Tibetans cannot understand it. English is the medium of instruction in schools, so most educated people speak it fluently. There are English signboards, books and menus throughout the country. Road signs and government documents are all written in both English and Dzongkha. The national newspaper, *Kuensel*, is published in three languages: English, Dzongkha and Nepali. In the monastic schools, Choekey, the classical Tibetan language, is taught.

In eastern Bhutan most people speak Sharchop (language of the east), which is totally different from Dzongkha. In the south, most people speak Nepali. As a result of the isolation of many parts of the country, a number of languages other than Dzongkha and Sharchop survive. Some are so different that people from different parts of the country can't understand each other. Bumthangkha is a language of the Bumthang region, and most regional minorities have their own language. Other tongues in Bhutan's Tower of Babel are Khengkha from Zhamgang, Kurtoep from Lhuentshe, Mangdep from Trongsa and Dzala from Trashi Yangtse.

The Dzongkha Development Commission has established a system for transliterating Dzongkha into Roman script. This official system uses three accent marks: the apostrophe to represent a high tone (eg, **'ne**) or a 'soft' consonant (eg, **g'**); a circumflex accent (eg, **ê**) to represent long vowels; and a diaeresis (eg, **ö** – see 'Pronunciation'). The system also attempts to represent sounds in Dzongkha that don't occur in English, such as retroflex and aspirated consonants. In this language guide, a simpler system is used with the primary aim being ease of communication at the risk of imperfect pronunciation. In the rest of this book, no accent marks are used.

Pronunciation
Vowels
a	as in 'father'
ä	as the 'a' in 'hat'
e	as the 'ey'in 'hey'
i	as in 'hit'
o	as in 'go'
ö	as the 'ir' in 'dirt' (without the 'r' sound)
u	as in 'jute'
ü	like saying 'i' with the lips stretched back

The circumflex accent marks a long vowel.

Consonants
Most consonants in Roman Dzongkha are pronounced as in English. The following guide covers letters and sounds that are likely to cause confusion.

An 'h' after the consonants **c**, **d**, **g**, **l**, **p** and **t** indicates that they are 'aspirated', ie, released with a slight puff of air – listen to the 'p' sounds in 'pip'; the first is aspirated, the second is not. Getting aspiration wrong can have a direct impact on the meaning, but it shouldn't be a problem with the words and phrases in this guide.

c	as the 'ch' in 'church'
ng	as in 'sing'; practise using the 'ng' sound at the beginning of a word, eg, *ngawang* (a name)
sh	as in 'ship'
t, th	'dental' consonants, pronounced with the tongue tip against the teeth
zh	as the 's' in 'measure'

Greetings & Civilities
Hello.	*kuzuzangbo la*
Goodbye.	
(person leaving)	*läzhimbe jön*
(person staying)	*läzhimbe zhû*
Good luck.	*trashi dele*
Thank you.	*kadriche*
Yes.	*ing/yö*
No.	*mê*
Maybe.	*im ong*

Small Talk

Hello, how are you?	*chö gadebe yö?*
I'm fine.	*nga läzhimbe ra yö*
Where are you going?	*chö gâti jou mo?*
What's your name?	*chö meng gaci mo?*
My name is ...	*ngê meng ... ing*
Where are you from?	*chö gâti lä mo?*
I'm from ...	*nga ... lä ing*
I'm staying at ...	*nga ... döp ing*
What is this?	*di gaci mo?*
It's cold today.	*dari jâm-mä*
It's raining.	*châp cap dowä*
I know.	*nga shê*
I don't know.	*nga mi shê*
May I take your photo?	*chögi pâ ci tapge mä?*
That's OK.	*di tupbä*

Directions

What time does the bus leave?	*drülkhor chutshö gademci kha jou inna?*
I want to get off here.	*nga nâ dögobe*
Is it near?	*bolokha in-na?*
Is it far?	*tha ringsa in-na?*
Go straight ahead.	*thrangdi song*
left	*öm*
right	*yäp*
in front of	*dongkha*
next to	*bolokha*
behind	*japkha*
opposite	*dongko/dongte*
north	*bjang*
south	*lho*
east	*shâ*
west	*nup*

Around Town

The word *khang* means building; in many cases it's only necessary to add the kind of building.

Where is a ...?	*... gâti mo?*
bank	*ngükha*
book shop	*pekha*
cinema	*loknyen*
hospital	*menkha*
market	*throm*
monastery	*goemba*
police station	*thrimsung gakpi mâkha*
post office	*dremkha*
public telephone	*manggi jüthrin tangsi*
shop	*tshongkha*
temple	*lhakhang*
toilet	*chapsa*

Where is the toilet?	*chapsa gâti in-na?*
How far is the ...?	*... gadeci tha ringsa mo?*
I want to see ...	*nga ... tagobe*
I'm looking for ...	*nga ... tau ing*
What time does it open?	*chutshö gademci lu go pchiu mo?*
What time does it close?	*chutshö gademci lu go dam mo?*
Is it still open?	*datoya pchidi ong ga?*
What is this?	*di gaci mo?*
I want to change money.	*nga tiru sôgobä*

Food Words & Phrases

Where is a ... ?	*... gâti mo?*
local bar	*changkha*
restaurant	*zakha*

I don't eat meat.	*nga sha miza*
This is too spicy.	*di khatshi dû*
I don't like food with chillies.	*nga zhêgo êma dacikha miga*
Is the food good?	*zhêgo zhim-mä ga?*
This is delicious.	*di zhim-mä*
Please give me a cup of tea.	*ngalu ja phôp gang nang*
Do you have food now?	*chö dato to za-wigang in-na?*
It's enough.	*digi lâm-mä*

beer (local)	*bang chhang*
whisky (local)	*ârra*
tea	*ja*
water	*chhu*
hot water	*chhu tshatom*
cold water	*chhu khöm*
boiled water	*chhu kököu*
cabbage	*banda kopi*
cauliflower	*meto kopi*
cheese	*datse*
chicken (meat)	*bja sha*
chilli	*êma*
cooked vegetable	*tshöse tsotsou*
corn (maize)	*gäza/gesasip*
egg	*gongdo*
food	*zhêgo/to*
meat	*sha*
mushroom	*shamu*
mustard	*päga*
noodles	*thukpa*
potatoes	*kewa*
radish	*laphu*
rice (cooked)	*to*
turnips	*öndo*
vegetable	*tshöse*
hot	*tshatom*
hot (spicy)	*khatshi yömi*
tasty	*zhimtoto*

Shopping

Bargaining is not a Bhutanese tradition, but if you are buying Bhutanese handicrafts at the weekend market, you might be able to lower the price a bit.

How much is it?	*dilu gadeci mo?*
That's too much.	*gong bôm mä*
I'll give you no more than ...	*ngâgi ... anemci lä trö mitshube*
What's your best price?	*gong gademcibe bjinni?*

Trekking Words & Phrases

Which trail goes to ...?
    ... josi lam gâti mo?
Is the trail steep?
    lam zâdra yö-ga?
Where is my tent?
    ngê gû di gâti in-na?

What's the name of this village?
    Ani ügi meng gaci zeu mo?

house	*chim*
steep uphill	*khagen gâdra*
steep downhill	*lam khamâ zâdra*
tired	*udû/thangche*
cold (weather)	*sîtraktra*
warm (weather)	*drotokto/tshatokto*

Other Useful Words

happy	*gatokto*
enough	*tupbä/lâmmä*
cheap	*khetokto*
expensive	*gong bôm*
big	*bôm*
small	*chungku*
clean	*tsangtokto*
dirty	*khamlôsisi*
good	*läzhim*
not good	*läzhim mindu*
heavy	*jice*
this	*di*
that	*aphidi*
mine	*ngêgi*
yours	*chögi*
his/hers	*khogi/mogi*
here	*nâ/nâlu*
there	*phâ/phâlu*
where	*gâti*
which	*gade*

Family

mother	*ama*
father	*apa*
daughter	*bum*
son	*bu*
elder sister	*azhim*
younger sister	*num/sîm*
elder brother	*phôgem*
younger brother	*nucu*
friend	*totsha/châro*

Animals & Crops

bird, chicken	*bja*
cow	*ba*
dog	*rochi/chi*
horse	*ta*
pig	*phap*
water buffalo	*mahe*

yak (male/female)	*yâ/jim*
barley	*nâ*
buckwheat	*bjô*
corn (maize)	*gäza/gesasip*
millet	*membja*
standing rice	*bjâ*
husked rice	*chum*
wheat	*kâ*

Places

alpine hut	*bjobi gâ*
alpine pasture	*la nogi tsamjo*
bridge	*zam*
hills	*ri*
lake	*tsho*
mountain	*gangri*
mountain pass	*la*
mule track	*ta lam*
plain or meadow	*thang*
prayer flag	*dâshi*
river	*chhu/tsangchhu*
stone carved with prayers	*dogi mani*
trail	*lam/kanglam*
village	*ü*

Time & Dates

What is the time?	*chutshö gademci mo?*
Five o'clock.	*chutshö nga*
today	*dari*
tomorrow	*nâba*
day after tomorrow	*nâtshe*
yesterday	*khatsha*
sometime	*retshe kap*
morning	*drôba*
afternoon	*pchiru*
day	*nyim, za*
night	*numu*

Days of the Week

Sunday	*za dau*
Monday	*za mîma*
Tuesday	*za lhap*
Wednesday	*za phup*
Thursday	*za pâsa*
Friday	*za pêm*
Saturday	*za nyim*

Numbers

1	*ci*
2	*nyî*
3	*sum*
4	*zhi*
5	*nga*
6	*drû*
7	*dün*
8	*gä*
9	*gu*
10	*cuthâm*
11	*cûci*
12	*cunyî*
13	*cûsu*
14	*cüzhi*
15	*cänga*
16	*cûdru*
17	*cupdü*
18	*côpgä*
19	*cügu*
20	*nyishu/khächi*
25	*nyishu tsanga*
30	*sumcu* or *khä pcheda nyî*
40	*zhipcu/khänyî*
50	*ngapcu* or *khä pcheda sum*
60	*drukcu/khäsum*
70	*düncu* or *khä pcheda zhi*
80	*gepcu/khäzhi*
90	*gupcu* or *khä pcheda nga*
100	*cikja/khänga*
1000	*ciktong* or *tongthra ci*
10,000	*cikthri*
100,000	*cikbum/bum*
one million	*saya ci*

Health & Emergencies

I'm ill.	*nga nau mä*
I feel nauseous.	*nga cûni zum beu mä*
I feel weak.	*nga thangchep mä*
I keep vomiting.	*nga cûp cûsara döp mä*
I feel dizzy.	*nga guyu khôu mä*
I'm having trouble breathing.	*nga bung tang mit shubä*
doctor	*drungtsho*
fever	*jangshu*
pain	*nazu*

Glossary

ABTO – Association of Bhutanese Tour Operators
anim – Buddhist nun
anim goemba – nunnery
arra – home-made spirit distilled from barley, wheat or rice
ashi – title for a queen or lady of aristocracy

bangchung – round bamboo basket with a tight-fitting cover
BHU – Basic Health Unit
bodhisattva – a being who has the capacity of gaining Buddhahood in this life but who refuses it in order to be reincarnated in the world to help other beings
Bon – ancient, pre-Buddhist, animistic religion of Tibet; its practitioners are called Bon-po
Brokpa – minority group in eastern Bhutan
BTCL – Bhutan Tourism Corporation Limited
bukhari – wood-burning stove
bumpa – vase, usually used to contain holy water in *goembas*

cairn – pile of stones marking a trail or pass
carom – a game similar to snooker or pool played on a small wooden board using checkers instead of billiard balls
cham – dance
chang – north
chappati – flat unleavened bread
chhang – beer made from rice, corn or millet, pronounced as 'chung'
chhu – river, also water
chilip – foreigner
chimi – member of the National Assembly
Choekey – classical Tibetan (the language of religion)
choesham – altar or shrine room
choesum – chapel
chorten – stone Buddhist monument, often containing relics
chugo – hard, dried yak cheese

dal – lentil soup

Dantak – Indian Border Roads Task Force
dasho – honorary title conferred by the king
deb raja – British term for the *desi* during the period 1652–1907
desi – secular ruler of Bhutan
dharma – Buddhist teachings
dharma raja – British name for the Shabdrung, the religious ruler, during period from 1652 to 1907
dochey – inner courtyard of a *dzong*
doma – beetel nut, also known by its Indian name, paan
dorji – a stylised thunderbolt used in rituals; 'vajra' in Sanskrit
DOT – Department of Tourism
dratshang – central monk body
driglam chhoesum – code of etiquette
driglam namzha – traditional values and etiquette
drubda – meditation centre for monks
Druk Gyalpo – the King of Bhutan
Drukpa Kagyu – the official religion of Bhutan, a school of tantric *Mahayana* Buddhism
drungkhag – subdistrict
dukhang – assembly hall in a *goemba*; also called a *tshokhang*
dungpa – head of a subdistrict
dzong – fort-monastery
dzongdag – district administrator
Dzongkha – national language of Bhutan
dzongkhag – district
dzongpen – old term for lord of the *dzong*

gakpa – police
gangri – snow mountain
gewog – block, the lowest administrative level
gho – traditional dress for men
global positioning system (GPS) – a device that calculates position and elevation by reading and decoding signals from satellites
goemba – a *Mahayana* Buddhist monastery
goenkhang – chapel devoted to protective and terrifying deities, usually *Mahakala*

gorikha – porch of a *lhakhang*, literally 'mouth of the door'
GSI – Geological Survey of India
gup – elected leader of a village
Guru Rinpoche – the common name of Padmasambhava, the founder of *Mahayana* Buddhism
gyalpo – ruler or king
himal – Sanskrit word for mountain
hot-stone bath – bath heated by hot stones sizzling in the water

IMTRAT – Indian Military Training Team

Je Khenpo – Chief Abbot of Bhutan

kabney – scarf worn over the shoulder on formal occasions
khandrom – a female celestial being; 'dakini' in Sanskrit
khenpo – abbot
khonying – archway chorten
kira – traditional dress for women
kora – circumambulation

la – mountain pass
lam – path or road
lama – *Mahayana* Buddhist teacher or priest
lha – god or deity
lhakhang – temple, literally 'god house'
lhentshog – commission
lho – south
lopon – Senior monk or teacher
Losar – Bhutanese and Tibetan New Year
lu – serpent deities, called 'naga' in Sanskrit
lyonpo – government minister

Mahakala – Yeshe Goenpo, the guardian god of Bhutan, who manifests himself as a raven
Mahayana – school of Buddhism, literally 'great vehicle'
mandala – cosmic diagram; *'kyilkhor'* in *Dzongkha*
mani stone – stone carved with the Buddhist mantra *'om mani peme hum'*
mantra – prayer formula or chant
momo – a steamed or fried dumpling
moraine – ridge of rocks that a glacier pushed up along its edges (a medial moraine) or at its foot (a terminal moraine)

naktshang – temple dedicated to warlord or protective deity, literally 'place of vows'
NCCA – National Commission for Cultural Affairs
ney – sacred site
NGO – nongovernmental organisation
ngultrum – unit of Bhutanese currency
nup – west
NWAB – National Womens' Association of Bhutan
Nyingma – lineage of Himalayan Buddhism; its practitioners are Nyingmapa

om mani peme hum – sacred Buddhist mantra, roughly translates as 'hail to the jewel in the lotus'
outreach clinic – health posts in remote villages

PCO – Public Call Office
penlop – regional governor, literally lord-teacher
phajo – priest
prayer flag – long strips of cloth printed with prayers that are 'said' whenever the flag flaps in the wind
prayer wheel – cylindrical wheel inscribed with, and containing, prayers
PWD – Public Works Department

rabdey – district monk body
rachu – shoulder cloth worn by women on formal occasions
RBA – Royal Bhutan Army
RBG – Royal Body Guard
RBP – Royal Bhutan Police
rigney – name used for a school for traditional studies
rinpoche – reincarnate lama, usually the abbot of a *goemba*
river left – the left bank of a river when facing downstream
river right – the right bank of a river when facing downstream
RSPN – Royal Society for Protection of Nature

SAARC – South Asia Association for Regional Cooperation. This includes the seven countries of Bangladesh, Bhutan, India, Maldives, Nepal, Pakistan and Sri Lanka.

Sakyamuni – another name for Gautama Buddha, the Historical Buddha
Shabdrung, the – title of the reincarnations of the Shabdrung Ngawang Namgyal
shar – east
shedra – Buddhist college
shing – wood
shunglam – highway
sonam – good luck
stupa – hemispherical Buddhist structure from which the *chorten* evolved

terma – texts and artefacts hidden by *Guru Rinpoche*
terton – discoverer of *terma*
thang – plain
thangka – painted or embroidered religious picture
thondrol – huge *thangka* that is unfurled on special occasions, literally 'liberation on sight'
thos – a heap of stones representing the guardians of the four directions
thukpa – noodles, often served in a soup
torma – ritual cake made of *tsampa*, butter and sugar
trulku – a reincarnation; the spiritual head of a *goemba*

Tsa-Wa-Sum – Government, Country and King
tsachhu – hot spring
tsampa – barley flour, a staple food in hill villages
tseri – the practice of shifting cultivation
tshamkhang – small meditation quarters
tsha-tsha – small images moulded in clay
tsho – lake
Tshogdu – National Assembly
tshokhang – assembly hall in a *lhakhang*

UNCDF – United Nations Capital Development Fund
utse – the central tower that houses the *lhakhang* in a *dzong*

WWF – World Wide Fund for Nature (known as the World Wildlife Fund in North America)

yak – main beast of burden and form of cattle above 3000m elevation
yathra – strips of woven woollen cloth
yeti – the abominable snowman

Zangto Pelri – the celestial abode or paradise of *Guru Rinpoche*

LONELY PLANET

ON THE ROAD

Travel Guides explore cities, regions and countries, and supply information on transport, restaurants and accommodation, covering all budgets. They come with reliable, easy-to-use maps, practical advice, cultural and historical facts and a rundown on attractions both on and off the beaten track. There are over 200 titles in this classic series, covering nearly every country in the world.

 Lonely Planet Upgrades extend the shelf life of existing travel guides by detailing any changes that may affect travel in a region since a book has been published. Upgrades can be downloaded for free from **www.lonelyplanet.com/upgrades**

For travellers with more time than money, **Shoestring** guides offer dependable, first-hand information with hundreds of detailed maps, plus insider tips for stretching money as far as possible. Covering entire continents in most cases, the six-volume shoestring guides are known around the world as 'backpackers bibles'.

For the discerning short-term visitor, **Condensed** guides highlight the best a destination has to offer in a full-colour, pocket-sized format designed for quick access. They include everything from top sights and walking tours to opinionated reviews of where to eat, stay, shop and have fun.

CitySync lets travellers use their Palm™ or Visor™ hand-held computers to guide them through a city with handy tips on transport, history, cultural life, major sights, and shopping and entertainment options. It can also quickly search and sort hundreds of reviews of hotels, restaurants and attractions, and pinpoint their location on scrollable street maps. CitySync can be downloaded from **www.citysync.com**

MAPS & ATLASES

Lonely Planet's **City Maps** feature downtown and metropolitan maps, as well as transit routes and walking tours. The maps come complete with an index of streets, a listing of sights and a plastic coat for extra durability.

Road Atlases are an essential navigation tool for serious travellers. Cross-referenced with the guidebooks, they also feature distance and climate charts and a complete site index.

LONELY PLANET

ESSENTIALS

Read This First books help new travellers to hit the road with confidence. These invaluable predeparture guides give step-by-step advice on preparing for a trip, budgeting, arranging a visa, planning an itinerary and staying safe while still getting off the beaten track.

Healthy Travel pocket guides offer a regional rundown on disease hot spots and practical advice on predeparture health measures, staying well on the road and what to do in emergencies. The guides come with a user-friendly design and helpful diagrams and tables.

Lonely Planet's **Phrasebooks** cover the essential words and phrases travellers need when they're strangers in a strange land. They come in a pocket-sized format with colour tabs for quick reference, extensive vocabulary lists, easy-to-follow pronunciation keys and two-way dictionaries.

Miffed by blurry photos of the Taj Mahal? Tired of the classic 'top of the head cut off' shot? **Travel Photography: A Guide to Taking Better Pictures** will help you turn ordinary holiday snaps into striking images and give you the know-how to capture every scene, from frenetic festivals to peaceful beach sunrises.

Lonely Planet's **Travel Journal** is a lightweight but sturdy travel diary for jotting down all those on-the-road observations and significant travel moments. It comes with a handy time-zone wheel, a world map and useful travel information.

Lonely Planet's eKno is an all-in-one communication service developed especially for travellers. It offers low-cost international calls and free email and voicemail so that you can keep in touch while on the road. Check it out on **www.ekno.lonelyplanet.com**

FOOD & RESTAURANT GUIDES

Lonely Planet's **Out to Eat** guides recommend the brightest and best places to eat and drink in top international cities. These gourmet companions are arranged by neighbourhood, packed with dependable maps, garnished with scene-setting photos and served with quirky features.

For people who live to eat, drink and travel, **World Food** guides explore the culinary culture of each country. Entertaining and adventurous, each guide is packed with detail on staples and specialities, regional cuisine and local markets, as well as sumptuous recipes, comprehensive culinary dictionaries and lavish photos good enough to eat.

LONELY PLANET

OUTDOOR GUIDES

For those who believe the best way to see the world is on foot, Lonely Planet's **Walking Guides** detail everything from family strolls to difficult treks, with 'when to go and how to do it' advice supplemented by reliable maps and essential travel information.

Cycling Guides map a destination's best bike tours, long and short, in day-by-day detail. They contain all the information a cyclist needs, including advice on bike maintenance, places to eat and stay, innovative maps with detailed cues to the rides, and elevation charts.

The **Watching Wildlife** series is perfect for travellers who want authoritative information but don't want to tote a heavy field guide. Packed with advice on where, when and how to view a region's wildlife, each title features photos of over 300 species and contains engaging comments on the local flora and fauna.

With underwater colour photos throughout, **Pisces Books** explore the world's best diving and snorkelling areas. Each book contains listings of diving services and dive resorts, detailed information on depth, visibility and difficulty of dives, and a roundup of the marine life you're likely to see through your mask.

LONELY PLANET

OFF THE ROAD

Journeys, the travel literature series written by renowned travel authors, capture the spirit of a place or illuminate a culture with a journalist's attention to detail and a novelist's flair for words. These are tales to soak up while you're actually on the road or dip into as an at-home armchair indulgence.

The range of lavishly illustrated **Pictorial** books is just the ticket for both travellers and dreamers. Off-beat tales and vivid photographs bring the adventure of travel to your doorstep long before the journey begins and long after it is over.

Lonely Planet **Videos** encourage the same independent, tough-minded approach as the guidebooks. Currently airing throughout the world, this award-winning series features innovative footage and an original soundtrack.

Yes, we know, work is tough, so do a little bit of deskside dreaming with the spiral-bound Lonely Planet **Diary** or a Lonely Planet **Wall Calendar**, filled with great photos from around the world.

TRAVELLERS NETWORK

Lonely Planet Online. Lonely Planet's award-winning Web site has insider information on hundreds of destinations, from Amsterdam to Zimbabwe, complete with interactive maps and relevant links. The site also offers the latest travel news, recent reports from travellers on the road, guidebook upgrades, a travel links site, an online book-buying option and a lively travellers bulletin board. It can be viewed at **www.lonelyplanet.com** or AOL keyword: lp.

Planet Talk is a quarterly print newsletter, full of gossip, advice, anecdotes and author articles. It provides an antidote to the being-at-home blues and lets you plan and dream for the next trip. Contact the nearest Lonely Planet office for your free copy.

Comet, the free Lonely Planet newsletter, comes via email once a month. It's loaded with travel news, advice, dispatches from authors, travel competitions and letters from readers. To subscribe, click on the Comet subscription link on the front page of the Web site.

Lonely Planet Guides by Region

Lonely Planet is known worldwide for publishing practical, reliable and no-nonsense travel information in our guides and on our Web site. The Lonely Planet list covers just about every accessible part of the world. Currently there are 16 series: Travel guides, Shoestring guides, Condensed guides, Phrasebooks, Read This First, Healthy Travel, Walking guides, Cycling guides, Watching Wildlife guides, Pisces Diving & Snorkeling guides, City Maps, Road Atlases, Out to Eat, World Food, Journeys travel literature and Pictorials.

AFRICA Africa on a shoestring • Botswana • Cairo • Cairo City Map • Cape Town • Cape Town City Map • East Africa • Egypt • Egyptian Arabic phrasebook • Ethiopia, Eritrea & Djibouti • Ethiopian Amharic phrasebook • The Gambia & Senegal • Healthy Travel Africa • Kenya • Malawi • Morocco • Moroccan Arabic phrasebook • Mozambique • Namibia • Read This First: Africa • South Africa, Lesotho & Swaziland • Southern Africa • Southern Africa Road Atlas • Swahili phrasebook • Tanzania, Zanzibar & Pemba • Trekking in East Africa • Tunisia • Watching Wildlife East Africa • Watching Wildlife Southern Africa • West Africa • World Food Morocco • Zambia • Zimbabwe, Botswana & Namibia
Travel Literature: Mali Blues: Traveling to an African Beat • The Rainbird: A Central African Journey • Songs to an African Sunset: A Zimbabwean Story

AUSTRALIA & THE PACIFIC Aboriginal Australia & the Torres Strait Islands •Auckland • Australia • Australian phrasebook • Australia Road Atlas • Cycling Australia • Cycling New Zealand • Fiji • Fijian phrasebook • Healthy Travel Australia, NZ & the Pacific • Islands of Australia's Great Barrier Reef • Melbourne • Melbourne City Map • Micronesia • New Caledonia • New South Wales • New Zealand • Northern Territory • Outback Australia • Out to Eat – Melbourne • Out to Eat – Sydney • Papua New Guinea • Pidgin phrasebook • Queensland • Rarotonga & the Cook Islands • Samoa • Solomon Islands • South Australia • South Pacific • South Pacific phrasebook • Sydney • Sydney City Map • Sydney Condensed • Tahiti & French Polynesia • Tasmania • Tonga • Tramping in New Zealand • Vanuatu • Victoria • Walking in Australia • Watching Wildlife Australia • Western Australia
Travel Literature: Islands in the Clouds: Travels in the Highlands of New Guinea • Kiwi Tracks: A New Zealand Journey • Sean & David's Long Drive

CENTRAL AMERICA & THE CARIBBEAN Bahamas, Turks & Caicos • Baja California • Belize, Guatemala & Yucatán • Bermuda • Central America on a shoestring • Costa Rica • Costa Rica Spanish phrasebook • Cuba • Cycling Cuba • Dominican Republic & Haiti • Eastern Caribbean • Guatemala • Havana • Healthy Travel Central & South America • Jamaica • Mexico • Mexico City • Panama • Puerto Rico • Read This First: Central & South America • Virgin Islands • World Food Caribbean • World Food Mexico • Yucatán
Travel Literature: Green Dreams: Travels in Central America

EUROPE Amsterdam • Amsterdam City Map • Amsterdam Condensed • Andalucía • Athens • Austria • Baltic States phrasebook • Barcelona • Barcelona City Map • Belgium & Luxembourg • Berlin • Berlin City Map • Britain • British phrasebook • Brussels, Bruges & Antwerp • Brussels City Map • Budapest • Budapest City Map • Canary Islands • Catalunya & the Costa Brava • Central Europe • Central Europe phrasebook • Copenhagen • Corfu & the Ionians • Corsica • Crete • Crete Condensed • Croatia • Cycling Britain • Cycling France • Cyprus • Czech & Slovak Republics • Czech phrasebook • Denmark • Dublin • Dublin City Map • Dublin Condensed • Eastern Europe • Eastern Europe phrasebook • Edinburgh • Edinburgh City Map • England • Estonia, Latvia & Lithuania • Europe on a shoestring • Europe phrasebook • Finland • Florence • Florence City Map • France • Frankfurt City Map • Frankfurt Condensed • French phrasebook • Georgia, Armenia & Azerbaijan • Germany • German phrasebook • Greece • Greek Islands • Greek phrasebook • Hungary • Iceland, Greenland & the Faroe Islands • Ireland • Italian phrasebook • Italy • Kraków • Lisbon • The Loire • London • London City Map • London Condensed • Madrid • Madrid City Map • Malta • Mediterranean Europe • Milan, Turin & Genoa • Moscow • Munich • Netherlands • Normandy • Norway • Out to Eat – London • Out to Eat – Paris • Paris • Paris City Map • Paris Condensed • Poland • Polish phrasebook • Portugal • Portuguese phrasebook • Prague • Prague City Map • Provence & the Côte d'Azur • Read This First: Europe • Rhodes & the Dodecanese • Romania & Moldova • Rome • Rome City Map • Rome Condensed • Russia, Ukraine & Belarus • Russian phrasebook • Scandinavian & Baltic Europe • Scandinavian phrasebook • Scotland • Sicily • Slovenia • South-West France • Spain • Spanish phrasebook • Stockholm • St Petersburg • St Petersburg City Map • Sweden • Switzerland • Tuscany • Ukrainian phrasebook • Venice • Vienna • Wales • Walking in Britain • Walking in France • Walking in Ireland • Walking in Italy • Walking in Scotland • Walking in Spain • Walking in Switzerland • Western Europe • World Food France • World Food Greece • World Food Ireland • World Food Italy • World Food Spain **Travel Literature:** After Yugoslavia • Love and War in the Apennines • The Olive Grove: Travels in Greece • On the Shores of the Mediterranean • Round Ireland in Low Gear • A Small Place in Italy

Lonely Planet Mail Order

Lonely Planet products are distributed worldwide. They are also available by mail order from Lonely Planet, so if you have difficulty finding a title please write to us. North and South American residents should write to 150 Linden St, Oakland, CA 94607, USA; European and African residents should write to 10a Spring Place, London NW5 3BH, UK; and residents of other countries to Locked Bag 1, Footscray, Victoria 3011, Australia.

INDIAN SUBCONTINENT & THE INDIAN OCEAN Bangladesh • Bengali phrasebook • Bhutan • Delhi • Goa • Healthy Travel Asia & India • Hindi & Urdu phrasebook • India • India & Bangladesh City Map • Indian Himalaya • Karakoram Highway • Kathmandu City Map • Kerala • Madagascar • Maldives • Mauritius, Réunion & Seychelles • Mumbai (Bombay) • Nepal • Nepali phrasebook • North India • Pakistan • Rajasthan • Read This First: Asia & India • South India • Sri Lanka • Sri Lanka phrasebook • Tibet • Tibetan phrasebook • Trekking in the Indian Himalaya • Trekking in the Karakoram & Hindukush • Trekking in the Nepal Himalaya • World Food India **Travel Literature:** The Age of Kali: Indian Travels and Encounters • Hello Goodnight: A Life of Goa • In Rajasthan • Maverick in Madagascar • A Season in Heaven: True Tales from the Road to Kathmandu • Shopping for Buddhas • A Short Walk in the Hindu Kush • Slowly Down the Ganges

MIDDLE EAST & CENTRAL ASIA Bahrain, Kuwait & Qatar • Central Asia • Central Asia phrasebook • Dubai • Farsi (Persian) phrasebook • Hebrew phrasebook • Iran • Israel & the Palestinian Territories • Istanbul • Istanbul City Map • Istanbul to Cairo • Istanbul to Kathmandu • Jerusalem • Jerusalem City Map • Jordan • Lebanon • Middle East • Oman & the United Arab Emirates • Syria • Turkey • Turkish phrasebook • World Food Turkey • Yemen **Travel Literature:** Black on Black: Iran Revisited • Breaking Ranks: Turbulent Travels in the Promised Land • The Gates of Damascus • Kingdom of the Film Stars: Journey into Jordan

NORTH AMERICA Alaska • Boston • Boston City Map • Boston Condensed • British Columbia • California & Nevada • California Condensed • Canada • Chicago • Chicago City Map • Chicago Condensed • Florida • Georgia & the Carolinas • Great Lakes • Hawaii • Hiking in Alaska • Hiking in the USA • Honolulu & Oahu City Map • Las Vegas • Los Angeles • Los Angeles City Map • Louisiana & the Deep South • Miami • Miami City Map • Montreal • New England • New Orleans • New Orleans City Map • New York City • New York City City Map • New York City Condensed • New York, New Jersey & Pennsylvania • Oahu • Out to Eat – San Francisco • Pacific Northwest • Rocky Mountains • San Diego & Tijuana • San Francisco • San Francisco City Map • Seattle • Seattle City Map • Southwest • Texas • Toronto • USA • USA phrasebook • Vancouver • Vancouver City Map • Virginia & the Capital Region • Washington, DC • Washington, DC City Map • World Food New Orleans **Travel Literature:** Caught Inside: A Surfer's Year on the California Coast • Drive Thru America

NORTH-EAST ASIA Beijing • Beijing City Map • Cantonese phrasebook • China • Hiking in Japan • Hong Kong & Macau • Hong Kong City Map • Hong Kong Condensed • Japan • Japanese phrasebook • Korea • Korean phrasebook • Kyoto • Mandarin phrasebook • Mongolia • Mongolian phrasebook • Seoul • Shanghai • South-West China • Taiwan • Tokyo • Tokyo Condensed • World Food Hong Kong • World Food Japan **Travel Literature:** In Xanadu: A Quest • Lost Japan

SOUTH AMERICA Argentina, Uruguay & Paraguay • Bolivia • Brazil • Brazilian phrasebook • Buenos Aires • Buenos Aires City Map • Chile & Easter Island • Colombia • Ecuador & the Galapagos Islands • Healthy Travel Central & South America • Latin American Spanish phrasebook • Peru • Quechua phrasebook • Read This First: Central & South America • Rio de Janeiro • Rio de Janeiro City Map • Santiago de Chile • South America on a shoestring • Trekking in the Patagonian Andes • Venezuela **Travel Literature:** Full Circle: A South American Journey

SOUTH-EAST ASIA Bali & Lombok • Bangkok • Bangkok City Map • Burmese phrasebook • Cambodia • Cycling Vietnam, Laos & Cambodia • East Timor phrasebook • Hanoi • Healthy Travel Asia & India • Hill Tribes phrasebook • Ho Chi Minh City (Saigon) • Indonesia • Indonesian phrasebook • Indonesia's Eastern Islands • Java • Lao phrasebook • Laos • Malay phrasebook • Malaysia, Singapore & Brunei • Myanmar (Burma) • Philippines • Pilipino (Tagalog) phrasebook • Read This First: Asia & India • Singapore • Singapore City Map • South-East Asia on a shoestring • South-East Asia phrasebook • Thailand • Thailand's Islands & Beaches • Thailand, Vietnam, Laos & Cambodia Road Atlas • Thai phrasebook • Vietnam • Vietnamese phrasebook • World Food Indonesia • World Food Thailand • World Food Vietnam

ALSO AVAILABLE: Antarctica • The Arctic • The Blue Man: Tales of Travel, Love and Coffee • Brief Encounters: Stories of Love, Sex & Travel • Buddhist Stupas in Asia: The Shape of Perfection • Chasing Rickshaws • The Last Grain Race • Lonely Planet ... On the Edge: Adventurous Escapades from Around the World • Lonely Planet Unpacked • Lonely Planet Unpacked Again • Not the Only Planet: Science Fiction Travel Stories • Ports of Call: A Journey by Sea • Sacred India • Travel Photography: A Guide to Taking Better Pictures • Travel with Children • Tuvalu: Portrait of an Island Nation

LONELY PLANET

You already know that Lonely Planet produces more than this one guidebook, but you might not be aware of the other products we have on this region. Here is a selection of titles that you may want to check out as well:

South-West China
ISBN 1 86450 370 X
US$21.99 • UK£13.99

Bangkok
ISBN 1 86450 285 1
US$15.99 • UK£9.99

Nepal
ISBN 1 86450 247 9
US$19.99 • UK£12.99

Tibet
ISBN 1 86450 162 6
US$19.99 • UK£12.99

Bangladesh
ISBN 0 86442 667 4
US$17.99 • UK£11.99

India
ISBN 1 86450 246 0
US$24.99 • UK£14.99

Thailand
ISBN 1 86450 251 7
US$24.99 • UK£14.99

North India
ISBN 1 86450 330 0
US$21.99 • UK£13.99

India & Bangladesh Road Atlas
ISBN 1 74059 019 8
US$15.99 • UK£9.99

Read This First: Asia & India
ISBN 1 86450 049 2
US$14.95 • UK£8.99

Healthy Travel Asia & India
ISBN 1 86450 051 4
US$5.95 • UK£3.99

Available wherever books are sold

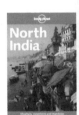

Index

Text

Bold indicates maps.

Bold indicates maps.

Boxed Text

MAP LEGEND

CITY ROUTES

Freeway .... Freeway
Highway .... Primary Road
Road .... Secondary Road
Street .... Street
Lane .... Lane
.... On/Off Ramp

═ ═ ═ ═......Unsealed Road
............One Way Street
............Pedestrian Street
............Stepped Street
⟩═ ═......................Tunnel
..........................Footbridge

REGIONAL ROUTES

..................Freeway
...........Primary Road
........Secondary Road
= = = =......Unsealed Road

BOUNDARIES

── · ── · ──........International
── · · ── · · ·..................State
─ ─ ─..................Disputed
..................Fortified Wall

TRANSPORT ROUTES & STATIONS

──── ◯ ─......................Train
─ ╫ ─ 🚉 ─ ╫ ─...............Ropeway
─ ─ ─ ─ ─..........Walking Trail

· · · · · · · ·......Walking Tour
..........................Path
..........Pier or Jetty

HYDROGRAPHY

.................River; Creek
.................Rapids
◉ ──⟩ ◁......Waterfalls
◉ .....Spring/Watering Hole

..................Lake
..................Dry Lake
..................Salt Lake
..................Swamp

AREA FEATURES

...................Building
❀ ......Park, Gardens
...................Market
..........Sports Ground
.........Beach
+ + +......Cemetery
...................Campus
.......................Rock

POPULATION SYMBOLS

✪ **CAPITAL** ....National Capital
◉ **Capital** ....State Capital
● **City** ....City
● **Town** ....Town
● Village ....Village
○ Place Name ....Uninhabited Town

MAP SYMBOLS

✈ ....Airport
⊖ ....Bank
卍 ....Buddhist Temple
🚌 🚏 ....Bus Station/Stop
△ ....Camping Area
⟁ ....Chorten
✝ ....Church
🎬 ....Cinema
🏯 ....Dzong
☎ .Embassy/Consulate

🛗 ....Goemba
❶ ....Golf Course
✛ ....Hospital
🖥 ....Internet Cafe
※ 📷 ....Lookout
✖ ....Mine
⚑ ....Monument
☪ ....Mosque
▲ ....Mountain
⌒ ⌒⌒ .....Mountain Range

🏛 ....Museum
🅿 ....Parking
)(.......................La
◉ ....Petrol
▼ ....Place to Eat
● ....Place to Stay
● ......Point of Interest
✪ ....Police Station
🅿 ....Pool
▣ ....Post Office

🍺 ....Pub or Bar
✖ ....Ruins
⊗ ....Shopping Centre
🏠 ....Stately Home
🚖 ....Taxi Rank
⊖ ....Toilet
ℹ .Tourist Information
🛐 ....Trailhead
🚍 .Transport (general)
🦁 ....Zoo

Note: Not all symbols displayed above appear in this book

LONELY PLANET OFFICES

Australia
Locked Bag 1, Footscray, Victoria 3011
☎ 03 8379 8000 fax 03 8379 8111
email: talk2us@lonelyplanet.com.au

UK
10a Spring Place, London NW5 3BH
☎ 020 7428 4800 fax 020 7428 4828
email: go@lonelyplanet.co.uk

USA
150 Linden St, Oakland, CA 94607
☎ 510 893 8555 TOLL FREE: 800 275 8555
fax 510 893 8572
email: info@lonelyplanet.com

France
1 rue du Dahomey, 75011 Paris
☎ 01 55 25 33 00 fax 01 55 25 33 01
email: bip@lonelyplanet.fr
www.lonelyplanet.fr

World Wide Web: www.lonelyplanet.com *or* AOL keyword: lp
Lonely Planet Images: lpi@lonelyplanet.com.au